AMERICAN VOICES

AMERICAN VOICES

Multicultural Literacy and Critical Thinking

DOLORES LAGUARDIA
University of San Francisco

HANS P. GUTH
San Jose State University

Mayfield Publishing Company
Mountain View, California
London • Toronto

To our children

Copyright © 1993 by Mayfield Publishing Company

LIBRARY OF CONGRESS CATALOGING-IN-PUBLICATION DATA
laGuardia, Dolores.
    American voices : multicultural literacy and critical thinking /
Dolores laGuardia, Hans P. Guth.
        p.   cm.
    ISBN 1-55934-185-8
    1. Readers — United States.   2. Pluralism (Social sciences) —
Problems, exercises, etc.   3. Ethnology — United States — Problems,
exercises, etc.   4. Ethnic groups — Problems, exercises, etc.
5. Culture — Problems, exercises, etc.   6. English language —
Rhetoric.   7. Critical thinking.   8. College readers.   I. Guth,
Hans Paul.   II. Title.
PE1127.H5L25   1992
808'.0427 — dc20   92-26825
                                                            CIP

Manufactured in the United States of America
10   9   8   7   6

Mayfield Publishing Company
1240 Villa Street
Mountain View, California 94041

Sponsoring editor, James Bull; managing editor, Linda Toy; manuscript editor, Margaret Moore; text designer, TS Design Group; cover designer, Donna Davis; cover artist, Lawrence Ferlinghetti; manufacturing manager, Martha Branch. The text was set in 10.5/12 Bembo by Thompson Type and printed on 50# Finch Opaque by the Maple-Vail Book Manufacturing Group.

Acknowledgments and copyrights continue at the back of the book on pages 681–685, which constitute an extension of the copyright page.

TO THE INSTRUCTOR

American Voices is a textbook for the courses in composition and critical thinking that are at the core of the student's general education. We aim at helping students become alert readers, more purposeful and effective writers, and thinking members of the larger community. We focus on issues that define our multicultural society as it charts its future. The book is built around selections by committed writers who demonstrate the power of the written word to record, interpret, and change the social and cultural reality in which we live.

The Goals of *American Voices*

REDEFINING AMERICA This book is part of the search for a new multicultural definition of American society. The text explores the promise of a multicultural America, examining the issues that confront us on the way to a richer pluralistic meeting of majority and minority cultures. A major theme of the book is diversity and community—the challenge of honoring diversity while searching for the common center.

TEACHING CRITICAL THINKING Instruction in critical thinking aims at developing our students' ability to re-examine familiar ideas, to take a serious look at issues, and to make up their own minds. Critical thinking requires the willingness to confront opposing views or play off differing perspectives on major issues. The readings in this text invite students to participate in the dialogue, introducing them to the dialectic of pro and con.

EXPLORING TODAY'S ISSUES The book is organized around major themes in our changing social and cultural awareness. Successive chapters focus on

- exploring the diverse settings of American lives;
- reassessing the immigrant experience;
- rereading our contested history;
- hearing the unheard voices;
- relating gender and race to the search for identity;
- searching for role models;
- probing how language shapes our reality;
- thinking about living at risk in a divided world;
- watching the media mold social and cultural attitudes;

v

- seeking alternative cultural perspectives on the environment;
- confronting Utopian and dystopian visions of the future.

FOSTERING STUDENT PARTICIPATION The apparatus in *American Voices* is designed to promote students' involvement in their reading and to provoke classroom interaction. Headnotes go beyond routine biography to highlight an author's experience and commitment. **Thought Starters** focus students' attention and activate what they bring to a selection. The after-selection apparatus validates the range of reader response by asking questions that do not have a single correct answer. Questions labeled **The Responsive Reader** direct attention to key points. Questions and suggested topics labeled **Talking, Listening, Writing** encourage students to formulate their own personal reactions and to engage in a dialogue with their classmates, often in preparation for both informal and more structured writing assignments. **Projects** for group work encourage collaborative learning.

INTEGRATING READING AND WRITING A writing workshop follows each chapter, with guidelines and activities in each workshop focused on a major writing or thinking strategy. The emphasis is on the learning, thinking, and shaping that are at the heart of the writing process. The text provides a range of imaginative writing assignments, including journal writing, papers based on interviews, letters-to-the-editor, investigative papers, and collaborative writing projects. A rich sampling of student papers helps instructors bridge the gap between professional and student writing and encourages students to find their own voices, to trust their own authority as witnesses and thoughtful observers.

RECOGNIZING THE IMAGINATIVE DIMENSION In *American Voices*, imaginative literature enriches and dramatizes major themes. Typically, the essays in each chapter are followed by a poem and a short story or a one-act play. The book encourages students to think of expository and imaginative writing as parts of a continuum, with passion and imagination playing a role in both nonfiction and fiction, in both prose and poetry.

Special Features of *American Voices*

In preparing this book, we have learned from the successes and difficulties of the first wave of multicultural readers. Our text is designed to help teachers deal with familiar teaching issues that arise in courses with a multicultural theme and a critical-thinking emphasis:

MOVING FROM EXPERIENCE TO EXPOSITION We help teachers move from personal narrative toward more balanced representation of exposition and argument. We help teachers provide the bridge from personal-experience writing to more academic, more public forms of discourse.

GUARDING AGAINST STEREOTYPES Promoting multicultural awareness requires openness to complexity. *American Voices* counteracts the tendency to reduce multifaceted cultural traditions to well-intended ethnic or cultural stereotypes (for example, "How Asians think"; "How Latinos act").

VALIDATING THE STUDENT'S INDEPENDENT JUDGMENT On politically sensitive topics, we try to guard against presenting the textbook authors' views as the only approved or correct slant on an issue. Ultimately, the test of instruction in critical thinking is whether students are learning to think for themselves.

INTEGRATING THEMATIC AND RHETORICAL CONCERNS We have correlated issues–oriented readings with the concerns of a writing course. The writing workshop following each chapter focuses on an aspect of critical thinking or on a writing strategy for which the chapter provides models and materials. An alternative rhetorical table of contents enables instructors to shift from a thematic, issues-oriented emphasis to an emphasis on rhetorical strategies. The writing workshops are self-contained — they may be assigned as needed to suit the sequence of writing assignments in a particular course.

SUGGESTING A SYLLABUS We have designed a text that is easily compatible with prevailing course patterns. *American Voices* sets up a framework for a typical semester-length or quarter-length course. The text suggests a workable sequence of topics for reading, writing, and class discussion. At the same time, we have aimed at maximum flexibility: Chapters, selections, and workshops are self-contained and may be rearranged to suit the objectives or needs of different classes.

Acknowledgments

It has been a pleasure to work on this book with Tom Broadbent, Jim Bull, and Linda Toy, the dedicated professionals at Mayfield Publishing. We owe a special debt to colleagues in the writing movement who have made the core courses in the general education curriculum more responsive to the needs of today's students and of a society facing the challenges of an uncertain future. We have taken to heart excellent advice from our reviewers: Frances Jorjorian, West Los Angeles College; Molly Travis, Tulane University; and Mark Wiley, California State University, Long Beach. Above all, we have learned much from our students. Often, struggling against odds, they have maintained their faith in American education; their candid and intelligent questions have made us think; and their earnestness and idealism have been a marvelous antidote to burnout and apathy.

D. laGuardia
H. Guth

TO THE STUDENT

This book will ask you to read, think, and write about your identity as an individual and as part of a nation. What makes us the people we are? Where do we come from, and where are we going? The readings in this book will invite you to think about how your sense of self is shaped by sometimes conflicting influences: gender, ethnic or national origin, religious ties, racial identity, sexual preference, or social status. You will have a chance to read, talk, and write about what you have in common with others and what separates you from them. How real are the barriers that seem to divide you from others?

Traditionally, Americans have prided themselves on being independent individuals, making their own choices. We each have the right to be our "own person" — not just a cog in the machine or a social security number in the college computer. As Americans, we have the right to say no to government officials, elders in the family, peer groups at school or college, preachers, teachers, advocates of causes — whoever wants to tell us what we should think and do.

Nevertheless, the choices we make are shaped by the culture in which we live. We have the option of conforming to the traditional lifestyles of our families or our parts of the country. We can accept or reject our native or immigrant heritage. We each in our own way come to terms with our inherited religious faiths. A culture is a traditional way of living, of thinking and feeling. A culture, for better or for worse, provides traditional answers to many basic questions: How important am I as an individual compared with the survival of society? What are my obligations to family — to parents, to siblings, to relatives in need? What jobs are open to me — to someone of my family background, gender, or social status? How am I expected to love, court, marry, have children? Is it all right to divorce? to have an abortion? What is valued in my culture? Who is judged successful and why? Who is considered beautiful and why? What is considered sinful, offensive, taboo?

In these and similar matters, many people adopt the traditions of their families, their neighborhoods, or their churches. They swim in a traditional lifestyle the way fish swim in the sea. However, for many others, part of growing up is to face the need to move on and, if necessary, to make their own personal "declaration of independence." They find themselves reexamining their roots, their assumptions, their loyalties. They reach a point in their lives where they have to decide. Should they work in the family's hardware store or go to college? Should they leave the church of their parents? Should they marry one of "their own kind" or someone from a different background or religion? Should they enter a profession where people of their gender, skin color, or ethnic background are still a rarity?

American culture is not a single monolithic culture where everybody has to think, talk, and act the same. A commuter might start the day in a mainly Spanish-speaking Texas country town and drive through predominantly white suburbs to a predominantly black downtown, interspersed with areas where shop signs are mostly in Chinese or Vietnamese. America is a multicultural society, with many of its citizens now, as always in the past, bilingual. Many Americans have always used another language (or a downhome dialect) in their families or neighborhoods, in addition to the standard American English of school, city hall, and office.

Americans do not all have names like Harriman or Saltonstall. The *Mayflower*, bringing dissident English Puritans to New England, was a small boat. Many Americans are descended from exploited Irish peasants driven out of their country by famine, from orthodox Jews, from freed slaves, or from displaced persons — Ukrainians, Poles, Lithuanians — uprooted by Hitler's war machine. Many Americans are descended from the refugees of failed revolutions (Germany in 1848; Hungary in the first stirrings of revolt against Stalinism). Many (perhaps two million or more) trace their ancestry at least in part to Native Americans living on the fringes of the white society that drove them from their land. Many Americans have Mexican ancestors who lived in the Southwest before the gringos came or who came across the border in search of work. Other Americans are descended from Puerto Ricans, or from Chinese laborers who built the railroads of the West, or from Japanese families who were taken to relocation camps in the desert during World War II.

As our country approaches the twenty-first century, Americans face fateful questions: Are the forces that divide us becoming stronger? Will racial strife make us a nation divided into hostile armed camps? Are class distinctions — layers of wealth and privilege — resurfacing that many of the immigrants from traditional societies thought they had left behind? Or can we achieve a richer new synthesis? What would it take to achieve a true pluralism? Can we envision a pluralistic society that values the contributions of many different strands, with people of different ties and backgrounds respecting and learning from one another? This book will ask you to read, think, and write about questions such as these.

CONTENTS

ALTERNATIVE RHETORICAL TABLE OF CONTENTS

AMERICAN VOICES

INTRODUCTION

Reading, Writing, and Critical Thinking

What is this book supposed to do for you? This book should help you become a more alert reader, getting more out of your reading. It should help turn you into a better writer — putting your ideas effectively into words and making your voice heard. It should nudge you toward thinking more critically — to help you reexamine familiar ideas, take a serious look at serious issues, and make up your own mind.

Reading, writing, and thinking are intertwined. Much of what writers write about comes from their reading. True, good writers draw on what they have seen with their own eyes. They write with special conviction when they draw on what they have witnessed. However, to understand their society and the larger world, they do more than listen to the seven o'clock news — they read. They keep up with current events. They turn to experts who can explain past history and new trends. They rely on insiders to take them behind the scenes.

In fact, even the way writers look at firsthand experience is shaped by their reading. They know how to make the personal connection: They come to understand their own lives better in the light of what they read. Their reading may help them see the importance in their own lives of gender roles, communication problems in relationships, or the embattled traditional family. Their reading may help them see the influence on their own lives of the immigrant experience, racial stereotypes, or the aftermath of divorce.

At the same time, writers read with the writer's eye. They look at something they read as the work of a fellow writer. How did the author get the audience to pay attention? How did she or he dramatize the issue — bring the topic to life? How carefully or how aggressively does the writer state the main point? What backup is there — personal witnessing, facts or hard data, expert testimony, inside information? How does the piece as a whole take shape?

Finally, good readers are thinking readers — who pay close attention but by no means believe everything they read. Good writers are thinking writers — who investigate and weigh the pro and con before they take a stand. When you do an honest piece of writing, you are likely to learn as much as your readers will. You do not just learn to write; you write to learn. People who do not think for themselves are doomed to repeat all their lives what the party line or corporate policy tells them. They are like television newscasters, reading forever the cue cards other people have written for them.

PREVIEW: THE RESPONSIVE READER

How do you define an educated person? First of all, an educated person is someone who reads. Readers have a chance to go beyond the headline news to the why, the so what, and the what now. Readers have a chance to go beyond a candidate's endorsement of a strong and prosperous America to a study of the candidate's background, funding, voting record, political alliances, and personal convictions. When they have company policy or a party line dinned into their ears, readers can find out how the issue looks from the other side of the negotiating table, the other side of the gender gap, or the other side of the aisle. Readers have a chance to find out what is behind the buzzwords: *pro-life, multicultural, alternative lifestyles, global competition.*

How do you become a better reader? A good reader has developed two basic skills that are tightly interrelated — like being a caring cook and an appreciative taster and eater of food. First, a good reader is a *receptive* reader. Receptive readers read along carefully and attentively, taking in what the writer is trying to say. The ideal reader, in the words of the English novelist Virginia Woolf, is the author's "fellow-worker and accomplice." The ideal reader tries to make sense of what the author is trying to communicate — at times perhaps in a fumbling or inarticulate way.

Second, however, a good reader is at the same time a *responsive* reader. Responsive readers make what they read their own. They do not accept everything the writer says at face value or as gospel truth. As you read along, there should be a running commentary going on in your mind. What is new here, and what is familiar? What assumptions do you bring to this topic, and which seem to be shared by the writer? Where do *you* stand on this issue? What do *you* know that perhaps the writer did not know? What would *you* say if you were asked to testify on this topic?

Remember: Listen first before you start talking back. Before you argue with a writer, before you reject or endorse what a writer says, take in what the writer is trying to say. Be alert to how a piece of writing develops. As an alert reader, you need to keep questions like the following in mind:

- What is the key issue or key question? How is it introduced?
- Is there an early statement or an early hint of the author's answer to the central question? Is there a **thesis**? (Where is the author's message stated most directly or most eloquently?)
- Does the argument hinge on a key term like *culture, assimilation,* or

affirmative action? Where and how is it defined? (Are there key examples or test cases that clarify the term?)

- Where are we headed? Is there an early hint of an overall plan or organizing strategy? For instance, is an article going to contrast the then and now? Is it going to start with surface first impressions and then take a look behind the scenes? Is the writer going to look first at arguments pro and then at arguments con?

- How solid is the array of examples or evidence that the author presents to support a general point? Which are most striking or convincing? (Which are drawn from personal experience or observation?)

- Does the author bring in expert testimony, insider's information, or eyewitness reports? Where and how?

- Does the author recognize possible objections or counterarguments? How are they handled or disposed of?

- Does the conclusion merely summarize, or does it go a step beyond what the author said before?

Assume you are reading an essay by Richard Rodriguez entitled "Children of a Marriage." The comments after each of the following excerpts illustrate how an alert reader might interact with the text:

> What is culture?
> The immigrant shrugs. Latin American immigrants come to the United States with only the things they need in mind — not abstractions like culture. Money. They need dollars. They need food. Maybe they need to get out of the way of bullets.
> Most of us who concern ourselves with Hispanic-American culture, as painters, musicians, writers — or as sons and daughters — are the children of immigrants. We have grown up on this side of the border, in the land of Elvis Presley and Thomas Edison; our lives are prescribed by the mall, by the DMV and the Chinese restaurant.

(It might seem strange that immediately after asking the key question — "What is culture?" — the author would mention immigrants too concerned about the necessities of life to worry about the issue. However, this reference serves to put the question in *perspective*. It is the sons and daughters of immigrants who face the question of what is "Hispanic American culture." So especially do painters, musicians, and writers.)

> Hispanics fear losing ground in any negotiation with the American city. We come from an expansive, an intimate culture that has been judged second-rate by the United States of America. For reasons of pride, therefore, as much as of affection, we are reluctant to give up our past. Hispanics often express a fear of "losing" culture. Our fame in the United States has been our resistance to assimilation.

> The symbol of Hispanic culture has been the tongue of flame—
> Spanish. But the remarkable legacy Hispanics carry from Latin
> America is not language—an inflatable skin—but breath itself, ca-
> pacity of soul, an inclination to live. The genius of Latin America is
> the habit of synthesis.

(By now the writer, a Mexican American himself, has focused on what he
sees as the central difference between Americans of Spanish-speaking
descent and other minority groups. Hispanic or Latino Americans want
to "belong to America" without *giving up* their distinctive history and
their distinctive culture. This passage already introduces the author's answer to this dilemma. The key word is *synthesis*—the gift of creating a
richer blend from diverse materials. The reader will now expect some
striking or convincing examples of what the author means by synthesis.)

> What Latin America knows is that people create one another as they
> marry. In the music of Latin America you will hear the litany of
> bloodlines—the African drum, the German accordion, the cry from
> the minaret.
>   The United States stands as the opposing New World experiment.
> In North America the Indian and the European stood apace. Whereas
> Latin America was formed by a medieval Catholic dream of one
> world—of meltdown conversion—the United States was built up
> from Protestant individualism. The American melting pot washes
> away only embarassment; it is the necessary initiation into public life.
> The American faith is that our national strength derives from sepa-
> rateness, from "diversity." The glamour of the United States is a
> carnival promise: You can lose weight, get rich as Rockefeller, touch
> up your roots, get a divorce.

(As expected, this passage gives examples of how in Latin America strands
from different cultures have combined in a richer new blend, or synthesis.
The author reinforces this point by *contrasting* the Catholic Latin American
tradition, with its dream of one world, with the Protestant North American tradition of individualism—of striking out on your own, of leaving
your past behind.)

> Immigrants still come for the promise. But the United States
> wavers in its faith. As long as there was space enough, sky enough,
> as long as economic success validated individualism, loneliness was
> not too high a price to pay. (The cabin on the prairie or the Sony
> Walkman.)
>   As we near the end of the American century, two alternative cul-
> tures beckon the American imagination—both highly communal
> cultures—the Asian and the Latin American. The United States is a
> literal culture. Americans devour what we might otherwise fear to
> become. Sushi will make us corporate warriors. Combination Plate
> #3, smothered in mestizo gravy, will burn a hole in our hearts. . . .

Latin America offers communal riches: an undistressed leisure, a kitchen table, even a full sorrow.

(As the traditional American ideal of "everyone for himself" no longer works in our crowded interdependent world, Americans have a choice of two possible models for a more "communal" culture—the Asian and the Latin American. The author is now ready for his conclusion, in which he redefines the familiar term *assimilation* so that it will no longer stand for a one-way street. It will no longer mean the assimilation or takeover of one culture by another. It will stand for a mutual influencing and richer new blend. As the author says at the end of his essay: "Expect bastard themes, expect ironies, comic conclusions. For we live on this side of the border, where Kraft manufactures bricks of "Mexican style" Velveeta, and where Jack in the Box serves "Fajita Pita." . . . Expect marriage. We will change America even as we will be changed."

Remember: Reading an essay attentively does not commit you to endorsing the author's opinions. True, an articulate and persuasive writer is likely to make you reconsider your own views. (Sometimes, a piece of writing may sweep you along by the sheer force of its eloquence.) But ultimately, you have to make up your own mind.

Where do you stand on the issue of a multicultural America that will be a rich blend of different cultural strands? The commitments of Rodriguez' readers are likely to range over a whole spectrum of opinion. At one end of the spectrum might be people with Anglo-Saxon names who carry "English Only" buttons and who wish they could build electrified barbed wire fences along the Mexican border high enough to keep out any further migrants to the north. At the other end of the spectrum might be people who have decided that for minorities to try to join the "mainstream" is a mirage. The only hope is for people to band together with those of their own race or culture to advance their cause.

As a responsive reader, you will be asking yourself questions like the following:

- How does my own experience compare with that of the author?
- How much of this article is fact or hard data, and how much is one person's opinion?
- When the author cites authorities and insiders, do I accept them as authoritative sources? (Do I "take their word for it"?)
- Is the author's argument balanced or one-sided? Is there something to be said on the other side?
- How much of this piece of writing is special pleading? (Is this author beholden to a party line? Does the author sound like a spokesperson for a special interest?)
- How narrow or how broad is this writer's appeal? (Does the writer write off a whole group of people because of ethnicity, race, gender, or lifestyle?)

A good reader is not simply a passive reader, dutifully taking notes. Ideally, your reading will trigger your writing. You will be moved to write in order to talk back. You may want to clarify something that the writer obscured or glossed over. You may feel the need to correct a stereotype or a misrepresentation. You may want to pay tribute to someone the writer ignored. Whether or not you agree with it, a strong reading selection will make you think. It will stimulate you to think the matter through.

YOUR TURN: How Well Do You Read

Use the following (slightly shortened) essay by a well-known columnist to test your capacity for close, responsive reading. The questions that precede the text will walk you through the essay. They will ask you to pinpoint the ideas and the features that give the essay shape and direction. How well do you follow the author's trend of thought? How quick are you to take in key points and key examples?

Answer the following questions as you work your way through the essay. Note that major links have been italicized.

- What does the *title* make you expect?
- What is the common pattern in the examples Goodman uses for her *introduction*? What word provides the common thread? (What meanings or associations does it have for you?)
- How does the introduction lead up to the central idea, or *thesis*? How does the thesis serve as a preview of the basic contrast that shapes much of the essay?
- What kind of *support* does Goodman offer to clarify and develop the basic contrast? How does she use material from personal experience or observation? How does she go beyond it?
- Where does Goodman offer a *concession* — anticipating possible objections, admitting that there are exceptions to her claims?
- What does the *conclusion* add to the essay? Does it merely summarize, or does it go beyond what the author has already said? (How does the last sentence circle back to the title of the essay?)
- Can you relate Goodman's points in any way to your personal experience or observation? (Can you make a *personal connection*?)
- Do you agree with the author wholeheartedly, or do you want to take issue with any of her points? What would you say if you were asked to respond to her or talk back?

Ellen Goodman
We Are What We Do

I have a friend who is a member of the medical community. It does not say that, of course, on the stationery that bears her home address. This membership comes from her hospital work.

I have another friend who is a member of the computer community. This is a fairly new subdivision of our economy, and yet he finds his sense of place in it.

Other friends and acquaintances of mine are members of the academic community, or the business community, or the journalistic community. Though you cannot find these on any map, we know where we belong.

None of us, mind you, was born into these communities. Nor did we move into them, U-Hauling our possessions along with us. None has papers to prove we are card-carrying members of one such group or another. *Yet it seems that more and more of us are identified by work these days, rather than by street.*

In the past, most Americans lived in neighborhoods. We were members of precincts or parishes or school districts. My dictionary still defines community first of all in geographic terms, as "a body of people who live in one place."

But today fewer of us do our living in that one place; more of us just use it for sleeping. Now we call our towns "bedroom suburbs," and many of us, without small children as icebreakers, would have trouble naming all the people on our street.

It's not that we are more isolated today. It's that many of us have transferred a chunk of our friendships, a major portion of our everyday social lives, from home to office. As more of our neighbors work away from home, the work place becomes our neighborhood. . . .

We may be strangers at the supermarket that replaced the corner grocer, but we are known at the coffee shop in the lobby. We share with each other a cast of characters from the boss in the corner office to the crazy lady in Shipping, to the lovers in Marketing. It's not surprising that *when researchers ask Americans* what they like best about work, they say it is "the shmooze (chatter) factor." When they ask young mothers at home what they miss most about work, it is the people.

Not all the neighborhoods are empty, nor is every work place a friendly playground. Most of us have had mixed experiences in these environments. *Yet* as one woman told me recently, she knows more about the people she passes on the way to her desk than on her way around the block. . . .

It's not unlike the experience of our immigrant grandparents. Many who came to this country still identified themselves as members of the Italian community, the Irish community, the Polish community. They sought out and assumed connections with people from the old country. Many of us have updated that experience. We have replaced ethnic identity with professional identity, the way we replaced neighborhoods with the work place. . . .

I don't think that there is anything massively disruptive about this shifting sense of community. The continuing search for connection and shared enterprise is very human. *But I do feel uncomfortable with our shifting identity.* The balance has tipped and we seem increasingly dependent on work for our sense of self.

If our offices are our new neighborhoods, if our professional titles are our new ethnic tags, then how do we separate ourselves from our jobs? Self-worth isn't just something to measure in the marketplace. But in these new communities, it becomes harder and harder to tell who we are without saying what we do.

PREVIEW: THE PROCESS OF WRITING

When you read an article or a book, you see the finished product. Everything seems to be in place. Supporting evidence follows key assertions. Facts and figures march down the page. Key points are stated clearly or forcefully, so that the reader may feel: "Well said!" "This is a pleasure to read!"

However, studying such finished writing can be misleading. You should not get discouraged when structured writing does not surface on a blank sheet or on your computer screen ready-made. The real question for you as a writer is: How was this beautiful finished piece *produced*? Remember that the beautiful Greek vase you see on display in a museum was once a lump of clay. It went through a process of shaping and finishing that took time and care. (And the same artist who produced beautiful finished specimens probably botched a few.)

Substantial, worthwhile writing — writing worth reading — similarly goes through a process. It goes through stages of focusing, gathering, shaping, revising, and final editing. Experienced writers make allowance for trial and error, for promising leads that do not work out, and for second thoughts or last-minute adjustments. Major stages in the writing process overlap — for instance, we start revising or working in second thoughts while still hunting for further material. Besides, different writers have their own ways of picking a subject, working up materials, and pulling them into shape.

However, the following stages of the process represent dimensions to which productive writers do justice in one way or another:

TRIGGERING What makes writers write? What triggers writing — what brings it on? On the most basic level, we may write because of an immediate practical need. We write a résumé because we need a job. We write to a judge or a planning commission to head off a decision that would hurt. But such practical writing easily shades over into other kinds. A woman who writes to complain about job discrimination is likely to find herself talking not just about her own case but about other cases as well. She will find herself writing about a topic that matters to more than one person.

Writers write because they have something to say to other people. Here are some of the motives that may trigger purposeful writing:

- *Writers write to explain.* When they have studied a complicated subject, they want to share the answers they have found with a larger audience. They write about acid rain, the ozone layer, global warming, desertification in Africa, youth gangs in Los Angeles, the causes of homelessness, or our overcrowded jails. They turn to their readers to say: "Listen! It's important! I want to explain it to you."

▪ *Writers write to talk back.* Suppose the governor of the state identifies a major problem of American education: Teachers care only about fat paychecks. A language arts teacher who was hired at a salary lower than the garbage collector's or the bus driver's may feel moved to pen his or her thoughts on this topic. A writing teacher who spends two or three hours each day commuting between two low-paying jobs may feel moved to write on the subject.

▪ *Writers write to set the record straight.* They read about how Southern whites supposedly feel about Southern blacks, or about how American males allegedly feel about women, and they find themselves saying: "That's not the way it is! I know something about this from firsthand experience! Let me set you straight."

▪ *Writers write to air grievances.* They protest against injustice; they appeal to their readers' sense of fairness. They write to promote the good cause. They write to register their solidarity with the exploited or the oppressed.

▪ *Writers write to commemorate.* They do not want the Japanese Americans in the internment camps, or the Vietnamese boat people, or the Lithuanians deported to Siberia to be forgotten.

Whatever the purpose, good writing is done with conviction. If your paper sounds like a dutiful exercise—something you were reluctant to write—your readers will be twice as reluctant to read it. No one wants to read writing that the author did not want to write—any more than people want to eat in a restaurant where the chef hates to cook. Discover the range of purposes that activate real writing. Discover the rewards of saying something that you can stand up for or that you honestly believe.

GATHERING To write an authentic, convincing paper, you have to immerse yourself in the subject. You may start by calling up from the memory bank of past experience the images, events, buzzwords, and arguments that cluster around your topic. You may follow up by reading up on it, discussing it with friends and roommates, or interviewing people who might have the inside story. Your finished paper should show that you are an attentive reader, an alert listener, a scribbler of notes, a collector of newspaper clippings, and a patron of the photocopy machine.

Develop the habit of taking notes. (According to temperament, these might range from rough jottings on scratch paper to neatly filed and inventoried background material.) Here are some **prewriting** techniques that can help you work up a rich fund of material for a paper:

▪ **Brainstorming** roams freely over a topic, dredging up any memories, images, events, or associations that might prove useful. Exploring the ideas related to the word *macho,* for instance, you jot down anything that the word brings to mind. You write quickly and freely, allowing one idea to lead to another. There will be time later to sort out these preliminary jottings — to see how they add up, to see what goes with what. Right now, the idea is to mobilize everything you already know, to bring to the surface anything you remember.

The following result of a brainstorming exercise has already brought together much promising material for a paper:

Macho: Big, muscular, unfeeling, rough—harsh, moves to kill. (Sylvester Stallone: I hate what he promotes.) Negative impression. Hard craggy faces with mean eyes that bore holes in you.

Men who have to prove themselves through acts of violence. The man who is disconnected from his feelings, insensitive to women's needs—cannot express himself in a feeling manner.

The word seems to have negative connotations for me because I work part-time in a bar. I am forever seeing these perfectly tanned types who come on to a woman. As a child, macho meant a strong male type who would take care of me—paternal, warmth in eyes. John Wayne: gruff, yet you feel secure knowing someone like this was around.

Crude, huge—the body, not the heart—tendency to violence always seems close to the surface. Looks are very important. Craggy face. Bloodshed excites them. Arnold Schwarzenegger muscles, gross.

Tend to dominate in relationships—desire for control. "Me Tarzan—you Jane."

As you sort out this preliminary collection of material, a number of major points for a paper may come into focus: (1) Macho is much a matter of external appearance — the tough, craggy, mean look. (2) However, what is behind the swaggering exterior of the macho male is the need to prove himself — the fear of being thought weak or a "sissy." (3) A major downside is that the macho proves what a tough he-man he is by brutal destructive violence. (4) A second major downside is that the macho's toughness translates into insensitivity toward women and the need to be the dominant, bullying partner in a relationship. (5) At the same time, the writer is already groping for an alternative warmer and more paternal model of manliness. Perhaps a man could be manly and gruff but caring, like a character played by John Wayne.

• **Clustering** is a different method of letting your mind bring to the surface a rich sampling of memories and associations. Instead of letting the items that come to mind march down the page, clustering makes them branch out from a central core. You pursue different chains of association started by a key word or stimulus word. More so than in brainstorming, a pattern takes shape. You begin to see connections; different items begin to fall into place. Here is a simple sample cluster from Gabriele Rico's *Writing the Natural Way:*

Here is writing based on this cluster, by a very young person who had had her share of trouble:

Flame

Flame is how I feel right now—so bitter I can taste it. I can't tell you how upset and fed up with life I am. I feel something is tearing up inside me. If I look back on the reasons, I guess it's all my own fault. People light their own fires.

Here is a more detailed cluster exploring the associations of the word *tradition*. It is followed by a write-up of the material generated by the cluster:

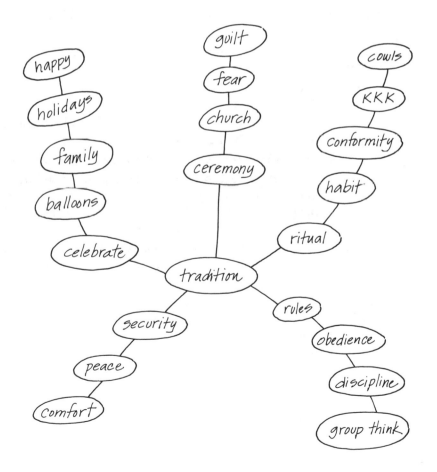

Tradition to many of us means first of all nostalgic memories of Christmas or Easter or Passover, happy hours spent with family and friends, birthday celebrations with balloons and ice cream cake and candles. In the traditional family, there is a sense of security — of knowing what to do, of relying on the tried and true. However, we also feel the weight of tradition — feeling guilty about not going to mass, feeling fear of retribution for our sins and backslidings. The inherent danger in tradition is the reliance on groupthink. Blind obedience to traditional rules and regulations can lead to unquestioned acceptance of cruel or idiotic practices. When we look at the dual nature of tradition, we see interlocking elements that can suddenly cover the face of love with a cowl of enmity and violence.

▪ **Discovery frames** are sets of questions that can guide you in exploring a topic systematically. For instance, you may be working toward a definition of feminism. This is a large umbrella term, covering many people and initiatives. It has a history. It has been the subject of debate and attack. What kind of tentative materials could you fill in under each of the following tentative headings?

1. What popular associations cluster around the term? What stereotypes does it bring to mind?

2. What is the history of feminism? What have been some outstanding leaders, role models, and key events?

3. How is the word related to similar terms — *emancipation, women's liberation, the women's movement*?

4. What is current media coverage of the movement? What images of women are projected in the news, in movies, in advertising?

5. What role have feminist concerns played in your own experience?

6. What seems to be the core meaning? What is the common thread in your various examples?

7. What does the future hold?

SHAPING How does a writer turn a rich collection of unsorted material into a coherent paper? Successful writers again and again employ four basic organizing strategies:

▪ *Bring a limited topic or a central issue into focus.* A focused paper does not roam over a variety of topics, allowing the writer to voice opinions about this and that. Instead, an effective paper zeroes in on an issue or a limited area and does it justice.

▪ *Push toward a central idea or thesis.* Ask: What is my paper as a whole going to say? What is the paper as a whole going to prove? After exploring the topic, looking at the evidence, reading and talking about the issue, you need to move toward a summing up. What conclusion or conclusions do your findings point to? What is going to be your main point? What is going to be your **thesis** — your central idea, your unifying overarching thought?

Try summing up the central message of your paper in a single sentence that will serve as your thesis statement. (Then use the next few sentences to spell out the full meaning of what you claim or assert.)

> THESIS: Vocational education, many experts claim, is forever trying to catch up with the real world. The educational system is preparing people for jobs that have already been taken by robots. . . .

> THESIS: American business is "downsizing," causing a rapid decline in employee loyalty. Executives improve a company's balance sheet by slashing payrolls, leaving insecure workers alienated from a company and a system that has no regard for their interests. . . .

> THESIS: Faulty communication torpedoes relationships. The authors of several recent bestsellers claim it's not that people dislike each other or develop diverging interests. It's simpler than that: They misunderstand or misread what the other person is saying. . . .

The traditional standard model for a short paper is **thesis-and-support**. Early in the paper, you stake out a claim. You make an assertion. Then you go on to support it. You follow it up with convincing backup material: examples, evidence, statistics, expert testimony, insiders' insights, firsthand personal experience.

▪ *Work out a meaningful overall plan.* If you are to take your readers with you, they need to feel that you have a planned itinerary. How are you going to lay out your material? What is your program? Your readers need to feel that you know where you are headed — and they appreciate early hints of what lies ahead. Often an effective thesis statement already hints at the overall plan:

> THESIS: Race relations in this country have moved from legally sanctioned discrimination, through the legal outlawing of discrimination, to the struggle to change deeply ingrained personal attitudes about race.

(The reader will expect that a major section of the paper will be devoted to each of these three stages.)

Each paper is different, but some tried-and-true organizing strategies prove useful again and again. Perhaps you are going to discuss familiar, reassuring examples first. Then perhaps you are going to tackle examples that are more controversial. (Writers often go from **simple to complex**, leading up by easy steps to the difficult parts.) Or perhaps you will organize your paper around a **contrast** of then and now. (What did your parents' generation expect of marriage? What do people expect of marriage now?)

In an early stage of your writing project, start jotting down a scratch outline or **working outline**. A working outline helps you visualize your tentative plan. It helps you become aware of any snags or awkward back-trackings. By definition a working outline is subject to revision.

▪ *Line up your supporting material.* Support any points you make with key examples, relevant evidence, material from interviews, quotable quotes. (As people advise proposal writers, "Have all your ducks in a row.")

REVISING When you finish the first run-through of a paper, you are entitled to a sigh of relief. However, you also need to remind yourself: This is a first draft. Whenever possible, allow a day or more before you go back to an early draft for rereading and revision. Genuine revision goes beyond surface corrections — correcting misspelled words or names, putting in missing commas. It involves some real rethinking. When you come back to a paper after a time, you are likely to see missing links, exaggerated claims, or detours and backtrackings.

Each paper is different, and each paper has its own strengths and weaknesses. Even so, teachers, reviewers, and editors often find themselves repeating familiar advice. Many of your papers will profit from your considering guidelines like the following:

▪ *Sharpen your focus.* An early draft often seems to take up several related issues in turn, without giving its readers a clear sense of where the paper is headed. Try to bring a central issue or key question clearly into focus. Ask yourself: What is the basic problem, and what are the two or three possible answers? What is the striking contrast or contradiction that your paper will try to resolve? Look at the before-and-after versions of title and introduction of a paper on rape. In revising the beginning of the paper, what did the writer do to sharpen its focus? (What sentence in the revised version can serve as a central thesis? What kind of program or agenda is the revised version setting up for the rest of the paper?)

BLURRED: Rape: An Examination of Data

    In recent years, the subject of rape has become more and more frequently discussed and analyzed. A growing number of women seem to believe that rape is statistically on the rise. Men often seem to view claims of vastly increased occurrence of rape with skepticism, finding themselves cast in the position of having to defend themselves against often-quoted statistics that tag them as dangerous to women. Conversely, women often seem to view a vast portion of the male population with suspicion and fear.

FOCUSED: Rape: A Growing Division Between the Sexes?

Men and women increasingly seem to react differently to the subject of rape. Women seem to view the incidence of rape as growing at a fearful rate. They seem to regard a large portion if not a majority of the male population with fear and suspicion. Men, on the other hand, often seem to view the current spate of statistics and reports with skepticism, suspecting that the media are sensationalizing the topic. They often find themselves in the position of having to defend themselves against the image of the male as predatory and dangerous toward women.

▪ *Review your organizing strategy.* Are you going in a clear enough sequence from the simpler to the more difficult or from problem to solution? Are you taking up a controversial point too early — before you have established yourself as an authority on the subject? Are you starting on your rebuttal of a new theory before you have taken time to explain what it is?

▪ *Build up and develop your examples.* In the first-draft stage, student writing often stays on a very general level. Try to bring a general point to life by presenting a striking, dramatic example. Go from the general to the specific — and back again. How do your reactions differ for the before-and-after versions of the following passage?

GENERAL: In patriarchal societies, men are in a position of power where women are often powerless to confront an accuser. It is ironic that rape, a crime that often enables women to identify their attackers, at the same time often leaves them in a position that forces them to keep silent and not seek remedy. Many women keep their secret to themselves, afraid that they will not be believed.

SPECIFIC: It is ironic that rape, a crime that often enables women to identify the attacker, often leaves them in a position that forces them to keep silent and not seek remedy. About five years ago, one of my best friends and I were pulling into a gas station; standing at another pump was a medium built, thirtyish middle-class male. "Back up and get out of here. That man raped me," my friend blurted out. I was outraged. I wanted to stop the car, get out, confront him, spit on him, get his name into the paper, let everyone know. But all she wanted to do was hide, leave, deny, fade away, let go. I could feel her fear, her shame at the memory, her desire to put it behind her although it was glaring her in the face.

I was shocked, amazed, and saddened that not even I knew. She said that almost no one else did — a boyfriend at the time, the police. She was raped by an acquaintance; the gas station customer was a classmate. The police had discouraged her from pressing charges. The circumstances made a conviction too precarious to attempt. She asked me not to tell anyone.

▪ *Add a striking firsthand quote.* Issues come to life when we hear the authentic voices of the people involved.

> SECOND-HAND: The headline in USA Today read "Rape Victim Speaks Out on 20/20." After emotional weeks in the courtroom, the victim in a celebrity rape trial told her side of the story.
>
> FIRSTHAND QUOTATION: The headline in USA Today read, "Rape Victim Speaks Out on 20/20." After emotional weeks in the courtroom, the victim in a celebrity rape trial was ready to be heard—ready to tell the world her story. "People have judged me without knowing all the facts, without knowing me as a person. I want to clear it up," she said in the interview. Why is this woman being judged? Why does she have to "clear" things up?

▪ *Show that you have listened to the other side.* When accusations become too sweeping, they may not merely alienate people who feel accused and who are being put on the defensive. They may also alienate fair-minded readers who try to see the other side. Do you think the following revision would strengthen or weaken a paper on sexual harassment?

> ONE-SIDED: Men use their traditional positions of power to exploit vulnerable women in the workplace. Men have been conditioned to consider women fair game.
>
> BALANCED: Some of the men I talked to seemed genuinely frustrated about changing definitions of sexual harassment. According to them, if the woman likes the man, advances are welcome; otherwise, the advances are unwelcome and are defined as sexual harassment. No wonder that men are confused about the role of their gender in courtship situations.

EDITING Final editing is your chance to take care of misspellings, awkwardly punctuated or garbled sentences, and confused or misused words. Make sure you have not misspelled the "unforgivables": *receive, definite, believe, similar, separate, used to, a lot* (two words). Save yourself grief by changing any *it's* to *it is* (if that is what you mean) or to *its* if that is what it should be (the band and *its* vocalist). Look for sentence fragments that should be linked to a preceding sentence from which they have been split off *(To fight disease. Living in the city. Which proved untrue.).* Use the semicolon as your handbook instructs you *(Speed kills; caution saves lives.).* Remember that text on a computer screen or printout looks deceptively neat and finished. Proofread carefully, checking your text line by line and word by word.

YOUR TURN: Responding to Peer Review

How do you react to comments on your writing? (Do they make you feel defensive or hostile?) Remember that **feedback** is an important

stage of the writing process. Much business writing is reworked in response to comments from coworkers, superiors, or consultants. Much
professional writing is revised in response to criticism from editors or
reviewers. Many writing classes today adopt a workshop format, with
students rewriting early drafts in response to comments from instructors
and peers.

Feedback can be painful. Critical readers may concentrate on the
negatives: what is missing, what is misleading, or what is ill-advised.
Even so, feedback helps make a writer audience-conscious. Writers have
to learn to ask themselves: "This seems obvious to me, but will it be
obvious to other people?" "This is the way I use this term — but would it
mean the same thing to someone else?" "People who agree with me will
like this part — but will it change the minds of others?"

When you participate in **peer review** (oral or written) in class, try
to combine the two basic functions of a good editor: First, recognize and
reinforce what a writer does well. Second, offer constructive suggestions
for improving what is weak or has gone wrong. Pay attention to larger
questions of purpose, audience, and organization as well as to spelling and
punctuation. You might use the following questions as a guide for your
participation in peer review:

1. What is the writer trying to do?

2. Does the writer bring a limited topic into focus? How does the
    writer lead up to the key issue or the key point?

3. How well does the writer bring the topic or the issue to life?
    How real does it become for the reader?

4. Is there a central idea, or thesis? (If not, should there be?) Is the
    thesis stated clearly or forcefully enough?

5. Is there a preview or an overview of the overall plan? Do readers
    get a sense of the writer's strategy? Does the plan seem to work?

6. How solid is the writer's followup or backup of major points?
    What is the quality of examples, evidence, or support from au-
    thorities? Which examples are strong? Which are weak?

7. Are there effective transitions — does the writer take the reader
    along from point to point? Are turning points or major stages in
    the argument signaled clearly enough?

8. What is confusing, and what is especially clear? What words
    seem vague? What sentences seem muddy?

9. What problems are there with spelling or punctuation?

10. Who might be the ideal reader for this paper? Who is ignored or
    left out?

11. Where do you agree? Where do you disagree, and why?

12. What would you say or write if you had a chance to respond to the writer?

Prepare a peer review of the following paper, and compare your responses with those of others.

No Heroes

In todays society young people find few worthy objects for loyalty or outlets for devotion. They join groups ranging from neighborhood gangs to Neo-nazi groups because they need something to be loyal to or to believe in. To better understand this assessment we must look at the past and try to determine what worthy objects used to be available for young people to pledge their support.

The traditional symbols for hero worship fall into three categories: political, military, and sports figures. These seem to reflect well the more popular forms of hero worship in our society—unless we count such idols as rock musicians, movie stars, or outlaws (Jesse James, Bonnie and Clyde).

In the past young adults had political figures to look up to and respect. Respect is the important word here. Today the offices and titles are still there, but much of the dignity attached to them has been lost. Political leaders like Franklin Roosevelt and Harry Truman were admired by millions. John Kennedy still lives on in people's memories as a symbol of idealism and a new Camelot. Nixon ("I am not a crook") did much to cheapen the office of the president with the Watergate scandal. Recently we have had the Iran-Contra scandal or the Congressional scandal with members of Congress routinely overdrawing their bank accounts. Politician has become a dirty word for many voters.

The decline in loyalty towards the military is due largely to unpopular wars like those fought in Korea and Vietnam. We were no longer rallying around the flag as we had done for World War I and World War II. People blamed the Cold War for drawing funds away from domestic programs into a huge arms buildup. Many people object to money spent on foreign aid. Why should we help others when our own country has unsolved problems?

It has also become increasingly difficult to hero-worship athletes in todays society. In baseball, we no longer have athletes like Babe Ruth, Lou Gehrig, Willie Mays, Stan Musial, or Mickey Mantle. Players who played the game with respect for the sport and a love of simply playing. Today we have players who hold out for million-dollar salaries with no concern for the fans. We have players who are in trouble with the law and perform below the standards their million-dollar contracts seem to call for.

With all these problems in our society today, one can understand why young people seach for new outlets for their loyalties. Instead of Little League baseball, they get involved in neighborhood gangs. They make heroes of rap singers who glorify violence against women. Young people have lost faith in the values of the establishment and are finding it hard to find worthy alternatives.

PREVIEW: WRITING AND CRITICAL THINKING

What is the relationship between writing and thinking? What kind of thinking helps give shape to your writing? When readers tell you that you "didn't think," what do they mean? How can you make your writing more thoughtful and convincing?

Many observers of the way our minds work are like Mr. Spock, in the original *Star Trek*; they marvel at the failure of human beings to be logical. What advice would they give to promote critical thinking — thinking that questions stale familiar ideas and traditional think schemes? How would they foster the kind of thinking that encourages investigation and discovery? How would they promote thinking that generates new ideas for new situations?

Efforts to promote critical thinking tend to adopt a two-prong strategy. One is to have people develop an inquiring attitude and practice productive procedures for thinking straight. For instance, what are productive **problem-solving** strategies? The problem might be how to dispose of a city's garbage at a time when people do not want garbage dumps or landfills or incinerators in their neighborhoods. How do we move from problem to solution? One productive procedure is to brainstorm possible solutions, however farfetched. (Maybe we could load the garbage on a train and take it to the desert.) Then, by ourselves or in a group, we look at the various options. We start to put aside those that for one reason or another seem wrong. Various alternatives might prove too expensive or too unpopular. They might be too experimental, or they may have been tried before and failed. By a process of elimination, we might arrive at the option that would solve the problem, at least for a time.

The second prong for promoting critical thinking is to make people wary of familiar fallacies — familiar kinds of shortcut thinking. Sometimes these are the product of our natural tendency to go for the simple answer or the quick fix. Sometimes they are the result of our being manipulated. How are our reactions being steered when the cutting down of trees is described as "harvesting"? The word *harvest* might lead us to believe that in a few years the trees will grow again. They would provide another crop — although, in the case of redwood trees, the last "crop" took between two hundred and eight hundred years to grow.

STRATEGIES FOR THINKING How can we study and practice effective thinking strategies? Our thoughts do not stand still so that we could easily chart or schematize them. Our thinking proceeds at lightning speed. Ideas come to us in a flash. Sometimes, when we are stymied, it seems the mind was "cooking" while we were thinking about something else. Suddenly we hit upon a solution to a problem or see a missing link. Nevertheless, we can chart some basic thinking strategies that we see at work again and again when people face a problem or try to think through a subject.

Several major think schemes provide models for the kind of reasoning that leads to sound conclusions. Often the writer presents the conclusions first and then shows the reasoning that led up to them. But sometimes the writer takes the readers along on an intellectual journey, helping them reach the same conclusions as the writer.

MODEL 1 The **inductive** model goes from the specific to the general. It is a discovery mode, starting from careful observation and finding the common pattern, the connecting thread. A good writer is first of all a faithful observer, who generalizes cautiously on the basis of authentic observation or patient data-gathering. The inductive model puts input first: We do not launch unsupported opinions but *earn* the right to have an opinion. Before we generalize, we take a close look at our experience, our observation, our data.

Some powerful writing follows the inductive model. James Baldwin, in his classic essay, "Notes of a Native Son," takes us on a journey of discovery to make us see the workings of racial discrimination in World War II New Jersey. Baldwin first re-creates his experiences with hallucinatory intensity:

he is refused service at a place called "The American Diner"
the waitress in a fancy restaurant tells him, almost apologetically, "We
  don't serve Negroes here"
in an outburst of uncontrollable rage he hurls a water pitcher at the
  waitress
he is chased from the restaurant by a murderous mob
a friend misdirects the pursuers and saves Baldwin's life
he goes over the experience again and again in his mind ("the way
  one relives an automobile accident after it has happened and one
  finds oneself alone and safe")

He then, after pondering the experience, draws his conclusion:

"I could not get over two facts, both equally difficult for the imagination to grasp, and one was that I could have been murdered. But the other was that I had been ready to commit murder."

The strength of the inductive model is that it stays close to firsthand experience or close to the facts. It shows a respect for the readers, who are invited to look for themselves, to reach their own conclusions. A standard application of the inductive pattern is to lay several related incidents end to end to show the common pattern. This is how a typical inductive paper might proceed:

A Tale of Three Cities

Incident 1: One of the major parties holds its national convention in a big city. The city authorities busily clean up the litter. They pick up the homeless and put them in shelters.

Incident 2: The other major party holds its convention in a big city.
The city authorities spruce up the city. Filth is picked up; beggars and
homeless people are made to move on or are moved to temporary shelters.
Incident 3: An important foreign visitor — the Pope, the Queen of
England — arrives. The city authorities spruce up the city; they make
beggars and the homeless less visible, as above.

CONCLUSION: We treat the homeless not as fellow human beings but as
an embarrassment; we hide them for appearances' sake.

MODEL 2 The **deductive** model starts with a general principle
and applies it to a specific situation. (This model reverses the itinerary of
the inductive model.) When we argue from principle, we start from basic
assumptions and apply them to specific cases. If we grant that life starts at
conception, various conclusions concerning abortion and the rights of the
unborn follow. If we start from a woman's right to make decisions concerning her own body, other very different conclusions will be the logical
result.

Writers who argue from principle appeal to shared values. Much
depends on the reader's accepting the basic assumptions, or **premises**. On
the topic of capital punishment, for instance, accepting premises like the
following is likely to make you agree with a writer rejecting the death
penalty:

PREMISE 1: The poor must have the equal protection of the law
(but they cannot afford the best, expensive legal help and therefore
are much more likely to receive the death penalty than the rich).

PREMISE 2: Minorities deserve equal treatment before the law (but
the death penalty is applied to them much more often than to
whites).

PREMISE 3: People innocently convicted must have a chance to be
rehabilitated (but the mistake cannot be rectified if the people are
dead).

Deductive arguments proceed from common base. Underlying
much argument and persuasion is a question on the model of "Don't you
agree that . . . ?"

MODEL 3 The play of **pro and con** makes us explore both sides
of an issue. We often feel that to arrive at a balanced conclusion we have to
line up arguments in favor and arguments against. We can then weigh
their respective merits. Often a convincing piece of writing moves from
point to counterpoint and from there to a reasonable conclusion. The play
of pro and con allows us to weigh the evidence and balance conflicting
claims. It is a safeguard against narrow, one-sided views; it keeps us from
jumping to conclusions.

The playing off of conflicting ideas, of point and counterpoint, is
the method of **dialectic**. The classic scheme for a dialectic argument is

thesis (first major point) — *antithesis* (counterpoint) — *synthesis* (a richer balanced view taking both sides into account).

The following might be a student writer's rough notes for a pro-and-con paper:

TOPIC: Should motorcycle riders have to wear safety helmets?

    CON — arguments against helmets

    freedom of the open road, sense of liberation, free spirits

    outdoor types: exhilaration of being exposed to the elements vs. isolation in excessively cushioned metal cage

    cost and inconvenience in dragging/storing the clumsy helmets

    principle of choice vs. state interference

    PRO — arguments in favor of helmets

    severe nature of injuries, often more ghastly than in car accidents

    strain on hospitals, rehabilitation services, horrendous cost to community

    trauma to the other motorist (who knows he/she is implicated in the death or maiming of another human being)

CONCLUSION: need to protect the public and fellow motorists should overrule the individual's desire for freedom

The pro-and-con approach is especially appropriate to thorny, hotly debated issues: abortion, affirmative action, English only, bilingual education, censorship. The commitment to listen to the other side counteracts our tendency to raise our voices and shout people down. The willingness to reconsider, to take a second look, is a prerequisite of rational discussion.

LOGIC AND LOGICAL FALLACIES Students of logic have paid much attention to how our minds work when at their best. However, they have also taken careful inventory of how logical arguments go wrong. They warn us against shortcut thinking, the way road signs warn us of hazards ahead in the road. For instance, a sound **syllogism** is a formal deductive argument that moves from a first premise through a second premise to a valid conclusion. The first premise is the more general or more inclusive one (major premise): "All human beings are mortal." The second premise is the more limited or specific one (minor premise): "Socrates is a human being." The justified logical conclusion is: "Socrates is mortal."

You can chart a formal syllogism like this:

FIRST PREMISE: Women are not eligible to join the Troglodyte Club.

SECOND PREMISE: Luisa is a woman.

CONCLUSION: Therefore, Luisa is not eligible to join the Troglodyte Club.

A **faulty syllogism** results when we try to get more out of our premises than they warrant:

```
FIRST PREMISE:  All human beings are mortal.
SECOND PREMISE:  My dog is mortal.
CONCLUSION:  Therefore, my dog is a human being.
```

Here, we are misreading the first premise. It is not exclusive; it does not say: "All human beings *and no other kinds of living beings* are mortal." We should really read it to mean: "All human beings (and perhaps also many other beings) are mortal." Here is a common faulty syllogism:

```
FIRST PREMISE:  All Marxists quote Marx.
SECOND PREMISE:  Professor Guth quotes Marx.
CONCLUSION:  Therefore, Professor Guth is a Marxist.
              (What is wrong here?)
```

Advocates of straight thinking warn us to avoid other similar pitfalls. Some of these are familiar **logical fallacies** — predictable ways of reaching the wrong conclusion. Others are familiar ploys that work with the unwary.

hasty generalization After knowing a few Vietnamese students, we don't really have the right to generalize about "how Asians think." (Filipino, Japanese, Chinese, and Vietnamese students might think alike in some ways, but it would be a formidable task to pinpoint the similarities and test our conclusions.) Similarly, we should not make sweeping generalizations about "what the American people want." Elections are designed to provide a rough measure of what people want, and often it is different from what we had hoped for. (And often these elections are decided by a few percentage points.)

unrepresentative sample We cannot determine student sentiment on current issues by talking only to members of fraternities and sororities. We need to listen as well to coop dwellers, people living on their own close to the campus, and commuters.

post-hoc fallacy *Post hoc* is short for the Latin for "after this, therefore because of this." "First this and then that" does not always mean cause and effect. If it rained after the rainmaker performed a ceremony, it might have rained anyway without his help. If a hurricane strikes after a nuclear test, there might or might not be a causal connection.

false analogy Is our nation like a lifeboat — with only so many spaces? Would it be swamped if we allowed an unlimited number of the people floundering in the water to climb aboard? It is true that no nation has unlimited resources, and absorbing too many immigrants might "swamp" cities and institutions. However, sooner or later the analogy breaks down. Immigrants have often developed new resources and taken new initiatives (which newcomers to a lifeboat could not do). And as a nation, we depend on people *outside* the lifeboat for resources and for trade that brings employment.

rationalization When we rationalize, we go for creditable explanations. When something goes wrong, we look for explanations that sound reasonable and at the same time clear us of blame. When you do poorly in a class with a teacher of a different gender or ethnicity, the reason may well be that the teacher is prejudiced against your kind. But the reason may also be that the subject is difficult or that you did not have enough time to study. When you become wary of rationalization, you try to distinguish between a legitimate grievance and an excuse.

slanting Court procedures require prosecutors and defense attorneys to share evidence favoring the other side. The wary reader knows that interested parties tend to slant the data or suppress damaging evidence. They exaggerate everything that favors their cause and simply leave out complicating or contrary testimony. Skeptical readers have learned to ask: Who on this issue has an axe to grind? Who has an interest in tampering with the evidence or cooking the books?

bandwagon Advertisers and public relations experts try to sway us by letting us know that "everybody does it" or "everyone thinks so." What is fashionable or trendy carries people along when it comes to selling ideas as well as shoes.

smokescreen Propagandists know how to hide damaging or disturbing information behind a verbal smokescreen. "Collateral damage" stands for civilians killed, maimed, and bombed out in attacks officially aimed at military targets. "Ethnic cleansing" stands for the practice of loading women, old men, and children into cattle cars after burning down their homes.

YOUR TURN: Assessing Arguments

How do you react to the following arguments? Which do you think are sound? Where would you take issue with the speaker or writer — and on what grounds?

1. Professor Minkin is from a middle-class background. She can't be expected to sympathize with the poor.

2. Where there is smoke, there is fire. There would not be charges of corruption against the mayor if he were totally innocent.

3. Only people born in the U.S. can be elected President. Henry Kissinger was born in Germany. He cannot become President of the United States.

4. In some state universities, tuition fees have gone up by as much as forty percent in the last few years. What we witness here is a concerted attempt to deprive minority students of an education.

5. Just about everyone agrees that the current welfare system perpetuates the cycle of dependency. We need to get able-bodied adults off the welfare rolls and stop rewarding welfare mothers for having additional children.

6. Students work best in a relaxed, supportive atmosphere. Tests generate anxiety and lead to cramming and abuse of coffee, pills, and other stimulants. Therefore, tests work against true learning.

7. Newspapers have been piling up on the driveway across the street. It looks as if the people went away on vacation. Or perhaps someone is sick and does not come out to pick up the papers.

8. The police found empty beer cans in the back of the overturned car. The driver must have been drinking.

9. In the local high schools, the dropout rates for minority students are at an all-time high. A recent study showed that fewer black or Hispanic candidates are about to receive advanced degrees than two or three years ago. At prestige institutions like the Harvard Law School, minority representation has hardly budged in recent years. America's minorities are not winning the race for equal educational opportunity.

10. Two of my coworkers at the chemical factory died of lung cancer. The safety precautions at the plant are totally inadequate.

WRITING
WORKSHOP

Starting a Journal

To help make writing a habit, start a journal or writer's log. Write in your journal two or three times a week, writing entries ranging from half a single-spaced page to a page or more. Your first entries might be about yourself — your roots, your family background, your memories (happy or unhappy) of school, or your major interests. Gradually, use your journal to record a running commentary on what you observe, view, and read. Write about incidents that make you think. Write about people who matter to you and about news stories that make you angry or glad. Record conversations that touched a nerve. Write about visits to the theater or to a museum.

In your journal, you will be writing spontaneously and informally. Your instructor may ask to read all or a sampling of it — but mainly as an interested reader, without a red pencil in hand. You may share entries with your classmates. You will be able to be somewhat more candid or unguarded than in formal papers, putting down first impressions as well as second thoughts, puzzling questions as well as tentative answers.

In addition to giving you practice in verbalizing your thoughts and feelings, your journal will serve you as a source of material for more structured papers. Often an entry will already contain the germ of an idea for a paper.

Use the first few entries of your journal for a **personal résumé**. Write entries under headings like the following:

- Roots — family background, ethnic or racial identity, the meeting of cultures
- Schooling — teachers and classmates, goals and obstacles, triumphs and failures
- Flashlight memories — vividly remembered incidents that have a special meaning for you
- Jobs — part-time jobs, experiences as counselor or mentor, initiation to the workplace
- Personal issues — personal goals and commitments, causes you support, unresolved problems in your life

Study the following sample journal entries. What might each writer do to expand the entry into a fully developed paper?

Roots

I lived with my family in Saigon, South Vietnam, until the age of six, when the communist government took over. The situation at that time was very tense; some people lost their lives, families, or property. My family lost everything but our lives, and we moved to a small town, where I went to school and spent the rest of the day helping my parents at home. Unfortunately, our lives got worse and worse and my parents decided to sell their last valuables and try to escape to seek a better life. My parents had hoped to be able to afford for all of us to escape, but unfortunately my father and brother had to be left behind at the last. This was against my hope and that of my parents. During our escape, I had to hide from the police beneath the deck of a small boat. We spent nine days on the ocean and were robbed by Thai pirates. They raped most of the women. One girl was killed, but four of us were safe, including my mother and me. We were hiding under the men's bodies, and luckily the pirates did not see us. After reaching Malaysia, I spent four months in a small refugee camp, where I suffered from loneliness, hunger, and lack of water. We were finally transferred to the Philippines for another six months. Finally, we were accepted as residents in America. Now I realized that I, as well as my parents, had paid so much for a word—freedom.

Schooling

I am a Hispanic woman and proud of who I am. But there was a time of my life when I was ashamed of myself. I went to a primarily white elementary school, but there were a few blacks, Hispanics, and Asians. The white kids would call the Hispanics beaners and greasers. I didn't understand the words exactly, but I knew they were aimed at my kind. Once at lunch time, I opened my lunch box, which contained two pieces of white bread with smashed beans in between them. One blond blue-eyed boy with red pants and striped shirt said to me: "Yuck! What is that brown junk in your sandwich?" Thereafter I would eat by myself or open my lunch box slowly to see what was in it first. I wanted to be just like the rest of the kids and not be called names or have different food and a different skin color. When the class put on a play called Sleeping Beauty, I was the witch's crow, with my face painted green and my nose with a black beak. I always wondered why I didn't get better parts, like the princess or even the witch. After I graduated from high school and was on my own, I realized I didn't have time to feel sorry for myself. I started to research my background as a Hispanic woman and found my culture to be interesting and inspiring. I know only that parents should raise their children with love and free of racism, realizing that we are all the same. Now I am proud and not afraid of names.

Flashlight Memories

Autumns in southern California are mild, so it wasn't odd that while the Thanksgiving turkey roasted, most of the family was out back eating antipasta beneath the avocado and fruit trees. Granma always cooked too much—everybody said so—and every holiday the tables groaned with turkey, ham, and ricotta ravioli, sweet bell peppers and dried tomatoes soaked in wine and garlic, apple and pecan pies. One year—I must have been twelve—while the rest of the family was out back drinking Granpa's wine, I was in front reading. I didn't immediately notice the woman coming up the walk until she was right in front of me. She explained that she was from the downtown mission and was collecting donations to feed the hungry—did we have any extra food? It seemed logical to me, so I suggested that she take the turkey; after all, I explained, we had plenty. She was skeptical but I insisted. (I remember thinking how awful it must be to be hungry.) Shortly thereafter I heard all kinds of yelling and Granpa came running out of the house yelling that we'd been robbed, that some bastard had stolen our turkey. I tried to explain but before I could finish, everyone was cursing and screaming about how stupid I was. My aunt shook me until my glasses fell off my face. I didn't have a chance to say anything else but I remember thinking that they didn't see me; all they could see was the empty turkey platter. Now, everybody laughs about the year I gave away the turkey.

Personal Issues

I guess you could say that I am an African-American, at least that's what we are calling ourselves these days. It seems our title keeps changing. Just last week, while cleaning out a file cabinet, I found a copy of my birth certificate. The word "Negro" was typed neatly in the "race" box. A person might become confused being referred to as "Colored" one day, "Negro" the next, and "Black and I'm Proud" in the sixties and seventies. Now it is "African-American," and although some of the Africans might not agree with it, I guess this is for the best because I've never felt comfortable calling myself "Black." I've never felt comfortable calling my friends "White" for that matter. Being a very light-skinned person my mother never felt comfortable with people calling her "yellow." It was more than just the name-calling though that made her pack us, her four daughters ranging from ages seven down to three, in a small car and drive over three thousand miles across country. We left Chesapeake, Virginia that day on a one-way trip that landed us in San Diego, California. My mother did not have a high school diploma at that time, nor did she know anyone in San Diego. But I can remember that she worked hard to not only receive her high school diploma, but her BA and Masters as well. I guess I don't need to say more. It is obvious who my role model is.

1

Initiation:
Growing Up American

I never write about anything I have not experienced myself.
                                                          Shelby Steele

*One writes out of one thing only — one's own experience. Everything
depends on how relentlessly one forces from this experience the last
drop, sweet or bitter, it can possibly give.*
                                                          James Baldwin

*There are so many young brothers and sisters coming to the forefront,
writers who have decided that we can tell our stories any way we
damn well please.*
                                                          Terry McMillan

Gabriele Rico, author of *Writing the Natural Way,* says that everyone
has a story. We all have a story to tell that reveals who we are and how we
became who we are. When we trust the listener or reader enough, we may
tell that story. Many such stories are stories of growing up, of initiation.
We move from an earlier stage (maybe of happy childhood days) to a new
stage that requires us to learn. We awaken to new demands. We face a
challenge that may seem new and overwhelming to us but that (we discover later) many others before us had to face in their own way. We find
ourselves reliving an archetypal experience — reliving a pattern that has
been played out by many earlier generations.

For many young Americans, that archetypal experience has been a
move from one world to another — from country to city or from the old-
country ways of immigrant parents to the American world of school and
profession. Often that move is a time of confusion, of divided loyalties. It
is a time of breaking away and searching for a new identity. People find
themselves torn between conflicting loyalties — to different cultures, different ways of life, and often different languages. Sometimes the initiation
or awakening centers on the rediscovery of a culture or a language that

29

was part of the family's past but that had been buried in the attempt to assimilate, to become part of the mainstream of American life. Many of the following selections tell the story of such a journey in quest of the writer's identity.

LAKOTA WOMAN

Mary Crow Dog

Lakota Woman *(written with Richard Erdoes) is the story of Mary Crow Dog, who grew up on a reservation in South Dakota in a one-room cabin, without a father in the house and without running water or electricity. Her publisher said about her, "Rebelling against the aimless drinking, punishing missionary school, narrow strictures for women, and violence and hopelessness of reservation life, she joined the new movement of tribal pride sweeping Native American communities in the sixties and seventies and eventually married Leonard Crow Dog, the movement's chief medicine man, who revived the outlawed Ghost Dance." William Kunstler has called the book the "moving story of a Native American woman who fought her way out of bitterness and despair to find the righteous ways of her ancestors." When she was a child on the reservation, Mary Crow Dog says, "Indian religion was forbidden. Children were punished for praying Indian, men were jailed for taking a sweat bath. Our sacred pipes were broken, our medicine bundles burned or given to museums." For a time, before she set out in search of the native traditions of her people, she conformed to the image of the Christian convert. She remembers being confirmed in a white dress, with veil and candle — "white outside and red inside, the opposite of an apple."*

Thought Starters: What in the following account fits in with what you know about the indigenous peoples of North America? What changes your mind about the experience of Native Americans? What new perspectives does this selection present to you; what windows does it open on a part of the American experience?

It is not the big, dramatic things so much that get us down, but just being Indian, trying to hang on to our way of life, language, and values while being surrounded by an alien, more powerful culture. It is being an iyeska, a half-blood, being looked down upon by whites and full-bloods alike. It is being a backwoods girl living in a city, having to rip off stores in order to survive. Most of all it is being a woman. Among Plains tribes, some men think that all a woman is good for is to crawl into the sack with them and mind the children. It compensates for what white society has done to them. They were famous warriors and hunters once, but the buffalo is gone and there is not much rep in putting a can of spam or an occasional rabbit on the table.

As for being warriors, the only way some men can count coup nowadays is knocking out another skin's teeth during a barroom fight. In the old days a man made a name for himself by being generous and wise, but now he has nothing to be generous with, no jobs, no money; and as far as our traditional wisdom is concerned, our men are being told by the white missionaries, teachers, and employers that it is merely savage superstition they should get rid of if they want to make it in this world. Men are forced to live away from their children, so that the family can get ADC — Aid to Dependent Children. So some warriors come home drunk and beat up their old ladies in order to work off their frustration. I know where they are coming from. I feel sorry for them, but I feel even sorrier for their women.

To start from the beginning, I am a Sioux from the Rosebud Reservation in South Dakota. I belong to the "Burned Thigh," the Brule Tribe, the Sicangu in our language. Long ago, so the legend goes, a small band of Sioux was surrounded by enemies who set fire to their tipis and the grass around them. They fought their way out of the trap but got their legs burned and in this way acquired their name. The Brules are part of the Seven Sacred Campfires, the seven tribes of the Western Sioux known collectively as Lakota. The Eastern Sioux are called Dakota. The difference between them is their language. It is the same except that where we Lakota pronounce an *L,* the Dakota pronounce a *D.* They cannot pronounce an *L* at all. In our tribe we have this joke: "What is a flat tire in Dakota?" Answer: "A b*d*owout."

The Brule, like all Sioux, were a horse people, fierce riders and raiders, great warriors. Between 1870 and 1880 all Sioux were driven into reservations, fenced in and forced to give up everything that had given meaning to their life — their horses, their hunting, their arms, everything. But under the long snows of despair the little spark of our ancient beliefs and pride kept glowing, just barely sometimes, waiting for a warm wind to blow that spark into a flame again.

My family was settled on the reservation in a small place called He-Dog, after a famous chief. There are still some He-Dogs living. One, an old lady I knew, lived to be over a hundred years old. Nobody knew when she had been born. She herself had no idea, except that when she came into the world there was no census yet, and Indians had not yet been given Christian first names. Her name was just He-Dog, nothing else. She always told me, "You should have seen me eighty years ago when I was pretty." I have never forgotten her face — nothing but deep cracks and gullies, but beautiful in its own way. At any rate very impressive.

On the Indian side my family was related to the Brave Birds and Fool Bulls. Old Grandpa Fool Bull was the last man to make flutes and play them, the old-style flutes in the shape of a bird's head which had the elk power, the power to lure a young girl into a man's blanket. Fool Bull lived a whole long century, dying in 1976, whittling his flutes almost until his last day. He took me to my first peyote meeting while I was still a kid.

He still remembered the first Wounded Knee, the massacre. He was a young boy at that time, traveling with his father, a well-known medicine

5

man. They had gone to a place near Wounded Knee to take part in a Ghost Dance. They had on their painted ghost shirts which were supposed to make them bulletproof. When they got near Pine Ridge they were stopped by white soldiers, some of them from the Seventh Cavalry, George Custer's old regiment, who were hoping to kill themselves some Indians. The Fool Bull band had to give up their few old muzzle-loaders, bows, arrows, and even knives. They had to put up their tipis in a tight circle, all bunched up, with the wagons on the outside and the soldiers surrounding their camp, watching them closely. It was cold, so cold that the trees were crackling with a loud noise as the frost was splitting their trunks. The people made a fire the following morning to warm themselves and make some coffee and then they noticed a sound beyond the crackling of the trees: rifle fire, salvos making a noise like the ripping apart of a giant blanket; the boom of cannon and the rattling of quick-firing Hotchkiss guns. Fool Bull remembered the grown-ups bursting into tears, the women keening: "They are killing our people, they are butchering them!" It was only two miles or so from where Grandfather Fool Bull stood that almost three hundred Sioux men, women, and children were slaughtered. Later grandpa saw the bodies of the slain, all frozen in ghostly attitudes, thrown into a ditch like dogs. And he saw a tiny baby sucking at his dead mother's breast.

I wish I could tell about the big deeds of some ancestors of mine who fought at the Little Big Horn, or the Rosebud, counting coup during the Grattan or Fetterman battle, but little is known of my family's history before 1880. I hope some of my great-grandfathers counted coup on Custer's men, I like to imagine it, but I just do not know. Our Rosebud people did not play a big part in the battles against generals Crook or Custer. This was due to the policy of Spotted Tail, the all-powerful chief at the time. Spotted Tail had earned his eagle feathers as a warrior, but had been taken East as a prisoner and put in jail. Coming back years later, he said that he had seen the cities of the whites and that a single one of them contained more people than could be found in all the Plains tribes put together, and that every one of the wasičuns' factories could turn out more rifles and bullets in one day than were owned by all the Indians in the country. It was useless, he said, to try to resist the wasičuns. During the critical year of 1876 he had his Indian police keep most of the young men on the reservation, preventing them from joining Sitting Bull, Gall, and Crazy Horse. Some of the young bucks, a few Brave Birds among them, managed to sneak out trying to get to Montana, but nothing much is known. After having been forced into reservations, it was not thought wise to recall such things. It might mean no rations, or worse. For the same reason many in my family turned Christian, letting themselves be "whitemanized." It took many years to reverse this process.

My sister Barbara, who is four years older than me, says she remembers the day when I was born. It was late at night and raining hard amid thunder and lightning. We had no electricity then, just the old-style kerosene lamps with the big reflectors. No bathroom, no tap water, no car. Only a few white teachers had cars. There was one phone in He-Dog, at the trading post. This was not so very long ago, come to think of it. Like most Sioux at that time my mother was supposed to give birth at home, I think, but something went wrong, I was pointing the wrong way, feet first or stuck sideways. My mother was in great pain, laboring for hours, until finally somebody ran to the trading post and called the ambulance. They took her — us — to Rosebud, but the hospital there was not yet equipped to handle a complicated birth, I don't think they had surgery then, so they had to drive mother all the way to Pine Ridge, some ninety miles distant, because there the tribal hospital was bigger. So it happened that I was born among Crazy Horse's people. After my sister Sandra was born the doctors there performed a hysterectomy on my mother, in fact sterilizing her without her permission, which was common at the time, and up to just a few years ago, so that it is hardly worth mentioning. In the opinion of some people, the fewer Indians there are, the better. As Colonel Chivington said to his soldiers: "Kill 'em all, big and small, nits make lice!"

I don't know whether I am a louse under the white man's skin. I   *10* hope I am. At any rate I survived the long hours of my mother's labor, the stormy drive to Pine Ridge, and the neglect of the doctors. I am an iyeska, a breed, that's what the white kids used to call me. When I grew bigger they stopped calling me that, because it would get them a bloody nose. I am a small woman, not much over five feet tall, but I can hold my own in a fight, and in a free-for-all with honkies I can become rather ornery and do real damage. I have white blood in me. Often I have wished to be able to purge it out of me. As a young girl I used to look at myself in the mirror, trying to find a clue as to who and what I was. My face is very Indian, and so are my eyes and my hair, but my skin is very light. Always I waited for the summer, for the prairie sun, the Badlands sun, to tan me and make me into a real skin.

The Crow Dogs, the members of my husband's family, have no such problems of identity. They don't need the sun to tan them, they are full-bloods — the Sioux of the Sioux. Some Crow Dog men have faces which make the portrait on the buffalo Indian nickel look like a washed-out white man. They have no shortage of legends. Every Crow Dog seems to be a legend in himself, including the women. They became outcasts in their stronghold at Grass Mountain rather than being whitemanized. They could not be tamed, made to wear a necktie or go to a Christian church. All during the long years when practicing Indian beliefs was forbidden and could be punished with jail, they went right on having their ceremonies, their sweat baths and sacred dances. Whenever a Crow Dog got together with some relatives, such as those equally untamed, unregenerated Iron Shells, Good Lances, Two Strikes, Picket Pins, or Hollow Horn Bears, then you could hear the sound of the can gleska, the drum, telling all the world that a Sioux ceremony was in the making. It took courage and suffering to keep the flame alive, the little spark under the snow.

The first Crow Dog was a well-known chief. On his shield was the design of two circles and two arrowheads for wounds received in battle—two white man's bullets and two Pawnee arrow points. When this first Crow Dog was lying wounded in the snow, a coyote came to warm him and a crow flew ahead of him to show him the way home. His name should be Crow Coyote, but the white interpreter misunderstood it and so they became Crow Dogs. This Crow Dog of old became famous for killing a rival chief, the result of a feud over tribal politics, then driving voluntarily over a hundred miles to get himself hanged at Deadwood, his wife sitting beside him in his buggy; famous also for finding on his arrival that the Supreme Court had ordered him to be freed because the federal government had no jurisdiction over Indian reservations and also because it was no crime for one Indian to kill another. Later, Crow Dog became a leader of the Ghost Dancers, holding out for months in the frozen caves and ravines of the Badlands. So, if my own family lacks history, that of my husband more than makes up for it.

Our land itself is a legend, especially the area around Grass Mountain where I am living now. The fight for our land is at the core of our existence, as it has been for the last two hundred years. Once the land is gone, then we are gone too. The Sioux used to keep winter counts, picture writings on buffalo skin, which told our people's story from year to year. Well, the whole country is one vast winter count. You can't walk a mile without coming to some family's sacred vision hill, to an ancient Sun Dance circle, an old battleground, a place where something worth remembering happened. Mostly a death, a proud death or a drunken death. We are a great people for dying. "It's a good day to die!" that's our old battle cry. But the land with its tar paper shacks and outdoor privies, not one of them straight, but all leaning this way or that way, is also a land to live on, a land for good times and telling jokes and talking of great deeds done in the past. But you can't live forever off the deeds of Sitting Bull or Crazy Horse. You can't wear their eagle feathers, freeload off their legends. You have to make your own legends now. It isn't easy.

The Responsive Reader

1. Mary Crow Dog says, "As a young girl I used to look at myself in the mirror, trying to find a clue as to who and what I was." Who is she? What are key elements in her sense of self?
2. What is her attitude toward Native American men? How does she describe and explain their behavior? How does she contrast their past and their present?
3. What do you learn here about the buried or half-forgotten past that, the author says, was for many years "not thought wise to recall"?

What is the author's relation to "our people's story"? What do you learn about customs, traditions, beliefs?

Talking, Listening, Writing

4. Some writers speak for themselves as individuals; others give voice to the experience of many. They speak for a group, for a region, or for a generation. Would you consider Mary Crow Dog an effective and representative spokesperson for Native Americans? Why or why not?

5. A later essay in this book examines the issue of "White Guilt" (Shelby Steele, p. 321). Do you think white Americans today should feel guilty about the treatment of Native Americans now and in the past? Why or why not?

6. Are you in favor of people like Mary Crow Dog restoring the forgotten or formerly banned culture and religion of their group?

7. Mary Crow Dog says, "You have to make your own legends now. It isn't easy." What does she mean?

Projects

8. How much do you know about the American Indian Movement or other organizations dedicated to recovering the cultural heritage of a group in American society? Are there comparable organizations for Spanish-speaking Americans (Chicanos, Latinos), for blacks or African Americans, or for Asian Americans? Pool your knowledge or relevant background with that of other students in your class.

STEP FORWARD IN THE CAR, PLEASE
Maya Angelou

Maya Angelou has had a spectacular career as writer, poet, singer, dancer, actor (she acted in Roots*), and writer-producer of a ten-part television series. She was part of the civil rights movement, working as the Northern coordinator for the Southern Leadership Conference. She lived for several years in Ghana editing the* African Review. *Angelou has told her story in a series of autobiographical volumes including* I Know Why the Caged Bird Sings *(which first introduced her to a large audience),* Gather Together in My Name, Singin', Swingin' and Gettin' Merry Like Christmas, *and* The Heart of a Woman. *She was born in 1928 in St. Louis, Missouri; after the breakup of her parents' marriage, she went to live with her grandmother in Arkansas among Southern rural blacks who, she says, valued age more than wealth and religious piety more than beauty. She early came to know poverty, segregated schools, and the fear of violence at the hands of white people and of abuse by her own people as well. She became an unmarried mother at age sixteen. Her grandmother ran a country store in Sparks, Arkansas, a small Southern town where many of her contemporaries knew only to "chop cotton, pick cotton, and hoe potatoes," all the while dreaming of being "free, free from this town, and crackers, and farming, and yes-sirring and no-sirring." They all "needed to believe that a land existed somewhere, even beyond the Northern star, where Negroes were treated as people." The following excerpt focuses on a crucial stage of Angelou's journey toward making this dream come true.*

Thought Starters: What does the term *racism* mean to you? What face of racism does the young black woman encounter in the following pages? (How does it work? What are its roots? How does she try to overcome?)

My room had all the cheeriness of a dungeon and the appeal of a   *1*
tomb. It was going to be impossible to stay there, but leaving held no attraction for me, either. The answer came to me with the suddenness of a collision. I would go to work. Mother wouldn't be difficult to convince; after all, in school I was a year ahead of my grade and Mother was a firm believer in self-sufficiency. In fact, she'd be pleased to think that I had that much gumption, that much of her in my character. (She liked to speak of herself as the original "do-it-yourself girl.")

Once I had settled on getting a job, all that remained was to decide which kind of job I was most fitted for. My intellectual pride had kept me from selecting typing, shorthand, or filing as subjects in school, so office work was ruled out. War plants and shipyards demanded birth certificates, and mine would reveal me to be fifteen, and ineligible for work. So the well-paying defense jobs were also out. Women had replaced men on the streetcars as conductors and motormen, and the thought of sailing up and down the hills of San Francisco in a dark-blue uniform, with a money changer at my belt, caught my fancy.

Mother was as easy as I had anticipated. The world was moving so fast, so much money was being made, so many people were dying in Guam, and Germany, that hordes of strangers became good friends overnight. Life was cheap and death entirely free. How could she have the time to think about my academic career?

To her question of what I planned to do, I replied that I would get a job on the streetcars. She rejected the proposal with: "They don't accept colored people on the streetcars."

I would like to claim an immediate fury which was followed by the noble determination to break the restricting tradition. But the truth is, my first reaction was one of disappointment. I'd pictured myself, dressed in a neat blue serge suit, my money changer swinging jauntily at my waist, and a cheery smile for the passengers which would make their own work day brighter.

From disappointment, I gradually ascended the emotional ladder to haughty indignation, and finally to that state of stubbornness where the mind is locked like the jaws of an enraged bulldog.

I would go to work on the streetcars and wear a blue serge suit. Mother gave me her support with one of her usual terse asides, "That's what you want to do? Then nothing beats a trial but a failure. Give it everything you've got. I've told you many times, 'Can't Do is like Don't Care.' Neither of them has a home."

Translated, that meant there was nothing a person can't do, and there should be nothing a human being didn't care about. It was the most positive encouragement I could have hoped for.

In the offices of the Market Street Railway Company, the receptionist seemed as surprised to see me there as I was surprised to find the interior dingy and drab. Somehow I had expected waxed surfaces and carpeted floors. If I had met no resistance, I might have decided against working for such a poor-mouth-looking concern. As it was, I explained that I had come to see about a job. She asked, was I sent by an agency, and when I replied that I was not, she told me they were only accepting applicants from agencies.

The classified pages of the morning papers had listed advertisements for motorettes and conductorettes and I reminded her of that. She gave me a face full of astonishment that my suspicious nature would not accept.

"I am applying for the job listed in this morning's *Chronicle* and I'd like to be presented to your personnel manager." While I spoke in supercilious accents, and looked at the room as if I had an oil well in my own backyard, my armpits were being pricked by millions of hot pointed needles. She saw her escape and dived into it.

"He's out. He's out for the day. You might call him tomorrow and if he's in, I'm sure you can see him." Then she swiveled her chair around on its rusty screws and with that I was supposed to be dismissed.

"May I ask his name?"

She half turned, acting surprised to find me still there.

"His name? Whose name?"   15

"Your personnel manager."

We were firmly joined in the hypocrisy to play out the scene.

"The personnel manager? Oh, he's Mr. Cooper, but I'm not sure you'll find him here tomorrow. He's . . . Oh, but you can try."

"Thank you."

"You're welcome."   20

And I was out of the musty room and into the even mustier lobby. In the street I saw the receptionist and myself going faithfully through paces that were stale with familiarity, although I had never encountered that kind of situation before and, probably, neither had she. We were like actors who, knowing the play by heart, were still able to cry afresh over the old tragedies and laugh spontaneously at the comic situations.

The miserable little encounter had nothing to do with me, the me of me, any more than it had to do with that silly clerk. The incident was a recurring dream concocted years before by whites, and it eternally came back to haunt us all. The secretary and I were like people in a scene where, because of harm done by one ancestor to another, we were bound to duel to the death. (Also because the play must end somewhere.)

I went further than forgiving the clerk; I accepted her as a fellow victim of the same puppeteer.

On the streetcar, I put my fare into the box and the conductorette looked at me with the usual hard eyes of white contempt. "Move into the car, please move on in the car." She patted her money changer.

Her Southern nasal accent sliced my meditation and I looked deep   25
into my thoughts. All lies, all comfortable lies. The receptionist was not innocent and neither was I. The whole charade we had played out in that waiting room had to do with me, black, and her, white.

I wouldn't move into the streetcar but stood on the ledge over the conductor, glaring. My mind shouted so energetically that the announcement made my veins stand out, and my mouth tighten into a prune.

I WOULD HAVE THE JOB. I WOULD BE A CONDUCTOR-ETTE AND SLING A FULL MONEY CHANGER FROM MY BELT. I WOULD.

The next three weeks were a honeycomb of determination with apertures for the days to go in and out. The Negro organizations to whom I appealed for support bounced me back and forth like a shuttlecock on a badminton court. Why did I insist on that particular job? Openings were going begging that paid nearly twice the money. The minor officials with whom I was able to win an audience thought me mad. Possibly I was.

Downtown San Francisco became alien and cold, and the streets I had loved in a personal familiarity were unknown lanes that twisted with malicious intent. My trips to the streetcar office were of the frequency of a person on salary. The struggle expanded. I was no longer in conflict only with the Market Street Railway but with the marble lobby of the building which housed its offices, and elevators and their operators.

During this period of strain Mother and I began our first steps on   30 the long path toward mutual adult admiration. She never asked for reports and I didn't offer any details. But every morning she made breakfast, gave me carfare and lunch money, as if I were going to work. She comprehended that in the struggle lies the joy. That I was no glory seeker was obvious to her, and that I had to exhaust every possibility before giving in was also clear.

On my way out of the house one morning she said, "Life is going to give you just what you put in it. Put your whole heart in everything you do, and pray, then you can wait." Another time she reminded me that "God helps those who help themselves." She had a store of aphorisms which she dished out as the occasion demanded. Strangely, as bored as I was with clichés, her inflection gave them something new, and set me thinking for a little while at least. Later when asked how I got my job, I was never able to say exactly. I only knew that one day, which was tiresomely like all the others before it, I sat in the Railway office, waiting to be interviewed. The receptionist called me to her desk and shuffled a bundle of paper to me. They were job application forms. She said they had to be filled out in triplicate. I had little time to wonder if I had won or not, for the standard questions reminded me of the necessity for lying. How old was I? List my previous jobs, starting from the last held and go backward to the first. How much money did I earn, and why did I leave the position? Give two references (not relatives). I kept my face blank (an old art) and wrote quickly the fable of Marguerite Johnson, aged nineteen, former companion and driver for Mrs. Annie Henderson (a White Lady) in Stamps, Arkansas.

I was given blood tests, aptitude tests, and physical coordination tests, then on a blissful day I was hired as the first Negro on the San Francisco streetcars.

Mother gave me the money to have my blue serge suit tailored, and I learned to fill out work cards, operate the money changer and punch transfers. The time crowded together and at an End of Days I was swinging on the back of the rackety trolley, smiling sweetly and persuading my charges to "step forward in the car, please."

For one whole semester the streetcars and I shimmied up and scooted down the sheer hills of San Francisco. I lost some of my need for the black ghetto's shielding-sponge quality, as I clanged and cleared my way down Market Street, with its honky-tonk homes for homeless sailors, past the quiet retreat of Golden Gate Park and along closed undwelled-in-looking dwellings of the Sunset District.

My work shifts were split so haphazardly that it was easy to believe that my superiors had chosen them maliciously. Upon mentioning my suspicions to Mother, she said, "Don't you worry about it. You ask for what you want, and you pay for what you get. And I'm going to show you that it ain't no trouble when you pack double." *35*

She stayed awake to drive me out to the car barn at four-thirty in the mornings, or to pick me up when I was relieved just before dawn. Her awareness of life's perils convinced her that while I would be safe on the public conveyances, she "wasn't about to trust a taxi driver with her baby."

When the spring classes began, I resumed my commitment with formal education. I was so much wiser and older, so much more independent, with a bank account and clothes that I had bought for myself, that I was sure I had learned and earned the magic formula which would make me a part of the life my contemporaries led.

Not a bit of it. Within weeks, I realized that my schoolmates and I were on paths moving away from each other. They were concerned and excited over the approaching football games. They concentrated great interest on who was worthy of being student body president, and when the metal bands would be removed from their teeth, while I remembered conducting a streetcar in the uneven hours of the morning.

The Responsive Reader

1. Angelou once described herself as a young Southern woman who grew up determined to "defy the odds." What kind of person is speaking to you in this selection? What are key traits? What kind of voice do you hear?
2. What does the writer want you to learn from this account about the workings of racism — its motives, its ploys, its repercussions?
3. If you were a sociologist, what in this account would you accept as an objective reporting of the facts? How much is the writer's interpretation — her personal slant on what happened to her? (Do you agree or disagree with the way she interprets the facts?)

Talking, Listening, Writing

4. How much of what you read here has to be understood in the context of a black woman's experience? How much of it has parallels in the experience of other groups?
5. What is the author's purpose — to encourage others, to "get even," to assert her pride?
6. What has been your own experience with prejudice — as a target or as a perpetrator? Describe a key incident or several learning experiences in vivid detail. What did you learn from your experience?

7. What's in a name? One teacher reported that students in his classes were uncomfortable with being called "white people." Why do you think they were? What are the pros and cons of other possible labels — *Caucasian, Anglo, European, European American?* (What are the pros and cons of *black, Afro-American, African, African American, people of color?*)

8. Tell the story of a challenge or an obstacle that you have faced and overcome or by which you were defeated.

Projects

9. Is the discrimination that Angelou faced a thing of the past? As one of several possible projects suggested in this chapter, you may want to work alone or in a group to quiz students from diverse cultural or ethnic backgrounds concerning this question. What are their perceptions of the obstacles and opportunities they encounter in looking for jobs?

BORN AMONG THE BORN-AGAIN

Garrison Keillor

Garrison Keillor became legendary in the Midwest as the host of A Prairie Home Companion, *a live radio show originating in St. Paul, Minnesota. He later took his show on the road to different regions of the country, giving audiences the same nostalgic mix of old-style storytelling, savvy appeals to local pride, the sentimental songs of barbershop quintets and crooners, and homespun humor delighting in the quirks and foibles of family and neighbors. Keillor is a master at creating a nostalgic vision of a small-town American past removed from the upheavals and paranoias of the twentieth century. He collected many of the stories he told on his show in* Lake Wobegon Days *(1985), explaining that many were "true stories from my childhood, dressed . . . up as fiction." He said in an interview in* Time *magazine that he looked to the stories he heard in his family as a child "as giving a person some sense of place," reassuring us "that we were not just chips floating on the waves, that in some way we were meant to be here, and had a history. That we had standing."*

Thought Starters: In the selection that follows, Keillor replays a classic story of growing up: A youngster growing up in a family with strong religious views (or other strong beliefs) starts to rebel against having to be "different" from his peers. How much in this story shows Keillor's home-spun sense of humor? How much is serious or thought-provoking?

In a town where everyone was either Lutheran or Catholic, our   1
family was not and never had been. We were Sanctified Brethren, a sect so tiny that nobody but us and God knew about it, so when kids asked what I was, I just said Protestant. It was too much to explain, like having six toes. You would rather keep your shoes on.

Grandpa Cotten was once tempted toward Lutheranism by a preacher who gave a rousing sermon on grace that Grandpa heard as a young man while taking Aunt Esther's dog home who had chased a Model T across town. He sat down on the church steps and listened to the voice boom out the open windows until he made up his mind to go in and unite with the truth, but he took one look from the vestibule and left. "He was dressed up like the Pope of Rome," said Grandpa, "and the altar and paintings and the gold candlesticks — my gosh, it was just a big show. And he was reading the whole darn thing off a page, like an actor."

Jesus said, "Where two or three are gathered together in my name, there am I in the midst of them," and the Brethren believed that was enough. We met in Uncle Al and Aunt Flo's bare living room, with plain folding chairs arranged facing in toward the middle. No clergyman in a black smock. No organ or piano, for that would make one person too prominent. No upholstery—it would lead to complacence. No picture of Jesus—He was in our Hearts. The faithful sat down at the appointed hour and waited for the Spirit to move one of them to speak or to pray or to give out a hymn from our Little Flock hymnal. No musical notation, for music must come from the heart and not off a page. We sang the texts to a tune that fit the meter, of the many tunes we all knew. The idea of reading a prayer was sacrilege to us—"If a man can't remember what he wants to say to God, let him sit down and think a little harder," Grandpa said.

"There's the Lord's Prayer," said Aunt Esther meekly. We were sitting on the porch after Sunday dinner. Esther and Harvey were visiting from Minneapolis and had attended Lake Wobegon Lutheran, she having turned Lutheran when she married him, a subject that was never brought up in our family.

"You call that prayer? Sitting and reciting like a bunch of school-children?" 5

Harvey cleared his throat and turned to me and smiled, "Speaking of school, how are you doing?" he asked.

There was a lovely silence in the Brethren assembled on Sunday morning as we waited for the Spirit. Either the Spirit was moving someone to speak who was taking his sweet time or else the Spirit was playing a wonderful joke on us and letting us sit, or perhaps silence was the point of it. We sat listening to rain on the roof, distant traffic, a radio playing from across the street, kids whizzing by on bikes, dogs barking, as we waited for the Spirit to inspire us. It was like sitting on the porch with your family, when nobody feels that they have to make talk. So quiet in church. Minutes drifted by in silence that was sweet to us. The old Regulator clock ticked, the rain stopped, and the room changed light as the sun broke through—shafts of brilliant sun through the windows and motes of dust falling through it—the smell of clean clothes and floor wax and wine and the fresh bread of Aunt Flo, which was Christ's body given for us. Jesus in our midst, who loved us. So peaceful; and we loved each other, too. I thought perhaps the Spirit was leading me to say that, but I was just a boy, and children were supposed to keep still.

And my affections were not pure. They were tainted with a sneaking admiration of Catholics—Catholic Christmas, Easter, the Living Rosary, and the Blessing of the Animals, all magnificent. Everything we did was plain, but they were regal—especially the Feast Day of Saint Francis, which they did right out in the open, a feast for the eyes. Cows, horses, some pets, right on the church lawn. The turmoil, animals bellowing and barking and clucking and a cat scheming how to escape and suddenly leaping out of the girl's arms who was holding on tight, the cat dashing through the crowd, dogs straining at the leash, and the ocarina band of third graders playing a song, and the great calm of the sisters, and the flags, and the Knights of Columbus decked out in their handsome black suits — the whole thing was gorgeous. I stared at it until my eyes almost fell out, and then I wished it would go on much longer.

"Christians," my Uncle Al used to say, "do not go in for show," referring to the Catholics. We were sanctified by the blood of the Lord; therefore we were saints, like Saint Francis, but we didn't go in for feasts or ceremonies, involving animals or not. We went in for sitting, all nineteen of us, in Uncle Al and Aunt Flo's living room on Sunday morning and having a plain meeting and singing hymns in our poor thin voices, while not far away the Catholics were whooping it up. I wasn't allowed inside Our Lady, of course, but if the Blessing of the Animals on the Feast Day of Saint Francis was any indication, Lord, I didn't know but what they had elephants in there and acrobats. I sat in our little group and envied them for the splendor and gorgeousness, as we tried to sing without even so much as a harmonica to give us the pitch. Hymns, Uncle Al said, didn't have to be sung perfect, because God looks on the heart, and if you are In The Spirit, then all praise is good.

The Brethren, also known as The Saints Gathered in the Name of   *10* Christ Jesus, who met in the living room were all related to each other and raised in the Faith from infancy except Brother Mel, who was rescued from a life of drunkenness, saved as a brand from the burning, a drowning sailor, a sheep on the hillside, whose immense red nose testified to his previous condition. I envied his amazing story of how he came to be with us. Born to godly parents, Mel left home at fifteen and joined the Navy. He sailed to distant lands in a submarine and had exciting experiences while traveling the downward path, which led him finally to the Union Gospel Mission in Minneapolis, where he heard God's voice "as clear as my voice speaking to you." He was twenty-six, he slept under bridges and in abandoned buildings, he drank two quarts of white muscatel every day, and then God told him that he must be born again, and so he was, and became the new Mel, except for his nose.

Except for his nose, Mel Burgess looked like any forty-year-old Brethren man: sober, preferring dark suits, soft-spoken, tending toward girth. His nose was what made you look twice: battered, swollen, very red with tiny purplish lines, it looked ancient and dead on his otherwise fairly handsome face, the souvenir of what he had been saved from, the "Before" of his "Before . . . and After" advertisement for being born again.

For me, there was nothing before. I was born among the born-again. This living room so hushed, the Brethren in their customary places on folding chairs (the comfortable ones were put away on Sunday morning) around the end table draped with a white cloth and the glass of wine and loaf of bread (unsliced), was as familiar to me as my mother and father, before whom there was nobody. I had always been here.

I never saw the "Before" until the Sunday we drove to St. Cloud for dinner and traipsed into a restaurant that a friend of Dad's had recommended, Phil's House of Good Food. The waitress pushed two tables together and we sat down and studied the menu. My mother blanched at the prices. A chicken dinner went for $2.50, the roast beef for $3.75. "It's a nice place," Daid said, multiplying the five of us times $2.50. "I'm not so hungry, I guess," he said. "Maybe I'll just have soup." We weren't restaurantgoers — "Why pay good money for food you could make better at home?" was Mother's philosophy — so we weren't at all sure about restaurant customs. For example, could a person who had been seated in a restaurant simply get up and walk out? Would it be proper? Would it be *legal*?

The waitress came and stood by Dad. "Can I get you something from the bar?" she said. Dad blushed a deep red. The question seemed to imply that he looked like a drinker.

"No," he whispered, as if he were turning down her offer to take off   15
her clothes and dance on the table.

Then another waitress brought a tray of glasses to a table of four couples next to us. "Martini," she said, setting the drink down, "whiskey sour, whiskey sour, Manhattan, whiskey sour, gin and tonic, martini, whiskey sour."

"Ma'am? Something from the bar?" Mother looked at her in disbelief.

Suddenly the room changed for us. Our waitress looked hardened, rough, cheap; across the room a woman laughed obscenely, "Haw, haw, haw"; the man with her lit a cigarette and blew a cloud of smoke; a swearword drifted out from the kitchen like a whiff of urine; even the soft lighting seemed suggestive, diabolical. To be seen in such a place on the Lord's Day — *what had we done?*

"Ed," my mother said, rising.

"We can't stay. I'm sorry," Dad told the waitress. We all got up and   20
put on our coats. Everyone in the restaurant had a good long look at us. A bald little man in a filthy white shirt emerged from the kitchen, wiping his hands. "Folks? Something wrong?" he said.

"We're in the wrong place," Mother told him. Mother always told the truth, or something close to it.

"This is *humiliating*," I said out on the sidewalk. "I feel like a *leper* or something. Why do we always have to make such a big production out of everything? Why can't we be like regular people?"

She put her hand on my shoulder. "Be not conformed to this world," she said. I knew the rest by heart ". . . but be ye transformed by the renewing of your mind, that ye may prove what is that good and acceptable and perfect will of God."

"Where we gonna eat?" Phyllis asked.

"We'll find someplace reasonable," said Mother, and we walked six   25
blocks across the river and found a lunch counter and ate sloppy joes

(called Maid-Rites) for fifteen cents apiece. They did not agree with us, and we were aware of them all afternoon through prayer meeting and Young People's.

The Responsive Reader

1. How does Keillor take you into the Brethren's world of attitudes and beliefs? What would you stress in trying to initiate an unsympathetic listener into their lifestyle, their way of thinking and feeling? (What role does Brother Mel play in this story? What does he contribute to your understanding of the family's religion?)
2. For the author, what was the appeal of the strange and different Catholic tradition?
3. The story leads up to a high point—to a climactic incident that dramatizes the boy's feelings about his background, about his family. What *are* the boy's feelings? Where do you first become aware of them? Do you sympathize with him?

Talking, Listening, Writing

4. Religion often seems a taboo subject in our society. Why? Courts ban displays of the Christmas scene on public property as well as prayers in public schools or at commencement ceremonies. Why? Where do you stand?
5. Have you ever felt the urge to speak up on behalf of a group considered different or alien or undesirable in our society? Speak or write in defense of the group.
6. Has the awareness of being "different" played a role in your life or in the life of someone you know well? (Or have you ever worried about being too much the *same* as everyone else?)

Projects

7. Is there a "religious revival" among the young? What kind of religious ideas or religious affiliations appeal to young people today? Help organize an informal poll of your classmates that would shed light on these questions.

FIFTH CHINESE DAUGHTER
Jade Snow Wong

> *In her much-honored* Fifth Chinese Daughter, *Jade Snow Wong told a classic story of American adolescence. In her introduction to a new 1989 edition, Wong said that at the time she first wrote her book "nothing had been published from a female Chinese American perspective." She grew up as the daughter of immigrant parents who preserved the values, customs, and language of their native country in the home. However, gradually she discovered a different world beyond the home and neighborhood. The following excerpt leads up to a classic confrontation between the generations as the young woman declares her independence and strikes out in search of her own identity. Wong grew up in Chinatown in San Francisco in a traditional family unit that was part of a larger clan, with many close relatives. People honored their parents and their ancestors; children were taught obedience and filial respect — the respect of a dutiful daughter or son for the parents. Wong graduated from Mills College, a woman's college with a proud independent tradition. She published* No Chinese Stranger *in 1975; her* Fifth Chinese Daughter *was made into a PBS television special in 1976. Today's most successful Chinese American authors — Maxine Hong Kingston, Amy Tan — have acknowledged her as a role model and source of inspiration.*

Thought Starters: What is the essential conflict between the Chinese parents' traditional way of life and the American lifestyle the daughter discovers outside the home? Do you find yourself identifying with the daughter? Why or why not?

From infancy to my sixteenth year, I was reared according to nine- 1
teenth-century ideals of Chinese womanhood. I was never left alone, though it was not unusual for me to feel lonely, while surrounded by a family of seven others, and often by ten (including bachelor cousins) at meals.

My father (who enjoyed our calling him Daddy in English) was the unquestioned head of our household. He was not talkative, being preoccupied with his business affairs and with reading constantly otherwise. My mother was mistress of domestic affairs. Seldom did these two converse before their children, but we knew them to be a united front, and suspected that privately she both informed and influenced him about each child.

In order to support the family in America, Daddy tried various occupations — candy making, the ministry to which he was later ordained — but finally settled on manufacturing men's and children's denim garments. He leased sewing equipment, installed machines in a basement where rent was cheapest, and there he and his family lived and worked. There was no thought that dim, airless quarters were terrible conditions for living and working, or that child labor was unhealthful. The only goal was for all in the family to work, to save, and to become educated. It was possible, so it would be done.

My father, a meticulous bookkeeper, used only an abacus, a brush, ink, and Chinese ledgers. Because of his newly learned ideals, he pioneered for the right of women to work. Concerned that they have economic independence, but not with the long hours of industrial home work, he went to shy housewives' apartments and taught them sewing.

My earliest memories of companionship with my father were as his passenger in his red wheelbarrow, sharing space with the piles of blue-jean materials he was delivering to a worker's home. He must have been forty. He was lean, tall, inevitably wearing blue overalls, rolled shirt sleeves, and high black kid shoes. In his pockets were numerous keys, tools, and pens. On such deliveries, I noticed that he always managed time to show a mother how to sew a difficult seam, or to help her repair a machine, or just to chat.

I observed from birth that living and working were inseparable. My mother was short, sturdy, young looking, and took pride in her appearance. She was at her machine the minute housework was done, and she was the hardest-working seamstress, seldom pausing, working after I went to bed. The hum of sewing machines continued day and night, seven days a week. She knew that to have more than the four necessities, she must work and save. We knew that to overcome poverty, there were only two methods: working and education.

Having provided the setup for family industry, my father turned his attention to our education. Ninety-five percent of the population in his native China had been illiterate. He knew that American public schools would take care of our English, but he had to nurture our Chinese knowledge. Only the Cantonese tongue was ever spoken by him or my mother. When the two oldest girls arrived from China, the schools of Chinatown received only boys. My father tutored his daughters each morning before breakfast. In the midst of a foreign environment, he clung to a combination of the familiar old standards and what was permissible in the newly learned Christian ideals.

My eldest brother was born in America, the only boy for fourteen years, and after him three daughters — another older sister, myself, and my younger sister. Then my younger brother, Paul, was born. That older brother, Lincoln, was cherished in the best Chinese tradition. He had his own room; he kept a German shepherd as his pet; he was tutored by a Chinese scholar; he was sent to private school for American classes. As a male Wong, he would be responsible some day for the preservation of and

5

pilgrimages to ancestral graves—his privileges were his birthright. We girls were content with the unusual opportunities of working and attending two schools. By day, I attended American public school near our home. From 5:00 P.M. to 8:00 P.M. on five weekdays and from 9:00 A.M. to 12 noon on Saturdays, I attended the Chinese school. Classes numbered twenty to thirty students, and were taught by educated Chinese from China. We studied poetry, calligraphy, philosophy, literature, history, correspondence, religion, all by exacting memorization.

Daddy emphasized memory development; he could still recite fluently many lengthy lessons of his youth. Every evening after both schools, I'd sit by my father, often as he worked at his sewing machine, sing-songing my lessons above its hum. Sometimes I would stop to hold a light for him as he threaded the difficult holes of a specialty machine, such as one for bias bindings. After my Chinese lessons passed his approval, I was allowed to attend to American homework. I was made to feel luckier than other Chinese girls who didn't study Chinese, and also luckier than Western girls without a dual heritage.

There was little time for play, and toys were unknown to me. In any *10* spare time, I was supplied with embroidery and sewing for my mother. The Chinese New Year, which by the old lunar calendar would fall sometime in late January or early February of the Western Christian calendar, was the most special time of the year, for then the machines stopped for three days. Mother would clean our living quarters very thoroughly, decorate the sitting room with flowering branches and fresh oranges, and arrange candied fruits or salty melon seeds for callers. All of us would be dressed in bright new clothes, and relatives or close friends, who came to call, would give each of us a red paper packet containing a good luck coin—usually a quarter. I remember how my classmates would gleefully talk of *their* receipts. But my mother made us give our money to her, for she said that she needed it to reciprocate to others.

Yet there was little reason for unhappiness. I was never hungry. Though we had no milk, there was all the rice we wanted. We had hot and cold running water—a rarity in Chinatown—as well as our own bathtub. Our sheets were pieced from dishtowels, but we had sheets. I was never neglected, for my mother and father were always at home. During school vacation periods, I was taught to operate many types of machines—tacking (for pockets), overlocking (for the raw edges of seams), buttonhole, double seaming; and I learned all the stages in producing a pair of jeans to its final inspection, folding, and tying in bundles of a dozen pairs by size, ready for pickup. Denim jeans are heavy—my shoulders ached often. My father set up a modest nickel-and-dime piecework reward for me, which he recorded in my own notebook, and paid me regularly.

My mother dutifully followed my father's leadership. She was extremely thrifty, but the thrifty need pennies to manage, and the old world had denied her those. Upon arrival in the new world of San Francisco, she accepted the elements her mate had selected to shape her new life: domestic duties, seamstress work in the factory-home, mothering each child in turn, church once a week, and occasional movies. Daddy frowned upon the community Chinese operas because of their very late hours (they did not finish till past midnight) and their mixed audiences.

Very early in my life, the manners of a traditional Chinese lady were taught to me. How to hold a pair of chopsticks (palm up, not down); how to hold a bowl of rice (one thumb on top, not resting in an open palm); how to pass something to elders (with both hands, never one); how to pour tea into the tiny, handleless porcelain cups (seven-eighths full so that the top edge would be cool enough to hold); how to eat from a center serving dish (only the piece in front of your place; never pick around); not to talk at table, not to show up outside of one's room without being fully dressed; not to be late, ever; not to be too playful — in a hundred and one ways, we were molded to be trouble-free, unobtrusive, cooperative.

We were disciplined by first being told, and then by punishment if we didn't remember. Punishment was instant and unceremonious. At the table, it came as a sudden whack from Daddy's chopsticks. Away from the table, punishment could be the elimination of a privilege or the blow on our legs from a bundle of cane switches.

Only Daddy and Oldest Brother were allowed individual idiosyn-   15 crasies. Daughters were all expected to be of one standard. To allow each one of many daughters to be different would have posed enormous problems of cost, energy, and attention. No one was shown physical affection. Such familiarity would have weakened my parents and endangered the one-answer authoritative system. One standard from past to present, whether in China or in San Francisco, was simpler to enforce. My parents never said "please" and "thank you" for any service or gift. In Chinese, both "please" and "thank you" can be literally translated as "I am not worthy" and naturally, no parent is going to say that about a service which should be their just due.

Traditional Chinese parents pit their children against a standard of perfection without regard to personality, individual ambitions, tolerance for human error, or exposure to the changing social scene. It never occurred to that kind of parent to be friends with their children on common ground.

During the Depression, my mother and father needed even more hours to work. Daddy had been shopping daily for groceries (we had no icebox) and my mother cooked. Now I was told to assume both those duties. My mother would give me fifty cents to buy enough fresh food for dinner and breakfast. In those years, twenty-five cents could buy a small chicken or three sanddabs, ten cents bought three bunches of green vegetables, and fifteen cents bought some meat to cook with these. After American school I rushed to the stores only a block or so away, returned and cleaned the foods, and cooked in a hurry in order to eat an early dinner and get to Chinese school on time. When I came home at 8:00 P.M., I took care of the dinner dishes before starting to do my homework. Saturdays and Sundays were for housecleaning and the family laundry, which I scrubbed on a board, using big galvanized buckets in our bathtub.

I had no sympathetic guidance as an eleven-year-old in my own reign in the kitchen, which lasted for four years. I finished junior high school, started high school, and continued studying Chinese. With the small earnings from summer work in my father's basement factory (we moved back to the basement during the Depression), I bought materials to sew my own clothes. But the routine of keeping house only to be dutiful, to avoid tongue or physical lashings, became exasperating. The tiny space which was the room for three sisters was confining. After I graduated from Chinese evening school, I began to look for part-time paying jobs as a mother's helper. Those jobs varied from cleaning house to baking a cake, amusing a naughty child to ironing shirts, but wearying, exhausting as they were, they meant money earned for myself.

As I advanced in American high school and worked at those jobs, I was gradually introduced to customs not of the Chinese world. American teachers were mostly kind. I remember my third-grade teacher's skipping me half a year. I remember my fourth-grade teacher — with whom I am still friendly. She was the first person to hold me to her physically and affectionately — because a baseball bat had been accidentally flung against my hand. I also remember that I was confused by being held, since physical comfort had not been offered by my parents. I remember my junior high school principal, who skipped me half a grade and commended me before the school assembly, to my great embarrassment.

In contrast, Chinese schoolteachers acted as extensions of Chinese   20
parental discipline. There was a formal "disciplinarian dean" to apply the cane to wayward boys, and girls were not exempt either. A whisper during chapel was sufficient provocation to be called to the dean's office. No humor was exchanged; no praise or affection expressed by the teachers. They presented the lessons, and we had to learn to memorize all the words, orally, before the class. Then followed the written test, word for word. Without an alphabet, the Chinese language requires exact memorization. No originality or deviation was permitted and grading was severe. One word wrong during an examination could reduce a grade by 10 percent. It was the principle of learning by punishment.

Interest and praise, physical or oral, were rewards peculiar to the American world. Even employers who were paying me thanked me for a service or complimented me on a meal well cooked, and sometimes helped me with extra dishes. Chinese often said that "foreigners" talked too much about too many personal things. My father used to tell me to think three times before saying anything, and if I said nothing, no one would say I was stupid. I perceived a difference between two worlds.

By the time I was graduating from high school, my parents had done their best to produce an intelligent, obedient daughter, who would know more than the average Chinatown girl and should do better than average at a conventional job, her earnings brought home to them in repayment for their years of child support. Then, they hoped, she would marry a nice Chinese boy and make him a good wife, as well as an above-average mother for his children. Chinese custom used to decree that families should "introduce" chosen partners to each other's children. The groom's family should pay handsomely to the bride's family for rearing a well-bred daughter. They should also pay all bills for a glorious wedding banquet for several hundred guests. Then the bride's family could consider their job done. Their daughter belonged to the groom's family and must hence-forth seek permission from all persons in his home before returning to her parents for a visit.

But having been set upon a new path, I did not oblige my parents with the expected conventional ending. At fifteen, I had moved away from home to work for room and board and a salary of twenty dollars per month. Having found that I could subsist independently, I thought it regrettable to terminate my education. Upon graduating from high school at the age of sixteen, I asked my parents to assist me in college expenses. I pleaded with my father, for his years of encouraging me to be above mediocrity in both Chinese and American studies had made me wish for some undefined but brighter future.

My father was briefly adamant. He must conserve his resources for my oldest brother's medical training. Though I desired to continue on an above-average course, his material means were insufficient to support that ambition. He added that if I had the talent, I could provide for my own college education. When he had spoken, no discussion was expected. After his edict, no daughter questioned.

But this matter involved my whole future — it was not simply asking for permission to go to a night church meeting (forbidden also). Though for years I had accepted the authority of the one I honored most, his decision that night embittered me as nothing ever had. My oldest brother had so many privileges, had incurred unusual expenses for luxuries which were taken for granted as his birthright, yet these were part of a system I had accepted. Now I suddenly wondered at my father's interpretation of the Christian code: was it intended to discriminate against a girl after all, or was it simply convenient for my father's economics and cultural preju-dice? Did a daughter have any right to expect more than a fate of obedi-ence, according to the old Chinese standard? As long as I could remember, I had been told that a female followed three men during her lifetime: as a girl, her father; as a wife, her husband; as an old woman, her son.

My indignation mounted against that tradition and I decided then that my past could not determine my future. I knew that more education would prepare me for a different expectation than my other female school-mates, few of whom were to complete a college degree. I, too, had my father's unshakable faith in the justice of God, and I shared his unconcern with popular opinion.

her feelings about the patriarchal tradition? Had her parents moved
away from the tradition in any way?

5. What are the gist and the outcome of the author's climactic confrontation with her father?
6. What is the author's tone? Does she sound bitter to you? Is she talking
about "bad parenting"?

Talking, Listening, Writing

7. A dual or divided cultural heritage is sometimes considered a liability — a source of problems, doubts, divided loyalties, or a lacking
sense of belonging. Sometimes it is considered an asset — a chance
for a richer, fuller identity drawing on what is best in two different
ways of realizing one's human potential. In the case of the young
woman speaking to you in this excerpt, do you think her dual
heritage will prove a liability or an asset?
8. In your own experience, have you encountered the clash or the
merging of two different traditions, two different lifestyles, two
different cultures?

Projects

9. How do students on your campus feel about allegiance to a distinctive heritage? Working with a group, you may want to organize a
survey of attitudes, trying to make your sample representative of a
cross section.

Thinking about Connections

Maxine Hong Kingston's "Warrior Woman" (p. 300) tells a later
story of a young Chinese woman rebelling against tradition and trying to
come to terms with a new American identity. How much do Wong's and
Kingston's stories have in common? How are the motives, targets, and
results of their rebellions similar or different?

CHILDREN OF THE HARVEST
Lois Phillips Hudson

*Many modern societies have or have had migrant populations. In this
country, seasonal workers from the rural South came to work in the factories
of the North. In the thirties, rural Midwesterners driven from their farms by
the dust storms and the Great Depression came to the migrant camps of the
West and Northwest. Called "Okies" even when they were not from Oklahoma, they were always on the move — looking for a job to do, a crop to pick,
a place to stay, a place to send children to school. They were watched suspi-
ciously by the locals and nudged by the local police to move on. In the West
today, Mexican agricultural workers, often officially classified as illegal
aliens, live in camps that show on no county map and would pass no health
inspection if any official were to seek them out. Born in North Dakota, Lois
Phillips Hudson published a novel about the Midwest of the thirties,* The
Bones of Plenty, *in 1962; she published* Reapers of the Dust: A Prairie
Chronicle *in 1965. In the following autobiographical essay, she tells her
story of growing up as a child of migrant workers on the wrong side of the
tracks, finding herself among the uprooted, the displaced, the dispossessed.*

Thought Starters: Readers have often liked the accounts of young naive
observers finding themselves in a different new world and looking at it
through wide-open wondering eyes. What are the things that the young
girl telling the following story wonders at? What are basic contrasts between her Midwestern origins and the new world in which she finds
herself?

On a suffocating summer day in 1937, the thirteenth year of drought
and the seventh year of depression, with our mouths, nostrils, and eyes
full of the dust blowing from our bare fields, my family sold to our
neighbors at auction most of the accoutrements of our existence. Then we
loaded what was left into a trailer my father had made and drove West to
find water and survival on the Washington coast.

During the auction the two classmates with whom I had just finished
the fourth grade hung about the desultory bidders giving me looks of
respect and undisguised envy. They envied me not so much for the things
they could imagine as for the things they couldn't — the unimaginable
distance I was going and the unimaginable things along it and at the
end of it.

How could any of us have imagined an end to the prairie's limitless
sky and the giddy encroachments rising higher and higher against that sky

that were the Rocky Mountains? How could we have imagined how in burning summer the forested profiles of the Cascades could echo everywhere the shouts of white falls above us and green rivers below? Who could have imagined, once confronted with their gray expanse, that the waters of Puget Sound were not actually the Pacific, but only a minute stray squiggle of it? Who, finally, could have imagined that there were so many people in the world or that the world could offer them so hospitable a habitation?

There were so many things I could scarcely believe even when I was doing them or looking at them or eating them. We lived in a cabin on an island for a few weeks after we arrived, and it always seemed impossible to me that we could be surrounded by so much water. I spent every moment of the hour-long ferry trip from the mainland hanging over the rail gazing down at the exhilarating wake of my first boat ride. The island was exactly what any island should be — lavish green acres covered with woods and orchards and fields of berries, ringed by glistening sandy beaches richly stocked with driftwood. Once in North Dakota my aunt had brought a very small basket of black cherries to my grandfather's house, and I had made the four or five that were my share last all afternoon. I would take tiny bites of each cherry, then suck the pit and roll it around with my tongue to get the faint remaining taste, till it came out as clean and smooth as a brook-bottom pebble. But on the island I would climb into the trees with my five-year-old sister and have contests with her, seeing which of us could get the most cherries in our mouths at once. Then we would shoot the wet pits, no longer hungrily scoured of their slipperiness, at each other and at the robins who perched above us. Sometimes I would go into the fields with my mother and father and spend an hour helping pick raspberries or blackberries or loganberries or any of the other things they worked in, but there were really only two important things to do — play on the beaches and eat fruit.

It didn't occur to me that things would ever be different again, but one day early in August the last berry was picked and we took the ferry into Seattle, where we bought a big brown tent and a gas stove. We added them to our trailer load and drove back over the green-and-white Cascades, beneath the glacial sunrise face of Mount Rainier, and down into the sweaty outdoor factory that is the Yakima Valley. There the Yakima River is bled for transfusions to the millions of rows of roots, its depleted currents finally dragging themselves muddily to their relieved merger with the undiminishable Columbia. One can follow the Yakima for miles and miles and see nothing but irrigated fields and orchards — and the gaunt camps of transient laborers.

The workers come like a horde of salvaging locusts, stripping a field, moving to the next, filling their boxes or crates or sacks, weighing in, collecting the bonuses offered to entice them to stay till the end of the season, and disappearing again. They spend their repetitive days in rows

5

of things to be picked and their sweltering nights in rows of tents and trailers. We pitched our tent beside the others, far from our pleasant island where the owners of the fields were neighbors who invited my sister and me among their cherry trees. Here the sauntering owners and their bristling foremen never smiled at those children who ran through the fields playing games and only occasionally at those who worked beside their parents.

In North Dakota I had worked on our farm — trampling hay, driving a team of horses, fetching cows, feeding calves and chickens — but of course that had all been only my duty as a member of the family, not a way to earn money. Now I was surrounded by grown-ups who wanted to pay me for working, and by children my own age who were stepping up to the pay window every night with weighing tags in their hands and collecting money. I saw that the time had come for me to assume a place of adult independence in the world.

I made up my mind I was going to earn a dollar all in one day. We were picking hops then, and of all the rows I have toiled my way up and down, I remember hop rows the most vividly. Trained up on their wires fifteen feet overhead, the giant vines resemble monster grape arbors hung with bunches of weird unripe fruit. A man who does not pick things for a living comes and cuts them down with a knife tied to a ten-foot pole so the people below can strip them off into sacks. Hops don't really look like any other growing thing but instead like something artificially constructed — pine cones, perhaps, with segments cleverly cut from the soft, limp, clinging leaves that lie next to the kernels of an ear of corn. A hop in your hand is like a feather, and it will almost float on a puff of air. Hops are good only for making yeast, so you can't even get healthily sick of them by eating them all day long, the way you can berries or peas.

Pickers are paid by the pound, and picking is a messy business. Sometimes you run into a whole cluster that is gummy with the honeydew of hop aphids, and gray and musty with the mildew growing on the sticky stuff. Tiny red spiders rush from the green petals and flow up your arms, like more of the spots the heat makes you see.

The professionals could earn up to six dollars a day. One toothless   *10* grandmother discouraged us all by making as much as anybody in the row and at the same time never getting out of her rocking chair except to drag it behind her from vine to vine. My father and mother each made over three dollars a day, but though I tried to work almost as long hours as they did, my pay at the end of the day would usually be somewhere between eighty and ninety cents.

Then one day in the second week of picking, when the hops were good and I stayed grimly sweating over my long gray sack hung on a child-sized frame, I knew that this was going to be the day. As the afternoon waned and I added the figures on my weight tags over and over again in my head, I could feel the excitement begin making spasms in my stomach. That night the man at the pay window handed me a silver dollar and three pennies. He must have seen that this was a day not for paper but for silver. The big coin, so neatly and brightly stamped, was coolly distant from the blurred mélange of piled vines and melting heat that had put it into my hand. Only its solid heaviness connected it in a businesslike way with the work it represented. For the first time in my life I truly comprehended the relationship between toil and media of exchange, and I saw how exacting and yet how satisfying were the terms of the world. Perhaps because of this insight, I did not want the significance of my dollar dimmed by the common touch of copper pettiness. I gave the vulgar pennies to my little sister, who was amazed but grateful. Then I felt even more grown-up than before, because not everybody my age was in a position to give pennies to kids.

That night I hardly slept, lying uncovered beside my sister on our mattress on the ground, sticking my hand out under the bottom of the tent to lay it on the cooling earth between the clumps of dry grass. Tired as I was, I had written post cards to three people in North Dakota before going to bed. I had told my grandmother, my aunt, and my friend Doris that I had earned a dollar in one day. Then, because I did not want to sound impolitely proud of myself, and to fill up the card, I added on each one, "I'm fine and I plan to pick again tomorrow. How are you?"

I couldn't wait to get to the field the next day and earn another dollar. Back home none of my friends would have dreamed of being able to earn so much in one day. The only thing to do back there for money was to trap gophers for the bounty; and even the big kids, who ran a fairly long trap line and had the nerve to cut the longest tails in half, couldn't make more than twenty cents on a good day, with tails at two cents apiece. I earned a dollar and forty cents the next day and the day after that, and at least a dollar every day for another week until we moved to another place of picking — a pear orchard.

By that time it was September, and most of us children from the rows of tents stood out at the gateway of the camp and waited each day for the long yellow school bus. I had never seen a school bus before, and my sister and I were shy about how to act in such a grand vehicle. We sat together, holding our lunch buckets on our knees, looking out at the trees beside the roads, trying to catch a glimpse of our mother and father on the ladders.

The school had about three times as many pupils in it as there were *15* people in the town back in North Dakota where we used to buy coal and groceries. The pupils who were planning to attend this school all year were separated from those who, like me, did not know how many days or weeks we would be in that one spot. In our special classes we did a great deal of drawing and saw a number of movies. School was so luxurious in comparison with the hard work I had done in North Dakota the previous year that I wrote another post card to Doris, telling her that we never had to do fractions and that we got colored construction paper to play with almost every day. I copied a picture of a donkey with such accuracy that my teacher thought I had traced it until she held the two to the window and saw that the lines were indisputably my own. After that I got extra drawing periods and became very good at copying, which always elicited more praise than my few original compositions.

I was understandably sad when we left that school after two weeks and went to Wenatchee. For the first time, we were not in a regular camp. The previous year my father, recognizing that the crops had not brought in enough to get us through the winter, had taken the train to Wenatchee after the sparse harvest was in and picked apples for a man named Jim Baumann. Baumann wanted him back, so he let us pitch our tent on his land not far from his house. We made camp, and after supper Baumann came down to talk about the next day's arrangements. The school was not so large as the other one, and there was no school bus for us because we were only a half mile away from it. Baumann was shorthanded in the packing shed and needed my mother early in the morning. Besides, there was no reason why she should have to take us to school, because he had a daughter who was in my grade who could walk with us and take us to our respective rooms.

"Why, isn't that lovely!" my mother exclaimed with unwonted enthusiasm. "Now you'll have a nice little girl to play with right here and to be your friend at school."

Her excitement was rather remarkable, considering the dubious reaction she had to everybody else I had played with since we started camping. It hadn't seemed to me that she had liked even the boy who made me a pair of stilts and taught me to walk them. Now here she was favorably predisposed toward somebody I didn't even know. I agreed that it would be nice to have a nice little girl to play with.

The next morning my sister and I sat on the steps of the Baumanns' front porch, where Barbara's mother had told us to make ourselves at home, waiting for her to finish her breakfast. We had already been up so long that it seemed to me we must surely be late for school; I began picturing the humiliating tardy entrance into a roomful of strange faces.

Two of Barbara's friends came down the driveway to wait for her. *20* They both wore the kind of plaid skirts I had been wondering if I could ask my mother about buying — after all, she *had* said all my dresses were too short this fall because of all the inches I'd grown in the summer. The two girls looked at us for a moment, then uncoiled shiny-handled jump ropes and commenced loudly shouting two different rhymes to accompany their jumping.

Barbara came out on the porch, greeted her friends with a disconcerting assurance, jumped down the steps past us, insinuated herself between them, and clasped their hands. "I have to show these kids where the school is," she told them. Turning her head slightly she called, "Well,

take them to the front of the room. Then she told everybody in my row to pack up his books and move one seat back. My heart banged alarmingly up in my throat and I nearly gagged from the sudden acute sensations in my viscera. In North Dakota such drastic action was taken only when an offender, after repeated warnings, had proved too incorrigible to sit anywhere except right in front of the teacher's desk. The fact that I had no idea of why I was now classified as such an incorrigible only augmented my anguish. While books banged and papers and pencils fell to the floor and boys jostled each other in the aisle, I managed to sidle numbly up to the front. I sat down in my new seat, trying not to notice how shamefully close it was to the big desk facing it, and I was careful not to raise my eyes higher than the vase of zinnias standing on the corner nearest me.

When school was out I hurried to find my sister and get out of the schoolyard before seeing anybody in my class. But Barbara and her friends had beaten us to the playground entrance and they seemed to be waiting for us. We started to walk around them but they fell into step with us. Barbara said, "So now you're in the 'A' class. You went straight from the 'C' class to the 'A' class." She sounded impressed.

"What's the 'A' class?" I asked. 35

Everybody made superior yet faintly envious giggling sounds. "Well, why did you think the teacher moved you to the front of the room, dopey? Didn't you know you were in the 'C' class before, 'way in the back of the room?"

Of course I hadn't known. The Wenatchee fifth grade was bigger than my whole school had been in North Dakota, and the idea of subdivisions within a grade had never occurred to me. The subdividing for the first marking period had been done before I came to the school, and I had never, in the six weeks I'd been there, talked to anyone long enough to find out about the "A," "B," and "C" classes.

I still could not understand why that had made such a difference to Barbara and her friends. I didn't yet know that it was disgraceful and dirty to be a transient laborer and ridiculous to be from North Dakota. I thought living in a tent was more fun than living in a house. I didn't know that we were gypsies, really (how that thought would have thrilled me then!), and that we were regarded with the suspicion felt by those who plant toward those who do not plant. It didn't occur to me that we were all looked upon as one more of the untrustworthy natural phenomena, drifting here and there like mists or winds, that farmers of certain crops are resentfully forced to rely on. I didn't know that I was the only child who had camped on the Baumanns' land ever to get out of the "C" class. I did not know that school administrators and civic leaders held conferences to talk about how to handle the problem of transient laborers.

I only knew that for two happy days I walked to school with Barbara and her friends, played hopscotch and jump rope with them at recess, and was even invited into the house for some ginger ale — an exotic drink I had never tasted before.

Then we took down our tent and packed it in the trailer with our   40
mattresses and stove and drove on, because the last apples were picked and
sorted and boxed and shipped to the people all over the world, whoever
they were, who could afford to buy them in 1937. My teacher wrote a
letter for me to take to my next school. In it, she told me, she had informed
my next teacher that I should be put in the "A" class immediately. But
there wasn't any "A" class in my room, the new teacher explained.

By then I was traveled enough to realize that it was another special
class for transients. The teacher showed us movies almost every day.

The Responsive Reader

1. What details, what sights or events, help you relive the experience
   of the girl telling her story? Which of her experiences or observations
   in the fields are especially striking or memorable for you?
2. The girl telling her story sees herself as moving toward self-reliance
   and maturity. In what ways?
3. What is the author's attitude toward or understanding of the larger
   economic or social system?
4. Does this essay make you think about the schooling of the children
   of migrant workers? How or why?

Talking, Listening, Writing

5. Is the significance of Hudson's story limited by time and place? Do
   you think young people have comparable experiences today?
6. In your experience, do teachers and schools treat well-to-do and
   poor children differently?
7. What parallels are there in the role of the traditional work ethic in
   the essays by Wong and Hudson?

Projects

8. What can you find out about the role and lives of migrant workers
   or illegal aliens in your community, county, or state? What do you
   know from personal experience or observation? Working with a
   group, try to bring together information from official agencies,
   news reports, or studies.

DONALD DUK AND THE WHITE MONSTERS

Frank Chin

> *Frank Chin was one of the first Asian American writers to become known to a wide audience. He attended the University of California at Berkeley in the sixties; in the seventies, he was the first Chinese American to have a play produced on the New York stage. His plays* Chickencoop Chinaman *and* Year of the Dragon *attacked the familiar stereotype of Asian males as sinister villains in the Fu Manchu mode. Maxine Hong Kingston, probably the best-known Chinese writer in America, has said of him that "the main energy that goes through his work is anger." He has been angry at publishers for publishing four female Asian writers for every Asian male; he has criticized other Chinese American writers for mispresenting and putting down the traditional culture. His spiritual roots are in Chinese myth and in the martial ideal of strong masculine archetypes — independent of state and bureaucracy and trusting "no one." His novel* Donald Duk *(1991) shows another side of his gift for inspiring controversy and mixed reviews. It has been called a "devilishly wild and wacky tale by a word-and-sword slinger of wit, audacity, and intelligence" (Michi Weglyn). The following excerpt — the opening pages of the novel — show his talent for seeing the humor in issues of ethnic identity that are usually treated in more solemn fashion.*

Thought Starters: Writers acknowledging the humorous side of the minority experience run a risk: They may be considered secure enough in their pride to acknowledge the sad and funny side of the rich collective experience of their group. Or they may be accused of perpetuating the self-contempt that makes members of minorities play the clown for a white audience. As you read the following pages, what kind of humor do you encounter? Do you consider it demeaning or offensive? Why or why not?

Who would believe anyone named Donald Duk dances like Fred Astaire? Donald Duk does not like his name. Donald Duk never liked his name. He hates his name. He is not a duck. He is not a cartoon character. He does not go home to sleep in Disneyland every night. The kids that laugh at him are very smart. Everyone at his private school is smart. Donald Duk is smart. He is a gifted one, they say.

No one in school knows he takes tap dance lessons from a man who calls himself "The Chinese Fred Astaire." Mom talks Dad into paying for the lessons and tap shoes.

Fred Astaire. Everybody everywhere likes Fred Astaire in the old black-and-white movies. Late at night on TV, even Dad smiles when Fred Astaire dances. Mom hums along. Donald Duk wants to live the late night life in old black-and-white movies and talk with his feet like Fred Astaire, and smile Fred Astaire's sweet lemonade smile.

The music teacher and English teacher in school go dreamy eyed when they talk about seeing Fred Astaire and Ginger Rogers on the late-night TV. "Remember when he danced with Barbara Stanwyck? What was the name of that movie . . . ?"

"Barbara Stanwyck?"   5

"Did you see the one where he dances with Rita Hayworth?"

"Oooh, Rita Hayworth!"

Donald Duk enjoys the books he reads in school. The math is a curious game. He is not the only Chinese in the private school. But he is the only Donald Duk. He avoids the other Chinese here. And the Chinese seem to avoid him. This school is a place where the Chinese are comfortable hating Chinese. "Only the Chinese are stupid enough to give a kid a stupid name like Donald Duk," Donald Duk says to himself. "And if the Chinese were that smart, why didn't they invent tap dancing?"

Donald Duk's father's name is King. King Duk. Donald hates his father's name. He hates being introduced with his father. "This is King Duk, and his son Donald Duk." Mom's name is Daisy. "That's Daisy Duk, and her son Donald." Venus Duk and Penny Duk are Donald's sisters. The girls are twins and a couple of years older than Donald.

His own name is driving him crazy! Looking Chinese is driving him   10
crazy! All his teachers are making a big deal about Chinese stuff in their classes because of Chinese New Year coming on soon. The teacher of California History is so happy to be reading about the Chinese. "The man I studied history under at Berkeley authored this book. He was a spellbinding lecturer," the teacher throbs. Then he reads, "The Chinese in America were made passive and nonassertive by centuries of Confucian thought and Zen mysticism. They were totally unprepared for the violently individualistic and democratic Americans. From their first step on American soil to the middle of the twentieth century, the timid, introverted Chinese have been helpless against the relentless victimization by aggressive, highly competitive Americans.

"One of the Confucian concepts that lends the Chinese vulnerable to the assertive ways of the West is 'the mandate of heaven.' As the European kings of old ruled by divine right, so the emperors of China ruled by the mandate of heaven." The teacher takes a breath and looks over his spellbound class. Donald wants to barf pink and green stuff all over the teacher's teacher's book.

"What's he saying?" Donald Duk's pal Arnold Azalea asks in a whisper.

"Same thing as everybody — Chinese are artsy, cutesy and chickendick." Donald whispers back.

Oh, no! Here comes Chinese New Year again! It is Donald Duk's worst time of year. Here come the stupid questions about the funny things Chinese believe in. The funny things Chinese do. The funny things Chinese eat. And, "Where can I buy some Chinese firecrackers?"

And in Chinatown it's *Goong hay fot choy* everywhere. And some gang kids do sell firecrackers. And some gang kids rob other kids looking for firecrackers. He doesn't like the gang kids. He doesn't like speaking their Chinese. He doesn't have to — this is America. He doesn't like Chinatown. But he lives here.

The gang kids know him. They call him by name. One day the Frog Twins wobble onto the scene with their load of full shopping bags. There is Donald Duk. And there are five gang boys and two girlfriends chewing gum, swearing and smirking. The gang kids wear black tanker jackets, white tee shirts and baggy black denim jeans. It is the alley in front of the Chinese Historical Society Museum. There are fish markets on each side of the Chinatown end of the alley. Lawrence Ferlinghetti's famous City Lights Bookstore is at the end that opens on Columbus Street. Suddenly there are the Frog Twins in their heavy black overcoats. They seem to be wearing all the clothes they own under their coats. Their coats bulge. Under their skirts they wear several pairs of trousers and slacks. They wear one knit cap over the other. They wear scarves tied over their heads and shawls over their shoulders.

That night, after he is asleep, Dad comes home from the restaurant and wakes him up. "You walk like a sad softie," Dad says. "You look like you want everyone to beat you up."

"I do not!" Donald Duk says.

"You look at yourself in the mirror," Dad says, and Donald Duk looks at himself in his full-length dressing mirror. "Look at those slouching shoulders, that pouty face. Look at those hands holding onto each other. You look scared!" Dad's voice booms and Donald hears everyone's feet hit the floor. Mom and the twins are out in the hall looking into his open door.

"I am scared!" Donald Duk says.

"I don't care if you are scared," Dad says. His eyes sizzle into Donald Duk's frightened pie-eyed stare. "Be as scared as you want to be, but don't look scared. Especially when you walk through Chinatown."

"How do I look like I'm not scared if I *am* scared?" Donald Duk asks.

"You walk with your back straight. You keep your hands out of your pockets. Don't hunch your shoulders. Think of them as being down. Keep your head up. Look like you know where you're going. Walk like you know where you're going. And you say, 'Don't mess with me, horse-puckie! Don't mess with me!' But you don't say it with your mouth. You say it with your eyes. You say it with your hands where everybody can see them. Anybody get two steps in front of you, you zap them with your eyes, and they had better nod at you or look away. When they nod, you nod. When you walk like nobody better mess with you, nobody will mess with you. When you walk around like you're walking now, all rolled up in a little ball and hiding out from everything, they'll get you for sure."

Donald does not like his dad waking him up like that and yelling at him. But what the old man says works. Outside among the cold San Francisco shadows and the early morning shoppers, Donald Duk hears his father's voice and straightens his back, takes his hands out of his pockets, says "Don't mess with me!" with his eyes and every move of his body. And, yes, he's talking with his body the way Fred Astaire talks, and shoots every gang kid who walks toward him in the eye with a look that says, "Don't mess with me." And no one messes with him. Dad never talks about it again.

Later, gang kids laugh at his name and try to pick fights with him   25
during the afternoon rush hour, Dad's busy time in the kitchen. Donald is smarter than these lowbrow beady-eyed goons. He has to beat them without fighting them because he doesn't know how to fight. Donald Duk gets the twins to talk about it with Dad while they are all at the dining room table working on their model airplanes.

Dad laughs. "So he has a choice. He does not like people laughing at his name. He does not want the gangsters laughing at his name to beat him up. He mostly does not want to look like a sissy in front of them, so what can he do?"

"He can pay them to leave him alone," Venus says.

"He can not! That is so chicken it's disgusting!" Penelope says.

"So, our little brother is doomed."

"He can agree with them and laugh at his name," Dad says. "He can   30
tell them lots of Donald Duk jokes. Maybe he can learn to talk that quack-quack Donald Duck talk."

"Whaaat?" the twins ask in one voice.

"If he keeps them laughing," Dad says, "even if he can just keep them listening, they are not beating him up, right? And they are not calling him a sissy. He does not want to fight? He does not have to fight. He has to use his smarts, okay? If he's smart enough, he makes up some Donald Duck jokes to surprise them and make them laugh. They laugh three times, he can walk away. Leave them there laughing, thinking Donald Duk is one terrific fella."

"So says King Duk," Venus Duk flips. The twins often talk as if everything they hear everybody say and see everybody do is dialog in a memoir they're writing or action in a play they're directing. This makes Mom feel like she's on stage and drives Donald Duk crazy.

"Is that Chinese psychology, dear?" Daisy Duk asks.

"Daisy Duk inquires," says Penelope Duk.   35

"And little Donnie Duk says, *Oh, Mom!* and sighs."

"I do not!" Donald Duk yelps at the twins.

"Well, then, say it," Penelope Duk says. "It's a good line. So *you* you, you know."

FREEWAY 280

Lorna Dee Cervantes

The Mexican American poet who revisits a childhood setting in the follow-ing poem was born in San Francisco and attended San Jose State University. She published her first volume of poetry, Empulmada, *in 1981. In the following poem she revisits a place where she used to live and finds only empty fenced-in lots under a raised freeway (Freeway 280). The houses are gone, and the fruit trees and vegetable patches are running wild. Like other Spanish-speaking Americans, Cervantes slides easily from English into Spanish (the language of her childhood) and back.*

Thought Starters: Many adults remember childhood scenes with mixed feelings — intense positive and negative memories that may haunt them in their dreams. What are the mixed or contradictory emotions the speaker expresses in this poem?

Las casitas near the gray cannery   *1*   *the little houses*
nestled amid wild abrazos of climbing roses   *hugs*
and man–high red geraniums
are gone now. The freeway conceals it
all beneath a raised scar.   *5*

But under the fake windsounds of the open lanes,
in the abandoned lots below, new grasses sprout,
wild mustard remembers, old gardens
come back stronger than they were,
trees have been left standing in their yards.   *10*
Albaricoqueros, cerezos, nogales . . .   *apricot, cherry, and walnut*
Viejitas come here with paper bags to gather greens.   *little old women*
Espinaca, verdolagas, yerbabuena . . .   *spinach, purslane, mint*

I scramble over the wire fence
that would have kept me out.   *15*
Once, I wanted out, wanted the rigid lanes
to take me to a place without sun,
without the smell of tomatoes burning
on swing shift in the greasy summer air.

Maybe it's here
en los campos extranos de esta ciudad
where I'll find it, that part of me
mown under
like a corpse
or a loose seed.

20

in the strange fields of
this city

25

The Responsive Reader

1. How does the speaker in this poem feel about the freeway? (What does she make you see and feel when she calls it a "raised scar"? What are the "windsounds," and why are they "fake"?)
2. What were the poet's feelings about this place when she left there? What are her feelings now?
3. Do you think the part of her or her past that was "mown under" here will prove a "corpse" or a "seed"?

Talking, Listening, Writing

4. Linguists — scientists studying language — use the term *code-switching* for the practice of moving back and forth from one language, or linguistic code, to another. Where and when in the poem does the poet shift to Spanish? (Can you try to explain why?) What would have been lost if the poet had used English instead of the interspersed Spanish phrases?
5. What childhood settings or childhood scenes call up intense memories or mixed emotions for you? Bring them to life for your reader.

Projects

6. Are you or any members of your family bilingual? If not, do you know any bilingual Americans? When and how do bilingual Americans use their first and second languages? If you can, talk to speakers of more than one language about how they use one language or the other.

WRITING
WORKSHOP 1

Writing from Experience

Good writing is often rooted in personal experience. This is true obviously for autobiographical writing — for instance, the life story of someone like Maya Angelou, overcoming the obstacles in her path, prevailing against odds. However, writing that is much less personal often owes its power to its roots in firsthand experience. When we read about discrimination, affirmative action, gender roles, or the immigrant experience, we prefer that the writer know the subject at first hand. We like to think that the author "was there" — as a target, a beneficiary, a witness, a close caring observer. We want the writer to show what theories or statistics mean by recreating in vividly remembered detail a relevant incident from personal experience. Words are just words until we can relate them to the experience of someone who is involved or who cares.

Writing based on personal experience has special strengths:

- When you take stock of your own personal experience, you write about what you know best. No one is more of an expert than you are on what matters to you as a person. No one knows more about where and how you grew up. Nobody knows better what home or family meant to you or what helped and hindered you in school or on the job.

- Writing from experience sets up a special confidential relationship between writer and reader. As the writer, you show that you trust your readers enough to share with them your personal thoughts and feelings. Writing from personal experience often seems less audience-conscious than other kinds of writing — especially those aimed at getting something from the reader, whether a sale or a vote. But the basic assumption in writing that takes stock honestly of the author's own experience is that the readers will be able to relate — to see the connection with what matters in their own lives.

TRIGGERING Papers based on personal experience often seem better motivated than other kinds. Here are some reasons to do this kind of writing:

- People often feel the need to unburden their hearts. When they have experienced a serious challenge, they need to tell somebody — if only a diary or journal. Becoming uprooted, suffering serious illness, being an outsider, coming to terms with divorce, living with disability — these are experiences that may make you want to tell your story. Many people find that writing about something helps them cope.

▪ When people have experienced divided loyalties or contradictory emotions, writing gives them a chance to sort things out in their own minds. When people have had difficult relationships with family, or when they had to break with an organization or abandon a cause, writing about the experience gives them a chance to come to terms with what happened.

▪ When people have been wronged, they may feel the need to go on record. When people see injustice, they may want to bear witness (rather than "not get involved"). The first step toward the correction of grievances often is for those concerned to make their voices heard.

▪ People experience pleasure in sharing what is good — discovering the rewards of tutoring or being a mentor, for instance. They get a satisfaction from paying tribute to someone who served as a role model or helped them in time of need.

GATHERING What does it take to make a reader share in your experience, thoughts, and feelings? What will make a paper become real for your reader? One crucial part of the answer is: Work up a rich fund of material. You will need to call up from the memory bank of your brain sights, sounds, emotions. You need to jog your memory, starting the chains of association that will gradually bring back a whole incident from one vividly remembered detail. Learn to draw on the rich backlog of what you have witnessed, thought, and felt.

An important requirement is to be honest with yourself: You are embarking on an honest exploration of "inner space." You need to start putting thoughts and feelings that may have been confused and inarticulate down on paper. You start putting into words what matters to you. If you are like most writers, you will begin by saying to yourself, "It is impossible to say just what I mean." Then slowly you will start finding the right words.

The following passage by a student of Japanese descent does not play games with the reader. It records powerful authentic personal feelings:

"What are you?" I have often been at a loss for words as to how to answer this question. Should I answer, Japanese? American? Japanese American? I do not consider myself fully Japanese, since I have not been brought up with the language and the strict traditional culture. I am not an ordinary American because of obvious visible differences. Trying to answer this question has often left me in an awkward position and has sometimes led me to regret my existence.

Remember, however, that *telling* your readers about your feelings is not enough. The second requirement is to make these feelings real for your reader by anchoring them to concrete incidents and situations. It is not enough to tell your readers that you are happy or in pain — make them share your happiness or help them share the pain. Recreate the people and situations that inspired your feelings and shaped your thoughts. Recreate the people, the places, the events in telling detail so that words will not just remain words. The following passage acts out and brings back to life an incident that was an eye-opener for the student writer:

> I remember several incidents that helped me see the truth about race relations. Once my family was traveling across the country to South Carolina to visit relatives. I recall our stopping at a small broken-down gas station. We waited and waited for service. My father even backed up the car and went forward to the pump again to make the bell ring the second time. I remember the attendant, wearing a white T-shirt and open red-checkered flannel jacket, leaning back in his chair, looking out at us, and then continuing to read his Field and Stream magazine. I asked my father what the problem was, and he replied that it must be closing time. I suspiciously looked out the back window as we pulled away. I saw another car pull up with a white driver, and the attendant, throwing down his magazine, jogged out to pump gas.

In this paragraph, a significant incident is told straight — in graphic revealing detail. We can see the country bumpkin in his red-checkered jacket, reading his magazine, ignoring customers merely because they are not white. In this paragraph, no one is called names; no one makes any speeches. The word *prejudice* is not even mentioned. The incident speaks for itself. (How would you spell out in so many words what it says?)

SHAPING   To turn a stream of jostling memories into a paper, you need to focus on what matters and lay out the material in an order that makes sense. Unsorted, unedited experience tends to be miscellaneous. One thing happens after another; people are often at cross purposes, thinking about several things at the same time. Avoid papers that fall into the "and-then" pattern: This happened, and then this happened, and then this happened (one thing after another). An effective paper has brought a key issue or concern into focus. It may highlight a major strand in your life, leaving much else aside. From a sequence of events, it pulls out high points that together tell a story. Details fall into place; they form a pattern.

An excellent exercise in focusing and channeling is to write a **story with a point**. You focus on one single incident dramatizing something that was an issue or a concern in your life. You tell the story in vivid detail. Then, at the end, you spell out what the incident meant to you. Perhaps the incident served as a warning, as a turning point, or as a revelation. Here is an example of a story with a point. How well does it lead up to the point it makes?

Hell in Suburbia

Crank (the street name for methamphetamine), also called poor man's cocaine, is a stimulant. Its main effect is sleep deprivation. One day while at work, having not slept for three days, I was experiencing "brownouts," lapses in concentration. I was using the forklift to pull a two-thousand pound pallet of copy paper off the top shelf fifteen feet in the air when I blanked out. The forks were not all the way into the pallet as I began to pull it from the shelf. It lurched and almost came down on me. Shaken, I went to the bathroom, splashed water on my face. Back in the warehouse, the pallet was still there, leaning dangerously against the forks. The rest of the crew had gone home for the day, and so I was alone. There was no way to bring the pallet down intact. Finally, I jerked the pallet hard with the forklift to straighten it and brought it down, losing about half of the fifty-pound cartons. They fell all around me. Had I not straightened the pallet out, the ton of paper would all have fallen on top of me.

This one incident worked on me like no other. I had been ready to quit for a long time. I knew the damage crank was doing to me mentally. Had the incident happened earlier I would have most likely shrugged it off and done another line. I needed a catalyst to help me make a decision I obviously didn't have the strength of character to make on my own.

A familiar criticism of personal writing is that it stays too much in the "let's-see-what-happens,-let's-see-what-develops" mode. It tends to stay too close to simple **chronological** order — the sequence of events in time. Part of your job is to wean yourself from a simple "and-then" kind of writing.

For a full-length personal experience paper, try to work out a stronger overall pattern. For instance, try to think in terms of major stages or of major **turning points** — turns in the road toward maturity or independence. You may want to use a strong **then-and-now** pattern to organize your paper. What were assumptions about gender roles when you grew up, and what are they now? How did people feel about divorce then, and what is their thinking now? Or you might trace the **point-counterpoint** of two strong conflicting influences in your growing up. Perhaps your allegiance was divided between two parents very different in their personalities and commitments. Perhaps you experienced a strong pull between the traditional culture of the home and the peer culture of the neighborhood or school.

What gave shape and direction to the following student paper? Is there an underlying chronological sequence — does it move roughly from the distant past closer to the more recent past and the present? How does the play of opposites help organize the paper as a whole?

My Parents, Myself

Last week I heard the poet Etheridge Knight speak to a group of
students and teachers. He said there were only two things he knew for
certain in his life, and the rest was all just his opinion. He said he
knew who his mother was—and he knew who his father was.

What I have often questioned is whether I am more like one parent
than the other. There were two different people inside my father, or so
it seemed to me. My early memories of him are positive: He made ships
with intricate detail, and he made a butterfly collection of specimens he
had caught himself. He took us to the beach. He looked self-assured; he
looked strong. He was a tall, slender man who had come from an English
middle-class background, and who had bettered himself through higher
education. He met my mother while he was going to law school.

She was of pure Irish stock, and very much a working-class girl
with a little style or class. Once Joe Dimaggio had sent her a drink from
across the bar, or so she said. Though she was short, she had a perfect
figure and dressed well on her modest income. She had a pretty smile
and baby-fine blonde hair which she always wore in a bun on top of her
head. My mother was an only child and her mother died when she was
fifteen, leaving her to be cared for by her aunt. At the age of twenty-
seven, she married my father, believing in family and hard work and all
the prospects a good marriage would bring. They moved to San Francisco
at my father's request and rapidly had nine children.

When I was young, I favored my father because his attention was
harder won and therefore more desirable. I remember choosing his home
state for my sixth grade report. But, as I grew older, I did not want
anything to do with him. I was no longer as sweet or as pretty, and
he was no longer as kind or as safe. I resented his rules—his strict
attention to "form." We were expected to dress before coming downstairs
in the morning; we were expected to say good night to our father, even if
he was passed out in his chair. As a young adult in my teens, I felt as if
I could never do anything right. For instance, I could never remember
how to set a table properly. More importantly, I could not choose the
"right" vocation. I wanted to be an artist, and he did not have the
confidence that I would succeed.

As an adult, I understand why I despaired so much of becoming like
him. I understand his failures in the light of my mother's success. He
shut people out of his life. He was a loner and he became an alcoholic,
a word I did not know the meaning of until I was twenty-five. I can
remember sitting in the half-lit kitchen waiting for my mom to come
home from work. Earlier in the evening, my father had come back from
Thrifty's as he always did on the weekends, with soda and potato chips
for us kids, and a bottle for himself. He would empty the bag on the
counter, putting his beer in the refrigerator, and carrying his bourbon
to the den. I would sit on the stool and wait to watch his tall figure
stumble towards the bathroom and complain about this or that.

People always moved toward my mother. I remember working with
her at the Pacific Telephone Company, and watching the women she

worked with treat her with respect and affection. Some girls called her "Mom," which pained me very much. Though I was like my father, I wanted my mother's closeness. When she died there were hundreds of people at her funeral. When my father died there were only a dozen people—men he had worked with and a few neighbors that had never known him well.

I remember the Christmas days that followed my mother's death and how my father tried to manage. I came to know who he was with some clarity three months before he died. I see him lacing red and green ribbons through the chandelier that hung over the dining room table, and putting out dishes of candy for us kids. I see him standing in the living room looking around at us, attempting a few pleasant comments, and then retreating awkwardly to his den where he sat with his books and the red curtains that hung down from the tall windows.

My mother was so different. She lacked pretenses and did not expect life to give her a lot. She gave to life instead. She gave her time to the infants at the Sunday school. She gave her home to a young girl of my own age when that girl's mother could give her neither a home nor a family. She gave her home to a young man she met in an English class who was drifting. My father did not know how to gather life towards him.

I have often feared not finding my mother's goodness inside myself. I have fought off the separateness my father carried inside himself, his failures, and his reserve which people see in me and mistake for calm. I loved them both very much.

REVISING Always make time for revision. Revising gives you a chance to look at your own writing with the reader's eye. Check a first draft for predictable weaknesses:

- *Build up concrete detail.* Even in a fairly well-developed paper, the texture of concretely observed detail is often too thin. Move in for the closer look. Add lifelike detail to make your readers visualize the setting or the people. Act out key events in more striking detail.

- *Look for places where you have fallen back on clichés.* Ready-made phrases are handy: "the need to find oneself," "the need for personal space," "the fear of commitment." However, make sure such phrases do not sound too interchangeable and secondhand. Try to find your own way of saying what you feel—which may be partly similar to but also partly different from what others have felt before you.

- *Check for overgeneralizing.* It is easy to read too much into a single incident. A key incident may dramatize a pattern—but it may also have resulted from an unusual combination of circumstances. (A teacher or a police officer may have had a bad day—just as a heart-warming gesture may have been a once-in-a-lifetime event.)

- *Try not to sound too one-sided or self-righteous.* Readers get wary when everything that went wrong in your life was someone else's fault. You may have to make an attempt to see the legitimate concerns or genuine misunderstandings of other people involved.

▪ *Revise for a strained facetiousness.* Some writers feel the compulsion to make everything sound bright, zany, hectic, funny. Readers tire of a strained facetious tone. A good tone to aim at is to be basically serious with an occasional lighter touch.

Topics for Experience Papers (A Sampling)

1. Have you ever rebelled against (or returned to) tradition? What led up to your change of attitude? Was there a turning point? What was the outcome?
2. Have you ever been aware of competing or conflicting influences on your life or your thinking? Have you ever experienced divided loyalties? How did you sort them out?
3. Have you experienced a change in your religious outlook?
4. Have you encountered special obstacles or opportunities because of who or what you are? What is your experience with discrimination, prejudice, favoritism, or having the "inside track"?
5. Have you felt on the defensive about your identity or your background? How did you cope?
6. In your growing up, has a major problem or issue presented a challenge to your sense of identity or your sense of self-worth? Has a problem in your family or personal life affected your outlook or helped shape your personality?
7. Where and how did you become aware of race or of varying ethnic origins? What difference have they made in your life?
8. Have you ever discovered a new lifestyle or rediscovered a cultural identity? What difference has it made in your life?
9. Have you ever changed your mind (or have you ever had a major change of heart) on a subject like marriage, having children, or divorce?
10. What shaped your views on what it means to be a man or a woman? Have you had occasion to reexamine or revise your views?

2

This Land:
Landscape/Cityscape

*Once in their lives, people ought to concentrate their minds upon the
remembered earth. They ought to give themselves up to a particular
landscape in their experience, to look at it from as many angles as they
can, to wonder upon it, to dwell upon it. . . . They ought to imagine
the creatures there and all the faintest motions of the wind.*

N. Scott Momaday

Where people live — city, small town, backwoods, suburb — shapes
their outlook and their lives. (What are familiar stereotypes about city
dwellers and country people? Is there a grain of truth in them?) Although
most Americans now live in cities, much American folklore and political
oratory hark back to a simpler rural past. A central American myth is the
pull of the "wide open spaces." Many Americans imagine a simpler existence in a less crowded, less hectic setting — where rugged Marlboro men
roamed the range and where sturdy pioneer women kept hostiles at bay.
Closer to everyday reality for many Americans is a rural and small-town
America created by early waves of immigrants. We like to envision the
people there as self-reliant and close to the basic necessities of life, maintaining traditional religious and family ties, close to nature and the changing seasons, dependent on the weather, learning about the realities of life
and disease and death from caring for crops and livestock.

How much of the vision of an idealized small-town America is only
nostalgia? Millions of Americans are crowded into the big cities. In the
cities, traditions of civic pride and cultural vitality are increasingly threatened by decay. Civic leaders face poverty, overcrowding, unemployment,
dirt, noise, crime, drugs, and the fear of violence. Millions of Americans
have headed for the suburbs, living in or commuting from a world of
shopping malls and movie theaters that often look the same from coast to
coast.

How does the setting in which Americans live shape their lives, their
thoughts, and their feelings? How do they live together or apart in their
neighborhoods? Is there an answer to urban blight? Is there hope for our
cities?

ALONG THE PLATTE
Ursula K. Le Guin

Ursula Le Guin is an intensely curious, observant, and politically active writer who finds it hard to make neat distinctions between "being a woman and being a feminist," between "art and politics," and between high culture and popular culture. She has described herself as an "angry woman laying mightily about me with my handbag, fighting hoodlums off" — doing battle against machos, pro-lifers, enemies of the environment, world hunger, and obliterators of the Native American past. Le Guin is a native of Berkeley, California, and studied at Radcliffe and Columbia. She is best known as a writer of science fiction (the Earthsea Trilogy *and many other books). In her science fiction novels and short stories, she deals not in futuristic technology and little green men but instead uses the imaginary future to make us ponder the perennial human condition. Her talks and essays have been collected in several volumes, including* Dancing at the Edge of the World *(1989). She often writes about her travels through the American countryside and loves the endangered, semi-extinct trains whose lonesome whistles tell about far places.*

Thought Starters: Le Guin loves the country and its people and yet is a sharp-eyed critic at the same time. What does she like about what she sees on the trip she describes in the following essay? What does she criticize?

Some people fly to Tierra del Fuego and Katmandu; some people   *1*
drive across Nebraska in a VW bus.

Living in Oregon, with family in Georgia, we drive the United States corner to corner every now and then. It takes a while. On the fifth day out of Macon, just crossing the Missouri, we look up to see a jet trail in the big sky. That plane going west will do two thousand miles while we do two hundred. A strange thought. But the strangeness works both ways. We'll drive about four hundred miles today. On foot with an ox-drawn wagon, that distance would take up to a month.

These are some notes from a day and a half on the Oregon Trail.

About ten in the morning we cross the wide Missouri into the West. Nebraska City looks comfortable and self-reliant, with its railyards and grain elevators over the big brown river. From it we drive out into rolling, spacious farmlands, dark green corn, pale yellow hay stubble, darkening gold wheat. The farmhouses, with big barns and a lot of outbuildings, come pretty close together: prosperous land. The signs say: Polled Short-horns . . . Hampshire Swine . . . Charolais . . . Yorkshire and Spotted Swine.

We cross the North Fork of the Little Nemaha. The rivers of America   5
have beautiful names. What was the language this river was named in?
Nemaha — Omaha — Nebraska . . . Eastern Siouan, I guess. But it's a
guess. We don't speak the language of this country.

Down in the deep shade of trees in high thick grass stand three
horses, heads together, tails swishing, two black and one white with black
tail and mane. Summertime . . .

Around eleven we're freewaying through Lincoln, a handsome city,
the gold dome on its skyscraper capitol shining way up in the pale blue
sky, and on our left the biggest grain elevator I ever saw, blocks long, a
cathedral of high and mighty cylinders of white. On KECK, Shelley and
Dave are singing, "Santa Monica freeway, sometimes makes a country
girl blue . . ." After a while the DJ does the announcements. There will
be a State Guernsey Picnic on Saturday, if I heard right.

Now we're humming along beside the Platte — there's a language I
know. Platte means Flat. It's pretty flat along the Platte, all right, but there
are long swells in this prairie, like on the quietest sea, and the horizon isn't
forever: it's a blue line of trees way off there, under the farthest line of
puffball fair-weather clouds.

We cross some channels of the braided Platte at Grand Island and
stop for lunch at a State Wayside Park called Mormon Island, where it
costs two bucks to eat your picnic. A bit steep. But it's a pretty place,
sloughs or channels of the river on all sides, and huge black dragonflies
with silver wingtips darting over the shallows, and blue darning-needles
in the grass. The biggest mosquito I ever saw came to eat my husband's
shoulder. I got it with my bare hand, but a wrecking ball would have been
more appropriate. There used to be buffalo here. They were replaced by
the mosquitoes.

On along the Platte, which we're going to cross and recross eleven   10
times in Nebraska and one last time in Wyoming. The river is in flood,
running hard between its grey willows and green willows, aspens and big
cottonwoods. Some places the trees are up to their necks in water, and
west of Cozad the hayfields are flooded, hayrolls rotting in the water,
grey-white water pouring through fields where it doesn't belong.

The cattle are in pure herds of Black Angus, Aberdeen, Santa Ger-
trudis, and some beautiful mixed herds, all shades of cream, dun, brown,
roan. There's a Hereford bull in with his harem and descendants, big,
frowning, curly-headed, like an angry Irishman.

In 1976 Nebraska commissioned ten sculptures for the roadside rest
areas along Interstate 80, and going west you see five of them; we stop at
each one to see and photograph it, as does the grey-haired man with two
daughters who pose with the sculpture for his photograph. The pieces are
all big, imaginative, bold. The one we like best resides in a pond a couple
miles west of Kearny. It's aluminum in planes and curves and discs; parts
of it are balanced to move softly, without sound; all of it floats on the
flickering, reflecting water. It's called *The Nebraska Wind Sculpture*. "What

is it?" says a grinning man. I say, "Well, the AAA tourbook says it looks like H. G. Wells's Time Machine." He says, "O.K., but what *is* it?" — and I realize he thinks it may be "something," not "just" a work of art; and so he's looking at it and grinning, enjoying the damfool thing. If he knew it was Art, especially Modern Art, would he be afraid of it and refuse to see it at all? A fearless little boy, meanwhile, haunts the pool and shouts, "Look! A lobster!" pointing at a crayfish, and nearly falls into the scummy shallows reflecting the silver Nebraska Wind.

Down the road a town called Lexington advertises itself:

ALL-AMERICAN CITY
ALL-NEBRASKA COMMUNITY

Those are some kind of national and state awards for something, I suppose, but how disagreeable, how unfriendly and exclusive they sound. But then, what other state of the union thought of celebrating the Bicentennial with big crazy sculptures right out for every stranger driving I-80 to see? Right on, Nebraska!

We pull in for the night at a motel in North Platte, a town that has a rodeo every night of every summer every year, and we sure aren't going to miss that. After dinner we drive out Rodeo Road to Buffalo Bill Avenue to the Cody Arena (by now we have the idea that that old fraud came from around here), and the nice cowgirl selling tickets says, trying to give us a senior citizen savings, "Would you be over sixty at all?" No, we can't manage that yet, so she gives us full-price tickets and a beautiful smile. All the seats are good. It's a warm dry prairie evening, the light getting dusty and long. Young riders on young horses mill around the arena enjoying the attention till the announcer starts the show the way all rodeos start, asking us to salute "the most beautiful flag in the world," a pleasure, while the horses fidget and the flag bearer sits stern, but the announcer goes on about how this flag has been "spat and trampled and mocked and burned on campuses," boy, does he have it in for campuses, what decade is he living in? The poison in his voice is pure Agent Orange. More of this "patriotism" that really means hating somebody. Shut up, please, and let's get on with what all us Americans are here to see — and here to do, for ten bucks prize money.

The first cowboy out of the chute, bareback bronc-riding, gets thrown against the fence, and another gets his leg broken right under the stands. Rodeos are hard on horses, hard on cattle, hard on men. A lousy way to earn ten bucks. Ladies, don't let your sons grow up to be cowboys, as the song says. But the calf-roping is done for the joy of skill, of team-work, horse and man, and the barrel-riding girls are terrific, whipping around those barrels like the spinning cars on a fairground octopus, and then the quirt flicks and the snorting pony lays out blurry-legged and belly to the ground on the home stretch with the audience yipping and yahooing all the way. By now the lady from Longview, Washington, with the six-pack on the next bench is feeling no pain. A bull is trying to destroy the chutes before the rider even gets onto him. The rodeo is one of the few places where people and animals still fully interact. How vain and gallant horses are, not intelligent, but in their own way wise; how fine the scared, wily vigor of the calves and the power of the big Brahma bulls—the terrific vitality of cattle, which we raise to kill. People who want matadors mincing around can have them, there's enough moments of truth for me in a two-bit rodeo.

Driving back after the show over the viaduct across Bayley Yard, a huge Union Pacific switching center, we see high floodlights far down the line make gold rivers of a hundred intertwining tracks curving off into the glare and dazzling dark. Trains are one of the really good things the Industrial Revolution did—totally practical and totally romantic. But on all those tracks, one train.

Next morning we stop at Ogallala for breakfast at the Pioneer Trails Mall. I like that name. Two eggs up, hashbrowns, and biscuits. The restaurant radio loudspeaker plays full blast over the South Platte River roaring past full of logs and junk and way over the speed limit for rivers.

We leave that river at last near where the Denver road splits off, and come into the low, bare hills across it. As the water dries out of the ground and air, going west, the blur of humidity is gone; colors become clear and pale, distance vivid. Long, light-gold curves of wheat and brown plowed land stripe the hills. At a field's edge the stiff wheat sticks up like a horse's mane cropped short. The wind blows in the tall yellow clover on the roadsides. Sweet air, bright wind. Radio Ogallala says that now is the time to be concerned about the European corn borer.

Between the wheat and corn fields scarped table-lands begin to rise, and dry washes score the pastures. The bones of the land show through, yellowish-white rocks. There's a big stockyard away off the road, the cattle, dark red-brown, crowded together, looking like stacked wood in a lumberyard. Yucca grows wild on the hills here; this is range land. Horses roam and graze far off in the soft-colored distances. We're coming to the Wyoming border, leaving this big, long, wide, bright Nebraska; a day and a half, or forty minutes, or a month in the crossing. From a plane I would remember nothing of Nebraska. From driving I will remember the willows by the river, the sweet wind. Maybe that's what they remembered when they came across afoot and horseback, and camped each night a few miles farther west, by the willows and the cottonwoods down by the Platte.

The Responsive Reader

1. What are striking sights and sounds that an attentive reader might remember after reading this essay? Of which does the author seem particularly fond? Which, in the words of one student reader, have a special "Midwest flavor"?
2. Where does Le Guin show her fascination with the names of trees,

animals, and rivers? Where does her description show a lively imagination? (For instance, the barrel–riders whip around the barrel like spinning cars on a fairground octopus.) What other examples of vivid imaginative comparisons can you find? (What do grain elevators have to do with cathedrals? What do Hereford bulls have to do with Irishmen?)

3. Writers of chamber-of-commerce brochures often seem to love everything about the places they tout. Le Guin is often critical in her essay — where and why? What are her standards? (How does her account of the rodeo show both her love of American popular culture and her criticism of it?)

4. What does Le Guin mean when she calls trains "totally practical and totally romantic"?

5. One student reader said, "Le Guin likes the country, and it is not just a long drive to her." What is the secret of Le Guin's positive relationship to the heartland setting she describes? Is there a common denominator — a common thread?

Talking, Listening, Writing

6. Would you call the sights and sounds Le Guin describes typically American?

7. Have you had any experience with patriotism that "really means hating somebody"?

8. What kind of traveler are you? Do you have a love-hate relationship with the places and people you visit?

9. Write a guide to a part of the country that you but perhaps not many other people know well. Bring the sights and sounds to life for your reader.

Projects

10. Many observers are more critical of the lifestyle of ordinary Americans than Le Guin is. Are you? As your choice of several projects suggested in this chapter, you may want to scout an example of Americana — American popular culture in its natural habitat. Visit a rodeo, county fair, parade, firefighters' picnic, rock concert, blues festival, or the like. Take copious notes; bring back a detailed report. Can you draw any general conclusions about heartland America or ordinary Americans? (Your class may want to stage a panel discussion of students pooling their observations of the different events they have scouted.)

THE EMMA CHASE CAFÉ
William Least Heat-Moon

William Least Heat-Moon is the pen name of William Trogdon, whose degrees are from the University of Missouri and who is descended from Irish-English and Osage ancestors. His Blue Highways *(1982) chronicled a journey he took across the country to Oregon. The following is part of his second book,* PrairyErth *(1991), which explores a Kansas county, "the most easterly piece of the American Far West . . . the last remaining grand expanse of tallgrass prairie in America."*

Thought Starters: What is the double identity of the women in this story — born in a small farming community, returning to work there, then heading back to the larger world? In what way are they country people, in what way city people?

Broadway, west side, a storefront window, and painted on the plate glass a cup of steaming coffee; morning, Cottonwood Falls, the Emma Chase Café, November: I'm inside and finishing a fine western omelet and in a moment will take on the planks of homemade wheat bread — just as soon as the shadow from the window coffee cup passes across my little notebook. The men's table (a bold woman sometimes sits at it, but rare is the man who sits at the women's table) has already emptied, and now the other one does too. On the west wall hangs a portrait of a woman from the time of Rutherford B. Hayes, and she, her hair parted centrally, turns a bit to the left, as if to answer someone in the street, her high collar crisp, her eyebrow ever so slightly raised, her lips pursed as if she's about to speak. (And now someone calls out from the kitchen to the new waitress, "On your ticket, what's this U.P.?" and the girl says, "Up," and from the kitchen, "You can't have scrambled eggs up.") The portrait is of "the woman history forgot" — Emma Chase, who said, "You can't start a revolution on an empty stomach." She was not wife, daughter, sister, or mother to Salmon P. Chase, the great enemy of slavery and Lincoln's Chief Justice, whose name the county carries. Emma stands in no man's shadow but in the dark recess that the past mostly is. In this county she's famous for having been forgotten; after all, who remembers that it was on the back of one of Emma's envelopes that Lincoln outlined his Emancipation Proclamation? That's been the story in the Falls, anyway.

Most countians now understand that Emma "A-Cookie-in-Every-Jar" Chase has the reality of an idea and an ideal, even if she had to be invented. When Linda Pretzer Thurston decided to open the café, a couple of years ago, she cast about for a name, something local, something feminine, and she searched the volumes of the *Chase County Historical Sketches* for an embodiment of certain values but came away unsatisfied by or unaware of the facts, such as those of 1889 about Minnie Morgan, of Cottonwood, one of the first women in the country to be elected mayor and *the* first — and probably the only one — to serve with an all-female city council. Minnie has stood in a few dark historical corridors herself: her daughter's biography of the family in the *Sketches* speaks of wild plums and a neighbor who threw the family's clothes down the cistern to save them from a prairie fire, and it mentions her father's founding of the county newspaper *The Leader* (of many papers, the only one still alive) and her brother's "Jayhawker in Yurrup" travel books, but it says not one word about Minnie's mayoralty. There has not been a female mayor since.

So the café had no name until one night, at the family supper table, Linda and her identical twin said simultaneously in response to something she's now forgotten, "The Emma Chase!" Soon newspaper ads for the café printed Emma's chocolate-chip-cookie recipe, and asked townspeople to search their attic trunks for information about her. One day the president of the county historical society, Whitt Laughridge, came in with a large framed portrait of an unidentified woman he'd found in the vault. Thurston cried, "Yes! At last we have Emma!" Unsatisfied with history, she had invented a persona and then had to invent ways to get people to accept the name. Her ads and fabricated history worked so well that *she,* who grew up five miles west, in Elmdale, became to the citizens "Emma down at the café," and she doesn't mind.

There are other things she does object to, such as the racist joke a fellow told a while ago at the men's table, and to which she said loudly from across the room, "Did you hear that one at church, Ray?" and sometimes in answer to sexist comments she'll recite from the café refrigerator, covered with stick-on slogans like a large, upright bumper: THE ROOSTER CROWS BUT THE HEN DELIVERS, or WOMEN'S RIGHTS — REAGAN'S WRONGS.

Linda Thurston is trim and pretty, a dark strawberry blonde given   5
to large, swinging earrings; today she wears a pair of silvery stars almost of a size to be hoisted atop the courthouse cupola for Christmas. She sits down across from me to see what I'm scratching in my notebook. I'm copying what is on her coffee mug:

> I HAVE A B.A., M.A., PH.D.
> ALL I NEED NOW IS A GOOD J.O.B.

Her doctorate is in child psychology. She is thirty-nine, divorced, and has a son, John. She calls across the little café to the new waitress, "We can't do scrambled eggs over easy."

She pushes the guest book toward me. In it are names from many states and also from Russia, Italy, Israel. She says, "My friends say I'm the white Aunt Jemima of the women's movement, a radicalized storefront feminist whose job is to get cowboys to eat quiche Lorraine even if they call it 'quick lorn.' I'm an aproned militant known for scratch pies, soups, and breads, the one who's taught a waitress Lamaze breathing on a café floor."

A man, his spine crumbling with age, his eyesight almost gone, comes up and holds out a palm of change for his coffee, and Linda takes out thirty-five cents, forget the tax. Three years ago she and her young son lived near Kansas City, Kansas, where she worked with battered women and handicapped children, some of whose fathers couldn't remember their child's name; they all were poor city people who lived anonymously. She was also the president of a large chapter of the National Organization for Women, and she campaigned and typed and marched. When Ronald Reagan became President and inner-city social programs started disappearing, she found herself depressed and beginning to wonder who the enemy was, where the battlefield was, and she didn't understand why ideas so apparently democratic and humane were so despised, and she was no longer sure what it meant to help anyone disadvantaged or to be a feminist. Women seemed in retreat from action to the easier, safer battles of awareness. Things were retrogressing.

On a trip home to Elmdale she learned that the old and closed Village Inn Café was for sale, and she looked it over, found a broken-down and fouled building. Suddenly a fight against dirt and dilapidation, enemies you could lay your rubber-gloved hands on, looked good, especially when she heard that the county-seat citizens wanted a pleasant place once again to sit down with a coffee and find out whose cattle it was that went through the ice, whose horse had sent him over the fence. A group of Broadway business people met in Bell's western-clothing store and offered to buy the café building and lease it to her—after all, she was a native—and so Linda Thurston decided to live out her fantasy of running a homey little restaurant, and she moved back to Chase County, where, she hoped, "the Hills could heal." Her friend Linda Woody, a state lobbyist for NOW, had also wearied of the struggle against Reaganism, and joined her, and the once dingy, moribund café became unofficially the Retreat for Burned-Out Social Activists, a place where the women could serve homilies, history, and cold pasta salad.

Linda Thurston says: "I saw it as a haven of rest from political struggles, a place I'd have time to write up my research. If we could undermine a few stereotypes along the way and wake up a few people, that was fine too. I've never seen my return as going home so much as going forward to my roots, and I don't think I'll stay long enough to grow old here—unless I already have—and I believe when the time comes to go back to whatever, I'll know where that is. I've learned you can go home again, but I don't know whether you can stay home again."

Refurbishing the café became a community task: the seventy-eight-   10
year-old furniture dealer power-sanded the chipped floor, the clothier painted, a dry-waller showed the women how to mud wallboard, and they came to love the exhaustion of such work. Then they got to the Wolf stove, which yielded its encrusted grease to no woman or man or method from scrapers to torches. One day two fellows came in with an idea: they dismantled the range, put it in the back of a pickup, hauled it to the county highway yard, turned a steam hose on it, and reassembled it into the beauty of new sculpture, and someone happily wrote on the blackboard Thurston had set up to list possible names for the place: The Clean Stove Café. Also on the board were The Double L, The Quarthouse, and Soup and Psychological Services, this last already beginning to have some meaning.

The women did not flaunt their politics, and the town was enough impressed with their hard work to ignore their ERA NOW! bumper stickers, and strollers stopped in to watch the work or help out or just pour themselves a cup of free coffee. After six weeks of reconstruction, the women papered over the street windows to create a little suspense for the opening, a couple of days later, while they completed last details. In a county where beef stands second only to Christianity, where gravy and chicken-fried steak are the bases from which all culinary judgments proceed, the women offered eggplant Parmesan, clam linguine, gazpacho, fettuccine Alfredo, and chicken-fried steak. Business was excellent, and the first day they sold out of pasta primavera, and the women were certain they could keep their pledge never to serve french fries or factory white bread. All their eggs came from Chase farms; on weekends, in season, they prepared calf fries fresh from county pastures (and tolerated jokes attendant to feminists grilling ballocks), and they catered meals to businessmen in lodge meetings and ranch hands at corrals.

Linda says to me: "Scratch cooking all the way. The highest compliment is a woman saying, 'This is as good as I make at home.' But the men bitched all the time about no french fries or white bread, so we gave in and cut our own fry potatoes and baked our own white bread, but still, today, if you want your grilled cheese on Rainbo bread, you'll just have to go someplace else. That's the only thing we haven't compromised on. We've never altered our deeper values, because we refuse to divorce being café owners from our feminism. We're tolerated for it and sometimes we're explained by it: I heard a man ask his friend what a crepe was and why something like that would even be on the menu, and the waitress explained, 'They're for the ERA.' And that's right. We employ only women, and we try to bring to them what we've learned. In the first days of the café a wealthy lady told me there were no battered women in the county, and she believed that, but she's been misled—the problem is just buried.

Not long ago, at the health fair in the school gym, we sponsored a display about services for abused women and children, and we found out later that some people were afraid to stand in front of it because a neighbor might think they were abused. And one day a woman, holding back tears, said to me, 'You ought to get out of here — the longer you stay, the worse you'll feel about yourself as a woman.' Maybe that's a minority view, but it's valid. The other side is that people here are still close to their pioneer ancestors, and they all can tell stories about strong and capable grandmothers. For a long time women have owned businesses in the county, so we're accepted, but then the café isn't a hardware store or a transmission shop."

The young waitress has just given a single check to a man sitting with two women, and Linda explains to her that she should give a check to each person and says, "Don't assume the male always pays," and to me, "Separate checks also protect privacy — people will watch and read something into who picks up the tab," and I ask whether lack of privacy isn't the worst thing about a small town, and she says, "And also the best: I love going to the post office in the morning and knowing everybody. The only time we honk a car horn is with a wave. It's touching when somebody asks about my son or my dad's health. We can't afford not to care about other people in a place this small. Our survival, in a way, depends on minimizing privacy, because the lack of it draws us into each other's lives, and that's a major resource in a little town where there aren't a thousand entertainments. There's an elderly man who lost his little granddaughter to a drunk, a hit-and-run driver, a few months ago. Every time the old fellow comes into the Emma, he retells the story, and every time people listen. What's that worth to a person? Or to a community? A café like this serves to bond us."

I'm scribbling things down, and she watches and says, "Growing up in this county, I learned not to ask questions. If people want you to know something, they'll tell you," and I say that I must be a popular fellow, what with a question mark in every sentence, and she says, "You don't count. You don't live here. Besides, the word is out that you're in the county. You'll be tolerated even if they do think you're about a half bubble off plumb." She watches me write that down, and she says, "We can't afford to ostracize each other just because we don't like this one's politics or the way that one raises her kids. You can get away with it in a city — picking and choosing — but here we're already picked. Participation by everybody discourages change, and the radical gets cut off. But if we give aberrant behavior a wide berth, we don't usually reject it completely. Every merchant on Broadway can tell a story about some petty shoplifter whose pilfering has been ignored to avoid a bigger problem. For an outsider, it's different: if you would espouse something terribly unpopular, like government ownership of land, they'll just question your sanity, but if you pocket a candy bar, they'll have you arrested. If *I* do either one, it would be just the reverse. We have limits, of course. The first and most powerful enforcement is gossip and scorn, the sap and sinew of a small town."

When she gets up to ready the kitchen for lunch, I ask whether she 15 or the Emma Chase has ever been scorned, and she says, "You'd be more likely to hear that than I would."

Now, late afternoon, a year later: the painted coffee cup still steams on the window, and stalwart Emma Chase looks over the stacked chairs and onto Broadway, and the dank odor of an old and unused building slips between the locked twin doors. The café has been closed for nearly a year, and there's nothing more than a hope of somebody's reopening it, although everyone is tired of coffee in foam cups and factory cookies in the Senior Citizen's Center, a few doors down. Linda Woody has gone to Washington as a NOW lobbyist, and Linda Thurston is sixty miles up the road, at Kansas State University, an assistant professor in rural special education. The café is for sale, and she's asking $8,000 less than she paid for it, in spite of its having become known as one of the best small-town eateries in the state, in spite of a Kansas Citian's offer to underwrite the franchising of Emma Chase cafés.

I've just returned from lunch with her in the student union, where she said, "Standing in front of that big Wolf stove, I kept remembering my degree and how useless it was getting with every fried egg. I'm ten years behind my colleagues. I worked hard at the café, and my feet hurt all the time, and I got arthritis in my hands, and finally I realized I didn't want to work that hard day after day and still not earn enough money to send my son to college. Every other business person on Broadway has at least one additional source of income — the furniture dealer runs a funeral parlor, the owners of the two women's dress shops have their husbands' income, the filling-station man has another in Strong City. The Emma Chase would support one frugal person, but it wouldn't even do that without weekend city people. Tourists coming to see the Hills, bicycle clubs — they kept us alive after we earned a name around the state by being special. But there were local folks who never came in, and I'd ask them what it would take to get them inside, and they'd say, 'We let the kids decide where we're going to eat out, and they choose McDonald's.' How does a box of toys in the Emma Chase compete against television commercials? And there's something else: good home cooking is common in the county. Franchise food is the novelty, especially when it's twenty miles away. What our café offered, city people wanted, but they also wanted clean floors, and the cowboys were afraid to come in and get the floor dirty."

I asked, Was it a loss? and she said, "I lost some money and something professionally, because I never found time to write, but I realized my fantasy, and I was at home for the last two years of my father's life. And I got to live again according to the dictates of rainfall and the price of cattle and grain and the outbreaks of chicken pox. I was part of a community rebuilding its café, and working with those helpers got me to see men again as people instead of the enemy, and it meant something for my son to go to school with children of people I went to school with. And—I think I can say this—because of the Emma Chase, I see my femaleness differently; now I think feminism means being connected with other people, not just with other feminists."

She was quiet for some time, and then she said, "There were losses, no question, but there was only one real failure—we never did get the farmers to eat alfalfa sprouts. They know silage when they see it. Maybe we should have tried it with gravy."

The Responsive Reader

1. What do you hear in this essay about local history? What do you learn about the private history of the women running the café? How is their history related to the recent history of the women's movement? (How are public and private history intertwined in this essay?)
2. What do you learn from the story of the café about country or small-town ways, customs, beliefs? How do the women relate to them, accept them, or clash with them? (What contradictory glimpses are there of how women are treated in this small country town?)
3. What, in this essay, is the connection between food and politics? How serious is it?
4. At the end, the writer asks about the experience of running the café, "Was it a loss?" What is the answer? Do you consider the experience the story of a defeat?

Talking, Listening, Writing

5. What has been your experience with the kind of country setting here described? Would you want to live in the kind of place you see here? What values or benefits do you see in this way of life? (Or what shortcomings would make you want to leave?)
6. Write about a person (or about several people) who seem to you characteristic or typical of a place you know well. What makes them typical or representative?
7. Rewrite the story of the Emma Chase Café as it might have been told from a different point of view. Assume the identity of one of the local men or one of the local women. What would the person have noticed, thought, and felt?

Projects

8. You may want to collaborate with other students to investigate the politics of food and restaurants in your community. Organize with your classmates to send out scouts investigating different places to

eat or different aspects of the situation. (For instance, are there places with a strong vegetarian philosophy? a strong health-food emphasis? a strong antismoking stand? Are there old-fashioned steak-and-potato places? Is there yuppie cuisine?)

_____

Thinking about Connections

How do Ursula Le Guin and William Least Heat-Moon compare as observers of rural American scenes? Are their perspectives similar or different? Do they focus on similar or different things? Are their preferences and commitments similar or different?

_____

HELL IN A VERY TALL PLACE

Camilo José Vergara

> *Camilo José Vergara is a documentary photographer who wrote the follow-*
> *ing article after visiting sixty public-housing complexes in poor neighborhoods*
> *of New York City. (He toured 140 separate buildings.) Vergara photographed*
> *the Kingsborough Houses in the Brownsville section of Brooklyn and a South*
> *Bronx high-rise project surrounded by blighted older housing. He photo-*
> *graphed doors used for target practice and steel "bird cages" protecting vehicles*
> *of the Housing Authority from vandals. He talked to employees of the Housing*
> *Authority, to tenants, and to the homeless. The editor of the* Atlantic, *where*
> *this article was first published, says that the places the author surveyed are*
> *considered some of the best public housing in the country.*

Thought Starters: Are our inner cities in a downward spiral that cannot
be arrested? Has our society given up on fighting the chronic ills of our
large cities?

It was my need for high places from which to photograph the land-   *1*
scape of the ghetto that led me to approach the New York City Housing
Authority (NYCHA) for permission to visit its projects. The roofs of the
buildings offered excellent area views. The management was concerned
enough about my safety to send an employee with me as I made my
rounds; my guides were familiar with the buildings and could answer
questions as we made our way to the roof. I had put my camera inside a
shopping bag, as I had been told to do. Under this arrangement I was not
afraid to walk past the dealers and the addicts. A typical visit began in the
waiting room of the management office, which might be presided over
by the image of a skull on a yellow background bearing the words CRACK
KILLS. Other signs warned against the sale of narcotics in public-housing
buildings and also about accidents occurring in elevators, offered aid to
victims of spouse abuse, and informed residents of cultural and social
activities. In this neat room, a place of official normalcy, tenants make
their rent payments, request repairs, and lodge complaints. But not even
here can they escape graphic reminders of the plague in their midst, the
drug epidemic shaping daily life.

Sometimes to get to the management office I had to make a long
detour around the perimeter of the complex; I had been warned to stay
clear of the center. In the South Bronx an administrator of the Andrew
Jackson Houses told a caretaker who was to walk with me through the

grounds, "Don't let him go through the projects with this [camera bag] or they'll kill him!" In Brownsville, the poorest section of Brooklyn, the supervisor of grounds loudly yelled "Move!" as I lingered to take notes in front of the northernmost tower, one of three twenty-two-story buildings of the Langston Hughes Houses. He later explained that two of his workers had been hit by bottles hurled from the upper floors of the buildings, and had required hospitalization.

The tallest buildings and those located on corners at the perimeter of the project grounds were usually the best suited to my purposes. My visits took place between 10:00 A.M. and 3:00 P.M., hours when drug dealing is at a low point.

Entering a project during the day, accompanied by a housing-authority employee, gives one a view of public housing at its best. I usually saw the buildings' public spaces soon after the caretaker had done the morning cleaning and at a time when school was in session and few children were around. My first impression was one of clean floors and quiet buildings.

But actually these massive buildings — typically they are more than twelve stories tall — are quite vulnerable. Nothing highlights this more clearly than the lack of secure front doors. Entrances almost always have broken locks, missing windowpanes, and vandalized intercoms. A key was necessary to come in by the main entrance in less than five percent of the buildings I visited, and I saw tenant patrols in only three percent. A young woman who was a caretaker in Brownsville reported, "Every time we put a new lock in, they break it. Everybody just comes and goes, comes and goes. They don't even live in the building."

"There is only one disease here: crack," says José Rodriguez, an assistant superintendent at the Mill Brook Houses, in the South Bronx. The tall, isolated, wide-open, and fully occupied buildings of public-housing complexes offer drug dealers a secure and accessible base of operations and a place to recruit staff and customers. Tenants fear to report them. In particular, the tree-lined inner courtyards of these projects, hidden from the streets, which were intended as urban oases for outdoor play, picnics, and socializing, now serve as open-air drug markets. The manager of the East River Houses, in East Harlem, characterizes the courtyard in her complex as "designed for escape." According to NYCHA workers I spoke with, many of the recent killings in such projects have taken place in the courtyards.

The most effective force for keeping drugs out of the public areas of buildings is organized groups of tenants who will call the police to arrest the dealers and their customers, and who are willing to testify in court against them. But organizing is becoming harder, as the most stable and active residents move out of the projects. The housing authority cannot afford twenty-four-hour security, and it lacks the funds to erect fences that might help control the flow of people in and out of the buildings.

5

Maintenance personnel are perhaps the closest and most knowledge-able observers of the present crack epidemic. They know in detail the history, mechanics, and social costs of addiction in their work areas. When asked why drugs are so popular, these people give answers that fit into three categories. Some lay the blame for addiction on the tenants' bleak prospects for the future. They argue that many turn to drugs for relief, particularly discouraged youths who are prone to depression. Others cite peer-group pressure: "Everybody is doing it." Youths use drugs first to be like their friends and later because they have become addicted. Still others bitterly blame the welfare system and the idleness it fosters: "People here don't have to strive. They clothe them, they feed them; this makes them lose their self-respect. You see grown-ups just hanging around the lobbies all day with nothing to do, except maybe going to the check-cashing place, always the same crowd, and they make fun of the people going to work. If they were busy doing something, they would not take drugs."

A popular opinion among maintenance personnel is that the federal government allows drugs to be sold openly in ghetto neighborhoods. I was repeatedly told that the U.S. Army and Navy have the power to stop the drug trade, and that since they do not use it, important people must be involved, making profits. Housing-authority workers complain that out-siders, by coming to the projects to buy, encourage drug dealing; they rightly feel that the police would not tolerate such blatant commerce in middle-class neighborhoods.

Many open lobbies of public-housing buildings have become crack   *10* supermarkets. A caretaker at the Seth Low Houses, in Brownsville, sadly pointed to the building he is responsible for and said, "This place is dis-tinctive. You go to the lobby and there is nothing but junkies down there. You see a lot of crackheads moving back and forth." He drew attention to the broken windows and missing signs, saying that addicts sometimes steal the front doors of buildings to sell as scrap metal. At the Langston Hughes Houses a big hole in a pillar in the lobby of a building had been made in order to steal a bronze pump. With impunity, apparently in clear sight or within earshot of hundreds of residents, someone had worked for several hours destroying part of their lobby.

The ubiquitous drug addicts often die, or go to jail or the hospital; their bony faces and starved bodies are soon replaced by others on street corners, in lobbies, behind buildings, and on stairways, their strange, dematerialized presence a constant reminder of death.

In entryways I found elderly tenants patiently waiting for somebody they trusted to ride the elevator with them to their apartments. The ele-vators are slow and sometimes need carefully placed kicks and a helping hand to get started, and their walls are full of bumps, bearing witness to rough treatment. In the Martin Luther King, Jr., Houses, in Harlem, for example, one elevator had several bullet holes in it. A long, slow elevator ride in complete darkness is a dreaded experience associated with the worst housing projects; muggers, a maintenance man explained, "put the elevator lights out to rob you."

Reaching one's floor unharmed does not necessarily mean that one is safe: muggings occur frequently in the corridors. A maintenance man at the J. Weldon Johnson Houses, in East Harlem, explained that if tenants see addicts on their floor, they will often go back down and call the police. Some mothers even fear being robbed by their own drug-addicted children. To protect themselves, they request that their door locks be changed. Forced out of their homes, the teenagers move in with friends or share the public spaces of their building with other homeless people. At a project in Brooklyn a mother locked her four addicted children out of her top-floor apartment; to get in, her sons made a hole in the roof.

The stairway walls serve as bulletin boards. There, in the E. R. Moore Houses, in the South Bronx, "K.C." chose to announce that after eight years he was "back from jail, 1-25-89." On the fourteenth-floor landing of one of the buildings of the notorious Marcus Garvey Houses, in Brownsville, someone had written, "Bob and I was walking down the Ave. smoking on a blunt and we saw this crab. The crab walked-up and this is what she said: Give me five dollars and I buff your head." Another inscription, in the Bronxchester Houses, in the South Bronx, warned, "Crack is wack. You use crack today, tomorrow you be bumming. That's word experience talk." Yet another, in the Patterson Houses, in the South Bronx, consisted of this cryptic sentence: "misty blue is the place to be." Many of the steps and landings were strewn with empty crack vials, used condoms, and excrement.

While opening the top-floor doors leading to the roof, caretakers _15_ often spoke loudly, started singing, or banged the door, to warn of our coming. A maintenance man at the Polo Grounds Towers, in Harlem, went ahead of me, explaining, "I have to watch and see if somebody is smoking crack." The wisdom of this became apparent when I saw people up there sleeping, reading, sitting, and talking, with empty vials next to them.

The roofs of projects showed many signs of drug activity, and there were often bullet holes in the vandalized metal doors and ventilation systems. At the Abraham Lincoln Houses, in Harlem, I saw a U.S. Army manual describing how to take apart and clean a high-powered rifle. At the Bushwick Houses, in Brooklyn, I found a door with a life-sized drawing of a deranged-looking man on it that had been used for target practice. A caretaker at the Albany Houses, in Brooklyn, explained to me that gun sellers take their clients to the tops of buildings to demonstrate their wares. If they can hit something in a nearby building, the guns fetch high prices.

The Narcotics Task Force of NYCHA recently began a campaign of subway advertising called "A Message for Drug Dealers," which warns, "Stay the hell _out_ of public housing or we'll _nail_ you." This "get tough" message is regarded as useless by NYCHA employees, who, in the midst of a raging crack epidemic, see these warnings and the attempts to implement them as ineffective. Residents themselves, fed up with the fear and violence imposed on them by the drug trade, have started a grass-roots graffiti campaign warning junkies to stay out of the projects. For example, at the Mill Brook Houses someone has written on an elevator wall, "I hate all the crackheads in this world. If I see one tonight, I am going to fuck them up, O.K. bitch."

NYCHA workers with whom I spoke were almost unanimous in the opinion that the crime in their projects was getting worse and their work was getting more difficult. For thirty-five years William Monroe, a housing-authority maintenance man, has lived and worked at the Marcy Houses, in the Bedford-Stuyvesant section of Brooklyn. He has seen many industries in the area move away and once-busy factories reduce their activities so much that the buildings seem deserted. "No work, no money, except from what comes from welfare, Social Security, and drugs," he says, and then asks, "How can you run a city without money?" Today, he observes, even the army is not taking the youngsters most in need of work—the high school dropouts. He calls the neighborhood "dead man's city." He has seen the children he coached in baseball and took on field trips grow discouraged. Yet William Monroe is proud of having raised nine children in the Marcy Houses, not one of whom has become an addict. "It can be done," he says.

At the Samuel J. Tilden Houses, in Brooklyn, I overheard a caretaker complaining, "With all the crack and stuff that is going on, you only can do the best you can. This is Brownsville, not the Waldorf-Astoria." Several caretakers told me that they would not live in the complexes where they work even if they got a rent-free apartment. One said that he would rather take his chances in the Bowery than live there. Others complained that NYCHA was rehabilitating additional buildings in the neighborhood instead of concentrating on improving troubled projects. A caretaker at the Patterson Houses felt that the only solution would be to sell the apartments as co-ops. In two exceptional projects, in Brooklyn, the Van Dyke Houses and the Marcy Houses, maintenance men told me that during the past year or so conditions had improved—fewer killings had occurred.

Nothing, perhaps, affects the morale of public-housing employees *20* more than the growing violence that engulfs them. On several visits I was accompanied by victims of recent muggings, and I observed fear in their actions and in their words. One likable young caretaker, at the Mill Brook Houses, had been badly beaten during a robbery. He talked obsessively about his request for a transfer out of the South Bronx, a place of strangers, to Brooklyn, where he lives and where he feels that everybody knows him. Even though he and his family live in the notorious Walt Whitman Houses, he finds security in the fact that his building is near the police station and the project's management office. There the dealers and addicts know him, and when they see him outside a store or on a street corner, they greet him and never bother him. Things are different in the Bronx, he said. "People saw me on the streets all bloodied up and they wouldn't help me. They don't know me here; I don't even want them to know me here."

Despite their pessimistic outlook, however, workers and officials made lists of things that needed to be done, picked up garbage left behind by careless residents, and addressed tenants politely. Not one expressed the desire to look for other work. As they passed by the crackheads and the pushers, the housing-authority employees did not look at them, perhaps to avoid a confrontation, or perhaps as a sign that the public areas of the buildings were out of their control.

New York City's public housing is a precious resource, especially in the present housing crisis. Yet the conditions in most projects are worsening. NYCHA buildings, maintenance people report, are only as good as the neighborhoods they are in. This year more than 33,000 families are sharing apartments without authorization, and thousands of people are sleeping on roofs, on stairways, in basements, and even in elevators. In this way public housing, at a great cost to itself, helps contain the flood of homelessness.

Beginning in the mid-1930s, the NYCHA projects were seen as a vast improvement over the crowded, unsanitary tenements and decrepit wooden houses they replaced. The projects boasted fireproof construction and sunny, ventilated apartments with hot running water. Life in them had, moreover, a provisional character: the complexes were designed to provide decent, sanitary housing for families until rising income and an increasing supply of private housing permitted them to move to more desirable dwellings. In 1989, however, life in public housing is vastly different from what it was expected to be. Projects have increasingly become permanent residences for the indigent.

Most of the developments in ghetto areas of the city are part of the legacy of Robert Moses, New York City's construction coordinator from 1946 to 1960. They reflect his preference for large complexes of more than a thousand units and for towers seven or more stories high. Arnold Vollmer, his longtime associate, recently told me that Moses had wanted "a project that would not be swamped, that could have an impact in the area." Vollmer said that Moses's view was "If you cannot do something that is really substantial, it is not worth doing." Moses's policies led to great concentrations of public housing. NYCHA became a model for the nation, with similar complexes arising from St. Louis to Boston.

Even after Moses's influence waned, NYCHA continued to build 25 new complexes near or immediately adjacent to existing ones, resulting in clusters of as many as half a dozen housing projects. Today, twenty years after their completion, these modern agglomerations are surrounded by specially designed schools, post offices, libraries, police precinct head-quarters, health facilities, and stores. But much of the city fabric around the complexes has been destroyed, and because, for the most part, the buildings contain no commercial facilities, the projects have become highly distinct urban environments, consisting of cores of housing ringed by businesses and services catering exclusively to the needs of the poor.

In the poorest and most crime-ridden and devastated areas of the city, NYCHA has more than 90,000 apartments, constituting more than 50 percent of its total stock. This is about twice as many apartments as the Chicago Housing Authority, the second-largest public-housing agency in the country, has altogether. And the poverty of the residents will continue to grow, since of the 180,000 families on the waiting list, 45 percent are welfare recipients.

Joseph Shuldiner, the general manager of NYCHA, would have been more at home in the Great Society than in an era of public stinginess toward the poor. Asking for real solutions to problems like homelessness, drug addiction, and crime, all of which have a devastating effect on public housing, he finds Washington unresponsive. It is "unfair to ask landlords to solve these problems," he says.

Shuldiner thinks that NYCHA, which already manages some 178,000 units, has no recourse in the present housing crisis but to extend itself. He continues to add to his stock rehabilitated buildings that are scattered and difficult to manage. And he would not consider evicting substantial numbers of tenants in order to improve the conditions in the projects. Shuldiner asks, "Do you know what effect it would have in the city if we evicted the 33,000 families now doubling up in our buildings? Where would they go? Our job is to provide housing for people, not to evict. We are not going to do it." But nothing is gained by adding new public-housing stock while allowing the existing dwellings to be de-stroyed by drugs.

The main source of funding for public housing, the federal govern-ment, today supports almost no new construction. The cuts in funds for services and community centers have worsened the health, education, employment, recreation, and safety problems faced by public-housing residents. The dwindling resources that Washington still provides are di-rected toward the poorest of the poor, thus accelerating a change in tenants from a mixed-income, mostly working population to dependent female-headed families, one of the most troubled of social groups. Working fam-ilies, lacking subsidies of any kind and perceiving that the "market rate" rents they pay for their apartments in dangerous surroundings are already too high and are increasing, are moving to private housing in better neighborhoods.

To really gauge the social horror represented by these projects, one   *30* must climb up for a view of the roof, where one sees blankets, mattresses, large pieces of cardboard, even tables and chairs. During the winter people prefer to sleep inside the building, or inside the shed that holds the elevator machinery, referred to without irony as the penthouse. People also live beneath the water tanks, where they arrange their belongings in a small space as if it were their private bedroom. The buildings being wide open, this practice has become accepted as inevitable. At the Bushwick Houses, for instance, a homeless man told the caretaker to stop placing new light bulbs on the stairway landing where he sleeps. "You put a light there and I will bust it. This is my house and I don't want a light there," he said.

Most homeless people taking shelter in public-housing buildings come at night and leave early in the morning, so as not to be found by the maintenance workers. But at the Patterson Houses a suddenly awakened man threatened me with a large knife, which he held by the blade as he sprang from a top-floor landing. After our quick retreat the caretaker with me commented, "We surprised him, and surprise brings out the devil in people." At the Jefferson Houses, in Manhattan, while accompanied by two supervisors, I encountered a sleeping man on the roof landing. One of the supervisors, while he was ordering the man out of the building, held a knife ready halfway out of his coat pocket. Weapons are increasingly among the tools of the public-housing trade; maintenance workers carry knives, heavy wrenches, golf clubs, and on pay day, I was told, even guns.

About half a dozen men live on each roof of the Polo Grounds public-housing complex—four thirty-story buildings. Located between the bluffs of Washington Heights and the Harlem River, in a magnificent natural setting, these giant buildings offer a breathtaking view of Manhattan, its pointed skyline, misty parks, and silvery bodies of water. From the tops of the buildings one can see the backs of hawks and seagulls as they fly below. Spanning the river are several magnificent bridges, and on highways along the perimeter of the project thousands of vehicles move rapidly by.

Contrasting with the panorama of the city are the sights that greet a manager who told me that he visits these roofs in the early morning: he sees a line of men defecating alongside a wall and others sleeping nearby. In this, the richest of cities in the richest of countries, in buildings of advanced late-twentieth-century technology, men who own nothing sleep under the open sky on a windswept roof three hundred feet above the ground.

The Responsive Reader

1. What does Vergara set his readers up for when he starts his article with a description of a typical project office, "a place of official normalcy"? What makes the signs he sees there ironic—how soon in this article do the grim realities of the situation clash with the official stance?

2. What makes the projects Vergara visited "vulnerable"? What has gone wrong? What is Vergara's diagnosis of the causes and effects

of the crack epidemic on the projects? According to the people he talked to, what other trends have contributed to the present situation?

3. What light does this article shed on the political history of these public-housing projects — their original goals, government policies past and present?

4. Why does Vergara end his article with his account of the people on the roofs?

5. Does Vergara offer any glimpses of hope? Does he offer any glimpse of advice for the future or of possible solutions?

Talking, Listening, Writing

6. Do you find this article believable or realistic? Is it an old story, or does it tell you anything new?

7. Reactions to truth-tellers like Vergara range from "Tell me it isn't so" to "I wish you hadn't told me" or "There isn't anything anyone can do." What is *your* reaction?

Projects

8. What is the official thinking about how to combat drugs and violence? What can you find out about current publicity campaigns, police efforts, or undercover operations? What do government officials or law-enforcement officers in your community think? What is their estimate of current efforts? (Your class may want to organize a task force to compile current information.)

THE NEW VIGILANTES

Kenneth T. Walsh

U.S. News & World Report *is the more conservative of the leading newsmagazines. The following article represents a format that has gradually replaced the anonymous, homogenized newsmagazine articles of earlier days. The article is attributed to a senior author, who wrote the article with input from contributing authors and from "bureau reports." The article makes a point of balancing the pro and con on current action designed to address a serious social problem. It tries to find a reasonable middle ground. (Does it succeed?)*

Thought Starters: This article focuses on the "understandable" impulse among law-abiding citizens "to take matters in their own hands" to stop neighborhood crime. Do you understand their motives? Do you sympathize with their efforts? Do you think their efforts can make a difference?

Their menacing brand of quiet belligerence is a welcome if somewhat   1
incongruous sight on the mean streets around Northeast Washington's Mayfair Mansions. It is one of the nation's most high-crime ghettos, but the dapper, bow-tied young men patrolling the neighborhood are out to change all that, slashing back at the drug trade that has all but strangled the impoverished, inner-city community. And for residents, that's all that matters: Pushers have fled to other areas of the city, the elderly no longer fear the night so much, and children play, once again, on the sidewalks. To most people who have lived in submission to the drug dealers for so long here, there is but one opinion of the young men from the neighborhood mosque: They are heroes.

From Manhattan to Miami, and in cities as varied as Houston and Los Angeles, similar scenes are being repeated this spring, as hybrids of Washington's do-it-yourself drug busters bloom in America's ghettos, and beleaguered police, unable to establish an effective presence, seem more and more willing to accept the unorthodox help. The Muslim presence, particularly in Washington and New York, is the most extreme example of citizen frustration over rampant inner-city drug districts. But it is emblematic of a growing restiveness in many urban areas with big drug problems. "We've told drug dealers," says Lillian Ray, a resident of the Grays Ferry section of South Philadelphia and one of the founders of the Direct Truth Anti-Drug Coalition, "that we're going to tear their kingdom down."

Where the Muslims are the most out-front groups, patrolling dark corners of dangerous neighborhoods late at night, other citizens' groups like Ray's have adopted less risky but still extraordinary strategies. In Houston last month, a crowd of about 1,000 people reclaimed Carver Park, one of three city parks that had become centers of street drug sales. In an effort to push drug dealers out, Houston police sought volunteers from the affected communities for the march. Most residents responded enthusiastically, and they say the effort is working in the 12-acre park, at least for now. "But police have to stay out [there] around the clock," says Ransom Craddock, who lives near Carver. "If they don't, the cars come in just like it's a hotel."

The ultimate response. Certainly, the impulse among many law-abiding inner-city blacks and Hispanics to take matters into their own hands is an understandable one. It is they, after all, who are most imperiled and frustrated by the drug scourge. And many residents of drug-infested neighborhoods feel that the billions of dollars the federal government throws at the problem have little impact on their lives. "If the system fails," says Hubert Williams, former Newark, N.J., police chief and now president of the Police Foundation, a Washington-based research group, "self-help is the ultimate response."

Some self-help approaches to the drug problem, like the one at May-   5
fair Mansions, are succeeding. Such operations work because the Muslims, carrying nightsticks and walkie-talkies, are often ex-hustlers and local toughs who know both the streets and the drug dealers. Supremely motivated by their religion, based on self-reliance, discipline and black pride (in the Washington case, they are followers of Louis Farrakhan, who has been accused of anti-Semitism and reverse racism), the patrollers sometimes broadcast religious slogans from loudspeakers mounted on vans or cars. Just as important, they are willing to put themselves at risk to clean up their communities — and the pushers steer clear. In the Bedford-Stuyvesant ghetto, Muslims from the At-Taqwa Mosque, who aren't Farrakhan followers, have virtually driven drugs from the immediate area since their patrols, with police backing, started in January. "Those drug houses have remained closed," says Capt. Tom Baumann of Brooklyn's 79th Precinct, "since the Muslims began their patrols. We've never seen anything like that before." But when such groups take matters into their own hands, they can create more problems than they solve. "When they seek to mete out justice," says Mayor Ed Koch, "[it's] unacceptable."

Even the normally disciplined Muslims can get carried away. In Washington, they disarmed, beat and kicked a man carrying a sawed-off shotgun, then injured a reporter for a local TV station who was filming the episode. And even as the patrols have dramatically reduced drug dealing in the immediate area of Mayfair Mansions, nearby residents complain that the drug traffic has simply been pushed into adjacent communities.

Whatever their nature, urban-affairs specialists point out, citizen patrols can't be sustained indefinitely. Participants are generally working-class people who have jobs and families, and they simply can't devote too much time to volunteer law enforcement — which may be a good thing, in the view of many police experts and urban-affairs specialists. "We're talking about the Beiruts of America," says urbanologist James Q. Wilson of the University of California at Los Angeles. "The police *have* to retake control of the streets. And until they do, the citizens can't do much by themselves."

Yet, such is the desperation in many drug-infested inner cities that citizen action, even outright vigilantism going well beyond Muslim patrols, seems to be increasingly common — sometimes with tragic consequences. In Miami, officials say well-meaning citizens have torched seven crack houses since January, including three wooden, two-story apartment buildings gutted on March 17 and one structure destroyed April 20. Five firemen were injured in one blaze, and the flames threatened innocent people in adjacent buildings. In Opa-Locka, Fla., after the Yahwehs, a black Hebrew sect that wears white robes and turbans, agreed to buy and patrol a drug-afflicted apartment complex, two tenants were shot to death. And in East Harlem, a man said to be a drug addict was fatally beaten by a mob after he allegedly grabbed $20 from a woman in a bakery, prompting an outcry from civil libertarians and civic leaders about vigilante violence. "Even the police are outgunned and outmanned," says Dade County, Fla., Police Chief Fred Taylor. "How can citizens do any better?"

Yet the drug plague appears to be, in some ways, improving the relationship between police and inner-city minorities. Many blacks who only a few years ago complained about police brutality and insensitivity now *demand* tougher police protection, ranging from antidrug sweeps to foot patrols in high-crime areas. True, the number of black officers has greatly increased over the years — a helpful trend in minority communities. But it's the drug trade that has, ironically, done most to defuse long-standing tensions between police and law-abiding blacks, as both sides struggle to clean up the streets in Houston, Jersey City, N.J., and many other cities.

In addition, police leaders and officers show increased acceptance of citizen patrols, even those of the Muslims, who once were considered anathema. Today, the same concerns that once worried police — the Muslims' reputation as tough, martial-arts experts who personally know drug dealers and their families — now seem like advantages in intimidating the pushers. Even so, city leaders remain nervous about both vigilantism and demands for a tougher police response to drugs. "The police department can't go in and kick butt," says Washington Police Chief Maurice Turner. "We have to stay within the law."

Muscle and money. What, then, is the answer? Some urbanologists say the long-term solution is to create more and better jobs for ghetto young people. Wilson calls for more police officers, more-effective police-community relations to enlist local support in identifying drug dealers and gathering evidence against them, more willingness by prosecutors to put offenders in jail, even for only a few days, and additional "creativity" in state legislatures to enact laws making it easier to jail gang members. But Wilson is pessimistic that such steps will be taken soon.

There also is some inner-city resistance to cracking down on drugs, because of money and fear. Gang members can ingratiate themselves with neighbors by paying their rent, and, in return, they receive a base of operations or a large degree of acceptance. In other cases, drug kingpins and their subalterns can impose a reign of terror, forcing residents to live in constant fear of reprisal.

But the inner-city drug war is so pervasive that many residents will settle for any short-term respite, such as the one provided by the Muslims at Mayfair Mansions, whatever the consequences. "Many people are living in a state of anarchy," says Robert Woodson, president of the National Center for Neighborhood Enterprise, "and the police are powerless to do anything about it." Adds Mayfair Mansions resident Melvin Jones: "The Muslims have done more in one day than the police in 22 years."

The Responsive Reader

1. How does this writer, in newsmagazine style, dramatize the issue? How does he lead up to the keynote of the article?
2. What, according to this article, are the arguments in favor of "self-help" as the "ultimate response"?
3. What, according to this article, are the second thoughts or objections that the trend toward neighborhood self-help inspires? What does the article say about the danger of "outright vigilantism"?
4. What alternatives to taking the law in our own hands does the article explore? How real or convincing do they become?

Talking, Listening, Writing

5. Have you had any experience with neighborhood efforts to combat crime? Have you read about them? What seems to be their chance of success or failure?
6. This article touches on three options for dealing with neighborhood crime: improved police protection, neighborhood vigilance, and violent vigilantism. Which option do you favor yourself? What are the pros and cons of each option?

Projects

7. Are the students on your campus following the trend away from complaints about police brutality to demands for tougher police protection? Working with other students, you may want to organize a survey or an opinion poll on this issue.

A CITY OF NEIGHBORHOODS
Harvey Milk

> *Harvey Milk was an articulate and influential gay member of the Board of Supervisors in San Francisco, a city of great ethnic and cultural diversity. He represented for many the hope for a tolerant and livable city at a time when the values he stood for were threatened by high-rise development destroying the texture of traditional neighborhoods, by urban decay in areas like the Tenderloin, or by poverty and violence in the projects of Hunters Point. (Milk mentions both these areas of the city in the following speech.) Milk and the popular mayor, George Moscone, were gunned down in City Hall in November 1978 by Dan White, a fellow member of the Board of Supervisors who was engaged in a bitter feud with them. As word of the assassination spread, Milk's admirers and supporters came out into the streets in an outpouring of rage and mourning. The following excerpts from a speech given by Harvey Milk were chosen by Diane Ravitch for her* American Reader *(1990).*

Thought Starters: Does Milk sound like a politician to you? Does he say things that other politicians also say? Does he seem different?

Let's make no mistake about this: The American Dream starts with the neighborhoods. If we wish to rebuild our cities, we must first rebuild our neighborhoods. And to do that, we must understand that the quality of life is more important than the standard of living. To sit on the front steps — whether it's a veranda in a small town or a concrete stoop in a big city — and talk to our neighborhoods is infinitely more important than to huddle on the living-room lounger and watch a make-believe world in not-quite living color.

Progress is not America's only business — and certainly not its most important. Isn't it strange that as technology advances, the quality of life so frequently declines? Oh, washing the dishes is easier. Dinner itself is easier — just heat and serve, though it might be more nourishing if we ate the ads and threw the food away. And we no longer fear spots on our glassware when guests come over. But then, of course, the guests don't come, because our friends are too afraid to come to our house and it's not safe to go to theirs.

And I hardly need to tell you that in that 19- or 24-inch view of the world, cleanliness has long since eclipsed godliness. So we'll all smell, look, and actually be laboratory clean, as sterile on the inside as on the out. The perfect consumer, surrounded by the latest appliances. The perfect audience, with a ringside seat to almost any event in the world, without smell, without taste, without feel—alone and unhappy in the vast wasteland of our living rooms. I think that what we actually need, of course, is a little more dirt on the seat of our pants as we sit on the front stoop and talk to our neighbors once again, enjoying the type of summer day where the smell of garlic travels slightly faster than the speed of sound.

There's something missing in the sanitized life we lead. Something that our leaders in Washington can never supply by simple edict, something that the commercials on television never advertise because nobody's yet found a way to bottle it or box it or can it. What's missing is the touch, the warmth, the meaning of life. A four-color spread in *Time* is no substitute for it. Neither is a 30-second commercial or a reassuring Washington press conference.

I spent many years on both Wall Street and Montgomery Street and   5
I fully understand the debt and responsibility that major corporations owe their shareholders. I also fully understand the urban battlefields of New York and Cleveland and Detroit. I see the faces of the unemployed—and the unemployable—of the city. I've seen the faces in Chinatown, Hunters Point, the Mission, and the Tenderloin . . . and I don't like what I see.

Oddly, I'm also reminded of the most successful slogan a business ever coined: The customer is always right.

What's been forgotten is that those people of the Tenderloin and Hunters Point, those people in the streets, are the customers, certainly potential ones, and they must be treated as such. Government cannot ignore them and neither can business ignore them. What sense is there in making products if the would-be customer can't afford them? It's not alone a question of price, it's a question of ability to pay. For a man with no money, 99¢ reduced from $1.29 is still a fortune.

American business must realize that while the shareholders always come first, the care and feeding of their customer is a close second. They have a debt and a responsibility to that customer and the city in which he or she lives, the cities in which the business itself lives or in which it grew up. To throw away a senior citizen after they've nursed you through childhood is wrong. To treat a city as disposable once your business has prospered is equally wrong and even more short-sighted.

Unfortunately for those who would like to flee them, the problems of the cities don't stop at the city limits. There are no moats around our cities that keep the problems in. What happens in New York or San Francisco will eventually happen in San Jose. It's just a matter of time. And like the flu, it usually gets worse the further it travels. Our cities must not be abandoned. They're worth fighting for, not just by those who live in them, but by industry, commerce, unions, everyone. Not alone because they represent the past, but because they also represent the future. Your children will live there and hopefully, so will your grandchildren. For all practical purposes, the eastern corridor from Boston to Newark will be one vast strip city. So will the area from Milwaukee to Gary, Indiana. In California, it will be that fertile crescent of asphalt and neon that stretches from Santa Barbara to San Diego. Will urban blight travel the arteries of the freeways? Of course it will — unless we stop it.

So the challenge of the 80s will be to awaken the consciousness of   10
industry and commerce to the part they must play in saving the cities which nourished them. Every company realizes it must constantly invest in its own physical plant to remain healthy and grow. Well, the cities are a part of that plant and the people who live in them are part of the cities. They're all connected; what affects one affects the others.

In short, the cheapest place to manufacture a product may not be the cheapest at all if it results in throwing your customers out of work. There's no sense in making television sets in Japan if the customers in the United States haven't the money to buy them. Industry must actively seek to employ those without work, to train those who have no skills. "Labor intensive" is not a dirty word, not every job is done better by machine. It has become the job of industry not only to create the product, but also to create the customer.

Costly? I don't think so. It's far less expensive than the problem of fully loaded docks and no customers. And there are additional returns: lower rates of crime, smaller welfare loads. And having your friends and neighbors sitting on that well-polished front stoop. . . .

Many companies feel that helping the city is a form of charity. I think it is more accurate to consider it a part of the cost of doing business, that it should be entered on the books as amortizing the future. I would like to see business and industry consider it as such, because I think there's more creativity, more competence perhaps, in business than there is in government. I think that business could turn the south of Market Area not only into an industrial park but a neighborhood as well. To coin a pun, too many of our cities have a complex, in fact, too many complexes. We don't need another concrete jungle that dies the moment you turn off the lights in the evening. What we need is a neighborhood where people can walk to work, raise their kids, enjoy life. . . .

The cities will be saved. The cities will be governed. But they won't be run from three thousand miles away in Washington, they won't be run from the statehouse, and most of all, they won't be run by the carpetbaggers who have fled to the suburbs. You can't run a city by people who don't live there, any more than you can have an effective police force made up of people who don't live there. In either case, what you've got is an occupying army. . . .

The cities will not be saved by the people who feel condemned to   15
live in them, who can hardly wait to move to Marin or San Jose — or Evanston or Westchester. The cities will be saved by the people who like it here. The people who prefer the neighborhood stores to the shopping mall, who go to the plays and eat in the restaurants and go to the discos and worry about the education the kids are getting even if they have no kids of their own.

That's not just the city of the future; it's the city of today. It means new directions, new alliances, new solutions for ancient problems. The typical American family with two cars and 2.2 kids doesn't live here anymore. It hasn't for years. The demographics are different now and we all know it. The city is a city of singles and young marrieds, the city of the retired and the poor, a city of many colors who speak in many tongues.

The city will run itself, it will create its own solutions. District elections was not the end. It was just the beginning. We'll solve our problems — with your help, if we can, without it if we must. We need your help. I don't deny that. But you also need us. We're your customers. We're your future.

I'm riding into that future and frankly I don't know if I'm wearing the fabled helm of Mambrino on my head or if I'm wearing a barber's basin. I guess we wear what we want to wear and we fight what we want to fight. Maybe I see dragons where there are only windmills. But something tells me the dragons are for real and if I shatter a lance or two on a whirling blade, maybe I'll catch a dragon in the bargain. . . .

Yesterday, my esteemed colleague on the Board said we cannot live on hope alone. I know that, but I strongly feel the important thing is not that we cannot live on hope alone, but that life is not worth living without it. If the story of Don Quixote means anything, it means that the spirit of life is just as important as its substance. What others may see as a barber's basin, you and I know is that glittering, legendary helmet.

The Responsive Reader

1. Why does Milk ask his listeners to reexamine their ideas about progress? How does he ask business to look at their customers and at the "cost of doing business" in a different new light?
2. Where and how does Milk describe his city in the present? What are essential ingredients in his vision of the future? What is his attitude toward people living in the suburbs?
3. What does Milk mean when he says, "The quality of life is more important than the standard of living"?
4. Does the speaker sound sincere to you? (How can you judge?)

Talking, Listening, Writing

5. Are you inclined to agree that there is "more creativity, more competence perhaps, in business than in government"?
6. Would you call Milk a realist or an idealist? Is he a dreamer? (Who was Don Quixote, and what is the story of the helmet to which Milk alludes?)
7. Where have you encountered some of the warmth and human quality that Milk seeks? Try to bring the settings, the events, or the occasions to life for your listeners or readers.

8. Give some serious thought to one major change or development that would make a difference — that would help your community move into a better future. Do everything you can to convince a skeptical audience of the merit of your choice.

Projects

9. Are our cities (or is your city) doomed? Working with a group, look for recent and current statistics that might help provide a partial answer to this question. Interpret your findings for your listeners or readers.

Thinking about Connections

One reader said after reading the selections in this chapter that they were unfair to city life and slanted in favor of rural America. Do you think this charge is true?

STALKING

Joyce Carol Oates

The following short story takes a probing look at the world of suburbia, to which many Americans moved in order to escape from the congestion and violence of the cities. Joyce Carol Oates was thirty-one when she received the National Book Award for fiction in 1970. She has published over twenty novels and over fifteen collections of short stories, as well as poems, plays, articles, and reviews. Her best-known novel, Them *(1961), is set in a violent urban landscape in Detroit, where she taught. Oates has a knack for upsetting readers by confronting them with realities that they might prefer to ignore or block out. She once said, "Writers are always under attack, usually for not being 'moral' enough. . . . There is insufficient recognition of the fact that one of the traditional roles of the writer is to bear witness — not simply to the presumably good things in life, the uplifting, life-enhancing, happy things, but to their polar opposites as well."*

Thought Starters: Oates' stories often force us to try out a new and different point of view. In this story, we see the world through Gretchen's, the central character's, eyes. What kind of universe does she live in? Do you recognize her, the suburban setting in which she moves, or the way she feels and acts?

The Invisible Adversary is fleeing across a field.   1

Gretchen, walking slowly, deliberately, watches with her keen unblinking eyes the figure of the Invisible Adversary some distance ahead. The Adversary has run boldly in front of all the traffic — on long spiky legs brisk as colts' legs — and jumped up onto a curb of new concrete, and now is running across a vacant field. The Adversary glances over his shoulder at Gretchen.

Saturday afternoon. November. A cold gritty day. Gretchen is out stalking. She has hours for her game. Hours. She is dressed for the hunt, her solid legs crammed into old blue jeans, her big, square, strong feet jammed into white leather boots that cost her mother forty dollars not long ago, but are now scuffed and filthy with mud. Hopeless to get them clean again, Gretchen doesn't care. She is wearing a dark-green corduroy jacket that is worn out at the elbows and the rear, with a zipper that can be zipped up or down, attached to a fringed leather strip. On her head nothing, though it is windy today.

She has hours ahead.

Cars and trucks and buses from the city and enormous interstate   5
trucks hauling automobiles pass by on the highway; Gretchen waits until
the way is nearly clear, then starts out. A single car is approaching. *Slow
down,* Gretchen thinks; and like magic he does.

Following the footprints of the Invisible Adversary. There is no
sidewalk here yet, so she might as well cut right across the field. A gigantic
sign announces the site of the new Pace & Fischbach Building, an office
building of fifteen floors to be completed the following year. The land
around here is all dug up and muddy; she can see the Adversary's footsteps
leading right past the gouged-up area . . . and there he is, smirking back
at her, pretending panic.

I'll get you. Don't worry. Gretchen thinks carefully.

Because the Adversary is so light-footed and invisible, Gretchen
doesn't make any effort to be that way. She plods along as she does at
school, passing from classroom to classroom, unhurried and not even
sullen, just unhurried. She knows she is very visible. She is thirteen years
old and weighs one hundred and thirty-five pounds. She's only five feet
three — stocky, muscular, squat in the torso and shoulders, with good
strong legs and thighs. She could be good at gym, if she bothered; instead,
she just stands around, her face empty, her arms crossed and her shoulders
a little slumped. If forced, she takes part in the games of volleyball and
basketball, but she runs heavily, without spirit, and sometimes bumps
into other girls, hurting them. *Out of my way,* she thinks; at such times her
face shows no expression.

And now? . . . The Adversary is peeking out at her from around the
corner of a gas station. Something flickers in her brain. *I see you,* she thinks,
with quiet excitement. The Adversary ducks back out of sight. Gretchen
heads in the direction, plodding through a jumbled, bulldozed field of
mud and thistles and debris that is mainly rocks and chunks of glass. The
gas station is brand-new and not yet opened for business. It is all white
tile, white concrete, perfect plate-glass windows with whitewashed X's
on them, a large driveway and eight gasoline pumps, all proudly erect and
ready for business. But the gas station has not opened since Gretchen and
her family moved here — about six months ago. Something must have
gone wrong. Gretchen fixes her eyes on the corner where the Adversary
was last seen. He can't escape.

One wall of the gas station's white tile has been smeared with some-   10
thing like tar. Dreamy, snakelike, thick twistings of black. Black tar.
Several windows have been broken. Gretchen stands in the empty driveway, her hands jammed into her pockets. Traffic is moving slowly over
here. A barricade has been set up that directs traffic out onto the shoulder
of the highway, on a narrow, bumpy, muddy lane that loops out and back
again onto the pavement. Cars move slowly, carefully. Their bottoms
scrape against the road. The detour signs are great rectangular things,
bright yellow with black zigzag lines. SLOW DETOUR. In the two center

lanes of the highway are bulldozers not being used today, and gigantic concrete pipes to be used for storm sewers. Eight pipes. They are really enormous; Gretchen's eyes crinkle with awe, just to see them.

She remembers the Adversary.

There he is — headed for the shopping plaza. *He won't get away in the crowds,* Gretchen promises herself. She follows. Now she is approaching an area that is more completed, though there are still no sidewalks and some of the buildings are brand-new and yet unoccupied, vacant. She jumps over a concrete ditch that is stained with rust-colored water and heads up a slight incline to the service drive of the Federal Savings Bank. The drive-in tellers' windows are all dark today, behind their green-tinted glass. The whole bank is dark, closed. Is this the bank her parents go to now? It takes Gretchen a minute to recognize it.

Now a steady line of traffic, a single lane, turns onto the service drive that leads to the shopping plaza. BUCKINGHAM MALL. 101 STORES. Gretchen notices a few kids her own age, boys or girls, trudging in jeans and jackets ahead of her, through the mud. They might be classmates of hers. Her attention is captured again by the Invisible Adversary, who has run all the way up to the Mall and is hanging around the entrance of the Cunningham Drug Store, teasing her.

You'll be sorry for that, Gretchen thinks with a smile.

Automobiles pass her slowly. The parking lot for the Mall is enor-   15
mous, many acres. A city of cars on a Saturday afternoon. Gretchen sees a car that might be her mother's, but she isn't sure. Cars are parked slanted here, in lanes marked LOT K, LANE 15; LOT K, LANE 16. The signs are spheres, bubbles, perched up on long slender poles. At night they are illuminated.

Ten or twelve older kids are hanging around the drugstore entrance. One of them is sitting on top of a mailbox, rocking it back and forth. Gretchen pushes past them — they are kidding around, trying to block people — and inside the store her eye darts rapidly up and down the aisles, looking for the Invisible Adversary.

Hiding here? Hiding?

She strolls along, cunning and patient. At the cosmetics counter a girl is showing an older woman some liquid makeup. She smears a small oval onto the back of the woman's hand, rubs it in gently. "That's Peach Pride," the girl says. She has shimmering blond hair and eyes that are penciled to show a permanent exclamatory interest. She does not notice Gretchen, who lets a hand drift idly over a display of marked-down lipsticks, each only $1.59.

Gretchen slips the tube of lipstick into her pocket. Neatly. Nimbly. Ignoring the Invisible Adversary, who is shaking a finger at her, she drifts over to the newsstand, looks at the magazine covers without reading them, and edges over to another display. Packages in a cardboard barrel, out in the aisle. Big bargains. Gretchen doesn't even glance in the barrel to see what is being offered . . . she just slips one of the packages in her pocket. No trouble.

She leaves by the other door, the side exit. A small smile tugs at her   20
mouth.

The Adversary is trotting ahead of her. The Mall is divided into geometric areas, each colored differently; the Adversary leaves the blue pavement and is now on the green. Gretchen follows. She notices the Adversary going into a Franklin Joseph store.

Gretchen enters the store, sniffs in the perfumy, overheated smell, sees nothing that interests her on the counters or at the dress racks, and so walks right to the back of the store, to the ladies' room. No one inside. She takes the tube of lipstick out of her pocket, opens it, examines the lipstick. It has a tart, sweet smell. A very light pink: *Spring Blossom.* Gretchen goes to the mirror and smears the lipstick onto it, at first lightly, then coarsely; part of the lipstick breaks and falls into a sink littered with hair. Gretchen goes into one of the toilet stalls and tosses the tube into the toilet bowl. She takes handfuls of toilet paper and crumbles them into a ball and throws them into the toilet. Remembering the package from the drugstore, she takes it out of her pocket—just toothpaste. She throws it, cardboard package and all, into the toilet bowl, then, her mind glimmering with an idea, she goes to the apparatus that holds the towel—a single cloth towel on a roll—and tugs at it until it comes loose, then pulls it out hand over hand, patiently, until the entire towel is out. She scoops it up and carries it to the toilet. She pushes it in and flushes the toilet.

The stuff doesn't go down, so she tries again. This time it goes partway down before it gets stuck.

Gretchen leaves the rest room and strolls unhurried through the store. The Adversary is waiting for her outside—peeking through the window—wagging a finger at her. *Don't you wag no finger at me,* she thinks, with a small tight smile. Outside, she follows him at a distance. Loud music is blaring around her head. It is rock music, piped out onto the colored squares and rectangles of the Mall, blown everywhere by the November wind, but Gretchen hardly hears it.

Some boys are fooling around in front of the record store. One of   25
them bumps into Gretchen and they all laugh as she is pushed against a trash can. "Watch it, babe!" the boy sings out. Her leg hurts. Gretchen doesn't look at them but, with a cold, swift anger, her face averted, she knocks the trash can over onto the sidewalk. Junk falls out. The can rolls. Some women shoppers scurry to get out of the way and the boys laugh.

Gretchen walks away without looking back.

She wanders through Sampson Furniture, which has two entrances. In one door and out the other, as always, it is a ritual with her. Again she notices the sofa that is like the sofa in their family room at home—covered with black and white fur, real goatskin. All over the store there are sofas, chairs, tables, beds. A jumble of furnishings. People stroll around them, in and out of little displays, displays meant to be living rooms, dining

rooms, bedrooms, family rooms. . . . It makes Gretchen's eyes squint to
see so many displays: like seeing the inside of a hundred houses. She slows
down, almost comes to a stop. Gazing at a living-room display on a raised
platform. Only after a moment does she remember why she is here —
whom she is following — and she turns to see the Adversary beckoning
to her.

She follows him outside again. He goes into Dodi's Boutique and,
with her head lowered so that her eyes seem to move to the bottom of her
eyebrows, pressing up against her forehead, Gretchen follows him. *You'll
regret this,* she thinks. Dodi's Boutique is decorated in silver and black.
Metallic strips hang down from a dark ceiling, quivering. Salesgirls
dressed in pants suits stand around with nothing to do except giggle with
one another and nod their heads in time to the music amplified throughout
the store. It is music from a local radio station. Gretchen wanders over to
the dress rack, for the hell of it. Size 14. "The time is now 2:35," a radio
announcer says cheerfully. "The weather is 32 degrees with a chance of
showers and possible sleet tonight. You're listening to WCKK, Radio Wonderful. . . ." Gretchen selects several dresses and a salesgirl shows her to a
dressing room.

"Need any help?" the girl asks. She has long swinging hair and a
high-shouldered, indifferent, bright manner.

"No," Gretchen mutters.   *30*

Alone, Gretchen takes off her jacket. She is wearing a navy blue
sweater. She zips one of the dresses open and it falls off the flimsy plastic
hanger before she can catch it. She steps on it, smearing mud onto the
white wool. She lets it lie there and holds up another dress, gazing at
herself in the mirror.

She has untidy, curly hair that looks like a wig set loosely on her
head. Light brown curls spill out everywhere, bouncy, a little frizzy, a
cascade, a tumbling of curls. Her eyes are deep set, her eyebrows heavy
and dark. She has a stern, staring look, like an adult man. Her nose is
perfectly formed, neat and noble. Her upper lip is long, as if it were
stretched to close with difficulty over the front teeth. She wears no
makeup, her lips are perfectly colorless, pale, a little chapped, and they are
usually held tight, pursed tightly shut. She has a firm, rounded chin. Her
facial structure is strong, pensive, its features stern and symmetrical as a
statue's, blank, neutral, withdrawn. Her face is attractive. But there is a
blunt, neutral stillness to it, as if she were detached from it and somewhere
else, uninterested.

She holds the dress up to her body, smooths it down over her chest,
staring at herself.

After a moment she hangs the dress up again, and runs down the
zipper so roughly that it breaks. The other dress she doesn't bother with.
She leaves the dressing room, putting on her jacket.

At the front of the store the salesgirl glances at her . . . "—Didn't   *35*
fit?—"

"No," says Gretchen.

She wanders around for a while, in and out of Carmichael's, the Mall's big famous store, where she catches sight of her mother on an escalator going up. Her mother doesn't notice her. She pauses by a display of "winter homes." Her family owns a home like this, in the Upper Peninsula, except theirs is larger. This one comes complete for only $5330: PACKAGE ERECTED ON YOUR LOT — YEAR–ROUND HOME FIBER GLASS IN-SULATION — BEAUTIFUL ROUGH-SAWN VERTICAL B. C. CEDAR SIDING WITH DEEP SIMULATED SHADOW LINES FOR A RUGGED EXTERIOR.

Only 3:15. Gretchen goes into the Big Boy restaurant and orders a ground-round hamburger with French fries. Also a Coke. She sits at the crowded counter and eats slowly, her jaws grinding slowly, as she glances at her reflection in the mirror directly in front of her — her mop of hair moving almost imperceptibly with the grinding of her jaws — and occa-sionally she sees the Adversary waiting outside, coyly. *You'll get yours,* she thinks.

She leaves the Big Boy and wanders out into the parking lot, eating from a bag of potato chips. She wipes her greasy hands on her thighs. The afternoon has turned dark and cold. Shivering a little, she scans the maze of cars for the Adversary — yes, there he is — and starts after him. He runs ahead of her. He runs through the parking lot, waits teasingly at the edge of a field, and as she approaches he runs across the field, trotting along with a noisy crowd of four or five loose dogs that don't seem to notice him.

Gretchen follows him through that field, trudging in the mud, and through another muddy field, her eyes fixed on him. Now he is at the highway — hesitating there — now he is about to run across in front of traffic — now, now — now he darts out —   40

Now! He is struck by a car. His body knocked backward, spinning backward. Ah, now, *now how does it feel?* Gretchen asks.

He picks himself up. Gets to his feet. Is he bleeding? Yes, bleeding! He stumbles across the highway to the other side, where there is a side-walk. Gretchen follows him as soon as the traffic lets up. He is staggering now, like a drunken man. *How does it feel? Do you like it now?*

The Adversary staggers along the sidewalk. He turns onto a side street, beneath an archway, *Piney Woods.* He is leading Gretchen into the Piney Woods subdivision. Here the homes are quite large, on artificial hills that show them to good advantage. Most of the homes are white colonials with attached garages. There are no sidewalks here, so the Adversary has to walk in the street, limping like an old man, and Gretchen follows him in the street, with her eyes fixed on him.

Are you happy now? Does it hurt? Does it?

She giggles at the way he walks. He looks like a drunken man. He   45 glances back at her, white-faced, and turns up a flagstone walk . . . goes right up to a big white colonial house. . . .

Gretchen follows him inside. She inspects the simulated brick of the foyer: yes, there are blood spots. He is dripping blood. Entranced, she follows the splashes of blood into the hall, to the stairs . . . forgets her own boots, which are muddy . . . but she doesn't feel like going back to wipe her feet.

Nobody seems to be home. Her mother is probably still shopping, her father is out of town for the weekend. The house empty, Gretchen goes into the kitchen, opens the refrigerator, takes out a Coke, and wanders to the rear of the house, to the family room. It is two steps down from the rest of the house. She takes off her jacket and tosses it somewhere. Turns on the television set. Sits on the goatskin sofa and stares at the screen: a return of a Shotgun Steve show, which she has already seen.

If the Adversary comes crawling behind her, groaning in pain, weeping, she won't even bother to glance at him.

The Responsive Reader

1. What are striking features of the suburban landscape through which Gretchen wanders? Do you see any connecting thread? Is there a keynote — a recurrent note struck more than once?
2. Do you understand Gretchen? What is her problem? What explains her "attitude"? What are telling details about the way she dresses, the way she acts toward others, or the way she acts in the stores and in the bathroom? (Do you feel you are getting an insight into teenage vandalism in the story?)
3. What is Gretchen's relation to school? to home and family?
4. Who or what is the invisible adversary? What role does he play in her fantasy life and in the story as a whole?

Talking, Listening, Writing

5. Do you consider Gretchen a freak, or does she represent the alienation of suburban youth?
6. The story presents Gretchen without comment — without editorializing or moralizing by the author. For you, what is the point of the story?
7. Rewrite Gretchen's story, telling it from the point of view of her mother or of a schoolmate. Or rewrite the story with Gretchen speaking in the first person to reveal her true thoughts and feelings.

Projects

8. You may want to look for another story Oates wrote about suburban or urban youth. Does it deal with similar or related themes as "Stalking"?

Thinking about Connections

Oates' "Stalking" and Hudson's "Children of the Harvest" (p. 57) each in their own way get us into the head of a young woman who finds herself at odds with her environment. Each young woman finds herself in a setting in which she is an alien — a setting of which she is not a congenial, accepted part. What is the key difference in the way the two relate to the world in which they find themselves? Do they represent two different generations?

YELLOW LIGHT
Garrett Hongo

> *Garrett Hongo is a Japanese American poet who writes about the places*
> *where he was born and grew up. He came from the big island of Hawaii to*
> *Southern California; later, he went to teach English and creative writing at*
> *the University of Oregon. The following poem is the title poem of his volume*
> Yellow Light. *His second book of poems,* The River of Heaven, *received*
> *the 1987 Lamont Poetry Prize, awarded by the American Academy of Poets.*
> *Maxine Hong Kingston has said of Hongo that his poetry "searches out those*
> *who inhabit alleys, islands, old graveyards, piers and learns that 'splendor*
> *must be something of what we all want.'"*

Thought Starters: What ideas or images does the word *barrio* bring to
mind? What kind of barrio do you see in the following poem?

One arm hooked around the frayed strap   1
of a tar–black patent–leather purse,
the other cradling something for dinner:
fresh bunches of spinach from a J–Town *yaoya*,
sides of split Spanish mackerel from Alviso's,   5
maybe a loaf of Langendorf; she steps
off the hissing bus at Olympic and Fig,
begins the three–block climb up the hill,
passing gangs of schoolboys playing war,
Japs against Japs, Chicanas chalking sidewalks   10
with the holy double–yoked crosses of hopscotch,
and the Korean grocer's wife out for a stroll
around this neighborhood of Hawaiian apartments
just starting to steam with cooking
and the anger of young couples coming home   15
from work, yelling at kids, flicking on
TV sets for the Wednesday Night Fights.

If it were May, hydrangeas and jacaranda
flowers in the streetside trees would be
blooming through the smog of late spring.   20
Wisteria in Masuda's front yard would be
shaking out the long tresses of its purple hair.
Maybe mosquitoes, moths, a few orange butterflies
settling on the lattice of monkey flowers
tangled in chain–link fences by the trash.   25

But this is October, and Los Angeles
seethes like a billboard under twilight.
From used-car lots and the movie houses uptown,
long silver sticks of light probe the sky.
From the Miracle Mile, whole freeways away,   30
a brilliant fluorescence breaks out
and makes war with the dim squares
of yellow kitchen light winking on
in all the side streets of the Barrio.

She climbs up the two flights of flagstone   35
stairs to 201–B, the spikes of her high heels
clicking like kitchen knives on a cutting board,
props the groceries against the door,
fishes through memo pads, a compact,
empty packs of chewing gum, and finds her keys.   40

The moon then, cruising from behind
a screen of eucalyptus across the street,
covers everything, everything in sight,
in a heavy light like yellow onions.

The Responsive Reader

1. What is the ethnic mix of the neighborhood in which the woman
   lives? What is the physical setting? Would you want to live there?
2. What role does the contrast between spring and fall play in the
   poem?
3. What is the attitude of the poet toward the woman? What is his
   interest in her?

Talking, Listening, Writing

4. Write about your discovery of a neighborhood very different from
   your own.

Projects

5. Working with a group, you may want to prepare a reading of poems
   by American poets of similar ethnic or regional background — Japanese American, Spanish American, Southern, African American,
   or the like.

WRITING
WORKSHOP 2

Writing from Observation

Good writers are alert observers. They profit from the open eye and the willing ear. They take in features that people in a hurry are likely to miss. They can call our attention to revealing details — details that tell us much about a person or a situation. When confronted with a new and difficult subject, they are likely to say: "I don't know much about this, but I can find out." When they are tired of hearsay, they are likely to say: "I am going to see for myself."

TRIGGERING What motivates writing based on close observation? Many writers get satisfaction from sharing with others what they have observed or discovered.

▪ Travel writers and nature writers marvel at the sights and sounds of the world around them. They seem more open or more receptive to their environment than ordinary people are. They know how to take us to places we have never been — whether the wide open spaces of Wyoming or a deteriorating neighborhood in the city — and bring them to life before our eyes. They get satisfaction from opening our eyes, extending our horizons.

▪ Much sharp-eyed observation, instead of taking us to places different and new, makes us revisit places that are familiar. It makes us look at our familiar everyday reality and really notice what is going on. Sometimes it makes us face up to realities to which we have deliberately closed our eyes.

GATHERING Writing from observation is an antidote to the repetition of secondhand ideas. Practice paying attention to "what is there." Go downtown, or uptown, or out into the country with a pad and pencil, jotting down faithfully what you see. Pretend to be the **camera eye**, which records impartially the revealing details and telltale features that keep people and places from seeming homogenized and interchangeable. Learn to go beyond the blurred general impression to the authentic specific detail:

GENERAL: I remember seeing one of the street people pushing her supermarket cart filled with cans for recycling down the street.

SPECIFIC: On a hot August afternoon on First Street, I saw a gray-haired woman in a ragged woollen coat and black basketball shoes pushing a supermarket wire basket filled with crumpled cans, her head hung low.

To collect the material for a paper, you would keep your eyes open for other sights and sounds that might reinforce or counteract your first impressions. What are the striking details in the following additional street scenes captured by an alert observer?

An old lady stops to put on her mantilla before she drags herself into St. Joseph's. Massive white pillars, stained glass windows, and silver domes are what I notice first. When I look more closely, I see that the pillars are chipped and worn and the sidewalks and steps are spattered with bird droppings and chewing gum.

On the corner, there is a condemned thrift shop with a painting on the wall that has a tree on it and some writing saying, "If you love me, feed my sheep."

Some local boys lean toward me and unconvincingly ask me for a cigarette, as though this was a programmed question that they ask any likely-looking person. Several others are hanging around the pawnshop with their black leather jackets, contemplating the knives.

Is there a common thread beginning to emerge in these snapshots of street scenes? How would you spell out the unifying overall impression that might become the keynote of a paper?

SHAPING What will tie authentic observations together in a coherent paper? Among tried-and-true strategies might be the setting up of a **before-and-after** contrast: a redwood forest before and after logging, a neighborhood before and after redevelopment (or gentrification), a factory town before and after the factory closed down. Or a paper might follow a journey down the river or a hike from the outskirts of civilization to the wilderness.

One student writer led his readers through the hospital where he worked by taking his readers along on his daily round as a gatherer of dirty dishes for his dishwashing job. Like other similar papers, the paper used a striking opening scene to establish the prevailing mood:

Quickly walking through the unending maze of ivory-white hallways, I see the familiar rectangular sign on the wall, "This elevator for employee use only." I press the plastic button, suddenly the bell sounds, and the down arrow above the elevator turns a bright red. Making sure I do not

overturn my shoulder-high polished-aluminum food tray cart, I watch that
the small black plastic wheels of the cart do not get caught in the crack
between the elevator and the tiled floor. Already in the capacious elevator
is an orderly dressed in blue from cap to booties, standing next to a
gurney with an unwrinkled snow-white sheet over the patient. As the
elevator door opens to the first floor, I pull my cart into the hallway. As
I turn to hold the door open, I notice a green tag dangling from the toe
of the patient, and I hear the orderly's voice: "Thanks, but I'm getting off
in the basement."

The writer then used his second paragraph to sum up the unifying
overall impression. His statement of the prevailing mood became the
thesis, or central idea, of the paper as a whole:

The depression I always felt as a dietary technician (actually a
dishwasher and gatherer of dirty dishes) at the Valley Hospital was
a result of the dejecting atmosphere. Every day's sights and sounds
reinforced my feeling of helplessness when confronted with pain and
misery.

The rest of the paper then fulfilled the expectations set up by this
preview. Prepared by it for the day's "sights and sounds," the reader
followed the writer to such places as the intensive-care unit or the "community kitchen" of the locked psychiatric ward —

nothing more than a green sink, a light green refrigerator, a green
formica table, and white plastic chairs. Four expressionless people sit
around the table, as if they were not of this planet. They look as if they
had been awake for days without sleep. They do not utter a word as I
walk by.

Like other effective conclusions, the wrap-up of this paper did not
just lamely restate the already familiar main point. It added a positive
note, however limited, to counterbalance at least somewhat the prevailing
somber mood:

After working in this environment for a time, I became used and
perhaps immune to the depressing sights I saw around me. I gradually
began to see the invigorating parts of life in the hospital, such as the
maternity ward and the miracle of a patient's fighting and conquering a
lethal disease. But these positive impressions could never quite balance
the feelings of depression and helplessness that I felt in the beginning.

REVISING When you revise a first draft, you may want to make
sure that the prevailing mood or the forward movement of the paper
becomes clearer or stronger for the reader. Especially, however, look for

features of style that blur the reader's vision or that make for a fuzzy picture:

Take out interchangeable labels. Declare a moratorium on paste–on labels such as *interesting, beautiful, spectacular, majestic, magnificent,* or *picturesque.* They do not conjure up actual scenes before the reader's eyes, and they make you sound like a travel folder or chamber–of–commerce brochure.

Tone down purple prose. A sentence like the following tries too hard and delivers too little: "I *greedily* pick the *luscious* ripe berries and savor them as they *explode* in my mouth with a taste of *total* refreshment."

Add striking details in strategic places. Individualize, dramatize. Build up the texture of real–life details:

> THIN: The saloon has the old-fashioned swinging doors familiar from Western movies.
>
> REVISED: The saloon has old-fashioned swinging doors. When someone enters, one can hear the doors flop back and forth, hitting each other until they come to rest.

Study the following sample paper. What are telling details that show the student writer to be an alert observer? What is the overall plan of the paper — what accounts for its purposeful forward movement? Do you sympathize with the writer's feelings and reactions, or would you have reacted differently?

Fourth of July

On the Fourth of July of last year, I was in New York City, specifically downtown and in Greenwich Village. The city was really alive as the day's festivities were getting under way. I expected the holiday to be a high point of my vacation, but it actually turned out to be a turning point in my education.

It was very hot and humid, a day when your clothes melt onto your body. Downtown streets were closed to traffic, so the multitudes of people swarmed in the streets. Vendors shouted about, trying to sell tee shirts and green foam crowns. The streets in the Village were also busy. People were sitting on fire escapes, while others sat on stoops or at cafe tables. There was a strange quiet as the traffic and its usual honking horns and screaming brakes were absent. Only a rare siren and a few street musicians were audible.

The general crowd downtown was basically a mob of families, friends, and sightseers. But up in Greenwich Village the people became a bit more visible. Washington Square was crowded with its normal leather-clad punks and skins, plus the oddly assorted stragglers looking for some place to be seen. A few bag ladies were searching trash cans and bearded men were lying on a patch of lawn with bottle in hand. The person who had a large effect on me was a girl in a total punk dress. She was quite tall

and while not what I would call fat, she seemed large. She had her head
shaved on the sides with a very thin mohawk which probably measured
about ten inches in height. It was a very hot day but she was in heavy
black leather pants and jacket, just the same as other days I had seen her
there.

Since it was the Fourth of July, I was feeling very patriotic and
proud to be in this great country. I had stood in Battery Park looking
out at the Statue of Liberty. I was in the city that I loved so much. Sure
it has problems, but there was nowhere else I would have rather been. I
loved going to the Village for lunch or for a shopping spree away from
Bloomies and Macys. I loved being around the unique people who hung
out under the Washington Arch. I admit I always had a somewhat
romantic notion of the punks. But it only took a glimpse of the real life
of one person there to open my mind to a grim reality.

What took place that day in the public restroom in Washington
Square did what no article or documentary ever could. As I had little
other option, I headed for the restroom which I had never been in before.
The room was hot and sticky. Water and trash covered the floor. Several
of the stalls had no door on them. I waited for one that did. In the stall
on my right there was a girl who was vomiting. The odor was horrid.
Her moaning was drowned out by two other girls who were shouting
obscenities at one another. I was almost afraid to come out of my stall.
When I did, I walked out to a sight I had not been prepared for. The
stall across from mine was doorless. In it was the girl with the mohawk
I had seen so often. Her jacket was off now. She had a strip of cloth
tied around her upper arm. I stood and watched as she put a needle into
her arm and shot it full of heroin. She withdrew the needle and took
notice of me. Her eyes looked empty. I felt empty.

Here was the birthday of our great nation—a place where everyone
was free. But was that girl free? Or was she a slave to a gross power?
My eyes opened that day. Until then I had not seen the hard, cold reality
that was out there. There was nothing romantic about this "rebel" girl.
It is painful to look back on how naive I had been. Never again would I
see the place or people in the same way.

Topics for Observation Papers (A Sampling)

1. City dwellers spend much time deploring or defending the city.
   Bring the city or town you know best to life for your readers,
   emphasizing what you hate or what you love about it.
2. Scout a nearby but out-of-the-way place that has been bypassed by
   development and that many commuters never see. Take your readers to such an undiscovered place: mudflats, foothills, a decaying
   waterfront, an out-of-the-way beach, a bird refuge, a park that has
   seen better days, an abandoned factory in the rust belt.
3. Recent immigration has transformed many inner-city neighborhoods, creating new Japantowns, Chinatowns, Little Saigons,
   New Havanas, or other areas with a strong ethnic emphasis. Bring

one of these places to life for your readers: the people, the shops, the institutions, the characteristic lifestyle.

4. Many of us at some point "do time" in camps, army barracks, hospitals, or jails. Make the characteristic feel or atmosphere of such a place real for your readers.

5. Have you ever gone in search of roots — visiting a place or places where you grew up or where your family used to live? What did you find?

6. How much of a contrast is there in your community between affluent and poor neighborhoods?

7. Have you ever lived in or visited a migrant camp, a reservation, a border town? What is it like to live there?

8. Many recent immigrants work in sweatshops or in the fields. What is it like to work there?

9. Much sociological research focuses on life in the ghetto or barrio. Can you provide an insider's guide to such a place for the outsider?

10. Have you ever lived in or visited a place that represents your idea of an ideal community?

3

New World: Diversity and Community

I am giving you a version of America, your America, that you may not have chosen to see or may have missed. I used to travel on the train going out to my job in Queens from the Upper West Side. After a certain subway stop, the entire train is filled with nonwhites. And those people are the people I am writing about, saying they have huge interesting lives.

Bharati Mukherjee

For many years, the official ideology of the United States was that of the melting pot. People would come to this country from across the seas and make a new start — with the promise of equal opportunity regardless of class, religion, or ethnic origin. Arriving on these shores, the immigrants would leave old allegiances and old hatreds behind to form a new nation. The American historian Arthur Schlesinger stated a widely held belief when he said in 1959,

> America has been in the best sense of the term a melting pot, every element adding its particular element of strength. The constant infusion of new blood has enriched our cultural life, speeded our material growth, and produced some of our ablest statesmen. Over 17 million immigrants arrived in the single period from the Civil War to World War I. . . . The very nationalities which had habitually warred with one another in the Old World have lived together in harmony in the New. America has demonstrated for everyone with eyes to see that those things which unite peoples are greater than those which divide them, that war is not the inevitable fate of mankind.

The policy implementing this belief was assimilation — "Americanizing" new immigrants and especially their children as quickly as possible, making them share in a common language and a common culture.

129

In the years since Schlesinger wrote the preceding statement, the melting-pot metaphor and the policy of assimilation have come in for much reexamination and revision. The melting-pot theory had not worked for large segments of American society: Native Americans on reservations; blacks segregated in the inner cities; Mexicans and Puerto Ricans living in Spanish-speaking neighborhoods with strong ties to their own culture; a large new Asian immigration that transformed parts of the cities into new Chinatowns or Little Saigons. Minority leaders and teachers started to teach black pride, pride in the Chicano heritage or *la raza,* and the preservation of Native American traditions. Sociologists and political leaders called for a new recognition of diversity, of pluralism. They asked for recognition of different languages and cultural strands existing side by side in a new American "mosaic" — with many different particles fitted together in a rich larger pattern, a larger whole.

How will tomorrow's Americans think of diversity and community? How much diversity will our society welcome or accommodate? Will a multicultural society lose its common center?

THE MOSAIC VS. THE MYTH
Anna Quindlen

> *Anna Quindlen is a widely syndicated columnist for the* New York Times. *Like other columnists, she writes about the issues of the day not as an expert—a political scientist, sociologist, or psychologist—but rather as a shrewd, informed observer who helps her readers make sense of the news. Like other columnists, Quindlen is a trend watcher who sizes up and explains the changes in awareness and public consciousness that slowly become part of the way we think about the world in which we live. In the following sample column, she comments on the gradual change from the melting-pot ideal of American society to a new outlook more tolerant or accepting of diversity.*

Thought Starters: How is American society like a melting pot? How is it like a mosaic? (How is it like a "tossed salad"?)

There is some disagreement over which wordsmith first substituted "mosaic" for "melting pot" as a way of describing America, but it is undoubtedly a more apt description. And it undoubtedly applies in Ms. Miller's third-grade class and elsewhere in the Lower East Side's Public School 20.

The neighborhood where the school is located is to the immigrant experience what Broadway is to actors. Past Blevitzky Bros. Monuments ("at this place since 1914"), past Katz's Delicatessen with its fan mail hung in the window, past the tenement buildings where fire escapes climb graceful as cat burglars, P.S. 20 holds the corner of Essex and Houston.

Its current student body comes from the Dominican Republic, Cambodia, Bangladesh, Puerto Rico, Colombia, mainland China, Vietnam and El Salvador. In Ms. Miller's third-grade class these various faces somehow look the same, upturned and open, as though they were cups waiting for the water to be poured.

There's a spirit in the nation now that's in opposition to these children. It is not interested in your tired, your poor, your huddled masses. In recent days it has been best personified by a candidate for governor and the suggestion in his campaign that there is a kind of authentic American. That authentic American is white and Christian (but not Catholic), ethnic origins lost in the mists of an amorphous past, not visible in accent, appearance or allegiance.

This is not a new idea, this resilient form of xenophobia. "It is but too common a remark of late, that the American character has within a short time been sadly degraded by numerous instances of riot and lawless violence," Samuel F. B. Morse wrote in an 1835 treatise called "Imminent Dangers to the Free Institutions of the United States through Foreign Immigration," decrying such riffraff as Jesuits.

Times are bad, and we blame the newcomers, whether it's 1835 or 1991. Had Morse had his way, half of me would still be in Italy; if some conservatives had their way today, most of the children at P.S. 20 would be, in that ugly phrase, back where they came from. So much for lifting a lamp beside the golden door.

They don't want to learn the language, we complain, as though the old neighborhoods were not full of Poles and Italians who kept to their mother tongue. They don't want to become American, we say, as though there are not plenty of us who believe we lost something when we renounced ethnicity. "Dagos," my mother said the American kids called them, American being those not Italian. "Wops." How quickly we forget as we use pejoratives for the newest newcomers.

Our greatest monument to immigration, the restored Ellis Island, seems to suggest by its display cases that coming to America is a thing nostalgic, something grandparents did. On the Lower East Side it has never been past tense, struggling with English and poverty, sharing apartments with the bathroom in the hall and the bathtub in the kitchen.

They send their children to school with hopes for a miracle, or a job, which is almost the same thing. This past week the School Volunteer Program, which fields almost 6,000 volunteer tutors, sponsored the first citywide Read Aloud: 400 grown-ups reading to thousands of kids in 90 schools. In P.S. 20, as so many have done before, the kids clutched their books like visas.

It is foolish to forget where you come from, which, in the case of the   10 United States, is almost always somewhere else. The true authentic American is a pilgrim with a small "p," armed with little more than the phrase "I wish. . . ." New ones are being minted in Ms. Miller's class, bits of a mosaic far from complete.

The Responsive Reader

1. Why is the term *mosaic* "a more apt description" for what Quindlen saw on the Lower East Side than *melting pot*? (Or is it?)
2. What does Quindlen say about the nature and history of "xenophobia" — the fear of foreigners — in this country? (Is it alive in your own community?)
3. How does Quindlen forge links between the present wave of immigration and America's past? What is her idea of the "true authentic American"?

Talking, Listening, Writing

4. Do you consider yourself a "true authentic American" in Quindlen's terms? Or are you one of those whose ethnic origins are "lost in the mists of an amorphous" — shapeless, indistinct — past?

Projects

5. You may want to work on a family history, with special attention to ethnic or regional origins. (Your class may decide to bring these family histories together as a class publication.)

COMING BACK ACROSS THE RIVER

José Luís and Rosa María Urbina

> *In his* New Americans: An Oral History *(1988), Al Santoli recorded the results of a nine-month journey across the United States, during which he talked to immigrant families from sixteen countries. He listened to refugees from Afghanistan and Ethiopia, to a Cuban immigrant who became the mayor of West Miami, to a former member of the independent Solidarity labor union that defied the Communist Polish government, and to Guatemalan Indians living in a migrant labor camp. The following testimony tells the story of a couple who came across the river from Juarez in Mexico to El Paso in Texas. Like many other "new Americans" before them, they came as illegal immigrants, outwitting border patrols or immigration authorities in the search for a place to live and work.*

Thought Starters: How typical or how untypical of the current wave of immigration do you think is the couple telling their story?

JOSÉ: The majority of the people in our apartment building have the same   1
problem as my family. All of us are in El Paso without legal papers. I have
been living here since 1981.

ROSA: I came in 1984, to find work. After José and I were married and we
found a place to live, I brought my children from a previous marriage. We
lived across the river, in Juárez. But I was born further south, in Zacatecas.

JOSÉ: My hometown is Juárez. Since I was nine years old, I've been coming to El Paso to work. At first I did gardening in people's yards, but I
have stayed in El Paso constantly since 1981, going out to the fields to do
farm work. I used to go to Juárez to visit my relatives at least one day each
month. But in the last year, I haven't gone, because of the new immigration law. To visit Juárez I have to swim across the river. I can't cross the
bridge or the *"migra"* [Border Patrol officers] can catch me right there.

During the past few months, the river has been very high and fast.
That's one reason why not so many people have been crossing lately. I am
not working now, because it isn't the growing or harvesting season on the
big farms. On February 15, we usually begin to plant onions. That is when
the main agricultural season begins. But during a three-month period
between planting and harvesting, there is no work.

We haven't paid our rent since December. If we're lucky, I can find   5
some part-time work to pay for food. Our baby, José Luís, is two months
old. Because he was born in El Paso, he is an American citizen. We can
only get food assistance for him. Once in a while, I find a job as a construc-

tion laborer, house painter, whatever is available. We use the money to buy food for the baby and the other three children first.

ROSA: I haven't been able to work lately, because the baby is so small. My other children are all in school. Lorenzo is twelve years old, José Rubén is ten, and Miriam is seven. From the time I came to El Paso, I have worked as a housekeeper and minding homes for people. I am not used to staying in the apartment every day, but I have no other choice, because of my small baby.

JOSÉ: Were we ever caught by the *migra* when we crossed the river to-gether? Oh, yes. [Laughs] Lots of times. But the patrolmen are really okay people. They arrest you, ask the usual questions. If you get rough, they will get rough, too. Otherwise they are fine. It all depends on the person who arrests you. If he has a mean personality, he will treat you rudely, whether you are impolite or not. But most of the time, it is a routine procedure.

When the *migra* catch us, they just put us in their truck and take us to their station. They ask our name, address, where we were born. They keep us in a cell maybe three or four hours. Then they put us in a bus and drive us back to Juárez. They drop the women off very near the main bridge. The men are taken a little further away from town.

Our favorite place to cross the river is close to the Black Bridge, which is not far from downtown El Paso. Many of us would stand on the Juárez riverbank and wait for the change of Border Patrol shifts. Each morning, the shift changes between seven-thirty and eight-thirty, some-times nine-thirty. We learn by observing over long periods of time. And all of our friends have been held in the immigration station. We observed certain patrolmen coming in to work and others checking out after their shifts.

Experienced river crossers pass this information to new people who   *10* are just learning the daily routines. Over a period of time, we learn the shift changes by recognizing different officers' faces. Some Mexican peo-ple even know the *migra* by name.

ROSA: Suppose I am caught by the patrolmen at seven-thirty in the morn-ing. They will take me to the station and hold me for a few hours, then bus me back to Juárez. I would walk back to a crossing point and try once again. It is like a game. I think the most times I was ever caught by the *migra* was six times in one day. No matter how many times they catch me, I keep coming back.

The majority of the people in the *colonia* where I lived in Juárez worked in El Paso, mostly as housekeepers, construction workers, or helpers in the fields. In the United States there is a lot of work, but in Mexico we have nothing.

JOSÉ: The men, like myself, who work in the fields come across the river at around 2:30 A.M. to meet the buses that take us to the fields from El Paso. The transportation is owned by the *padrone* of the farms, or by the labor-crew chiefs who hire and pay the workers. In the evenings, we ride the buses back to the river. Sometimes I work twelve hours in a day and earn $20. I've learned to check around to see which farms pay the best. Some pay up to $35 a day.

Farm-labor jobs are not very steady. We just grab whatever is open at the moment. I accept anything, any time, as long as it is work. But suppose I take a job that only pays me $12 a day. It would only be enough to cover my transportation and meals in the field. I must find jobs that pay enough to feed my family.

In order to make $25, I must pick seventy-two buckets of chili peppers. That could take me four or five hours; it depends on how fast my hands are. The total amount of buckets we pick depends upon the amount contracted by the big companies in California. For a big contract, we work as long as necessary to complete the order. But the most I can earn in a day is $35.

During the summer, it gets very hot in the fields, up to 110 degrees. We work for eight hours with a half-hour break for lunch. To save money, I bring my lunch from home. The companies usually provide us with a thermos bottle of cold water. The farthest we travel from El Paso is to Lordsburg, New Mexico. That is around three and a half hours by bus. We leave El Paso at 3:00 A.M. For Las Cruces we leave at 5:00 or 5:30 A.M.

ROSA: To my housekeeping jobs I can take a regular El Paso city bus at 7:00 or 8:00 A.M. I usually come home around 3:30 or 4:00 P.M. each day. For a long while, I worked at one house — a Mexican-American family. They started me at $20 a day. Eventually they increased my wages to $25. They live near a large shopping center in the eastern part of town. The job was a little bit easier than working in the factory in Juárez, and paid much better.

In the factory, a whistle blows to let us know when to start, when to stop, when to eat dinner, and when to resume work. Doing housecleaning, I can rest a little when I need to take a short break.

To compare our apartment in El Paso with where I lived in Juárez, I prefer it a little better over there, because in the *colonia* I had a place to hang my clothes after I washed them. The bathroom was outside of the house. But we don't have a bathroom in our apartment here, either. All of the apartments in this part of the building share a toilet on the back stairwell. But in this apartment we have electric appliances, which makes life better than my previous home.

JOSÉ: The landlord who owns this building is very generous. He lets us owe him rent for the months that I am not working. He understands how tough our life is. We pay whatever we can, even if it's only $50. And he knows that, if the day comes where we are raided by immigration officers, we will run.

The rent for this apartment is $125 a month plus electricity. We all live and sleep in this one room. The two boys sleep on the couch. Our daughter, Miriam, sleeps with us on the bed. And the baby sleeps in a crib next to our bed. Fortunately, we have a kitchen, and a closet in this room. Living conditions in Juárez were better, but there was no work at all.

If it is possible, Rosa and I would like to become American citizens. I would have my documents, and the government wouldn't be after us. All we want is to be able to work in peace.

Our dream is to be able to give the children the best of everything. We know that, for them to have a better future and purpose in life, they need a good education. Of the three children in school now, Miriam is the fastest learner. She received an award for being an honor student, the best in her classroom.

We hope the children can finish high school and have the career of their choice. We are going to sacrifice for them, so that they can have the profession that they desire.

I was only allowed to finish grammar school. I am the oldest in my family, of five sisters and two boys. I had to stop going to school when I was twelve, to work with my father to support the family. I would have liked to finish school, but my parents needed me to work. They chose my sisters to study. So I gave up my studies to support my sisters.

At first, I liked working better than going to school. But after a while, I wanted to attend junior high school. But my mother told me that the family couldn't afford for me to go, and she said my sisters seemed to like the books better than I did. So I continued working. My father had a fruit-and-vegetable business. We sold from a pushcart in downtown Juárez, and I came across the river to do some gardening.

Even though I've come to work in Texas and New Mexico for many years, I've never learned to speak much English. I would like to learn, but I've never had the chance to study. I have a lot of responsibility now to provide for the children. It is more important that they have school, so I must work.

The dreams that Rosa María and I had of living in the U.S. and reality are not the same. We hoped to find a job and live comfortably. Now that we are here, our main purpose is to survive.

I worry about our status under the new immigration law. In the previous place where I lived, I paid the rent all the time, but the landlord threw away all of the receipts. So we have no proof that we have been living here enough years to qualify for amnesty.

On the farms where I worked, my employers or crew bosses didn't keep pay records, because I only worked temporarily at each place. And, besides, I was illegal. So what was the use? If the police showed up, we would be in trouble whether or not the employer had a record. And the employers wanted to protect themselves. They didn't pay us with checks; it was always cash.

Fortunately, the last farmer I worked for took taxes and Social Security out of our wages. He is sending me a W-2 form as proof. I am waiting for it now. But things are getting worse, because the immigration police are putting pressure on people who hire undocumented workers. If the police catch illegals on a job site, the boss can be arrested under the new law. So most places have stopped hiring illegals. For example, my last job in El Paso, I was fired because the *migra* would raid the construction site every day. We would have to stop working and run.

When the planting season begins on the farms, I hope the immigration police don't show up. They raid a farm with a truck and four or five police cars. They position themselves outside the entrance to the farm and wait for us to walk by. They ask us for identification. If we cannot show proof that we are legal, we've had it. They'll take us away.

On the farms where I work, some people are legal and others aren't. If you drive your own car, the police usually won't question you. But if you come to work in the employer's bus, they'll take you away.

ROSA: In town, we don't feel comfortable walking on the street. If the immigration officers see us, they will grab us. We are not afraid for ourselves, because we are accustomed to it. But I worry about the children. They have just begun studying in school here in El Paso. They like it very much. My sons are in the sixth and fifth grades, and Miriam is in second grade. They are learning English very quickly. My oldest boy, Lorenzo, likes social studies and mathematics; he would like to be a doctor. My other son likes the army a lot. He could probably be a good soldier.

JOSÉ: If we become citizens and the United States government asks them to spend time in the army, we would be honored if they are chosen to serve. We would be very proud of our children for doing their duty for their country.

ROSA: My daughter, Miriam, received a certificate from her teacher. You can ask her what she would like to do when she finishes school.

MIRIAM: [Big grin] I like to study English and mathematics. Some day I would like to be a teacher.

ROSA: In the buildings on this block, the majority of the people are families. In each apartment there are three or four children. This is the only area we found where the landlords don't mind renting to families with kids. The kids play outside, in the alley behind our building. Not many cars pass on this street at night, so it is pretty quiet. But other neighborhoods are more active and there is more crime on the streets.

We would like to have an ordinary life, but our problems with the *migra* are nothing new. If they catch me again and send me back to Juárez, I will just come back across the river.

The Responsive Reader

1. For you, what in this account is a familiar story? What is different from what you might have expected? What is hard to believe or explain?
2. How traditional are the gender roles in this account?

Talking, Listening, Writing

3. The *Chicago Tribune* reviewer of Santoli's book said that "new im-migrants are as American as apple pie." Do you think the couple speaking in this account will become "Americanized"? Will their children?
4. As a citizen and taxpayer, do you feel responsible for this couple and their children?

Projects

5. How much do you know about immigration and the law? What does it take to get into the country legally? What is the treatment of illegal aliens in your community or state? You may want to work with a group to investigate legal aspects of immigration.

DIVERSITY AND ITS DISCONTENTS
Arturo Madrid

> *Arturo Madrid is a native of New Mexico who studied at the University of New Mexico and at UCLA. His first teaching assignment was at Dartmouth; he later became president of the Thomas Rivera Center at the Claremont Graduate School in California. He represents Spanish-speaking Americans of the Southwest who live in lands that were once part of Mexico and for whom the Anglos, or* americanos, *were the "immigrants" or new arrivals. The following article is excerpted from a speech he gave at the National Conference of the American Association of Higher Education in 1988. He urged his audience of educators to recognize excellence in workers as well as managers, in people who are not glib or superficially sophisticated, and in people regardless of class, gender, race, or national origin.*

Thought Starters: What does it mean to be "different"? How does it shape a person's outlook and personality? What do you learn from this article about the feeling of being the "other"?

My name is Arturo Madrid. I am a citizen of the United States, as   *1*
are my parents and as were my grandparents and my great-grandparents. My ancestors' presence in what is now the United States antedates Plymouth Rock, even without taking into account any American Indian heritage I might have.

I do not, however, fit those mental sets that define America and Americans. My physical appearance, my speech patterns, my name, my profession (a professor of Spanish) create a text that confuses the reader. My normal experience is to be asked, "And where are *you* from?" My response depends on my mood. Passive-aggressive, I answer, "From here." Aggressive-passive, I ask, "Do you mean where I am originally from?" But ultimately my answer to those follow-up questions that will ask about origins will be that we have always been from here.

Overcoming my resentment I try to educate, knowing that nine times out of ten my words fall on inattentive ears. I have spent most of my adult life explaining who I am not. I am exotic, but — as Richard Rodriguez of *Hunger of Memory* fame so painfully found out — not exotic enough . . . not Peruvian, or Pakistani, or whatever. I am, however, very clearly the *other*, if only your everyday, garden-variety, domestic *other*. I will share with you another phenomenon that I have been a part of, that of being a missing person, and how I came late to that awareness. But I've always known that I was the *other,* even before I knew the vocabulary or understood the significance of otherness.

I grew up in an isolated and historically marginal part of the United States, a small mountain village in the state of New Mexico, the eldest child of parents native to that region, whose ancestors had always lived there. In those vast and empty spaces people who look like me, speak as I do, and have names like mine predominate. But the *americanos* lived among us: the descendants of those nineteenth-century immigrants who dispossessed us of our lands; missionaries who came to convert us and stayed to live among us; artists who became enchanted with our land and humanscape and went native; refugees from unhealthy climes, crowded spaces, unpleasant circumstances; and, of course, the inhabitants of Los Alamos, whose sociocultural distance from us was accentuated by the fact that they occupied a space removed from and proscribed to us. More importantly, however, they—*los americanos*—were omnipresent (and almost exclusively so) in newspapers, newsmagazines, books, on radio, in movies, and, ultimately, on television.

Despite the operating myth of the day, school did not erase my otherness. It did try to deny it, and in doing so only accentuated it. To this day what takes place in schools is more socialization than education, but when I was in elementary school—and given where I was—socialization was everything. School was where one became an American, because there was a pervasive and systematic denial by the society that surrounded us that we were Americans. That denial was both explicit and implicit.

Quite beyond saluting the flag and pledging allegiance to it (a very intense and meaningful action, given that the United States was involved in a war and our brothers, cousins, uncles, and fathers were on the frontlines), becoming American was learning English, and its corollary: not speaking Spanish. Until very recently ours was a proscribed language, either *de jure*—by rule, by policy, by law—or *de facto*—by practice, implicitly if not explicitly, through social and political and economic pressure. I do not argue that learning English was not appropriate. On the contrary. Like it or not, and we had no basis to make any judgments on that matter, we were Americans by virtue of having been born Americans and English was the common language of Americans. And there was a myth, a pervasive myth, to the effect that if only we learned to speak English well—and particularly without an accent—we would be welcomed into the American fellowship.

Sam Hayakawa and the official English movement folks notwithstanding, the true text was not our speech, but rather our names and our appearance, for we would always have an accent, however perfect our pronunciation, however excellent our enunciation, however divine our diction. That accent would be heard in our pigmentation, our physiognomy, our names. We were, in short, the *other.*

Being the *other* involves contradictory phenomena. On the one hand being the *other* frequently means being invisible. Ralph Ellison wrote eloquently about that experience in his magisterial novel, *Invisible Man.* On the other hand, being the *other* sometimes involves sticking out like a sore thumb. What is she/he doing here?

For some of us being the *other* is only annoying; for others it is debilitating; for still others it is damning. Many try to flee otherness by taking on protective colorations that provide invisibility, whether of dress or speech or manner or name. Only a fortunate few succeed. For the majority of us otherness is permanently sealed by physical appearance. For the rest, otherness is betrayed by ways of being, speaking, or doing.

The first half of my life I spent downplaying the significance and consequences of otherness. The second half has seen me wrestling to understand its complex and deeply ingrained realities; striving to fathom why otherness denies us a voice or visibility or validity in American society and its institutions; struggling to make otherness familiar, reasonable, even normal to my fellow Americans.

I spoke earlier of another phenomenon that I am a part of: that of being a missing person. Growing up in northern New Mexico I had only a slight sense of us being missing persons. *Hispanos,* as we called (and call) ourselves in New Mexico, were very much a part of the fabric of the society, and there were *hispano* professionals everywhere about me: doctors, lawyers, schoolteachers, and administrators. My people owned businesses, ran organizations, and were both appointed and elected public officials.

My awareness of our absence from the larger institutional life of the society became sharper when I went off to college, but even then it was attenuated by the circumstances of history and geography. The demography of Albuquerque still strongly reflected its historical and cultural origins, despite the influx of Midwesterners and Easterners. Moreover, many of my classmates at the University of New Mexico were *hispanos,* and even some of my professors. I thought that would obtain at UCLA, where I began graduate studies in 1960. Los Angeles had a very large Mexican population and that population was visible even in and around Westwood and on the campus. Many of the groundskeepers and food-service personnel at UCLA were Mexican. But Mexican-American students were few and mostly invisible, and I do not recall seeing or knowing a single Mexican-American (or, for that matter, African-American, Asian, or American Indian) professional on the staff or faculty of that institution during the five years I was there. Needless to say, people like me were not present in any capacity at Dartmouth College, the site of my first teaching appointment, and of course were not even part of the institutional or individual mind-set. I knew then that we — a we that had come to encompass American Indians, Asian-Americans, African-Americans, Puerto Ricans, and women — were truly missing persons in American institutional life.

Over the past three decades the *de jure* and *de facto* types of segregation that have historically characterized American institutions have been under assault. As a consequence, minorities and women have become part of American institutional life. Although there are still many areas where we are not to be found, the missing persons phenomenon is not as pervasive as it once was. However, the presence of the *other,* particularly minorities, in institutions and in institutional life resembles what we call in Spanish a *flor de tierra* (a surface phenomenon): we are spare plants whose roots do not go deep, vulnerable to inclemencies of an economic, or political, or social, nature.

Our entrance into and our status in institutional life are not unlike a scenario set forth by my grandmother's pastor when she informed him that she and her family were leaving their mountain village to relocate to the Rio Grande Valley. When he asked her to promise that she would remain true to the faith and continue to involve herself in it, she asked why he thought she would do otherwise. "Doña Trinidad," he told her, "in the Valley there is no Spanish church. There is only an American church." "But," she protested, "I read and speak English and would be able to worship there." The pastor responded, "It is possible that they will not admit you, and even if they do, they might not accept you. And that is why I want you to promise me that you are going to go to church. Because if they don't let you in through the front door, I want you to go in through the back door. And if you can't get in through the back door, go in the side door. And if you are unable to enter through the side door I want you to go in through the window. What is important is that you enter and stay."

Some of us entered institutional life through the front door; others through the back door; and still others through side doors. Many, if not most of us, came in through windows, and continue to come in through windows. Of those who entered through the front door, some never made it past the lobby; others were ushered into corners and niches. Those who entered through back and side doors inevitably have remained in back and side rooms. And those who entered through windows found enclosures built around them. For, despite the lip service given to the goal of the integration of minorities into institutional life, what has frequently oc-curred instead is ghettoization, marginalization, isolation.

Not only have the entry points been limited, but in addition the dynamics have been singularly conflictive. Gaining entry and its corollary, gaining space, have frequently come as a consequence of demands made on institutions and institutional officers. Rather than entering institutions more or less passively, minorities have of necessity entered them actively,

15

even aggressively. Rather than waiting to receive, they have demanded. Institutional relations have thus been adversarial, infused with specific and generalized tensions.

The nature of the entrance and the nature of the space occupied have greatly influenced the view and attitude of the majority population within those institutions. All of us are put into the same box; that is, no matter what the individual reality, the assessment of the individual is inevitably conditioned by a perception that is held of the class. Whatever our history, whatever our record, whatever our validations, whatever our accomplishments, by and large we are perceived unidimensionally and dealt with accordingly. I remember an experience I had in this regard, atypical only in its explicitness. A few years ago I allowed myself to be persuaded to seek the presidency of a well-known state university. I was invited for an interview and presented myself before the selection committee, which included members of the board of trustees. The opening question of that brief but memorable interview was directed at me by a member of that august body. "Dr. Madrid," he asked, "why does a one-dimensional person like you think he can be the president of a multidimensional institution like ours?"

Over the past four decades America's demography has undergone significant changes. Since 1965 the principal demographic growth we have experienced in the United States has been of peoples whose national origins are non-European. This population growth has occurred both through birth and through immigration. A few years ago discussion of the national birthrate had a scare dimension: the high — "inordinately high" — birthrate of the Hispanic population. The popular discourse was informed by words such as "breeding." Several years later, as a consequence of careful tracking by government agencies, we now know that what has happened is that the birthrate of the majority population has decreased. When viewed historically and comparatively, the minority populations (for the most part) have also had a decline in birthrate, but not one as great as that of the majority.

There are additional demographic changes that should give us something to think about. African-Americans are now to be found in significant numbers in every major urban center in the nation. Hispanic-Americans now number over 15 million people, and although they are a regionally concentrated (and highly urbanized) population, there is a Hispanic community in almost every major urban center of the United States. American Indians, heretofore a small and rural population, are increasingly more numerous and urban. The Asian-American population, which has historically consisted of small and concentrated communities of Chinese-, Filipino-, and Japanese-Americans, has doubled over the past decade, its complexion changed by the addition of Cambodians, Koreans, Hmongs, Vietnamese, et al.

Prior to the Immigration Act of 1965, 69 percent of immigration was   *20*
from Europe. By far the largest number of immigrants to the United
States since 1965 have been from the Americas and from Asia: 34 percent
are from Asia; another 34 percent are from Central and South America; 16
percent are from Europe; 10 percent are from the Caribbean; the remaining
6 percent are from other continents and Canada. As was the case with
previous immigration waves, the current one consists principally of young
people: 60 percent are between the ages of 16 and 44. Thus, for the next
few decades, we will continue to see a growth in the percentage of non-
European-origin Americans as compared to European-Americans.

To sum up, we now live in one of the most demographically diverse
nations in the world, and one that is increasingly more so.

During the same period social and economic change seems to have
accelerated. Who would have imagined at mid-century that the prototyp-
ical middle-class family (working husband, wife as homemaker, two children) would for all intents and purposes disappear? Who could have
anticipated the rise in teenage pregnancies, children in poverty, drug use?
Who among us understood the implications of an aging population?

We live in an age of continuous and intense change, a world in which
what held true yesterday does not today, and certainly will not tomorrow.
What change does, moreover, is bring about even more change. The only
constant we have at this point in our national development is change. And
change is threatening. The older we get the more likely we are to be
anxious about change, and the greater our desire to maintain the status quo.

Evident in our public life is a fear of change, whether economic or
moral. Some who fear change are responsive to the call of economic
protectionism, others to the message of moral protectionism. Parentheti-
cally, I have referred to the movement to require more of students without
in turn giving them more as academic protectionism. And the pronouncements of E. D. Hirsch and Allan Bloom are, I believe, informed by intellectual protectionism. Much more serious, however, is the dark side of the
populism which underlies this evergoing protectionism — the resentment
of the *other*. An excellent and fascinating example of that aspect of populism is the cry for linguistic protectionism — for making English the official
language of the United States. And who among us is unaware of the
tensions that underlie immigration reform, of the underside of demographic protectionism?

A matter of increasing concern is whether this new protectionism,   *25*
and the mistrust of the *other* which accompanies it, is not making more
significant inroads than we have supposed in higher education. Specifically, I wish to discuss the question of whether a goal (quality) and a reality
(demographic diversity) have been erroneously placed in conflict, and, if
so, what problems this perception of conflict might present.

As part of my scholarship I turn to dictionaries for both origins and meanings of words. Quality, according to the *Oxford English Dictionary,* has multiple meanings. One set defines quality as being an essential character, a distinctive and inherent feature. A second describes it as a degree of excellence, of conformity to standards, as superiority in kind. A third makes reference to social status, particularly to persons of high social status. A fourth talks about quality as being a special or distinguishing attribute, as being a desirable trait. Quality is highly desirable in both principle and practice. We all aspire to it in our own person, in our experiences, in our acquisitions and products, and of course we all want to be associated with people and operations of quality.

But let us move away from the various dictionary meanings of the word and to our own sense of what it represents and of how we feel about it. First of all we consider quality to be finite; that is, it is limited with respect to quantity; it has very few manifestations; it is not widely distributed. I have it and you have it, but they don't. We associate quality with homogeneity, with uniformity, with standardization, with order, regularity, neatness. All too often we equate it with smoothness, glibness, slickness, elegance. Certainly it is always expensive. We tend to identify it with those who lead, with the rich and famous. And, when you come right down to it, it's inherent. Either you've got it or you ain't.

Diversity, from the Latin *divertere,* meaning to turn aside, to go different ways, to differ, is the condition of being different or having differences, is an instance of being different. Its companion word, diverse, means differing, unlike, distinct; having or capable or having various forms; composed of unlike or distinct elements. Diversity is lack of standardization, of regularity, of orderliness, homogeneity, conformity, uniformity. Diversity introduces complications, is difficult to organize, is troublesome to manage, is problematical. Diversity is irregular, disorderly, uneven, rough. The way we use the word diversity gives us away. Something is too diverse, is extremely diverse. We want a little diversity.

When we talk about diversity, we are talking about the *other,* whatever that other might be: someone of a different gender, race, class, national origin; somebody at a greater or lesser distance from the norm; someone outside the set; someone who possesses a different set of characteristics, features, or attributes; someone who does not fall within the taxonomies we use daily and with which we are comfortable; someone who does not fit into the mental configurations that give our lives order and meaning.

In short, diversity is desirable only in principle, not in practice. Long   30
live diversity . . . as long as it conforms to my standards, my mind set, my view of life, my sense of order. We desire, we like, we admire diversity, not unlike the way the French (and others) appreciate women; that is, *Vive la différence!* — as long as it stays in its place.

What I find paradoxical about and lacking in this debate is that diversity is the natural order of things. Evolution produces diversity. Margaret Visser, writing about food in her latest book, *Much Depends on Dinner,* makes an eloquent statement in this regard:

> Machines like, demand, and produce uniformity. But nature loathes it: her strength lies in multiplicity and in differences. Sameness in biology means fewer possibilities and therefore weakness.

The United States, by its very nature, by its very development, is the essence of diversity. It is diverse in its geography, population, institutions, technology; its social, cultural, and intellectual modes. It is a society that at its best does not consider quality to be monolithic in form or finite in quantity, or to be inherent in class. Quality in our society proceeds in large measure out of the stimulus of diverse modes of thinking and acting; out of the creativity made possible by the different ways in which we approach things; out of diversion from paths or modes hallowed by tradition.

One of the principal strengths of our society is its ability to address, on a continuing and substantive basis, the real economic, political, and social problems that have faced and continue to face us. What makes the United States so attractive to immigrants is the protections and opportunities it offers; what keeps our society together is tolerance for cultural, religious, social, political, and even linguistic difference; what makes us a unique, dynamic, and extraordinary nation is the power and creativity of our diversity.

The true history of the United States is one of struggle against intolerance, against oppression, against xenophobia, against those forces that have prohibited persons from participating in the larger life of the society on the basis of their race, their gender, their religion, their national origin, their linguistic and cultural background. These phenomena are not consigned to the past. They remain with us and frequently take on virulent dimensions.

If you believe, as I do, that the well-being of a society is directly related to the degree and extent to which all of its citizens participate in its institutions, then you will have to agree that we have a challenge before us. In view of the extraordinary changes that are taking place in our society we need to take up the struggle again, irritating, grating, troublesome, unfashionable, unpleasant as it is. As educated and educator members of this society we have a special responsibility for ensuring that all American institutions, not just our elementary and secondary schools, our juvenile halls, or our jails, reflect the diversity of our society. Not to do so is to risk greater alienation on the part of a growing segment of our society; is to risk increased social tension in an already conflictive world; and, ultimately, is to risk the survival of a range of institutions that, for all their defects and deficiencies, provide us the opportunity and the freedom to improve our individual and collective lot.

Let me urge you to reflect on these two words — quality and diversity — and on the mental sets and behaviors that flow out of them. And let me urge you further to struggle against the notion that quality is finite in quantity, limited in its manifestations, or is restricted by considerations of class, gender, race, or national origin; or that quality manifests itself only in leaders and not in followers, in managers and not in workers, in breeders and not in drones; or that it has to be associated with verbal agility or elegance of personal style; or that it cannot be seeded, nurtured, or developed.

Because diversity — the *other* — is among us, will define and determine our lives in ways that we still do not fully appreciate, whether that other is women (no longer bound by tradition, house, and family); or Asians, African-Americans, Indians, and Hispanics (no longer invisible, regional, or marginal); or our newest immigrants (no longer distant, exotic, alien). Given the changing profile of America, will we come to terms with diversity in our personal and professional lives? Will we begin to recognize the diverse forms that quality can take? If so, we will thus initiate the process of making quality limitless in its manifestations, infinite in quantity, unrestricted with respect to its origins, and more importantly, virulently contagious.

I hope we will. And that we will further join together to expand — not to close — the circle.

The Responsive Reader

1. What does it mean to Madrid to be the "other"? What is or was the role of such factors as history, genealogy, appearance (or "physiognomy"), and language in his sense of being different?
2. What was Madrid's experience with or perception of the *americanos*?
3. What was Madrid's experience with the school as the institution most directly representing American society? What was its goal? What was its governing myth? Did it fail or succeed?
4. What are different ways of dealing with minority identity or minority status? How did (and does) Madrid react or cope? Did his attitude or awareness change at different stages in his life?
5. What is Madrid's account of the changes as American colleges and universities try to deal with the issue of diversity? Have the changes been for the better?
6. What is Madrid's last word on the role of diversity in American society?

Talking, Listening, Writing

7. On balance, what do you think predominates in this essay — the "discontents" of the past or the challenges of the future?
8. Have you ever tried to put yourself in the shoes of someone with a history or with grievances and aspirations very different from your own? Tell the story of an experience that opened up for you a new perspective or opened a new window on the world. What did you learn from the experience?
9. Have you ever had difficulty answering the question "Who are you?" or "What are you?"

Projects

10. Has the hiring and retention of minority faculty been an issue at your own institution? You and classmates may want to arrange interviews with people who are in a position to know.

MULTICULTURALISM AND THE COMMON CENTER

Diane Ravitch

> *Diane Ravitch is an influential voice in the debate about the history and future of American education. She is a graduate of the Houston public schools who now teaches history and education at Teachers College, Columbia University. She became known for her book* The Troubled Crusade: American Education, 1945–1980 *and for other books about the dilemmas and needs of the American educational system. In 1990 she published* The American Reader: Words That Moved a Nation, *a book collecting classic speeches, poems, songs, arguments, and landmark court decisions that mirror Americans' understanding of themselves as a nation. Representing eloquent voices from Thomas Jefferson, Tom Paine, and Frederick Douglass to Alice Walker, Harvey Milk, and Lorna Dee Cervantes, the book has been called "a journey through the American democratic experience" (Albert Shanker).*

Thought Starters: How far has our society moved toward "cultural pluralism"? What kind of stock-taking takes place in the following article? What second thoughts about multiculturalism does it present?

As a result of the political and social changes of recent decades, cultural pluralism is now generally recognized as an organizing principle of this society. In contrast to the idea of the melting pot, which promised to erase ethnic and group differences, children now learn that variety is the spice of life. They learn that America has provided a haven for many different groups and has allowed them to maintain their cultural heritage or to assimilate, or — as is often the case — to do both; the choice is theirs, not the state's. They learn that cultural pluralism is one of the norms of a free society; that differences among groups are a national resource rather than a problem to be solved. Indeed, the unique feature of the United States is that its common culture has been formed by the interaction of its subsidiary cultures. It is a culture that has been influenced over time by immigrants, American Indians, Africans (slave and free) and by their descendants. American music, art, literature, language, food, clothing, sports, holidays, and customs all show the effects of the commingling of diverse cultures in one nation. Paradoxical though it may seem, the United States has a common culture that is multicultural.

Our schools and our institutions of higher learning have in recent years begun to embrace what Catherine R. Stimpson of Rutgers University has called "cultural democracy," a recognition that we must listen to a "diversity of voices" in order to understand our culture, past and present. This understanding of the pluralistic nature of American culture has taken a long time to forge. It is based on sound scholarship and has led to major revisions in what children are taught and what they read in school. The new history is — indeed, must be — a warts-and-all history; it demands an unflinching examination of racism and discrimination in our history. Making these changes is difficult, raises tempers, and ignites controversies, but gives a more interesting and accurate account of American history. Accomplishing these changes is valuable, because there is also a useful lesson for the rest of the world in America's relatively successful experience as a pluralistic society. Throughout human history, the clash of different cultures, races, ethnic groups, and religions has often been the cause of bitter hatred, civil conflict, and international war. The ethnic tensions that now are tearing apart Lebanon, Sri Lanka, Kashmir, and various republics of the Soviet Union remind us of the costs of unfettered group rivalry. Thus, it is a matter of more than domestic importance that we closely examine and try to understand that part of our national history in which different groups competed, fought, suffered, but ultimately learned to live together in relative peace and even achieved a sense of common nationhood.

Alas, these painstaking efforts to expand the understanding of American culture into a richer and more varied tapestry have taken a new turn, and not for the better. Almost any idea, carried to its extreme, can be made pernicious, and this is what is happening now to multiculturalism. Today, pluralistic multiculturalism must contend with a new, particularistic multiculturalism. The pluralists seek a richer common culture; the particularists insist that no common culture is possible or desirable. The new particularism is entering the curriculum in a number of school systems across the country. Advocates of particularism propose an ethnocentric curriculum to raise the self-esteem and academic achievement of children from racial and ethnic minority backgrounds. Without any evidence, they claim that children from minority backgrounds will do well in school *only* if they are immersed in a positive, prideful version of their ancestral culture. If children are of, for example, Fredonian ancestry, they must hear that Fredonians were important in mathematics, science, history, and literature. If they learn about great Fredonians and if their studies use Fredonian examples and Fredonian concepts, they will do well in school. If they do not, they will have low self-esteem and will do badly.

At first glance, this appears akin to the celebratory activities associated with Black History Month or Women's History Month, when schoolchildren learn about the achievements of blacks and women. But the point of those celebrations is to demonstrate that neither race nor gender is an

obstacle to high achievement. They teach all children that everyone, regardless of their race, religion, gender, ethnicity, or family origin, can
achieve self-fulfillment, honor, and dignity in society if they aim high and
work hard.

By contrast, the particularistic version of multiculturalism teaches   5
children that their identity is determined by their "cultural genes." That
something in their blood or their race memory or their cultural DNA
defines who they are and what they may achieve. That the culture in which
they live is not their own culture, even though they were born here. That
American culture is "Eurocentric," and therefore hostile to anyone whose
ancestors are not European. Perhaps the most invidious implication of
particularism is that racial and ethnic minorities are not and should not try
to be part of American culture; it implies that American culture belongs
only to those who are white and European; it implies that those who are
neither white nor European are alienated from American culture by virtue
of their race or ethnicity; it implies that the only culture they do belong to
or can ever belong to is the culture of their ancestors, even if their families
have lived in this country for generations.

The war on so-called Eurocentrism is intended to foster self-esteem
among those who are not of European descent. But how, in fact, is self-
esteem developed? How is the sense of one's own possibilities, one's potential choices, developed? Certainly, the school curriculum plays a relatively small role as compared to the influence of family, community, mass
media, and society. But to the extent that curriculum influences what
children think of themselves, it should encourage children of all racial and
ethnic groups to believe that they are part of this society and that they
should develop their talents and minds to the fullest. It is enormously
inspiring, for example, to learn about men and women from diverse backgrounds who overcame poverty, discrimination, physical handicaps, and
other obstacles to achieve success in a variety of fields. Behind every such
biography of accomplishment is a story of heroism, perseverance, and
self-discipline. Learning these stories will encourage a healthy spirit of
pluralism, of mutual respect, and of self-respect among children of different backgrounds. The children of American society today will live their
lives in a racially and culturally diverse nation, and their education should
prepare them to do so.

The pluralist approach to multiculturalism promotes a broader interpretation of the common American culture and seeks due recognition for
the ways that the nation's many racial, ethnic, and cultural groups have
transformed the national culture. The pluralists say, in effect, "American
culture belongs to us, all of us; the U.S. is us, and we remake it in every
generation." But particularists have no interest in extending or revising
American culture; indeed, they deny that a common culture exists. Particularists reject any accommodation among groups, any interactions that
blur the distinct lines between them. The brand of history that they es-

pouse is one in which everyone is either a descendant of victims or oppressors. By doing so, ancient hatreds are fanned and recreated in each new generation. Particularism has its intellectual roots in the ideology of ethnic separatism and in the black nationalist movement. In the particularist analysis, the nation has five cultures: African American, Asian American, European American, Latino/Hispanic, and Native American. The huge cultural, historical, religious, and linguistic differences within these categories are ignored, as is the considerable intermarriage among these groups, as are the linkages (like gender, class, sexual orientation, and religion) that cut across these five groups. No serious scholar would claim that all Europeans and white Americans are part of the same culture, or that all Asians are part of the same culture, or that all people of Latin-American descent are of the same culture, or that all people of African descent are of the same culture. Any categorization this broad is essentially meaningless and useless.

Several districts — including Detroit, Atlanta, and Washington, D.C. — are developing an Afrocentric curriculum. *Afrocentricity* has been described in a book of the same name by Molefi Kete Asante of Temple University. The Afrocentric curriculum puts Africa at the center of the student's universe. African Americans must "move away from an [*sic*] Eurocentric framework" because "it is difficult to create freely when you use someone else's motifs, styles, images, and perspectives." Because they are not Africans, "white teachers cannot inspire in our children the visions necessary for them to overcome limitations." Asante recommends that African Americans choose an African name (as he did), reject European dress, embrace African religion (not Islam or Christianity) and love "their own" culture. He scorns the idea of universality as a form of Eurocentric arrogance. The Eurocentrist, he says, thinks of Beethoven or Bach as classical, but the Afrocentrist thinks of Ellington or Coltrane as classical; the Eurocentrist lauds Shakespeare or Twain, while the Afrocentrist prefers Baraka, Shange, or Abiola. Asante is critical of black artists like Arthur Mitchell and Alvin Ailey who ignore Afrocentricity. Likewise, he speaks contemptuously of a group of black university students who spurned the Afrocentrism of the local Black Student Union and formed an organization called Inter-race: "Such madness is the direct consequence of self-hatred, obligatory attitudes, false assumptions about society, and stupidity."

The conflict between pluralism and particularism turns on the issue of universalism. Professor Asante warns his readers against the lure of universalism: "Do not be captured by a sense of universality given to you by the Eurocentric viewpoint; such a viewpoint is contradictory to your own ultimate reality." He insists that there is no alternative to Eurocentrism, Afrocentrism, and other ethnocentrisms. In contrast, the pluralist says, with the Roman playwright Terence, "I am a man: nothing human is alien to me." A contemporary Terence would say "I am a person" or might be a woman, but the point remains the same: You don't have to be black to love Zora Neale Hurston's fiction or Langston Hughes's poetry or Duke Ellington's music. In a pluralist curriculum, we expect children to learn a broad and humane culture, to learn about the ideas and art and animating spirit of many cultures. We expect that children, whatever their color, will be inspired by the courage of people like Helen Keller, Vaclav Havel, Harriet Tubman, and Feng Lizhe. We expect that their response to literature will be determined by the ideas and images it evokes, not by the skin color of the writer. But particularists insist that children can learn only from the experiences of people from the same race.

Particularism is a bad idea whose time has come. It is also a fashion 10 spreading like wildfire through the education system, actively promoted by organizations and individuals with a political and professional interest in strengthening ethnic power bases in the university, in the education profession, and in society itself. One can scarcely pick up an educational journal without learning about a school district that is converting to an ethnocentric curriculum in an attempt to give "self-esteem" to children from racial minorities. A state-funded project in a Sacramento high school is teaching young black males to think like Africans and to develop the "African Mind Model Technique," in order to free themselves of the racism of American culture. A popular black rap singer, KRS-One, complained in an op-ed article in the *New York Times* that the schools should be teaching blacks about their cultural heritage, instead of trying to make everyone Americans. "It's like trying to teach a dog to be a cat," he wrote. KRS-One railed about having to learn about Thomas Jefferson and the Civil War, which had nothing to do (he said) with black history.

Pluralism can easily be transformed into particularism, as may be seen in the potential uses in the classroom of the Mayan contribution to mathematics. The Mayan example was popularized in a movie called *Stand and Deliver,* about a charismatic Bolivian-born mathematics teacher in Los Angeles who inspired his students (who are Hispanic) to learn calculus. He told them that their ancestors invented the concept of zero; but that wasn't all he did. He used imagination to put across mathematical concepts. He required them to do homework and to go to school on Saturdays and during the Christmas holidays, so that they might pass the Advanced Placement mathematics examination for college entry. The teacher's reference to the Mayans' mathematical genius was a valid instructional device: It was an attention-getter and would have interested even students who were not Hispanic. But the Mayan example would have had little effect without the teacher's insistence that the class study hard for a difficult examination.

Ethnic educators have seized upon the Mayan contribution to mathematics as the key to simultaneously boosting the ethnic pride of Hispanic children and attacking Eurocentrism. One proposal claims that Mexican-American children will be attracted to science and mathematics if they study Mayan mathematics, the Mayan calendar, and Mayan astronomy. Children in primary grades are to be taught that the Mayans were first to discover the zero and that Europeans learned it long afterwards from the Arabs, who had learned it in India. This will help them see that Europeans were latecomers in the discovery of great ideas. Botany is to be learned by study of the agricultural techniques of the Aztecs, a subject of somewhat limited relevance to children in urban areas. Furthermore, "ethnobotanical" classifications of plants are to be substituted for the Eurocentric Linnaean system. At first glance, it may seem curious that Hispanic children are deemed to have no cultural affinity with Spain; but to acknowledge the cultural tie would confuse the ideological assault on Eurocentrism.

This proposal suggests some questions: Is there any evidence that the teaching of "culturally relevant" science and mathematics will draw Mexican-American children to the study of these subjects? Will Mexican-American children lose interest or self-esteem if they discover that their ancestors were Aztecs or Spaniards, rather than Mayans? Are children who learn in this way prepared to study the science and mathematics that are taught in American colleges and universities and that are needed for advanced study in these fields? Are they even prepared to study the science and mathematics taught in *Mexican* universities? If the class is half Mexican-American and half something else, will only the Mexican-American children study in a Mayan and Aztec mode or will all the children? But shouldn't all children study what is culturally relevant for them? How will we train teachers who have command of so many different systems of mathematics and science?

The efficacy of particularist proposals seems to be less important to their sponsors than their value as ideological weapons with which to criticize existing disciplines for their alleged Eurocentric bias. In a recent article titled "The Ethnocentric Basis of Social Science Knowledge Production" in the *Review of Research in Education*, John Stanfield of Yale University argues that neither social science nor science are objective studies, that both instead are "Euro-American" knowledge systems which reproduce "hegemonic racial domination." The claim that science and reason are somehow superior to magic and witchcraft, he writes, is the product of Euro-American ethnocentrism. According to Stanfield, current fears about the misuse of science (for instance, "the nuclear arms race, global pollution") and "the power-plays of Third World nations (the Arab oil boycott and the American-Iranian hostage crisis) have made Western people more aware of nonscientific cognitive styles. These last events are beginning to demonstrate politically that which has begun to be understood in intellectual circles: namely, that modes of social knowledge such as theology, science, and magic are different, not inferior or superior. They represent different ways of perceiving, defining, and organizing knowledge of life experiences." One wonders: If Professor Stanfield broke his leg, would he go to a theologian, a doctor, or a magician?

The Responsive Reader

1. What is Ravitch's opening account of the general movement toward recognizing diversity in our society? How convincing is it? Is there anything new or debatable?
2. The turning point of the essay comes when Ravitch talks about the downside of the "clash of cultures." What is the basis of her warnings?
3. The heart of this essay is in the distinctions between *pluralism, particularism,* and *universalism* that the author works out. How does she define these terms? What is the gist of her argument concerning them? What are her objections to "particularism"?
4. Does Ravitch seem to do justice to the current objections to a "Eurocentric" tradition in education or American culture?
5. Extended debate about an issue like multiculturalism is often precipitated by a test case that becomes a *cause célèbre*—a much-debated, much-analyzed case in point. Is there such a test case in this essay? What role does it play?

Talking, Listening, Writing

6. How "Eurocentric" or how open to diversity has your own schooling been? How much ethnic or cultural diversity have you seen in the teaching in school or college? (How did you react to this aspect of your educational experience?)
7. What has been your observation of the self-image or self-identity of white ethnics—descendants of European immigrants other than English? (For instance, how Polish and how American are Polish Americans?)

Projects

8. Recent years have seen a backlash against the movement toward multiculturalism in American education and society. You may want to work with other students to investigate the phenomenon. If you can, interview faculty or officials with reservations or objections on the subject.

Thinking about Connections

Working with other students, you may want to script and stage an imaginary dialogue between Arturo Madrid and Diane Ravitch on the subject of diversity.

WHY THEY EXCEL
Fox Butterfield

Fox Butterfield won the National Book Award for his book China: Alive in the Bitter Sea *(1982). He first became intrigued by the motivation and academic performance of Asian students when he was a young journalist in Taiwan. The young Vietnamese student he interviewed for the following article had left Vietnam ten years earlier and had not heard from her parents, who stayed behind, for three years. However, their admonitions to be a good daughter and a good student were still ringing in her ears. One of the sayings she remembered from her childhood said, "If you don't study, you will never become anything. If you study, you will become what you wish." In his article about why Asian students excel, Butterfield draws on a mix of personal experience, firsthand investigation, and expert opinion. He makes use of a range of oral and written sources.*

Thought Starters: Asians are often called the "model minority" — who work hard, study hard, and enter college and graduate in large numbers. How does this article support and explain the idea of the model minority?

Kim-Chi Trinh was just 9 in Vietnam when her father used his   1
savings to buy a passage for her on a fishing boat. It was a costly and risky sacrifice for the family, placing Kim-Chi on the small boat, among strangers, in hopes she would eventually reach the United States, where she would get a good education and enjoy a better life. Before the boat reached safety in Malaysia, the supply of food and water ran out.

Still alone, Kim-Chi made it to the United States, coping with a succession of three foster families. But when she graduated from San Diego's Patrick Henry High School in 1988, she had a straight-A average and scholarship offers from Stanford and Cornell universities.

"I have to do well — it's not even a question," said the diminutive 19-year-old, now a sophomore at Cornell. "I owe it to my parents in Vietnam."

Kim-Chi is part of a tidal wave of bright, highly motivated Asian-Americans who are suddenly surging into our best colleges. Although Asian-Americans make up only 2.4 percent of the nation's population, they constitute 17.1 percent of the undergraduates at Harvard, 18 percent at the Massachusetts Institute of Technology and 27.3 percent at the University of California at Berkeley.

With Asians being the fastest-growing ethnic group in the coun-   5
try — two out of five immigrants are now Asian — these figures will increase. At the University of California at Irvine, a staggering 35.1 percent

of the undergraduates are Asian-American, but the proportion in the freshman class is even higher: 41 percent.

Why are the Asian-Americans doing so well? Are they grinds, as some stereotypes suggest? Do they have higher IQs? Or are they actually teaching the rest of us a lesson about values we have long treasured but may have misplaced — like hard work, the family and education?

Not all Asians are doing equally well. Poorly educated Cambodian and Hmong refugee youngsters need special help. And Asian-Americans resent being labeled a "model minority," feeling that is just another form of prejudice by white Americans, an ironic reversal of the discriminatory laws that excluded most Asian immigration to America until 1965.

But the academic success of many Asian-Americans has prompted growing concern among educators, parents and other students. Some universities have what look like unofficial quotas, much as Ivy League colleges did against Jews in the 1920s and '30s. Berkeley Chancellor Ira Heyman apologized last spring for an admissions policy that, he said, had "a disproportionately negative impact on Asian-Americans."

I have wondered about the reason for the Asians' success since I was a fledgling journalist on Taiwan in 1969. That year, a team of boys from a poor, isolated mountain village on Taiwan won the annual Little League World Series at Williamsport, Pa. Their victory was totally unexpected. At the time, baseball was a largely unknown sport on Taiwan, and the boys had learned to play with bamboo sticks for bats and rocks for balls. But since then, teams from Taiwan, Japan or South Korea have won the Little League championship in 16 out of the 21 years. How could these Asian boys beat us at our own game?

Fortunately, the young Asians' achievements have led to a series of intriguing studies. "There is something going on here that we as Americans need to understand," said Sanford M. Dornbusch, a professor of sociology at Stanford. Dornbusch, in surveys of 7000 students in six San Francisco-area high schools, found that Asian-Americans consistently get better grades than any other group of students, regardless of their parents' level of education or their families' social and economic status, the usual predictors of success. In fact, those in homes where English is spoken often, or whose families have lived longer in the United States, do slightly less well. 10

"We used to talk about the American melting pot as an advantage," Dornbusch said. "But the sad fact is that it has become a melting pot with low standards."

Other studies have shown similar results. Perhaps the most disturbing have come in a series of studies by a University of Michigan psychologist, Harold W. Stevenson, who has compared more than 7000 students in kindergarten, first grade, third grade and fifth grade in Chicago and Minneapolis with counterparts in Beijing; Sendai, Japan; and Taipei, Taiwan. On a battery of math tests, the Americans did worst at all grade levels.

Stevenson found no differences in IQ. But if the differences in performance are showing up in kindergarten, it suggests something is happening in the family, even before the children get to school.

It is here that the various studies converge: Asian parents are able to instill more motivation in their children. "My bottom line is, Asian kids work hard," said Professor Dornbusch.

In his survey of San Francisco-area high schools, for example, he   15
reported that Asian-Americans do an average of 7.03 hours of homework a week. Non-Hispanic whites average 6.12 hours, blacks 4.23 hours and Hispanics 3.98 hours. Asians also score highest on a series of other measures of effort, such as fewer class cuts and paying more attention to the teacher.

Don Lee, 20, is a junior at Berkeley. His parents immigrated to Torrance, Calif., from South Korea when he was 5, so he could get a better education. Lee said his father would warn him about the danger of wasting time at high school dances or football games. "Instead," he added, "for fun on weekends, my friends and I would go to the town library to study."

The real question, then, is how do Asian parents imbue their offspring with this kind of motivation? Stevenson's study suggests a critical answer. When the Asian parents were asked why they think their children do well, they most often said "hard work." By contrast, American parents said "talent."

"From what I can see," said Stevenson, "we've lost our belief in the Horatio Alger myth that anyone can get ahead in life through pluck and hard work. Instead, Americans now believe that some kids have it and some don't, so we begin dividing up classes into fast learners and slow learners, where the Chinese and Japanese believe all children can learn from the same curriculum."

The Asians' belief in hard work also springs from their common heritage of Confucianism, the philosophy of the 5th-century B.C. Chinese sage who taught that man can be perfected through practice. "Confucius is not just some character out of the past—he is an everyday reality to these people," said William Liu, a sociologist who directs the Pacific Asian-American Mental Health Research Center at the University of Illinois in Chicago.

Confucianism provides another important ingredient in the Asians'   20
success. "In the Confucian ethic," Liu continued, "there is a centripetal family, an orientation that makes people work for the honor of the family, not just for themselves." Liu came to the United States from China in 1948. "You can never repay your parents, and there is a strong sense of guilt," he said. "It is a strong force, like the Protestant Ethic in the West."

Liu has found this in his own family. When his son and two daughters were young, he told them to become doctors or lawyers—jobs with the best guaranteed income, he felt. Sure enough, his daughters have gone into law, and his son is a medical student at UCLA, though he really wanted to be an investment banker. Liu asked his son why he picked medicine. The reply: "Ever since I was a little kid, I always heard you tell your friends their kids were a success if they got into med school. So I felt guilty. I didn't have a choice."

Underlying this bond between Asian parents and their children is yet another factor I noticed during 15 years of living in China, Japan, Taiwan and Vietnam. It is simply that Asian parents establish a closer physical tie to their infants than do most parents in the United States. When I let my baby son and daughter crawl on the floor, for example, my Chinese friends were horrified and rushed to pick them up. We think this constant attention is overindulgence and old-fashioned, but for Asians, who still live through the lives of their children, it is highly effective.

Yuen Huo, 22, a senior at Berkeley, recalled growing up in an apartment above the Chinese restaurant her immigrant parents owned and operated in Millbrae, Calif. "They used to tell us how they came from Taiwan to the United States for us, how they sacrificed for us, so I had a strong sense of indebtedness," Huo said. When she did not get all A's her first semester at Berkeley, she recalled, "I felt guilty and worked harder."

Here too is a vital clue about the Asians' success: Asian parents expect a high level of academic performance. In the Stanford study comparing white and Asian students in San Francisco high schools, 82 percent of the Asian parents said they would accept only an A or a B from their children, while just 59 percent of white parents set such a standard. By comparison, only 17 percent of Asian parents were willing to accept a C, against 40 percent of white parents. On the average, parents of black and Hispanic students also had lower expectations for their children's grades than Asian parents.

Can we learn anything from the Asians? "I'm not naïve enough to think everything in Asia can be transplanted," said Harold Stevenson, the University of Michigan psychologist. But he offered three recommendations.   25

"To start with," he said, "we need to set higher standards for our kids. We wouldn't expect them to become professional athletes without practicing hard."

Second, American parents need to become more committed to their children's education, he declared. "Being understanding when a child doesn't do well isn't enough." Stevenson found that Asian parents spend many more hours really helping their children with homework or writing to their teachers. At Berkeley, the mothers of some Korean-American students move into their sons' apartments for months before graduate school entrance tests to help by cooking and cleaning for them, giving the students more time to study.

And, third, schools could be reorganized to become more effective — without added costs, said Stevenson. One of his most surprising findings is that Asian students, contrary to popular myth, are not just rote learners subjected to intense pressure. Instead, nearly 90 percent of Chinese youngsters said they actually enjoy school, and 60 percent can't wait for school vacations to end. These are vastly higher figures for such attitudes than are found in the United States. One reason may be that students in China and Japan typically have a recess after each class, helping them to relax and to increase their attention spans. Moreover, where American teachers spend almost their entire day in front of classes, their Chinese and Japanese counterparts may teach as little as three hours a day, giving them more time to relax and prepare imaginative lessons.

Another study, prepared for the U.S. Department of Education, compared the math and science achievements of 24,000 13-year-olds in the United States and five other countries (four provinces of Canada, plus South Korea, Ireland, Great Britain and Spain). One of the findings was that the more time students spent watching television, the poorer their performance. The American students watched the most television. They also got the worst scores in math. Only the Irish students and some of the Canadians scored lower in science.

"I don't think Asians are any smarter," said Don Lee, the Korean-   *30* American at Berkeley. "There are brilliant Americans in my chemistry class. But the Asian students work harder. I see a lot of wasted potential among the Americans."

The Responsive Reader

1. Have you encountered the idea of the "model minority"? Do you remember any evidence, ideas, explanations? (Have you encountered challenges or rebuttals to this idea?)
2. The author dramatizes the issue by using Kim-Chi Trinh as a case in point. What key details and key ideas does the author want you to take in and remember?
3. How does the author use key statistics, expert testimony, and his "insider's" knowledge of the Confucian heritage to support his points?
4. What recommendations is Butterfield's article designed to support? Are they surprising or predictable? Which are strongest or most convincing? (Who has the last word in this article?)

Talking, Listening, Writing

5. Does this article change your ideas or preconceptions? Does it make you think? Why and how — or why not?
6. Do you want to take issue with all or part of this article? On what grounds? Where would you turn for supporting evidence?
7. What has shaped your own ideas about success and failure in our system of education? In your experience as a student, what have you learned about learning?
8. Some people support admission quotas to ensure fair representation

of minority students in colleges and universities. Do you agree with them? Do you think there should be quotas to prevent *over*represen- tation of groups like the Asian students described in Butterfield's article?

Projects

9. Why do model students do well? Why do dropouts fail? How many dropouts are really pushouts — pushed out by educational policies or economic pressures that defeat them? How many dropouts drop back in for a second (or third) chance? You may want to focus on one of these questions. Working with a group, quiz students, teach- ers, counselors, or others in a position to know. Find some current articles or new reports. What conclusions do your explorations sug- gest? Is there a consensus among your sources?

AMERICANIZATION IS TOUGH ON "MACHO"

Rose Del Castillo Guilbault

> *Rose Del Castillo Guilbault is director of editorials and public affairs at a television station in San Francisco and an associate editor at Pacific News Service. She writes a monthly column on the Hispanic experience, focusing on issues of special concern to Spanish-speaking Americans. In the column that follows, she targets the misunderstandings that can result when words travel from one language to another and when cultural traits are transplanted to another culture. She tries to reclaim the word* macho *from its present use to label the Sylvester Stallones and Charles Bronsons of our world.*

Thought Starters: Do you use the word *macho,* and if so, how? How does your use of the word contrast with the way the author says it is used in her family?

What is *macho*? That depends which side of the border you come   *1*
from.

Although it's not unusual for words and expressions to lose their subtlety in translation, the negative connotations of *macho* in this country are troublesome to Hispanics.

Take the newspaper descriptions of alleged mass murderer Ramon Salcido. That an insensitive, insanely jealous, hard-drinking, violent Latin male is referred to as *macho* makes Hispanics cringe.

"Es muy macho," the women in my family nod approvingly, describing a man they respect. But in the United States, when women say, "He's so macho," it's with disdain.

The Hispanic *macho* is manly, responsible, hardworking, a man in   *5*
charge, a patriarch. A man who expresses strength through silence. What the Yiddish language would call a *mensch*.

The American *macho* is a chauvinist, a brute, uncouth, selfish, loud, abrasive, capable of inflicting pain, and sexually promiscuous.

Quintessential *macho* models in this country are Sylvester Stallone, Arnold Schwarzenegger, and Charles Bronson. In their movies, they exude toughness, independence, masculinity. But a closer look reveals their machismo is really violence masquerading as courage, sullenness disguised as silence and irresponsibility camouflaged as independence.

If the Hispanic ideal of *macho* were translated to American screen roles, they might be Jimmy Stewart, Sean Connery, and Laurence Olivier.

In Spanish, *macho* ennobles Latin males. In English it devalues them. This pattern seems consistent with the conflicts ethnic minority males experience in this country. Typically the cultural traits other societies value don't translate as desirable characteristics in America.

I watched my own father struggle with these cultural ambiguities. 10
He worked on a farm for 20 years. He laid down miles of irrigation pipe, carefully plowed long, neat rows in fields, hacked away at recalcitrant weeds and drove tractors through whirlpools of dust. He stoically worked 20-hour days during harvest season, accepting the long hours as part of agricultural work. When the boss complained or upbraided him for minor mistakes, he kept quiet, even when it was obvious the boss had erred.

He handled the most menial tasks with pride. At home he was a good provider, helped out my mother's family in Mexico without complaint, and was indulgent with me. Arguments between my mother and him generally had to do with money, or with his stubborn reluctance to share his troubles. He tried to work them out in his own silence. He didn't want to trouble my mother—a course that backfired, because the imagined is always worse than the reality.

Americans regarded my father as decidedly un-*macho*. His character was interpreted as non-assertive, his loyalty non-ambition, and his quietness, ignorance. I once overheard the boss's son blame him for plowing crooked rows in a field. My father merely smiled at the lie, knowing the boy had done it, but didn't refute it, confident his good work was well known. But the boss instead ridiculed him for being "stupid" and letting a kid get away with a lie. Seeing my embarrassment, my father dismissed the incident, saying "They're the dumb ones. Imagine, me fighting with a kid."

I tried not to look at him with American eyes because sometimes the reflection hurt.

Listening to my aunts' clucks of approval, my vision focused on the qualities America overlooked. "He's such a hard worker. So serious, so responsible," my aunts would secretly compliment my mother. The unspoken comparison was that he was not like some of their husbands, who drank and womanized. My uncles represented the darker side of *macho*.

In a patriarchal society, few challenge their roles. If men drink, it's 15
because it's the manly thing to do. If they gamble, it's because it's how men relax. And if they fool around, well, it's because a man simply can't hold back so much man! My aunts didn't exactly meekly sit back, but they put up with these transgressions because Mexican society dictated this was their lot in life.

In the United States, I believe it was the feminist movement of the early '70s that changed *macho's* meaning. Perhaps my generation of Latin women was in part responsible. I recall Chicanas complaining about the chauvinistic nature of Latin men and the notion they wanted their women barefoot, pregnant, and in the kitchen. The generalization that Latin men embodied chauvinistic traits led to this interesting twist of semantics. Suddenly a word that represented something positive in one culture became a negative prototype in another.

The problem with the use of *macho* today is that it's become an accepted stereotype of the Latin male. And like all stereotypes, it distorts truth.

The impact of language in our society is undeniable. And the misuse of *macho* hints at a deeper cultural misunderstanding that extends beyond mere word definitions.

The Responsive Reader

1. Do you recognize the current American use of *macho* as it is described by Guilbault? What are key features or ingredients? What are key examples? (Who, according to the author, helped give the word its current American meaning?)
2. What contrasting Spanish or Mexican definition of *macho* emerges from Guilbault's portrait of her father? How did he look when seen "through American eyes"? Who or what was he in the eyes of his family?
3. Is there any connection between the traditional Mexican and the modern American senses of *macho*?

Talking, Listening, Writing

4. Have you had any experience with, or do you have feelings about, the macho male in the current American sense?
5. Observers of social trends have written much about a trend toward the androgynous male—a man who combines traditionally male and female qualities. The androgynous male has left the he-man image behind to become more sensitive; he is more in touch with his emotions; he relates to women. To judge from your own experience and observation, is there a trend toward the androgynous male in our society?

Projects

6. Do definitions of the ideal male or ideal female vary for different ethnic or cultural groups? Or are they highly personal? Working with other students, you might organize a panel discussion that would shed light on this question.

SEVENTEEN SYLLABLES

Hisaye Yamamoto

The seventeen syllables referred to in the title of the following short story are those of the traditional Japanese haiku. These short poems have only three lines that follow a short-long-short pattern (five syllables, then seven syllables, then five syllables). A famous example by the seventeenth-century poet Basho runs like this in a modern translation:

An old quiet pond —	*5*
Frog splashes into water	*7*
Breaking the silence	*5*

A modern student-written haiku runs like this:

A seed yearning for	*5*
the dark warm earth to moisten	*7*
must practice patience	*5*

In the short story that follows, an American woman of Japanese ancestry tries to give us a sense of what it is like to grow up in a family with immigrant parents rooted in another culture. During World War II, like thousands of other Americans of Japanese ancestry, Hisaye Yamamoto was detained in camps, or "relocation centers," justified by the U.S. government as a precaution against sabotage or support for the Japanese war effort by Japanese Americans.

Thought Starters: We sometimes talk about cultural traditions as if they were a mold that creates people with identical values. But the two Japanese American parents in the following story are very different people. How and why?

The first Rosie knew that her mother had taken to writing poems 1
was one evening when she finished one and read it aloud for her daughter's approval. It was about cats, and Rosie pretended to understand it thoroughly and appreciate it no end, partly because she hesitated to disillusion her mother about the quantity and quality of Japanese she had learned in all the years now that she had been going to Japanese school every Saturday (and Wednesday, too, in the summer). Even so, her mother must have been skeptical about the depth of Rosie's understanding, because she explained afterwards about the kind of poem she was trying to write.

See, Rosie, she said, it was a *haiku,* a poem in which she must pack all her meaning into seventeen syllables only, which were divided into three lines of five, seven, and five syllables. In the one she had just read, she had tried to capture the charm of a kitten, as well as comment on the superstition that owning a cat of three colors meant good luck.

"Yes, yes, I understand. How utterly lovely," Rosie said, and her mother, either satisfied or seeing through the deception and resigned, went back to composing.

The truth was that Rosie was lazy; English lay ready on the tongue but Japanese had to be searched for and examined, and even then put forth tentatively (probably to meet with laughter). It was so much easier to say yes, yes, even when one meant no, no. Besides, this was what was in her mind to say: I was looking through one of your magazines from Japan last night, Mother, and towards the back I found some *haiku* in English that delighted me. There was one that made me giggle off and on until I fell asleep —

> *It is morning, and lo!*
> *I lie awake, comme il faut,*
> *sighing for some dough.*

Now, how to reach her mother, how to communicate the melancholy   5
song? Rosie knew formal Japanese by fits and starts, her mother had even less English, no French. It was much more possible to say yes, yes.

It developed that her mother was writing the *haiku* for a daily news-paper, the *Mainichi Shimbun,* that was published in San Francisco. Los Angeles, to be sure, was closer to the farming community in which the Hayashi family lived and several Japanese vernaculars were printed there, but Rosie's parents said they preferred the tone of the northern paper. Once a week, the *Mainichi* would have a section devoted to *haiku,* and her mother became an extravagant contributor, taking for herself the blossoming pen name, Ume Hanazono.

So Rosie and her father lived for awhile with two women, her mother and Ume Hanazono. Her mother (Tome Hayashi by name) kept house, cooked, washed, and, along with her husband and the Carrascos, the Mexican family hired for the harvest, did her ample share of picking tomatoes out in the sweltering fields and boxing them in tidy strata in the cool packing shed. Ume Hanazono, who came to life after the dinner dishes were done, was an earnest, muttering stranger who often neglected speaking when spoken to and stayed busy at the parlor table as late as midnight scribbling with pencil on scratch paper or carefully copying characters on good paper with her fat, pale green Parker.

The new interest had some repercussions on the household routine. Before, Rosie had been accustomed to her parents and herself taking their hot baths early and going to bed almost immediately afterwards, unless her parents challenged each other to a game of flower cards or unless company dropped in. Now if her father wanted to play cards, he had to resort to solitaire (at which he always cheated fearlessly), and if a group of friends came over, it was bound to contain someone who was also writing *haiku,* and the small assemblage would be split in two, her father entertaining the non-literary members and her mother comparing ecstatic notes with the visiting poet.

If they went out, it was more of the same thing. But Ume Hanazono's life span, even for a poet's, was very brief—perhaps three months at most.

One night they went over to see the Hayano family in the neighboring town to the west, an adventure both painful and attractive to Rosie. It was attractive because there were four Hayano girls, all lovely and each one named after a season of the year (Haru, Natsu, Aki, Fuyu), painful because something had been wrong with Mrs. Hayano ever since the birth of her first child. Rosie would sometimes watch Mrs. Hayano, reputed to have been the belle of her native village, making her way about a room, stooped, slowly shuffling, violently trembling (*always* trembling), and she would be reminded that this woman, in this same condition, had carried and given issue to three babies. She would look wonderingly at Mr. Hayano, handsome, tall, and strong, and she would look at her four pretty friends. But it was not a matter she could come to any decision about.

On this visit, however, Mrs. Hayano sat all evening in the rocker, as motionless and unobtrusive as it was possible for her to be, and Rosie found the greater part of the evening practically anaesthetic. Too, Rosie spent most of it in the girls' room, because Haru, the garrulous one, said almost as soon as the bows and other greetings were over, "Oh, you must see my new coat!"

It was a pale plaid of grey, sand, and blue, with an enormous collar, and Rosie, seeing nothing special in it, said, "Gee, how nice."

"Nice?" said Haru, indignantly. "Is that all you can say about it? It's gorgeous! And so cheap, too. Only seventeen-ninety-eight, because it was a sale. The saleslady said it was twenty-five dollars regular."

"Gee," said Rosie. Natsu, who never said much and when she said anything said it shyly, fingered the coat covetously and Haru pulled it away.

"Mine," she said, putting it on. She minced in the aisle between the two large beds and smiled happily. "Let's see how your mother likes it."

She broke into the front room and the adult conversation and went to stand in front of Rosie's mother, while the rest watched from the door. Rosie's mother was properly envious. "May I inherit it when you're through with it?"

Haru, pleased, giggled and said yes, she could, but Natsu reminded gravely from the door, "You promised me, Haru."

10

15

Everyone laughed but Natsu, who shamefacedly retreated into the bedroom. Haru came in laughing, taking off the coat. "We were only kidding, Natsu," she said. "Here, you try it on now."

After Natsu buttoned herself into the coat, inspected herself solemnly in the bureau mirror, and reluctantly shed it, Rosie, Aki, and Fuyu got their turns, and Fuyu, who was eight, drowned in it while her sisters and Rosie doubled up in amusement. They all went into the front room later, because Haru's mother quaveringly called to her to fix the tea and rice cakes and open a can of sliced peaches for everybody. Rosie noticed that her mother and Mr. Hayano were talking together at the little table — they were discussing a *haiku* that Mr. Hayano was planning to send to the *Mainichi,* while her father was sitting at one end of the sofa looking through a copy of *Life,* the new picture magazine. Occasionally, her father would comment on a photograph, holding it toward Mrs. Hayano and speaking to her as he always did — loudly, as though he thought someone such as she must surely be at least a trifle deaf also.

The five girls had their refreshments at the kitchen table, and it was   20
while Rosie was showing the sisters her trick of swallowing peach slices without chewing (she chased each slippery crescent down with a swig of tea) that her father brought his empty teacup and untouched saucer to the sink and said, "Come on, Rosie, we're going home now."

"Already?" asked Rosie.

"Work tomorrow," he said.

He sounded irritated, and Rosie, puzzled, gulped one last yellow slice and stood up to go, while the sisters began protesting, as was their wont.

"We have to get up at five-thirty," he told them, going into the front room quickly, so that they did not have their usual chance to hang onto his hands and plead for an extension of time.

Rosie, following, saw that her mother and Mr. Hayano were sipping   25
tea and still talking together, while Mrs. Hayano concentrated, quivering, on raising the handleless Japanese cup to her lips with both her hands and lowering it back to her lap. Her father, saying nothing, went out the door, onto the bright porch, and down the steps. Her mother looked up and asked, "Where is he going?"

"Where is he going?" Rosie said. "He said we were going home now."

"Going home?" Her mother looked with embarrassment at Mr. Hayano and his absorbed wife and then forced a smile. "He must be tired," she said.

Haru was not giving up yet. "May Rosie stay overnight?" she asked, and Natsu, Aki, and Fuyu came to reinforce their sister's plea by helping her make a circle around Rosie's mother. Rosie, for once having no desire to stay, was relieved when her mother, apologizing to the perturbed Mr.

and Mrs. Hayano for her father's abruptness at the same time, managed to shake her head no at the quartet, kindly but adamant, so that they broke their circle and let her go.

Rosie's father looked ahead into the windshield as the two joined him. "I'm sorry," her mother said. "You must be tired." Her father, stepping on the starter, said nothing. "You know how I get when it's *haiku*," she continued, "I forget what time it is." He only grunted.

As they rode homeward silently, Rosie, sitting between, felt a rush *30* of hate for both — for her mother for begging, for her father for denying her mother. I wish this old Ford would crash, right now, she thought, then immediately, no, no, I wish my father would laugh, but it was too late: already the vision had passed through her mind of the green pick-up crumpled in the dark against one of the mighty eucalyptus trees they were just riding past, of the three contorted, bleeding bodies, one of them hers.

Rosie ran between two patches of tomatoes, her heart working more rambunctiously than she had ever known it to. How lucky it was that Aunt Taka and Uncle Gimpachi had come tonight, though, how very lucky. Otherwise she might not have really kept her half-promise to meet Jesus Carrasco. Jesus was going to be a senior in September at the same school she went to, and his parents were the ones helping with the tomatoes this year. She and Jesus, who hardly remembered seeing each other at Cleveland High where there were so many other people and two whole grades between them, had become great friends this summer — he always had a joke for her when he periodically drove the loaded pick-up up from the fields to the shed where she was usually sorting while her mother and father did the packing, and they laughed a great deal together over infinitesimal repartee during the afternoon break for chilled watermelon or ice cream in the shade of the shed.

What she enjoyed most was racing him to see which could finish picking a double row first. He, who could work faster, would tease her by slowing down until she thought she would surely pass him this time, then speeding up furiously to leave her several sprawling vines behind. Once he had made her screech hideously by crossing over, while her back was turned, to place atop the tomatoes in her green-stained bucket a truly monstrous, pale green worm (it had looked more like an infant snake). And it was when they had finished a contest this morning, after she had pantingly pointed a green finger at the immature tomatoes evident in the lugs at the end of his row and he had returned the accusation (with justice), that he had startlingly brought up the matter of their possibly meeting outside the range of both their parents' dubious eyes.

"What for?" she had asked.

"I've got a secret I want to tell you," he said.

"Tell me now," she demanded. *35*

"It won't be ready till tonight," he said.

She laughed. "Tell me tomorrow then."

"It'll be gone tomorrow," he threatened.

"Well, for seven hakes, what is it?" she had asked, more than twice, and when he had suggested that the packing shed would be an appropriate place to find out, she had cautiously answered maybe. She had not been certain she was going to keep the appointment until the arrival of mother's sister and her husband. Their coming seemed a sort of signal of permission, of grace, and she had definitely made up her mind to lie and leave as she was bowing them welcome.

So as soon as everyone appeared settled back for the evening, she 40 announced loudly that she was going to the privy outside, "I'm going to the *benjo*!" and slipped out the door. And now that she was actually on her way, her heart pumped in such an undisciplined way that she could hear it with her ears. It's because I'm running, she told herself, slowing to a walk. The shed was up ahead, one more patch away, in the middle of the fields. Its bulk, looming in the dimness, took on a sinisterness that was funny when Rosie reminded herself that it was only a wooden frame with a canvas roof and three canvas walls that made a slapping noise on breezy days.

Jesus was sitting on the narrow plank that was the sorting platform and she went around to the other side and jumped backwards to seat herself on the rim of a packing stand. "Well, tell me," she said without greeting, thinking her voice sounded reassuringly familiar.

"I saw you coming out the door," Jesus said. "I heard you running part of the way, too."

"Uh-huh," Rosie said. "Now tell me the secret."

"I was afraid you wouldn't come," he said.

Rosie delved around on the chicken-wire bottom of the stall for 45 number two tomatoes, ripe, which she was sitting beside, and came up with a left-over that felt edible. She bit into it and began sucking out the pulp and seeds. "I'm here," she pointed out.

"Rosie, are you sorry you came?"

"Sorry? What for?" she said. "You said you were going to tell me something."

"I will, I will," Jesus said, but his voice contained disappointment, and Rosie fleetingly felt the older of the two, realizing a brand-new power which vanished without category under her recognition.

"I have to go back in a minute," she said. "My aunt and uncle are here from Wintersburg. I told them I was going to the privy."

Jesus laughed. "You funny thing," he said. "You slay me!" 50

"Just because you have a bathroom *inside*," Rosie said. "Come on, tell me."

Chuckling, Jesus came around to lean on the stand facing her. They still could not see each other very clearly, but Rosie noticed that Jesus became very sober again as he took the hollow tomato from her hand and dropped it back into the stall. When he took hold of her empty hand, she could find no words to protest; her vocabulary had become distressingly constricted and she thought desperately that all that remained intact now was yes and no and oh, and even these few sounds would not easily out. Thus, kissed by Jesus, Rosie fell for the first time entirely victim to a helplessness delectable beyond speech. But the terrible, beautiful sensation lasted no more than a second, and the reality of Jesus' lips and tongue and teeth and hands made her pull away with such strength that she nearly tumbled.

Rosie stopped running as she approached the lights from the windows of home. How long since she had left? She could not guess, but gasping yet, she went to the privy in back and locked herself in. Her own breathing deafened her in the dark, close space, and she sat and waited until she could hear at last the nightly calling of the frogs and crickets. Even then, all she could think to say was oh, my, and the pressure of Jesus' face against her face would not leave.

No one had missed her in the parlor, however, and Rosie walked in and through quickly, announcing that she was next going to take a bath. "Your father's in the bathhouse," her mother said, and Rosie, in her room, recalled that she had not seen him when she entered. There had been only Aunt Taka and Uncle Gimpachi with her mother at the table, drinking tea. She got her robe and straw sandals and crossed the parlor again to go outside. Her mother was telling them about the *haiku* competition in the *Mainichi* and the poem she had entered.

Rosie met her father coming out of the bathhouse. "Are you through,   *55* Father?" she asked. "I was going to ask you to scrub my back."

"Scrub your own back," he said shortly, going toward the main house.

"What have I done now?" she yelled after him. She suddenly felt like doing a lot of yelling. But he did not answer, and she went into the bathhouse. Turning on the dangling light, she removed her denims and T-shirt and threw them in the big carton for dirty clothes standing next to the washing machine. Her other things she took with her into the bath compartment to wash after her bath. After she had scooped a basin of hot water from the square wooden tub, she sat on the grey cement of the floor and soaped herself at exaggerated leisure, singing "Red Sails in the Sunset" at the top of her voice and using da-da-da where she suspected her words. Then, standing up, still singing, for she was possessed by the notion that any attempt now to analyze would result in spoilage and she believed that the larger her volume the less she would be able to hear herself think, she obtained more hot water and poured it on until she was free of lather. Only then did she allow herself to step into the steaming vat, one leg first, then the remainder of her body inch by inch until the water no longer stung and she could move around at will.

She took a long time soaking, afterwards remembering to go around outside to stoke the embers of the tin-lined fireplace beneath the tub and to throw on a few more sticks so that the water might keep its heat for her mother, and when she finally returned to the parlor, she found her mother still talking *haiku* with her aunt and uncle, the three of them on another round of tea. Her father was nowhere in sight.

At Japanese school the next day (Wednesday, it was), Rosie was grave and giddy by turns. Preoccupied at her desk in the row for students on Book Eight, she made up for it at recess by performing wild mimicry for the benefit of her friend Chizuko. She held her nose and whined a witticism or two in what she considered was the manner of Fred Allen; she assumed intoxication and a British accent to go over the climax of the Rudy Vallee recording of the pub conversation about William Ewart Gladstone; she was the child Shirley Temple piping, "On the Good Ship Lollipop"; she was the gentleman soprano of the Four Inkspots trilling, "If I Didn't Care." And she felt reasonably satisfied when Chizuko wept and gasped, "Oh, Rosie, you ought to be in the movies!"

Her father came after her at noon, bringing her sandwiches of *60* minced ham and two nectarines to eat while she rode, so that she could pitch right into the sorting when they got home. The lugs were piling up, he said, and the ripe tomatoes in them would probably have to be taken to the cannery tomorrow if they were not ready for the produce haulers tonight. "This heat's not doing them any good. And we've got no time for a break today."

It *was* hot, probably the hottest day of the year, and Rosie's blouse stuck damply to her back even under the protection of the canvas. But she worked as efficiently as a flawless machine and kept the stalls heaped, with one part of her mind listening in to the parental murmuring about the heat and the tomatoes and with another part planning the exact words she would say to Jesus when he drove up with the first load of the afternoon. But when at last she saw that the pick-up was coming, her hands went berserk and the tomatoes started falling in the wrong stalls, and her father said, "Hey, hey! Rosie, watch what you're doing!"

"Well, I have to go to the *benjo*," she said, hiding panic.

"Go in the weeds over there," he said, only half-joking.

"Oh, Father!" she protested.

"Oh, go on home," her mother said. "We'll make out for awhile." *65*

In the privy Rosie peered through a knothole toward the fields, watching as much as she could of Jesus. Happily she thought she saw him look in the direction of the house from time to time before he finished unloading and went back toward the patch where his mother and father worked. As she was heading for the shed, a very presentable black car purred up the dirt driveway to the house and its driver motioned to her. Was this the Hayashi home, he wanted to know. She nodded. Was she a Hayashi? Yes, she said, thinking that he was a good-looking man. He got

given premature birth to a stillborn son, who would be seventeen now. Her family did not turn her out, but she could no longer project herself in any direction without refreshing in them the memory of her indiscretion. She wrote to Aunt Taka, her favorite sister in America, threatening to kill herself if Aunt Taka would not send for her. Aunt Taka hastily arranged a marriage with a young man of whom she knew, but lately arrived from Japan, a young man of simple mind, it was said, but of kindly heart. The young man was never told why his unseen betrothed was so eager to hasten the day of meeting.

The story was told perfectly, with neither groping for words nor untoward passion. It was as though her mother had memorized it by heart, reciting it to herself so many times over that its nagging vileness had long since gone.

"I had a brother then?" Rosie asked, for this was what seemed to matter now; she would think about the other later, she assured herself, pushing back the illumination which threatened all that darkness that had hitherto been merely mysterious or even glamorous. "A half-brother?"

"Yes."

"I would have liked a brother," she said.

Suddenly, her mother knelt on the floor and took her by the wrists. "Rosie," she said urgently, "Promise me you will never marry!" Shocked more by the request than the revelation, Rosie stared at her mother's face. Jesus, Jesus, she called silently, not certain whether she was invoking the help of the son of the Carrascos or of God, until there returned sweetly the memory of Jesus' hand, how it had touched her and where. Still her mother waited for an answer, holding her wrists so tightly that her hands were going numb. She tried to pull free. Promise, her mother whispered fiercely, promise. Yes, yes, I promise, Rosie said. But for an instant she turned away, and her mother, hearing the familiar glib agreement, released her. Oh, you, you, you, her eyes and twisted mouth said, you fool. Rosie, covering her face, began at last to cry, and the embrace and consoling hand came much later than she expected.

90

The Responsive Reader

1. How does Rosie in this story relate to her bilingual and bicultural background? How does she relate to the two languages she is expected to understand and use? What are differences between her own world and the traditional ways and old-country memories of her parents?

2. What is at the heart of the conflict between the parents? What is the story of their marriage? What kind of person is the mother, and what does poetry mean to her? What kind of person is the father? What does he expect of his wife and daughter? What explains his violent actions at the end?

3. Where in this story does Rosie say what she is expected to say rather than what she really feels? What do you think are her real thoughts and feelings? Is she taking sides in the conflict between her father and mother?

Talking, Listening, Writing

4. Imaginative literature, and especially modern literature, often prefers not to preach or explain. Yamamoto, like many modern writers, lets her story speak for itself. What for you is the meaning of the story? Is it mainly about the role of cultural traditions? differences in personality? the gap between the generations?
5. How much in this story has to be explained in terms of the cultural background of the parents? How much is generally human or universal and could apply to families from other backgrounds?
6. What has been a major source of conflict in your own life? Do you have any thoughts about causes, wrong choices, possible remedies?

Projects

7. For a major group project, you might decide to research the story of the World War II relocation camps. If possible, interview survivors or their children, World War II veterans, and others who might have information or opinions on the subject.

PERSIMMONS

Li-Young Lee

Li-Young Lee, born to Chinese parents in Indonesia, at an early age fled with his family from persecution, moving from country to country in search of a place to live and be safe. His family finally came to the United States, where his father became a Presbyterian minister in Pennsylvania. Lee published Rose, *a book of poems, in 1986. He is one of the best known of a new generation of bilingual American poets whose poems often explore the meeting of two cultures, two worlds.*

Thought Starters: In the meeting of two worlds in this poem, what is the symbolic role of the persimmon (the fruit after which the poem is named), the father's scroll paintings in a centuries-old Chinese tradition, and the monolingual American teacher?

In sixth grade Mrs. Walker   1
slapped the back of my head
and made me stand in the corner
for not knowing the difference
between *persimmon* and *precision*.   5
How to choose

persimmons. This is precision.
Ripe ones are soft and brown-spotted.
Sniff the bottoms. The sweet one
will be fragrant. How to eat: 10
put the knife away, lay down newspaper.
Peel the skin tenderly, not to tear the meat.
Chew the skin, suck it,
and swallow. Now, eat
the meat of the fruit,   15
so sweet,
all of it, to the heart.

Donna undresses, her stomach is white.
In the yard, dewy and shivering
with crickets, we lie naked,   20
face-up, face-down.
I teach her Chinese.
Crickets: *chiu chiu.* Dew: I've forgotten.
Naked: I've forgotten.

Ni, wo: you and me.   *25*
I part her legs,
remember to tell her
she is beautiful as the moon.

Other words
that got me into trouble were   *30*
fight and *fright, wren* and *yarn.*
Fight was what I did when I was frightened,
fright was what I felt when I was fighting.
Wrens are small, plain birds,
yarn is what one knits with.   *35*
Wrens are soft as yarn.
My mother made birds out of yarn.
I loved to watch her tie the stuff;
a bird, a rabbit, a wee man.

Mrs. Walker brought a persimmon to class   *40*
and cut it up
so everyone could taste
a *Chinese apple.* Knowing
it wasn't ripe or sweet, I didn't eat
but watched the other faces.   *45*

My mother said every persimmon has a sun
inside, something golden, glowing,
warm as my face.

Once, in the cellar, I found two wrapped in newspaper,
forgotten and not yet ripe.   *50*
I took them and set both on my bedroom windowsill,
where each morning a cardinal
sang, *The sun, the sun.*

Finally understanding
he was going blind,   *55*
my father sat up all one night
waiting for a song, a ghost.
I gave him the persimmons,
swelled, heavy as sadness,
and sweet as love.   *60*

This year, in the muddy lighting
of my parents' cellar, I rummage, looking
for something I lost.
My father sits on the tired, wooden stairs,

black cane between his knees,   *65*
hand over hand, gripping the handle.

He's so happy that I've come home.
I ask how his eyes are, a stupid question.
All gone, he answers.

Under some blankets, I find a box.   *70*
Inside the box I find three scrolls.
I sit beside him and untie
three paintings by my father:
Hibiscus leaf and a white flower.
Two cats preening.   *75*
Two persimmons, so full they want to drop from the cloth.

He raises both hands to touch the cloth,
asks, *Which is this?*

This is persimmons, Father.

Oh, the feel of the wolftail on the silk,   *80*
the strength, the tense
precision in the wrist.
I painted them hundreds of times
eyes closed. These I painted blind.
Some things never leave a person: *85*
scent of the hair of one you love,
the texture of persimmons,
in your palm, the ripe weight.

The Responsive Reader

1. Like other central symbols in poetry, the persimmon in this poem is rich in associations and symbolic significance. How often does the fruit come up in the poem? What does the fruit mean to the person speaking in the poem? What memories and associations does it bring to the speaker's mind?
2. What is the role of the teacher in this poem?
3. What is the poet's relation to the scroll paintings and to his father?
4. How does the poem touch on the difficulties and challenges faced by the bilingual student?

Talking, Listening, Writing

5. Can you understand and sympathize with the poet's thoughts and feelings in this poem? Or does the speaker seem a stranger to you?

6. As you look back over your own memories, is there an object, a place, or an event that is rich in symbolic meaning for you? Write about it, bringing memories and associations to life for your reader.

Projects

7. Do a Quaker reading of this poem with your classmates. (Someone starts reading a stanza, or group of lines, and then stops, with the neighbor picking up the thread.)

WRITING
WORKSHOP 3

Writing from Interviews

Good writers are often good listeners. Before they speak up themselves, they take in what other people have to say. When official pronouncements or statistics leave key questions unanswered, they talk to people who have relevant information. Before they jump into the fray, they listen and get their bearings. They may listen during the course of informal conversations. Or they may set up formal interviews, leading the interviewee through a series of pointed questions (sometimes submitted in advance). When we read the writing of good listeners, we can see that they know what is involved, what they are up against in promoting a new or different point of view. A writer who knows how to listen can make readers feel that they are not simply being preached at from on high but are being addressed by someone who understands what they think and feel.

TRIGGERING You will often want to talk to someone in the know when you wonder: What's the human meaning of these statistics? What's behind this bland public relations announcement? What's behind official denials or alibis? When someone has been accused of wrongdoing, what is that person's side of the story? Here are some sample questions on which a productive interview (or interviews) might shed light:

- What's behind the faceless current immigration statistics? What brought recent immigrants here from a country like Cambodia, Somalia, or the former Soviet Union?
- Do students from diverse ethnic, racial, or cultural backgrounds feel accepted on your campus?
- What happened when separate men's and women's physical education departments were abolished in colleges? What happened to the women who headed the separate women's departments? What happened to the women's teams?
- How do charges of police brutality look from the other side of the desk — from the point of view of police officers or their superiors?

GATHERING   When you write a paper on a subject of public interest, you may get helpful ideas from talking with a roommate, a family
member, a teacher, a coworker, or a friend. At times your paper may profit
from informal conversations with strangers or an exchange overheard on
a bus. However, often the most productive source of information and
opinion for a paper may be a formal interview or a series of interviews.

When you first approach people to set up an interview, you may find
a natural reluctance to set aside time to talk to a stranger. However, once
you explain why you value their input, you may find that people love to
be consulted as an authority. Many will go on at length on a subject dear
to them. Some of the most informative books about what America is and
where it is going are published by writers who get Americans to talk —
freely, candidly, from the heart. Classics of this genre include such books
as Jonathan Kozol's *Rachel and Her Children,* Robert Coles' *Children of
Crisis,* Al Santoli's *The New Immigrants,* and Studs Terkel's *Race.*

You will typically prepare a *set of questions* designed to give focus and
direction to an interview. (You should, however, be flexible enough to
adapt your prepared questions as promising areas of talk open up.) If you
are investigating life after retirement, you might come to an interview
with a tentative set of questions like the following:

- Is it true that the elderly are a privileged group in our society?
- What did you do before you retired?
- Were you ready for retirement?
- How or why did you retire?
- What do you think about mandatory retirement?
- What about retirement was least like what you expected or the
  hardest to handle?
- What was best about retirement?
- What advice would you give people starting to plan for retirement?
- If you could turn the clock back thirty years, what would you do
  differently?

The following is part of a fact-finding interview. The interviewer
asked businesslike, open questions. The student interviewer had heard
about the superior academic performance of Asian students, and he went
to a math teacher to get an insider's point of view. What kind of questions
did the interviewer ask? What is the flow of the questions — does one
naturally lead to another? How informative and how straightforward are
the answers?

QUESTION: On the average, what percentage of your classes is made up of
Asian students?

ANSWER: Well, the lower-level courses have very few, but the higher-level courses have many. Of all the students I've taught during the last five years, maybe forty percent have been Asian.

QUESTION: hen you say higher-level courses, what classes are you referring to?

ANSWER: Calculus, trigonometry, differential equations.

QUESTION: As for the students in these higher-level math classes, are most of them American-born Asian students, or were they born in other countries?

ANSWER: Many of my students are immigrants, born in Asia. Many of them have come to this country within the last two to ten years.

QUESTION: Do your Asian students tend to score higher on tests and get better grades than other groups of students?

ANSWER: All of us teachers say the same thing to ourselves and to each other. There are more good grades going to Asians than to any other ethnic, racial, or cultural group.

QUESTION: Do you discuss this trend with your peers on an informal or formal basis, say, in staff or departmental meetings?

ANSWER: We discuss it informally. It's hard to discuss it formally with a chairperson sitting in because it seems almost racist to discuss the subject in those terms. We talk informally about what we have noticed and how we feel.

QUESTION: Have you talked to the students about why they do well?

ANSWER: I get various answers, but it boils down to that they learn to use their minds earlier. I don't think that they are necessarily born with higher intelligence, but they are pushed hard from the earliest years. In their home countries, they had to cram and memorize their books. Their curriculum moved faster, so that by the seventh grade they were doing algebra and by the ninth grade they were doing calculus.

QUESTION: What is the driving force or incentive for their success?

ANSWER: They work a lot harder, although we have to remember that others have dropped out along the way, and we see only the hardest workers or better students. The ones that do reach us do better than their American counterparts. Why? I think culturally they have a great respect for learning and for teachers. At home their parents would never think of saying something critical about a teacher.

Many interviewers today cultivate a more aggressive, participatory interviewing style. They may ask provocative questions designed to draw a cautious interviewee out. They may challenge the answers they receive in order to trigger a vigorous exchange of ideas. In the following excerpt from an interview, Frances Lear, publisher of *Lear's* magazine, prods Kate Michelman, president of the National Abortion Rights League, to take a more aggressive stand.

Question: I think a lot of people are pro–choice intellectually but not emotionally. Is that right?

Answer: That's right. Most people agree that women have the right to choose. But some think that means they have to be in favor of abortion. There's a lot of ambivalence about abortion. There's a big difference between being pro-abortion and pro-choice.

Question: Well, why don't you clarify it? Why aren't you as articulate as the other side?

Answer: I think we are. But for the past eighteen years our efforts were focused mostly in the courts, while our opposition concentrated on political organizing and on communicating to the public, defining the images and the symbols. We haven't been as graphic as they are.

Question: Why not? The pro-choice movement is loaded with journalists.

Answer: But the other side captured the attention of the media because they were on the offensive and we were on the defensive.

Question: You have been at this for a long, long time. Why haven't you come up with a message just as strong and emotional as the right-to-lifers have? Why are you so pure?

Answer: We're not so pure. But we tried to argue in a rational, legal way, and it made the issue abstract for people. . . . Listen, if I wanted to get really emotional and sensationalistic I could show you pictures of women bleeding to death from illegal abortions.

Question: Why don't you?

Answer: I could show pictures of children with cigarette burns all over their bodies — born unwanted, unloved, which is the critical issue here.

From *Lear's,* August 1992

SHAPING Most published interviews have been more or less extensively edited. The interviewer may have taken a rambling conversation and concentrated on hot current topics and on statements that seem revealing, provocative, or new. (Sometimes the material has been edited to the point where the interviewee says: "I never said that!")

When you write a paper *integrating* the results of an interview, you have a chance to sort out and rearrange the material. You can use revealing comments by your subject to set the scene or to provide biographical background. You can bring out strongly a connecting thread or recurrent theme. How does the writer of the following student paper use revealing details about the person interviewed? What is the connecting strand or the keynote that the writer used to unify the paper?

Picking Up Garbage

Gabriel was born the youngest of thirteen children. He grew up in the old country and has been in the United States for three years. Every morning he goes to his job in the waste land-fill area. When I ask him about his work, he says: "I used to pick up papers in the area. Everybody starts out with that job. Some people are able to save some money that way. Then they go back to the old country, drink and relax for a few months, and then, when they run out of money, come back here. They will always be picking up papers. I don't want to go back. I drive a truck now, and I crush the garbage. I save money."

I ask him about the place where he lives. He is not living with family. "It is a small place with fifteen people living there. I feel bad because we all sleep together in two rooms. I am the first one to go to work in the morning. So when my alarm goes off at 5:30 A.M., everybody is disturbed. I feel bad that everybody wakes up because of the noise from my alarm. But what can I do? I have to work."

Gabriel spends little time at the place where he "lives." He usually works more than five days and goes to school four evenings a week. What does he like least about his job? He says that he does a lot of thinking while he drives the truck. "You know that the American people throw out many things. Much of it is good stuff. I see toys that are brand new. I see radios that are not broken. I see many things that I would like to send to people in my own country. But I cannot pick up any of the things. There is a rule. The driver is not allowed to get out of the truck."

I assume that the company is trying to protect the drivers' health by not letting them handle items from the garbage cans. But Gabriel says that the rule is intended for the driver's safety: Once a driver who climbed out of the truck to pick up something was run over by another driver who did not see him.

"A few times," Gabriel says, "I have taken the chance of losing my job. I got out and picked up a tape recorder once. I brought it home, and it worked perfectly. The Americans throw away so many things like that. It's like throwing away money. Americans are very rich. The people in my country are very poor. Every day I see good things thrown away, and it breaks my heart to crush them. I am destroying what my people could use."

I am looking at the job of the garbage collector from a different perspective since I talked to Gabriel. I used to think that the filth and the smell would bother me most about the job. I found that what bothers Gabriel most is the idea of looking at "waste" all day.

REVISING AND EDITING An interview paper presents some special problems of format and mechanics. In editing your paper, check whether you have made it clear who says what. You will often vary **direct quotation**—material quoted verbatim, word for word—and **paraphrase**, which puts someone else's ideas into your own words. Put all material quoted verbatim—word for word—in quotation marks. (Remember to close the quotation marks at the point where direct quotation, or verbatim quotation, ends.)

STANDARD QUOTE: Dr. So-and-So, Professor of What-Is-It at Where-Is-It College, said about such-and-such a topic, "There is something to be said on both sides."

At times you will use a **block quotation** (or chunk quotation) to present a substantial portion of material (four lines or more). Indent a block quotation ten spaces, with no additional indent for an initial paragraph break. (Don't use quotation marks — extra indenting signals direct quotation.) For instance, you might quote Professor So-and-So as saying,

> In the language of today's spin doctors and practitioners of doublespeak, the bottom line is that the window of opportunity that enabled us to push the envelope has developed a downside that will negatively impact the parameters of future growth.

In an effective paper, such block quotations are often used sparingly — at strategic places. For the smooth flow of a paper, make sure that much of your quoted material takes the form of **partial quotation** worked organically into your own text. In revising a paper, look for passages that might need rewriting to integrate quotations better into your own sentences.

PARTIAL QUOTATION: "Equestrian sports are ideally suited to become a leading women's sport," Coach Hiernan claims. Women have an "intuitive understanding" with the animals they train, and they have the patience often lacking in male riders, who "tend to force the issue."

Topics for Interview Papers (A Sampling)

1. What is it like to be a refugee? an illegal alien? a recent immigrant?
2. What is it like to be a foreign student on your campus?
3. What is it like to grow up in an orthodox Jewish family? in the Mormon church? in a devout Catholic family? in an atheist family?
4. What is it like to be of African American, Asian American, Latino, or other non-Anglo descent in a predominantly Anglo society?
5. What is it like to be a single parent?
6. What is the self-image of police officers today?
7. How do women athletes feel about the role of women's sports at your school?
8. What is it like to live at the minimum-wage level of income? What is it like to live on welfare? What is it like to be unemployed?
9. What is it like to marry someone from a different cultural, ethnic, or racial background?
10. What is it like to live as an American in a foreign country?

4

Contested History: Rediscovering America

Come, my tan-faced children,
Follow well in order, get your weapons ready;
Have you your pistols? have you your sharp-edged axes?
Pioneers! O Pioneers!

Walt Whitman

Nations look in the mirror of their history to understand who they are. They look for inspiration for what lies ahead. However, what they see in the mirror of history is shaped by the agendas, loyalties, and perceptions of those who do the writing. American history at one time was the story of explorers discovering new continents. It told the story of pioneers settling the great empty spaces. It told of great white men with Anglo-Saxon names like Lincoln and Grant and Lee making the speeches and riding great horses to glorious victories or defeats. American history was the story of a new nation civilizing the wilderness, throwing off the chains of the feudal European past.

Much of that history is now being rewritten. It is rewritten to take into account the point of view of the conquered, the dispossessed, the enslaved. The tide of white invaders that swept over the Americas did not fill an empty space—"virgin land." In the Caribbean islands, the native population, doomed to extinction by the arrival of Columbus and the Spaniards, is variously estimated to have numbered as much as ten million people. Millions of people were brought to the land of the free in chains to work as slaves. California and the Southwest were Mexican before they were annexed to the United States. The great American cities have large numbers of blacks and Hispanics, as well as large populations of white ethnics who are not white Anglo-Saxon Protestants. (Chicago is one of the largest Polish and Boston is one of the largest Italian cities in the world.)

How much of what is in traditional history books is fact? How much is legend or myth? What new countermyths are taking hold? How much of a revised, or "revisionist," history are Americans ready to accept?

189

in museums and educational institutions than there are live ones today. Most of us are in economic survival mode on a daily basis, and many of us are bobbing about in the middle of the mainstream just treading water. This leaves precious few against great odds to do our part to change the world.

It is necessary and well past time for others to amplify our voices and find their own to tell their neighbors and institutions that 500 years of this history is more than enough and must come to an end.

This year, Native people will memorialize those who did not survive the invasion of 1492. It is fitting for others to join us at this time to begin an era of respect and rediscovery, to find a new world beyond 1992.

The Responsive Reader

1. How does Harjo employ the rhetoric of protest, the language of dissent? How are the terms she uses to describe this nation's early history different from what you remember from your schooling or early reading? What grievances does she stress? What are major points in her indictment?
2. For you, is there any part of the article that is particularly telling or thought-provoking? Is there any part that you think is particularly unfair?
3. Which of Harjo's charges and arguments are familiar, and which are new to you?

Talking, Listening, Writing

4. What has been your experience with the current rewriting of American history? Have you encountered examples of history revised to reflect the point of view of the exploited, the dispossessed? Explore the contrast between what you might have been taught earlier and the changes now seen in many courses and textbooks.

Projects

5. The current rethinking of the nation's early history has produced reevaluations of figures like Christopher Columbus, Thomas Jefferson, and Father Junipero Serra. For use in a future research project, you may want to look for a recent book or article on one of these or a similar figure. How do current attitudes compare with earlier, more worshipful ones? (Your class may want to organize a panel discussion to pool findings on one or several of these figures.)

WERE THE SPANIARDS *THAT* CRUEL?

Gregory Cerio

> *In the following article, a contributor to a special issue of* Newsweek
> *comes to the defense of his Spanish ancestors, trying to clear them of charges
> of genocide in the conquered lands of the Americas. He tries to show that*
> *history is more complex than acknowledged by those who look for clear-cut
> confrontations of good and evil. The story of colonization is more involved
> than current attacks on the European invaders lead us to believe: The Spanish
> conquistadors conquered in alliance with native tribes rebelling against their
> Aztec or Inca overlords. The European invaders of the Americas were not
> united in a common quest; Catholic Spaniards were locked in a murderous
> struggle with the Protestant English. In Spain the treatment of the natives
> was a matter of disagreement and debate. (Queen Isabella of Spain liberated
> and sent back to the West Indies a group of Taino natives that Spaniards had
> brought back to Spain with them as their property.)*

Thought Starters: How convincing or effective is Cerio's effort to ex-
onerate his forebears? What is his line of defense?

For the Spanish, the Columbus Quincentennial stirs an ambivalent 1
nostalgia, blending pride and pain. Spain's shining memories of its Golden
Age, when the nation stood at the summit of world power, have been
tarnished by critics who call the 1492 arrival of the Spanish in the New
World "an invasion" fueled by greed and leading to "genocide." In their
words, Spaniards hear echoes of age-old malevolence: a body of anti-
Spanish prejudices they know as *la leyenda negra,* the Black Legend, that
tarred the Spanish as incomparably savage and avaricious. It created a
national image that Spain is still trying to dispel.

The Black Legend was born in the 16th century, when Spain controlled the greatest empire the West had ever known, stretching from
Holland to Austria to Italy, and westward across the Atlantic to the Americas. The Spanish were prosperous, powerful and smug. And almost
everyone else in Europe hated them.

Fearful and envious of Spain but poorer and militarily inferior, rival
European nations resorted to a paper war, the first modern propaganda
campaign. Throughout the century and beyond it, pamphleteers from
London to Frankfurt made malice toward the Spanish a byword of patriotism. Their tracts depicted the Spanish as a people inherently barbaric,
corrupt and intolerant; lovers of cruelty and bloodshed. "Tyranny," one
1597 French screed began, "is as proper and natural to a Spaniard as

laughter is to a man." Others warned that if Europeans had been outraged by the Inquisition, or by Spain's expulsion of the Jews in 1492 (two centuries, it should be noted, after they were expelled from England), these were kindnesses compared to what Spain did in the Americas. William of Orange, the Dutch nobleman who led the Protestants of Holland in revolt against Spanish authority, railed in 1580 that Spain "committed such horrible excesses that all the barbarities, cruelties and tyrannies ever perpetrated before are only games in comparison to what happened to the poor Indians."

Were the Spanish that bad? Well, there's no reason to print up I LOVE THE CONQUEST bumper stickers. As with most legends, la leyenda negra has some basis in fact. Like many invaders, the Spanish committed horrifying atrocities. But savagery was not the norm for the Spanish, or even commonplace. To understand their conduct in the Americas, one must look at the world as the Spanish did in the 15th century. By their standards, they acted with moderation. When the English and French arrived in the Americas, they systematically drove the natives from their land. The Spanish accepted the Indians into their society — however rudely — and sought to provide a philosophical and moral foundation for their actions in the New World.

If that isn't the history presented in many American schoolbooks, novels and films, it is perhaps because the attitudes of most North Americans are a cultural legacy from the same people — English, German, Dutch, French — who fought Spain for 300 years. Varnished and repeated through those centuries, the Black Legend continues to distort our vision of the past, as well as the present, in repugnant stereotypes of Hispanics in both hemispheres, from the vicious *cholo* to the "lazy wetback." 5

Politics and religion, those two tinderbox subjects, gave the Black Legend its momentum and its staying power. Rivals like France — where even today Spain is sometimes dismissed with the jeer "Africa begins at the Pyrenees" — resented Spanish domination and coveted its empire. Religion added a more visceral animus. Charles V began his reign as King of Spain in 1517, the same year that Martin Luther launched the Protestant Reformation. He was also Holy Roman Emperor, the anointed protector of Christianity, and saw it as his duty to purge the heresy from the Continent. Leading the bloody Counter-Reformation, Spain fought in Germany in the 1540s, began an 80-year war with Holland in 1568 and sent the disastrous Armada against England in 1588. Protestants saw Spain as the agent of the Devil; its extermination was an article of faith. Opening Parliament in 1656, Oliver Cromwell called Spain the "enemy abroad, who is head of the Papal interest, the head of that anti-Christian interest, that is so described in Scripture . . . and upon this account you have a quarrel with the Spaniard. And truly he hath an interest in your bowels."

Ironically, it was Spain's sense of religious mission, and the broad freedom of speech it permitted in its colonies, that helped foster the Black

Legend. From Ferdinand onward, Spanish monarchs encouraged candid reports, favorable or unfavorable, on conditions in the Americas. One of the most tireless critics of Spanish rule was a Dominican bishop, Bartolomé de Las Casas, who worked for 50 years to improve the treatment of the Indians. A skilled politician, in 1552 he published a passionate tract called "A Brief Account of the Destruction of the Indies." In graphic and sometimes exaggerated detail, he recounted Spanish cruelties to the Indians, describing, in one instance, how Spaniards hanged natives in groups of 13, "thus honoring our Redeemer and the twelve apostles," then lit fires beneath them.

Spain's enemies ate it up. In the next 100 years, 42 editions of Las Casas's "Brief Account" appeared in Germany, France, Holland and England, some illustrated with lurid engravings by the Dutch artist Theodore DeBry, who had never crossed the Atlantic. One English edition was subtitled "A Faithful Narrative of the Horrid and Unexampled Massacres, Butcheries, and all Manner of Cruelties that Hell and Malice could invent, committed by the Popish Spanish." A U.S. edition of Las Casas was even published in 1898, to bolster support for the Spanish-American War.

Yet, as historian William Maltby points out, "the most powerful indictment of Spain's cruelty and avarice is at the same time a monument to its humanitarianism and sense of justice." Las Casas, other Spanish clergy and their sympathizers were not lonely do-gooders. They embodied a Spanish moral impulse that led the royal court to conduct a soul-searching ethical inquiry into the Spanish Conquest throughout the 16th century. "Spain was constantly debating with itself: 'Am I right, am I wrong? What is it I'm doing with these peoples?'" notes Mexican writer Carlos Fuentes in his television documentary "The Buried Mirror: Reflections on Spain and the New World."

From the beginning of their conquest, the Spanish recognized the need to mediate between the conflicting demands of Christianity and profit. Bernal Díaz, a soldier in the army of Cortés who later wrote a history of the conquest of Mexico, explained the motives of the conquistadors: "We came here to serve God, and also to get rich." It is easy to view the former as a rationale for the latter. But the 16th-century Spanish lived in an age of devotion, when every aspect of life was examined through the lens of religious faith. Spaniards believed they offered the Indians a gift worth any earthly pain: eternal life in heaven.

God had ordained a social hierarchy, most Renaissance Spaniards thought. They accepted Aristotle's concept of "natural slavery"—that large masses of humanity are simply born to serve. The papacy sanctioned slavery and was a large slaveholder. But where the Indians fit in the ranks of mankind baffled the Spanish.

Early on, Isabella of Castile established the policy that Indians who accepted Christianity were free crown subjects. (Those who didn't could be sold into slavery.) But like other subjects, they were expected to pay royal tribute, which could be extracted in the form of labor. With so few colonists, Indian labor was a necessity, but one which, Isabella's counselors reasoned, could teach the natives useful habits of industry. The Spanish devised the *encomienda,* a labor system intended as a sort of trusteeship. A deserving Spaniard was given Indians to use for mining gold or silver or growing cash crops. In return, he would feed the Indians, provide for their instruction in the faith and defend them.

That was the theory. In practice the encomienda varied with the agenda of each Spaniard. Most conquistadors were ex-soldiers, merchants, craftsmen, ex-convicts — "nobodies who wanted to become somebodies," as historian L. B. Simpson put it. Those who wanted to get rich quick and return to Spain drove the Indians hard. Others saw the New World as a permanent home and the Indians as future clients who should be treated well. The encomienda was always, if sometimes only marginally, better than outright slavery. "The people remained in a community even if they were exploited," explains Yale historian David Brion Davis. "They had a certain cultural integrity; their family structure and customs weren't, for the most part, interfered with."

Out of Christian duty, and to keep a close rein on its New World colonies, the Spanish throne consistently ordained that the natives be treated with humane respect. In 1512, Ferdinand's Laws of Burgos provided, among other things, that "no Indian shall be whipped or beaten or called 'dog' or any other name, unless it is his proper name." These and later laws were often ignored or watered down, but under them many Spaniards were punished for mistreating Indians.

Spanish monarchs were also willing to experiment with new systems   15
of government and labor. Las Casas was given a chance to convert an area of Guatemala without the interference of soldiers and met with mixed success. There were four separate, failed experiments on Caribbean islands to see if, given the tools, Indians could live alone like civilized people — that is, like Spaniards. In 1530, Vasco de Quiroga, a Mexican bishop, established a cooperative society in Michoacán, with communal property and what we would call social-welfare benefits.

If these experiments treated the natives as naive children, that is perhaps no more offensive than today's tendency to believe the Indians were helpless before the Spanish. In fact, they were quite resourceful, argues historian Steve Stern: "Indigenous peoples shaped everyday life and social structures much more than our stereotyped imagery would have it." Cortés could not have conquered Mexico without the aid of tribes dominated by the Aztecs. For their help, these natives happily accepted titles, coats of arms and encomiendas from the Spanish crown. The encomienda itself was molded by tributary labor practices long established among the Indians. In many regions, Indians dictated to Spaniards the form and amount of payment to be given. A group of Peruvian Indian chiefs hired a lawyer and sailed to Spain in the 1560s to make a case before

Philip II for curtailing the encomienda. In the best political tradition, they even offered him a bribe. "Indians entered into the Spanish legal system to use it for their own purposes," says Stern. "And to some effect."

Always a legalistic people, the Spanish created General Indian Courts where the natives aired their grievances. As historian Philip Wayne Powell wrote, "Spaniards did not try to impose upon America something hypocritically foreign or inferior to what they lived with at home." Spain's rulers taxed the New World colonists less heavily than their European subjects. In America, the Spanish built schools — 23 universities in the New World — that graduated white, mestizo and Indian alike, along with some blacks. They established hospitals to provide the Indians with medical care, such as it was in the era of barber-surgeons and leeches.

If only for economic reasons, the Spanish cared deeply for the welfare of the natives. "Genocide," in fact, may be the unfairest of all the accusations leveled at Spain — if the term is used in its proper sense, to describe the intentional, systematic eradication of a race. Millions of Indians died after the arrival of the Spanish. But a host of pestilences brought from Europe wiped out the vast majority, not war or abuse. The whole of Spain's treatment of the Indians seems almost beneficent compared with the way other colonial powers dealt with natives. "The Spanish made a place for the Indians — as part of the lowest order, but at least they had a place," says Woodrow Borah of the University of California, Berkeley. "North Americans in many cases simply exterminated the Indians." The Spanish mingled with the Indians, at times with the encouragement of the crown. "The Spanish were conquered in turn by those they conquered," says Mexican poet Homero Aridjis. The marriage of blood and cultures created *la raza* — the new mestizo people who compose most of today's Latin Americans. North America, where the natives were excluded, driven off their land and eventually hunted down, remained white. The United States elected several presidents — Andrew Jackson, William Henry Harrison, Zachary Taylor — who first made a name for themselves as Indian fighters. It is a piece of our heritage that may help explain the potency of U.S. racism.

Today, Spain has invested $20 billion worldwide in Columbus Quincentennial projects, still hoping to escape the distortions of the Black Legend. But if the 16th-century Spanish can be granted motives beyond profit, they appear no worse — and often far better — than the nations who castigated them for their sins. Spain committed terrible deeds while bringing "the light of Christianity" to the New World. But history offers no shortage of acts of cruelty performed in the service of religious, social, political and economic ideals. Susan Milbrath, a Florida museum curator whose recent Quincentennial exhibit was greeted with pickets, asks why people concentrate on the morality of Columbus and the Spanish: "The big question to me is, are *human beings* good?" The Black Legend casts a shadow on us all.

The Responsive Reader

1. How real do the ancient religious quarrels between Catholic Spain and Protestant European countries become in this account? What are key historical facts? What are interesting sidelights?
2. How convincing is Cerio's defense or rehabilitation of Spain's role in the New World? What, according to him, were the contemporary justifications or rationalizations for Spain's behavior in the new territories? What is the evidence he presents for soul-searching and humane objectives on the part of the Spaniards?
3. How much of a case does Cerio build for his claim that other colonial powers treated Native Americans worse than the Spaniards did?

Talking, Listening, Writing

4. Does the Cerio article change your mind? In what ways does it make you revise your own thinking?
5. Do you think there is a possible middle ground between the anti-Columbus and the pro-Columbus factions?
6. What have been your opportunities to study and understand the "marriage of blood and cultures" that Cerio calls *la raza*?

Projects

7. Writers including Octavio Paz, Pablo Neruda, Carlos Fuentes, and Richard Rodriguez have written about the joint Spanish and Indian heritage of Latin America. You may want to look for commentary on the mestizo heritage in the writings of one such writer and report your findings to your classmates.

Thinking about Connections

For you, does Cerio provide a satisfactory answer to the charges brought by Harjo in "I Won't Be Celebrating Columbus Day" (p. 190)? How strong or convincing is his defense?

THE EARTH IS ALL THAT LASTS

Black Elk

> *The following selection tells the story of General Custer's Last Stand from the point of view of a young Lakota fighting on the other side. Custer had served on the Union side in the American Civil War and assumed command of the U.S. Seventh Cavalry in 1866. A few years later, he destroyed an Indian camp after the people there had been promised safety by a military agent. He had a son by a girl who was taken captive there, along with other Cheyenne women and children. Black Elk, who is speaking in this selection, was a teenage boy when Custer, or "Long Hair," with his soldiers (the Wasichus of the story) attacked a large Sioux encampment on the Little Big Horn in 1876. In the ensuing fight, Custer and many of his soldiers lost their lives. Black Elk, a Lakota holy man, told his story many years later when living as a lonely old man in a one-room log cabin among barren hills. John G. Neihardt, who recorded Black Elk's story, was the author of books and poems about Native Americans and the American West.*

Thought Starters: What shaped your ideas about the role of the U.S. military in the conquest of the West? Have you recently seen movies or read books that made you reexamine your ideas about Native Americans and the U.S. Cavalry?

It was the next summer, when I was eleven years old (1874), that the first sign of a new trouble came to us. Our band had been camping on Split-Toe Creek in the Black Hills; and from there we moved to Spring Creek, then to Rapid Creek where it comes out into the prairie. That evening just before sunset, a big thundercloud came up from the west, and just before the wind struck, there were clouds of splittail swallows flying all around above us. . . . The boys tried to hit the swallows with stones and it hurt me to see them doing this, but I could not tell them. I got a stone and acted as though I were going to throw, but I did not. The swallows seemed holy. Nobody hit one, and when I thought about this I knew that of course they could not.

The next day some of the people were building a sweat tepee for a medicine man by the name of Chips, who was going to perform a ceremony and had to be purified first. They say he was the first man who made a sacred ornament for our great chief, Crazy Horse. While they were heating the stones for the sweat tepee, some boys asked me to go with them to shoot squirrels. We went out, and when I was about to shoot at one, I felt very uneasy all at once. So I sat down, feeling queer, and wondered about it. While I sat there I heard a voice that said: "Go at once! Go home!" I told the boys we must go home at once, and we all hurried. When we got back, everybody was excited, breaking camp, catching the ponies, and loading the drags; and I heard that while Chips was in the sweat tepee a voice had told him that the band must flee at once because something was going to happen there.

It was nearly sundown when we started, and we fled all that night on the back trail toward Spring Creek, then down that creek to the south fork of the Good River. I rode most of the night in a pony drag because I got too sleepy to stay on a horse. We camped at Good River in the morning, but we stayed only long enough to eat. Then we fled again, upstream, all day long until we reached the mouth of Horse Creek. We were going to stay there, but scouts came to us and said that many soldiers had come into the Black Hills; and that was what Chips saw while he was in the sweat tepee. So we hurried on in the night towards Smoky Earth River (the White), and when we got there, I woke up and it was daybreak. We camped a while to eat, and then went up the Smoky Earth, two camps, to Robinson, for we were afraid of the soldiers up there.

Afterward I learned that it was Pahuska (Long Hair, General Custer) who had led his soldiers into the Black Hills that summer to see what he could find. He had no right to go in there, because all that country was ours. Also the Wasichus had made a treaty with Red Cloud (1868) that said it would be ours as long as grass should grow and water flow. Later I learned too that Pahuska had found there much of the yellow metal that makes the Wasichus crazy; and that is what made the bad trouble, just as it did before, when the hundred were rubbed out.

Our people knew there was yellow metal in little chunks up there; *5* but they did not bother with it, because it was not good for anything.

We stayed all winter at the Soldiers' Town,[1] and all the while the bad trouble was coming fast; for in the fall we heard that some Wasichus had come from the Missouri River to dig in the Black Hills for the yellow metal, because Pahuska had told about it with a voice that went everywhere. Later he got rubbed out for doing that.

The people talked about this all winter. Crazy Horse was in the Powder River country and Sitting Bull was somewhere north of the Hills. Our people at the Soldiers' Town thought we ought to get together and do something. Red Cloud's people said that the soldiers had gone in there to keep the diggers out, but we, who were only visiting, did not believe it. We called Red Cloud's people "Hangs-Around-the-Fort," and our people said they were standing up for the Wasichus, and if we did not do something we should lose the Black Hills.

---

[1] [Soldiers' Town: Fort Robinson, in western South Dakota.]

In the spring when I was twelve years old (1875), more soldiers with many wagons came up from the Soldiers' Town at the mouth of the Laramie River and went into the Hills.

There was much talk all summer, and in the Moon of Making Fat (June) there was a sun dance there at the Soldiers' Town to give the people strength, but not many took part; maybe because everybody was so excited talking about the Black Hills. I remember two men who danced together. One had lost a leg in the Battle of the Hundred Slain and one had lost an eye in the Attacking of the Wagons, so they had only three eyes and three legs between them to dance with. We boys went down to the creek while they were sun dancing and got some elm leaves that we chewed up and threw on the dancers while they were all dressed up and trying to look their best. We even did this to some of the older people, and nobody got angry, because everybody was supposed to be in a good humor and to show their endurance in every kind of way; so they had to stand teasing too.

In the Moon When the Calves Grow Hair (September) there was a   *10* big council with the Wasichus on the Smoky Earth River at the mouth of White Clay Creek. I can remember the council, but I did not understand much of it then. Many of the Lakotas were there, also Shyelas and Blue Clouds (Cheyennes and Arapahoes); but Crazy Horse and Sitting Bull stayed away. In the middle of the circle there was a shade made of canvas. Under this the councilors sat and talked, and all around them there was a crowd of people on foot and horseback. They talked and talked for days, but it was just like wind blowing in the end. I asked my father what they were talking about in there, and he told me that the Grandfather at Washington wanted to lease the Black Hills so that the Wasichus could dig yellow metal, and that the chief of the soldiers had said if we did not do this, the Black Hills would be just like melting snow held in our hands, because the Wasichus would take that country anyway.

It made me sad to hear this. It was such a good place to play and the people were always happy in that country. . . .

After the council we heard that creeks of Wasichus were flowing into the Hills and becoming rivers, and that they were already making towns up there. It looked like bad trouble coming, so our band broke camp and started out to join Crazy Horse on Powder River. We camped on Horsehead Creek, then on the War Bonnet after we crossed the old Wasichu's road[2] that made the trouble that time when the hundred were rubbed out. Grass was growing on it. Then we camped at Sage Creek, then on the Beaver, then on Driftwood Creek, and came again to the Plain of Pine Trees at the edge of the Hills.

---

[2][Wasichu's road: the Bozeman Trail, which began in Colorado and went to the mining town of Virginia City, in Montana.]

six-shooter like the soldiers had, and told me I was a man now. I was thirteen years old and not very big for my age, but I thought I should have to be a man anyway. We boys had practiced endurance, and we were all good riders, and I could shoot straight with either a bow or a gun.

We were a small band, and we started in the night and traveled fast. Before we got to War Bonnet Creek, some Shyelas joined us, because their hearts were bad like ours and they were going to the same place. Later I learned that many small bands were doing the same thing and coming together from everywhere.

Just after we camped on the War Bonnet, our scouts saw a wagon train of the Wasichus coming up the old road that caused the trouble before.[3] They had oxen hitched to their wagons and they were part of the river of Wasichus that was running into the Black Hills. They shot at our scouts, and we decided we would attack them. When the war party was getting ready, I made up my mind that, small as I was, I might as well die there, and if I did, maybe I'd be known. I told Jumping Horse, a boy about my age, that I was going along to die, and he said he would too. So we went, and so did Crab and some other boys.

When the Wasichus saw us coming, they put their wagons in a circle and got inside with their oxen. We rode around and around them in a wide circle that kept getting narrower. That is the best way to fight, because it is hard to hit ponies running fast in a circle. And sometimes there would be two circles, one inside the other, going fast in opposite directions, which made us still harder to hit. The cavalry of the Wasichus did not know how to fight. They kept together, and when they came on, you could hardly miss them. We kept apart in the circle. While we were riding around the wagons, we were hanging low on the outside of the ponies and shooting under their necks. This was not easy to do, even when your legs were long, and mine were not yet very long. But I stuck tight and shot with the six-shooter my aunt gave me. Before we started the attack I was afraid, but Big Man told us we were brave boys, and I soon got over being frightened. The Wasichus shot fast at us from behind the wagons, and I could hear bullets whizzing, but they did not hit any of us. I do not know whether we killed any Wasichus or not. We rode around several times, and once we got close, but there were not many of us and we could not get at the Wasichus behind their wagons; so we went away. This was my first fight. When we were going back to camp, some Shyela warriors told us we were very brave boys, and that we were going to have plenty of fighting.

We were traveling very fast now, for we were in danger and wanted to get back to Crazy Horse. He had moved over west to the Rosebud River, and the people were gathering there. As we traveled, we met other

[3][the old road: the Bozeman Trail. The Indians opposed the use of it by gold seekers.]

little bands all going to the same place, until there were a good many of us all mixed up before we got there. Red Cloud's son was with us, but Red Cloud stayed at the Soldiers' Town.

When we came to the ridge on this side of the Rosebud River, we could see the valley full of tepees, and the ponies could not be counted. Many, many people were there—Oglalas, Hunkpapas, Minneconjous, Sans Arcs, Blackfeet, Brules, Santees, and Yanktonais; also many Shyelas and Blue Clouds had come to fight with us. The village was long, and you could not see all the camps with one look. The scouts came out to meet us and bring us in, and everybody rejoiced that we had come. Great men were there: Crazy Horse and Big Road of the Oglalas; Sitting Bull and Gall and Black Moon and Crow King of the Hunkpapas; Spotted Eagle of the Sans Arcs; the younger Hump and Fast Bull of the Minneconjous; Dull Knife and Ice Bear of the Shyelas; Inkpaduta with the Santees and Yanktonais. Great men were there with all those people and horses. Hetchetu aloh! [It is so indeed!]

About the middle of the Moon of Making Fat (June) the whole village moved a little way up the River to a good place for a sun dance. The valley was wide and flat there, and we camped in a great oval with the river flowing through it, and in the center they built the bower of branches in a circle for the dancers, with the opening of it to the east whence comes the light. Scouts were sent out in all directions to guard the sacred place. Sitting Bull, who was the greatest medicine man of the nation at that time, had charge of this dance to purify the people and to give them power and endurance. It was held in the Moon of Fatness because that is the time when the sun is highest and the growing power of the world is strongest. I will tell you how it was done.

First a holy man was sent out all alone to find the *waga chun,* the holy tree that should stand in the middle of the dancing circle. Nobody dared follow to see what he did or hear the sacred words he would say there. And when he had found the right tree, he would tell the people, and they would come there singing, with flowers all over them. Then when they had gathered about the holy tree, some women who were bearing children would dance around it, because the Spirit of the Sun loves all fruitfulness. After that a warrior, who had done some very brave deed that summer, struck the tree, counting coup upon it; and when he had done this, he had to give gifts to those who had least of everything, and the braver he was, the more he gave away.

After this, a band of young maidens came singing, with sharp axes in their hands; and they had to be so good that nobody there could say anything against them, or that any man had ever known them; and it was the duty of anyone who knew anything bad about any of them to tell it right before all the people there and prove it. But if anybody lied, it was very bad for him.

The maidens chopped the tree down and trimmed its branches off. Then chiefs, who were the sons of chiefs, carried the sacred tree home, stopping four times on the way, once for each season, giving thanks for each.

Now when the holy tree had been brought home but was not yet set up in the center of the dancing place, mounted warriors gathered around the circle of the village, and at a signal they all charged inward upon the center where the tree would stand, each trying to be the first to touch the sacred place; and whoever was the first could not be killed in war that year. When they all came together in the middle, it was like a battle, with the ponies rearing and screaming in a big cloud of dust and the men shouting and wrestling and trying to throw each other off the horses.

After that there was a big feast and plenty for everybody to eat, and a big dance just as though we had won a victory.

The next day the tree was planted in the center by holy men who sang sacred songs and made sacred vows to the Spirit. And the next morning nursing mothers brought their holy little ones to lay them at the bottom of the tree, so that the sons would be brave men and the daughters the mothers of brave men. The holy men pierced the ears of the little ones, and for each piercing the parents gave away a pony to someone who was in need.

The next day the dancing began, and those who were going to take part were ready, for they had been fasting and purifying themselves in the sweat lodges, and praying. First, their bodies were painted by the holy men. Then each would lie down beneath the tree as though he were dead, and the holy men would cut a place in his back or chest, so that a strip of rawhide, fastened to the top of the tree, could be pushed through the flesh and tied. Then the man would get up and dance to the drums, leaning on the rawhide strip as long as he could stand the pain or until the flesh tore loose.

We smaller boys had a good time during the two days of dancing, for we were allowed to do almost anything to tease the people, and they had to stand it. We would gather sharp spear grass, and when a man came along without a shirt, we would stick him to see if we could make him cry out, for everybody was supposed to endure everything. Also we made popguns out of young ash boughs and shot at the men and women to see if we could make them jump; and if they did, everybody laughed at them. The mothers carried water to their holy little ones in bladder bags, and we made little bows and arrows that we could hide under our robes so that we could steal up to the women and shoot holes in the bags. They were supposed to stand anything and not scold us when the water spurted out. We had a good time there.

Right after the sun dance was over, some of our scouts came in from the south, and the crier went around the circle and said: "The scouts have returned and they have reported that soldiers are camping up the river. So, young warriors, take courage and get ready to meet them."

While they were all getting ready, I was getting ready too, because Crazy Horse was going to lead the warriors and I wanted to go with him; but my uncle, who thought a great deal of me, said: "Young nephew, you must not go. Look at the helpless ones. Stay home, and maybe there will be plenty of fighting right here." So the war parties went on without me. Maybe my uncle thought I was too little to do much and might get killed.

Then the crier told us to break camp, and we moved over west   *40* towards the Greasy Grass (Little Big Horn) and camped at the head of Spring Creek while the war parties were gone. We learned later that it was Three Stars (General Crook) who fought with our people on the Rosebud that time. He had many walking soldiers and some cavalry, and there were many Crows and Shoshones with him. They were all coming to attack us where we had the sun dance, but Crazy Horse whipped them and they went back to Goose Creek where they had all their wagons.

Crazy Horse whipped Three Stars on the Rosebud that day, and I think he could have rubbed the soldiers out there. He could have called many more warriors from the villages and he could have rubbed the soldiers out at daybreak, for they camped there in the dark after the fight.

He whipped the cavalry of Three Stars when they attacked his village on the Powder that cold morning in the Moon of the Snowblind (March). Then he moved farther west to the Rosebud; and when the soldiers came to kill us there, he whipped them and made them go back. Then he moved farther west to the valley of the Greasy Grass. We were in our own country all the time and we only wanted to be let alone. The soldiers came there to kill us, and many got rubbed out. It was our country and we did not want to have any trouble.

We camped there in the valley along the south side of the Greasy Grass before the sun was straight above; and this was, I think, two days before the battle. It was a very big village and you could hardly count the tepees. Farthest up the stream toward the south were the Hunkpapas, and the Oglalas were next. Then came the Minneconjous, the Sans Arcs, the Blackfeet, the Shyelas; and last, the farthest toward the north, were the Santees and Yanktonais. Along the side towards the east was the Greasy Grass, with some timber along it, and it was running full from the melting of the snow in the Big Horn Mountains. If you stood on a hill you could see the mountains off to the south and west. On the other side of the river, there were bluffs and hills beyond. Some gullies came down through the bluffs. On the westward side of us were lower hills, and there we grazed our ponies and guarded them. There were so many they could not be counted.

There was a man by the name of Rattling Hawk who was shot through the hip in the fight on the Rosebud, and people thought he could not get well. But there was a medicine man by the name of Hairy Chin who cured him.

The day before the battle I had greased myself and was going to   *45*
swim with some boys, when Hairy Chin called me over to Rattling Hawk's tepee, and told me he wanted me to help him. There were five other boys there, and he needed us for the bears in the curing ceremony, because he had his power from a dream of the bear. He painted my body yellow, and my face too, and put a black stripe on either side of my nose from the eyes down. Then he tied my hair up to look like bear's ears, and put some eagle feathers on my head.

Hairy Chin, who wore a real bear skin with the head on it, began to sing a song that went like this:

At the doorway, sacred herbs are rejoicing.

While he sang, two girls came in and stood one on either side of the wounded man; one had a cup of water and one some kind of an herb. They gave the cup and the herb to Rattling Hawk while Hairy Chin was singing. Then they gave him a red cane, and right away he stood up with it. The girls then started out of the tepee, and the wounded man followed, leaning on the sacred red stick; and we boys, who were the little bears, had to jump around him and make growling noises toward the man. When we did this, you could see something like feathers of all colors coming out of our mouths. Then Hairy Chin came out on all fours, and he looked just like a bear to me. Then Rattling Hawk began to walk better. He was not able to fight next day, but he got well in a little while.

After the ceremony, we boys went swimming to wash the paint off, and when we got back many of the people were dancing and having kill talks all over the village, remembering brave deeds done in the fight with Three Stars on the Rosebud.

When it was about sundown we boys had to bring the ponies in close, and when this was done it was dark and the people were still dancing around fires all over the village. We boys went around from one dance to another, until we got too sleepy to stay up any more.

My father woke me at daybreak and told me to go with him to take   *50*
our horses out to graze, and when we were out there he said: "We must have a long rope on one of them, so that it will be easy to catch; then we can get the others. If anything happens, you must bring the horses back as fast as you can, and keep your eyes on the camp."

Several of us boys watched our horses together until the sun was straight above and it was getting very hot. Then we thought we would go swimming, and my cousin said he would stay with our horses till we got back. When I was greasing myself, I did not feel well; I felt queer. It seemed that something terrible was going to happen. But I went with the boys anyway. Many people were in the water now and many of the women were out west of the village digging turnips. We had been in the water quite a while when my cousin came down there with the horses to give them a drink, for it was very hot now.

Just then we heard the crier shouting in the Hunkpapa camp, which was not very far from us: "The Chargers are coming! They are charging! The chargers are coming!" Then the crier of the Oglalas shouted the same words; and we could hear the cry going from camp to camp northward clear to the Santees and the Yanktonais.

Everybody was running now to catch the horses. We were lucky to have ours right there just at that time. My older brother had a sorrel, and he rode away fast toward the Hunkpapas. I had a buckskin. My father came running and said: "Your brother has gone to the Hunkpapas without his gun. Catch him and give it to him. Then come right back to me." He had my six-shooter too—the one my aunt gave me. I took the guns, jumped on my pony and caught my brother. I could see a big dust rising just beyond the Hunkpapa camp and all the Hunkpapas were running around and yelling, and many were running wet from the river. Then out of the dust came the soldiers on their big horses. They looked big and strong and tall and they were all shooting. My brother took his gun and yelled for me to go back. There was a brushy timber just on the other side of the Hunkpapas, and some warriors were gathering there. He made for that place, and I followed him. By now women and children were running in a crowd downstream. I looked back and saw them all running and scattering up a hillside down yonder.

When we got into the timber, a good many Hunkpapas were there already and the soldiers were shooting above us so that leaves were falling from the trees where the bullets struck. By now I could not see what was happening in the village below. It was all dust and cries and thunder; for the women and children were running there, and the warriors were coming on their ponies.

Among us there in the brush and out in the Hunkpapa camp a cry went up: "Take courage! Don't be a coward! The helpless are out of breath!" I think this was when Gall stopped the Hunkpapas, who had been running away, and turned them back.

Then another great cry went up out in the dust: "Crazy Horse is coming! Crazy Horse is coming!" Off toward the west and north they were yelling "Hoka hey!" like a big wind roaring, and making the tremolo; and you could hear eagle bone whistles screaming.

The valley went darker with dust and smoke, and there were only shadows and a big noise of many cries and hoofs and guns. On the left of where I was I could hear the shot hoofs of the soldiers' horses going back into the brush and there was shooting everywhere. Then the hoofs came out of the brush, and I came out and was in among men and horses weaving in and out and going upstream, and everybody was yelling, "Hurry! Hurry!" The soldiers were running upstream and we were all mixed there in the twilight and the great noise. I did not see much; but once I saw a

Lakota charge at a soldier who stayed behind and fought and was a very brave man. The Lakota took the soldier's horse by the bridle, but the soldier killed him with a six-shooter. I was small and could not crowd in to where the soldiers were, so I did not kill anybody. There were so many ahead of me, and it was all dark and mixed up.

Soon the soldiers were all crowded into the river and many Lakotas too; and I was in the water awhile. Men and horses were all mixed up and fighting in the water, and it was like hail falling in the river. Then we were out of the river, and people were stripping dead soldiers and putting the clothes on themselves. There was a soldier on the ground and he was still kicking. A Lakota rode up and said to me, "Boy, get off and scalp him." I got off and started to do it. He had short hair and my knife was not very sharp. He ground his teeth. Then I shot him in the forehead and got his scalp.

Many of our warriors were following the soldiers up a hill on the other side of the river. Everybody else was turning back down stream, and on a hill away down yonder above the Santee camp there was a big dust, and our warriors whirling around in and out of it just like swallows, and many guns were going off.

I thought I would show my mother my scalp, so I rode over toward 60 the hill where there was a crowd of women and children. On the way down there I saw a very pretty young woman among a band of warriors about to go up to the battle on the hill, and she was singing like this:

> Brothers, now your friends have come!
> Be brave! Be brave!
> Would you see me taken captive?

When I rode through the Oglala camp I saw Rattling Hawk sitting up in his tepee with a gun in his hands, and he was all alone there singing a song of regret that went like this:

> Brothers, what are you doing that I can not do?

When I got to the women on the hill they were all singing and making the tremolo to cheer the men fighting across the river in the dust on the hill. My mother gave a big tremolo just for me when she saw my first scalp.

I stayed there awhile with my mother and watched the big dust whirling on the hill across the river, and horses were coming out of it with empty saddles. . . .

By then our scouts had reported that more soldiers were coming upstream; so we all broke camp. Before dark we were ready and we started up the Greasy Grass, heading for Wood Louse Creek in the Big Horn Mountains. We fled all night, following the Greasy Grass. My two younger brothers and I rode in a pony drag, and my mother put some young pups in with us. They were always trying to crawl out and I was always putting them back in, so I didn't sleep much.

By morning we reached a little dry creek and made camp and had a   65
big feast. The meat had spots of fat in it, and I wish I had some of it right
now.

When it was full day, we started again and came to Wood Louse
Creek at the foot of the mountains, and camped there. A badly wounded
man by the name of Three Bears had fits there, and he would keep saying:
"Jeneny, jeneny." I do not know what he meant. He died, and we used to
call that place the camp where Jeneny died.

That evening everybody got excited and began shouting: "The soldiers are coming!" I looked, and there they were, riding abreast right
toward us. But it was some of our own men dressed in the soldiers' clothes.
They were doing this for fun.

The scouts reported that the soldiers had not followed us and that
everything was safe now. All over the camp there were big fires and dances
all night long.

I will sing you some of the songs that our people made up and sang
that night. Some of them went like this:

> Long Hair has never returned,
> So this woman is crying, crying.
> Looking over here, she cries.
> . . . .
> Long Hair, guns I had none.
> You brought me many. I thank you!
> You make me laugh!
> . . . .
> Long Hair, horses I have none,
> You brought me many. I thank you!
> You make me laugh!
> . . . .
> Long Hair, where he lies nobody knows.
> Crying, they seek him.
> He lies over here.
> . . . .
> Let go your holy irons (guns).
> You are not men enough to do any harm.
> Let go your holy irons!

After awhile I got so tired dancing that I went to sleep on the ground   70
right where I was.

My cousin, Black Wasichu, died that night.

The Responsive Reader

1. What do you learn from this account about the lifestyle of Black
   Elk's people? What do you learn about customs, beliefs, legends,
   ceremonies, treatment of women?
2. The Sioux were legendary as a warrior nation. To judge from this
   account, how did they think of war? Were their ideas, ceremonies,
   and customs connected with war similar to or different from ours?

3. What role does Crazy Horse play in this story? What kind of leader is he? What leadership qualities does he have that would be understood or go unrecognized in our society today?

Talking, Listening, Writing

4. *Empathy* is a currently fashionable word for the ability to enter imaginatively into the thoughts and feelings of people from backgrounds different from our own. Can you identify with the world view of the young Lakota whose experience is being remembered in this selection? Why or why not?
5. Throughout history, people have painted their enemies as savage and inhuman (or, to use the word first employed by the ancient Greeks, "barbarian"). In rare instances, cultures have developed traditions allowing them to honor the "noble foe." What is the record of American culture on this score? Do we tend to recognize our enemies as human beings?

Projects

6. How have the movies shaped your view of Native Americans' first encounters and last battles with the whites? How did Westerns stereotype Native Americans? (What image or images of them emerge from more modern treatments like *Dances with Wolves* or the Canadian *Black Robe*?) Your class might want to stage a panel discussion on Native Americans as seen in the mirror of the movies.

DEATH VALLEY EARNS ITS NAME
Irving Stone

Soon, notice was formally circulated among the emigrants that a certain man, whose name I forget, professing to be an experienced traveler, and explorer of the Great Basin, would lead a company to California by a route far south of the one followed by emigrants thus far.

Immigrants are people who come into a place (where they are often not wanted). Emigrants are people who are coming out of a place, often embarking on an uncertain journey. The quote above is from the diary of Sarah Royce, who survived the journey across the mountains and the "Great American Desert" during the great westward trek of 1849. Many perished from accidents, thirst, or exhaustion; many lost their cattle and wagons to escape with their bare lives. Some, like the ill-fated Donner Party, were surprised by winter and trapped by the deep snow blocking the mountain passes. The author telling the story of one party of emigrants in the following selection is Irving Stone, best-selling author of Lust for Life *(a biography of the French painter Vincent van Gogh) and* The Agony and the Ecstasy *(a biography of the Italian Renaissance painter and sculptor Michelangelo).*

Thought Starters: What motivated the pioneers who went west, facing legendary hardships? What went on in their minds?

In October of 1849 there assembled at Provo on Utah Lake, some   1
sixty miles south of Salt Lake, a number of traveling groups, families and young men on horseback, unknown to each other prior to this meeting, which would make up the Death Valley Party. The majority of the party had come south to Provo instead of north around Salt Lake to join the California Trail because they had heard the grisly details of the Donner Party. Judging that it was too late to risk the winter snows of the Sierra Nevada, they decided to take the longer but safer route into southern California, then north to the mines. Word had been spread that there would be a rendezvous at Provo for all wishing to travel the Old Spanish Trail.

In the party when it started for Los Angeles on October 9 there were eighty wagons, two hundred fifty people, and one thousand head of horses and cattle. For their guide they hired Captain Jefferson Hunt, a member of the Mormon Battalion who was being sent to California to buy cattle and seed for the community in Salt Lake. Hunt imposed Mormon military discipline on the train: it moved like an army, divided into seven divisions, each under its captain. The train named itself the Sand Walking Company.

No crueler nor more accurate title could be divined.

Captain Hunt made an early error: he took a wrong turning. Though he was soon back on the main trail this undermined confidence in him, and when a Captain Smith with a party of nine Mormons heading for the California mines rode up with a map or waybill which claimed that there was a cutoff, what James Reed of the Donner Party had called "a nigher way," over Walker's Pass from which they could descend into the Tulare Valley close to the mines, and save themselves four hundred wearisome miles, the Sand Walking Company went into a Committee of the Whole around a campfire to debate the desirability of taking Smith's cutoff. When Captain Hunt was asked his opinion, he said he doubted if any white man had ever traveled it; that young men alone might make it but families with wagons would have serious trouble:

"If you all wish to go and follow Smith I will go also. But if even one 5 wagon decides to go the original route, I shall feel bound by my promise to go with that lone wagon."

The Reverend John W. Brier, described in the journal of one of the listeners as a "man who always liked to give his opinion on every subject," declared forcibly for the cutoff, despite the fact he was traveling with a wife and three young sons. So did a number of others.

The next morning, as the wagons and men came to the fork in the road, Smith and the Reverend Mr. Brier prevailed, even as Lansford Hastings and James Reed had helped make the decision for the Donners over the advice of experienced mountain men. Only seven wagons continued on the known trail with Captain Hunt. A hundred wagons seceded, including the Briers, Bennetts, and Arcanes, the Wade and Dale families, all of whom had children, and the entire Jayhawker[1] party of single men.

For two days Smith's party crossed green valleys with plenty of water. But that was as far as the anonymous mapmaker had traveled. Caught in an impassable canyon, with evidence of worse terrain ahead, seventy-two wagons turned back to the Old Spanish Trail. Though they never caught up with Hunt, they followed him into southern California, and arrived in Los Angeles before the seceders had even reached the heart of their inferno.

Smith had also thought better of his decision; he cut back with his mounted Mormons to the Old Spanish Trail and safety without informing the remaining eighty-five emigrants that he had changed his mind. Meeting about their campfire at Misery Mountain, guideless, they too seemed to have little choice but to turn back, when scouts rode into the camp with the message that they had seen a good pass which would carry them into California.

They decided to plunge ahead, but not as a unified train with a leader; 10 instead they split into three separate groups. The Jayhawkers, young,

[1] [Jayhawker: antislavery guerrillas in Kansas and Missouri before and during the Civil War.]

unencumbered, started out first and fast; the Reverend Mr. Brier's party came next with his three children and two young men who were part of their mess; third, and bringing up the rear, the Bennett, Arcane, and Wade families, the two Earhart brothers with two sons, several unattached men, and twenty-one-year-old William Manly, who was to be their guide. It was Manly's first trip west.

Juliet Brier was born in Bennington, Vermont, September 26, 1813, and educated at a seminary. She was a wisp of a woman, nervous by nature, the mother of three sons, aged eight, seven, and four. The first white woman to enter Death Valley, the sight that greeted her eyes from the ridge of the eastern range was one to strike terror into the stoutest heart: utter, hopeless, unalleviated desolation: eight to fourteen miles wide, one hundred thirty miles long, with the lower-lying, aptly named Funeral Range in the center. There was nothing living as far as the eye could sweep, only windblown and rippled Sahara wastes of sunbaked sand and crusted salt-mud flats, with mountains surrounding on all sides and bearing not a tree, bush, or blade of grass; what H. H. Bancroft, historian of the West, calls:

"The region of mirage, accursed to all living things, its atmosphere destructive even to the passing bird."

When the Reverend Mr. Brier went ahead looking for water, says Mrs. Brier, "I was left with our three little boys to help bring up the cattle. Poor little Kirke gave out and I carried him on my back, barely seeing where I was going."

She stumbled on, hour after hour, in the hot choking dust, the cattle bellowing for water. When darkness fell she lost the two men of the group and had to get on her knees to search out the ox tracks in the starlight. Not until three in the morning did she reach camp, where the men had found hot and cold springs.

It was Christmas morning. At the springs, which they named Furnace Creek, one of the men asked, "Don't you think you and the children better remain here?" 15

"I have never kept the company waiting," replied Mrs. Brier. "Neither have my children. *Every step I take will be towards California.*"

The next morning when they reached the Jayhawker camp the Briers found the young men burning their wagons in order to travel faster: for it needed only one surveying look about them to know that they all faced imminent death.

The Briers also abandoned their wagons, packing their rapidly vanishing foodstuffs on the failing oxen. The Reverend Mr. Brier asked the Jayhawkers for permission to travel with them; the Jayhawkers did not want to be encumbered by a woman and small children, and objected. Then they looked at Mrs. Brier, all skin and bones, and relented. William Manly, leading the Bennett Party, also arrived at the springs. He reports:

"She was the one who put the packs on the oxen in the morning. She it was who took them off at night, built the fires, cooked the food, helped

then borrowed horses to load with oranges and other foodstuffs, and spent the next week retracing their steps, exploring for better passes and water holes. When they got their first view of the camp not a soul was in sight; they concluded they had made the journey for nothing.

Manly fired a shot. From under a wagon a man emerged. He threw his arms high over his head and shouted:

"The boys have come! The boys have come!"

They were saved.

The Brier party also emerged, as images of death, onto the opulent   45
hospitality of the Californios who owned San Francisquito ranch. Mrs. Brier came down out of the San Gabriel Mountains, leading her three sons, in rags, the last of the moccasins she had made of the hides of dead oxen worn through; seventy pounds of bone, grit, and indestructibility.

Thirteen men had lost their lives in the Sand Walking Company. The women were tougher; they endured. Juliet Brier's inner strength saved not only her own family but several of the Jayhawkers as well.

The Responsive Reader

1. Stone's account is in part a story of weak and strong leaders. (What is wrong with the guides that fail the emigrants?) What leadership qualities did Stone see in Juliet Brier?
2. Hardship puts people to the test. How do the people in the Sand Walking Party pass the test?

Talking, Listening, Writing

3. Is the pioneering spirit dead in American society today?
4. Try to put yourself in the shoes of one of the anonymous travelers in the story. Write a diary entry sharing your thoughts and feelings.
5. What attracts readers to stories of hardship and disaster? Is the kind of documentary literature represented by this article flourishing or languishing in America today?

Projects

6. Does your community keep alive the memory of pioneers or founders? Can you find brochures or other sources commemorating early settlers, early builders? Your class may decide to collaborate on a project devoted to the people involved in the early history of your community.

THE DAY THE SLAVES GOT THEIR WAY

Matthew Kauffman

> *Newspapers, Sunday supplements, and large-circulation magazines have in recent years often turned to a forgotten page from American history. An article might discuss ancient treaty rights that a tribe is trying to recover; another article might focus on the role of black soldiers during the Civil War, or War Between the States. The following selection focuses on the legal aftermath of a slave rebellion that is also treated in Robert Hayden's poem "Middle Passage" and in a book that Howard Jones wrote in 1987. The article was first published in Hartford, Connecticut, in the* Hartford Courant. *It appeared on the occasion of the 150th anniversary of the court case that lined up American abolitionists in support of Africans who had staged a successful mutiny on a slave ship bound for Cuba.*

Thought Starters: What expectations or assumptions do you bring to an article about a mutiny aboard a slave ship? Would you be inclined to consider the story unlikely? Are you predisposed to take sides? How does the article change or add to your understanding of the history of slavery in the Americas?

For weeks in the summer of 1839, seafarers along the East Coast had spotted a sleek, black schooner with no national flag waving above its tattered sails. The ship moved slowly, seemingly with no destination, and those who approached the mysterious vessel reported that the crew was composed almost entirely of half-naked black men.

When the crew of a Coast Guard cutter boarded the vessel near Montauk Point, N. Y., on Long Island, they found that the men were slaves who had overpowered their captors at sea, killed four white men and commandeered the schooner. The captain ordered the ship towed to New London, Conn., where, he expected, the slaves would be tried as murderers and mutineers.

But the seizure of the Amistad, as the schooner was called, touched off a two-year legal battle that pitted the governments of two nations against a small group of feisty abolitionists determined to prove that the Africans were enslaved illegally and should be freed.

A celebration of the 150th anniversary of that legal struggle has been planned in New Haven, where the Africans were jailed for much of the time their fate was argued in the courts. The city has scheduled lectures, exhibits, school essay contests, artistic performances, outdoor events and a community dinner.

The case will be celebrated as the first major court victory for the   5
anti-slavery forces and as an early example of the involvement of blacks
on the frontline of the battle against slavery.

Americans were riveted by the case, but the fate of the Africans is
less well-known today. In the early 1970s, Amistad House opened in
Hartford as a group home for troubled teenage girls, but the house closed
in 1983. One of the men who kidnapped Patricia Hearst 15 years ago called
himself Cinque after Joseph Cinque, the leader of the rebellion.

Organizers hope the celebration will revive interest in the saga.

"What I would love to see is that it become an integral part of
Connecticut history," said Alfred Marder, a New Haven peace worker and
a member of the 100-member committee planning the celebration.

The 52 slaves aboard the schooner undoubtedly had little concern
for their place in history when they rose up against their Cuban captors.
They wanted to go home, so they spared the lives of two men and ordered
them to sail east toward Africa. But during the night, the Cubans secretly
turned the ship around, and spent nearly two months zig-zagging north
along the East Coast, hoping to be rescued.

The Cubans had documents indicating that the Africans were ladi-   10
nos, Africans taken to Cuba before the importation of slaves to the island
was outlawed in 1817, but abolitionists suspected that the papers were
fraudulent. If the blacks had been illegally imported from Africa, the
abolitionists argued in court, then they were not slaves guilty of murder,
but kidnap victims who acted reasonably to regain their liberty.

The case became a lightning rod for those who opposed slavery,
including Roger Sherman Baldwin, who later became governor of Connecticut and a U.S. senator, and former President John Quincy Adams,
who argued the case before the U.S. Supreme Court. A leading abolitionist declared the Amistad case a "providential occurrence" delivered to
force a nationwide hearing on the evils of slavery.

Abolitionists, who were determined to keep the Africans, and the
issue of slavery, on the minds of Americans, embarked on a tremendous
public relations drive, inviting people to visit the Africans in jail, delivering lectures across the country and arranging to have life-size wax dum-
mies made of Cinque and others.

Hundreds and sometimes thousands of people visited the Africans in
jail each day. In Hartford, an especially entrepreneurial jailer charged visitors 12½ cents each for a peek at the captives.

Despite the excitement, lawyers for the Africans knew they had an
uphill battle. The administration of President Martin Van Buren, bowing
to pressure from the Spanish government and pro-slavery forces in America, worked against the Africans.

Despite Van Buren's inclinations, the Africans won in the lower   15
court. But the case was appealed to the Supreme Court, and lawyers for
the Africans knew that only two of the nine men on the court opposed
slavery. Nevertheless, in March 1841, the court granted the Africans the

wish expressed by Cinque, who knew only enough English to utter in court the simple plea, "Give me free."

The Africans, the court ruled, were not slaves and were not criminals.

The Africans from the Amistad returned to their homeland 10 months later, but before leaving, the prominent New Haven lawyers who had arranged their defense sought to turn the Africans into Christian missionaries. Cinque and the others took up residence in Farmington, Conn., and spent six hours a day in a classroom. They also cultivated a 15-acre farm and participated in a nationwide tour to help raise money for their voyage home.

The Amistad rebellion rates only a few paragraphs in most encyclopedias and is rarely taught in schools or included in textbooks, said Howard Jones, a University of Alabama history professor who wrote a 1987 book on the case.

New Haven schools, however, are ordering 2,000 booklets on the Amistad affair, and an effort is under way to have the Amistad rebellion featured on a U.S. postage stamp during the sesquicentennial of the Supreme Court decision.

New Haven also hopes to raise $100,000 for a statue of Cinque, *20* which would be erected on the street where the town jail stood.

The Responsive Reader

1. How much do you learn from this article about the Amistad rebellion and its legal aftermath? (What are some of the "hard facts"?)
2. How much knowledge of slavery and the abolitionist movement does the writer assume? How much does he add to your understanding of slavery and of the antislavery forces? (One hundred fifty years later, can you get into the spirit of the abolitionist movement?)

Talking, Listening, Writing

3. What shaped your own views of slavery and abolition? What was the role of teachers, books, the media?
4. Prepare a defense (or an indictment) of the accused "murderers and mutineers."
5. As a member of a school board or similar body, would you vote in favor of commemorating the Amistad affair or a similar historical episode? Why or why not?

Projects

6. Your class may want to stage a mock trial of the Amistad group. (You may want to turn to the Hayden poem and the Jones book or to other sources — history books, encyclopedias — for additional information.)

THE WAY TO RAINY MOUNTAIN

N. Scott Momaday

In the sixties and seventies, many Americans set out in search of their roots. They tried to retrace the journey that had brought them to where they were — before records and the testimonies of old-timers became erased. N. Scott Momaday is a Kiowa who was born in Lawton, Oklahoma, and studied at the University of New Mexico and Stanford University. He became a professor of English first at the University of California at Santa Barbara and then at the University of New Mexico. He first became known when he published a collection of Kiowa tales, The Journey of Tai-me *(1968), later republished as* The Way to Rainy Mountain. *His novel* The House Made of Dawn *won the Pulitzer Prize in 1969. Many of his poems, which appeared in collections like* The Gourd Dancer *(1976), recreate the songs and legends of his people.*

Thought Starters: What memories does this essay retrieve from the past? What is their special meaning for the writer?

A single knoll rises out of the plain in Oklahoma, north and west of   *1*
the Wichita range. For my people, the Kiowas, it is an old landmark, and they gave it the name Rainy Mountain. The hardest weather in the world is there. Winter brings blizzards, hot tornadic winds arise in the spring, and in the summer the prairie is an anvil's edge. The grass turns brittle and brown, and it cracks beneath your feet. There are green belts along the rivers and creeks, linear groves of hickory and pecan, willow and witch hazel. At a distance in July or August the steaming foliage seems almost to writhe in fire. Great green and yellow grasshoppers are everywhere in the tall grass, popping up like corn to sting the flesh, and tortoises crawl about on the red earth, going nowhere in the plenty of time. Loneliness is an aspect of the land. All things in the plain are isolate; there is no confusion of objects in the eye, but *one* hill or *one* tree or *one* man. To look upon that landscape in the early morning, with the sun at your back, is to lose the sense of proportion. Your imagination comes to life, and this, you think, is where Creation was begun.

I returned to Rainy Mountain in July. My grandmother had died in the spring, and I wanted to be at her grave. She had lived to be very old and at last infirm. Her only living daughter was with her when she died, and I was told that in death her face was that of a child.

I like to think of her as a child. When she was born, the Kiowas were living the last great moment of their history. For more than a hundred

years they had controlled the open range from the Smoky Hill River to
the Red, from the headwaters of the Canadian to the fork of the Arkansas
and Cimarron. In alliance with the Comanches, they had ruled the whole
of the Southern Plains. War was their sacred business, and they were the
finest horsemen the world has ever known. But warfare for the Kiowas
was pre-eminently a matter of disposition rather than of survival, and they
never understood the grim, unrelenting advance of the U.S. Cavalry.
When at last, divided and ill provisioned, they were driven onto the Staked
Plains in the cold of autumn, they fell into panic.[1] In Palo Duro Canyon
they abandoned their crucial stores to pillage and had nothing then but
their lives. In order to save themselves, they surrendered to the soldiers at
Fort Sill and were imprisoned in the old stone corral that now stands as a
military museum. My grandmother was spared the humiliation of those
high gray walls by eight or ten years, but she must have known from birth
the affliction of defeat, the dark brooding of old warriors.

　　Her name was Aho, and she belonged to the last culture to evolve in
North America. Her forebears came down from the high country in western Montana nearly three centuries ago. They were a mountain people, a
mysterious tribe of hunters whose language has never been classified in
any major group. In the late seventeenth century they began a long migration to the south and east. It was a journey toward the dawn, and it led to
a golden age. Along the way the Kiowas were befriended by the Crows,
who gave them the culture and religion of the Plains. They acquired
horses, and their ancient nomadic spirit was suddenly free of the ground.
They acquired Tai-me, the sacred sun-dance doll, from that moment the
object and symbol of their worship, and so shared in the divinity of the
sun. Not least, they acquired the sense of destiny, therefore courage and
pride. When they entered upon the Southern Plains they had been transformed. No longer were they slaves to the simple necessity of survival;
they were a lordly and dangerous society of fighters and thieves, hunters
and priests of the sun. According to their origin myth, they entered the
world through a hollow log. From one point of view, their migration was
the fruit of an old prophecy, for indeed they emerged from a sunless world.

　　Though my grandmother lived out her long life in the shadow of   5
Rainy Mountain, the immense landscape of the continental interior lay
like memory in her blood. She could tell of the Crows, whom she had
never seen, and of the Black Hills, where she had never been. I wanted to
see in reality what she had seen more perfectly in the mind's eye, and drove
fifteen hundred miles to begin my pilgrimage.

　　Yellowstone, it seemed to me, was the top of the world, a region of
deep lakes and dark timber, canyons and waterfalls. But, beautiful as it is,
one might have the sense of confinement there. The skyline in all directions is close at hand, the high wall of the woods and deep cleavages of

[1][The Staked Plains, English for the Spanish *Llano Estacado*, is the name of the great
arid plateau of southeast New Mexico, northwest Oklahoma, and west Texas.]

burned gray and the grain appears and the nails turn red with rust. The window panes are black and opaque; you imagine there is nothing within, and indeed there are many ghosts, bones given up to the land. They stand here and there against the sky, and you approach them for a longer time than you expect. They belong in the distance; it is their domain.

Once there was a lot of sound in my grandmother's house, a lot of coming and going, feasting and talk. The summers there were full of excitement and reunion. The Kiowas are a summer people; they abide the cold and keep to themselves, but when the season turns and the land becomes warm and vital they cannot hold still; an old love of going returns upon them. The aged visitors who came to my grandmother's house when I was a child were made of lean and leather, and they bore themselves upright. They wore great black hats and bright ample shirts that shook in the wind. They rubbed fat upon their hair and wound their braids with strips of colored cloth. Some of them painted their faces and carried the scars of old and cherished enmities. They were an old council of warlords, come to remind and be reminded of who they were. Their wives and daughters served them well. The women might indulge themselves; gossip was at once the mark and compensation of their servitude. They made loud and elaborate talk among themselves, full of jest and gesture, fright and false alarm. They went abroad in fringed and flowered shawls, bright beadwork and German silver. They were at home in the kitchen, and they prepared meals that were banquets.

There were frequent prayer meetings, and nocturnal feasts. When I was a child I played with my cousins outside, where the lamplight fell upon the ground and the singing of the old people rose up around us and carried away into the darkness. There were a lot of good things to eat, a lot of laughter and surprise. And afterwards, when the quiet returned, I lay down with my grandmother and could hear the frogs away by the river and feel the motion of the air.

Now there is a funeral silence in the rooms, the endless wake of some final word. The walls have closed in upon my grandmother's house. When I returned to it in mourning, I saw for the first time in my life how small it was. It was late at night, and there was a white moon, nearly full. I sat for a long time on the stone steps by the kitchen door. From there I could see out across the land; I could see the long row of trees by the creek, the low light up on the rolling plains, and the stars of the Big Dipper. Once I looked at the moon and caught sight of a strange thing. A cricket had perched upon the handrail, only a few inches away. My line of vision was such that the creature filled the moon like a fossil. It had gone there, I thought, to live and die, for there, of all places, was its small definition made whole and eternal. A warm wind rose up and purled like the longing within me.

The next morning, I awoke at dawn and went out on the dirt road to Rainy Mountain. It was already hot, and the grasshoppers began to fill the air. Still, it was early in the morning, and birds sang out of the shadows. The long yellow grass on the mountain shone in the bright light, and a scissortail hied above the land. There, where it ought to be, at the end of a long and legendary way, was my grandmother's grave. She had at last succeeded to that holy ground. Here and there on the dark stones were ancestral names. Looking back once, I saw the mountain and came away.

The Responsive Reader

1. What is the keynote in Momaday's opening description of the Oklahoma setting? What are striking details?
2. How does Momaday retell the history of his people? What is most meaningful to him about his heritage?
3. In his description of life at his grandmother's house, how does Momaday recreate the vanished past? What kind of person was his grandmother, and what does she mean to him? What was the role of women in the traditional setting?

Talking, Listening, Writing

4. How much in this essay is nostalgia for a past that is gone forever? How much has meaning for the present or the future?
5. Are there common elements in the search for the Native American past in the selections by Mary Crow Dog, Black Elk, and N. Scott Momaday in this book? What are recurrent notes, common areas of concern?

Projects

6. Controversies have in recent years swirled around Native American artifacts in museums or remains in cemeteries. Do you remember news reports bearing on these controversies? Can you find newspaper and magazine articles on the subject? What are the issues?

MISTER TOUSSAN

Ralph Ellison

> *Ralph Ellison, born in Oklahoma City, became famous for his novel* Invisible Man *(1952). His semi-autobiographical hero embarked on an archetypal journey of a Southern black in search of his true identity. He experienced segregated schools in the South. He rebelled against white co-workers considering him inferior ("Were they all Ph.D.s?"). In the big Northern city, he first tried to deny and then came to accept his southern roots—grits and hot yams and all ("I yam what I yam!"). He watched political groups—communists, black nationalists—trying to use him for their own purposes. Everywhere he felt no one saw him as a human being in his own right. He was typed as a member of a racial group—he was invisible as his own person. In the following short story, two young boys are learning pride in who they are. The "Mister Toussan" of the title is Toussaint L'Ouverture (1743–1803), who led the people of Haiti in their fight against French colonial rule. Napoleon was rising to power as emperor of France at the time.*

Thought Starters: What do you know about the colonial history of the Caribbean?

> Once upon a time
> The goose drink wine
> Monkey chew tobacco
> And he spit white lime.
> — *Rhyme used as a prologue*
> *to Negro slave stories*

"I hope they all gits rotten and the worms git in 'em," the first boy   1
said.

"I hopes a big windstorm comes and blows down all the trees," said
the second boy.

"Me too," the first boy said. "And when old Rogan comes out to see
what happened I hope a tree falls on his head and kills him."

"Now jus' look a-yonder at them birds," the second boy said, "they
eating all they want and when we asked him to let us git some off the
ground he had to come calling us names and chasing us home!"

"Doggonit," said the second boy, "I hope them birds got poison in   5
they feet!"

The two small boys, Riley and Buster, sat on the floor of the porch,
their bare feet resting upon the cool earth as they stared past the line on

the paving where the sun consumed the shade, to a yard directly across the street. The grass in the yard was very green and a house stood against it, neat and white in the morning sun. A double row of trees stood alongside the house, heavy with cherries that showed deep red against the dark green of the leaves and dull dark brown of the branches. They were watching an old man who rocked himself in a chair as he stared back at them across the street.

"Just look at him," said Buster. "Ole Rogan's so scared we gonna git some of his ole cherries he ain't even got sense enough to go in outa the sun!"

"Well, them birds is gitting theirs," said Riley.

"They mockingbirds."

"I don't care what kinda birds they is, they sho in them trees."   10

"Yeah, old Rogan don't see *them*. Man, white folks ain't got no sense."

They were silent now, watching the darting flight of the birds into the trees. Behind them they could hear the clatter of a sewing machine: Riley's mother was sewing for the white folks. It was quiet and, as the woman worked, her voice rose above the whirring machine in song.

"Your mamma sho can sing, man," said Buster.

"She sings in the choir," said Riley, "and she sings all the leads in church."

"Shucks, I know it," said Buster. "You tryin' to brag?"   15

As they listened they heard the voice rise clear and liquid to float upon the morning air:

I got wings, you got wings,
All God's chillun got a-wings
When I git to heaven gonna put on my wings
Gonna shout all ovah God's heaven.
Heab'n, heab'n
Everybody talkin' bout heab'n ain't going there
Heab'n, heab'n, Ah'm gonna fly all ovah God's heab'n. . . .

She sang as though the words possessed a deep and throbbing meaning for her, and the boys stared blankly at the earth, feeling the somber, mysterious calm of church. The street was quiet and even old Rogan had stopped rocking to listen. Finally the voice trailed off to a hum and became lost in the clatter of the busy machine.

"Sure wish I could sing like that," said Buster.

Riley was silent, looking down to the end of the porch where the sun had eaten a bright square into the shade, fixing a flitting butterfly in its brilliance.

"What would you do if you had wings?" he said.   20

"Shucks, I'd outfly an eagle, I wouldn't stop flying till I was a million, billion, trillion, zillion miles away from this ole town."

"Where'd you go, man?"

"Up north, maybe to Chicago."

"Man, if I had wings I wouldn't never settle down."

"Me, neither. With wings you could go anywhere, even up to the sun if it wasn't too hot. . . ."

". . . I'd go to New York. . . ."

"Even around the stars . . ."

"Or Dee–troit, Michigan . . ."

"You could git some cheese off the moon and some milk from the Milky Way. . . ."

"Or anywhere else colored is free. . . ." 30

"I bet I'd loop–the–loop. . . ."

"And parachute. . . ."

"I'd land in Africa and git me some diamonds. . . ."

"Yeah, and them cannibals would eat you too," said Riley.

"The heck they would, not fast as I'd fly away. . . ." 35

"Man, they'd catch you and stick soma them long spears in you!" said Riley.

Buster laughed as Riley shook his head gravely: "Boy, you'd look like a black pin cushion when they got through with you," said Riley.

"Shucks, man, they couldn't catch me, them suckers is too lazy. The geography book says they 'bout the most lazy folks in the whole world," said Buster with disgust, "just black and lazy!"

"Aw naw, they ain't neither," exploded Riley.

"They is too! The geography book says they is!" 40

"Well, my ole man says they ain't!"

"How come they ain't then?"

"'Cause my ole man says that over there they got kings and diamonds and gold and ivory, and if they got all them things, all of 'em cain't be lazy," said Riley. "Ain't many colored folks over here got them things."

"Sho ain't, man. The white folks won't let 'em," said Buster.

It was good to think that all the Africans were not lazy. He tried to 45 remember all he had heard of Africa as he watched a purple pigeon sail down into the street and scratch where a horse had passed. Then, as he remembered a story his teacher had told him, he saw a car rolling swiftly up the street and the pigeon stretching its wings and lifting easily into the air, skimming the top of the car in its slow, rocking flight. He watched it rise and disappear where the taut telephone wires cut the sky above the curb. Buster felt good. Riley scratched his initials in the soft earth with his big toe.

"Riley, you know all them African guys ain't really that lazy," he said.

"I know they ain't," said Riley, "I just tole you so."

"Yeah, but my teacher tole me, too. She tole us 'bout one of them African guys named Toussan what she said whipped Napoleon!"

Riley stopped scratching the earth and looked up, his eyes rolling in disgust:

"Now how come you have to start lying?"   50

"Thass what she said."

"Boy, you oughta quit telling them things."

"I hope God may kill me."

"She said he was a *African*?"

"Cross my heart, man. . . ."   55

"Really?"

"Really, man. She said he come from a place named Hayti."

Riley looked hard at Buster and seeing the seriousness of the face felt the excitement of a story rise up within him.

"Buster, I'll bet a fat man you lyin'. What'd that teacher say?"

"Really, man, she said that Toussan and his men got up on one of   60
them African mountains and shot down them peckerwood soldiers fass as they'd try to come up. . . ."

"Why good-a-mighty!" yelled Riley.

"Oh boy, they shot'em down!" chanted Buster.

"Tell me about it, man!"

"And they throwed 'em all off the mountain. . . ."

". . . Goool-leee! . . ."   65

". . . And Toussan drove 'em cross the sand. . . ."

". . . Yeah! And what was they wearing, Buster? . . ."

"Man, they had on red uniforms and blue hats all trimmed with gold, and they had some swords, all shining what they called sweet blades of Damascus. . . ."

"Sweet blades of Damascus! . . ."

". . . They really had 'em," chanted Buster.   70

"And what kinda guns?"

"Big, black cannon!"

"And where did ole what-you-call-'im run them guys? . . ."

"His name was Toussan."

"Toussan! Just like Tarzan . . ."   75

"Not *Taar*-zan, dummy, *Toou*-zan!"

"Toussan! And where'd ole Toussan run 'em?"

"Down to the water, man . . ."

". . . To the river water . . ."

". . . Where some great big ole boats was waiting for 'em. . . ."   80

". . . Go on, Buster!"

"An' Toussan shot into them boats. . . ."

". . . He shot into 'em. . . ."

"With his great big cannons . . ."

". . . Yeah! . . ."   85

". . . Made a-brass . . ."

". . . Brass . . ."

". . . An' his big black cannonballs started killin' them pecker-woods. . . ."

". . . Lawd, Lawd . . ."

". . . Boy, till them peckerwoods hollowed *'Please, please, Mister* 90
Toussan, we'll be good!'"

"An' what'd Toussan tell em, Buster?"

"'Boy,' he said in his big deep voice, *'I oughta drown all a-you.'*"

"An' what'd the peckerwoods say?"

"They said, 'Please, Please, *Please, Mister Toussan . . .'*"

". . . 'We'll be good,'" broke in Riley. 95

"Thass right, man," said Buster excitedly. He clapped his hands and kicked his heels against the earth, his black face glowing in a burst of rhythmic joy.

"Boy!"

"And what'd ole Toussan say then?"

"He said in his deep voice: 'You all peckerwoods better be good, *'cause this is sweet Papa Toussan talking and my men is crazy 'bout white meat!'*"

"Ho, ho, ho!" Riley bent double with laughter. The rhythm still 100 throbbed within him and he wanted the story to go on and on. . . .

"Buster, you know didn't no teacher tell you that lie," he said.

"Yes she did, man."

"That teacher said there was really a guy like that what called hisself Sweet Papa Toussan?"

Riley's voice was unbelieving and there was a wistful expression in his eyes which Buster could not understand. Finally he dropped his head and grinned.

"Well," he said, "I bet thass what ole Toussan said. You know how 105 grown folks is, they cain't tell a story right, 'cepting real old folks like grandma."

"They sho cain't," said Riley. "They don't know how to put the right stuff to it."

Riley stood, his legs spread wide, and stuck his thumbs in the top of his trousers, swaggering sinisterly.

"Come on, watch me do it now, Buster. Now I bet ole Toussan looked down at them white folks standing just about like this and said in a soft easy voice: 'Ain't I done begged you white folks to quit messin' with me? . . .'"

"Thass right, quit messing with 'im," chanted Buster.

"'But naw, you-all had to come on anyway. . . .'" 110

". . . Jus' 'cause they was black . . ."

"Thass right," said Riley. "Then ole Toussan felt so bad and mad the tears come a-trickling down. . . ."

". . . He was really mad."

"And then, man, he said in his big bass voice: 'white folks, how come you-all cain't let us colored alone?'"

". . . An' he was crying. . . ." 115

". . . An' Toussan tole them peckerwoods: 'I been beggin' you-all to quit bothering us. . . .'"

"... Beggin' on his bended knees! ..."

"Then, man, Toussan got real mad and snatched off his hat and started stompin' up and down on it and the tears was tricklin' down and he said: 'You-all come tellin' me about Napoleon. ...'"

"They was tryin' to make him scared, man. ..."

"Toussan said: 'I don't care about no Napoleon. ...'"   120

"... Wasn't studyin' 'bout him. ..."

"... Toussan said: 'Napoleon ain't nothing but a man!' Then Toussan pulled back his shining sword like this, and twirled it at them pecker-woods' throats so hard it z-z-z-zinged in the air!"

"Now keep on, finish it, man," said Buster. "What'd Toussan do then?"

"Then you know what he did, he said: 'I oughta beat you peckerwoods!'"

"Thass right, and he did it too," said Buster. He jumped to his feet   125
and fenced violently with five desperate imaginary soldiers, running each through with his imaginary sword. Buster watched from the porch, grinning.

"Toussan musta scared them white folks almost to death!"

"Yeah, thass 'bout the way it was," said Buster. The rhythm was dying now and he sat back upon the porch, breathing tiredly.

"It sho is a good story," said Riley.

"Heck, man, all the stories my teacher tells us is good. She's a good ole teacher — but you know one thing?"

"Naw; what?"   130

"Ain't none of them stories in the books! Wonder why?"

"You know why, ole Toussan was too hard on them white folks, thass why."

"Oh, he was a hard man!"

"He was mean. ..."

"But a good mean!"   135

"Toussan was clean. ..."

"... He was a good, clean mean," said Riley.

"Aw, man, he was sooo-preme," said Buster.

"Riiiley!!"

The boys stopped short in their word play, their mouths wide.   140

"Riley I say!" It was Riley's mother's voice.

"Ma'am?"

"She musta heard us cussin'," whispered Buster.

"Shut up, man. ... What you want, Ma?"

"I says I wants you-all to go around in the backyard and play, you   145
keeping up too much fuss out there. White folks says we tear up a neigh-borhood when we move in it and you-all out there jus' provin' them out true. Now git on round in the back."

"Aw, ma, we was jus' playing, ma. ..."

"Boy, I said for you-all to go on."

"But, ma . . ."

"You hear me, boy!"

"Yessum, we going," said Riley. "Come on, Buster." 150

Buster followed slowly behind, feeling the dew upon his feet as he walked upon the shaded grass.

"What else did he do, man?" Buster said.

"Huh? Rogan?"

"Heck, naw! I mean Toussan."

"Doggone if I know, man — but I'm gonna ask that teacher." 155

"He was a fightin' son-of-a-gun, wasn't he, man?"

"He didn't stand for no foolishness," said Riley reservedly. He thought of other things now, and as he moved along he slid his feet easily over the short-cut grass, dancing as he chanted

Iron is iron,
And tin is tin,
And that's the way
The story . . .

"Aw come on man," interrupted Buster. "Let's go play in the alley. . . ."

And that's the way . . .

"Maybe we can slip around and git some cherries," Buster went on. 160

". . . the story ends," chanted Riley.

The Responsive Reader

1. In much of his fiction, Ellison has fought racial stereotypes. How does he do so in this story?
2. The boys in this story delight in word play, in playing games with words. Can you describe their way of talking, their use of language?
3. What is the role of the mother in the story?

Talking, Listening, Writing

4. The boys claim that stories like the ones about Toussaint are not in their school books. Should they be?
5. Are treatments of black history in the media too downbeat? Are blacks or other minorities too often associated in the viewers' or readers' minds with problems or trouble?
6. Have you observed or participated in recent efforts to help African Americans or members of other groups to overcome a sense of inferiority and to feel pride? What are these efforts? How successful are they?

Projects

7. You may want to do some background reading for a capsule portrait of, or short tribute to, one of the following famous people: Paul Laurence Dunbar, Harriet Tubman, Frederick Douglass, Sojourner Truth, William E. B. DuBois, Marian Anderson, Paul Robeson, Leontyne Price, Mahalia Jackson, Alexander Haley, Thurgood Marshall, Lorraine Hansberry, Cicely Tyson. (You may want to start with but also go beyond entries in encyclopedias or biographical dictionaries.)

Writing about Your Reading

Good writers tend to be good readers. When they take a break from working at the keyboard, they are likely to pick up a magazine or a book. They browse; they look something up; they take notes. They are compulsive underliners and collectors of clippings from newspapers. At the right point in a paper, they refer to an event currently in the news. To clinch an argument, they cite authoritative statistics or bring in a quotable quote from a media guru like Ellen Goodman or George Will.

TRIGGERING Writers interact with their reading in a number of ways.

• Reading helps us give shape to tentative ideas. We write to show that our reading confirmed an idea that was at first only a hunch. What was only a tentative theory was validated by the testimony of experts or insiders. When we quote, interpret, and integrate what we have read, we can show that our ideas are more than superficial impressions. They have the backing of qualified observers.

• One of the most reliable motives for writing is the urge to talk back. Much writing is triggered when we say: "Just a minute! That is simply not so" or "That is badly oversimplified!" We then write to set the record straight. We write to show where we agree with other writers and where we think they go wrong. We might be reading a reassuring discussion of slaves' living conditions in the Old South (because slaves were valuable property, owners were not likely to jeopardize their health etc.). We might agree up to a point but finally say: "Yes — but! Look at what has been left out here!"

• Reading can raise important questions in our minds. An author writing about the need to save the spotted owl or to protect the whales can bring an important question into focus while leaving us dissatisfied with the answer he or she provides. We can then set out in search of a better answer.

GATHERING Good writers are not passive readers who read quickly to get "the general idea." Early in an article or a book, they get the drift of the argument. They size up the writer's agenda. They follow an argument point by point, noting the supporting evidence (or lack of it). They underline or highlight key points; they put question marks or exclamation marks in the margin. They take notes, making sure not to pounce on some minor point or to mispresent the author's intention.

The following might be a student reader's annotated text of a key passage about the traditional struggle between "evolutionists" and "creationists" over what to tell students about the origin of life. Why do many parents object to having students in biology classes study Darwin's account of evolution but not the biblical account of creation?

And what if the creationists win? They might, you know, for there are millions who, faced with the choice between science and their interpretation of the Bible, will choose the Bible and reject science, regardless of the evidence.

eynote: "*Fear*" *science*

This is not entirely because of a traditional and unthinking reverence for the literal works of the Bible; there is also a pervasive uneasiness— even an <u>actual fear</u>—of science that will drive even those who care little for Fundamentalism into the arms of the creationists. For <u>one thing</u>,

hanging cientific neories

science is <u>uncertain</u>. Theories are subject to revision; observations are open to a variety of interpretations, and <u>scientists quarrel among themselves</u>. This is disillusioning for those untrained in the scientific method, who thus turn to the rigid certainty of the Bible instead. . . .

"Cold" entific niverse

Second, science is complex and chilling. The mathematical language of science is understood by very few. The <u>vistas it presents are scary</u>—an <u>enormous universe ruled by chance and impersonal rules, empty and uncaring, ungraspable and vertiginous</u>. How comfortable to turn instead to a small world, only a few thousand years old, and under God's personal and immediate care. . . .

structive ential cience

Third, science is dangerous. There is no question but that <u>poison gas, genetic engineering and nuclear weapons and power stations are terrifying.</u> It may be that civilization is falling apart and the world we know is coming to an end. In that case, why not turn to religion and look forward to the Day of Judgment, in which you and your fellow believers will be uplifted into eternal bliss. Isaac Asimov, "The 'Threat' of Creationism," <u>New York Times</u>

SHAPING In papers interpreting or arguing with a single source, the basic "Yes, but" pattern often provides the key to the writer's overall plan. For perhaps two-thirds of the paper, you might present, explain, and illustrate the author's position. However, your paper then might reach a turning point where you start saying, "Yes — but." After being a receptive reader for most of the paper, you may feel entitled to voice doubts and reservations about what you have read.

In papers using material from several sources, you need to guard against presenting undigested chunks of material. In an effective paper, the materials you have brought in mesh — without the seams showing. Make sure you integrate — correlate — material from your different sources. Here is an example of how a student reader pulled relevant material from several different sources and then worked them into a smoothly flowing paragraph:

("Man-Made Hearts: A Grim Prognosis," U.S. News & World Report)
"Two winters ago, as William Schroeder sat in his hospital bed sipping a beer and declaring it 'the Coors cure,' the future looked good for permanent artificial hearts. Supporters said the devices might someday become as much of a long-term lifesaver as plastic valves and pacemakers. But by the time Schroeder died on August 6, that talk had all but vanished."

(Robert Bazell, "Hearts of Gold," The New Republic)
"Exotic medical procedures certainly make compelling news stories, and for a time they can elevate relatively unknown medical institutions such as Loma Linda and Humana from obscurity. The trouble is that they are indeed experimental, and often they do not work. In the end they run the risk of attracting considerably more bad publicity than good. Despite hopes to the contrary, it takes more than one operation to make any medical establishment 'number one.'"

(Kathleen Deremy and Alan Hall, "Should Profit Drive Artificial Hearts?" Business Week)
"Experts on medical ethics and health care costs are also questioning the wisdom of the current tests. If the use of artificial hearts becomes widespread it could add up to $3 billion a year to U.S. health care costs. And that will raise some onerous questions, says Henry Aaron, an economist at Brookings Institution. 'The funding mechanisms are open-ended. The dilemma is: Does everybody get it? If not, who does?'"

(Beth Vaughan-Cole and Helen Lee, "A Heart Decision," American Journal of Nursing)
"Finally, life-extending technology raises the 'right to die' issue. The committee drew the Clarks' attention to the clause in the consent form that stated that the subject could withdraw from the experiment at any time. If the recipient should be crippled physically or psychologically, the extension of life might be more of a curse than a blessing. Who could predict what the patient might want to do if he found himself in an inescapable position in which the activities that make life worthwhile might be impossible? The Clarks understood the alternative and could face that choice if necessary.
The moral issue of suicide arises, too: The artificial heart recipient has the key that turns off the machinery."

In the finished paragraph, the student writer has used input from these notes to support the central point about the second thoughts that replaced the initial euphoria about the artificial heart:

People have long had false teeth, artificial limbs, and pacemakers—
why not an artificial heart? For a while, the future looked bright for
another "breakthrough" or a "medical miracle." However, after the death
of artificial-heart recipient William Schroeder, many observers had second
thoughts about the outlook for the permanent artificial heart as "a long-
term lifesaver." Doubts and reservations multiplied. As Robert Bazell said
in The New Republic, "Exotic medical procedures make compelling news
stories" but the "trouble is that they are indeed experimental, and often
they do not work." The costs are horrendous: In an article in Business
Week, Kathleen Deremy and Alan Hall estimated that the widespread use
of artificial hearts could add up to $3 billion to the nation's health costs.
And the procedure raises thorny questions of medical ethics: Who decides
who gets the artificial heart and who is left out? What stand do we take
on the "right-to-die" issue—does the patient have the right to suicide?
(As Beth Vaughan-Cole and Helen Lee pointed out in The American
Journal of Nursing, "The artificial heart recipient has the key that turns
off the machinery.")

REVISING When you reread a first draft of a paper drawing on
your reading, pay special attention to how you have introduced and identified quoted material. In revising the paper, make sure your reader will
have clear answers to questions like the following: Who said this and
where? Why are you quoting this person? (What makes this author an
authority or a reliable source? What are the quoted author's credentials?)
What is the point of the quotation — why are you using it here?

Here is a sampling of **credit tags** (brief informative lead-ins to a
quotation):

> SOURCE: Rachel Carson said in Silent Spring that "only within
> the moment of time represented by the present century" has one
> species—ours—acquired the power to alter the nature of the world.

> CREDENTIALS: Garrett Hardin, author of "The Tragedy of the
> Commons" and many other articles and books on "human ecology,"
> has attacked "suicidal policies for sharing our resources through
> uncontrolled immigration and foreign aid."

> POINT: Garrett Hardin has used the lifeboat analogy to dramatize
> our limited capacity for helping the world's poor: "Our survival
> demands that we govern our actions by the ethics of a lifeboat,
> harsh though they may be."

Read the following sample paper. What use does it make of the
student's reading?

Pink Collar Workers

Many women, like myself, when hearing the word "feminist" try to
stay as far away as possible. Images of protests, marching libbers on
the war path, and loud radical women come to mind. I held many

misconceptions about the Women's Movement. (I thought that as many as 80% of these women hated men.) However, after having a Women's Studies class, I feel I understand much more about what the movement is trying to accomplish. After reading about the injustices that women are faced with, I can say without a doubt that I, too, am a feminist.

A conference at Seneca Falls in 1848 represented the first wave of feminism in the U.S. A small assembly affirmed their belief in equality of men and women and wanted to pursue the struggle for sex equality. The first wave of feminism was led by women activists of the antislavery movement. Some extremely outspoken feminists were Susan B. Anthony, Elizabeth Cady Stanton, Lucretia Mott, and Matilda Joslyn Gage. They all agreed that the women's right to vote was the first priority. This was not achieved until 1920, after some seventy-two years of struggle. There was only one single woman of those who had attended the Seneca Falls Convention who was still alive to cast her first vote. The following quote is from Elizabeth Cady Stanton, writing to Lucretia Mott:

> The more I think on the present condition of woman, the more I am oppressed with the reality of her degradation. The laws of our country, how unjust they are! Our customs, how vicious! What God has made sinful, both in man and woman, custom has made sinful in woman alone.

The next quote is from Susan B. Anthony from a letter she wrote to her sister, urging her to join the movement:

> We need not wait for one more generation to pass away in order to find a race of women worthy to assert the humanity of women; and that is all we claim to do.

I grew up with a best friend whose parents, especially her mother, would tell her that as long as she found a "good" man, she wouldn't have to worry about college or a good job. At school, my friend took classes like sewing and cooking. I always felt really bad for her because my parents were exactly the opposite. They always encouraged me to take pre-college classes and to first finish college before settling down. Their philosophy was that I should first be strong in myself and have a good job then think about marriage. That way, if something was to end the marriage (divorce, death), I could take care of myself. While we were growing up, I was in after-school sports, but my friend wasn't allowed to so she'd go home and wait for me.

Everywhere we look, magazines and movies convey a message of how a woman should look and should be. I once saw an ad selling perfume where there was a beautiful woman's head attached to a snake's body with hands open towards a man. The caption read, "Dare to be tempted." This ad implied that women are like the snake in the garden trying to tempt and deceive men. If people keep seeing ads and movies like that, they will eventually begin to believe them.

Today's women of the second wave of feminism are asking how long before the struggle for equal rights — which has been pursued by feminists every year since 1920 — is won. While women have won important rights during the past, some of these rights are still under challenge (e.g., abortion). Statistics show that men's incomes have increased by about 5% over women's during the same period in which women supposedly have been making more marked advances toward equality than before. So, are women more liberated now than before? Until men and women promote support towards women's issues, there will not be any advances. Even if an issue doesn't affect you directly, feminists need to be supportive of each other if any advancements are to be made.

Topics for Papers Based on Reading (A Sampling)

1. Choose Harjo's "I Won't Be Celebrating Columbus Day" or Cerio's "Were the Spaniards *That* Cruel?" Write a "Yes, but" paper in which you first sketch any common ground you share with the author and then go on to present and defend your disagreements.
2. Compare the re-creation of the Native American past in Black Elk's "The Earth Is All That Lasts" and N. Scott Momaday's "The Way to Rainy Mountain." Focus on major similarities or differences (or both).
3. Read more about the Amistad rebellion, and correlate and interpret your findings.
4. Write a "Yes, but" paper in which you show where you agree or disagree with Arturo Madrid on diversity or with Diane Ravitch on multiculturalism.
5. Write a paper in which you discuss major themes or recurrent topics in readings by or about young Asian Americans. You may want to read or reread selections by Jade Snow Wong, Frank Chin, Fox Butterfield, and Hisaye Yamamoto.
6. People who distrust sociological theories are fascinated with oral history — the direct and minimally edited testimony of ordinary people. Look at such examples as the testimonies of José Luís and Rosa María Urbina, Black Elk, and Joe Gutierrez. In what they have to say, what might go beyond or counter familiar assumptions or often-cited theories?
7. Feminists represented in this volume include Maya Angelou, Ursula Le Guin, Patty Fisher, Alice Walker, Margaret Mead, Gloria Steinem, Judi Bari, and Barbara Ehrenreich. Study the essays by several of these to arrive at a composite portrait of a contemporary feminist.
8. History has often been the record of wars, revolutions, invasions, and great ideological confrontations. What dimension of history is represented by the writing of Lois Phillips Hudson, Garrison

Keillor, and Irving Stone in this volume? What do they remind us of that in conventional political and military history is left out?

9. Have you read about controversies regarding the preservation of Native American remains in museums and the preservation of Native American burial grounds or religious sites? Find several articles and write a paper that brings the issues into focus for your readers.

10. What is the history of popular or official attitudes toward people with disabilities in this country? Find several articles that examine changes in public awareness or public policy. Is there a consensus?

5

Outsiders:
Unheard Voices

I feel I am of them —
I feel I belong to those convicts and prostitutes myself,
And henceforth I will not deny them —
For how can I deny myself?

                                        Walt Whitman

The promise of America to successive waves of immigrants was that it had created a new classless society. No longer would society be run for the benefit of a small, privileged elite. The blessings of liberty would be available to all. No longer would the many toil so that the few could squander the fruits of honest labor. In some of the great movements of our history, the unfree and disenfranchised reminded American society of its unkept promise. Abolition, the civil rights movement, and the women's movement aimed to make the promise of equal rights come true.

Today, however, observers who care see everywhere growing evidence of inequality and the failure of human hopes. The United States, holding a sorry record, has a larger percentage of its population in jail than almost any other country. The gulf that separates a homeless encampment from the high-tech digs of a billionaire like Ross Perot seems as wide as the one that separated the hovel of the French peasant from the Sun King's ostentatious palace at Versailles. The horrendous dropout rates for minority students in high school and college are an unanswered challenge to the Jeffersonian ideal of an educated citizenry, of free universal education. The cities decay.

Is our society going to listen to the unheard voices of the disenfranchised and the dispossessed? Or are the affluent going to insulate themselves from the marginalized, the outsiders? Are we again, like Victorian England, going to be one state but "two nations" — the privileged and those society has written off?

243

HOMELESS WOMAN LIVING IN A CAR

Anonymous

> *The Diane who speaks to you in the following article is the pseudonym (an assumed name) of a woman from Orange County in California, who wrote her story for the* Los Angeles Times. *Although she joined the ranks of the homeless, she is not mentally ill. She is not an addict. She is holding on to a job, but like many jobs in today's America, it doesn't pay enough for a deposit on a place to live. As she says, "I was one of you." She gave up good earnings and a middle-class lifestyle when catastrophic illness struck her family. She is not without relatives — she lived with a son in Tennessee for a time.*

Thought Starters: What is it like to be homeless? Are you one of the "prosperous-looking people" who, Diane says, watch her with suspicion?

I need anonymity, so call me Diane.   1

I try not to be seen as I watch you prosperous-looking people walking from your cars to your offices. If you saw me, your faces would mirror your suspicion and disapproval.

Yet I was one of you. And at least some of you are dancing on the same tightrope over the same abyss into which I have fallen.

None of you know I am here in the car just a few feet away from you — or what it is like once you get here. I can tell you, courtesy of a typewriter for which no one would pay me five desperately needed dollars.

Last night my money added up to $38.67, so I found a cheaper motel.   5
But tonight I will start sleeping in my car. I must eat on $6.23 for the next 10 days. Then there will be a paycheck — enough to keep me in a motel again for about a week. After that, it will be back to the car until the next payday.

Yes, I work for a living, but this job may end soon. And since the pay isn't enough for a deposit on an apartment or even a room, it would be hard to mourn its loss. Except that I have no money, no home, no evident prospects.

My downward spiral from a middle-class Orange County lifestyle began a few years ago. I was divorced and in my 50s, earning $40,000 a year as an editor, when my mother died of cancer. As the only child, I was left to care for an aged father advancing steadily into the dementia of Alzheimer's.

I quit my job, moved to his apartment in Florida and cared for him for two years. We survived on my savings and his annuity. And in 1989 he died, leaving me broke and drained of self-confidence and the ability to concentrate.

News reports told of high unemployment among "older workers," meaning anyone over 40. I was 57. Where did I fit in?

I didn't.   10

Now I drive through the streets of Newport Beach looking for a place to spend the night.

There seems something wrong with each street-side parking space. Here is a house whose windows look directly into my car. Here a space is too near an intersection with heavy traffic. To remain anywhere, I must remain invisible. Yet the one quiet area is also isolated. There is danger in isolation.

Finally, I drive slowly past the Sheraton hotel, with its many parked cars and empty parking spaces. It seems so civilized. I used to come here for business lunches when I worked across the street. Aware of the irony, I check into a space facing the street.

The back seat of my 5-year-old Oldsmobile is too short for sleeping, but the front seats recline. My legs dangle toward the brake and accelerator, yet it seems comfortable enough to think of getting some sleep.

I drop my seat back, but tense whenever footsteps approach. I dread   15
waking to find someone staring at me, so a large, black, cotton knit jacket I place over my head makes me feel nicely invisible. If I were dressed entirely in black, I'd be even less visible. From now on I shall prepare for the night like a cat burglar.

I sleep soundly for two hours, then fitfully for the next hour and a half. To avoid discovery, I must leave before daylight.

This is the first night of what will become four months of living out of my car — long hours of solitude, physical discomfort, boredom and sometimes hunger.

But it will teach me much about myself — and that line beyond which lies permanent hopelessness.

When I awaken, the night sky is beginning to pale. I drive toward McDonald's and sit impatiently in a parking lot for its 6 o'clock opening. I can wait for coffee, but I need the restroom. I take my dish-washing detergent along and manage a passable sponge bath.

After one of the most boring days and nights of my life, I wake up   20
the next morning and drive to Ralph's and spend 69 cents of my remaining $2.56 for a can of tuna. Carrying my tuna back to the car, I find a wallet full of cash and credit cards in the parking lot. I take it to the market manager. As I walk back to my car, I wonder: How hungry or desperate would I have to be to have kept that wallet? I don't know, but I'm not there now and I'm thankful.

I awaken the next morning at 4:30 after sleeping almost five hours.

This is a go-to-work day for me. I work a 40-hour week in four days. But while most people yearn for quitting time, I now look forward to the hours in the office, that place of blissful luxury.

It has hot water, coffee, tea, drinking water, a newspaper, a restroom, my own chair and a place to leave the car. I hope I will be alert enough to do a good day's work.

I manage to perform well. Only in the warm, airless afternoon do I suddenly drop off over my papers and yank instantly awake. I pull through the fog, pour more coffee and focus on my work. The irony is I work for a firm that publishes books advertising apartment rentals and their vast array of comforts and amenities.

Back in my car, one night late, I awaken abruptly. I hear the sound   25
of a key being slowly worked into my door lock and turned, just inches from my ear. My scalp tingles. The key does not work and is slowly withdrawn. I listen warily. I can lunge for the horn if need be. That could bring someone out of the hotel — and probably end my tenancy at the Sheraton. I wait, unmoving and unseeing under my nighttime shroud.

In a few minutes, I hear a key working the lock of a nearby car door or trunk. It opens and soon closes softly. Then it is quiet. I lie awake, adrenaline rushing, and finally sleep fitfully. This is a cold wash of reality: I am no more immune from danger than anyone else.

This payday has loomed larger in my mind with each passing day. I feel increasing urgency to buy some fresh food, to have a bed to sleep in for a few nights, to soak in a tub. Such expectation allowed me very little sleep last night.

But the paychecks from out of state are delayed; they won't be here until tomorrow.

Tonight I eat my last saved slice of bread and margarine. And, with a wary eye on the gas tank, which reads empty, I drive to the Sheraton yet again.

The paychecks arrive. I check into a motel and almost instantly fall   30
asleep, unable to enjoy the luxury of tub and television until tomorrow.

I wish I had discovered earlier how much money can be saved by sleeping in the car. It's the only way I know now to save enough to rent a room near my office. Allowing for a night at a motel once a week to catch up on sleep, for laundry and for general self-repair, it will probably take two months or so to save up.

But will I be able to keep up the rent?

When I returned to California from Florida, I finally landed a low-paying but full-time job and was promised rapid advancement. Now I find that the promises are not going to be kept by the corporation that bought this company.

I decide to take a stand: Live up to the promises the company made me or I quit. They praise me but won't budge. I quit, and they look surprised. It was hardly noble or heroic. When you are already living out of your car, it is easier to give up a job. If you have a home, you can imagine losing it.

The downward spiral continues in earnest. The auto life had a   35
rhythm based on paydays. But now there are no more paychecks to come.

My son, who lives in Tennessee, is suspicious. He's been aware that I'm having money problems, but my lack of a permanent phone number and address prompts him to ask me outright if I'm sleeping in my car. I've tried carefully to keep this from him. I don't want to burden him and his family with my financial problems. So when he asks, I laugh it off.

The gas tank is precariously low. I start walking almost everywhere.

It's harder to look for a new job. Without motel room telephones and the workplace, there is no way to leave call-back numbers when respond-ing to ads. I can walk major distances, but it means arriving hot, sweaty and too tired to impress anybody.

I walk as much as 25 miles a day. Now, after seven days of exceptional walking, my left knee is stunningly painful, and the right knee echoes the pain. There are other unfamiliar pains running down the front of my legs. But if I don't start walking, I won't get a gallon of gas into the car and I won't get any food.

So I grit my teeth and walk, overriding the pain with necessity. For 40 the next three days, I continue to walk many miles. The pain fills every part of my brain.

Now I am hobbling, so crippled that I can hardly get in and out of the car. One day of rest makes no improvement, nor do two, nor three. Movement is excruciating.

I have come to a critical time. My days have become a self-defeating spiral of non-accomplishment. Everything I do now is devoted to simple survival. If I don't do something to halt it, I could be on my way into a rougher homelessness. But what can I do?

The Responsive Reader

1. Are you one of those who, in the words of Diane, "are dancing on the same tightrope over the same abyss into which I have fallen"?
2. Does this article change your thinking about the causes of home-lessness?
3. Many people block out unpleasant realities. How real does Diane make the problems, deprivations, and dangers of homelessness to you? Can you imagine yourself in her place?

Talking, Listening, Writing

4. How would you answer Diane's final question: "What can I do?"
5. Do you know anyone who is homeless, has no "permanent address," or lives out of a truck or car?

Projects

6. How do people in our society come to terms with the growing number of homeless in our midst? How do they explain, deplore, or rationalize what is happening? Have you and fellow students seen

the issue taken up in editorials, newspaper columns, letters to the editor, call-ins to talk shows, speeches by politicians, sermons? Can you and your classmates reach any general conclusions about the state of public opinion on this subject?

MY DAILY DIVES IN THE DUMPSTER
Lars Eighner

The author of the following article in Harper's Magazine *is a scavenger. He is thus a member of one of the world's oldest professions, which has made a spectacular comeback in our modern world. Like archeologists who reconstruct the lifestyle of whole societies from the refuse they left behind, the author analyzes and philosophizes about what we throw out.*

Thought Starters: Do you think this writer is serious? What insights, if any, do you glean concerning our "throw-it-away" society? What do you make of the "lessons" the writer learned from the study of garbage?

Eating from Dumpsters is the thing that separates the dilettanti from the professionals. Eating safely involves three principles: using the senses and common sense to evaluate the condition of the found materials; knowing the Dumpsters of a given area and checking them regularly; and seeking always to answer the question, Why was this discarded?

Perhaps everyone who has a kitchen and a regular supply of groceries has, at one time or another, eaten half a sandwich before discovering mold on the bread, or has gotten a mouthful of milk before realizing the milk had turned. Nothing of the sort is likely to happen to a Dumpster diver because he is constantly reminded that most food is discarded for a reason.

Yet perfectly good food can be found in Dumpsters. Canned goods, for example, turn up fairly often in the Dumpsters I frequent. All except the most phobic people would be willing to eat from a can even if it came from a Dumpster. I have few qualms about dry foods such as crackers, cookies, cereal, chips, and pasta if they are free of visible contaminates and still dry and crisp. Raw fruits and vegetables with intact skins seem perfectly safe to me, excluding, of course, the obviously rotten. Many are discarded for minor imperfections that can be pared away. Chocolate is often discarded only because it has become discolored as the cocoa butter de-emulsified.

I began scavenging by pulling pizzas out of the Dumpster behind a pizza delivery shop. In general, prepared food requires caution, but in this case I knew what time the shop closed and went to the Dumpster as soon as the last of the help left.

Because the workers at these places are usually inexperienced, pizzas are often made with the wrong topping, baked incorrectly, or refused on delivery for being cold. The products to be discarded are boxed up because inventory is kept by counting boxes: A boxed pizza can be written off; an unboxed pizza does not exist. So I had a steady supply of fresh, sometimes warm pizza.

The area I frequent is inhabited by many affluent college students. I am not here by chance; the Dumpsters are very rich. Students throw out many good things, including food, particularly at the end of the semester and before and after breaks. I find it advantageous to keep an eye on the academic calendar.

A typical discard is a half jar of peanut butter — though non-organic peanut butter does not require refrigeration and is unlikely to spoil in any reasonable time. Occasionally I find a cheese with a spot of mold, which, of course, I just pare off, and because it is obvious why the cheese was discarded, I treat it with less suspicion than an apparently perfect cheese found in similar circumstances. One of my favorite finds is yogurt — often discarded, still sealed, when the expiration date has passed — because it will keep for several days, even in warm weather.

I avoid ethnic foods I am unfamiliar with. If I do not know what it is supposed to look or smell like when it is good, I cannot be certain I will be able to tell if it is bad.

No matter how careful I am I still get dysentery at least once a month, oftener in warm weather. I do not want to paint too romantic a picture. Dumpster diving has serious drawbacks as a way of life.

Though I have a proprietary feeling about my Dumpsters, I don't   10
mind my direct competitors, other scavengers, as much as I hate the soda-can scroungers.

I have tried scrounging aluminum cans with an able-bodied com-panion, and afoot we could make no more than a few dollars a day. I can extract the necessities of life from the Dumpsters directly with far less effort than would be required to accumulate the equivalent value in alu-minum. Can scroungers, then, are people who *must* have small amounts of cash — mostly drug addicts and winos.

I do not begrudge them the cans, but can scroungers tend to tear up the Dumpsters, littering the area and mixing the contents. There are precious few courtesies among scavengers, but it is a common practice to set aside surplus items: pairs of shoes, clothing, canned goods, and such. A true scavenger hates to see good stuff go to waste, and what he cannot use he leaves in good condition in plain sight. Can scroungers lay waste to everything in their path and will stir one of a pair of good shoes to the bottom of a Dumpster to be lost or ruined in the muck. They become so specialized that they can see only cans and earn my contempt by passing up change, canned goods, and readily hockable items.

Can scroungers will even go through individual garbage cans, some-thing I have never seen a scavenger do. Going through individual garbage cans without spreading litter is almost impossible, and litter is likely to reduce the public's tolerance of scavenging. But my strongest reservation about going through individual garbage cans is that this seems to me a very personal kind of invasion, one to which I would object if I were a homeowner.

Though Dumpsters seem somehow less personal than garbage cans, they still contain bank statements, bills, correspondence, pill bottles, and other sensitive information. I avoid trying to draw conclusions about the people who dump in the Dumpsters I frequent. I think it would be unethical to do so, although I know many people will find the idea of scavenger ethics too funny for words.

Occasionally a find tells a story. I once found a small paper bag   *15* containing some unused condoms, several partial tubes of flavored sexual lubricant, a partially used compact of birth control pills, and the torn pieces of a picture of a young man. Clearly, the woman was through with him and planning to give up sex altogether.

Dumpster things are often sad — abandoned teddy bears, shredded wedding albums, despaired-of sales kits. I find diaries and journals. College students also discard their papers; I am horrified to discover the kind of paper that now merits an A in an undergraduate course.

Dumpster diving is outdoor work, often surprisingly pleasant. It is not entirely predictable; things of interest turn up every day, and some days there are finds of great value. I am always very pleased when I can turn up exactly the thing I most wanted to find. Yet in spite of the element of chance, scavenging, more than most other pursuits, tends to yield returns in some proportion to the effort and intelligence brought to bear.

I think of scavenging as a modern form of self-reliance. After ten years of government service, where everything is geared to the lowest common denominator, I find work that rewards initiative and effort refreshing. Certainly I would be happy to have a sinecure again, but I am not heartbroken to be without one.

I find from the experience of scavenging two rather deep lessons. The first is to take what I can use and let the rest go. I have come to think that there is no value in the abstract. A thing I cannot use or make useful, perhaps by trading, has no value, however fine or rare it may be. (I mean useful in the broad sense — some art, for example, I would think valuable.)

The second lesson is the transience of material being. I do not sup-   *20* pose that ideas are immortal, but certainly they are longer-lived than material objects.

The things I find in Dumpsters, the love letters and rag dolls of so many lives, remind me of this lesson. Many times in my travels I have lost everything but the clothes on my back. Now I hardly pick up a thing without envisioning the time I will cast it away. This, I think, is a healthy state of mind. Almost everything I have now has already been cast out at least once, proving that what I own is valueless to someone.

I find that my desire to grab for the gaudy bauble has been largely sated. I think this is an attitude I share with the very wealthy — we both know there is plenty more where whatever we have came from. Between

It isn't a reassuring line of thought. But I also understand that while living in a crowded cage awash in a sea of noise, I must acquire a caged mentality or I won't survive.

The two most devastating aspects of modern prisons are noise and overcrowding. Prisons are noisy places anyway, but when they become overcrowded, as most are now, the noise becomes unbearable, and there's no escape from it.

The din of an overcrowded prison puts a heavy burden of stress on us all. We become, among other things, tense, irritable, introverted, bitter, paranoid and violent.

A study of overcrowding done on a colony of laboratory mice back in the '50s uncovered many types of abnormal behavior. Cannibalism, self-mutilation, aggressive behavior (to the point of attacking any moving object), sexual ambiguity, introversion and homosexual behavior. Those characteristics were brought about by overcrowding, not by deprivation of food or other necessities. In our prisons, overcrowding results from legislative changes, and the effects on individuals can be painful to behold.

A 20-year-old man came here recently from the East Coast. He was 10 sentenced to 15 years with no possibility of parole under the new federal sentencing code. He was convicted of bank robbery, and it's his first trip to prison. The new sentencing code allows very little credit for good time, and he will have to serve about 13 years before his release.

Not long after he arrived here, he was placed in isolation by mistake when the authorities confused his name with that of a notorious stool pigeon. Soon after that incident, he was assigned a cell with a weightlifter twice his size who tried to force him into a homosexual act, then beat him within an inch of his life when he refused.

He approached a guard with one eye swollen shut, and through mangled, swollen lips, he mumbled that he'd like a cell change.

"There's no room," the guard replied. "You'll have to stay where you were assigned."

He then violated another rule so that he could be put back in isolation in order to get a cell change and a new cell partner.

"I never thought prison was this bad," he told me in the yard when 15 he was released from isolation.

I assured him that this prison is not as bad as maximum-security prisons like Leavenworth and Lompoc. He didn't seem to take much consolation from that fact.

Stories like that young man's will become more common as bewildered newcomers and cage-wise cons are pressed ever tighter because of tough new sentencing laws.

The small cell block I live in was designed for 60 men in single cells. There are more than 120 of us in here now, with all the cells doubled up.

We don't choose our cell partners. When a bunk becomes vacant, another convict is moved in.

When you live in a small cell with another convict, his presence is always there, whether you're using the toilet, writing a letter or reading a book. It's a much closer relationship than a marriage. But it's between two people who usually don't want to live with each other.

Outside the cell, the lines and lists go on forever. We stand in a long *20* line three times a day in order to eat. At the prison store, we wait in a raucous crowd until our name is called. We stand in line to be strip-searched before visits with people on the outside, then stand in line to be strip-searched after the visit. We line up at the laundry and line up to sign up for a phone call.

Anyone who wants to work in hobbycraft finds there's a three- or four-month waiting list for a hobby card. When the prison is over-crowded, all the lines and lists are longer.

I've seen convicts go crazy while standing in line; they begin hitting and kicking everyone they can reach. For someone with an aversion to lines, this aspect of prison is hell on Earth.

Many prisoners in this pressure-cooker environment develop anti-social coping mechanisms.

When people tour a prison, they see convicts nonchalantly making their way to jobs, or standing patiently in chow lines waiting to eat. In the cell blocks, they see us playing pinochle or lying in a cell reading a book. They go away thinking that we live a calm existence.

But the real world of convicts lies hidden from the view of a tourist. *25* These crowds of seemingly uniform prisoners are banded together in groups that work against the laws of the prison system itself.

Some convicts like to drink, and four or five of them will get together and make wine regularly. Others gamble and run betting pools. Stolen food and government merchandise are bought and sold. Drug users band together in schemes to obtain their drug of choice.

The guards don't see much more of our real world than the tourists, unless they happen to stumble upon someone using drugs or gambling.

We've developed codes and signals to protect our world. I can look at a convict across the building from me and put my right index finger under my eye, and he will nod his head and remain standing where he is while I go back into my cell.

I've just told him to watch for the guard, and he will stand there and watch until I come out and signal him that I'm finished with whatever I'm doing. A convict will do that for someone he doesn't even know, and we all know the signal. It's only one of many we use to communicate in our own world.

By nurturing our hidden life and being loyal to it, we find some relief *30* from the crowds and the noise. Even if it's only a drunk, a high or an exciting wager, it helps. The best of it all is that it's hidden from view and belongs to us alone.

Naturally, some of this goes on all the time in all prisons, but over-crowding encourages the climate of lawlessness; it spurs us to develop our subterranean activities.

When a 60-man cell block is made into a 120-man cell block, there is still only one guard. His job becomes twice as hard, even as the extra convicts help to develop more schemes.

The overcrowding pushes us further toward introversion, secretive-ness, clique mentality, violence and deceit. Those aren't the traits society wants to foster in a man headed back to the "free world" some day.

The new federal sentencing law, approved by the Supreme Court early this year, is adding another dimension of madness in already over-crowded prisons. Because of the "get-tough" legislation, judges will no longer have much of a say in sentencing. Whatever the circumstances of the crime, the sentence is definite and final. Parole is abolished. The basic unfairness of those harsh new sentences is hard to believe.

Every week, people are coming in here with 25- and 30-year sen-   35
tences with no chance of parole. Many of them are as young as 19 and 20. They are more abusive toward guards and violent toward fellow convicts. They don't have anything to lose. The courts have tattooed the term "criminal" on the foreheads of young men who might still have had a chance to take other routes.

Recently, at a 4 p.m. standing count here, a guard walked by a convict's cell and told him to stand up.

"F--- you!" was the reply.

The guard asked him again to stand up.

"I said f--- you!" the man replied and remained sitting down.

After the count, some guards came and led him off to isolation. A   40
few days later, when he was released from the hole, I asked him why he had done that.

"I have a 10-year sentence with no parole," he told me. "I only get one year good time, so I have to do nine years if I'm a good boy. Well, I'd rather lose that year of good time right now and do 10 years my way than nine their way. I'll stand up when I feel like it, and I meant exactly what I said: F--- him!"

Older convicts are in a state of shock right now because of the heavy impact on them of the new sentencing law. A 45-year-old man whom I've known for years just received a 30-year sentence for possession of a gun. His prior crimes were two second-degree burglaries and an assault that didn't involve a weapon. He will have to serve 25 years in prison before he's eligible to be released.

"I can't believe this," he says. "People don't do this much time for murder. If I do survive this sentence, I will be 70 years old when I get out."

"What if you do live through it?" I asked him. "What will you do at that age when you are released?"

"Man, if I have to do all that time and finally get back out, the only   45
thing I'll want to know is if that judge and that prosecutor are still alive,"
he replied.

A man here from Seattle pleaded guilty to a conspiracy to sell cocaine. It was a plea bargain, and he received 20 years, of which he will have to serve 18 years in prison. He is 47 years old.

I told him I couldn't understand how someone could plead guilty in exchange for 18 years in prison. I would take my chances in court.

"They held back another charge," he said. "If I refused the plea bargain, they were going to add that charge as well and give me 30 years."

Members of gangs from the inner cities are already arriving here in large numbers. Most of them were sentenced to long, nonparolable terms under the new sentencing guidelines. These are kids who grew up in ghettos bumming quarters to play Pac Man machines.

They've heard the slogans "War on Drugs" and "War on Crime"   50
used so often that now they believe it. When people go down on their turf, they are war casualties to them, not victims.

They wear their gang colors in prison yards now, and their young eyes burn with an old, hard look of having nothing much more to lose. It's as if they are saying:

"Well, you got tough on us. Now what?"

Not long ago at Phoenix, the isolation building became so full that convicts had to be put on a waiting list to go to the hole. Often, when a man finishes his isolation time, he has to languish in there another two weeks until a mainline cell comes open.

I sometimes wonder what happened to those deranged mice when the overcrowding study was completed. I doubt they were turned loose to roam in an innocent colony of field mice.

But most of these convicts with unnaturally long sentences will   55
survive and eventually be released. After 15 or 20 years in a noisy, violent, overcrowded prison, some of them are going to make Freddy Kreuger look like an Eagle Scout.

The Responsive Reader

1. Martin tells the stories of several of his fellow convicts. What is most thought-provoking or most real for you in these accounts? (Why does he start with the story of the stabbing? What do you learn from his capsule portrait of the twenty-year-old bank robber early in the article? Is there a common thread in the stories of convicts sentenced according to new "get-tough" sentencing laws?)
2. How does Martin take you into the hidden world of prison life?

What are some of the things that make his article truly an "inside story"?

3. Early in the article, Martin mentions the study of the laboratory mice, and he circles back to it at the end. What is the role of the mice in his article?

4. After pondering Martin's testimony, what conclusions do you draw about the way our society treats criminals? Is there a need for change?

Talking, Listening, Writing

5. If you were the judge in Martin's lawsuit, would you rule in favor of his First Amendment rights? Or would you agree with prison officials that convicts give up certain basic rights?

6. Do you believe in getting tough with criminals? Or do you believe in giving them a second chance? What has shaped your thinking on this central issue?

7. Imagine yourself as a convict in Martin's prison. Write an "A Day in the Life of Prisoner X" eyewitness account.

Projects

8. Have the justice system and prison officials given up on the idea of rehabilitation? If you can, raise the issue with people concerned with law enforcement whom you can reach on your campus or in your community.

ADDICT IS FINALLY A STAR AT HIS OWN FUNERAL

Herbert Gold

Novelist Herbert Gold is the author of books like The Age of Happy Problems *and, most recently,* Diane. *He has long been an observer of the passing scene, with a special sympathy for dropouts, dissenters, and people who exist on the margins of our go-getter society. He has a special gift for getting inside the heads of people whom we more often watch from the outside with suspicion and disapproval. In the following article, he reports on the losing battle of one of them with the drugs that were his demons.*

Thought Starters: Are you tired of the subject of drug addiction? Are you ready to turn your back on the issue and the people involved?

Gathered at the Swedenborgian Church in Pacific Heights, an intimate house of worship with its old wood and warm light, the mourners stood and listened uneasily. The church manages to combine something Scandinavian and something Californian. On this occasion it wasn't right for distant acquaintances to say, "Glad to see you again."

After an appointed leader made his little speech, sympathy to the wife and son — "I didn't know him personally, but now I know he has gone to find peace at last" — a few friends, who knew him personally, spoke up for Freddy. A fellow painter said, "I'll bet he's happy today. He always wanted to show in a nice place like this."

He died on the day I received a postcard from him, asking me to come to a South of Market gallery opening for a show of his paintings. He was an addict, supposedly clean now, but in recent months his friends had become suspicious of his behavior. He was quarreling with his family, complaining of illnesses requiring cough syrup, letting his life get away from him.

People accused him of using again. He denied it with all the fervor of a man wronged by those who loved him. There was a little-boy tone of injured pride in the denials. "Don't you trust me? Don't you trust me?"

"No," said his best friend, "I don't trust you anymore, Freddy."

Freddy fought back against himself and his past. He wanted to survive, he had a wife and son in San Francisco, he had other children back in the East Village, but if any normal trouble came his way — a fight with his wife, a suspicion that he wasn't Van Gogh or Jackson Pollock, or just the usual blahs and boredom or the kind of beat-up feeling a person can get—he looked for rapid relief. Cocaine spelled relief. Heroin spelled relief. Even alcohol would do in a pinch. But what he preferred was speed, to get up. He liked downers to sleep. He liked hallucinogens to give him his very own head movie.

When his friends yelled, "Freddy, you're doing it again," he got indignant.

"I have a cold, that's all."

"You have a craziness, Freddy. You're a s—-head."

He looked pained. "We call it angst now," he said. "And these days *10* I'm an artist."

There was no meanness in him. He looked on life as an unsolvable puzzle at his expense, but the way out of the puzzle involved chemical dreams. Other people make do with love, family, work, plans, ambitions. His soul was deceived by quicker solutions.

"Freddy, you're blowing it. You're going to blow it."

Some addicts are saved. Addiction is an aspect of the psychopathic personality. The addict uses energy, charm, even intelligence to quell the normal notions of how to deal with our time on Earth. He's found a way to end boredom. But it's an exhausting career to be continually in search of the next fix. When I used to ask William Burroughs why he was an addict, he'd say: "Gives me something to do."

The addict is never bored. He's always got an important task. He's moving on up to the next connection. Which suggests an element of bleak hope. If the psychopath survives into his 40s, he sometimes burns out that cool and self-serving despair. He learns to care for others, or he may. He learns to care for himself, or he may. The education can take place earlier, too, of course, in such tough-love family structures as Delancey Street.

Freddy was giving it a try. He married again, he had a child again, *15* he had other hopes. He thought he might be a painter, and he was working at it. When he quarrelled with his wife or the kid was a bother, he found himself tempted. When he didn't become a star right away, he was tempted. Sometimes he seemed to lapse into lethargic undersea motions, swimming in a place with no known shore.

In dreams, every adolescent is a star. With drugs, a grown man can rediscover this dream stardom. When a person nods out, it's not mere oblivion he sees. But that's usually what he finds.

Freddy found the final oblivion.

The bringing together of family and friends is essential in putting matters to a close. We might think we can mourn alone, but we can't even remember the dead properly without help. We can suffer alone, but we need to express and fulfill the suffering.

Once, when a friend died far away, I couldn't go to the funeral. On that day, distracted and sad in San Francisco, I called another friend of his whom I seldom saw. We didn't care for each other, but we decided to meet at Ocean Beach and talk about our buddy. For an afternoon we were friends, too. We portioned our griefs out into little anecdotes, memories, praisings. We sat over a mug of coffee in a fogged-in sandwich joint. We remembered why we liked our pal in New York and had no need to discuss why we didn't like each other. On that day we were grateful to find another who remembered.

Now, when we meet in North Beach, we hardly speak, but there is   *20* a shrug of mutuality. We shared something once.

As a child, I thought the institutions adults inflicted on us were all for the birds. I've learned by now how much church, temple and synagogue matter to me, and therefore can respect their mattering to others. Rituals are a form of communication; they do the work of poetry for groups.

Freddy's funeral at the Swedenborgian Church helped to send him on his way out of our lives and also to keep him there forever, as part of the archipelago of islands entire of themselves.

Later, back at the widow's house on Potrero Hill, their son, aged 11, kept passing plates of goodies to the mourners. Grinning through a mouth filled with cookies, he said, "Have some more. Dad would want you to have more."

The Responsive Reader

1. What is Gold's thinking about the psychology of addiction? How does he explain to himself and his readers the nature of Freddy's problem?
2. Does Freddy seem to you a special case or a typical case?
3. What does Gold say he learned about rituals of mourning?

Talking, Listening, Writing

4. Many observers in our society have become defeatist or disillusioned on the subject of drugs. They have more or less given up hope for a solution for the individual or society. Is Gold defeatist on this subject? Are you?
5. Some argue that the use of drugs by the younger generation is no different from the use of alcohol by the older generation. Do you agree or disagree? What arguments or evidence can you present to support your case?
6. Can you tell the story of an addict or alcoholic the way Gold did in his article?

Projects

7. Some of what we know about drug abuse may be the result of personal experience or observation. However, much of our thinking

is influenced by newspaper stories, media hype, or exploitation of the issue by interested parties. What attitudes, perspectives, or stereotypes predominate in current media treatment of the subject? You may want to farm out investigation of different areas of media coverage to individual members of a group or to different groups. Can you and your fellow students agree on some general conclusions?

MEMORIES OF FRANK

Mary Kay Blakely

Mary Kay Blakely is a free-lance writer whose work has appeared in many magazines and in the "Hers" column in the New York Times. *The following article from* Psychology Today *was adapted from her book* Wake Me When It's Over *(1989). Blakely here tells the story of her brother's descent into the hell of mental illness, a topic that in our society remains shrouded in superstition and prejudice. Patients and their families carry on an often desperate struggle against ignorance, the threat of indeterminate confinement or disabling "cures," legal obstacles to promising drugs or treatments, brutal side effects of medications, cutbacks in public health care, and the constant psychological and financial drain of catastrophic illness.*

Thought Starters: Relatives of people with apparently unsurmountable problems are sometimes told to "let go" and go on with their own lives. Would you have given this advice to the woman writing about her brother in this article?

Francis Jude, my eldest brother, was brilliant and witty, the leading   1
madman of my four eccentric siblings, and I miss him enormously. During his brief adult life, he suffered altogether eight nervous breakdowns, serving as many sentences — voluntary and not — in Chicago institutions. Whether his wild imagination caused the stunning chemical changes in his body or the other way around, he surged with inhuman energy during his manic periods, then was flattened for months with tremendous exhaustion. He committed suicide on Nov. 12, 1981.

His doctors diagnosed him as manic depressive, but Frank thought of his illness as a spiritual fever. After his boyhood years as a Catholic seminarian, followed by an earnest search for God in the writings of Buddhist monks, Jewish rabbis, Protestant pastors and, finally, Unitarian ministers, he'd formed a nonsectarian but wholly religious view of events. "We are all like bacteria in a banana," he once wrote after a manic episode, "each doing our own little thing, while the fruit is ripened for God's digestion." It was not unusual for Frank to see signs of God in a bunch of bananas — he saw God everywhere. At times he thought he was God himself, infused with a euphoric rhythm inside his head he called "the beat, the beat, the beat."

Normally reserved and shy, he was charismatic and demonstrative when he was high. Frank ran for governor of Illinois once, on orders from above. He broke through security at *The Chicago Sun Times*, where he brought columnist Mike Royko the good news that he was destined to become Frank's campaign manager. Royko called my parents, and Frank spent the rest of his campaign at the Reed Mental Health Center. The incident did prompt Royko to write a column about Frank, not endorsing his gubernatorial race, but pointing out the faulty security systems at hospitals and newspapers that allowed lunatics to roam freely about the city of Chicago.

Although I am an avowed agnostic myself, I thought Frank's spiritual diagnosis was as credible as anything else. Nevertheless, I felt obliged to argue with him. During his first breakdown in 1967, when he was wired with electrodes and given shock treatments at Loretto Hospital in Chicago, he reported that he'd received messages directly from God himself. The truth arrived in tremendous jolts, he said, just as he expected it would some day. I tried to help him unscramble his brain, pointing out the difference between electricity and divinity. It was machinery, not God, that sent the sizzling jolts through his mind, I explained.

"Truth doesn't fry your brain," I tried pointing out.   5

"Sometimes it *does*," he replied, wide-eyed, as surprised to report this revelation as I was to hear it. A look of sheer lucidity crossed his face, followed by sudden surprise and then vast confusion. It was a silent movie of the chaos inside his head—I could actually *watch* Frank losing his innocence. He shed a great quantity of that innocence in the shock-treatment room at Loretto Hospital, being electrified by truth.

The treatments halted his illness only temporarily. During subsequent breakdowns, he was studied and probed, tested and drugged, interviewed and examined by some of the most famous psychiatrists in Chicago, but no one could cure him. Attempts to stabilize his moods with lithium carbonate failed repeatedly, puzzling his physicians. Frank himself was amazed by the constant motion inside his mind. He said it felt like his head had been clapped between two powerful hands and was orbiting around a spinning discus thrower warming up for a mighty heave. He was anxious for the final thrust, releasing him from the dizzying spins into free flight.

I was one of Frank's main companions throughout his bouts of madness, when his mind rolled out to the ends of human passion. He would hear and see things I couldn't understand, and I spent countless hours arguing with him inside the wards of insane asylums. In polite company, they're referred to as mental health centers, but in the ravaged minds of the inmates, politeness was the first thing to go.

Spending time with Frank and his mad peers was disturbing, because they made the line between sanity and insanity become so murky. After an afternoon arguing with lunatics who spoke truth bluntly, I would go home and watch the evening news, where the president of the most powerful country in the world was declaring war on the tiny island of Grenada. Nobody suggested locking him up. It worried me that mental patients made perfect sense and the president of the United States seemed like a candidate for the Reed Mental Health Center.

Frank would come back from his journeys into madness radically   *10*
altered by what he had seen, and I understand now how much I relied on
his expeditions. I was too much of a coward to let my own mind roll out
full length, having witnessed the devastating price he paid.

His manic bouts were followed by long depressions, as he struggled
to apply his dreams to ordinary life. The messages he believed so ardently
during his seizures would melt into doubt, and he felt his otherness with
an excruciating loneliness. Paralyzed with indecision and fear, he would
sleep through those months, sometimes for 20 hours at a time. The fantastic energy abandoned him, and he lifted his thin body out of bed as if it
weighed 500 pounds. He described these terrible confrontations with his
conscience as "*grand mal* seizures of despair." They were a regular stop on
the circular course of his spiritual fevers.

In the spring of 1970, Frank was interned at the Illinois State Psychiatric Institute (ISPI) — it was his fourth breakdown, the most reckless one
so far. It was our mother, Kay, who arranged to get him into ISPI after
reading a newspaper report about two psychiatrists from the University
of Chicago who ran the experimental program. While it was still widely
believed among psychiatrists then that bad mothering caused most mental
problems, Dr. Herbert Y. Meltzer and Dr. Ronald Moline were among
the pioneers who explored manic depression as a result of a chemical
imbalance.

Their early experiments turned up evidence of faulty genetic wiring,
suggesting that biology, not socialization, triggered the disease. They'd
identified a muscle enzyme that seemed to play a role in manic depression,
and had been given the 9th floor of ISPI to test their hypothesis. When
Kay recognized her son's symptoms in the report — the stunning physical
changes Frank underwent during his breakdowns — she scheduled an
appointment.

To be admitted to the program, Frank had to submit to a muscle
biopsy on his left calf. Kay and I, as part of the "control group," reported
to the 9th floor one afternoon to surrender blood and urine samples, ride
exercise bikes for five miles, then surrender more samples.

"I'm not sure I belong in anyone's control group," I said to Kay   *15*
somewhere during our third stationary mile. I felt so closely related to
Frank, I suspected I bordered on manic depression myself. Every one of
my siblings lived with this fear. It seemed crazy, trying to retrieve him
from the seduction of his madness by pedaling hard for five nonlocomo-
tive miles. Maybe we were the lunatics — I mentioned this possibility to
Kay. She smiled, but didn't encourage a further critique of our going-
nowhere ride that afternoon.

Whenever my mother's pale-blue Irish eyes would darken, reflecting
her ardor for some imagined improvement in her children — whether it
was a cleaner room or better grades or another home permanent despite
former disasters — none of us was fool enough to try to dissuade her. She

was not a woman who gave up easily, and when madness claimed her eldest, most intelligent, most sensitive son, her eyes took on the deepest blue I'd seen so far. Her smile ruefully acknowledged the absurdity of our circumstances, but her eyes, those two Celtic oracles of unswerving faith, directed me to keep pedaling even harder.

Because the doctors were committed to a theory involving enzymes and brain cells, they couldn't have been counting heavily on answers from psychoanalysis. But because a cure was still unavailable through medicine, the ISPI program included weekly doses of psychotherapy.

I hated the Thursday night sessions, when the patients and their families were collectively grilled under the harsh fluorescent lights of the locked ward. Maybe somewhere in the pasts of these humbled people there were cases of bad mothering or absent fathering or emotional neglect — what family surviving the '50s was exempt? — but I couldn't believe these human errors brought the physical changes in Frank. I knew an unhappy childhood was not the problem. If anything, my parents' unstoppable affection had postponed Frank's crisis. He didn't have his first breakdown under their roof — it happened 240 miles away, at Southern Illinois University the year he left home.

Each week Kay, my father Jerry, my brother Paul and I joined the other families with members impounded on ISPI's 9th floor for a rigorous interrogation of our pasts. My parents exempted Kevin and Gina, the two youngest siblings, in an effort to spare them a direct confrontation with the terrifying look of mental illness, even though they had witnessed Frank's bizarre behavior. Whether obligation or tradition or just plain helplessness prompted this futile treatment, the sessions were unproductive if not outright harmful. One week, Jerry was questioned about his habit of shaking hands with his adult sons, replacing the childhood hugs. The therapist on duty that night suggested our father's formal handshakes had deprived Frank of his affectionate due. This was ridiculous, Paul and I knew.

While my father tried to practice the emotional reserve required of his generation of men, the disguise never completely covered him. I remembered a Saturday morning in June when Jerry paced back and forth across the living-room carpet in his tuxedo, anxiously rehearsing his immediate duties concerning the bride. The task of giving me away clashed with 22 years of loving me, and he was unable to form a single word when I emerged in my wedding dress. Instead, his eyes filled up and his face became bright red, then his smile finally appeared like a period at the end of a long, emotional speech. 20

I'd seen that expression repeatedly at baptisms and confirmations, basketball games and high-school plays. It was embarrassing to sit next to Jerry when one of his children was on stage because invariably, unable to hold out for the cover of final applause, he would pull out his handkerchief and alert the audience to his severely clogged-up condition. There were plenty of crosses the children of this complicated, emotional man had to bear during the John Wayne-worshipping '50s, but being insufficiently loved was never one of them. Yet in the spring of 1970, a therapist unfamiliar with this history sent Jerry home in despair. He spent the following months doubting himself, believing a dozen more hugs might have saved his son from madness.

Few participants emerged from those evenings without confessing to some charge, but the heaviest guilt was generally accepted by the mothers. During a luckless search for signs of "over-mothering" or "dominance" or "aggression" in Kay one evening, the therapist appeared ready to move on to more promising candidates when he raised a question about "rejection." My mother remembered a night in 1949, when Frank was 3, that still caused her some regrets.

A pediatrician had applied bindings around Frank's head during a visit that afternoon, to flatten the ears a bit. His tiny ears stuck out at what my mother thought was an adorable angle, but the doctor soon convinced her they wouldn't be so adorable when he was a young man. He suggested they would mar his attractiveness, possibly threaten his sex life. As the bindings were applied I imagine the pediatrician caught my mother wincing. That wince appeared hundreds of times as her five offspring somersaulted through childhood — when I got my hand caught in the wringer of the washing machine or one of my brothers had his head stitched in the emergency room. She usually followed the wince with a pat of sympathy, a gesture of comfort.

The doctor, an authoritative man, disapproved of her soft-touch approach. He warned her of the dangers of coddling, especially coddling boys. There were lots of stories then about men whose lives were wrecked by homosexuality because their mothers over-kissed them. Between his ears and his mother, the doctor believed my brother had a very narrow chance for a normal life.

Kay remembered being awake that whole night, listening to cries from the baby's room and wrestling with her urge to scoop him up and comfort him. It took tremendous discipline, but she accepted the punishment of the pediatrician's advice and resisted. She could still hear those cries, she told the therapist at ISPI 21 years later. She winced.

Perhaps that's when my brother may have felt rejected, she volunteered. How could he have known her longing to pick him up, to comfort him? How could he have known she was struggling to follow orders? Perceiving the fresh scent of guilt, the therapist probed deeper: Maybe she really did think he was homely — maybe she really was unconsciously rejecting him. My mother considered this suggestion for a moment. She looked across the room at my brother, then shook her head slowly. No, she said simply, without further explanation. Even ravaged by illness, even

listened politely–the poor are always polite. The poor always listen. They don't say that there is no money for iron pills, or better food, or worm medicine. The idea of an operation is frightening and costs so much that, if I had dared, I would have laughed. Who takes care of my children? Recovery from an operation takes a long time. I have three children. When I left them with "Granny" the last time I had a job, I came home to find the baby covered with fly specks, and a diaper that had not been changed since I left. When the dried diaper came off, bits of my baby's flesh came with it. My other child was playing with a sharp bit of broken glass, and my oldest was playing alone at the edge of a lake. I made twenty-two dollars a week, and a good nursery school costs twenty dollars a week for three children. I quit my job.

Poverty is dirt. You can say in your clean clothes coming from your clean house, "Anybody can be clean." Let me explain about housekeeping with no money. For breakfast I give my children grits with no oleo or cornbread without eggs and oleo. This does not use up many dishes. What dishes there are, I wash in cold water and with no soap. Even the cheapest soap has to be saved for the baby's diapers. Look at my hands, so cracked and red. Once I saved for months to buy a jar of Vaseline for my hands and the baby's diaper rash. When I had saved enough, I went to buy it and the price had gone up two cents. The baby and I suffered on. I have to decide every day if I can bear to put my cracked sore hands into the cold water and strong soap. But you ask, why not hot water? Fuel costs money. If you have a wood fire it costs money. If you burn electricity, it costs money. Hot water is a luxury. I do not have luxuries. I know you will be surprised when I tell you how young I am. I look so much older. My back has been bent over the wash tubs every day for so long, I cannot remember when I ever did anything else. Every night I wash every stitch my school age child has on and just hope her clothes will be dry by morning.

Poverty is staying up all night on cold nights to watch the fire know- 5 ing one spark on the newspaper covering the walls means your sleeping child dies in flames. In summer poverty is watching gnats and flies devour your baby's tears when he cries. The screens are torn and you pay so little rent you know they will never be fixed. Poverty means insects in your food, in your nose, in your eyes, and crawling over you when you sleep. Poverty is hoping it never rains because diapers won't dry when it rains and soon you are using newspapers. Poverty is seeing your children forever with runny noses. Paper handkerchiefs cost money and all your rags you need for other things. Even more costly are antihistamines. Poverty is cooking without food and cleaning without soap.

Poverty is asking for help. Have you ever had to ask for help knowing your children will suffer unless you get it? Think about asking for a loan from a relative, if this is the only way you can imagine asking for help. I will tell you how it feels. You find out where the office is that you are supposed to visit. You circle that block four or five times. Thinking of your children, you go in. Everyone is busy. Finally, someone comes out and you tell her that you need help. That never is the person you need to see. You go see another person, and after spilling the whole shame of your poverty all over the desk between you, you find that this isn't the right office after all — you must repeat the whole process, and it never is any easier at the next place.

You have asked for help, and after all it has a cost. You are again told to wait. You are told why, but you don't really hear because of the red cloud of shame and the rising cloud of despair.

Poverty is remembering. It is remembering quitting school in junior high because "nice" children had been so cruel about my clothes and my smell. The attendance officer came. My mother told him I was pregnant. I wasn't, but she thought I could get a job and help out. I had jobs off and on, but never long enough to learn anything. Mostly I remember being married. I was so young then. I am still young. For a time, we had all the things you have. There was a little house in another town, hot water and everything. Then my husband lost his job. There was unemployment insurance for a while and what few jobs I could get. Soon, all our nice things were repossessed and we moved back here. I was pregnant then. This house didn't look so bad when we first moved in. Every week it gets worse. Nothing is ever fixed. We now had no money. There were a few odd jobs for my husband, but everything went for food then, as it does now. I don't know how we lived through three years and three babies, but we did. I'll tell you something, after the last baby died I destroyed my marriage. It had been a good one, but could you keep on bringing children in this dirt? Did you ever think how much it costs for any kind of birth control? I knew my husband was leaving the day he left, but there were no goodbyes between us. I hope he has been able to climb out of this mess somewhere. He never could hope with us to drag him down.

That's when I asked for help. When I got it, you know how much it was? It was, and is, seventy-eight dollars a month for the four of us; that is all I ever can get. Now you know why there is no soap, no needles and thread, no hot water, no aspirin, no worm medicine, no hand cream, no shampoo. None of these things forever and ever and ever. So that you can see clearly, I pay twenty dollars a month rent, and most of the rest goes for food. For grits and cornmeal, and rice and milk and beans. I try my best to use only the minimum electricity. If I use more, there is that much less for food.

Poverty is looking into a black future. Your children won't play with 10 my boys. They will turn to other boys who steal to get what they want. I can already see them behind the bars of their prison instead of behind the bars of my poverty. Or will they turn to the freedom of alcohol or drugs, and find themselves enslaved. And my daughter? At best, there is for her a life like mine.

But you say to me, there are schools. Yes, there are schools. My children have no extra books, no magazines, no extra pencils, or crayons, or paper and most important of all, they do not have health. They have worms, they have infections, they have pink-eye all summer. They do not sleep well on the floor, or with me in my one bed. They do not suffer from hunger, my seventy-eight dollars keeps us alive, but they do suffer from malnutrition. Oh yes, I do remember what I was taught about health in school. It doesn't do much good. In some places there is a surplus commodities program. Not here. The county said it cost too much. There is a school lunch program. But I have two children who will already be damaged by the time they get to school.

But, you say to me, there are health clinics. Yes, there are health clinics and they are in the town. I live out here eight miles from town. I can walk that far (even if it is sixteen miles both ways), but can my little children? My neighbor will take me when he goes; but he expects to get paid, one way or another. . . . I bet you know my neighbor. He is that large man who spends his time at the gas station, the barbershop, and the corner store complaining about the government spending money on the immoral mothers of illegitimate children.

Poverty is an acid that drips on pride until all pride is worn away. Poverty is a chisel that chips on honor until honor is worn away. Some of you say that you would do something in my situation, and maybe you would, for the first week or the first month, but for year after year after year?

Even the poor can dream. A dream of a time when there is money. Money for the right kinds of foods, for worm medicine, for iron pills, for toothbrushes, for hand cream, for hammer and nails and a bit of screening, for a shovel, for a bit of paint, for some sheeting, for needles and thread. Money to pay in money for a trip to town. And, oh, money for hot water and money for soap. A dream of when asking for help does not eat away the last bit of pride. When the office you visit is as nice as the offices of other governmental agencies, when there are enough workers to help you quickly, when workers do not quit in defeat and despair. When you have to tell your story to only one person, and that person can send you for other help and you don't have to prove your poverty over and over again.

I have come out of my despair to tell you this. Remember I did not   *15* come from another place or another time. Others like me are all around you. Look at us with an angry heart, anger will help you help me. Anger that will let you tell of me. The poor are always silent. Can you be silent too?

The Responsive Reader

1. Parker re-creates for her readers the feel and smell of poverty. What for you is most unexpected or disturbing about the physical conditions of living "below the poverty line"?
2. Parker touches on familiar topics that crop up in discussions of poverty: trying to get a job; the workings of public assistance; help from private individuals; health care for the poor; birth control;

children without fathers. Does she change your assumptions on these topics? Does she make you rethink any of the issues?
3. Do you think this plea for understanding and help would move people you know? Why or why not? What do you think are its strong points or its weaknesses?

Talking, Listening, Writing

4. Do you think the conditions Parker describes are a thing of the past? Have things gotten better? Have they gotten worse?
5. How much do you know about currently fashionable proposed remedies for growing poverty? If you had a chance to make a plea for one of them, what would it be — workfare? breaking the cycle of dependency? retraining the unemployed? reindustrializing America? taxing the rich? Present a proposal that your fellow students would be able to take seriously.
6. Parker says, "The poor are always silent." In our society, are the voices of the poor ever heard? Do the poor have effective spokespersons or advocates? What do they say?

Projects

7. What level of subsistence is possible with welfare payments in your own area or community? What does it take to be eligible? What will a typical welfare check buy? Collaborating with others, try to get information from agencies, social workers, and aid recipients.

Thinking about Connections

A familiar question about the plight of the homeless, the poor, the mentally ill, the imprisoned, or the drug addicted is whether they are not in some way themselves to blame. Are they not to a larger or lesser extent responsible for their own condition? After reading the selections in this chapter, how would you answer this question? Would you answer it differently for different groups?

KAISER AND THE WAR
Simon J. Ortiz

> Simon J. Ortiz was born and grew up at the Acoma Pueblo in New
> Mexico. He has been called a part of a Native American Renaissance that
> has forced white writers to reevaluate the Native American's part in the
> American experience. Ortiz has worked as a laborer, teacher, journalist, and
> public relations director. In books like Going for the Rain (1976) and A
> Good Journey (1977), he has written about the lives and legends of the
> people of New Mexico. In the following story, he dramatizes the clash of
> cultures that occurs when two different ways of thinking, of looking at things,
> come into conflict. In our own group, we know the assumptions, the rules, the
> signals, the penalties. However, when we encounter people with different
> cultural conditioning, what they say and do may seem strange and wrong-
> headed to us. As a Native American says about the early Jesuit missionaries
> in the Canadian film Black Robe, "None of what the white men say makes
> any sense."

Thought Starters: This story offers several different perspectives on the
actions of the central character and on what happens to him. Which of
these different points of view seems most valid to you?

Kaiser got out of the state pen when I was in the fourth grade. I don't   1
know why people called him Kaiser. Some called him Hitler, too, since he
was Kaiser, but I don't think he cared at all what they called him. He was
probably just glad to get out of the state pen anyway.

Kaiser got into the state pen because he didn't go into the army.
That's what my father said anyway, and because he was a crazy nut according to some people, which was probably why he didn't want to go
into the army in the first place, which was what my father said also.

The army wanted him anyway, or maybe they didn't know he was
crazy or supposed to be. They came for him out at home on the reservation; and he said he wasn't going to go because he didn't speak good
English. Kaiser didn't go to school more than just the first or second
grade. He said what he said in Indian and his sister said it in English for
him. The army men, somebody from the county draft board, said they'd
teach him English, don't worry about it, and how to read and write and
give him clothes and money when he got out of the army so that he could
start regular as any American. Just like anybody else, and they threw in
stuff about how it would be good for our tribe and the people of the
U.S.A.

Well, Kaiser, who didn't understand that much English anyway, listened quietly to his sister telling him what the army draft-board men were saying. He didn't ask any questions, just once in a while said, "Yes," like he'd been taught to say in the first grade. Maybe some of the interpretation was lost the way his sister was doing it, or maybe he went nuts like some people said he did once in a while because the next thing he did was to burst out the door and start running for Black Mesa.

The draft-board men didn't say anything at first and then they got   5 pretty mad. Kaiser's sister cried because she didn't want Kaiser to go into the army but she didn't want him running out just like that either. She had gone to the Indian school in Albuquerque, and she learned that stuff about patriotism, duty, honor — even if you were said to be crazy.

At about that time, their grandfather, Faustin, cussed in Indian at the draft-board men. Nobody had noticed when he came into the house, but there he was, fierce-looking as usual, although he wasn't fierce at all. Then he got mad at his granddaughter and the men, asked what they were doing in his house, making the women cry and not even sitting down like friendly people did. Old Faustin and the army confronted each other. The army men were confused and getting more and more nervous. The old man told the girl to go out of the room and he'd talk to the army himself, although he didn't speak a word of English.

Those army men tried to get the girl to come back, but the old man wouldn't let her. He told her to get to grinding corn or something useful. They tried sign language and when Faustin figured out what they were waving their hands around for, he laughed out loud. He wouldn't even take the cigarettes offered him, so the army men didn't say anything more. The last thing they did though was give the old man a paper which they didn't try to explain what it was for. They probably hoped it would get read somehow.

Well, after they left, the paper did get read by the girl, and she told Faustin what it was about. The law was going to come and take Kaiser to jail because he wouldn't go into the army by himself. Grandfather Faustin sat down and talked quietly to himself for a while and then he got up to look for Kaiser.

Kaiser was on his way home by then, and his grandfather told him what was going to happen. They sat down by the side of the road and started to make plans. Kaiser would go hide up on Black Mesa and maybe go up all the way to Brushy Mountain if the law really came to poking around seriously. Faustin would take him food and tell him the news once in a while.

Everybody in the village knew what was going on pretty soon. Some   10 approved, and some didn't. Some thought it was pretty funny. My father, who couldn't go in the army even if he wanted to because there were too many of us kids, laughed about it for days. The people who approved of it and thought it funny were the ones who knew Kaiser was crazy and that

come by himself anyway. Let's go get him." He was a man who didn't like Kaiser. He looked around carefully when he got through speaking and sat down.

"Tell the Americans that is not the way," one of the chiefs said. "If our son wants to meet these men he will come." And the law was answered with the translation.

"I'll be switched," the sheriff said, and the Indians laughed quietly. *30* He glared at them and they stopped. "Let's go get him ourselves," he continued.

The man who had been interpreting said, "He is crazy."

"Who's crazy?" the sheriff yelled, like he was refuting an accusation. "I think you're all crazy."

"Kaiser, I think he is crazy," the interpreter said like he was ashamed of saying so. He stepped back, embarrassed.

Faustin then came to the front. Although he said he didn't want to talk with the law, he shouted, "Go get Kaiser yourself. If he's crazy, I hope he kills you. Go get him."

"Okay," the agent replied when the interpreter finished. "We'll go *35* get him ourselves. Where is he?" The agent knew no one would tell him, but he asked it anyway.

Upon that, the Indians assumed the business that the law came to do was over, and that the law had resolved what it came to do in the first place. The Indians began to leave.

"Wait," the agent said. "We need someone to go with us. He's up on Black Mesa, but we need someone to show us where."

The men kept on leaving. "We'll pay you. The government will pay you to go with us. You're deputized," the agent said. "Stop them, Sheriff," he said to the county sheriff, and the sheriff yelled, "Stop, come back here," and put a hand to his six-shooter. When he yelled, some of the Indians looked at him to laugh. He sure looked funny and talked funny. But some of them came back. "All right, you're deputies, you'll get paid," the sheriff said. Some of them knew what that meant, others weren't too sure. Some of them decided they'd come along for the fun of it.

The law and the Indians piled into the government car and a pickup truck which belonged to one of the deputies who was assured that he would get paid more than the others.

Black Mesa is fifteen miles back on the reservation. There are dirt *40* roads up to it, but they aren't very good, nobody uses them except sheep herders and hunters in the fall. Kaiser knew what he was doing when he went up there, and he probably saw them when they were coming. But it wouldn't have made any difference because when the law and the deputies come up to the foot of the mesa, they still weren't getting anywhere. The deputies, who were still Indians too, wouldn't tell or didn't really know where Kaiser was at the moment. So they sat for a couple of hours at the foot of the mesa, debating what should be done. The law tried to get the deputies to talk. The sheriff was boiling mad by this time, getting madder too, and he was for persuading one of the deputies into telling where Kaiser was exactly. But he reasoned the deputy wouldn't talk being that he was Indian too, and so he shut up for a while. He had figured out why the Indians laughed so frequently even though it was not as loud as before they were deputized.

Finally, they decided to walk up Black Mesa. It's rough going and when they didn't know which was the best way to go up they found it was even rougher. The real law dropped back one by one to rest on a rock or under a piñon tree until only the deputies were left. They watched the officer from the Indian Affairs office sitting on a fallen log some yards back. He was the last one to keep up so far, and he was unlacing his shoes. The deputies waited patiently for him to start again and for the others to catch up.

"It's sure hot," one of the deputies said.

"Yes, maybe it'll rain soon," another said.

"No, it rained for the last time last month, maybe next year."

"Snow then," another said.

They watched the sheriff and the Indian agent walking toward them half a mile back. One of them limped.

"Maybe the Americans need a rest," someone said. "We walked a long ways."

"Yes, they might be tired," another said. "I'll go tell that one that we're going to stop to rest," he said and walked back to the law sitting on the log. "We gonna stop to rest," he told the law. The law didn't say anything as he massaged his feet. And the deputy walked away to join the others.

They didn't find Kaiser that day or the next day. The deputies said they could walk all over the mesa without finding him for all eternity, but they wouldn't find him. They didn't mind walking, they said. As long as they got paid for their time, their crops were already in, and they'll just hire someone to haul winter wood for them now that they had the money. But they refused to talk. The ones who wanted to tell where Kaiser was, if they knew, didn't say so out loud, but they didn't tell anyway so it didn't make any difference. They were too persuaded by the newly found prosperity of being employed.

The sheriff, exhausted by the middle of the second day of walking the mesa, began to sound like he was going back to Albuquerque. Maybe Kaiser'd come in by himself, he didn't see any sense in looking for some Indian anyway just to get him into the army. Besides, he'd heard the Indian was crazy. When the sheriff had first learned the Indian's name was Kaiser he couldn't believe it, but he was assured that wasn't his real name, just something he was called because he was crazy. But the sheriff didn't feel any better or less tired, and he was getting jumpy about the crazy part.

45

50

At the end of the second day, the law decided to leave. Maybe we'll come back, they said; we'll have to talk this over with the Indian Affairs officials, maybe it'll be all right if that Indian didn't have to be in the army after all. And they left. The sheriff, his six-shooter off his hip now, was pretty tired out, and he didn't say anything.

The officials for the Indian Affairs didn't give up though. They sent back some more men. The county sheriff had decided it wasn't worth it, besides he had a whole county to take care of. And the Indians were deputized again. More of them volunteered this time, some had to be turned away. They had figured out how to work it: they wouldn't have to tell, if they knew, where Kaiser was. All they would have to do was walk and say from time to time, "Maybe he's over there by that canyon. Used to be there was some good hiding places back when the Apache and Navaho were raising Cain." And some would go over there and some in the other direction, investigating good hiding places. But after camping around Black Mesa for a week this time, the Indian Affairs gave up. They went by Faustin's house the day they left for Albuquerque and left a message: the government would wait and when Kaiser least expected it, they would get him and he would have to go to jail.

Kaiser decided to volunteer for the army. He had decided to after he had watched the law and the deputies walk all over the mesa. Grandfather Faustin had come to visit him up at one of the sheep camps, and the old man gave him all the news at home and then he told Kaiser the message the government had left.

"Okay," Kaiser said. And he was silent for a while and nodded his head slowly like his grandfather did. "I'll join the army."

"No," his grandfather said. "I don't want you to. I will not allow   *55*
you."

"Grandfather, I do not have to mind you. If you were my grandfather or uncle on my mother's side, I would listen to you and probably obey you, but you are not, and so I will not obey you."

"You are really crazy then," Grandfather Faustin said. "If that's what you want to do, go ahead." He was angry and he was sad, and he got up and put his hand on his grandson's shoulder and blessed him in the people's way. After that the old man left. It was evening when he left the sheep camp, and he walked for a long time away from Black Mesa before he started to sing.

The next day, Kaiser showed up at home. He ate with us, and after we ate we sat in the living room with my grandfather.

"So you've decided to go into the Americans' army," my grandfather said. None of us kids, nor even my parents, had known he was going but my grandfather had known all along. He probably knew as soon as Kaiser had walked into the house. Maybe even before that.

My grandfather blessed him then, just like Faustin had done, and he   *60*
talked to him of how a man should behave and what he should expect. Just

general things, and grandfather turned sternly toward us kids who are playing around as usual. My father and mother talked with him also, and when they were through, my grandfather put cornmeal in Kaiser's hand for him to pray with. Our parents told us kids to tell Kaiser good-bye and good luck and after we did, he left.

The next thing we heard was that Kaiser was in the state pen.

Later on, some people went to visit him up at the state pen. He was okay and getting fat, they said, and he was getting on okay with everybody and the warden told them. And when someone had asked Kaiser if he was okay, he said he was fine and he guessed he would be American pretty soon being that he was around them so much. The people left Kaiser some home baked-bread and dried meat and came home after being assured by the warden that he'd get out pretty soon, maybe right after the war. Kaiser was a model inmate. When the visitors got home to the reservation, they went and told Faustin his grandson was okay, getting fat and happy as any American. Old Faustin didn't have anything to say about that.

Well, the war was over after a while. Faustin died sometime near the end of it. Nobody had heard him mention Kaiser at all. Kaiser's sister and nephew were the only ones left at their home. Sometimes someone would ask about Kaiser, and his sister and nephew would say, "Oh, he's fine. He'll be home pretty soon, right after the war." But after the war was over, they just said he was fine.

My father and a couple of other guys went down to the Indian Affairs office to see what they could find out about Kaiser. They were told that Kaiser was going to stay in the pen longer now because he had tried to kill somebody. Well, he just went crazy one day, and he made a mistake so he'll just have to stay in for a couple more years or so, the Indian Affairs said. That was the first anybody heard of Kaiser trying to kill somebody, and some people said why didn't they put him in the army for that like they wanted to in the first place. So Kaiser remained in the pen long after the war was over and most of the guys who had gone into the army from the tribe had come home. When he was due to get out, the Indian Affairs sent a letter to the governor and several men from the village went to get him.

My father said Kaiser was quiet all the way home on the bus. Some of the guys tried to joke with him, but he just wouldn't laugh or say anything. When they got off the bus at the highway and began to walk home, the guys broke into song, but that didn't bring Kaiser around. He kept walking quiet and reserved in his gray suit. Someone joked that Kaiser probably owned the only suit in the whole tribe.

"You lucky so and so. You look like a rich man," the joker said. The others looked at him sharply and he quit joking, but Kaiser didn't say anything.

When they reached home, his sister and nephew were very happy to see him. They cried and laughed at the same time, but Kaiser didn't do

anything except sit at the kitchen table and look around. My father and
the other guys gave him advice and welcomed him home again and left.

After that, Kaiser always wore his gray suit. Every time you saw
him, he was wearing it. Out in the fields or at the plaza watching the
katzina, he wore the suit. He didn't talk much any more, my father said,
and he didn't come around home any more either. The suit was getting all
beat-up looking, but he just kept on wearing it so that some people began
to say that he was showing off.

"That Kaiser," they said, "he's always wearing this suit, just like he
was an American or something. Who does he think he is anyway?" And
they'd snicker, looking at Kaiser with a sort of envy. Even when the suit
was torn and soiled so that it hardly looked anything like a suit, Kaiser
wore it. And some people said, "When he dies, Kaiser is going to be
wearing his suit." And they said that like they wished they had gotten a
suit like Kaiser's.

Well, Kaiser died, but without his gray suit. He died up at one of his   70
distant relatives' sheep camps one winter. When someone asked about the
suit, they were told by Kaiser's sister that it was rolled up in some newspaper at their home. She said that Kaiser had told her, before he went up
to the sheep camp, that she was to send it to the government. But, she
said, she couldn't figure out what he meant, whether Kaiser had meant
the law or somebody, maybe the state pen or the Indian Affairs.

The person who asked about the suit wondered about this Kaiser's
instructions. He couldn't figure out why Kaiser wanted to send a beat-up
suit back. And then he figured, well, maybe that's the way it was when
you either went into the state pen or the army and became an American.

The Responsive Reader

1. There are divided opinions about Kaiser even before the army comes
   looking for him. What kind of person was he? Do you think he was
   crazy?
2. What are some of the misunderstandings or breakdowns in communication between the "law people" from the outside and Kaiser
   and the people in the village?
3. For the kind of problem that develops in this story, some tend to
   blame the system. Others tend to claim that in part it was the individual's own fault. For what happens in the story, would you blame
   society or the individual?

Talking, Listening, Writing

4. Do you think Kaiser was treated unjustly by the law?
5. Imagine that Kaiser were still in prison. Write a letter — to the governor, or to the editor of your newspaper — to call attention to his
   case.

6. Have you experienced or observed the clash of cultures and the misunderstandings or conflicts it can generate? If not, have you encountered striking or thought-provoking reading or viewing on the subject?
7. Have you ever rebelled against the rules or against the law?

Projects

8. Ortiz called the people he wrote about "the forgotten people." Does your state or area have reservations, migrant camps, or refugee camps? Working with other students, you may want to investigate one such place. (If you do not have a chance for firsthand investigation, go to such sources as news reports or television documentaries.) What conclusions can you draw about the people there? What is their legal status? What are their living conditions? How are they viewed by the authorities or by their neighbors?

INDIAN BOARDING SCHOOL: THE RUNAWAYS

Louise Erdrich

> *Louise Erdrich, of Chippewa and German-American descent, grew up in North Dakota and later went to live in New Hampshire. Her best-selling novel,* Love Medicine *(1984), won the National Book Critics Circle Award; her more recent books are* The Beet Queen *(1986) and* Tracks *(1988). Her poem is a vivid expression of rebellion against schooling that becomes forced conversion to a different way of life.*

Thought Starters: What are your thoughts about "Americanizing" cultural minorities?

Home's the place we head for in our sleep.   1
Boxcars stumbling north in dreams
don't wait for us. We catch them on the run.
The rails, old lacerations that we love,
soot parallel across the face and break   5
just under Turtle Mountains. Riding scars
you can't get lost. Home is the place they cross.

The lame guard strikes a match and makes the dark
less tolerant. We watch through cracks in boards
as the land starts rolling, rolling till it hurts   10
to be here, cold in regulation clothes.
We know the sheriff's waiting at midrun
to take us back. His car is dumb and warm.
The highway doesn't rock, it only hums
like a wing of long insults. The worn–down welts   15
of ancient punishments lead back and forth.

All runaways wear dresses, long green ones,
the color you would think shame was. We scrub
the sidewalks down because it's shameful work.
Our brushes cut the stone in watered arcs   20
and in the soak frail outlines shiver clear
a moment, things us kids pressed on the dark
face before it hardened, pale, remembering
delicate old injuries, the spines of names and leaves.

The Responsive Reader

1. What were the runaways running away from? What do you learn about their past history? What do you learn about the system against which they are rebelling? What is in store for them?
2. Much of what we observe in this poem has symbolic meanings and overtones. What vivid details in the runaways' surroundings mirror for them their thoughts and feelings?
3. One editor said that "the language of hurt and injury pervades this poem." What examples can you find? What role does each play in the poem?

Talking, Listening, Writing

4. Does the intense sense of grievance in this poem take you by surprise?
5. In your own experience, has schooling been a means of liberation, widening perspectives and extending opportunities? Or has it been an instrument of oppression — aiming at forced changes in attitudes, narrowing your outlook, or trying to make you over into something you did not want to be?
6. Is there something to be said in defense of policies of enforced Americanization?

Projects

7. In the school district(s) in the area where you live, what is the policy regarding cultural diversity? If you can, talk to teachers or administrators in a position to know.

WRITING
WORKSHOP 5

Drawing Conclusions

What kind of thinking shapes the ideas in an effective paper? Tracking the thought processes that produce a well-thought-out paper is difficult. The brain moves at computer speed, and ideas surface in our consciousness without our knowing exactly how they took shape. Nevertheless, we can reconstruct some of the most common thought patterns that help us make sense of the data we take in.

A very basic (or at any rate very productive) think scheme finds the common thread in a number of related events. It finds a pattern where at first there was a confusing collection of data. If you get violently ill every time you eat shrimp, you will sooner or later tag shellfish and your possible allergy to it as the likely culprit. If Asian American students consistently do better than Anglos on a math teacher's tests, she will start looking for some common element in the Asian Americans' backgrounds as the clue to their superior performance.

This kind of thinking is one of our most basic ways of moving from fact to **inference** — moving from raw data to what we think they mean. The technical term for thinking that looks for the common element in a set of observations is **induction**, or inductive thinking. If it weren't for inductive thinking, a person allergic to shellfish would keep eating it, and getting sick as a result, forever. Many solidly argued papers line up the examples, the evidence, that all point in the same direction. If it is an effective paper, the reader is likely to say: "Yes, I agree. Looking at the facts or the data, I would have drawn the same conclusion."

TRIGGERING The need to make sense of a rich array of data is one of the most basic human needs. Here are some situations that often trigger a search for general conclusions:

- Much writing aiming at general conclusions sets out to test stereotypes and clichés. For instance, is it true that, as many people in other countries think, Americans are incorrigible optimists? (What makes American peace corps volunteers go into distant villages thinking they will be able to change age-old patterns of behavior? Was it the experience of getting out from under the stifling tutelage of kings and aristocrats?

Was it the experience of being able to start all over somewhere in the wide-open spaces of the West? Is the tradition of American optimism wearing thin?)

▪ Much writing sets out to find answers to nagging questions. For instance, who are the homeless? Assuming that the homeless come from many different backgrounds, what are common factors in their histories? (If we could agree on some conclusions about how they got there, we might be able to agree on ways to keep others from traveling the same route.)

GATHERING When we first explore a topic, we may stumble onto related facts that all seem to point roughly in the same direction. Testing or following up our first hunches, we may soon be able to gather relevant information in a more systematic fashion. If you ask, "What is different about the Japanese?" data like the following may soon begin to tell their own story:

Students graduating from twelfth grade:	Japan	90%
	United States	77%
Average daily hours of homework during high school:	Japan	2.0
	United States	.5
Daily absentee rate:	Japan	very low
	United States	9%
Years required of high school mathematics:	Japan	3
	United States (typical)	1
Years required of foreign language (grades 7–12):	Japan	6
	United States	0–2
Engineering majors in undergraduate population:	Japan	20%
	United States	5%

SHAPING A focused paper or a coherent paragraph is often the result of funneling related observations into a general conclusion. The basic process producing a paragraph like the following is that a writer has laid related observations end to end:

I am a blonde. I have a soft musical voice. I have always had high grades, and I have worked as a tutor to help other students improve theirs. Still, some people do not take me seriously because of the way I look and sound. I have been told to put up my hair in a bun, wear glasses, quit wearing make-up, and work to lower the pitch of my voice. Men are not the only ones doing the stereotyping. I had a female instructor criticize my voice as unprofessional after an oral report. I had a female student tell me during a group project that my "Barbie Doll" voice would make the wrong impression on the audience.

The difference between the thinking that produced this passage and the actual paragraph printed here is a question of what comes first. During the thinking process, we start with the data and then draw a conclusion. However, in most of the writing that *presents* conclusions, we state the conclusion first and then marshal the evidence that led up to it. When we put the conclusion first in a paragraph, we call it the **topic sentence**. When we put the more general or overarching conclusion early in a paper, we call it the **thesis**. (Sometimes, you may want to lead your readers up to the conclusion, simulating the actual process of sorting the data and discovering the common thread.)

Often an effective paper is modeled on the inverted funnel. (What came out of the funnel comes first; what went into the funnel comes later.) The thesis comes first, and then the writer lays out the observations that were funneled into the general conclusion that the thesis sums up. The claim the writer makes comes first; the evidence comes second. The following might be the thesis of a paper about the lack of political involvement among the current generation of college students:

THESIS: A pervasive apathy about political issues marks today's generation of students.

The rest of the paper would then present the evidence that led to this conclusion. Successive paragraphs might focus on points like the following:

• Turnouts for controversial speakers invited to your campus have been small.

• Turnout for elections for student government has been dismal.

• Debates scheduled on topics like AIDS and safe sex have fizzled.

• Few students turned out for special events scheduled to honor minority authors or to recognize outstanding women on campus.

REVISING Whenever you claim to have found a general pattern, you have to guard against jumping to conclusions. Revision is a chance to rethink what your evidence really shows. It is a chance to reword sweeping generalizations. Keep in mind advice like the following:

▪ *Spell out your thesis.* What exactly are you claiming? It is a lame beginning to start a paper by saying that "certain factors" play a role in prejudice or homelessness. What are they? Which are the most important?

▪ *Limit your generalizations.* Obviously, readers will not sit still for claims that people of one nationality or religion are marvelously more gifted and generous than any other. Neither will educated readers listen patiently to sweeping claims that members of any one group are inherently lazy or violence-prone. But less provocative generalizations — about voter apathy, about immigrants on welfare — may also have to be worded more cautiously, with due consideration for exceptions and countertrends.

 ▪ *Build your case on representative examples.* Try to present a cross section of relevant instances. Try to listen to a cross section of witnesses, pro and con. Do not build your case on one outstanding case that might turn out to be a freak example.

What general conclusions does the author of the following sample paper present to her readers? How real or convincing are the observations on which she based her findings?

Child Care

When I quit work to return to school, I naively believed that I could keep my two-year-old daughter with me while I studied at home. During the hours I was away at school, I had planned to have her stay with a neighbor, who is also Korean and who also has a two-year-old (a boy). After about a month at school, I had learned the hard way how impractical my plans had been. There was no way to get my school work done while my daughter was awake. She would climb up on my back and hang on to my neck while I was reading. She would push several keys on the keyboard all at once while I was typing. At times, bored, she would simply lie on the floor and moan.

Since my plans for sending her to the neighbor fell through, I found myself embarking on a search for affordable day care where my daughter would receive adequate attention. Like other mothers before me, I discovered the frustrations of trying to find a place for the child so that the mother would be able to study or work.

I called every single daycare center within a ten-mile radius of where we lived, about twenty places in all. Most would not bother at all with toddlers, who might not be perfectly toilet-trained. I finally came up with three preschools that would accept two-year-olds. The first place I called was called Young Pioneers. A group of well over twenty two-year-old and three-year-old children were gathered in a circle to listen to a teacher describing different body parts. At a table, another teacher was sitting with four kids, helping them with pasting. Two other kids were crying, and a few more were sitting outside the circle or lying on the floor completely oblivious to what was going on. My feeling was that the two teachers were completely overwhelmed by the large number of students and that they were trying their best under the circumstances.

My next stop was at Loving Cup, where a class of two-year-olds had only twelve children in it; naturally I became more interested in this school. However, the teacher never looked at me or acknowledged me during the whole time I was there. When I went back to the school in the afternoon to talk to her, she had already left, handing the children over to the afternoon shift.

My final stop was at the Rainbow of Knowledge, where again two teachers were looking after a too large group of two-year-olds. While we were there during lunch time, the teacher assistant handed my daughter a carrot stick, and the head teacher took time to take a hamster out of its cage and let her pat it for a second or two. This might have been a possibility for my daughter if she had been older, had already known English, and could have followed the teacher's instructions, keeping herself occupied. But there was no way the teachers could have given her individual attention to help her adjust to a totally new environment.

After a week of hopping from one preschool to another, I found myself pretty much back where I started. Everywhere I looked, I saw a scarcity of adequate child care, with teachers overextended or already burnt out. For many mothers in my situation, child care remains a mirage.

Topics for Papers Drawing Conclusions (A Sampling)

1. Are students of your generation apathetic about political or social issues?
2. To judge from your own observation, is there such a thing as "recreational drug use" — by people who can take or leave it?
3. Have you observed common traits or a recurrent pattern in young people who get into trouble with the law?
4. Did your high school or does your college have cliques? Is there a common pattern in the behavior of cliques or of the people who belong to them?
5. We hear much talk about dysfunctional families. To judge from your own observation, how widespread is the phenomenon? What are key elements such families seem to share?
6. To judge from your own observation of our society, how large is the gap between the rich and the poor?
7. On your campus, do people of the same racial or ethnic background tend to flock together? How much mingling is there of people from diverse backgrounds?
8. Do women make better students than men?
9. When you see people fail or become marginalized, do you tend to say: "In some ways, it was their own fault"? Discuss some test cases you know well from personal observation and experience.
10. To judge from your own observation, which immigrant groups have the least (or the most) difficulty in adjusting to their new environment?

6

Identity: Gender and Race

*It took me a long time and much painful boomeranging of expectations
to achieve a realization everyone else seems to have been born with:
That I am nobody but myself.*

Ralph Ellison

We are so many selves.
Gloria Steinem

"Who am I?" The search for identity has for centuries been a major
theme in the imaginative literature of the West. How can we discover our
true selves? How can we realize our full human potential?

Many discover in this search that a crucial preliminary question is
not "*Who* am I?" but "*What* am I?" Being a dentist's son or daughter at
Stanford University is a different identity from being a student looking
for student loans at a community college. Going to a mainly black school
in a country town in the South is a different matter from attending a prep
school in the East. What parents, counselors, teachers, and employers
expect of a young woman may steer her toward options very different
from those open to a young man.

Who we can be is shaped and often limited by what we are. We
encounter expectations, pressures, barriers visible and invisible. Sometimes these barriers are crudely obvious, as when a country club does not
accept Jews. Sometimes they are more subtle, as when the Berlin Philhar-
monic Orchestra discourages women musicians. Sometimes the battle is
joined, as when gays and lesbians fight for the right to be accepted in the
military.

How do we become aware of the limits and opportunities that await
us when we are identified in terms of gender, race, ethnicity, or sexual
orientation? What chance do we have to shape our own destiny, to forge
our own identity? In her feminist rereading of Charlotte Brontë's novel
Jane Eyre, Adrienne Rich traces one young woman's journey toward self-
realization. Young Jane exercises the limited options open to her as a poor

293

young woman in nineteenth-century England. She goes to work as a governess in the mansion of Rochester, the gloomy aristocrat. When she finds he is married to a mentally ill woman, she refuses the temptation of an extramarital romance and leaves his employ. Later, she rejects the option of serving as a Platonic helpmate to a high-minded missionary on his way to convert the heathens. She discovers female friends and teachers who think of other women not as rivals but as sisters. She finally marries the widowed Rochester when she can join in the union as a partner, as an equal.

How optimistic or how realistic is the scenario acted out in Brontë's novel? What chance do people in our culture have to transcend the barriers created by gender, race, ethnicity, or sexual orientation?

HOW IT FEELS TO BE COLORED ME

Zora Neale Hurston

Zora Neale Hurston once said about the idea of democracy that she was all for trying it out. In fact, she couldn't wait to do so as soon as the Jim Crow laws that legalized discrimination against African Americans were a thing of the past. Hurston was born in Eatonville, an all-black town in Florida, and was working as a domestic when she managed to attend college. She finally went on to Howard University, which has been called "a center of black scholarship and intellectual ferment." As a scholarship student at Barnard College in New York City, she became an associate of the anthropologist Franz Boas, who asked her to return to the South to collect black folk tales. She had earlier published earthy slice-of-life sketches of black life; her classic collection of African American folklore, Mules and Men, *appeared in 1935. Like other students of black dialect and folk tradition, she was accused by militants of perpetuating damaging stereotypes of African Americans as uneducated and unsophisticated. Like other minority artists and writers dependent on white patronage, she was accused of selling out to the white establishment. Although for a time one of the best-known voices of the Harlem Renaissance of the twenties and thirties, she died in a county welfare home and was buried in an unmarked grave. In recent years, feminists have rediscovered her fiction; her masterpiece, the novel* Their Eyes Were Watching God *(1937), is now widely read in college classes. A recent biographer has called her "the most significant unread author in America."*

Thought Starters: How aware are people of their separate racial or ethnic identity? Is it constantly on their minds? When was Hurston most aware of being black? When least?

I am colored but I offer nothing in the way of extenuating circum-   *1*
stances except the fact that I am the only Negro in the United States whose grandfather on the mother's side was *not* an Indian chief.

I remember the very day that I became colored. Up to my thirteenth year I lived in the little Negro town of Eatonville, Florida. It is exclusively a colored town. The only white people I knew passed through the town going to or coming from Orlando. The native whites rode dusty horses, the Northern tourists chugged down the sandy village road in automobiles. The town knew the Southerners and never stopped cane chewing when they passed. But the Northerners were something else again. They were peered at cautiously from behind curtains by the timid. The more venturesome would come out on the porch to watch them go past and got just as much pleasure out of the tourists as the tourists got out of the village.

The front porch might seem a daring place for the rest of the town, but it was a gallery seat to me. My favorite place was atop the gate-post. Proscenium box for a born first-nighter. Not only did I enjoy the show, but I didn't mind the actors knowing that I liked it. I usually spoke to them in passing. I'd wave at them and when they returned my salute, I would say something like this: "Howdy-do-well-I-thank-you-where-you-goin'?" Usually the automobile or the horse paused at this, and after a queer exchange of compliments, I would probably "go a piece of the way" with them, as we say in farthest Florida. If one of my family happened to come to the front in time to see me, of course negotiations would be rudely broken off. But even so, it is clear that I was the first "welcome-to-our-state" Floridian, and I hope the Miami Chamber of Commerce will please take notice.

During this period, white people differed from colored to me only in that they rode through town and never lived there. They liked to hear me "speak pieces" and sing and wanted to see me dance the parse-me-la, and gave me generously of their small silver for doing these things, which seemed strange to me for I wanted to do them so much that I needed bribing to stop. Only they didn't know it. The colored people gave no dimes. They deplored any joyful tendencies in me, but I was their Zora nevertheless. I belonged to them, to the nearby hotels, to the county — everybody's Zora.

But changes came in the family when I was thirteen, and I was sent   *5* to school in Jacksonville. I left Eatonville, the town of the oleanders, as Zora. When I disembarked from the river-boat at Jacksonville, she was no more. It seemed that I had suffered a sea change. I was not Zora of Orange County any more, I was now a little colored girl. I found it out in certain ways. In my heart as well as in the mirror, I became a fast brown — warranted not to rub nor run.

But I am not tragically colored. There is no great sorrow dammed up in my soul, nor lurking behind my eyes. I do not mind at all. I do not belong to the sobbing school of Negrohood who hold that nature somehow has given them a lowdown dirty deal and whose feelings are all hurt about it. Even in the helter-skelter skirmish that is my life, I have seen that the world is to the strong regardless of a little pigmentation more or less. No, I do not weep at the world — I am too busy sharpening my oyster knife.

Someone is always at my elbow reminding me that I am the granddaughter of slaves. It fails to register depression with me. Slavery is sixty years in the past. The operation was successful and the patient is doing well, thank you. The terrible struggle that made me an American out of a potential slave said "On the line!" The Reconstruction said "Get set!"; and the generation before said "Go!" I am off to a flying start and I must not halt in the stretch to look behind and weep. Slavery is the price I paid for civilization, and the choice was not with me. It is a bully adventure and worth all that I have paid through my ancestors for it. No one on earth ever had a greater chance for glory. The world to be won and nothing to be lost. It is thrilling to think — to know that for any act of mine, I shall get twice as much praise or twice as much blame. It is quite exciting to hold the center of the national stage, with the spectators not knowing whether to laugh or to weep.

The position of my white neighbor is much more difficult. No brown specter pulls up a chair beside me when I sit down to eat. No dark ghost thrusts its leg against mine in bed. The game of keeping what one has is never so exciting as the game of getting.

I do not always feel colored. Even now I often achieve the unconscious Zora of Eatonville before the Hegira. I feel most colored when I am thrown against a sharp white background.

For instance at Barnard. "Beside the waters of the Hudson" I feel my   10
race. Among the thousand white persons, I am a dark rock surged upon, overswept by a creamy sea. I am surged upon and overswept, but through it all, I remain myself. When covered by the waters, I am; and the ebb but reveals me again.

Sometimes it is the other way around. A white person is set down in our midst, but the contrast is just as sharp for me. For instance, when I sit in the drafty basement that is The New World Cabaret with a white person, my color comes. We enter chatting about any little nothing that we have in common and are seated by the jazz waiters. In the abrupt way that jazz orchestras have, this one plunges into a number. It loses no time in circumlocutions, but gets right down to business. It constricts the thorax and splits the heart with its tempo and narcotic harmonies. This orchestra grows rambunctious, rears on its hind legs and attacks the tonal veil with primitive fury, rending it, clawing it until it breaks through to the jungle beyond. I follow those heathen — follow them exultingly. I dance wildly inside myself; I yell within, I whoop; I shake my assegai above my head, I hurl it true to the mark *yeeeeooww!* I am in the jungle and living in the jungle way. My face is painted red and yellow and my body is painted blue. My pulse is throbbing like a war drum. I want to slaughter something — give pain, give death to what, I do not know. But the piece ends. The men of the orchestra wipe their lips and rest their fingers. I creep back slowly to the veneer we call civilization with the last tone and find the white friend sitting motionless in his seat, smoking calmly.

"Good music they have here," he remarks, drumming the table with his fingertips.

Music! The great blobs of purple and red emotion have not touched him. He has only heard what I felt. He is far away and I see him but dimly across the ocean and the continent that have fallen between us. He is so pale with his whiteness then and I am *so* colored.

At certain times I have no race, I am *me*. When I set my hat at a certain angle and saunter down Seventh Avenue, Harlem City, feeling as snooty as the lions in front of the Forty-Second Street Library, for instance. So far as my feelings are concerned, Peggy Hopkins Joyce on the Boule Mich with her gorgeous raiment, stately carriage, knees knocking together in a most aristocratic manner, has nothing on me. The cosmic Zora emerges. I belong to no race nor time. I am the eternal feminine with its string of beads.

I have no separate feeling about being an American citizen and col-   15
ored. I am merely a fragment of the Great Soul that surges within the boundaries. My country, right or wrong.

Sometimes, I feel discriminated against, but it does not make me angry. It merely astonishes me. How *can* any deny themselves the pleasure of my company! It's beyond me.

But in the main, I feel like a brown bag of miscellany propped against a wall. Against a wall in company with other bags, white, red and yellow. Pour out the contents, and there is discovered a jumble of small things priceless and worthless. A first-water diamond, an empty spool, bits of broken glass, lengths of string, a key to a door long since crumbled away, a rusty knifeblade, old shoes saved for a road that never was and never will be, a nail bent under the weight of things too heavy for any nail, a dried flower or two, still a little fragrant. In your hand is the brown bag. On the ground before you is the jumble it held—so much like the jumble in the bags, could they be emptied, that all might be dumped in a single heap and the bags refilled without altering the content of any greatly. A bit of colored glass more or less would not matter. Perhaps that is how the Great Stuffer of Bags filled them in the first place—who knows?

The Responsive Reader

1. There has been much talk about the need for self-esteem — the need for women and minorities to overcome culturally conditioned feelings of inferiority and inadequacy. What is the secret of Hurston's self-esteem?
2. What were major stages in Hurston's awareness of race? (For instance, when was it that she "became" colored? How does she distance herself from other definitions of "Negrohood"? When is she least aware of racial difference?)

3. What is Hurston's last word on the role of race in her life and in the larger society? Do her words seem dated or still valid today?

Talking, Listening, Writing

4. How does Hurston's attitude toward race compare with what you think is predominant in today's generation?
5. What efforts have you observed to restore people's pride in their own racial or ethnic identity? Have you personally participated in such efforts? How successful are they?
6. Have you experienced self-doubt, feelings of inadequacy, or feelings of inferiority? What causes them? How do you cope with them?

Projects

7. How much do you know about the art and literature of diverse ethnic or cultural traditions? Your class may want to organize a presentation of poems, tales, songs, or music. (Will you encounter any questions about what is authentic, what is exploitative, or what is offensive or demeaning?)

Thinking about Connections

How does the self-image of a black woman in Hurston's essay compare with the self-image of the young black woman in Maya Angelou's "Step Forward in the Car, Please" (p. 37)?

THE WOMAN WARRIOR
Maxine Hong Kingston

> *Maxine Hong Kingston's powerful, disturbing prose differs from writing that sets out in search of a lost cultural heritage in order to find a more idyllic, romanticized past. She was born as the daughter of Chinese immigrants who ran a laundry in Stockton, California. Her autobiographical* The Woman Warrior: Memoirs of a Childhood Among Ghosts *won the National Book Critics' Circle award for nonfiction in 1976. In this intensely personal account, she wove a fascinating web of personal history, family tradition, and Chinese legend. She wrote with great bitterness about growing up as a girl within the narrow boundaries set for women by the traditional Chinese culture. She told the story of relatives who had stayed behind in China and were caught up in the turmoil of the Communist revolution. In Mao's China, class warfare against exploiters and ideological allies of the West destroyed landlords, property owners, shopkeepers, teachers, artists, and intellectuals and their families. She told the story of her own struggles with racism and sexism in what Chinese immigrants had called the land of the "Golden Mountains." In her* China Men *(1980), she chronicled the special barriers and humiliations that the earlier Chinese immigrants had experienced in America.*

Thought Starters: Kingston writes from a deep-rooted sense of injustice. What were its causes? How does she deal with it?

My American life has been such a disappointment.   1
"I got straight A's, Mama."
"Let me tell you a true story about a girl who saved her village."
I could not figure out what was my village. And it was important that I do something big and fine, or else my parents would sell me when we made our way back to China. In China there were solutions for what to do with little girls who ate up food and threw tantrums. You can't eat straight A's.
When one of my parents or the emigrant villagers said, "Feeding   5
girls is feeding cowbirds," I would thrash on the floor and scream so hard I couldn't talk. I couldn't stop.
"What's the matter with her?"
"I don't know. Bad, I guess. You know how girls are. 'There's no profit in raising girls. Better to raise geese than girls.'"
"I would hit her if she were mine. But then there's no use wasting all that discipline on a girl. 'When you raise girls, you're raising children for strangers.'"

"Stop that crying!" my mother would yell. "I'm going to hit you if you don't stop. Bad girl! Stop!" I'm going to remember never to hit or to scold my children for crying, I thought, because then they will only cry more.

"I'm not a bad girl," I would scream. "I'm not a bad girl. I'm not a   10
bad girl." I might as well have said, "I'm not a girl."

"When you were little, all you had to say was 'I'm not a bad girl,' and you could make yourself cry," my mother says, talking-story about my childhood.

I minded that the emigrant villagers shook their heads at my sister and me. "One girl—and another girl," they said, and made our parents ashamed to take us out together. The good part about my brothers being born was that people stopped saying, "All girls," but I learned new grievances. "Did you roll an egg on *my* face like that when *I* was born?" "Did you have a full-month party for *me*?" "Did you turn on all the lights?" "Did you send *my* picture to Grandmother?" "Why not? Because I'm a girl? Is that why not?" "Why didn't you teach me English?" "You like having me beaten up at school, don't you?"

"She is very mean, isn't she?" the emigrant villagers would say.

"Come, children. Hurry. Hurry. Who wants to go out with Great-Uncle?" On Saturday mornings, my great-uncle, the ex-river pirate, did the shopping. "Get your coats, whoever's coming."

"I'm coming. I'm coming. Wait for me."   15

When he heard girls' voices, he turned on us and roared, "No girls!" and left my sisters and me hanging our coats back up, not looking at one another. The boys came back with candy and new toys. When they walked through Chinatown, the people must have said, "A boy—and another boy— and another boy!" At my great-uncle's funeral I secretly tested out feeling glad that he was dead—the six-foot bearish masculinity of him.

I went away to college—Berkeley in the sixties—and I studied, and I marched to change the world, but I did not turn into a boy. I would have liked to bring myself back as a boy for my parents to welcome with chickens and pigs. That was for my brother, who returned alive from Vietnam.

If I went to Vietnam, I would not come back; females desert families. It was said, "There is an outward tendency in females," which meant that I was getting straight A's for the good of my future husband's family, not my own. I did not plan ever to have a husband. I would show my mother and father and the nosey emigrant villagers that girls have no outward tendency. I stopped getting straight A's.

And all the time I was having to turn myself American-feminine, or no dates.

There is a Chinese word for the female I—which is "slave." Break   20
the women with their own tongues!

I refused to cook. When I had to wash dishes, I would crack one or

simply ask but have to talk-story too. The revolutionaries had taken
Fourth Aunt and Uncle's store, house, and lands. They attacked the house
and killed the grandfather and oldest daughter. The grandmother escaped
with the loose cash and did not return to help. Fourth Aunt picked up her
sons, one under each arm, and hid in the pig house, where they slept that
night in cotton clothes. The next day she found her husband, who had
also miraculously escaped. The two of them collected twigs and yams to
sell while their children begged. Each morning they tied the faggots on
each other's back. Nobody bought from them. They ate the yams and
some of the children's rice. Finally Fourth Aunt saw what was wrong.
"We have to shout 'Fuel for sale' and 'Yams for sale,'" she said. "We can't
just walk unobtrusively up and down the street." "You're right," said my
uncle, but he was shy and walked in back of her. "Shout," my aunt
ordered, but he could not. "They think we're carrying these sticks home
for our own fire," she said. "Shout." They walked about miserably, silently, until sundown, neither of them able to advertise themselves.
Fourth Aunt, an orphan since the age of ten, mean as my mother, threw
her bundle down at his feet and scolded Fourth Uncle, "Starving to death,
his wife and children starving to death, and he's too damned shy to raise
his voice." She left him standing by himself and afraid to return empty-
handed to her. He sat under a tree to think, when he spotted a pair of
nesting doves. Dumping his bag of yams, he climbed up and caught the
birds. That was when the Communists trapped him, in the tree. They
criticized him for selfishly taking food for his own family and killed him,
leaving his body in the tree as an example. They took the birds to a
commune kitchen to be shared.

It is confusing that my family was not the poor to be championed.
They were executed like the barons in the stories, when they were not
barons. It is confusing that birds tricked us.

What fighting and killing I have seen have not been glorious but
slum grubby. I fought the most during junior high school and always
cried. Fights are confusing as to who has won. The corpses I've seen had
been rolled and dumped, sad little dirty bodies covered with a police khaki
blanket. My mother locked her children in the house so we couldn't look
at dead slum people. But at news of a body, I would find a way to get out;
I had to learn about dying if I wanted to become a swordswoman. Once
there was an Asian man stabbed next door, word on cloth pinned to his
corpse. When the police came around asking questions, my father said,
"No read Japanese. Japanese words. Me Chinese."

I've also looked for old people who could be my gurus. A medium ⁴⁵
with red hair told me that a girl who died in a far country follows me
wherever I go. This spirit can help me if I acknowledge her, she said.
Between the head line and heart line in my right palm, she said, I have the
mystic cross. I could become a medium myself. I don't want to be a
medium. I don't want to be a crank taking "offerings" in a wicker plate

from the frightened audience, who, one after another, asked the spirits how to raise rent money, how to cure their coughs and skin diseases, how to find a job. And martial arts are for unsure little boys kicking away under fluorescent lights.

I live now where there are Chinese and Japanese, but no emigrants from my own village looking at me as if I had failed them. Living among one's own emigrant villagers can give a good Chinese far from China glory and a place. "That old busboy is really a swordsman," we whisper when he goes by, "He's a swordsman who's killed fifty. He has a tong ax in his closet." But I am useless, one more girl who couldn't be sold. When I visit the family now, I wrap my American successes around me like a private shawl; I *am* worthy of eating the food. From afar I can believe my family loves me fundamentally. They only say, "When fishing for treasures in the flood, be careful not to pull in girls," because that is what one says about daughters. But I watched such words come out of my own mother's and father's mouths; I looked at their ink drawing of poor people snagging their neighbor's flotage with long flood hooks and pushing the girl babies on down the river. And I had to get out of hating range. I read in an anthropology book that Chinese say, "Girls are necessary too"; I have never heard the Chinese I know make this concession. Perhaps it was a saying in another village. I refuse to shy my way anymore through our Chinatown, which tasks me with the old sayings and the stories.

The swordswoman and I are not so dissimilar. May my people understand the resemblance soon so that I can return to them. What we have in common are the words at our backs. The ideographs for *revenge* are "report a crime" and "report to five families." The reporting is the vengeance — not the beheading, not the gutting, but the words. And I have so many words — "chink" words and "gook" words too — that they do not fit on my skin.

The Responsive Reader

1. Kingston has a way of letting people damn themselves with words from their own mouths. She takes her readers into her confidence with exceptionally honest, candid expressions of confused, hostile feelings. What are striking examples of both of these features of her style and strategy as a writer?

2. What was it like to be a young woman in a traditional Chinese family? How does Kingston deal with this recurrent strand in her early experiences? Is her perspective as an adult different from what it was as a child?

3. The transition from the home to the workplace often takes young people into a very different world. Was this true in Kingston's case? Is there a connection between her feelings about her family background and the world of work?

4. How does Kingston come to terms with the fate of her relatives in China? What is her perspective, her attitude?
5. What personal use does Kingston make of the world of traditional Chinese myth and legend?

Talking, Listening, Writing

6. Have there been parallels to the traditional misogyny or demeaning of women in your own background or in your own cultural tradition? How does the traditional Chinese treatment of women as described by Kingston compare with the treatment of women in *our* society?
7. How do you think male readers react to this essay?
8. Are sexism and racism related? Do they seem to spring from similar or different roots? Can you develop a detailed comparison and contrast of the two?
9. Do you have a strong sense of grievance? Do you have a strong sense of injustice? Focus on a grievance or an injustice that has played a major role in your life. How can you enlist the sympathies or support of your listeners or readers?

Projects

10. Kingston's prose is rich in far-ranging allusions to history, tradition, and legend. Working with other students, you could parcel out topics for mini-reports based on information in encyclopedias or other sources. Sample topics: foot-binding in China, Joan of Arc, tongs, martial arts, ideographs, CORE.

THE INJUSTICE SYSTEM:
WOMEN HAVE BEGUN TO FIGHT

Patty Fisher

> *Patty Fisher is an editorial writer for a major newspaper in California. In the article that follows, she focuses on the explosive issue of rape as a test of attitudes toward women in our society. She buttresses personal observation and her close professional following of the news with an array of authoritative sources: a law professor and former public defender; statistics compiled by concerned organizations. She writes with the passion of intense personal involvement: She voices her concerns about her daughters; she shares the testimony of a friend.*

Thought Starters: Is our justice system rigged against victims of rape? Does our culture encourage or condone violence against women?

They called it "Brock's problem." Sen. Brock Adams, a respected   1
Democrat, was known to make sexual advances toward young women assistants. For years, his staff and close friends protected him, even after a woman told police he had drugged and molested her in his Washington apartment.

Then, the *Seattle Times* printed allegations from eight unnamed women that Adams raped, fondled, drugged or sexually harassed them over a period of 20 years. Before the day was over, Adams abruptly withdrew from his race for re-election.

So clean, so neat. No criminal charges, no trial, no witnesses. Just like that, the man's career is over, his reputation is shattered.

Vigilante justice, certainly. But if you believe the women's stories — and I do — it is justice nonetheless. And if you understand how the official justice system fails in cases of crimes against women, you see why women long ago abandoned the courts and began to fight against rape, spouse abuse and sexual harassment with whatever tools they could find.

The FBI has estimated that only one in 10 cases of rape is reported to   5
the police. Why don't women report these crimes? Some are afraid. Some are ashamed. All too many have learned that the system serves the interests of men and puts women victims on trial.

Cookie Ridolfi, a professor at Santa Clara University law school, worked for eight years as a public defender in Philadelphia. In most of the criminal cases she tried, her client was at a disadvantage, even though the burden of proof was on the prosecution.

"There is enormous bias against the defendant simply because he was arrested," she said. "Juries assume that he must have done something wrong."

Except in rape.

In a rape trial, the defense attorney has the edge. Instead of assuming the defendant is guilty, the jury assumes the victim either provoked the attack or made it up. "I can't think of one other criminal offense where the victim is blamed so routinely," she said.

It might be difficult for a man to see a situation short of Kafka in which he, as an innocent victim, is blamed for the crime in court. But imagine this scenario: [10]

A man is robbed at gunpoint. At the trial, he positively identifies the defendant as the one who followed him into a parking garage late at night and robbed him. The prosecution produces the man's credit cards and wedding ring, which were found on the defendant.

An open and shut case.

Until the defense attorney goes to work. The alleged victim, he says, is a liberal, guilt-ridden yuppie with a history of giving to homeless shelters. He spotted the defendant on the street, saw that he hadn't eaten all day and gave him his valuables. Only later, when he had to explain to his wife about his missing wedding ring, did he make up the story about being robbed.

The defense attorney points out inconsistencies in the victim's story: Why did he go into the garage alone that night when he knew it might be dangerous? Why didn't he leave his car and take a cab home? Why did he wear an expensive suit and flashy diamond ring unless he wanted to draw attention to his wealth? Why didn't he scream, fight or try to run away instead of docilely handing over his money?

There were no witnesses. There's plenty of room for reasonable doubt. The jury returns a verdict of not guilty. [15]

Preposterous? Only because juries don't assume that people give away their money and then lie about it later. But juries do assume that women have sex and then lie about it, file rape charges, lie to prosecutors and convince them to go to court.

Rape is a problem for the justice system in part because it is a unique crime. The act of sexual intercourse can be love or it can be rape, depending upon whether both parties consent to it. So the prosecution in a rape trial must prove the woman did not consent. That is difficult if the victim knew the rapist, which usually is the case; if there were no witnesses, which is nearly always the case; or if there are no bruises or other signs of struggle.

If the rapist had a gun or knife, if there was a group of assailants, or if the woman decided it was fruitless to struggle, the case comes down to her word against his. And traditionally, juries believe him and not her.

In ancient times, when women were regarded as the property of first their fathers and then their husbands, "consent" had nothing to do with rape. A man who deflowered a virgin not his wife was guilty of rape. He was ordered to marry the girl and pay her father the equivalent of what an intact virgin would have brought on the marriage market.

There was no such thing as rape of a married woman. If attacked, she was expected to fight to the death rather than give up her precious virtue (and her husband's good name). If she was unfortunate enough to live through the attack, she was guilty of adultery. 20

How far have we come? Only within the past 20 years have rape shield laws barred a victim's past sexual relations from being introduced as evidence in a rape trial. It remains more difficult to convict a man of raping a divorced woman than an "innocent" one.

Rape is not the only crime in which the system fails to treat women fairly. Wife beating wasn't even a crime until the 1800s. Today it is estimated that between 2 million and 6 million women are battered each year in this country by their husbands or boyfriends. Often their attempts to get protection from the justice system fail. And when they fight back and kill their abusers, the courts treat them more harshly than they do men who kill their wives or girlfriends.

According to statistics compiled by the National Clearinghouse for Battered Women, the average prison sentence for abusive men who kill their mates is two to six years. The average sentence for women who kill abusive men is 15 years.

Apparently juries make allowances for the remorseful man who kills in a momentary fit of rage, but not for the woman who pulls a gun on an unarmed man who has beaten her senseless for years and threatened to kill her.

Without the justice system to protect them, women have found ways to protect themselves. They taught their daughters to be "good" and follow the rules: 25

Never talk to strangers. Never walk alone at night. Never wear revealing clothes. Never let a boy kiss you on the first date.

But even "nice" girls get raped. In a San Jose courtroom recently, a man who confessed to raping more than 20 women said he attacked a Japanese exchange student because he thought she was flirting with him at a bus stop. "We stared at each other for a second," Gregory Smith told the jury. He apparently interpreted that one second as an invitation to follow her off the bus, drag her into a school playground, brutally rape and murder her.

Never look at strangers. Never take buses. Never leave the house. Of course there's always the chance you will be raped at home. Better get married so you'll have a man around to protect you.

Since Susan Brownmiller's landmark book on rape, *Against Our Will:*

Men, Women and Rape, was published in 1975, women have recognized that fighting violence against women means more than avoiding dark alleys. Brownmiller dispelled the myth that women are better off if they submit to rapists. More women are taking self-defense classes and carrying guns. And they are fighting to change the system, through the courts, Congress and state legislatures.

Yet changing laws is only the first step in reforming the system. We   30
have to change attitudes. One attitude we have to change is the notion that when it comes to sex, "no" means "yes."

Men didn't make up the notion that "no" means "yes." Those parents who taught their daughters to be "good" fostered it. For generations, they raised girls to believe that only bad girls have sexual feelings. Consenting to sex or, heaven forbid, initiating it would be acknowledging "bad" feelings. What a way to mess with a normal adolescent's already fragile self-esteem.

For generations girls dealt with this dilemma by denying their sex drive. That was easy enough. Their boyfriends were willing to take all the necessary action, so the girls could feign resistance as a way of experimenting with sex without taking responsibility for it, without being bad girls.

Of course, once girls forfeited their integrity on the question of consent, it was difficult to get it back. Once boys got the word that "no" sometimes meant "yes," it was open season on resisting females.

Imagine a society in which when a woman says "no," a man stops. One man I spoke with suggested that in such a society there would be a lot less sex and a steep drop in the birth rate. I doubt it. I think that if men backed off from women who said no, more women would say yes.

It's hard to change 3,000 years of attitudes, but parents and teachers,   35
judges and lawmakers can help. We start by teaching little boys to respect the feelings — and words — of little girls. And what do we teach little girls?

I have two young daughters, and I want to protect them from harm just as my parents wanted to protect me. But the days are long gone when girls went directly from their father's house to their husband's.

I hope I can teach my daughters more than just how to avoid being alone with a man in an elevator. They will study karate as well as ballet. I want them to understand their own strength, the importance of knees and elbows, the power of a well-placed kick.

I want them to understand the difference between "no" and "yes." While I'll probably preach the virtue of "no," I hope I won't lead them to think that there is something wrong with them if they have sexual feelings.

I'll teach them that the justice system can be unjust. They should use the system, but not trust it, and work to reform it.

A woman was telling me about being raped many years ago. She   *40* was young and naive, she said. He invited her to a party at his mother's fancy apartment. When they got there she realized she was the party. The apartment was deserted. He showed her a gun and told her to do as he said. She did.

She saw no point in calling the police. He was wealthy, she had gone there on her own, he hadn't injured her. But she told the story to a friend, a man, who was furious. He had some vague mob connections. He offered to fix the guy for her. She declined.

"I figured somehow it was sort of my fault. I didn't think he deserved to die."

Today, she says, she wishes she had told her friend to go ahead. "What that man did to me was a crime."

Vigilante justice. It's not the best way, but sometimes it's the only way.

The Responsive Reader

1. As Fisher writes, with charges of rape and sexual molestation, the case often comes down to the woman's word against the man's. Do you think it is true that in our society we are more likely to believe the man than the woman?
2. How does Fisher challenge entrenched attitudes? Do you think she is successful?
3. What historical background does Fisher provide for our current attitudes toward rape? How helpful or instructive is it? Does she shed new light for you on the psychological and cultural causes of rape and of society's treatment of rape? (What, for instance, are the problems with the concept of "consent"?)
4. What is Fisher's outlook or advice for the future? (Is she serious about her endorsement of vigilante justice at the end? Do you see her point?)

Talking, Listening, Writing

5. Have you personally observed or heard about abuse, molestation, or rape? How has what you saw or heard changed your thinking?
6. Do you think men's perspective on rape is basically different from women's? Why and how? Or why not?
7. Males today often feel on the defensive. Write a reply to Fisher's article from a male point of view or from the point of view of a woman trying to see the man's side.
8. Write an imaginary letter to a daughter or son on the issue of rape, sexual abuse, or sexual harassment.

Projects

9. Collaborating with others, you may want to research widely publicized cases that have tested society's attitudes toward rape. Are attitudes changing? Are there new trends for the treatment of rape victims by law-enforcement officers and in court? You may want to look at cases of rape victims' charges believed or disbelieved by juries; you may want to examine reopenings of cases in which men were wrongfully convicted of rape.

Thinking about Connections

What comes first or is more important—changes in attitude or changes in the law? For different perspectives on this question, compare Fisher's perspective with views expressed in Margaret Mead's "We Need Taboos on Sex at Work" (p. 363) and in Barbara Ehrenreich's "The Next Wave" (p. 638).

DIVORCE: THE END THAT NEVER QUITE DOES

Kathleen Parker

> *One of the first questions on questionnaires designed to establish a person's official identity used to be "single, married, or divorced?" In recent decades, patterns of marriage and divorce have changed drastically, turning long-held assumptions about the sanctity of marriage and about the traditional family unit upside down. The author of the following article writes a lifestyle column for the Orlando* Sentinel *in Florida. She here attacks fashionable or "chic" attitudes toward divorce and tries to correct the belief that divorce can ever be "quick and easy."*

Thought Starters: Do you agree that "divorce, unlike marriage, persists"? Do you agree that the aftereffects of divorce are painful and lasting?

A friend with two children under age 5 calls to say she's getting a *1* divorce. Her husband has been seeing another woman — so what's new? — and she's taking the kids. So there.

Her announcement startles me not because of the circumstances — pretty commonplace these days — but because of her cavalier tone. She announces her divorce as she might a headache or a traffic jam. Just another inevitable inconvenience.

Sympathy surfaces reluctantly. For although nothing hurts quite like betrayal, it is but a hangnail compared to the pain of divorce. My immediate impulse is to offer not compassion but a dire warning: Don't do it.

The quick and easy divorce is one of the great myths of our time. We see it on television, in the movies; half our friends and parents are divorced; it's no big deal. Marriage in the '80s has the longevity of a Bic pen. When it runs out of ink, we don't bother to fix it. We just throw it away.

Divorce is never easy. It is physically and spiritually devastating, no *5* matter how congenial the players. There's also nothing quick about it, especially if you have children.

Divorce, unlike marriage, persists. It dwells in the heart of the child who asks tough questions about Daddy. Why isn't Daddy at the class play? Where is Daddy on Father's Day? It resurfaces on birthdays, anniversaries, graduations and weddings.

When we begin to consider divorce, all we can think about is escape, liberation from the immediate problem. We look around and see that others have survived. Divorce is so commonplace — and apparently so easy — that people throw parties to celebrate. There are even greeting cards for divorce announcements, just like the ones for births and weddings.

It is ironic and pitiable that divorce is chic in an age when we read daily about the problems of latchkey children, custody kidnappings, visitation disputes and deadbeat dads, single mothers and father-hungry infants.

A charitable alien visiting Earth might view us as we do a beached whale. How sad that these creatures, so full of grace and intelligence, should willingly invite their own premature end. One less charitable might conclude that we are not a very bright species.

What we with our limited vision fail to consider is that the decision   10
to divorce is only the first step, the easiest one we'll take for many years to come. The process of divorce — the actual division of family — wreaks havoc on the soul. The reality is not a court date and a document. The reality is hours sifting through drawers of old photographs, dividing up furniture and children, sitting late into the night — night after night — at the bedside of a young child who can't sleep because he misses his daddy or mommy.

The reality is going to work the next day without any sleep and without enough money to pay the bills and not enough hope to force a smile at dinner that night.

In a nutshell, "Divorce is hell," says Diane Medved, marriage counselor, psychologist and author of *The Case Against Divorce* (Fine, $18.95).

Medved points out that divorce may be the only recourse in cases of drug addiction, abuse or permanent abandonment. "But on balance, people could spare themselves enormous suffering if they scotched their permissive acceptance of divorce and viewed marriage as a lifelong commitment not to be entered into — or wriggled out of — lightly."

No one, says Medved, is suggesting a return to the sanctimonious 1950s, when divorced people were ostracized. No one is suggesting that men or women tolerate impossible circumstances. But it is worth mentioning that divorce, like most things fashionable, is overrated.

The Responsive Writer

1. How does Parker explain our current "permissive" attitudes toward divorce?
2. What, according to Parker, are the drawbacks of divorce? What are the penalties divorced people pay? (Which of these drawbacks, as here described, seem particularly vivid or new?)

Talking, Listening, Writing

3. Do you agree that "divorce wreaks havoc on the soul"? What has been your observation of its traumas or aftermath? What has been your observation of its benefits?
4. We hear much talk from politicians about "family values." Is it just

talk? What are they saying? Is it similar to or different from the points made by Parker?

5. Parker grants that divorce becomes necessary when men or women face "impossible circumstances." Where does she draw the line? Where would you draw the line? When, for you, does the continuation of a marriage become "impossible"?

6. Compare and contrast life in the traditional family and life after divorce.

Projects

7. Do differences in attitude toward divorce separate the generations? Talk informally with people of varying ages about changing attitudes toward divorce. You may want to arrange for members of your class to pool their findings.

ON THE JOB

Joe Gutierrez

> *Studs Terkel is known for several best-selling collections of interviews with*
> *ordinary Americans. He was born in 1912 and grew up in Chicago, attending*
> *the University of Chicago and the Chicago Law School. He has been a disk*
> *jockey, sports commentator, and television emcee; he has hosted a popular talk*
> *show for thirty-five years. In books like* Working, Hard Times, *and*
> American Dreams: Lost and Found, *he proved a good listener, getting*
> *the people he interviewed to cut through media hype and political slogans and*
> *to talk with amazing honesty about their lives, thoughts, and feelings. The*
> *following interview with a fifty-year-old steel worker is from Terkel's latest*
> *book,* Race: How Blacks and Whites Feel about the American Ob-
> session *(1992). A reviewer in the* Chicago Sunday Times *said about this*
> *book, "Studs Terkel has got people to say things in such a way that you know*
> *at once they have finally said their truth and said it better than they ever*
> *believed they could say it."*
>
> *Joe Gutierrez, the person interviewed in the following selection from*
> Race, *spent four years in a seminary preparing to be a priest but then quit to*
> *work in the steel mills like his father. Gutierrez said about his family:*
>
> > *My father worked at the Ford plant in Detroit when he first came from*
> > *Mexico. Then he came to Chicago and the steel mill and worked there as*
> > *far back as I can remember. . . . My mother was a hillbilly from Georgia.*
> > *She married at fourteen. We're fifteen children. She didn't speak Spanish*
> > *and he didn't speak English. I didn't know two words of Spanish until I*
> > *got out into the steel mill.*

Thought Starters: Gutierrez is of Mexican American descent, with a
Mexican father and a North American mother. He says of Spanish Americans, or Latinos, "Latins are right in the middle." In how many ways
does the person speaking to you in this interview find himself "right in
the middle"?

I didn't identify with Mexicans until people started throwing racism   1
around. My name is José but I've always been called Little Joe. The whites
didn't know my last name and thought I was Italian or Greek. So they let
out their true feelings.

I was not accepted by the Mexicans because I couldn't speak the
language: "You look white, so you don't want to be a Mexican." I forced
myself to learn the language so at least I could get by.

We were the only Mexican family in the neighborhood. The Mexicans, Puerto Ricans, and blacks lived on the East Chicago side by the mills. Now it's all changed. You've got a neighbor that's black, another Puerto Rican, another something else. All on our street.

We were about eight years old, my brother, Vince, and I when we went to a public swimming pool in a park in East Chicago. We took a black kid with us. This was 1948. As soon as we dove in the pool, everybody got out. The lifeguard got out, too, a female. They shut down the pool. I was never raised to be a racist, so I didn't know what it was all about.

There's a certain amount of racism among Mexicans against blacks,   5
and Mexicans against Puerto Ricans. But I see more racism with the blacks than with the white or Latin.

We went through a union election. We're about thirty percent black. Every time I ran for office, there was a solid black vote for the black, regardless of the person. It made no difference. Over the years, I felt it would change because people would look at the person's qualifications. For the most part, it hasn't changed. That's true among Latins also. They'll vote Latin just because he's Latin. Whites? Yeah, pretty much the same.

A good friend of mine, a white from Kentucky, just got elected griever in the metal-plate department. I said, "The black griever we have is simply unqualified; he's done a terrible job. I don't expect the blacks to vote for him. He won't get over twenty votes." He said, "The guy's gonna get a hundred votes." He was right. For three years, the guy did an awful job. They still came out and backed him. I understand the past injustices, but . . .

The guys who are honest say, "Look, we've been down so long, the first time we get somebody to represent the black community, he projects an image of leadership and we overlook the bad. We just want a black there."

It baffles my mind because I've had an ongoing fight in the mills: I don't care if you're black, brown, or white, we're all workers. I sometimes get chastised by the so-called leaders of the Latin community because I don't stand up and say we should all go for *la raza*. There are some Latins who always vote that way. I voted that way before I got involved with the union. I didn't know people. If I saw a Sánchez or Gonzalez or Rodríguez, I voted for him. I met a Cisneros who couldn't write his own name and didn't give a damn about the union, was a company guy. I said nah, nah, nah. He may be Latin but he doesn't represent the interests of working people. I don't care about image.

With whites, what comes first is my pocketbook. I can work with a   10
black, with a Latin, but as soon as I leave that steel mill, I get on South 41 and go back to my world. Here it's a temporary world for eight hours a day, five days a week. When you park your car and walk into that plant,

you walk into another world. All your prejudices, all your hates, you leave in the parking lot.

At the workplace, there's not much tension. You still have people who feel they're treated unfairly because they're black or Latin. When some whites get disciplined, they say, "I'm white, you didn't discipline the black guy." It's a crutch. But in general, it's not there. You're working around heavy equipment and you've got to look out for your buddy. It's very easy to get hurt in a steel mill.

As for whites, there's still a lot of prejudice out there. I know how to erase it. If you give other people a chance — if you give me the opportunity to present my views, maybe you'll get to know me and like me. Look, there's some people you just don't like. It's got nothing to do with color; it's got a lot to do with personality.

Latins are right in the middle. For the longest time, they were classified as blacks. You go to Texas, and Latinos are treated like blacks.

With people losing jobs, there's always got to be somebody to blame. We had nineteen thousand people at Inland Steel. Now we're below ten thousand. For years, whites had all the better jobs. In 1977, the government came in and said you've got to do something about discrimination in the workplace or we'll do it for you. They signed a Memorandum of Understanding that implemented plantwide seniority. It was good for everybody. Now a black or Latino as well as a white could transfer in any department and utilize seniority.

At the time, whites ran the trains, Latins worked on the tracks, and blacks worked in the coke plants. When the changes took place, there was a lot of hatred among whites against minorities in general. "I've worked in this mill for twenty-five years, and here's one of them coming over and bumping me out of a job." It didn't happen that way for the most part, because you still had contract language to go by. You couldn't leapfrog over somebody.

We had an election the other day and won by a landslide. I acted as a watcher. Some voted only for Latins, others only for blacks, and some whites only for whites. Our slate had a president who's white, a Latin who's vicepresident, and two black trustees. It was a mix all around. We voted for the person. We represented the rank-and-file against the old guys. For the most part, we're forty, forty-one years old. You don't have a younger crop because there are no jobs for them.

What's ahead doesn't look good. With a new power plant, a lot of departments will shut down. The coke plants will go. You'll see some of the old hatred coming back. Blacks will say, "You gave us the rotten jobs whites wouldn't take, working on batteries, causing cancer and so forth, and when things get bad, we're the first to go." We're hearing it now. With fewer and fewer jobs, it'll get worse.

I don't like racists — white, black, Latin, anybody. Life's too short for meanness. There was a lot in the army when I was in it. Sometimes it comes out of people you don't expect it from. There's a guy who's decent, a hard worker, a good family man, and he'll say, "That fuckin' nigger." It's like getting hit in the gut. I stop him: "Why do you say that?" He just shrugs. He's Mexican, a deacon in the church. I'm a lector there. I tell this guy, "If a white guy says nigger, the word you use, I bet he calls you spic, taco-bender. Cut out this bullshit."

What's happened is that people were getting tired of the sixties. There was a legitimate grievance among the blacks in this country and a lot of us took part in the marches. But about twelve, fifteen years ago, younger blacks started coming into the steel mills. The older guys found allies among the Latins on the shop floor. But the younger guys came in with one thought in mind: We've been screwed and if we don't keep on their backs, they're gonna screw us again. To them, we're no different than the whites. It started backfiring.

Those of us who were sympathetic are less that way today. I had 20
won over a lot of blacks because I did a good job. But there are some blacks, I swear to God, I don't care what you did, it made no difference. All they saw was black. It's damaging to themselves. What more can a boss wish for? — divide and conquer!

When the government came down with a consent decree, Inland Steel ignored it. Every other company — LTV, Bethlehem, USX — paid minorities monies — two, three thousand dollars apiece — on the basis of years of discrimination at work. Inland Steel paid not a penny. They had a sharp lawyer who said, "Look, people are tired of civil rights, of marches, of busing, of affirmative action. The mood of the country is changing. Let's fight it." The government didn't follow through, and they didn't pay a penny. It's the Reagan years, and Bush is going even further.

I don't think the company is racist. That's too simple. It's the bottom line, the dollar. They don't care about you, no matter what your color is. You're nothing to them. If you're black or Latin or white, if they can set you up against the other workers, they're going to use you. They don't give a damn what color you are. It's the profit.

We have to keep working together, and when we hear the word nigger or spic — or cracker — stand up and say, "I don't appreciate that. Enough of this bullshit!"

The Responsive Reader

1. Like many Americans, Gutierrez does not have a clear-cut racial or ethnic identity. What experiences shaped his sense of who he is or where he belongs?
2. What has shaped his perceptions of the role of race in American life — in the communities in which we live?
3. What are Gutierrez' observations of the role of race on the job? For instance, what does he say about the hierarchy, or pecking order, in

the distribution of jobs? What does he say about company policy on the subject of race? (Does he think it is racist?)

4. Readers of Studs Terkel's books marvel at the candor with which the people he interviews seem to talk about subjects on which many people hide their feelings or lie to both themselves and others. Does anything in this interview seem especially honest or candid? Is there anything that might make you question the speaker's sincerity?

Talking, Listening, Writing

5. What in this interview seems familiar; what seems different or new? Have you had experiences similar to those of Gutierrez — or other experiences that contrast with his?

6. Does this interview make you rethink some of your assumptions about ethnicity and race? How?

7. Would you call Gutierrez a typical American? Why or why not?

8. One reviewer said that Terkel's research "runs directly counter to the meanness of spirit so often expressed and exploited by today's politicians." She said that if Terkel's interviewees are representative, there is a far greater degree of "public consensus" and of "yearning for resolution" than one might imagine. What did she mean? Does this sample interview bear out her observations?

Projects

9. Studs Terkel started the book in which this interview appeared with a number of findings he had gleaned from reputable polls and surveys. Study the following sampling of the data he had collected. You may want to *interpret* these findings: What do they tell us? What do they mean? Or you may want to *challenge* these findings: What information can you find that would seem to contradict some of these data?

> Black males have the lowest life expectancy of any comparable group in the United States. Their unemployment rate is double that of white males; even black males with college degrees are three times as likely to be without jobs as white college graduates. One in four black men between the ages of twenty and twenty-nine is in jail. Since 1960, suicide rates for young black males have nearly tripled, and they have doubled for black females. Half of all black children are born in poverty. Many blacks die prematurely from preventable major diseases. More than half of non-blacks believe that African Americans are less intelligent than whites. Over sixty percent of nonblacks believe that African Americans are more likely to "prefer to live off welfare" and less likely to "prefer to be self-supporting."

WHITE GUILT

Shelby Steele

> *Shelby Steele is a professor at San Jose State University who has made many Americans rethink their assumptions about race and racism. He is the son of a black father and a white mother and experienced racism when attending a segregated school in South Chicago. He became an instant celebrity in 1990 when he published* The Content of Our Character: A New Vision of Race in America, *a collection of the essays that he first published in* Harper's *and* The American Scholar. *He appeared on talk shows and wrote and narrated a television special on the murder of a black teenager by a white mob in Bensonhurst. Steele sees race relations in this country as setting up a scenario in which both blacks and whites play familiar and predictable parts. Blacks play the part of the victim, pressing for redress of their grievances. Whites, suffering from white guilt, salve their consciences by setting up affirmative action programs that are largely ineffectual and counterproductive. Black students agitate against campus racism and are placated by "cheap buyoffs" like separate black dorms. When Steele was active in the civil rights movement in the sixties, all of the eighteen black students at his school, Coe College in Iowa, graduated. Today, at the university where he teaches, the dropout rate for African American students is seventy percent. To Steele, these figures mean that blacks must leave behind the politics of victimization and concentrate on maximizing the opportunities that exist.*

Thought Starters: According to Steele, when blacks continue to ask for compensation for past injustices, they perpetuate the wrong "paradigm" — the wrong established pattern to which everything is made to conform. What, according to him, is wrong with the paradigm?

I don't remember hearing the phrase "white guilt" very much before the mid-1960s. Growing up black in the 1950s, I never had the impression that whites were much disturbed by guilt when it came to blacks. When I would stray into the wrong restaurant in pursuit of a hamburger, it didn't occur to me that the waitress was unduly troubled by guilt when she asked me to leave. I can see now that possibly she was, but then all I saw was her irritability at having to carry out so unpleasant a task. If there was guilt, it was mine for having made an imposition of myself. I can remember feeling a certain sympathy for such people, as if I was victimizing them by drawing them out of an innocent anonymity into the unasked for role of racial policemen. Occasionally they came right out and asked me to feel sorry for them. A caddymaster at a country club told my brother and me that he was doing us a favor by not letting us caddy at this white club and that we should try to understand his position, "put yourselves in my shoes." Our color had brought this man anguish and, if a part of that anguish was guilt, it was not as immediate to me as my own guilt. I smiled at the man to let him know he shouldn't feel bad and then began my long walk home. Certainly I also judge him a coward, but in that era his cowardice was something I had to absorb.

In the 1960s, particularly the black-is-beautiful late 1960s, this absorption of another's cowardice was no longer necessary. The lines of moral power, like plates in the earth, had shifted. White guilt became so palpable you could see it on people. At the time what it looked like to my eyes was a remarkable loss of authority. And what whites lost in authority, blacks gained. You cannot feel guilty about anyone without giving away power to them. Suddenly, this huge vulnerability had opened up in whites and, as a black, you had the power to step right into it. In fact, black power all but demanded that you do so. What shocked me in the late 1960s, after the helplessness I had felt in the fifties, was that guilt had changed the nature of the white man's burden from the administration of inferiors to the uplift of equals — from the obligations of dominance to the urgencies of repentance.

I think what made the difference between the fifties and sixties, at least as far as white guilt was concerned, was that whites underwent an archetypal Fall. Because of the immense turmoil of the civil rights movement, and later the black-power movement, whites were confronted for more than a decade with their willingness to participate in, or comply with, the oppression of blacks, their indifference to human suffering and denigration, their capacity to abide evil for their own benefit and in the defiance of their own sacred principles. The 1964 Civil Rights Bill that bestowed equality under the law on blacks was also, in a certain sense, an admission of white guilt. Had white society not been wrong, there would have been no need for such a bill. In this bill the nation acknowledged its fallenness, its lack of racial innocence, and confronted the incriminating self-knowledge that it had rationalized for many years a flagrant injustice. Denial is a common way of handling guilt, but in the 1960s there was little will left for denial except in the most recalcitrant whites. With this defense lost there was really only one road back to innocence — through actions and policies that would bring redemption.

In the 1960s the need for white redemption from racial guilt became the most powerful, yet unspoken, element in America's social-policy-making process, first giving rise to the Great Society and then to a series of programs, policies, and laws that sought to make black equality and restitution a national mission. Once America could no longer deny its guilt, it went after redemption, or at least the look of redemption, and did so with a vengeance. Yet today, some twenty years later, study after study tells us that by many measures the gap between blacks and whites is widening rather than narrowing. A University of Chicago study indicates that segregation is more entrenched in American cities today than ever imagined. A National Research Council study notes the "status of blacks relative to whites (in housing and education) has stagnated or regressed since the early seventies." A follow-up to the famous Kerner Commission Report warns that blacks are as much at risk today of becoming a "nation within a nation" as we were twenty years ago, when the original report was made.

I think the white need for redemption has contributed to this tragic situation by shaping our policies regarding blacks in ways that may deliver the look of innocence to society and its institutions but that do very little actually to uplift blacks. The specific effect of this hidden need has been to bend social policy more toward reparation for black oppression than toward the much harder and more mundane work of black uplift and development. Rather than facilitate the development of blacks to achieve parity with whites, these programs and policies—affirmative action is a good example—have tended to give blacks special entitlements that in many cases are of no use because blacks lack the development that would put us in a position to take advantage of them. I think the reason there has been more entitlement than development is (along with black power) the unacknowledged white need for redemption—not true redemption, which would have concentrated policy on black development, but the appearance of redemption, which requires only that society, in the name of development, seem to be paying back its former victims with preferences. One of the effects of entitlements, I believe, has been to encourage in blacks a dependency both on entitlements and on the white guilt that generates them. Even when it serves ideal justice, bounty from another man's guilt weakens. While this is not the only factor in black "stagnation" and "regression," I believe it is one very potent factor.

It is easy enough to say that white guilt too often has the effect of bending social policies in the wrong direction. But what exactly is this guilt, and how does it work in American life?

I think white guilt, in its broad sense, springs from a knowledge of ill-gotten advantage. More precisely, it comes from the juxtaposition of this knowledge with the inevitable gratitude one feels for being white rather than black in America. Given the moral instincts of human beings, it is all but impossible to enjoy an ill-gotten advantage, much less to feel at least secretly grateful for it, without consciously or unconsciously experiencing guilt. If, as Kierkegaard writes, "innocence is ignorance," then guilt must always involve knowledge. White Americans *know* that their historical advantage comes from the subjugation of an entire people. So, even for whites today for whom racism is anathema, there is no escape from the knowledge that makes for guilt. Racial guilt simply accompanies the condition of being white in America.

I do not believe that this guilt is a crushing anguish for most whites, but I do believe it constitutes a continuing racial vulnerability–an openness to racial culpability—that is a thread in white life, sometimes felt, sometimes not, but ever present as a potential feeling. In the late 1960s almost any black could charge this vulnerability with enough current for a white person to feel it. I had a friend who had developed this activity into a sort of specialty. I don't think he meant to be mean, though certainly he was mean. I think he was, in that hyperbolic era, exhilarated by the discovery that his race, which had long been a liability, now gave him a certain edge — that white guilt was the true force behind black power. To feel this power he would sometimes set up what he called "race experiments." Once I watched him stop a white businessman in the men's room of a large hotel and convince him to increase his tip to the black attendant from one to twenty dollars.

My friend's tactic was very simple, even corny. Out of the attendant's earshot he asked the man simply to look at the attendant, a frail, elderly, and very dark man in a starched white smock that made the skin on his neck and face look as leathery as a turtle's. He sat listlessly, pathetically, on a straight-backed chair next to a small table on which sat a stack of hand towels and a silver plate for tips. Since the attendant offered no service whatever beyond the handing out of towels, one could only conclude the hotel management offered his lowly presence as flattery to their patrons, as an opportunity for that easy noblesse oblige that could reassure even the harried and weary traveling salesman of his superior station. My friend was quick to make this point to the businessman and to say that no white man would do in this job. But when the businessman put the single back in his wallet and took out a five, my friend only sneered. Did he understand the tragedy of a life spent this way, of what it must be like to earn one's paltry living as a symbol of inferiority? And did he realize that his privilege as an affluent white businessman (ironically he had just spent the day trying to sell a printing press to the Black Muslims for their newspaper *Mohammed Speaks*) was connected to the deprivation of this man and others like him?

But then my friend made a mistake that ended the game. In the heat   10
of argument, which until then had only been playfully challenging, he inadvertently mentioned his father. This stopped the victim cold and his eyes turned inward. "What about your father?" the businessman asked. My friend replied, "He had a hard life, that's all." "How did he have a hard life?" the businessman asked. Now my friend was on the defensive. I knew he did not get along with his father, a bitter man who worked nights in a factory and demanded that the house be dark and silent all day. My friend blamed his father's bitterness on racism, but I knew he had not meant to exploit his own pain in this silly "experiment." Things had gotten too close to home, but he didn't know how to get out of the situation without losing face. Now, caught in his own trap, he did what he least wanted to do. He gave forth the rage he truly felt to a white stranger in a public men's room. "My father never had a chance," he said with the kind of anger that could easily turn to tears. "He never had a

freakin' chance. Your father had all the goddamn chances, and you know he did. You sell printing presses to black people and make thousands and your father probably lives down in Fat City, Florida, all because you're white." On and on he went in this vein, using—against all that was honorable in him—his own profound racial pain to extract a flash of guilt from a white man he didn't even know.

He got more than a flash. The businessman was touched. His eyes became mournful, and finally he simply said, "You're right. Your people got a raw deal." He took a twenty dollar bill from his wallet and walked over and dropped it in the old man's tip plate. When he was gone my friend and I could not look at the old man, nor could we look at each other.

It is obvious that this was a rather shameful encounter for all concerned—my friend and I, as his silent accomplice, trading on our racial pain, tampering with a stranger for no reason, and the stranger then buying his way out of the situation for twenty dollars, a sum that was generous by one count and cheap by another. It was not an encounter of people but of historical grudges and guilts. Yet, when I think about it now twenty years later, I see that it had all the elements of a paradigm that I believe has been very much at the heart of racial policy-making in America since the 1960s.

My friend did two things that made this businessman vulnerable to his guilt—that brought his guilt into the situation as a force. First he put this man in touch with his own knowledge of his ill-gotten advantage as a white. The effect of this was to disallow the man any pretense of racial innocence, to let him know that, even if he was not the sort of white who used the word *nigger* around the dinner table, he still had reason to feel racial guilt. But, as disarming as this might have been, it was too abstract to do much more than crack open this man's vulnerability, to expose him to the logic of white guilt. This was the five-dollar, intellectual sort of guilt. The twenty dollars required something more visceral. In achieving this, the second thing my friend did was something he had not intended to do, something that ultimately brought him as much shame as he was doling out: He made a display of his own racial pain and anger. (What brought him shame was not the pain and anger, but his trading on them for what turned out to be a mere twenty bucks.) The effect of this display was to reinforce the man's knowledge of ill-gotten advantage, to give credibility and solidity to it by putting a face on it. Here was human testimony, a young black beside himself at the thought of his father's racially constricted life. The pain of one man evidenced the knowledge of the other. When the businessman listened to my friend's pain, his racial guilt—normally only one source of guilt lying dormant among others—was called out like a neglected debt he would finally have to settle. An ill-gotten advantage is not hard to bear—it can be marked up to fate—until it touches the genuine human pain it has brought into the world. This is the pain that hardens guilty knowledge.

Such knowledge is a powerful influence when it becomes conscious. What makes it so powerful is the element of fear that guilt always carries, the fear of what the guilty knowledge says about us. Guilt makes us afraid for ourselves, and thus generates as much self-preoccupation as concern for others. The nature of this preoccupation is always the redemption of innocence, the reestablishment of good feeling about oneself.

In this sense, the fear for the self that is buried in all guilt is a pressure toward selfishness. It can lead us to put our own need for innocence above our concern for the problem that made us feel guilt in the first place. But this fear for the self does not only inspire selfishness; it also becomes a pressure to *escape* the guilt-inducing situation. When selfishness and escapism are at work, we are no longer interested in the source of our guilt and, therefore, no longer concerned with an authentic redemption from it. Then we only want the look of redemption, the gesture of concern that will give us the appearance of innocence and escape from the situation. Obviously the businessman did not put twenty dollars in the tip plate because he thought it would uplift black Americans. He did it selfishly for the appearance of concern and for the escape it afforded him.

This is not to say that guilt is never the right motive for doing good works or showing concern, only that it is a very dangerous one because of its tendency to draw us into self-preoccupation and escapism. Guilt is a civilizing emotion when the fear for the self that it carries is contained — a containment that allows guilt to be more selfless and that makes genuine concern possible. I think this was the kind of guilt that, along with the other forces, made the 1964 Civil Rights Bill possible. But since then I believe too many of our social policies related to race have been shaped by the fearful underside of guilt.

Black power evoked white guilt and made it a force in American institutions, very much in the same way as my friend brought it to life in the businessman. Few people volunteer for guilt. Usually others make us feel it. It was the expression of black anger and pain that hardened the guilty knowledge of white ill-gotten advantage. And black power — whether from militant fringe groups, the civil rights establishment, or big city political campaigns — knew exactly the kind of white guilt it was after. It wanted to trigger the kind of white guilt in which whites fear for their own decency and innocence; it wanted the guilt of white self-preoccupation and escapism. Always at the heart of black power, in whatever form, has been a profound anger at what was done to blacks and an equally profound feeling that there should be reparations. But a sober white guilt (in which fear for the self is still contained) seeks a strict fairness — the 1964 Civil Rights Bill that guaranteed equality under the law. It is of little value when one is after more than fairness. So black power made its mission to have whites fear for their innocence, to feel a visceral guilt from which they would have to seek a more profound redemption. In such redemption was the possibility of black reparation. Black power upped the ante on white guilt.

With black power, all of the elements of the hidden paradigm that shape America's race-related social policy were in place. Knowledge of ill-gotten advantage could now be shown and deepened by black power into the sort of guilt from which institutions could only redeem themselves by offering more than fairness — by offering forms of reparation and compensation for past injustice. I believe this bent our policies toward racial entitlements at the expense of racial development. In 1964, one of the assurances Senator Hubert Humphrey and others had to give Congress to get the landmark Civil Rights Bill passed was that the bill would not in any way require employers to use racial preferences to rectify racial imbalances. But this was before the explosion of black power in the late 1960s, before the hidden paradigm was set in motion. After black power, racial preferences became the order of the day.

If this paradigm brought blacks entitlements, it also brought the continuation of the most profound problem in American society, the invisibility of blacks as a people. The white guilt that this paradigm elicits is the kind of guilt that preoccupies whites with their own innocence and pressures them toward escapism — twenty dollars in the plate and out the door. With this guilt, as opposed to the contained guilt of genuine concern, whites tend to see only their own need for quick redemption. Blacks then become a means to this redemption and, as such, they must be seen as generally "less than" others. Their needs are "special," "unique," "different." They are seen exclusively along the dimension of their victimization, so that they become "different" people with whom whites can negotiate entitlements but never fully see as people like themselves. Guilt that preoccupies people with their own innocence blinds them to those who make them feel guilty. This, of course, is not racism, and yet it has the same effect as racism since it makes blacks something of a separate species for whom normal standards and values do not automatically apply.

Nowhere is this more evident today than in American universities. [20] At some of America's most elite universities administrators have granted concessions in response to black student demands (black power) that all but sanction racial separatism on campus — black "theme" dorms, black student unions, black yearbooks, homecoming dances, and so forth. I don't believe administrators sincerely believe in these separatist concessions. Most of them are liberals who see racial separatism as wrong. But black student demands pull administrators into the paradigm of self-preoccupied white guilt, whereby they seek a quick redemption by offering special entitlements that go beyond fairness. As a result, black students become all but invisible to them. Though blacks have the lowest grade point average of any racial group in American universities, administrators never sit down with them and "demand" in kind that black students bring their grades up to par. The paradigm of white guilt makes the real problems of black students secondary to the need for white redemption. It also cuts administrators off from their own values, which would most certainly discourage racial separatism and encourage higher academic performance for black students. Lastly, it makes for escapist policies. There is no difference between giving black students a separate lounge and leaving twenty dollars in the tip plate on the way out the door.

The Responsive Reader

1. What is the basic contrast that Steele sees between racial attitudes when he grew up in the fifties and today? What brought the shift about? What to Steele was the symbolic significance of the civil rights legislation of the sixties? (How was the development of white guilt like the original biblical "fall" from innocence?)
2. What evidence does Steele see that the promise of the civil rights movement has not come true? Where does he think public policy took the wrong turn?
3. What makes the story of the tip for the restroom attendant a test case for Steele's view of race relations? How does it conform to his "paradigm" of black anger and white guilt? (Would you have interpreted the incident the same way Steele did?)
4. According to Steele, how have black militants traded on white guilt?
5. How or why, according to Steele, do racial preferences on and off campus have "the same effect as racism"?

Talking, Listening, Writing

6. Have you been the beneficiary of affirmative action? Or have you been disadvantaged by special preferences for others? What is your personal opinion regarding affirmative action to advance the cause of minorities who have experienced discrimination?
7. Steele endeared himself to white conservatives like the columnist George Will and alienated a large segment of the black community. Do you consider him a legitimate and effective voice for the concerns of African Americans?
8. Do you remember an earlier cycle when racial attitudes or race relations were different from what they are today? Work out a detailed comparison and contrast, drawing on vivid examples from your own experience and observation.

Projects

9. Is there a consensus or a majority opinion on your campus concerning special admission procedures and programs designed to help minority students? Working with others, you could try to sample the opinions of students, counselors, people working in or enrolled in mentor programs, or teachers and students in special classes.

AMERICA'S EMERGING GAY CULTURE
Randall E. Majors

> *Lesbians and gays are emerging from a long history during which they were forced to deny their identity. The struggle for recognition of gay rights continues in the military, in the Boy Scouts, and in campaigns to have gay rights ordinances enacted in communities and states. What kind of advocacy, what kind of political action, will further the cause of full acceptance of lesbians and gays in American society? Randall E. Majors, who teaches at California State University at Hayward, wrote the following article for a collection of readings on intercultural communication. He sees in the current movement toward a new sense of identity and solidarity in the gay community an affirmation of the "American vision of individual freedom and opportunity."*

Thought Starters: How, according to this article, are gays "solidifying a unique sense of identity"?

A gay culture, unique in the history of homosexuality, is emerging   1
in America. Gay people from all walks of life are forging new self-identity concepts, discovering new political and social power, and building a revolutionary new life style. As more people "come out," identify themselves as gay, and join with others to work and live as openly gay people, a stronger culture takes shape with each passing year.

There have always been homosexual men and women, but never before has there emerged the notion of a distinct "culture" based on being gay. A useful way to analyze this emerging gay culture is to observe the communication elements by which gay people construct their life styles and social institutions. Lesbians and gay men, hereafter considered together as gay people, are creating a new community in the midst of the American melting pot. They are building social organizations, exercising political power, and solidifying a unique sense of identity — often under repressive and sometimes dangerous conditions. The following essay is an analysis of four major communication elements of the American gay culture: the gay neighborhood, gay social groups, gay symbols, and gay meeting behavior. These communication behaviors will demonstrate the vibrancy and joy that a new culture offers the American vision of individual freedom and opportunity.

The Gay Neighborhood

Most cultural groups find the need to mark out a home turf. American social history has many examples of ethnic and social groups who create their own special communities, whether by withdrawing from the larger culture or by forming specialized groups within it. The utopian communities of the Amish or Shakers are examples of the first, and ghetto neighborhoods in large urban areas are examples of the latter.

This need to create a group territory fulfills several purposes for gay people. First, a gay person's sense of identity is reinforced if there is a special place that is somehow imbued with "gayness." When a neighborhood becomes the home of many gay people, the ground is created for a feeling of belonging and sharing with others. Signs of gayness, whether overt symbols like rainbow flags or more subtle cues such as merely the presence of other gay people on the street, create the feeling that a certain territory is special to the group and hospitable to the group's unique values.

How do you know when a neighborhood is gay? As with any generality, the rule of thumb is that "enough gay people in a neighborhood and it becomes a gay neighborhood." Rarely do gay people want to paint the streetlamps lavender, but the presence of many more subtle factors gives a gay character to an area. The most subtle cues are the presence of gay people as they take up residence in a district. Word spreads in the group that a certain area is starting to look attractive and open to gay members. There is often a move to "gentrify" older, more affordable sections of a city and build a new neighborhood out of the leftovers from the rush to the suburbs. Gay businesses, those operated by or catering to gay people, often develop once enough clientele is in the area. Social groups and services emerge that are oriented toward the members of the neighborhood. Eventually, the label of "gay neighborhood" is placed on an area, and the transformation is complete. The Castro area in San Francisco, Greenwich Village in New York, New Town in Chicago, the Westheimer district in Houston, and West Hollywood or Silver Lake in Los Angeles are examples of the many emergent gay neighborhoods in cities across America.

A second need fulfilled by the gay neighborhood is the creation of a meeting ground. People can recognize and meet each other more easily when a higher density of like population is established. It is not easy to grow up gay in America; gay people often feel "different" because of their sexual orientations. The surrounding heterosexual culture often tries to imprint on everyone sexual behaviors and expectations that do not suit gay natures. Because of this pressure, gay people often feel isolated and alienated, and the need for a meeting ground is very important. Merely knowing that there is a specific place where other gay people live and work and play does much to anchor the psychological aspect of gayness in a tangible, physical reality. A gay person's sense of identity is reinforced by knowing that there is a home base, or a safe place where others of a similar persuasion are nearby.

Gay neighborhoods reinforce individual identity by focusing activities and events for members of the group. Celebrations of group unity and pride, demonstrations of group creativity and accomplishment, and services to individual members' needs are more easily developed when they are centralized. Gay neighborhoods are host to all the outward elements of a community — parades, demonstrations, car washes, basketball games, petition signing, street fairs, and garage sales.

A critical purpose for gay neighborhoods is that of physical and psychological safety. Subcultural groups usually experience some degree of persecution and oppression from the larger surrounding culture. For gay people, physical safety is a very real concern — incidences of homophobic assaults or harassment are common in most American cities. By centralizing gay activities, some safeguards can be mounted, as large numbers of gay people living in proximity create a deterrence to violence. This may be informal awareness of the need to take extra precautions and to be on the alert to help other gay people in distress or in the form of actual street patrols or social groups, such as Community United Against Violence in San Francisco. A sense of psychological safety follows from these physical measures. Group consciousness raising on neighborhood safety and training in safety practices create a sense of group cohesion. The security inspired by the group thus creates a psychic comfort that offsets the paranoia that can be engendered by alienation and individual isolation.

Another significant result of gay neighborhoods is the political reality of "clout." In the context of American grassroots democracy, a predominantly gay population in an area can lead to political power. The concerns of gay people are taken more seriously by politicians and elected officials representing an area where voters can be registered and mustered into service during elections. In many areas, openly gay politicians represent gay constituencies directly and voice their concerns in ever-widening forums. The impact of this kind of democracy-in-action is felt on other institutions as well: police departments, social welfare agencies, schools, churches, and businesses. When a group centralizes its energy, members can bring pressure to bear on other cultural institutions, asking for and demanding attention to the unique needs of that group. Since American culture has a strong tradition of cultural diversity, gay neighborhoods are effective agents in the larger cultural acceptance of gay people. The gay rights movement, which attempts to secure housing, employment, and legal protection for gay people, finds its greatest support in the sense of community created by gay neighborhoods.

Gay Social Groups

On a smaller level than the neighborhood, specialized groups fulfill   10
the social needs of gay people. The need for affiliation — to make friends, to share recreation, to find life partners, or merely to while away the time — is a strong drive in any group of people. Many gay people suffer from an isolation caused by rejection by other people or by their own fear

of being discovered as belonging to an unpopular group. This homophobia leads to difficulty in identifying and meeting other gay people who can help create a sense of dignity and caring. This is particularly true for gay teenagers who have limited opportunities to meet other gay people. Gay social groups serve the important function of helping gay people locate each other so that this affiliation need can be met.

The development of gay social groups depends to a large degree on the number of gay people in an area and the perceived risk factor. In smaller towns and cities, there are often no meeting places, which exacerbates the problem of isolation. In some small towns a single business may be the only publicly known meeting place for gay people within hundreds of miles. In larger cities, however, an elaborate array of bars, clubs, social groups, churches, service agencies, entertainment groups, stores, restaurants, and the like add to the substance of a gay culture.

The gay bar is often the first public gay experience for a gay person, and it serves as a central focus for many people. Beyond the personal need of meeting potential relationship partners, the gay bar also serves the functions of entertainment and social activity. Bars offer a wide range of attractions suited to gay people: movies, holiday celebrations, dancing, costume parties, live entertainment, free meals, boutiques, and meeting places for social groups. Uniquely gay forms of entertainment, such as drag shows and disco dancing, were common in gay bars before spreading into the general culture. Bars often become a very central part of a community's social life by sponsoring athletic teams, charities, community services, and other events as well as serving as meeting places.

The centrality of the bar in gay culture has several drawbacks, however. Young gay people are denied entrance because of age restrictions, and there may be few other social outlets for them. A high rate of alcoholism among urban gay males is prominent. With the spread of Acquired Immune Deficiency Syndrome (AIDS), the use of bars for meeting sexual partners has declined dramatically as gay people turn to developing more permanent relationships.

Affiliation needs remain strong despite these dangers, however, and alternative social institutions arise that meet these needs. In large urban areas, where gay culture is more widely-developed, social groups include athletic organizations that sponsor teams and tournaments; leisure activity clubs in such areas as country-and-western dance, music, yoga, bridge, hiking, and recreation; religious groups such as Dignity (Roman Catholic), Integrity (Episcopal), and the Metropolitan Community Church (MCC); volunteer agencies such as information and crisis hotlines and charitable organizations; and professional and political groups such as the Golden Gate Business Association of San Francisco or the national lobby group, the Gay Rights Task Force. A directory of groups and services is usually published in urban gay newspapers, and their activities are reported on and promoted actively. Taken together, these groups compose a culture that supports and nourishes a gay person's life.

Gay Symbols

Gay culture is replete with symbols. These artifacts spring up and   15
constantly evolve as gayness moves from an individual, personal experience into a more complex public phenomenon. All groups express their
ideas and values in symbols, and the gay culture, in spite of its relatively
brief history, has been quite creative in symbol making.

The most visible category of symbols is in the semantics of gay
establishment names. Gay bars, bookstores, restaurants, and social groups
want to be recognized and patronized by gay people, but they do not want
to incur hostility from the general public. This was particularly true in the
past when the threat of social consequences was greater. In earlier days,
gay bars, the only major form of gay establishment, went by code words
such as "blue" or "other" — the Blue Parrot, the Blue Goose, the Other
Bar, and Another Place.

Since the liberalization of culture after the 1960s, semantics have
blossomed in gay place names. The general trend is still to identify the
place as gay, either through affiliation (Our Place or His 'N' Hers), humor
(the White Swallow or Uncle Charley's), high drama (the Elephant Walk
or Backstreet), or sexual suggestion (Ripples, Cheeks, or Rocks). Lesbians
and gay men differ in this aspect of their cultures. Lesbian place names
often rely upon a more personal or classical referent (Amanda's Place or
the Artemis Cafe), while hypermasculine referents are commonly used
for gay male meeting places (the Ramrod, Ambush, Manhandlers, the
Mine Shaft, the Stud, or Boots). Gay restaurants and nonpornographic
bookstores usually reflect more subdued names, drawing upon cleverness
or historical associations: Dos Hermanos, Women and Children First,
Diana's, the Oscar Wilde Memorial Bookstore, and Walt Whitman
Bookstore. More commonly, gay establishments employ general naming
trends of location, ownership, or identification of product or service similar to their heterosexual counterparts. The increasing tendency of business to target and cater to gay markets strengthens the growth and
diversity of gay culture.

A second set of gay symbols are those that serve as member-
recognition factors. In past ages such nonverbal cues were so popular as to
become mythical: the arched eyebrow of Regency England, the green
carnation of Oscar Wilde's day, and the "green shirt on Thursday" signal
of mid-century America. A large repertoire of identifying characteristics
has arisen in recent years that serves the functions of recognizing other
gay people and focusing on particular interests. In the more sexually
promiscuous period of the 1970s, popular identifying symbols were a ring
of keys worn on the belt, either left or right depending upon sexual passiv-
ity or aggressiveness, and the use of colored handkerchiefs in a rear pocket
coded to desired types of sexual activity. Political sentiments are commonly expressed through buttons, such as the "No on 64" campaign
against the LaRouche initiative in California in 1986. The pink triangle as

a political symbol recalls the persecution and annihilation of gay people in Nazi Germany. The lambda symbol, an ancient Greek referent, conjures up classical images of gay freedom of expression. Stud earrings for men are gay symbols in some places, though such adornment has evolved and is widely used for the expression of general countercultural attitudes. The rainbow and the unicorn, mythical symbols associated with supernatural potency, also are common signals of gay enchantment, fairy magic, and spiritual uniqueness to the more "cosmic" elements of the gay community.

Another set of gay symbols to be aware of are the images of gay people as portrayed in television, film, literature, and advertising. The general heterosexual culture controls these media forms to a large extent, and the representations of gay people in those media take on a straight set of expectations and assumptions. The results are stereotypes that often oversimplify gay people and their values and do not discriminate the subtleties of human variety in gay culture. Since these stereotypes are generally unattractive, they are often the target of protests by gay people. Various authors have addressed the problem of heterosexual bias in the areas of film and literature. As American culture gradually becomes more accepting of and tolerant toward gay people, these media representations become more realistic and sympathetic, but progress in this area is slow.

One hopeful development in the creation of positive gay role models 20 has been the rise of an active gay market for literature. Most large cities have bookstores that stock literature supportive of gay culture. A more positive image for gay people is created through gay characters, heroes, and stories that deal with the important issues of family, relationship, and social responsibility. This market is constantly threatened by harsh economic realities, however, and gay literature is not as well developed as it might be.

Advertising probably has done the most to popularize and integrate gay symbols into American culture. Since money making is the goal of advertising, the use of gay symbols has advanced more rapidly in ad media than in the arts. Widely quoted research suggests that gay people, particularly men, have large, disposable incomes, so they become popular target markets for various products: tobacco, body-care products, clothing, alcohol, entertainment, and consumer goods. Typical gay-directed advertising in these product areas includes appeals based upon male bonding, such as are common in tobacco and alcohol sales ads, which are attractive to both straight and gay men since they stimulate the bonding need that is a part of both cultures.

Within gay culture, advertising has made dramatic advances in the past ten years, due to the rise of gay-related businesses and products. Gay advertising appears most obviously in media specifically directed at gay markets, such as gay magazines and newspapers, and in gay neighborhoods. Gay products and services are publicized with many of the same means as are their straight counterparts. Homoerotic art is widely used in clothing and body-care product ads. The male and female body are displayed for their physical and sexual appeal. This eroticizing of the body may be directed at either women or men as a desirable sexual object, and perhaps strikes at a subconscious homosexual potential in all people. Prominent elements of gay advertising are its use of sexuality and the central appeal of hypermasculinization. With the rise of sexual appeals in general advertising through double entendre, sexual punning, subliminal seduction, and erotic art work, it may be that gay advertising is only following suit in its emphasis on sexual appeals. Hugely muscled bodies and perfected masculine beauty adorn most advertising for gay products and services. Ads for greeting cards, billboards for travel service, bars, hotels, restaurants, and clothing stores tingle to the images of Hot 'N' Hunky Hamburgers, Hard On Leather, and the Brothel Hotel or its cross-town rival, the Anxious Arms. Some gay writers criticize this use of advertising as stereotyping and distorting of gay people, and certainly, misconceptions about the diversity in gay culture are more common than understanding. Gay people are far more average and normal than the images that appear in public media would suggest.

Gay Meeting Behavior

The final element of communication in the gay culture discussed here is the vast set of behaviors by which gay people recognize and meet one another. In more sexually active days before the concern for AIDS, this type of behavior was commonly called cruising. Currently, promiscuous sexual behavior is far less common than it once was, and cruising has evolved into a more standard meeting behavior that helps identify potential relationship partners.

Gay people meet each other in various contexts: in public situations, in the workplace, in gay meeting places, and in the social contexts of friends and acquaintances. Within each context, a different set of behaviors is employed by which gay people recognize someone else as gay and determine the potential for establishing a relationship. These behaviors include such nonverbal signaling as frequency and length of interaction, posture, proximity, eye contact, eye movement and facial gestures, touch, affect displays, and paralinguistic signals. The constraints of each situation and the personal styles of the communicators create great differences in the effectiveness and ease with which these behaviors are displayed.

Cruising serves several purposes besides the recognition of other gay   25
people. Most importantly, cruising is an expression of joy and pride in being gay. Through cruising, gay people communicate their openness and willingness to interact. Being gay is often compared to belonging to a universal — though invisible — fraternity or sorority. Gay people are generally friendly and open to meeting other gay people in social contexts because of the common experience of rejection and isolation they have had growing up. Cruising is the means by which gay people communicate their gayness and bridge the gap between stranger and new-found friend.

Cruising has become an integral part of gay culture because it is such a commonplace behavior. Without this interpersonal skill — and newcomers to gay life often complain of the lack of comfort or ease they have with cruising — a gay person can be at a distinct disadvantage in finding an easy path into the mainstream of gay culture. While cruising has a distinctly sexual overtone, the sexual subtext is often a symbolic charade. Often the goals of cruising are no more than friendship, companionship, or conversation. In this sense, cruising becomes more an art form or an entertainment. Much as the "art of conversation" was the convention of a more genteel cultural age, gay cruising is the commonly accepted vehicle of gay social interaction. The sexual element, however, transmitted by double meaning, clever punning, or blatant nonverbal signals, remains a part of cruising in even the most innocent of circumstances.

In earlier generations, a common stereotype of gay men focused on the use of exaggerated, dramatic, and effeminate body language — the "limp wrist" image. Also included in this negative image of gay people was cross-gender dressing, known as "drag," and a specialized, sexually suggestive argot called "camp." Some gay people assumed these social roles because that was the picture of "what it meant to be gay," but by and large these role behaviors were overthrown by the gay liberation of the 1970s. Gay people became much less locked into these restraining stereotypes and developed a much broader means of social expression. Currently, no stereotypic behavior would adequately describe gay communication style — it is far too diverse and integrated into mainstream American culture. Cruising evolved from these earlier forms of communication, but as a quintessential gay behavior, cruising has replaced the bitchy camp of an earlier generation of gay people.

The unique factor in gay cruising, and the one that distinguishes it from heterosexual cruising, is the level of practice and refinement the process receives. All cultural groups have means of introduction and meeting, recognition, assessment, and negotiation of a new relationship. In gay culture, however, the "courtship ritual" or friendship ritual of cruising is elaborately refined in its many variants and contexts. While straight people may use similar techniques in relationship formation and development, gay people are uniquely self-conscious in the centrality of these signals to the perpetuation of their culture. There is a sense of adventure and discovery in being "sexual outlaws," and cruising is the shared message of commitment to the gay life style.

Conclusion

These four communication elements of gay culture comprise only a small part of what might be called gay culture. Other elements have been more widely discussed elsewhere: literature, the gay press, religion, politics, art, theater, and relationships. Gay culture is a marvelous and dynamic phenomenon, driven and buffeted by the energies of intense feeling and creative effort. Centuries of cultural repression that condemned gay people to disgrace and persecution have been turned upside down in a brief period of history. The results of this turbulence have the potential for either renaissance or cataclysm. The internalized fear and hatred of repression is balanced by the incredible joy and idealism of liberation. Through the celebration of its unique life style, gay culture promises to make a great contribution to the history of sexuality and to the rights of the individual. Whether it will fulfill this promise or succumb to the pressures that any creative attempt must face remains to be seen.

The Responsive Reader

1. What purpose does the creation of a gay neighborhood serve? What, for Randall, are some of the attitudes, activities, businesses, or civic efforts that give a gay character to an area? What does he say about the role of friendships, social groups, or institutions like the gay bar?
2. What does Randall say about the role of symbols in the gay lifestyle? How does he assess the ambivalent, two-sided role of the media in dealing with gays in our culture? (Are the media hostile to or supportive of the gay lifestyle?)
3. How or in what contexts does Randall touch on homophobia — the rejection, oppression, or persecution that gays experience? How, according to Randall, does it affect or shape their social behavior?
4. What, according to this article, are some of the stereotypes that gays are leaving behind as the result of gay liberation?

Talking, Listening, Writing

5. Are the purposes the gay neighborhood serves similar to or different from the purposes served by the "turf" staked out by other groups?
6. How does the struggle for gay rights compare with other struggles for civil rights? How is it similar to or different from the struggle for racial equality or for women's rights?
7. What has been your experience with or observation of homophobia? Is it abating, holding steady, or increasing in our society? What is your prediction for the future?

Projects

8. The Mapplethorpe exhibit, with the obscenity trial it triggered in Cincinnati, became a major media event. For many observers, the trial was not primarily about a museum director (threatened with a year in jail or a $2,000 fine). What was on trial was America and its commitment to accept diversity. Collaborating with others, you may want to research media coverage of the trial. What was the range of opinion? What was the range of perspectives on overtly homosexual art, on instigators like Senator Jesse Helms, on the role of the jury and the people of Cincinnati?

EVERYDAY USE

Alice Walker

Alice Walker's novel The Color Purple *(1982) established her as a dominant voice in the search for a new black identity and black pride. In her Pulitzer Prize–winning novel, as in some of her short stories, her heroines are black women struggling to emerge from a history of oppression by white society and abuse by black males who "had failed women — and themselves." Walker's women find strength in bonding with other women, and they turn to the African past in the search for alternatives to our exploitative technological civilization. Walker's more recent novel,* The Temple of My Familiar *(1989), has been called a book of "amazing, overwhelming" richness, with characters "pushing one another towards self-knowledge, honesty, engagement" (Ursula K. Le Guin). Born in Eatonton, Georgia, Walker knew poverty and racism as the child of sharecroppers in the Deep South. While a student at Spelman College in Atlanta, she joined in the rallies, sit-ins, and freedom marches of the civil rights movement, which, she said later, "broke the pattern of black servitude in this country." She worked as a social worker for the New York City Welfare Department and as an editor for* Ms. *magazine. In the following story, the older generation holds on to its hard-won pride and independence, while members of a younger generation assert their break with the past by adopting Muslim names and African greetings.*

Thought Starters: What do the quilts symbolize in the story? How do they bring the confrontation between the characters to a head?

for your grandmama

I will wait for her in the yard that Maggie and I made so clean and   1
wavy yesterday afternoon. A yard like this is more comfortable than most
people know. It is not just a yard. It is like an extended living room. When
the hard clay is swept clean as a floor and the fine sand around the edges
lined with tiny, irregular grooves, anyone can come and sit and look up
into the elm tree and wait for the breezes that never come inside the house.

Maggie will be nervous until after her sister goes: she will stand
hopelessly in corners, homely and ashamed of the burn scars down her
arms and legs, eyeing her sister with a mixture of envy and awe. She
thinks her sister has held life always in the palm of one hand, that "no" is
a word the world never learned to say to her.

You've no doubt seen those TV shows where the child who has "made it" is confronted, as a surprise, by her own mother and father, tottering in weakly from backstage. (A pleasant surprise, of course: What would they do if parent and child came on the show only to curse out and insult each other?) On TV mother and child embrace and smile into each other's faces. Sometimes the mother and father weep, the child wraps them in her arms and leans across the table to tell how she would not have made it without their help. I have seen these programs.

Sometimes I dream a dream in which Dee and I are suddenly brought together on a TV program of this sort. Out of a dark and soft-seated limousine I am ushered into a bright room filled with many people. There I meet a smiling, gray, sporty man like Johnny Carson who shakes my hand and tells me what a fine girl I have. Then we are on the stage and Dee is embracing me with tears in her eyes. She pins on my dress a large orchid, even though she has told me once that she thinks orchids are tacky flowers.

In real life I am a large, big-boned woman with rough, man-working   5 hands. In the winter I wear flannel nightgowns to bed and overalls during the day. I can kill and clean a hog as mercilessly as a man. My fat keeps me hot in zero weather. I can work outside all day, breaking ice to get water for washing; I can eat pork liver cooked over the open fire minutes after it comes steaming from the hog. One winter I knocked a bull calf straight in the brain between the eyes with a sledge hammer and had the meat hung up to chill before nightfall. But of course all this does not show on television. I am the way my daughter would want me to be: a hundred pounds lighter, my skin like an uncooked barley pancake. My hair glistens in the hot bright lights. Johnny Carson has much to do to keep up with my quick and witty tongue.

But that is a mistake. I know even before I wake up. Who ever knew a Johnson with a quick tongue? Who can even imagine me looking a strange white man in the eye? It seems to me I have talked to them always with one foot raised in flight, with my head turned in whichever way is farthest from them. Dee, though. She would always look anyone in the eye. Hesitation was no part of her nature.

"How do I look, Mama?" Maggie says, showing just enough of her thin body enveloped in pink skirt and red blouse for me to know she's there, almost hidden by the door.

"Come out into the yard," I say.

Have you ever seen a lame animal, perhaps a dog run over by some careless person rich enough to own a car, sidle up to someone who is ignorant enough to be kind to him? That is the way my Maggie walks. She has been like this, chin on chest, eyes on ground, feet in shuffle, ever since the fire that burned the other house to the ground.

Dee is lighter than Maggie, with nicer hair and a fuller figure. She's ₁₀
a woman now, though sometimes I forget. How long ago was it that the
other house burned? Ten, twelve years? Sometimes I can still hear the
flames and feel Maggie's arms sticking to me, her hair smoking and her
dress falling off her in little black papery flakes. Her eyes seemed stretched
open, blazed open by the flames reflected in them. And Dee. I see her
standing off under the sweet gum tree she used to dig gum out of; a look
of concentration on her face as she watched the last dingy gray board of
the house fall in toward the red-hot brick chimney. Why don't you do a
dance around the ashes? I'd wanted to ask her. She had hated the house
that much.

I used to think she hated Maggie, too. But that was before we raised
the money, the church and me, to send her to Augusta to school. She used
to read to us without pity; forcing words, lies, other folks' habits, whole
lives upon us two, sitting trapped and ignorant underneath her voice. She
washed us in a river of make-believe, burned us with a lot of knowledge
we didn't necessarily need to know. Pressed us to her with the serious way
she read, to shove us away at just the moment, like dimwits, we seemed
about to understand.

Dee wanted nice things. A yellow organdy dress to wear to her
graduation from high school; black pumps to match a green suit she'd
made from an old suit somebody gave me. She was determined to stare
down any disaster in her efforts. Her eyelids would not flicker for minutes
at a time. Often I fought off the temptation to shake her. At sixteen she
had a style of her own: and knew what style was.

I never had an education myself. After second grade the school was
closed down. Don't ask me why: in 1927 colored asked fewer questions
than they do now. Sometimes Maggie reads to me. She stumbles along
good-naturedly but can't see well. She knows she is not bright. Like good
looks and money, quickness passed her by. She will marry John Thomas
(who has mossy teeth in an earnest face) and then I'll be free to sit here and
I guess just sing church songs to myself. Although I never was a good
singer. Never could carry a tune. I was always better at a man's job. I used
to love to milk till I was hooked in the side in '49. Cows are soothing and
slow and don't bother you, unless you try to milk them the wrong way.

I have deliberately turned my back on the house. It is three rooms,
just like the one that burned, except the roof is tin; they don't make shingle
roofs any more. There are no real windows, just some holes cut in the
sides, like the portholes in a ship, but not round and not square, with
rawhide holding the shutters up on the outside. This house is in a pasture,
too, like the other one. No doubt when Dee sees it she will want to tear it
down. She wrote me once that no matter where we "choose" to live, she
will manage to come see us. But she will never bring her friends. Maggie

and I thought about this and Maggie asked me, "Mama, when did Dee ever *have* any friends?"

She had a few. Furtive boys in pink shirts hanging about on washday   15 after school. Nervous girls who never laughed. Impressed with her they worshiped the well-turned phrase, the cute shape, the scalding humor that erupted like bubbles in lye. She read to them.

When she was courting Jimmy T she didn't have much time to pay to us, but turned all her faultfinding power on him. He *flew* to marry a cheap city girl from a family of ignorant flashy people. She hardly had time to recompose herself.

When she comes I will meet — but there they are!

Maggie attempts to make a dash for the house, in her shuffling way, but I stay her with my hand. "Come back here," I say. And she stops and tries to dig a well in the sand with her toe.

It is hard to see them clearly through the strong sun. But even the first glimpse of leg out of the car tells me it is Dee. Her feet were always neat-looking, as if God himself had shaped them with a certain style. From the other side of the car comes a short, stocky man. Hair is all over his head a foot long and hanging from his chin like a kinky mule tail. I hear Maggie suck in her breath. "Uhnnnh," is what it sounds like. Like when you see the wriggling end of a snake just in front of your foot on the road. "Uhnnnh."

Dee next. A dress down to the ground, in this hot weather. A dress   20 so loud it hurts my eyes. There are yellows and oranges enough to throw back the light of the sun. I feel my whole face warming from the heat waves it throws out. Earrings gold, too, and hanging down to her shoulders. Bracelets dangling and making noises when she moves her arm up to shake the folds of the dress out of her armpits. The dress is loose and flows, and as she walks closer, I like it. I hear Maggie go "Uhnnnh" again. It is her sister's hair. It stands straight up like the wool on a sheep. It is black as night and around the edges are two long pigtails that rope about like small lizards disappearing behind her ears.

"Wa-su-zo-Tean-o!" she says, coming on in that gliding way the dress makes her move. The short stocky fellow with the hair to his navel is all grinning and he follows up with "Asalamalakim, my mother and sister!" He moves to hug Maggie but she falls back, right up against the back of my chair. I feel her trembling there and when I look up I see the perspiration falling off her chin.

"Don't get up," says Dee. Since I am stout it takes something of a push. You can see me trying to move a second or two before I make it. She turns, showing white heels through her sandals, and goes back to the car. Out she peeks next with a Polaroid. She stoops down quickly and lines up picture after picture of me sitting there in front of the house with Maggie cowering behind me. She never takes a shot without making sure the house is included. When a cow comes nibbling around the edge of the yard she snaps it and me and Maggie *and* the house. Then she puts the Polaroid in the back seat of the car, and comes up and kisses me on the forehead.

Meanwhile Asalamalakim is going through motions with Maggie's hand. Maggie's hand is as limp as a fish, and probably as cold, despite the sweat, and she keeps trying to pull it back. It looks like Asalamalakim wants to shake hands but wants to do it fancy. Or maybe he don't know how people shake hands. Anyhow, he soon gives up on Maggie.

"Well," I say. "Dee."

"No, Mama," she says. "Not 'Dee,' Wangero Leewanika Kemanjo!"   25

"What happened to 'Dee'?" I wanted to know.

"She's dead," Wangero said. "I couldn't bear it any longer, being named after the people who oppress me."

"You know as well as me you was named after your aunt Dicie," I said. Dicie is my sister. She named Dee. We called her "Big Dee" after Dee was born.

"But who was *she* named after?" asked Wangero.

"I guess after Grandma Dee," I said.   30

"And who was she named after?" asked Wangero.

"Her mother," I said, and saw Wangero was getting tired. "That's about as far back as I can trace it," I said. Though, in fact, I probably could have carried it back beyond the Civil War through the branches.

"Well," said Asalamalakim, "there you are."

"Uhnnnh," I heard Maggie say.

"There I was not," I said, "before 'Dicie' cropped up in our family,   35
so why should I try to trace it that far back?"

He just stood there grinning, looking down on me like somebody inspecting a Model A car. Every once in a while he and Wangero sent eye signals over my head.

"How do you pronounce this name?" I asked.

"You don't have to call me by it if you don't want to," said Wangero.

"Why shouldn't I?" I asked. "If that's what you want us to call you, we'll call you."

"I know it might sound awkward at first," said Wangero.   40

"I'll get used to it," I said. "Ream it out again."

Well, soon we got the name out of the way. Asalamalakim had a name twice as long and three times as hard. After I tripped over it two or three times he told me to just call him Hakim-a-barber. I wanted to ask him was he a barber, but I didn't really think he was, so I didn't ask.

"You must belong to those beef-cattle peoples down the road," I said. They said "Asalamalakim" when they met you, too, but they didn't shake hands. Always too busy: feeding the cattle, fixing the fences, putting up salt-lick shelters, throwing down hay. When the white folks poisoned some of the herd the men stayed up all night with rifles in their hands. I walked a mile and a half just to see the sight.

Hakim-a-barber said, "I accept some of their doctrines, but farming and raising cattle is not my style." (They didn't tell me, and I didn't ask, whether Wangero (Dee) had really gone and married him.)

We sat down to eat and right away he said he didn't eat collards and pork was unclean. Wangero, though, went on through the chitlins and corn bread, the greens and everything else. She talked a blue streak over the sweet potatoes. Everything delighted her. Even the fact that we still used the benches her daddy made for the table when we couldn't afford to buy chairs.

"Oh, Mama!" she cried. Then turned to Hakim-a-barber. "I never knew how lovely these benches are. You can feel the rump prints," she said, running her hands underneath her and along the bench. Then she gave a sigh and her hand closed over Grandma Dee's butter dish. "That's it!" she said. "I knew there was something I wanted to ask you if I could have." She jumped up from the table and went over in the corner where the churn stood, the milk in it clabber by now. She looked at the churn and looked at it.

"This churn top is what I need," she said. "Didn't Uncle Buddy whittle it out of a tree you all used to have?"

"Yes," I said.

"Uh huh," she said happily. "And I want the dasher, too."

"Uncle Buddy whittle that, too?" asked the barber.

Dee (Wangero) looked up at me.

"Aunt Dee's first husband whittled the dash," said Maggie so low you almost couldn't hear her. "His name was Henry, but they called him Stash."

"Maggie's brain is like an elephant's," Wangero said, laughing. "I can use the churn top as a centerpiece for the alcove table," she said, sliding a plate over the churn, "and I'll think of something artistic to do with the dasher."

When she finished wrapping the dasher the handle stuck out. I took it for a moment in my hands. You didn't even have to look close to see where hands pushing the dasher up and down to make butter had left a kind of sink in the wood. In fact, there were a lot of small sinks; you could see where thumbs and fingers had sunk into the wood. It was beautiful light yellow wood, from a tree that grew in the yard where Big Dee and Stash had lived.

After dinner Dee (Wangero) went to the trunk at the foot of my bed and started rifling through it. Maggie hung back in the kitchen over the dishpan. Out came Wangero with two quilts. They had been pieced by Grandma Dee and then Big Dee and me had hung them on the quilt frames on the front porch and quilted them. One was in the Lone Star pattern.

The other was Walk Around the Mountain. In both of them were scraps of dresses Grandma Dee had worn fifty and more years ago. Bits and pieces of Grandpa Jarrell's Paisley shirts. And one teeny faded blue piece, about the size of a penny matchbox, that was from Great Grandpa Ezra's uniform that he wore in the Civil War.

"Mama," Wangero said sweet as a bird. "Can I have these old quilts?"

I heard something fall in the kitchen, and a minute later the kitchen door slammed.

"Why don't you take one or two of the others?" I asked. "These old things was just done by me and Big Dee from some tops your grandma pieced before she died."

"No," said Wangero. "I don't want those. They are stitched around the borders by machine."

"That'll make them last better," I said.   60

"That's not the point," said Wangero. "These are all pieces of dresses Grandma used to wear. She did all this stitching by hand. Imagine!" She held the quilts securely in her arms, stroking them.

"Some of the pieces, like those lavender ones, come from old clothes her mother handed down to her," I said, moving up to touch the quilts. Dee (Wangero) moved back just enough so that I couldn't reach the quilts. They already belonged to her.

"Imagine!" she breathed again, clutching them closely to her bosom.

"The truth is," I said, "I promised to give them quilts to Maggie, for when she marries John Thomas."

She gasped like a bee had stung her.   65

"Maggie can't appreciate these quilts!" she said. "She'd probably be backward enough to put them to everyday use."

"I reckon she would," I said. "God knows I been saving 'em for long enough with nobody using 'em. I hope she will!" I didn't want to bring up how I had offered Dee (Wangero) a quilt when she went away to college. Then she had told me they were old-fashioned, out of style.

"But they're *priceless!*" she was saying now, furiously; for she has a temper. "Maggie would put them on the bed and in five years they'd be in rags. Less than that!"

"She can always make some more," I said. "Maggie knows how to quilt."

Dee (Wangero) looked at me with hatred. "You just will not under-   70
stand. The point is these quilts, *these* quilts!"

"Well," I said, stumped. "What would *you* do with them?"

"Hang them," she said. As if that was the only thing you *could* do with quilts.

Maggie by now was standing in the door. I could almost hear the sound her feet made as they scraped over each other.

"She can have them, Mama," she said, like somebody used to never winning anything, or having anything reserved for her. "I can 'member Grandma Dee without the quilts."

I looked at her hard. She had filled her bottom lip with checkerberry   75
snuff and it gave her face a kind of dopey, hangdog look. It was Grandma Dee and Big Dee who taught her how to quilt herself. She stood there with her scarred hands hidden in the folds of her skirt. She looked at her sister with something like fear but she wasn't mad at her. This was Maggie's portion. This was the way she knew God to work.

When I looked at her like that something hit me in the top of my head and ran down to the soles of my feet. Just like when I'm in church and the spirit of God touches me and I get happy and shout. I did something I never had done before: hugged Maggie to me, then dragged her on into the room, snatched the quilts out of Miss Wangero's hands and dumped them into Maggie's lap. Maggie just sat there on my bed with her mouth open.

"Take one or two of the others," I said to Dee.

But she turned without a word and went out to Hakim-a-barber.

"You just don't understand," she said, as Maggie and I came out to the car.

"What don't I understand?" I wanted to know.   80

"Your heritage," she said. And then she turned to Maggie, kissed her, and said, "You ought to try to make something of yourself, too, Maggie. It's really a new day for us. But from the way you and Mama still live you'd never know it."

She put on some sunglasses that hid everything above the tip of her nose and her chin.

Maggie smiled; maybe at the sunglasses. But a real smile, not scared. After we watched the car dust settle I asked Maggie to bring me a dip of snuff. And then the two of us sat there just enjoying, until it was time to go in the house and go to bed.

The Responsive Reader

1. What kind of person is the mother? What role do her daydreams play in the story? How does her initial self-portrait as the narrator, or person telling the story, prepare you for what happens later?
2. What is the contrasting history of the two sisters? What is most important in their earlier history?
3. What do Dee and her companion stand for in this story? Do you recognize their attitudes and way of talking?
4. How does the confrontation over the quilts bring things to a head? What is the history of the quilts and their symbolic meaning? How does the climactic ending resolve the conflict in this story?

Talking, Listening, Writing

5. If you had to choose a role model from this story, would you opt for the mother or for Dee? Defend your choice.

Projects

6. Do you ever chafe at being a passive reader — who cannot enter into the story to help it steer one way or another? Write a passage in which one daughter or the other tells her side of the story. Or rewrite the ending the way you would have preferred the story to come out. Or write a sequel to the story bringing it up to date. Arrange for members of the class to share their imaginative efforts.

NADINE, RESTING ON HER NEIGHBOR'S STOOP

Judy Grahn

Judy Grahn is a feminist and lesbian poet, some of whose earlier poems were collected in The Work of a Common Woman *(1978). More recently she has been working on a cycle of poems devoted to the Helen myth, taking it beyond the story of Helen of Troy, former Queen of Sparta, who as the "stolen queen" was "hated and blamed for the most famous war of western history and literature, the model war of Troy." Grahn makes Helen the archetypal creation goddess that appears in various forms in many early religions. Helen is the goddess of beauty and love, of the womb and the source of life, of life and fire. Grahn associates her with the tradition of the weaver, or webster, symbolized by the spider, from whose very body comes the cloth of life. The following is one of the poems in which Grahn pays tribute to "common women."*

Thought Starters: How common is the "common woman" in the following poem? How does she challenge traditional definitions of femininity or womanhood?

	1

She holds things together, collects bail,
makes the landlord patch the largest holes.
At the Sunday social she would spike
every drink, and offer you half of what she knows,
which is plenty. She pokes at the ruins of the city   *5*
like an armored tank; but she thinks
of herself as a ripsaw cutting through
knots in wood. Her sentences come out
like thick pine shanks
and her big hands fill the air like smoke.   *10*
She's a mud–chinked cabin in the slums,
sitting on the doorstep counting
rats and raising 15 children,
half of them her own. The neighborhood
would burn itself out without her;   *15*
one of these days she'll strike the spark herself.
She's made of grease
and metal, with a hard head
that makes the men around her seem frail.
The common woman is as common as a nail.   *20*

The Responsive Reader

1. What are striking images or details in this poem that the reader is likely to remember?
2. Do you recognize this person? Does she seem like a real person to you?
3. Compare and contrast what you take to be a more traditional "feminine image" with Grahn's portrait of a "common woman."

Talking, Listening, Writing

4. What images of femininity or womanhood are dominant in our culture? How obsolete or how alive are such stereotypes as the homemaker, the cover girl, the beauty queen, the cheerleader, the dumb blonde, the sex bomb? What, if anything, has taken their place?
5. Have you encountered "strong women" in your own family or as part of your observation of friends, neighbors, coworkers, business associates?

Projects

6. Working with a group, you may want to investigate changing definitions of femininity or changing images of womanhood in the media. Draw on such sources as reruns of television series and reissues of old movies for comparison and contrast with more recent media trends. (For instance, you might study differences between the role Mary Tyler Moore played in the old Dick Van Dyke show and in the later Mary Tyler Moore show.)

WRITING WORKSHOP 6

Comparing and Contrasting

Writers use comparison and contrast to make connections. Often they can help readers understand something new by showing in detail how it differs from something familiar. (Gentrification is different from earlier patterns of urban renewal — it does not raze existing structures; it renovates and upgrades them instead; it uses them to lure affluent buyers back to the city.) Purposeful comparison and contrast can help us put historical changes in perspective. It can help us make tricky choices between alternative careers, mates, places to live, or political candidates.

TRIGGERING Writers do not usually make comparisons merely as an intellectual exercise. They typically have an agenda.

- A writer who contrasts the stark glass-and-steel highrises of Bauhaus (early modern) architecture with the curves, step patterns, and curlicues of postmodern buildings is not likely to be a neutral observer. He or she is likely to consider the earlier style sterile and the newer style more imaginative and more human.

- A telling contrast can help nudge people toward needed changes. It might be an eye-opener to compare the cost and trauma of an elderly relative's terminal illness under two different systems of health insurance. In this country — with a largely privately operated system of health insurance — the death of an elderly relative might leave a family bankrupt and in disarray. In a country like Canada or Germany, where health care is considered a citizen's right, all costs might be assumed by the publicly financed system of universal insurance.

GATHERING For an informative (and not oversimplified) comparison and contrast, the preliminary stock-taking is especially important. A key part of your prewriting may be **brainstorming** notes: You jot down features that might prove important as you chart similarities and differences. Suppose you are working on a paper that will show how changing gender roles have transformed traditional assumptions about marriage. The following might be your first jotting down of possibly relevant points:

TRADITIONAL	MODERN
church wedding	live together first
till death do us part	high divorce rate
virgin bride	family planning
subservient wife	both work
husband works	backyard weddings
take the good with the bad	equal relationships
husband handles finances	supportive, caring male
housewife cleans and cooks	share chores
wait on the husband	mixed marriages
sex on demand	marriage contract
talk about sex is taboo	mutual sex
marry your own kind	discuss problems
feminine wife	

Even while you jot down these items, you will be mentally making connections. Revealing contrasts emerge as you connect contrasting items: (traditional) the wife cooks and cleans / (modern) both share chores; (traditional) the husband works / (modern) both work; (traditional) subservient wife / (modern) equal partners. What other items should be linked to show a striking contrast between the old and the new?

SHAPING How would you organize the brainstorming notes about changing gender roles in the modern marriage? These notes might lead naturally to a **point–by–point** comparison. As each question is raised, the writer would first show the traditional answer and then the contrasting modern one. The following sequence might prove workable as a general organizing strategy for the paper:

POINT 1: Who supports the family financially? Who "provides"?

POINT 2: Who is the dominant partner? Who is in charge?

POINT 3: Who does the housekeeping?

POINT 4: What is the role of sex? (And what are the sex roles of the spouses?)

POINT 5: Who is considered an "eligible" marriage partner in the first place?

However, sometimes a **parallel–order** comparison might prove more workable or instructive. To give your readers a clear picture of two things you are comparing, you might decide to give them a complete, rounded picture of first the one and then the other. However, you help your readers see the connections. You take up key points in the same or very similar order — in parallel order. Here is the skeleton for a parallel-order comparison of two day-care centers:

It's Your Choice

preview

... In the light of these findings, working parents can perhaps suspend some of their feelings of guilt and instead concentrate on the hardest task: finding the right place for their children. Three important qualities to look for in a day-care center are a stable staff, the right activities, and an active role for the parents.

EXAMPLE A

point 1

I have worked at two different centers. The first one I consider a bad example. The staff changed every few months, mainly because we were paid minimum wage. The teachers who stayed did so because they did not feel qualified to work for a higher salary elsewhere. . . .

point 2

The children's day was as follows: TV — inside play — outside play — lunch — nap — outside play — TV — parents' pick up. The main goal was to make the children follow the rules and keep quiet. I remember one small girl particularly who was a very active child. . . .

point 3

Parents were not encouraged to participate; their role was to drop off the children and pick them up. . . .

EXAMPLE B

point 1

The second school I worked at was quite different. There was a very low turnover of staff. . . .

point 2

The children's schedule was as follows: Play — story time — work time — music — outside play — lunch — nap — independent work or play — story time — outside play — art — parents' pickup. . . .

point 3

Parents joined in all the outside activities and often stopped for lunch with the children. Parents should be wary of any school that does not allow drop-in visits. . . .
In a world of two-career or single-parent families, day care is going to be part of growing up for thousands of children. Instead of dropping a child off at the nearest center, parents must shop around to find a place designed to help children grow.

Make sure your organizing strategy works for the job at hand. Instead of using the classic point-by-point or parallel-order patterns, you may want to start with strong similarities — but then alert your reader to important differences that do not meet the eye. Sometimes, you may want to start with deceptive surface differences. (For instance, race relations today are different than they were in the days of overt legalized segregation and officially condoned violence.) However, you might then go on to show that basic similarities remain, though the current version of racism takes a more subtle form. (For instance, there is de facto segregation in the schools; minorities hit a "glass ceiling" on their way up the promotion ladder; etc.)

REVISING The plan of a comparison-and-contrast paper is necessarily more complicated than a simple main-point-and-supporting-examples scheme. As you reread and revise a first draft, try to see if you have indeed taken your readers with you—or whether you might have lost them along the way. You may need stronger signposts; you may need to give your readers a stronger sense of direction.

▪ *Spell out clearly the main point of your comparison.* Have you really summed up in a unifying thesis what your paper as a whole is trying to show? You may also need a stronger conclusion to pull together various points you made along the way.

▪ *Give your readers a preview of the itinerary.* Try to word your thesis in such a way that it gives away your overall plan. Give your readers a hint: point-by-point? parallel-order? similarities first? (But avoid a stodgy "in-this-paper-I-plan-to-do-the-following" style.)

▪ *Strengthen your network of transitions.* Signal major turning points. Signal similarities by such phrases as *similarly, in parallel fashion, as an exact counterpart, pointing in the same direction,* or *along the same lines.* Signal contrasts by phrases like *however, by contrast, on the other hand, as the direct opposite,* or *providing a counterweight* (or *a counterpoint*).

What is the overall plan in the following sample paper? How does the plan become clear to the reader? How effectively has the student writer followed through?

Wolves Mate for Life—Do You?

It is believed that the wolf mates for life. Spring is the breeding season. Six to seven in a litter is usual, but there may be as many as fourteen. The pups are born with big blue eyes, which soon fade in color. The family remains together while the pups are young, even when the mother breeds in successive years, and all members help take care of the family.

This could be compared to the traditional marriages of earlier times—married for life with six to fourteen children, and the family was a unit—unlike some of today's modern marriages where divorce dismantles half of them. What are the differences between the old traditional marriage and the new modern one that is so prominent in today's society? Where do these differences lie? I believe the substantial differences lie in the three general areas of work, family, and education, each stemming from changes in economics, values, or morality (or the lack of it, depending upon your viewpoint).

My grandpa and grandma lived in the little town of Yuba City and carried on a very traditional marriage. My grandfather did all of the out-of-house work while Grandma preoccupied herself with the domestic duties such as cleaning, cooking, and taking care of the children. My grandfather was a farmer and grew fruit and nut trees. He "brought home the bacon," while Grandma did the frying. This was very common in the traditional marriage for the husband to work and the wife to stay at home, but this isn't too often seen in today's society anymore.

Now we see the modern marriage as the only way to go. Because of the high cost of living both partners must work to support themselves. No longer can the husband deal with the outside job while his wife deals with the household. When I was younger my parents operated on a traditional-style marriage, but when I became a freshman in college, my mother went to work as an accountant. Our family could no longer live on what my father brought home, so my mother's joining the labor force was the only answer.

Family life in the traditional marriage is quite different from that in the modern marriage. My grandparents had three children—two boys and one girl. Having three or more children was not uncommon, but now in a modern marriage the third is usually "a mistake." My grandparents considered the family to be a very important institution and thus had many family activities together that brought closeness and harmony to the family. They often went camping at a cabin in Mt. Lassen, fed the ducks Wonder Bread at Ellis Lake, and played at the Sutter County park which had four swings, a set of monkey bars, a slide, and a merry-go-round. Vacations were also family-oriented. They would pack the car and drive to Oklahoma to visit family out there, singing "She'll be comin' round the mountain" as they traveled.

In the modern marriage, people often forget the importance of the family. Often there isn't even a whole family present. Half of today's marriages end in divorce, thus leaving a single parent somewhere with children to take care of, and that parent working to support the children usually has little or no time for family activities. Even when both parents are present, often work schedules conflict, and differing individual wants and needs come into play. Dad's been working all week and wants to watch baseball and relax on Saturday, Mom has to work 10 to 6:30, the older child has a book report due on Monday, but the little six-year-old wants to feed the ducks the stale bread with the family. It just doesn't work as well as it used to. Families are lucky if they get a one-week vacation together at Big Basin to camp in an overcrowded tent and fight off savage ants and blood-sucking mosquitoes, eat overripe fruit, and use outhouses that reek and have doors that never quite latch.

Education is something that the whole family participates in in a traditional marriage. Not only do the children learn at school, but they are also taught important things at home. My grandma taught her daughter to cook, embroider, can fruits and vegetables, iron, and churn butter. She taught all her kids manners and how to behave. My grandpa taught all his children how to grade fruit—know what is acceptable for market—drive the vehicles, milk the cows, even ride a bike, swim and dive, hunt, and fish. He also taught his sons how to work on mechanical vehicles, prune trees, irrigate, and breed the livestock. He also took time to help his children learn the value of money, by helping them open up a savings account. Other relatives taught the children also. An aunt taught the girl to crochet and her great-grandmother taught her to sew and quilt. The boys' great-grandfather taught them to carve things out of wood.

Things are quite different in the modern marriages we see today. The parents have little time for teaching in the home because of their work responsibilities. Education occurs at school and through peers and other sources, and children learn more on their own without the family than ever before. They attend driving school to learn how to drive, and the local Parks and Recreation Department takes care of the swim lessons. Relatives aren't usually involved as much as in a traditional marriage either. As <u>Ms.</u> magazine says, "Grandma is 61. She looks 45, is divorced, has a job selling real estate, and spends her weekends with a retired banker whose wife died three years ago."

Why have marriages changed? Why aren't families the self-sufficient, close, "all for one and one for all" units they used to be? I believe the change stems from economics. Society hardly allows that type of lifestyle anymore. Values have changed also, along with changes in morality. I don't believe people put as high a priority on marriage and family as they used to. Maybe divorce, suicide, emotional breakdowns, and child abuse would decrease if people valued marriage and family more, and looked back to some of the traditional marriage ways, and even took after the wolf and mated for life, as it used to be.

Topics for Comparison-and-Contrast Papers (A Sampling)

1. Have you ever lived in a homogenous neighborhood (with people of very similar backgrounds or social status) — but also in a more diverse, mixed neighborhood? Write a paper working out the contrast between the two settings.
2. Have you ever attended a school with a very homogenous student body — but also a school with a more diverse population? Write a comparison-and-contrast paper about the two schools.
3. Have you ever converted from one religious or political group to another? How did they compare?
4. Have you ever experienced a major change in your lifestyle? Write a before-and-after paper on the subject.
5. Weigh the options: What is preferable — a problem marriage or a divorce? (Or choose another similar topic: What is preferable — single motherhood or an alternative?)
6. In the men you have a chance to observe, do you find both the macho and the sensitive male? What sets them apart?
7. In our society, is there a contrast between middle-class and lower-class lifestyles and values?
8. Do men and women feel differently about love?
9. Have you experienced the difference between blue-collar and white-collar jobs?
10. In your family or in other areas of your experience, is there a generation gap?

7

Role Models: Seers and Pioneers

When I hear the people praising greatness, then I know that I too shall be recognized; I too when my time comes shall achieve.

                                                      from the Chippewa

Our society finds it hard to worship heroes — or to find heroes to worship. Many voters look at their leaders with suspicion, and the media thrive on scandals. Offspring of celebrities publish books exposing the mean-spirited person behind the public façade of the kindly old poet, the twinkle-eyed storyteller, or the glamorous star. Some of America's best-known entrepreneurs or television evangelists are in jail.

Nevertheless, people who are struggling or faced with barriers have a need for someone to admire, to look up to, to emulate. They look for role models that can symbolize for them their hopes and aspirations. Eve Merriam said in her poem dedicated to Elizabeth Blackwell, who braved centuries of precedent to become a female M.D., "don't let it darken, / the spark of fire; / keep it aglow." Amelia Earhart, before she left on the flight around the world from which she did not return, wrote a letter that said:

> Please know that I am quite aware of the hazards. I want to do it because I want to do it. Women must try to do things as men have tried. When they fail, their failure must be but a challenge to others.

Thousands of Americans each year visit the Martin Luther King Memorial in Atlanta to remind themselves of the eloquence and vision of the preacher who spoke of his dream that "the rough places will be made plain, and the crooked places will be made straight, and the glory of the Lord shall be revealed, and all flesh shall see it together."

In our diverse culture, what role models do we have who are not athletes, generals, or astronauts? What do we hear when we do not merely put people we admire on a pedestal but listen to what they have to say?

355

A BLACK ATHLETE LOOKS AT EDUCATION

Arthur Ashe

> *Arthur Ashe was one of the first African Americans to achieve an international reputation in tennis, until then often thought of as a sport for white people with money and social aspirations. Althea Gibson had been the first black woman to win the English Wimbledon tournament in 1957 and 1958. Ashe defeated the seemingly invincible Jimmy Connors for the Wimbledon title in men's tennis in 1975. Ashe was ranked first in the world at the time, but injuries and finally a heart attack cut short his career. He used his influence as a sports celebrity to promote civil rights causes; he helped get South Africa banned from the Davis Cup because of the government's apartheid policies. The following is one of the articles he wrote for the* New York Times *and the* Washington Post, *often trying to convince "not only black athletes but young blacks in general to put athletics in its proper place."*

Thought Starters: Ashe said about this article, "Some teacher probably read it and put it on the bulletin board. . . . The people who have the problems may not read it, but the ones who are in a position to influence them will." Do you think the kind of advice Ashe gives in this article influences people?

Since my sophomore year at UCLA, I have become convinced that we blacks spend too much time on the playing fields and too little time in the libraries. Consider these facts: for the major professional sports of hockey, football, basketball, baseball, golf, tennis and boxing, there are roughly only 3170 major league positions available (attributing 200 positions to golf, 200 to tennis and 100 to boxing). And the annual turnover is small.

There must be some way to assure that those who try but don't make it to pro sports don't wind up on street corners or in unemployment lines. Unfortunately, our most widely recognized role models are athletes and entertainers — "runnin'" and "jumpin'" and "singin'" and "dancin'."

Our greatest heroes of the century have been athletes — Jack Johnson, Joe Louis, and Muhammad Ali. Racial and economic discrimination forced us to channel our energies into athletics and entertainment. These were the ways out of the ghetto, the ways to get that Cadillac, those regular shoes, that cashmere sport coat.

Somehow, parents must instill a desire for learning alongside the desire to be Walt Frazier. Why not start by sending black professional athletes into high schools to explain the facts of life?

I have often addressed high school audiences and my message is 5 always the same: "For every hour you spend on the athletic field, spend two in the library. Even if you make it as a pro athlete, your career will be over by the time you are 35. You will need that diploma."

Have these pro athletes explain what happens if you break a leg, get a sore arm, have one bad year or don't make the cut for five or six tournaments. Explain to them the star system, wherein for every star earning millions there are six or seven others making $15,000 or $20,000 or $30,000. Invite a bench-warmer or a guy who didn't make it. Ask him if he sleeps every night. Ask him whether he was graduated. Ask him what he would do if he became disabled tomorrow. Ask him where his old high school athletic buddies are.

We have been on the same roads — sports and entertainment — too long. We need to pull over, fill up at the library and speed away to Congress and the Supreme Court, the unions and the business world.

I'll never forget how proud my grandmother was when I graduated from UCLA. Never mind the Davis Cup. Never mind the Wimbledon title. To this day, she still doesn't know what those names mean. What mattered to her was that of her more than thirty children and grandchildren, I was the first to be graduated from college, and a famous college at that. Somehow, that made up for all those floors she scrubbed all those years.

The Responsive Reader

1. Where does Ashe state his central thesis? How does he echo or reinforce it? How does he support it with examples, explanations, statistics?
2. Does Ashe look at the larger political or cultural context of the issue? Does he try to get at underlying causes?

Talking, Listening, Writing

3. Do you think this article persuaded its intended audience? Why or why not?
4. Some observers say that the lionizing of black athletes and entertainers perpetuates damaging stereotypes: African Americans can succeed only as ballplayers, singers, or comedians. Others answer that successful athletes from nonwhite backgrounds give both nonwhite and white youngsters people from other backgrounds to admire. Widely admired athletes thus help break down the barriers of prejudice. What do you think? How would you defend your stand on this issue?

5. In 1992 Ashe announced at a news conference that he had been infected with the AIDS virus, apparently as the result of a blood transfusion during open-heart surgery. He made the announcement reluctantly, after *USA Today* confronted him with a rumor of his condition and asked him to confirm or deny. Anna Quindlen examined the questions of journalistic ethics involved when she wrote in her column in the *New York Times*:

> Anyone who tries to make readers believe the questions are simple ones, who automatically invokes freedom of the press and the public's right to know, is doing a disservice to America's newspapers. . . . Naming rape victims. Outing gay people. The candidate's sex life. The candidate's drug use. Editors are making decisions they have never made before, on deadline, with competitors breathing down their necks. . . . Like victims of rape, perhaps the victims of this illness deserve some special privacy. . . . The white light of the press and the closed doors of our homes are two of the most deeply prized assets of our lives as Americans. It just so happens that they are often in direct opposition.

Toward the end of her column, Quindlen asked: "Need we know the medical condition of every public figure? . . . What are the parameters?" How would you answer the questions raised by her column?

Projects

6. Critics attack the passive role of the audience in the popular spectator sports, which the fans follow from their seats in the stadium or from the couch in front of the small screen. On your campus or in your community, is there a trend away from spectator sports and toward more active participation in sports? Working with other students, you may want to organize an investigation or survey to find answers to this question.

VICTOR VILLASEÑOR AND THE LONG ROAD NORTH

Nora Villagrán

Victor Villaseñor succeeded as a Mexican American writer against formidable odds. Held back by undiagnosed dyslexia, a high school dropout at eighteen, he describes himself as "feeling like a bombshell, ready to explode and prepared to kill anyone who made me feel ashamed." He decided to become a writer after reading the Irish author James Joyce's A Portrait of the Artist as a Young Man, *the story of a young man's search for his true self in spite of the "nets" thrown over him by family, church, and country. After 260 rejections of his novels and stories, Villaseñor finally sold his first novel,* Macho!, *which was praised for its descriptions of violent encounters among men trying to get across the border from Mexico "in any way possible." His next success was* Jury: The People vs. Juan Corona, *followed by* The Ballad of Gregorio Cortez. *In 1981 his screenplay for the Cortez story won first place in the television drama competition of the National Endowment for the Humanities. In his* Rain of Gold, *he tells the story of three generations of his family and their journey from the violence of the Mexican Revolution to a new life in Southern California. He based the book on over two hundred hours of taped conversations with relatives and godparents who remembered the family history and the hardships they had endured on both sides of the border.*

Thought Starters: After a major publisher, G. P. Putnam's, had paid $75,000 for *Rain of Gold,* Villaseñor bought it back to have it published by Arte Publico at the University of Houston, which paid $1,500 for the rights. According to the following interview conducted by a staff writer for the *San Jose Mercury News,* why does the author feel he made the "right decision"?

Why did you buy back your book?   1
"Putnam wanted to call my book fiction and change the title to *Rio Grande* — which sounds like an old John Wayne movie — because they thought it more marketable. I love my book; I was willing to go to New York and kill my publisher.

"In a New York restaurant, I told her the relationship between a publisher and a writer is a marriage. You've been unfaithful. You loved my book as non-fiction when you bought it and now you want to change it and you'll ruin it. I want my child back."
And Arte Publico?

"The publisher, Nicolás Kanellos, understood my book. But at first   5
he said, 'I can't help you — you're too big.' I said, 'Stop telling me what
you can't do; tell me what your dreams are.' He shares my vision: to reach
mainstream America. Russian writers, black writers, Anglo writers are
read by everyone — why not Hispanic writers? At an autograph party in
Houston a woman hugged me, crying, 'You wrote about my grandmother — and I'm German.'"

Why is it important that it's nonfiction?

"If a little Latina reads it and knows it's non-fiction, she'll picture my
mother and realize: 'My God, if Lupe can do it — I can do it.' We need
positive self-images."

What was your self-image growing up?

"I was dying, brainwashed by society into thinking Mexicans could
only wash dishes, work in the fields. I'd been taught self-hate. It wasn't
until I saw the movie *Viva Zapata!* that I saw Mexicans could be heroes —
and also when I went to Mexico at 19.

"My year in Mexico, I realized our rich culture: art, literature, mu-   10
seums, schools, professionals. I finally felt pride — but I also felt so much
hate and anger, I went crazy. I said, 'Papa, if I come home and see another
person insult a Mexican, I'll kill them.' He said, 'Don't you think I have
rage? You come home and make a difference.' He challenged me; so I said,
'OK, I'll be a writer.'"

Why writing?

"I wanted to build heroes for our children to look up to — heroes for
Anglos, too. They like our food, but what about us? Enchiladas are
tasty — Mexicans are tasty, too."

Why do you think there is prejudice?

"Ignorance, fear, jealousy, feeling there's not enough to share. So
they try to make us feel bad about ourselves. When children are warned
not to speak Spanish, the message is their culture is bad. Violence comes
from a poor self-image.

"We'll soon be the largest minority. If we don't develop a good self-   15
image, we'll still have a powerful influence on this country — but it won't
be a positive one. Kids need to see us on TV, in movies, in books, in
newspapers, everywhere, or else, well, if I hadn't become a writer, I'd
probably be dead or in prison."

You see women as worthy heroes.

"Women are the heroes of my book because when everyone was
starving, the men gave up but the women kept going. Women are *el eje* —
the hub, the center. The power of a family radiates from the women in it.
My father always said, when you raise fighting cocks, you breed to the
female, not the male. You look to the hen, a powerful *gallina*."

What books influenced you?

"I was 20 when I really read my first book: *The Family of Man,* then
The Little Prince and *Tender Is the Night.* I told a friend, 'Now I want to read

an important book that talks of humanity, the spiritual world and has guts.' She said, 'That sounds like *The Iliad.*' Later I thought, 'This is magnificent; I want to write a book like Homer.'

"Then I read *A Portrait of the Artist as a Young Man.* I saw how Joyce   *20* took a little private thing—a boy wetting the bed like I did—and made it into a universal that anyone could identify with. I realized in writing you start with the particular and it becomes universal. Then I read *Crime and Punishment,* and I was blown away."

When did you realize you'd become a writer?

"I was so afraid to say the words even after five years of writing. Then one day running across the Wyoming plains, I came to some caves with bits of broken Indian pottery. I asked God for help. I realized I don't *want* to be a writer—I *am* a writer. That's what I do: I write. It is more difficult to change our self-image than (it is to write).

"Even then, I wrote for 10 years and got 260 rejections before my first book was published. The first hundred hurt the worst."

Tell me about your dyslexia.

"I didn't do well in school except at recess. I didn't know I had   *25* dyslexia. Teachers called me lazy; I felt embarrassed, ashamed. So I'd run home and take off on my horse and hunt with a bow and arrow in the hills."

You're comfortable in the physical world.

"I grew up on my parents' Oceanside ranch. I had space. I learned to control power. *Aprevinado* means to prepare yourself, so that you've pre-lived life by the time you've grown up. Expose your kids to real life; that's how they learn."

How do you feel about the excitement over your book?

"I'm so happy. In Houston, a jazz station asked for a late-night interview—or was I too tired? I said, 'Tired? I spent 16 years on this book—I'll be right there!'"

The Responsive Reader

1. What were the publisher's plans for making Villaseñor's book "marketable"? What was the author's reaction?
2. What does Villaseñor say about the need for a positive self-image? How did his own self-image change? What does he consider his contribution as a writer?
3. What is the meaning of *aprevinado?*

Talking, Listening, Writing

4. How important is it to have a positive self-image? How difficult is it to achieve? Has anything or anybody helped you develop a positive self-image?
5. Have you encountered a writer, an artist, or a thinker that became

an inspiration for you? (Or have you encountered one that disappointed your expectations?)

Projects

6. What Hispanic or Latino writers are today "read by everybody"? What books by such authors are in your college bookstore? Talk to people in the know—bookstore clerks, librarians, book lovers, teachers of literature.

WE NEED TABOOS ON SEX AT WORK
Margaret Mead

Margaret Mead was a pioneering American scientist who wrote some of the classics of American anthropology. At age twenty-four, she went to live among the indigenous people of the Pacific island of Samoa to come to know from the inside their ways of thinking and patterns of behavior. The book she wrote about the experience, Coming of Age in Samoa *(1928), became one of the most widely read books in the history of anthropology. She specialized in studying the patterns of growing up of adolescent girls in non-Western cultures; she published her findings in a succession of widely read books including* Growing Up in New Guinea *(1930) and* Male and Female *(1949). Mead grew up in New Jersey and Pennsylvania and moved frequently as made necessary by the studies or teaching jobs of her parents. After studying at Columbia University, she ignored the advice of a famous fellow anthropologist and linguist to stay home and have children. Instead, she embarked on years of pioneering anthropological fieldwork whose results were still debated, attacked, and defended half a century later.*

Thought Starters: Toward the end of her career, Mead wrote to provide young people, and especially young women, with guidance in times of rapid change. What kind of voice do you hear in the following article? Are you inclined to heed her advice?

What should we — what can we — do about sexual harassment on the job? 1

During the century since the first "type writer" — that is, the first young woman clerk who had mastered the operation of the mechanical writing machine — entered a business office and initiated a whole new female-male work relationship, women have had to struggle with the problem of sexual harassment at work. And we still are at a loss as to how to cope with it successfully.

Certainly no one of us — young or old, single or married, attractive or homely, naive or socially skilled — has escaped entirely unscathed. True, actual sexual assaults — rape and seduction — have been less common in almost any work situation than fathers and brothers once feared and predicted. But who among us hasn't met the male kiss-and-tell office flirt, the pinching prankster, the man in search of party girls, or the man who makes sex a condition for job promotion? Who has not known the man who thinks no task is too tedious, unpleasant, or demeaning for his "girl" to do in or out of office hours, the gossipmonger and — perhaps most dangerous — the apparently friendly man who subtly undercuts every direction given by a woman, depreciates every plan she offers, and devalues her every accomplishment? Some women get discouraged and give up; most women learn to be wary. But as long as so many men use sex in so many ways as a weapon to keep down the women with whom they work, how can we develop mature, give-and-take working relationships?

As I see it, it isn't more laws that we need now, but new taboos.

Not every woman — and certainly not every man — realizes and ac-   5 knowledges that the mid-1960s marked a watershed in the *legal* treatment of women in the working world. Beginning with the Equal Pay Act of 1963 and the Civil Rights Acts of 1964 (especially Title VII), legislation has been passed, executive orders have been issued, official guidelines have been established and decisions in a great many court cases have set forth a woman's right to be a first-class working citizen. Slowly but surely, using the new laws, women are making progress in their fight to gain what the law now so clearly defines as the right of every working person. And today almost half of all adult women are working persons.

But there are serious discrepancies. At home and at school we still bring up boys to respond to the presence of women in outmoded ways — to become men who cannot be trusted alone with a woman, who are angry and frustrated by having to treat a woman as an equal — either as a female with power who must be cajoled or as a female without power who can be coerced. But at the same time we are teaching our daughters to expect a very different working world, one in which both women and men are full participants.

In keeping with this goal, we are insistent that the rights women have gained must be spelled out and that women use every legal device to ensure that new rules are formulated and translated into practice. Why, then, do I think that the new laws will not be sufficient to protect women — and men too, for that matter — from the problems of sexual harassment on the job? Why do I think we need new taboos?

I realize that this must sound strange to a generation of young women who have felt the need to break and abandon taboos of many kinds — from taboos against the inappropriate use of four-letter words to taboos against petty pilfering; from taboos against the use of addictive drugs to taboos against the public display of the naked human body; from the taboo against the frank enjoyment of sex to the taboos against full sexual honesty.

In some circles it has even become fashionable to call incest taboos — the taboos against sex with close family members other than husband and wife — out of date and unimportant. Yet incest taboos remain a vital part of any society. They insure that most children can grow up safe in the household, learn to trust, to be loved and to be sexually safe, unexploited and unmolested within the family.

When we examine how any society works, it becomes clear that it is   *10* precisely the basic taboos — the deeply and intensely felt prohibitions against "unthinkable" behavior — that keep the social system in balance. Laws are an expression of principles concerning things we can and do think about, and they can be changed as our perception of the world changes. But a taboo, even against taking a human life, may or may not be formulated in legal terms in some societies; the taboo lies much deeper in our consciousness, and by prohibiting certain forms of behavior also affirms what we hold most precious in our human relationships. Taboos break down in periods of profound change and are re-created in new forms during periods of transition.

We are in such a period now. And like the family, the modern business and the modern profession must develop incest taboos. If women are to work on an equal basis with men, with men supervising women in some cases and women supervising men in others, we have to develop decent sex mores in the whole working world.

In the past, when women entered the working world as factory workers or clerks in shops, as typists or chorus girls, they entered at the bottom; their poverty and their need for the job were part of their helplessness. Like women in domestic service, they were very vulnerable to sexual advances and seduction by men in positions of power over them. But sex also presented a precarious ladder by which a girl just might climb to become the pampered mistress or even the wife of the boss, the producer, the important politician.

For a long time after women began to work away from home, people made a sharp distinction between women who virtuously lived at home and limited "work" to voluntary efforts and other women who, lacking the support and protection of a father, brother, husband, or son, were constrained to work for money. Wage-earning women were sexually vulnerable, and it was generally believed that the woman who was raped probably deserved it and that the woman who was seduced probably had tempted the man. By leaving home, a woman did not merely move beyond the range of the laws that protected her there, but beyond the areas of living made safe by the force of taboos.

In the primitive societies in which I worked and lived as a young woman and as an older one, women who obeyed the accepted rules of behavior were not molested. But a woman who broke the rules — went out in the bush at night, worked alone in a distant garden or followed a lonely path without even a child companion — was asking for trouble. In general, women and men knew what was expected of them — until their lives were shaken up by change through the coming of strangers and the introduction of new kinds of work and new expectations. Then, along with other sorts of confusion, there was confusion about the sex relations of men and women. Cases of sex molestation, attack, and rape reflected the breakdown of traditional security.

Everywhere and at all times, societies have developed ways of styl-   *15*
izing relations between women and men. Though the rules might be cruel
and exploitative, they defined with clarity the posture and gait, the costume and the conversation, that signaled a woman's compliance with the
rules as well as the circumstances in which a woman defined herself as a
whore. In our own society, when women first became nurses their costume, reminiscent of the dress of nuns, at once announced the virtue of
their calling. When a young American woman went away from home to
teach children in one of the thousands of one-room schoolhouses that
abounded in the countryside, the local community took charge of her
virtue. Sometimes the rules were broken — on purpose. But the rules that
protected men as well as women were known and agreed upon.

Today, with our huge and restless mobility from country to city,
from one city to another, from class to class and from one country to
another, most of the subtle ways in which women and men related to each
other in a more limited setting have broken down. And now a new element
has entered into their working relations with the demands that women
must be employed in unfamiliar occupations and at higher executive and
professional levels. Almost without warning, and certainly without considering the necessity for working out new forms of acceptable behavior,
men and women are confronting each other as colleagues with equal
rights.

And suddenly there is an outburst of complaints from women who
find themselves mistreated in ways to which they are quite unaccustomed,
as well as complaints from women who have suddenly discovered that
sexual harassment on the job no longer is part of the expected life of a
working woman. By banding together, organizing themselves and counseling one another, women are beginning to feel their strength and are
making themselves heard, loud and clear, on the job, in the media and in
the courts. Harassment on the job and wife beating at home have become
part of our public consciousness.

Now, how to deal with the problems, the social discord and disso-
nance, in the relations between women and men? The complaints, the
legal remedies and the support institutions developed by women all are
part of the response to the new conception of women's rights. But I believe
we need something much more pervasive, a climate of opinion that includes men as well as women, and that will affect not only adult relations
and behavior on the job but also the expectations about the adult world
that guide our children's progress into that world.

What we need, in fact, are new taboos that are appropriate to the
new society we are struggling to create — taboos that will operate within
the work setting as once they operated within the household. Neither men
nor women should expect that sex can be used either to victimize women
who need to keep their jobs or to keep women from advancement or to

help men advance their own careers. A taboo enjoins. We need one that says clearly and unequivocally, "You don't make passes at or sleep with the people you work with."

This means that girls and boys will have to grow up together expect-   *20* ing and respecting a continuous relationship, in season and out, alone together or in a mixed group, that can withstand tension and relaxation, stimulation and frustration, frankness and reserve, without breaking down. It will have something of the relationship of brothers and sisters who have grown up together safely within a household, but it also will be different. For where brother and sister have a lifelong relationship, women and men who work together may share many years or only a few weeks or days or even hours.

In the way in which societies do develop new ways of meeting new problems, I believe we are beginning to develop new ways of working together that carry with them appropriate taboos — new ways that allow women and men to work together effortlessly and to respect each other as persons.

The beginning was made not at work but in our insistence on coeducation in the earliest grades of school, and gradually at all levels. This has made it possible for women to have much greater freedom wherever they go — so much so that we take it almost wholly for granted. We know it is not always wholehearted, but it is a beginning we know well.

And now, in line with new attitudes toward sex and equality, many students have demanded, and obtained, coeducational dormitories. Their elders mistook this as a demand for freer sexual access; but student advocates said firmly that, as young men and women, they wanted to meet under more natural circumstances and get to know one another as friends.

Today, wherever there is coeducation with a fairly even ratio between the sexes and several years' experience of living in coeducational dormitories, a quiet taboo is developing without the support of formal rules and regulations, fines or public exposure, praise or censure — a taboo against serious dating within the dormitory. Young women and young men who later will have to work side by side, in superordinate and subordinate relations as well as equals and members of a team, are finding their way toward a kind of harmony in which exploitative sex is set aside in favor of mutual concern, shared interests and, it seems to me, a new sense of friendship.

This is just a beginning, and one that is far from perfect. But one of   *25* the very good things is that women are discovering they can be frank and outspoken without being shrill, just as men are discovering there are pleasures in friendships without domination.

It is just a beginning, but students can set a style that will carry over into working relations in which skill, ability, and experience are the criteria by which persons are judged, and appreciation of a woman or a man as a whole person will deeply modify the exploitation and the anguish of sexual inequality. Laws and formal regulations and the protection given by the courts are necessary to establish and maintain institutional arrangements. But the commitment and acceptance that are implied by taboos are critical in the formation and protection of the most meaningful human relations.

The Responsive Reader

1. How would you initially react to the idea of a taboo? What ideas or associations does the term bring to mind? How does Mead try to change your mind about the role taboos play in a culture? (Does she succeed?)
2. The term *sexual harassment* has become a buzzword in recent years. How does Mead bring it to life? How does she make sure her readers take it seriously? (What are her most telling or striking examples?)
3. Mead systematically analyzes the problem and possible alternative solutions. Which does she find wanting, and why? Which does she endorse, and why?
4. How instructive or helpful is Mead's look at the history of women's role in the workplace?
5. Mead wrote with great earnestness and conviction. What makes her concluding paragraphs seem especially intense or committed? Do you find them eloquent or persuasive? Why or why not?

Talking, Listening, Writing

6. Have you observed the traditional sex roles that Mead describes? When and where? Have you seen evidence of the changes she traces? When and where?
7. Some people put their faith in better laws; others believe we need fundamental changes in people's attitudes. Which to you seems more promising or more important?
8. Is Mead hostile toward men? Do you think men and women react differently to her article?
9. Some people believe that in principle personal relations are private and therefore none of the business of an employer or institution. Argue your own position on this issue.

Projects

10. How much movement has there been toward true acceptance of women or equality of the sexes on your own campus? Working

with others, check into such areas as athletics, teaching, administration, and treatment of students.

Thinking about Connections

Some readers of Mead's article have felt that her assumptions about
what happens in coed dorms and her banning of sex in the workplace are
unrealistic. For a perspective different from hers, see the next article, "Far
More Than Friendship," by David R. Eyler and Andrea P. Baridon. How
much merit is there in the dissenting view?

FAR MORE THAN FRIENDSHIP
David R. Eyler and Andrea P. Baridon

Psychology Today *presents current developments in psychology in a language accessible to the educated layperson or nonspecialist. It prints articles ranging from new insights into the workings of the central nervous system to reports on psychological experiments. The following article from the magazine is one of many studies that take stock of current changes in personal relationships as the traditional extended family or clan or the traditional nuclear family of provider, homemaker, and children become increasingly rare. The authors try to find a language for new kinds of relationships that evolve as men and women more and more find themselves working together as equals in the workplace. Like other investigators who venture beyond the limits of the tried and true to trace new trends, these writers find themselves navigating in uncharted waters and are likely to stir up controversy or incur hostility.*

Thought Starters: What is the essence of the relationship that the authors are trying to define? How does it counter conventional assumptions? Why do the authors endorse it?

Our ways of living and loving have changed radically in the last   1
decade. Today men and women are thrust together on the job, sharing the workplace in equal numbers and, increasingly often, as professional peers. Work is becoming a major source of intimate interaction between them as they daily share the physical proximity of working side by side, the stimulation of professional challenge, and the powerful passions of accomplishment and failure.

Like every other kind of intimacy, the workplace variety brings with it the likelihood of sexual attraction. It is natural. It is inevitable, hard-wired as we are to respond to certain kinds of stimuli, although it sometimes comes as a surprise to those it strikes. But sexual attraction in the office is virtually inevitable for other reasons as well: The workplace is an ideal pre-screener, likely to throw us together with others our own age having similar socioeconomic and educational backgrounds, similar sets of values, and similar aspirations.

It also offers countless opportunities for working friendships to develop. As teams come to dominate the structure of the business world, the other half of a business team is increasingly likely to be not only a colleague with complementary skills and interests, but an attractive member of the opposite sex. As close as the collaboration between men and women workers can get at the office, it may be even more so outside it, as workers today function in an extended workplace of irregular hours and non-office settings. We are now more likely than ever, for example, to share the intimate isolation of business travel.

Such opportunity for interaction between the sexes is, in the grand scheme of things, really rather new. Only in the last 20 years, particularly the last 10, have women worked in equal numbers with men, and as equals rather than subordinates. Traditionally, society limits the opportunities for relationships between the sexes — how it does so is typically one of the distinguishing features of a culture. Until recently, unmarried men and women who were attracted to each other could date, court, or marry without raising eyebrows. For attracted couples who were already committed to others, the only option was to avoid each other or give in to an affair that consumed great energy just to be kept secret. So new is our sharing of the workplace that we have not yet created rules or social structures for dealing with today's unfamiliar intermixture of men and women working together.

The problem is not that sexual attraction inhabits the workplace, but that the options we traditionally give ourselves for recognizing that passion are far too limited. Conventional thinking tells us there is only one place to take our sexual feelings — to bed together. The modern American mind equates sexual attraction with sexual intercourse — the word "sex" serves as a synonym for physical contact. But intercourse is only one possible outcome among many.

Sexual attraction can be managed. It is not only possible to acknowledge sexual attraction, but also to enjoy the energy generated by it — and without acting on it sexually. The positive energy of sexual attraction is instead focused on work as it pulls men and women into a process of discovery, creativity and productivity. This thinking is part of a broader ethic emerging in this country: It's possible to have a lot without having it all.

We propose a new, psychologically unique relationship for which no models currently exist in American culture. It is a positive way for men and women to share intimate feelings outside of marriage or an illicit affair. It rejects altogether the saint-or-sinner model of colleague relations as too simplistic for modern life. In our own work as management consultants, we see the new relationship slowly unfolding in the American workplace. Confused coworkers, lacking guidance of any kind but responding to today's workplace realities, are stumbling toward new ways of relating to each other as they find the old alternatives too confining or otherwise unacceptable. The relationship they are inventing is not quite romantic — but it's not Platonic, either. It adds a dimension of increased intimacy to friendship and removes the sexual aspect from love. We call this relationship More than Friends, Less than Lovers.

The new sexually energized but strictly working relationship has already been officially documented. In a study conducted recently by researchers at the University of Michigan, 22 percent of managers reported involvement in such a relationship. Moreover, the relationship, unleashing as it does a great deal of creative energy, was shown to benefit both "couple" and company. And a study at the University of North Dakota found that work teams composed of men and women were more productive than those of same-sex colleagues.

Whatever else, of this we are sure: The new nonsexual love lacks a place among people's traditional expectations. We find that women seem to intuitively understand this new relationship when they learn of it. They are often the ones who move to forge it, often out of the wreckage of a colleague's awkward attempts at something sexual. But men often have a hard time with the idea . . . at first. The conventional models for sexual behavior prescribe a course of sexual conquest for men (seduction for women) and, moreover, they have a large ego-investment in it. Men find it harder to give up the deeply ingrained macho model. They deny that they can be anything other than a successful lover. Nevertheless, we have often observed two people approach this new relationship with unmatched expectations and move to mutually acceptable middle ground — and both benefit. To men we say: Count to 10 and hear us through.

We believe that sexual attraction among certain coworkers is inevitable. The laws of probability alone guarantee that the new gender parity will create a lot of sexual attraction at work that will need an outlet. The new commonplace of shared assignments provides natural opportunities for intimate communication between men and women and nurtures attractions that might have languished for lack of proximity or initiative. As always, some people will pursue sexual attraction to love and/or marriage. Others will become involved in affairs that have potential costs to careers and to other, established relationships outside. But the vast majority will not want or need a romantic relationship at work. We think it is time to bring sexual attraction out of the office closet and let it find its motivational and creative application in people's professional lives. *10*

Left with the old thinking alone, however, in which the only outlet for sexual attraction is physical sex, frustrated attraction has an unwelcome way of turning up as sexual harassment. We all need a way of thinking about sexual attraction that offers us more of a choice than consummation or harassment.

There is another incentive for welcoming this new, intimate relationship. Traditional thinking assumes there is only one appropriate place for sexual attraction — between lovers or spouses. But that leads to an untenable burden on our primary relationships — the spouses or lovers with whom we share it all romantically and sexually. As seasoned observers, we believe that it is naive to assume that a single intimate relationship will fulfill us in every way. As busy people leading complex lives outside the home, we cannot expect our primary relationships to also bear the burden of providing total personal and professional satisfaction. We need to grow comfortable loving one person romantically and deeply valuing another intellectually, artistically, or in any of a variety of ways that do not diminish our commitment to a primary partner.

The term "consenting adults" needs broadening to include not just those who willingly share physical sex, but those who are open to the possibility of acknowledging their sexual attraction, communicating openly about their feelings, and enjoying their sexuality within mutually agreed-upon boundaries. Above all, the new relationship is a limited relationship. You may share moments of great personal revelation and intimacy, but you do not expect to share your bodies and souls. That leaves only one question: How do you get there?

Don and Alicia are attorneys with complementary specialties who work for the same firm and have for years criss-crossed the country taking depositions and building cases together. They share grueling work schedules, meals, hours of strapped-in airliner conversation, and even exercise regimens that overlap away from home. When they put away the briefcases, they look like a couple, and at times they act like one.

As is commonly the case, neither can cite any lightning bolts that signalled the beginning of an irresistible attraction between them. Because events dictated their time together, the attraction developed slowly and naturally; they didn't deliberately cultivate it. The fact that they found each other interesting was almost incidental—at the beginning. Now, either will admit the other is good company, attractive, and worthy of a fantasy from time to time. An affair is the last thing they need as partnership looms for each, Don awaits the birth of a child in a happy marriage, and Alicia knows in her heart that he isn't the right guy for her. 15

In the course of their relationship they talked about affairs, but consciously decided not to have one. At the same time, neither of them wanted a relationship that had been neutered, and both acknowledged a desire to enjoy the sexual spark between them, keep it within their chosen boundaries, and continue working together without falling in love or having sex. Instead, they deliberately cultivated an intimacy that everyone came to recognize as special but not romantic.

Neither partner had to overcome the clumsy advances of the other, yet this successful resolution of a modern-workplace attraction came about as the result of an emerging sexual etiquette. It says we can talk about sex without inviting advances or harassing one another. It offers mutual respect and open communication as alternatives to playing out the old stereotypes of seduction and conquest. It offers the interpersonal sophistication to deal with sexual feelings in other than a romance-novel mode.

Since 1983, we have been working together as management trainers.

As we traveled around the country, gathering experience with the problems people were having, meeting workers of all kinds, we learned some things about the new gender-mixed work force. Alicia and Don's experience is becoming increasingly common. Women like Alicia tell us, "With Don, it didn't happen overnight. We've spent enough time together to develop the kind of trust and mutual respect that will let us talk about it. I know how to say no, and he would never force himself on me. I trust him completely, and there's no reason we can't enjoy an attraction that's fun and energizing without ending up in bed."

And men like Don acknowledge that "part of me says it's all or nothing when I have sexual feelings about a woman. But another part of me says it's more complicated than that with someone like Alicia. Somehow it has to be possible to play safely with sexy feelings, enjoy them, and still not have to sleep together.

A New Sexual Etiquette

On the basis of our experience, we have developed a practical, two-person model of sexual etiquette for those who wish to exploit the energy of workplace attraction without physical sex or falling in love, or avoiding each other altogether and pretending that the workplace is genderless. At its heart is a consciously managed relationship founded on mutual trust, respect, and acceptable boundaries that are openly agreed on, communicated, and monitored by both parties. Unlike friends, these partners share moments of great personal revelation. But unlike lovers, they do not expect to share bodies and souls. They divulge only what they choose to. 20

Natural human desire is something any two people should be able to feel without guilt or awkwardness. Where we set our boundaries is what distinguishes committed, romantic relationships from the near-loving feeling of those who come to know each other intimately through work. These are the five keys to pulling off the new relationship:

• **Setting boundaries.** Our personal boundaries are the psychological barriers that define us as individuals. You need a strong sense of your own values and purpose to risk sharing them intimately with someone else — even more so when you rely on your boundaries to permit tremendous personal intimacy yet prevent its becoming physical. You and your partner openly discuss and decide what is and is not off-limits.

You establish boundaries and expectations for the relationship right at the outset, as a means for defining and consciously managing it. You agree that you will not develop a personal life together and that your relationship will not be allowed to become a love affair. Some boundaries, notably the sexual one, are lines you agree never to cross; they remain forever out of bounds. Similarly, neither physical contact nor the language of lovers has a place in the relationship — they will only send misunderstood signals.

Other boundaries may be set and changed as you grow safe and comfortable in this new, unfamiliar relationship: defining the kinds of situations in which you allow yourselves to be alone, discussing certain facets of your personal lives, the giving and accepting of compliments, allowing your partner to see you when you are not at your best, and admitting the high value you place on the relationship without fear of being misunderstood.

You will also have internal boundaries to contend with — very personal ones you set and maintain without the knowledge of your partner. These are the lines you draw for monitoring your own thoughts and behavior; coping with near-love feelings is a personal matter each partner handles in his/her own way.

Part of the contract between you is an agreement to respect each other's privacy and individual identities. Situations may arise when you feel you must reinforce a boundary; you can do it indirectly, by altering the direction of a conversation, or directly, by discussing the unwelcome inquiry openly, as part of the process of consciously managing your relationship.

• **Conscious management.** There are no sure paths to ideal relationships between mutually attracted men and women under any circumstances. But without conscious management of this relationship, personal attraction can lead to destructive consequences — from ruined marriages to tainted professional reputations. Consciously managed, the relationship becomes a series of purposeful, directed events, rather than random ones that could drift into unplanned physical intimacy. You expect to have differences that you will resolve openly, instead of dancing around issues and leaving them open to ambiguity.

Through discussion, you create a voluntary contract in which you both agree that you will divert your sexual energy from personal attraction between you to the working relationship supporting it. You agree that your attraction is a positive thing that makes your working relationship exciting. You define ways to behave that will help you maintain your mutual boundaries. You communicate honestly with each other about your feelings and expectation. You make no attempt to hide the relationship from your spouse or lover on the one hand, or your company managers on the other, although you maintain discretion.

At first, you will probably find it difficult and awkward to discuss the emotional issues involved in creating and managing this relationship. It's new and unfamiliar turf and you're not sure what constitutes the right measure of trust. Your best guide is to sense when tension builds — that's when something needs to be brought into the open for honest discussion.

• **Monitoring each other.** Two people seldom approach a relationship — any relationship — with perfectly matched expectations. You and your partner both know that adjustments in your behavior will sometimes be necessary to keep things on an even keel. You share the responsibility for keeping your own behavior, feelings and expectations in line with the boundaries you establish. Monitoring each other ensures that open communication takes place when you sense your partner may infringe on a boundary or yield to temptation.

Monitoring each other also sets the expectation of open communication. You come to your relationship with respect for each other's intellect, tastes, and competencies. You look to each other to supplement what you individually bring to your work — to stimulate your thinking and enhance your creativity.

• **Open discussion.** You are making deliberate use of sexual chemistry to become both more personally satisfied and more successful and productive. The overarching technique you use to keep behavior within the boundaries you set is open discussion. It short-circuits problems that tend to build with time. Instead of maintaining the relationship by one-sided internal coping, you raise concerns to the level of two-person reasoning.

You clarify areas of misunderstanding where individual interpretations of events or intentions may be wrong. In time, you'll probably be laughing at simple misunderstandings. You vent frustrations to each other as well as understanding and being understood — eliminating the need to reject and the pain of rejection. The secret is not some perfect progression through an ideal set of relationship-building steps, but rather in the openness that says, "Ask me. Let's talk about it. We can work this out."

• **Cooling-off periods.** Unlike husbands and wives, you have the advantage of regular time-outs from each other, away from a nonphysical but demanding association. In permanent relationships, a large tolerance quotient is both desirable and required. In this relationship, by contrast, you are not obligated to keep each other happy or to take care of each other or to tolerate differences in food or music or television preferences on a daily and nightly basis. You deny yourselves some of the privileges of a fully committed couple while you avoid some of their frictions.

On the rare occasions when work isn't going well, or your conscious management techniques are flagging, you can acknowledge this is not going to be the right day to accomplish much together and step back to a comfortable distance.

On the good days, this relationship fosters inspired work that is intense, demanding and fulfilling. When it ends, parting involves ambivalence. You enjoy what you do so you are reluctant to stop, but you feel a sense of relief in getting away for a time to relax and be nourished in different ways with your family and friends. Down time spent apart allows you to keep a view of your work partner as someone special.

The "Business Couple"

Nothing promises to replace the committed love of a primary relationship. But the bottom line is that men and women working closely together find themselves in relationships that in many ways mimic courtship and marriage. They ride the emotional roller coaster of success and failure side by side. They become interdependent. They think alike and share values. Common goals emerge and are met through mutual effort. They have a de facto marriage minus the morning breath, the kids' problems and the mortgage payments. Fresh tailored clothes, a perpetually clean-shaven face, and a crisp clean shirt spare coworkers the gritty reality that personal appearances take on at home.

As pretty as this picture looks, however, a review of life's priorities quickly suggests to participants what it lacks. Coworkers who are more than friends come to realize that their work partner is not the one who takes care of them when they are sick, who shares the joys of the children, who wakes them up on Christmas morning. They take part in none of the life activities that make their at-home romantic relationships primary and their work relationships secondary. Above all, the privilege of discarding boundaries that separate individuals, the free merging of two people, is exclusive to the primary relationship.

Loving center-of-our-lives arrangements remain the source of our deepest satisfactions sexually and otherwise, but secondary relationships provide treasured qualities of narrow depth and exclusive experience not found elsewhere, especially since professional interests are dominant factors in our identities. They allow discovery and elaboration of parts of ourselves that remain unexplored in other relationships — passions for art or music or sports, say. One very sober "business couple" we know discovered to their vast amusement that they are both avid Elvis fans. On a business trip to Memphis they decided to use their free time to visit Graceland, simply because it's there — something their mates wouldn't do for money.

Good Work Is Sexy

"Business couples" breathe life into their projects together. They find   *40*
themselves struggling to make them survive. They grieve when they fail. And they revel in the joy of what they've created in their intense interaction. They may travel together closing deals, winning accolades, recounting victorious days together. Good work is sexy!

Michelle and Kevin are intimates but not lovers. They are experimental chemists in the new-products division of a pharmaceutical company. They think and plan and dispute ideas together, then defend their ideas in the corporate world with an intensity known only to people who have shared insight. There is a magic between them that transcends chemical formulas and careers, and each of them knows it.

Sometimes they look at each other after completing an important thought in unison and, without words, communicate an appreciation for one another that unknowing observers might misconstrue as love. Their lab technique is a symphony of moves developed through countless hours of teamwork — they know each other's professional souls, anticipate their every move, and sometimes it looks and feels very personal. But it isn't, and they know it. When work ends, Michelle is totally absorbed in a life all her own with seldom a thought of her lab partner. In it she shares loving intimacy with another partner who doesn't know a beaker from a Petri dish, but knows her like no one else does, not even Kevin, who has a fulfilling personal life of his own.

The Responsive Reader

1. According to the authors, what features of today's workplace favor the kind of relationship they describe?
2. How does this article require readers to rethink conventional assumptions? How does it challenge ideas about the macho male, about Platonic (nonsexual) relationships, or about traditional romance?
3. What case do the authors make for the benefits of the relationships they describe? What parts of the article do most for you to make their ideas clear or persuasive?

Talking, Listening, Writing

4. Do you think a chemistry like the one described in this article could exist among male and female students who attend classes or study together?
5. Do you think employers should have the right to inquire into the personal lives or private history of employees?

Projects

6. You may want to work with a group of your fellow students to come up with suggested guidelines governing friendship and romantic or sexual relationships in the workplace or on a college campus.

Thinking about Connections

How does the authors' argument compare with the position taken by Margaret Mead in "We Need Taboos on Sex at Work"? Where they disagree, what side are you inclined to take? How would you support your position?

IN SEARCH OF OUR MOTHERS' GARDENS

Alice Walker

> *Alice Walker is the author of the novel* The Color Purple *and the short story "Everyday Use" (p. 338). She has written and lectured widely on the relationship between black and white men and women, and between her own writing and the work of African American writers—Jean Toomer, Zora Neale Hurston—who were her role models and inspiration. She has taught creative writing and black literature at colleges including Jackson State College, Wellesley, and Yale. Many of Walker's essays, articles, and reviews were collected in her* In Search of Our Mothers' Gardens *(1983). In the title essay, she paid tribute to women of her mother's and grandmother's generations. They channeled the creative and spiritual energies that were denied other outlets into their rich gardens and into the "fanciful, inspired, and yet simple" quilts they fashioned from "bits and pieces of worthless rags."*

Thought Starters: How does Walker answer her two basic questions: "What did it mean for a black woman to be an artist in our grandmothers' time?" What does it mean to be "an artist and black woman" today?

> I described her own nature and temperament. Told how they needed a larger life for their expression. . . . I pointed out that in lieu of proper channels, her emotions had overflowed into paths that dissipated them. I talked, beautifully I thought, about an art that would be born, an art that would open the way for women the likes of her. I asked her to hope, and build up an inner life against the coming of that day. . . . I sang, with a strange quiver in my voice, a promise song. (Jean Toomer, "Avey," *Cane*)

(The poet speaking to a prostitute who falls asleep while he's talking)[1]

When the poet Jean Toomer walked through the South in the early twenties, he discovered a curious thing: black women whose spirituality was so intense, so deep, so *unconscious* that they were themselves unaware of the richness they held. They stumbled blindly through their lives: creatures so abused and mutilated in body, so dimmed and confused by pain, that they considered themselves unworthy even of hope. In the

1

---

[1][Jean Toomer (1894–1967) was born in Washington, D.C., and published *Cane*, a collection of poems and stories, in 1923.]

selfless abstractions their bodies became to the men who used them, they became more than "sexual objects," more even than mere women: they became "Saints." Instead of being perceived as whole persons, their bodies became shrines: what was thought to be their minds became temples suitable for worship. These crazy Saints stared out at the world, wildly, like lunatics — or quietly, like suicides; and the "God" that was in their gaze was as mute as a great stone.

Who were these Saints? These crazy, loony, pitiful women?

Some of them, without a doubt, were our mothers and grandmothers.

In the still heat of the post-Reconstruction South, this is how they   5 seemed to Jean Toomer: exquisite butterflies trapped in an evil honey, toiling away their lives in an era, a century, that did not acknowledge them, except as "the *mule* of the world." They dreamed dreams that no one knew — not even themselves, in any coherent fashion — and saw visions no one could understand. They wandered or sat about the countryside crooning lullabies to ghosts, and drawing the mother of Christ in charcoal on courthouse walls.

They forced their minds to desert their bodies and their striving spirits sought to rise, like frail whirlwinds from the hard red clay. And when those frail whirlwinds fell, in scattered particles, upon the ground, no one mourned. Instead, men lit candles to celebrate the emptiness that remained, as people do who enter a beautiful but vacant space to resurrect a God.

Our mothers and grandmothers, some of them: moving to music not yet written. And they waited.

They waited for a day when the unknown thing that was in them would be made known; but guessed, somehow in their darkness, that on the day of their revelation they would be long dead. Therefore to Toomer they walked, and even ran, in slow motion. For they were going nowhere immediate, and the future was not yet within their grasp. And men took our mothers and grandmothers, "but got no pleasure from it." So complex was their passion and their calm.

To Toomer, they lay vacant and fallow as autumn fields, with harvest time never in sight: and he saw them enter loveless marriages, without joy; and become prostitutes, without resistance; and become mothers of children, without fulfillment.

For these grandmothers and mothers of ours were not Saints, but   10 Artists; driven to a numb and bleeding madness by the springs of creativity in them for which there was no release. They were Creators, who lived lives of spiritual waste, because they were so rich in spirituality — which is the basis of Art — that the strain of enduring their unused and unwanted talent drove them insane. Throwing away this spirituality was their pathetic attempt to lighten the soul to a weight their work-worn, sexually abused bodies could bear.

What did it mean for a black woman to be an artist in our grandmothers' time? In our great-grandmothers' day? It is a question with an answer cruel enough to stop the blood.

Did you have a genius of a great-great-grandmother who died under some ignorant and depraved white overseer's lash? Or was she required to bake biscuits for a lazy backwater tramp, when she cried out in her soul to paint watercolors of sunsets, or the rain falling on the green and peaceful pasturelands? Or was her body broken and forced to bear children (who were more often than not sold away from her) — eight, ten, fifteen, twenty children — when her one joy was the thought of modeling heroic figures of rebellion, in stone or clay?

How was the creativity of the black woman kept alive, year after year and century after century, when for most of the years black people have been in America, it was a punishable crime for a black person to read or write? And the freedom to paint, to sculpt, to expand the mind with action did not exist. Consider, if you can bear to imagine it, what might have been the result if singing, too, had been forbidden by law. Listen to the voices of Bessie Smith, Billie Holiday, Nina Simone, Roberta Flack, and Aretha Franklin, among others, and imagine those voices muzzled for life. Then you may begin to comprehend the lives of our "crazy," "Sainted" mothers and grandmothers. The agony of the lives of women who might have been Poets, Novelists, Essayists, and Short-Story Writers (over a period of centuries), who died with their real gifts stifled within them.

And, if this were the end of the story, we would have cause to cry out in my paraphrase of Okot p'Bitek's great poem:

> O, my clanswomen
> Let us all cry together!
> Come,
> Let us mourn the death of our mother,
> The death of a Queen
> The ash that was produced
> By a great fire!
> O, this homestead is utterly dead
> Close the gates
> With *lacari* thorns,
> For our mother
> The creator of the Stool is lost!
> And all the young women
> Have perished in the wilderness!

But this is not the end of the story, for all the young women — our   15
mothers and grandmothers, *ourselves* — have not perished in the wilderness. And if we ask ourselves why, and search for and find the answer, we will know beyond all efforts to erase it from our minds, just exactly who, and of what, we black American women are.

One example, perhaps the most pathetic, most misunderstood one, can provide a backdrop for our mothers' work: Phillis Wheatley, a slave in the 1700s.[2]

Virginia Woolf, in her book *A Room of One's Own,* wrote that in order for a woman to write fiction she must have two things, certainly: a room of her own (with key and lock) and enough money to support herself.[3]

What then are we to make of Phillis Wheatley, a slave, who owned not even herself? This sickly, frail black girl who required a servant of her own at times — her health was so precarious — and who, had she been white, would have been easily considered the intellectual superior of all the women and most of the men in the society of her day.

Virginia Woolf wrote further, speaking of course not of our Phillis, that "any woman born with a great gift in the sixteenth century [insert "eighteenth century," insert "black woman," insert "born or made a slave"] would certainly have gone crazed, shot herself, or ended her days in some lonely cottage outside the village, half witch, half wizard [insert "Saint"], feared and mocked at. For it needs little skill and psychology to be sure that a highly gifted girl who had tried to use her gift for poetry would have been so thwarted and hindered by contrary instincts [add "chains, guns, the lash, the ownership of one's body by someone else, submission to an alien religion"], that she must have lost her health and sanity to a certainty."

The key words, as they relate to Phillis, are "contrary instincts." For when we read the poetry of Phillis Wheatley — as when we read the novels of Nella Larsen or the oddly false-sounding autobiography of that freest of all black women writers, Zora Hurston — evidence of "contrary instincts" is everywhere.[4] Her loyalties were completely divided, as was, without question, her mind.

But how could this be otherwise? Captured at seven, a slave of wealthy, doting whites who instilled in her the "savagery" of the Africa they "rescued" her from . . . one wonders if she was even able to remember her homeland as she had known it, or as it really was.

Yet, because she did try to use her gift for poetry in a world that made her a slave, she was "so thwarted and hindered by . . . contrary instincts, that she . . . lost her health. . . ." In the last years of her brief life, burdened not only with the need to express her gift but also with a penniless, friendless "freedom" and several small children for whom she

20

[2][Phillis Wheatley (c. 1753–1794), an African slave, wrote *Poems on Various Subjects, Religious and Moral,* published in 1773.]
[3][Virginia Woolf (1882–1941) was a leading British novelist and critic whose best-known novels are *Mrs. Dalloway* (1925) and *To the Lighthouse* (1927).]
[4][Zora Neale Hurston (1901–1960) wrote *Mules and Men,* a collection of black legend and folklore. Her novels include *Their Eyes Were Watching God,* which Alice Walker has praised for its "sense of black people as complete, complex, *undiminished* human beings."]

was forced to do strenuous work to feed, she lost her health, certainly. Suffering from malnutrition and neglect and who knows what mental agonies, Phillis Wheatley died.

So torn by "contrary instincts" was black, kidnapped, enslaved Phillis that her description of the "Goddess" — as she poetically called the Liberty she did not have — is ironically, cruelly humorous. And, in fact, has held Phillis up to ridicule for more than a century. It is usually read prior to hanging Phillis's memory as that of a fool. She wrote:

> The Goddess comes, she moves divinely fair,
> Olive and laurel binds her *golden* hair.
> Wherever shines this native of the skies,
> Unnumber'd charms and recent graces rise. [My italics]

It is obvious that Phillis, the slave, combed the "Goddess's" hair every morning; prior, perhaps, to bringing in the milk, or fixing her mistress's lunch. She took her imagery from the one thing she saw elevated above all others.

With the benefit of hindsight we ask, "How could she?"   25

But at last, Phillis, we understand. No more snickering when your stiff, struggling, ambivalent lines are forced on us. We know now that you were not an idiot or a traitor; only a sickly little black girl, snatched from your home and country and made a slave; a woman who still struggled to sing the song that was your gift, although in a land of barbarians who praised you for your bewildered tongue. It is not so much what you sang, as that you kept alive, in so many of our ancestors, *the notion of song*.

Black women are called, in the folklore that so aptly identifies one's status in society, "the *mule* of the world," because we have been handed the burdens that everyone else — *everyone* else — refused to carry. We have also been called "Matriarchs," "Superwomen," and "Mean and Evil Bitches." Not to mention "Castraters" and "Sapphire's Mama." When we have pleaded for understanding, our character has been distorted; when we have asked for simple caring, we have been handed empty inspirational appellations, then stuck in the farthest corner. When we have asked for love, we have been given children. In short, even our plainer gifts, our labors of fidelity and love, have been knocked down our throats. To be an artist and a black woman, even today, lowers our status in many respects, rather than raises it: and yet, artists we will be.

Therefore we must fearlessly pull out of ourselves and look at and identify with our lives the living creativity some of our great-grandmothers were not allowed to know. I stress *some* of them because it is well known that the majority of our great-grandmothers knew, even without "knowing" it, the reality of their spirituality, even if they didn't recognize it beyond what happened in the singing at church — and they never had any intention of giving it up.

How they did it — those millions of black women who were not

Phillis Wheatley, or Lucy Terry or Frances Harper or Zora Hurston or Nella Larsen or Bessie Smith; or Elizabeth Catlett, or Katherine Dunham, either — brings me to the title of this essay, "In Search of Our Mothers' Gardens," which is a personal account that is yet shared, in its theme and its meaning, by all of us. I found, while thinking about the far-reaching world of the creative black woman, that often the truest answer to a question that really matters can be found very close.

In the late 1920s my mother ran away from home to marry my father.   *30*
Marriage, if not running away, was expected of seventeen-year-old girls. By the time she was twenty, she had two children and was pregnant with a third. Five children later, I was born. And this is how I came to know my mother: she seemed a large, soft, loving-eyed woman who was rarely impatient in our home. Her quick, violent temper was on view only a few times a year, when she battled with the white landlord who had the misfortune to suggest to her that her children did not need to go to school.

She made all the clothes we wore, even my brothers' overalls. She made all the towels and sheets we used. She spent the summers canning vegetables and fruits. She spent the winter evenings making quilts enough to cover all our beds.

During the "working" day, she labored beside — not behind — my father in the fields. Her day began before sunup, and did not end until late at night. There was never a moment for her to sit down, undisturbed, to unravel her own private thoughts; never a time free from interruption — by work or the noisy inquiries of her many children. And yet, it is to my mother — and all our mothers who were not famous — that I went in search of the secret of what has fed that muzzled and often mutilated, but vibrant, creative spirit that the black woman has inherited, and that pops out in wild and unlikely places to this day.

But when, you will ask, did my overworked mother have time to know or care about feeding the creative spirit?

The answer is so simple that many of us have spent years discovering it. We have constantly looked high, when we should have looked high — and low.

For example: in the Smithsonian Institution in Washington, D.C.,   *35*
there hangs a quilt unlike any other in the world. In fanciful, inspired, and yet simple and identifiable figures, it portrays the story of the Crucifixion. It is considered rare, beyond price. Though it follows no known pattern of quilt-making, and though it is made of bits and pieces of worthless rags, it is obviously the work of a person of powerful imagination and deep spiritual feeling. Below this quilt I saw a note that says it was made by "an anonymous Black woman in Alabama, a hundred years ago."

If we could locate this "anonymous" black woman from Alabama, she would turn out to be one of our grandmothers — an artist who left her mark in the only materials she could afford, and in the only medium her position in society allowed her to use.

As Virginia Woolf wrote further, in *A Room of One's Own*:

Yet genius of a sort must have existed among women as it must have existed among the working class. [Change this to "slaves" and "the wives and daughters of sharecroppers."] Now and again an Emily Brontë or a Robert Burns [change this to "a Zora Hurston or a Richard Wright"] blazes out and proves its presence. But certainly it never got itself on to paper. When, however, one reads of a witch being ducked, of a woman possessed by devils [or "Sainthood"], of a wise woman selling herbs [our root workers], or even a very remarkable man who had a mother, then I think we are on the track of a lost novelist, a suppressed poet, of some mute and inglorious Jane Austen. . . . Indeed, I would venture to guess that Anon, who wrote so many poems without signing them, was often a woman. . . .

And so our mothers and grandmothers have, more often than not anonymously, handed on the creative spark, the seed of the flower they themselves never hoped to see: or like a sealed letter they could not plainly read.

And so it is, certainly, with my own mother. Unlike "Ma" Rainey's songs, which retained their creator's name even while blasting forth from Bessie Smith's mouth, no song or poem will bear my mother's name. Yet so many of the stories that I write, that we all write, are my mother's stories. Only recently did I fully realize this: that through years of listening to my mother's stories of her life, I have absorbed not only the stories themselves, but something of the manner in which she spoke, something of the urgency that involves the knowledge that her stories — like her life — must be recorded. It is probably for this reason that so much of what I have written is about characters whose counterparts in real life are so much older than I am.

But the telling of these stories, which came from my mother's lips   40
as naturally as breathing, was not the only way my mother showed herself as an artist. For stories, too, were subject to being distracted, to dying without conclusion. Dinners must be started, and cotton must be gathered before the big rains. The artist that was and is my mother showed itself to me only after many years. This is what I finally noticed:

Like Mem, a character in *The Third Life of Grange Copeland*, my mother adorned with flowers whatever shabby house we were forced to live in. And not just your typical straggly country stand of zinnias, either. She planted ambitious gardens — and still does — with over fifty different varieties of plants that bloom profusely from early March until late November. Before she left home for the fields, she watered her flowers, chopped up the grass, and laid out new beds. When she returned from the fields she might divide clumps of bulbs, dig a cold pit, uproot and replant roses, or prune branches from her taller bushes or trees — until night came and it was too dark to see.

Whatever she planted grew as if by magic, and her fame as a grower of flowers spread over three counties. Because of her creativity with her flowers, even my memories of poverty are seen through a screen of blooms — sunflowers, petunias, roses, dahlias, forsythia, spirea, delphiniums, verbena . . . and on and on.

And I remember people coming to my mother's yard to be given cuttings from her flowers; I hear again the praise showered on her because whatever rocky soil she landed on, she turned into a garden. A garden so brilliant with colors, so original in its design, so magnificent with life and creativity, that to this day people drive by our house in Georgia — perfect strangers and imperfect strangers — and ask to stand or walk among my mother's art.

I notice that it is only when my mother is working in her flowers that she is radiant, almost to the point of being invisible — except as Creator: hand and eye. She is involved in work her soul must have. Ordering the universe in the image of her personal conception of Beauty.

Her face, as she prepares the Art that is her gift, is a legacy of respect she leaves to me, for all that illuminates and cherishes life. She has handed down respect for the possibilities — and the will to grasp them.

For her, so hindered and intruded upon in so many ways, being an artist has still been a daily part of her life. This ability to hold on, even in very simple ways, is work black women have done for a very long time.

This poem is not enough, but it is something, for the woman who literally covered the holes in our walls with sunflowers:

> They were women then
> My mama's generation
> Husky of voice — Stout of
> Step
> With fists as well as
> Hands
> How they battered down
> Doors
> And ironed
> Starched white
> Shirts
> How they led
> Armies
> Headragged Generals
> Across mined
> Fields
> Booby-trapped
> Kitchens
> To discover books
> Desks
> A place for us
> How they knew what we
> *Must* know

Without knowing a page
Of it
Themselves.

Guided by my heritage of a love of beauty and a respect for strength — in search of my mother's garden, I found my own.

And perhaps in Africa over two hundred years ago, there was just such a mother; perhaps she painted vivid and daring decorations in oranges and yellows and greens on the walls of her hut; perhaps she sang — in a voice like Roberta Flack's — *sweetly* over the compounds of her village; perhaps she wove the most stunning mats or told the most ingenious stories of all the village story-tellers. Perhaps she was herself a poet — though only her daughter's name is signed to the poems that we know.

Perhaps Phillis Wheatley's mother was also an artist. *50*

Perhaps in more than Phillis Wheatley's biological life is her mother's signature made clear.

The Responsive Reader

1. How would you sum up the central lesson or inspiration that Walker draws from her look at the past?
2. Which of the writers and singers whose memory Walker invokes do you recognize? What use does she make of the quotations from the African American writer Jean Toomer and the British novelist Virginia Woolf?
3. Walker has made her readers revise more conventional judgments of writers like Zora Neale Hurston, for instance. How does she want her readers to revise stereotyped views of Phillis Wheatley? What is the meaning of Wheatley's story for her?
4. What use does Walker make of her own family history in this essay? What makes her mother a role model for her?

Talking, Listening, Writing

5. Have people who played a central role in your own past been good role models? Or have they been negative examples? Where have you looked for or found sources of inspiration — in the family, in school, in church, among friends?
6. Has art or music played a major role in your own life? Does any traditional or modern art have spiritual or vital significance for you? What outlets for creative energy or talent have you encountered outside conventional art?
7. Have school books or the media presented believable role models for you or for others with similar background or of the same generation?
8. Write a tribute to someone who has made a major contribution to your life or to the shaping of your personality.

Projects

9. Who are the heroes for students of differing ethnic or cultural backgrounds? What role models do young people with minority backgrounds recognize? How do they explain their choices? What difficulties or disappointments do they encounter in the search for heroes? Work with others to find and interpret answers to these questions.

I HAVE A DREAM

Martin Luther King, Jr.

The Reverend Martin Luther King, Jr., gave his "I Have a Dream" speech in August 1963 after he led 200,000 people in a march on Washington, D.C., to commemorate the one-hundredth anniversary of Lincoln's proclamation freeing the slaves. King was born in Atlanta, Georgia, and became a Baptist minister like his father. He was the pastor of the Dexter Avenue Baptist Church in Montgomery, Alabama, when Rosa Parks challenged the blacks-to-the-back-of-the-bus rule of the city's bus system. King organized the boycott that brought the segregated transit system to its knees and marked the birth of the civil rights movement. He founded the Southern Christian Leadership Conference, preaching the philosophy of nonviolent revolution in books like Letter from a Birmingham Jail (1963) and Why We Can't Wait (1964). The movement he led brought about the 1964 Civil Rights Act and the 1965 Voting Rights Act and ended a century of legally sanctioned segregation. King was kept under surveillance as a suspected Communist sympathizer by the FBI under its notorious director, J. Edgar Hoover. He was struck down in Memphis on April 4, 1968, by the bullet of a cowardly assassin, who died in jail without revealing the identity of the instigators, if any, who put him to work. The Martin Luther King Memorial in Atlanta, Georgia, has become a shrine for visitors who remember King's courage and vision and will not forget.

Thought Starters: Like no other black leader before or after him, King stirred the consciences of white Americans. Why or how?

Five score years ago, a great American, in whose symbolic shadow we stand, signed the Emancipation Proclamation. This momentous decree came as a great beacon light of hope to millions of Negro slaves who had been seared in the flames of withering injustice. It came as a joyous daybreak to end the long night of captivity.

But one hundred years later, we must face the tragic fact that the Negro is still not free. One hundred years later, the life of the Negro is still sadly crippled by the manacles of segregation and the chains of discrimination. One hundred years later, the Negro lives on a lonely island of poverty in the midst of a vast ocean of material prosperity. One hundred years later, the Negro is still languishing in the corners of American society and finds himself an exile in his own land. So we have come here today to dramatize an appalling condition.

In a sense we have come to our nation's capital to cash a check. When the architects of our republic wrote the magnificent words of the Constitution and the Declaration of Independence, they were signing a promissory note to which every American was to fall heir. This note was a promise that all men would be guaranteed the unalienable rights of life, liberty, and the pursuit of happiness.

It is obvious today that America has defaulted on this promissory note insofar as her citizens of color are concerned. Instead of honoring this sacred obligation, America has given the Negro people a bad check; a check which has come back marked "insufficient funds." But we refuse to believe that the bank of justice is bankrupt. We refuse to believe that there are insufficient funds in the great vaults of opportunity of this nation. So we have come to cash this check — a check that will give us upon demand the riches of freedom and the security of justice. We have also come to this hallowed spot to remind America of the fierce urgency of *now*. This is no time to engage in the luxury of cooling off or take the tranquilizing drugs of gradualism. *Now* is the time to make real the promises of Democracy. *Now* is the time to rise from the dark and desolate valley of segregation to the sunlit path of racial justice. *Now* is the time to open the doors of opportunity to all of God's children. *Now* is the time to lift our nation from the quicksands of racial injustice to the solid rock of brotherhood.

It would be fatal for the nation to overlook the urgency of the moment and to underestimate the determination of the Negro. This sweltering summer of the Negro's legitimate discontent will not pass until there is an invigorating autumn of freedom and equality. 1963 is not an end, but a beginning. Those who hope that the Negro needed to blow off steam and will now be content will have a rude awakening if the nation returns to business as usual. There will be neither rest nor tranquility in America until the Negro is granted his citizenship rights. The whirlwinds of revolt will continue to shake the foundations of our nation until the bright day of justice emerges.

But there is something I must say to my people who stand on the warm threshold which leads into the palace of justice. In the process of gaining our rightful place we must not be guilty of wrongful deeds. Let us not seek to satisfy our thirst for freedom by drinking from the cup of bitterness and hatred. We must forever conduct our struggle on the high plane of dignity and discipline. We must not allow our creative protest to degenerate into physical violence. Again and again we must rise to the majestic heights of meeting physical force with soul force. The marvelous new militancy which has engulfed the Negro community must not lead us to a distrust of all white people, for many of our white brothers, as evidenced by their presence here today, have come to realize that their destiny is tied up with our destiny and their freedom is inextricably bound to our freedom. We cannot walk alone.

And as we walk, we must make the pledge that we shall march ahead. We cannot turn back. There are those who are asking the devotees of civil rights, "When will you be satisfied?" We can never be satisfied as long as the Negro is the victim of the unspeakable horrors of police brutality. We can never be satisfied as long as our bodies, heavy with the fatigue of travel, cannot gain lodging in the motels of the highways and the hotels of the cities. We cannot be satisfied as long as the Negro's basic mobility is from a smaller ghetto to a larger one. We can never be satisfied as long as a Negro in Mississippi cannot vote and a Negro in New York believes he has nothing for which to vote. No, no, we are not satisfied, and will not be satisfied until justice rolls down like waters and righteousness like a mighty stream.

I am not unmindful that some of you have come here out of great trials and tribulations. Some of you have come fresh from narrow jail cells. Some of you have come from areas where your quest for freedom left you battered by the storms of persecution and staggered by the winds of police brutality. You have been the veterans of creative suffering. Continue to work with the faith that unearned suffering is redemptive.

Go back to Mississippi, go back to Alabama, go back to South Carolina, go back to Georgia, go back to Louisiana, go back to the slums and ghettos of our northern cities, knowing that somehow this situation can and will be changed. Let us not wallow in the valley of despair.

I say to you today, my friends, that in spite of the difficulties and frustrations of the moment I still have a dream. It is a dream deeply rooted in the American dream. 10

I have a dream that one day this nation will rise up and live out the true meaning of its creed: "We hold these truths to be self-evident; that all men are created equal."

I have a dream that one day on the red hills of Georgia the sons of former slaves and the sons of former slaveowners will be able to sit down together at the table of brotherhood.

I have a dream that one day even the state of Mississippi, a desert state sweltering with the heat of injustice and oppression, will be transformed into an oasis of freedom and justice.

I have a dream that my four little children will one day live in a nation where they will not be judged by the color of their skin but by the content of their character.

I have a dream today. 15

I have a dream that one day the state of Alabama, whose governor's lips are presently dripping with the words of interposition and nullification, will be transformed into a situation where little black boys and black girls will be able to join hands with little white boys and white girls and walk together as sisters and brothers.

I have a dream today.

I have a dream that one day every valley shall be exalted, every hill and mountain shall be made low, the rough places will be made plain, and the crooked places will be made straight, and the glory of the Lord shall be revealed, and all flesh shall see it together.

This is our hope. This is the faith with which I return to the South. With this faith we will be able to hew out of the mountain of despair a stone of hope. With this faith we will be able to transform the jangling discords of our nation into a beautiful symphony of brotherhood. With this faith we will be able to work together, to pray together, to struggle together, to go to jail together, to stand up for freedom together, knowing that we will be free one day.

This will be the day when all of God's children will be able to sing   *20* with new meaning

> My country, 'tis of thee,
> Sweet land of liberty,
>   Of thee I sing:
> Land where my fathers died,
> Land of the pilgrims' pride,
> From every mountain-side
>   Let freedom ring.

And if America is to be a great nation this must become true. So let freedom ring from the prodigious hilltops of New Hampshire. Let freedom ring from the mighty mountains of New York. Let freedom ring from the heightening Alleghenies of Pennsylvania!

Let freedom ring from the snowcapped Rockies of Colorado!

Let freedom ring from the curvaceous peaks of California!

But not only that; let freedom ring from Stone Mountain of Georgia!

Let freedom ring from Lookout Mountain of Tennessee!   *25*

Let freedom ring from every hill and molehill of Mississippi. From every mountainside, let freedom ring.

When we let freedom ring, when we let it ring from every village and every hamlet, from every state and every city, we will be able to speed up that day when all of God's children, black men and white men, Jews and Gentiles, Protestants and Catholics, will be able to join hands and sing in the words of the old Negro spiritual, "Free at last! free at last! thank God almighty, we are free at last!"

The Responsive Reader

1. King in this speech invokes many of the weighty words that have played a role in the history of race relations in this country. What meanings, memories, and associations cluster around words like *emancipation, segregation, gradualism, brotherhood, militancy, civil rights, police brutality, the American dream, interposition,* or *nullification?* (Which of these do you have to look up? What do you learn from your dictionary or other reference source?)
2. King was speaking to a double audience: His aim was to mobilize the aspirations of African Americans and to appeal to the consciences

of the white majority. How does he appeal to shared values by using historical documents, the Bible, or Negro spirituals?

3. Where does King speak most directly for or to "my people"? Where does he most eloquently voice their grievances? What warnings does he address to them?

4. What principles does King appeal to in speaking to white Americans? How does he link the civil rights struggle and the American dream?

Talking, Listening, Writing

5. Although King preached nonviolent revolution, he also said: "A riot is the language of the unheard." Is the philosophy of nonviolence alive today? Or has it been left behind by events?

6. King exhorts members of American minorities who believe they have "nothing for which to vote." After the 1992 riots in South Central Los Angeles, the black congresswoman from the district said, "A third of my people vote." Do you believe that in today's America the individual vote makes a difference? Why or why not?

7. Among people you know best, is racism alive or on the wane? Is there such a thing as "reverse racism"?

Projects

8. What African American leaders, national or local, receive prominent media coverage today? Working with a group, you may want to study the media coverage of the current black leadership. For instance, look at news reports, editorials and columns, magazine articles, and documentary coverage of protest activities. What are recurrent images, familiar criticisms, or prevalent attitudes?

Thinking about Connections

Compare King's dream for a better future with the vision of the future in Harvey Milk's "A City of Neighborhoods" (p. 108).

I STAND HERE IRONING

Tillie Olsen

> *Tillie Olsen is a working-class woman who without benefit of a Radcliffe education, Guggenheim fellowships, or similar perks bestowed by an elitist establishment became a powerful writer and a force in the women's movement. She came to be widely admired for giving voice to the story of the unheard in American society. She has said, "The power and the need to create, over and beyond reproduction, is native in both women and men. Where the gifted among women (and men) have remained mute, or have never attained full capacity, it is because of circumstances, inner or outer, which oppose the needs of creation." Chronicling the Great Depression of the thirties, Olsen has written with bitter eloquence about poverty, illness, hunger, unemployment, and soul-deadening jobs. Her novel* Yonnondio: From the Thirties *(1974) paid tribute to people deprived of their chance to develop into full human beings "so that a few may languidly lie on couches and trill 'how exquisite' to paid dreamers." A native of Omaha, Nebraska, with only a high school education, she lived through grinding poverty to write powerful stories shaking up the complacency of the well-to-do. Her "Tell Me a Riddle" won the O. Henry Award as best short story of the year in 1961. She has since been much honored and has lectured at universities including Amherst and Stanford.*

Thought Starters: The following short story is the kind of intensely personal writing that stays close to lived experience. We look through the eyes of a mother at a daughter who was "the child of anxious, not proud, love." What world do we see through the mother's eyes? (The WPA referred to in the story is the Works Progress Administration, begun in 1935 to provide federally funded jobs for the unemployed during the Great Depression.)

I stand here ironing, and what you asked me moves tormented back and forth with the iron. 1

"I wish you would manage the time to come in and talk with me about your daughter. I'm sure you can help me understand her. She's a youngster who needs help and whom I'm deeply interested in helping."

"Who needs help." Even if I came, what good would it do? You think because I am her mother I have a key, or that in some way you could use me as a key? She has lived for nineteen years. There is all that life that has happened outside of me, beyond me.

And when is there time to remember, to sift, to weigh, to estimate, to total? I will start and there will be an interruption and I will have to gather it all together again. Or I will become engulfed with all I did or did not do, with what should have been and what cannot be helped.

She was a beautiful baby. The first and only one of our five that was   5
beautiful at birth. You do not guess how new and uneasy her tenancy in her now-loveliness. You did not know her all those years she was thought homely, or see her poring over her baby pictures, making me tell her over and over how beautiful she had been — and would be, I would tell her — and was now, to the seeing eye. But the seeing eyes were few or non-existent. Including mine.

I nursed her. They feel that's important nowadays. I nursed all the children, but with her, with all the fierce rigidity of first motherhood, I did like the books then said. Though her cries battered me to trembling, I waited until the clock decreed.

Why do I put that first? I do not even know if it matters at all, or if it explains anything.

She was a beautiful baby. She blew shining bubbles of sound. She loved motion, loved light, loved color and music and textures. She would lie on the floor in her blue overalls patting the surface so hard in ecstasy her hands and feet would blur. She was a miracle to me, but when she was eight months old I had to leave her daytimes with the woman downstairs to whom she was no miracle at all, for I worked or looked for work and for Emily's father, who "could no longer endure" (he wrote in his good-bye note) "sharing want with us."

I was nineteen. It was the pre-relief, pre-WPA world of the depression. I would start running as soon as I got off the streetcar, running up the stairs, the place smelling sour, and awake or asleep to startle awake, when she saw me she would break into a clogged weeping that could not be comforted, a weeping I can hear yet.

After a while I found a job hashing at night so I could be with her   10
days, and it was better. But it came to where I had to bring her to his family and leave her.

It took a long time to raise the money for her fare back. Then she got chicken pox and I had to wait longer. When she finally came, I hardly knew her, walking quick and nervous like her father, looking like her father, thin, and dressed in a shoddy red that yellowed her skin and glared at the pockmarks. All the baby loveliness gone.

She was two. Old enough for nursery school they said, and I did not know then what I know now — the fatigue of the long day, and the lacerations of group life in the kinds of nurseries that are only parking places for children.

Except that it would have made no difference if I had known. It was the only place there was. It was the only way we could be together, the only way I could hold a job.

And even without knowing, I knew. I knew the teacher that was evil because all these years it has curdled into my memory, the little boy hunched in the corner, her rasp, "why aren't you outside, because Alvin hits you? that's no reason, go out, scaredy." I knew Emily hated it even if she did not clutch and implore "don't go Mommy" like the other children, mornings.

She always had a reason why we should stay home. Momma, you look sick, Momma. I feel sick. Momma, the teachers aren't there today, they're sick. Momma, we can't go, there was a fire there last night. Momma, it's a holiday today, no school, they told me.   15

But never a direct protest, never rebellion. I think of our others in their three-, four-year-oldness — the explosions, the tempers, the denunciations, the demands — and I feel suddenly ill. I put the iron down. What in me demanded that goodness in her? And what was the cost, the cost to her of such goodness?

The old man living in the back once said in his gentle way: "You should smile at Emily more when you look at her." What *was* in my face when I looked at her? I loved her. There were all the acts of love.

It was only with the others I remembered what he said, and it was the face of joy, and not of care or tightness or worry I turned to them — too late for Emily. She does not smile easily, let alone almost always as her brothers and sisters do. Her face is closed and somber, but when she wants, how fluid. You must have seen it in her pantomimes, you spoke of her rare gift for comedy on the stage that rouses a laughter out of the audience so dear they applaud and applaud and do not want to let her go.

Where does it come from, that comedy? There was none of it in her when she came back to me that second time, after I had had to send her away again. She had a new daddy now to learn to love, and I think perhaps it was a better time.

Except when we left her alone nights, telling ourselves she was old enough.   20

"Can't you go some other time, Mommy, like tomorrow?" she would ask. "Will it be just a little while you'll be gone? Do you promise?"

The time we came back, the front door open, the clock on the floor in the hall. She rigid awake. "It wasn't just a little while. I didn't cry. Three times I called you, just three times, and then I ran downstairs to open the door so you could come faster. The clock talked loud. I threw it away, it scared me what it talked."

She said the clock talked loud again that night I went to the hospital to have Susan. She was delirious with the fever that comes before red measles, but she was fully conscious all the week I was gone and the week after we were home when she could not come near the new baby or me.

She did not get well. She stayed skeleton thin, not wanting to eat, and night after night she had nightmares. She would call for me, and I would rouse from exhaustion to sleepily call back: "You're all right, darling, go to sleep, it's just a dream," and if she still called, in a sterner voice, "now go to sleep, Emily, there's nothing to hurt you." Twice, only twice, when I had to get up for Susan anyhow, I went in to sit with her.

Now when it is too late (as if she would let me hold and comfort her *25*
like I do the others) I get up and go to her at once at her moan or restless stirring. "Are you awake, Emily? Can I get you something?" And the answer is always the same: "No, I'm all right, go back to sleep, Mother."

They persuaded me at the clinic to send her away to a convalescent home in the country where "she can have the kind of food and care you can't manage for her, and you'll be free to concentrate on the new baby." They still send children to that place. I see pictures on the society page of sleek young women planning affairs to raise money for it, or dancing at the affairs, or decorating Easter eggs or filling Christmas stockings for the children.

They never have a picture of the children so I do not know if the girls still wear those gigantic red bows and the ravaged looks on the every other Sunday when parents can come to visit "unless otherwise notified" — as we were notified the first six weeks.

Oh it is a handsome place, green lawns and tall trees and fluted flower beds. High up on the balconies of each cottage the children stand, the girls in their red bows and white dresses, the boys in white suits and giant red ties. The parents stand below shrieking up to be heard and the children shriek down to be heard, and between them the invisible wall "Not To Be Contaminated by Parental Germs or Physical Affection."

There was a tiny girl who always stood hand in hand with Emily. Her parents never came. One visit she was gone. "They moved her to Rose Cottage," Emily shouted in explanation. "They don't like you to love anybody here."

She wrote once a week, the labored writing of a seven-year-old. "I *30*
am fine. How is the baby. If I write my letter nicely I will have a star. Love." There never was a star. We wrote every other day, letters she could never hold or keep but only hear read — once. "We simply do not have room for children to keep any personal possessions," they patiently explained when we pieced one Sunday's shrieking together to plead how much it would mean to Emily, who loved so to keep things, to be allowed to keep her letters and cards.

Each visit she looked frailer. "She isn't eating," they told us.

(They had runny eggs for breakfast or mush with lumps, Emily said later, I'd hold it in my mouth and not swallow. Nothing ever tasted good, just when they had chicken.)

It took us eight months to get her released home, and only the fact that she gained back so little of her seven lost pounds convinced the social worker.

I used to try to hold and love her after she came back, but her body would stay stiff, and after a while she'd push away. She ate little. Food sickened her, and I think much of life too. Oh she had physical lightness and brightness, twinkling by on skates, bouncing like a ball up and down up and down over the jump rope, skimming over the hill; but these were momentary.

She fretted about her appearance, thin and dark and foreign-looking   35 at a time when every little girl was supposed to look or thought she should look a chubby blonde replica of Shirley Temple. The doorbell sometimes rang for her, but no one seemed to come and play in the house or be a best friend. Maybe because we moved so much.

There was a boy she loved painfully through two school semesters. Months later she told me how she had taken pennies from my purse to buy him candy. "Licorice was his favorite and I brought him some every day, but he still liked Jennifer better'n me. Why, Mommy?" The kind of question for which there is no answer.

School was a worry to her. She was not glib or quick in a world where glibness and quickness were easily confused with ability to learn. To her overworked and exasperated teachers she was an overconscientious "slow learner" who kept trying to catch up and was absent entirely too often.

I let her be absent, though sometimes the illness was imaginary. How different from my now-strictness about attendance with the others. I wasn't working. We had a new baby, I was home anyhow. Sometimes, after Susan grew old enough, I would keep her home from school, too, to have them all together.

Mostly Emily had asthma, and her breathing, harsh and labored, would fill the house with a curiously tranquil sound. I would bring the two old dresser mirrors and her boxes of collections to her bed. She would select beads and single earrings, bottle tops and shells, dried flowers and pebbles, old postcards and scraps, all sorts of oddments; then she and Susan would play Kingdom, setting up landscapes and furniture, peopling them with action.

Those were the only times of peaceful companionship between her   40 and Susan. I have edged away from it, that poisonous feeling between them, that terrible balancing of hurts and needs I had to do between the two, and did so badly, those earlier years.

Oh there are conflicts between the others too, each one human, needing, demanding, hurting, taking — but only between Emily and Susan, no, Emily toward Susan that corroding resentment. It seems so obvious on the surface, yet it is not obvious. Susan, the second child, Susan, golden- and curly-haired and chubby, quick and articulate and assured, everything in appearance and manner Emily was not; Susan, not able to resist Emily's precious things, losing or sometimes clumsily breaking them; Susan telling jokes and riddles to company for applause while Emily sat silent (to say to me later: that was *my* riddle, Mother, I told it to Susan); Susan, who for all the five years' difference in age was just a year behind Emily in developing physically.

I am glad for that slow physical development that widened the difference between her and her contemporaries, though she suffered over it. She was too vulnerable for that terrible world of youthful competition, of preening and parading, of constant measuring of yourself against every other, of envy, "If I had that copper hair," "If I had that skin. . . ." She tormented herself enough about not looking like the others, there was enough of the unsureness, the having to be conscious of words before you speak, the constant caring — what are they thinking of me? without having it all magnified by the merciless physical drives.

Ronnie is calling. He is wet and I change him. It is rare there is such a cry now. That time of motherhood is almost behind me when the ear is not one's own but must always be racked and listening for the child cry, the child call. We sit for a while and I hold him, looking out over the city spread in charcoal with its soft aisles of light. "*Shoogily,*" he breathes and curls closer. I carry him back to bed, asleep. *Shoogily.* A funny word, a family word, inherited from Emily, invented by her to say: *comfort.*

In this and other ways she leaves her seal, I say aloud. And startle at my saying it. What do I mean? What did I start to gather together, to try and make coherent? I was at the terrible, growing years. War years. I do not remember them well. I was working, there were four smaller ones now, there was not time for her. She had to help be a mother, and housekeeper, and shopper. She had to set her seal. Mornings of crisis and near hysteria trying to get lunches packed, hair combed, coats and shoes found, everyone to school or Child Care on time, the baby ready for transportation. And always the paper scribbled on by a smaller one, the book looked at by Susan then mislaid, the homework not done. Running out to that huge school where she was one, she was lost, she was a drop; suffering over the unpreparedness, stammering and unsure in her classes.

There was so little time left at night after the kids were bedded down. 45 She would struggle over books, always eating (it was in those years she developed her enormous appetite that is legendary in our family) and I would be ironing, or preparing food for the next day, or writing V-mail to Bill, or tending the baby. Sometimes, to make me laugh, or out of her despair, she would imitate happenings or types at school.

I think I said once: "Why don't you do something like this in the school amateur show?" One morning she phoned me at work, hardly understandable through the weeping: "Mother, I did it. I won, I won; they gave me first prize; they clapped and clapped and wouldn't let me go."

Now suddenly she was Somebody, and as imprisoned in her difference as she had been in anonymity.

She began to be asked to perform at other high schools, even in colleges, then at city and statewide affairs. The first one we went to, I only recognized her that first moment when thin, shy, she almost drowned herself into the curtains. Then: Was this Emily? The control, the command, the convulsing and deadly clowning, the spell, then the roaring, stamping audience, unwilling to let this rare and precious laughter out of their lives.

Afterwards: You ought to do something about her with a gift like that—but without money or knowing how, what does one do? We have left it all to her, and the gift has as often eddied inside, clogged and clotted, as been used and growing.

She is coming. She runs up the stairs two at a time with her light 50 graceful step, and I know she is happy tonight. Whatever it was that occasioned your call did not happen today.

"Aren't you ever going to finish the ironing, Mother? Whistler painted his mother in a rocker. I'd have to paint mine standing over an ironing board." This is one of her communicative nights and she tells me everything and nothing as she fixes herself a plate of food out of the icebox.

She is so lovely. Why did you want me to come in at all? Why were you concerned? She will find her way.

She starts up the stairs to bed. "Don't get me up with the rest in the morning." "But I thought you were having midterms." "Oh, those." she comes back in, kisses me, and says quite lightly, "in a couple of years when we'll all be atom-dead they won't matter a bit."

She has said it before. She *believes* it. But because I have been dredging the past, and all that compounds a human being is so heavy and meaningful in me, I cannot endure it tonight.

I will never total it all. I will never come in to say: She was a child 55 seldom smiled at. Her father left me before she was a year old. I had to work her first six years when there was work, or I sent her home and to his relatives. There were years she had care she hated. She was dark and thin and foreign-looking in a world where the prestige went to blondness and curly hair and dimples, she was slow where glibness was prized. She was a child of anxious, not proud, love. We were poor and could not afford for her the soil of easy growth. I was a young mother, I was a distracted mother. There were the other children pushing up, demanding. Her younger sister seemed all that she was not. There were years she did not let me touch her. She kept too much in herself, her life was such she had to keep too much in herself. My wisdom came too late. She has much to her and probably little will come of it. She is a child of her age, of depression, of war, of fear.

Let her be. So all that is in her will not bloom—but in how many does it? There is still enough left to live by. Only help her to know—help make it so there is cause for her to know—that she is more than this dress on the ironing board, helpless before the iron.

The Responsive Reader

1. Why do you think Olsen wrote this story? (Who is the *you* addressed in the story?) What do you think writing this story did for the writer?

2. How do the physical conditions, the circumstances of her life, shape the outlook of the woman telling the story? How does poverty shape her attitude and expectations?

3. What is the role of institutions in this story? (Why do they loom so large?) What is the role of individuals — for instance, the teacher, Emily's father, the old man who lives in the back?

4. What picture of Emily emerges from this story? Can you relate to her as a person? Do you think the picture her mother gives us of her is incomplete or one-sided?

5. What is the narrator's last word on her story and the story of Emily? How do you react to the way the story ends?

Talking, Listening, Writing

6. Some readers of this story empathize with the mother; others criticize her for failing her child. How would you defend the mother? Or how would you justify the charges some readers bring against her?

7. How do you think the situation or the child might have looked when seen from a different point of view? For instance, what might have been the perspective of a teacher or social worker?

8. Tell the story of Emily as she might have told it herself.

Projects

9. What are the current statistics about poverty in this country? Who compiles them, and what do they mean? Where do we draw the "poverty line," and how meaningful is the term? Collaborate with other students to explore the answers to these questions.

Thinking about Connections

How is the perspective on poverty in Olsen's story similar to or different from the perspective in Jo Goodwin Parker's "What Is Poverty?" (p. 271)?

TO A FRIEND WHOSE WORK HAS COME TO TRIUMPH

Anne Sexton

Anne Sexton started to write poetry in an adult education class suggested by her psychiatrist. She became a much-published poet admired for the bold, surreal quality of her poems in spite of lifelong "emotional problems" — her biographers' euphemism for the mental illness that left her a prey to periodic breakdowns and debilitating medications and finally led to her suicide in 1974. She wrote powerful provocative poems about the historical servitude and oppression of women. ("I have been her kind," she said about the "possessed" and persecuted witch in her poem "Her Kind.") A one-time fashion model and the mother of two children, she wrote about the tyranny of gender and was one of the first feminist poets to write "openly about menstruation, abortion, masturbation, incest, adultery, and drug addiction" (Maxine Kumin).

Thought Starters: One of the best-known myths of ancient Greece tells the story of the inventor Daedalus, who was prevented from leaving the island of Crete after he built the labyrinth — the maze that kept in the monstrous Minotaur, half man, half bull. To escape and return home to Athens with his son Icarus, Daedalus designed wings made from wax and feathers. As they were flying homeward, Icarus flew too close to the sun, causing the wax to melt and causing him to drown in the sea. What is the symbolic meaning of the story?

Consider Icarus, pasting those sticky wings on, 1
testing that strange little tug at his shoulder blade,
and think of that first flawless moment over the lawn
of the labyrinth. Think of the difference it made!
There below are the trees, as awkward as camels; 5
and here are the shocked starlings pumping past
and think of innocent Icarus who is doing quite well;
larger than a sail, over the fog and blast
of the plushy ocean he goes. Admire his wings!
Feel the fire at his neck and see how casually 10
he glances up and is caught, wondrously tunneling
into that hot eye. Who cares that he fell back into the sea?
See him acclaiming the sun and come plunging down
while his sensible daddy goes straight into town.

The Responsive Reader

1. To you, does Icarus represent overreaching human ambition, doomed to fail? Does he symbolize the heedless eagerness of youth, disregarding the voice of experience? Does he represent the tragedy of heroic effort that almost succeeds — and yet fails? Or does the story appeal to the strongest kind of love — the love of a parent for a child?
2. How does Sexton rewrite the ancient myth? What for her is the meaning of the Icarus story?
3. What informal touches make this modern retelling less solemn than most versions of the ancient myth? How serious is the poet?

Talking, Listening, Writing

4. Do you admire risk-takers? Why or why not? Are you like the son in this poem or like the "sensible daddy"?
5. What character from myth or legend would you choose as a role model or inspiration? What meanings and associations cluster around the mythical or legendary figure?

Projects

6. Can you find other Icarus poems for a class reading?

WRITING
WORKSHOP 7

Arguing from Principle

As rational, objective people, we pride ourselves on our ability to approach a subject with an open mind. We feel capable of looking at the evidence and drawing logical conclusions. This inductive think scheme, moving from fact to inference, has for centuries been the model for Western science. (Early scientists took in such facts as that the moon is kept in orbit around the earth, that pens fall to the floor and not to the ceiling, that apples drop to the ground instead of flying off toward the sky. They concluded that there was an all-pervading physical force — gravity — that pulled material objects toward one another.)

However, the inductive, generalizing kind of reasoning is only one of several procedures that our minds use to process information. Much of our actual reasoning follows the opposite, or deductive pattern. **Deduction** spells out something that we believe or accept as true. It then shows how the general principle applies to a specific situation. (The two kinds of reasoning work together if we first develop general physical laws or patterns of behavior and then use them to predict behavior in a specific situation. For instance, if the law of gravity holds true, a space module passing Venus or Mars should be pulled toward the planet or deflected into an orbit around the planet.)

Deductive reasoning moves from the general to the specific. It invokes principles that we expect the reader to share, and it then applies these to the situation in question. Many arguments concerning values or behavior follow a deductive pattern:

- If all human beings, regardless of race, are created equal, then slavery is evil.
- If we believe in the sanctity of life, and if life begins at conception, then abortion is a sin.
- If the foundation of democracy is an educated citizenry, then providing universal public education is a civic duty.
- If all Americans are equal before the law, then the son of a senator or corporation president should not get a special exemption from military service.

As you can see, many such arguments hinge on the initial *if*—the initial assumption, or **premise**. (If the masses are not intelligent enough to make informed political decisions, we are off the hook as far as free universal public education is concerned. We may then settle for minimal vocational training for those who need only basic skills and the ability to follow instructions.)

TRIGGERING As with other kinds of reasoning, we may think about the principles at stake in a current issue at least in part to make up our own minds. But more often we use a deductive argument to bring others around to our point of view.

In his famous "I Have a Dream" speech, Martin Luther King invoked some of the most basic principles of the American political tradition. In the country of the free, one large segment of the population should not be denied the freedom to live, eat, and go to school where they choose. In a country founded on the principle of human dignity, a large number of fellow citizens should not be subjected to demeaning restrictions and exclusions.

GATHERING To appeal effectively to shared values, you might need to invoke precedents and established legal principles. You might want to quote an eloquent statement by a widely respected leader or impressive evidence of public opinion.

Perhaps you want to appeal to the principle of compassion in arguing against "heroic" medical procedures that needlessly prolong the suffering of the terminally ill. Your paper will profit greatly if your reading notes for the paper include entries like the following:

> Public opinion polls show that most Americans oppose the use of "heroic measures" to keep patients alive when there is no hope of recovery. A Louis Harris poll found that 82% supported the idea of withdrawing feeding tubes if it was the patient's wish. . . .

> In many cases, the family and the staff agree that the patient in question "derives no comfort, no improvement, and no hope of improvement" from further medical treatment. . . .

> Many Americans linger in a hopeless twilight zone between life and imminent death. Recent studies show the tremendous financial burden and the anguish suffered by their families. . . .

SHAPING A classic pattern for an argument from principle first dramatizes the current situation that raised the issue. It then spells out the principle (or principles) involved, presented in such a way that the argument will speak strongly to the shared values of the intended audience. Then the writer applies the principle (or principles) to specific authentic examples.

What are the principles invoked in the following paper? Do you think they will command the assent or at least the respect of the intended readers? How authentic or convincing do the test cases or key examples seem to you? How do *you* react to this paper as a reader?

Thou Shalt Not

As we hear about prayer vigils and last-minute pleas protesting the current spate of executions, we realize that an issue that has lain dormant for many years is again dividing the citizens into hostile camps. The weakness of the passionate last-minute appeals for clemency played up by the media is that they tend to focus on the special circumstances of the individual case. A murderer was the victim of child abuse. A rapist suffered brain damage. By focusing on the individual history of those waiting on death row, we run the danger of losing sight of the basic principles at stake when a civilized society reinstitutes capital punishment.

In spite of strong current arguments in favor of the death penalty, capital punishment violates basic principles underlying the American system of justice. Most basic to our legal system is the commitment to even-handed justice. We believe that equal crimes should receive equal punishment. However, the death penalty has always been notorious for its "freakish unfairness." Some murderers walk the streets again after three or five or seven years, whereas others—because of ineffectual legal counsel, a vindictive prosecutor, or a harsh judge—join the inmates waiting out their appeals on death row. In one celebrated case, two partners in crime were convicted of the same capital crime on identical charges. One was executed; the other is in prison and will soon be eligible for parole. In the words of one study, "Judicial safeguards for preventing the arbitrary administration of capital punishment are not working." Judges and juries apply widely different standards.

We believe that all citizens are equal before the law. Justice should be blind to wealth, race, or ethnic origin. However, poor defendants are many times more likely to receive the death penalty than wealthy ones, protected by highly paid teams of lawyers whose maneuvers stymie the prosecution and baffle the jury. Minority defendants convicted of capital crimes have a much higher statistical chance of being executed than white defendants. A black person killing a white person is more likely to receive the death penalty than a white person killing a black person.

Fairness demands that the judicial system make provision for correcting its own mistakes. If someone has been unjustly convicted, there should be a mechanism for reversing the verdict and setting the person free. No one doubts that there are miscarriages of justice. Citizens of Northern Ireland convicted as terrorists are set free after many years because of evidence that they were framed and their confessions coerced by the police. Victims withdraw rape charges; witnesses admit to mistaken identification of suspects. A convict confesses on his deathbed to a crime for which someone else was convicted.

However, in the case of the death penalty, any such correction of error is aborted. We are left with futile regrets, like the prosecutor who said, "Horrible as it is to contemplate, we may have executed the wrong man."

REVISING When we write with real conviction, we are likely to come on strong. We use emotional language; we are impatient with the opposition; we sound very sure — probably too sure — of ourselves. Re-reading a paper in the sober light of the next morning, we have a chance to take some of the heat and steam out of the argument. We have a chance to make sure the argument stands *on its merits*. In revising your paper, consider advice like the following:

- *Try not to dismiss (or brush off) opposing points of view.* People who feel insulted or ignored are not likely to listen attentively — and perhaps change their minds. (Not everyone who — often only reluctantly — endorses the reinstatement of the death penalty is a fascist, a sadist, a vigilante, or a believer in primitive eye-for-an-eye justice.)

- *Tone down passages that make you sound bigoted or prejudiced.* ("The average criminal is a brutal individual who deserves exactly what he got." "To rid our streets of violent crime, we should lock up violent criminals and throw the key away.")

- *Strengthen logical links.* Insert a strategic *therefore, however,* or *nevertheless* to signal turns in the argument. Use links like *on the one hand* and *on the other hand* that hold an argument together.

Topics for Papers Arguing from Principle (A Sampling)

1. Do you endorse the principle of affirmative action in education or in employment? How should it be implemented and why?
2. Should a college ensure parity in funding for men's and women's sports? Why or why not? If you answer in the affirmative, how would parity be achieved?
3. Should schools do more to teach about role models for children from minority backgrounds?
4. Are the private lives of public figures their own business? On what principle or principles do you take your stand?
5. Should employers have the right to ban romantic relationships among employees? On what grounds?
6. Do traditional tests or qualifying exams work against equal opportunity for candidates from other than conventional white middle-class backgrounds? What principles are at stake?
7. In awarding custody of children in divorce cases, should the courts give preference to the mother? Why or why not?
8. Should colleges terminate their relationship with the ROTC? What are the principles at stake?
9. Should the military have the right to ban gays and lesbians?
10. Does the United States have the obligation to accept refugees from war, poverty, or repression?

8

Media Watch:
Image and Reality

*On the front page
of the daily fivestarfinal
***** Edition a child
is dying in the rubble
of newsprint.*
                    Olga Cabral

The media have a vast potential for educating us and broadening our views. However, they also have a frightening power to manipulate our minds. As some people are alcohol-dependent, so many of us are media-dependent. We choose political leaders in campaigns conducted in large part in the newspapers and on television. Our views on race relations may have been shaped by TV images of places that few viewers have actually visited: Watts, South Central L.A., Bensonhurst. Our fears and doubts about child molestation, rape, incest, or world hunger are aroused and fueled (and often again allowed to subside) by the media.

What we see and read on such subjects depends on editors' and network executives' judgment on what is newsworthy. Editorial and often marketing judgment decide what goes on page one and what is lost in the back pages. When the media focus on candidates for the Supreme Court or the presidency, the voter may learn more about their experiments with marijuana or the way they talk behind closed doors than about their stand on health insurance or abortion. For many viewers, the faces that people the small or the large screen — Madonna, Arnold Schwarzenegger, Elvis Presley, a favorite quarterback — are more real (not to mention interesting) than their coworkers or neighbors.

We know some of our world at first hand and much of it through the media. Viewers may know almost no African Americans personally but only media stereotypes: the smartass wise-cracking tough street kid, male or female; Bill Cosby (the kindly, ever-smiling, and self-deprecating entertainer); Mike Tyson (the violent and self-destructing black male). The news may play out in loving detail the personal disasters, heroic rescues, and petty scandals that viewers love. However, it may provide little insight into the politics of race, immigration, education, the national debt, recession, sexism, mental health, or unemployment.

How do the media shape or distort our reality? Do they always skim the surface, in sound bites that allow for no real thinking about cause and effect? Are we always helpless "target audiences," or can we influence the steady stream of images and ideas that the media present to us?

FIVE FRIENDS IN A CAR

Margaret Carlson

Time *magazine, started by the legendary Henry Luce, early developed a winning formula for presenting the week's news: A newsmagazine should not just present the dry facts; it should entertain and provoke. It should go for the dramatic story (and never be dull). It should look for the human angle while maintaining a slightly amused ironic distance. Its readers should feel knowledgeable, reasonable, and concerned (without being asked to pay higher taxes). The following article presents a savvy* Time*style mix of information and commentary. The following* Time *report, subtitled "A minor accident spirals tragically into robbery and death," is an example of the kind of human-interest story* Time*'s editors love.*

Thought Starters: What in the following article is fact? What is commentary? Does the incident have a point or a meaning? What did the writer for *Time* magazine think the incident showed? What do you think it shows?

Like many teenagers on a Friday night, James Cooney needed a car   1
to pick up his girlfriend. He borrowed his good friend Barry Bootan's father's Chevrolet, banged it into a pole and racked up $900 worth of body damage. To come up with the money, the two New York City prep school graduates hatched a bizarre robbery scheme. Over the next 48 hours, youngsters who had never been in trouble played out every parent's nightmare. A minor scrape gave way to panic, then to terror. All judgment vanished. At the end, Cooney, 18, was dead, and four other lives lay in ruins.

Frantic to get the car repaired before Bootan's father returned from a weekend fishing trip, Cooney and Bootan, 18, called three other classmates from Fordham Prep, a Jesuit school from which they were graduated on June 3. About 1 A.M. last Sunday, the five headed off in Jason Katanic's mother's Chrysler with three ski masks and a .22-cal. rifle. They drove to a late-night grocery, where Cooney held up the owner for $140. Buoyed by their success, the boys rode around looking for someone else to rob, shooting out the windows of about six empty cars before pulling alongside an auto parked on a deserted street with a couple inside.

Cooney leaned out the window of the Chrysler, pointed the rifle in the driver's face and demanded his wallet. He then fired two shots into the side of the car, and the boys' luck ran out. The driver turned out to be an off-duty policeman. Ducking down, the officer drew his .38 pistol, stuck it out the window and fired five times. At least one shot hit Cooney square in the face. Four more bullets strafed the Chrysler as it sped away, Cooney dying in the front seat.

Still thinking a cover-up possible, the panicked boys dumped Cooney's body in thick weeds and pledged one another to secrecy. They burned one boy's bloodstained clothing and somehow managed to get a replacement for the bullet-pocked rear window of the Chrysler. For almost three days, the boys acted as if nothing had happened, silent even in the face of Cooney's disappearance. Then Bootan told his girlfriend, who notified police. Bootan and Katanic were arrested on charges of armed robbery, attempted robbery and attempted murder. Brendan Moynihan, 16, and Danny Florio, 17, who reportedly cowered on the floor of the back seat, jackets over their heads during the robberies, have not yet been charged.

Horrible deeds done by good people prompt the most difficult ques-   5
tions. How did efforts to get the car fixed spiral into robbery and death, bad decisions made at every turn? Nothing about Cooney or his friends suggested they were capable of reckless, murderous behavior. So far, drinking and drugs do not appear to be a factor. Three of the boys came from working-class families who struggled to pay the $3,225 tuition at a strict private school where Catholic, not prep, is the defining sensibility. Cooney was the stepson of a police officer. Katanic's widowed mother is a clerical worker. All five boys were headed to college in the fall.

Fordham Headmaster Cornelius McCarthy is baffled as to how good kids could go so far wrong so fast. "James Patrick Cooney was a happy-go-lucky kid, confident of himself." Confident, perhaps cocksure. Away from the protection of adults, Cooney and his friends indulged the illusion they were exempt from death and other mortal coils, as the young tend to do, this time to a deadly end.

The Responsive Reader

1. How would you summarize the bare facts in this article? (Is anything puzzling, or does anything seem to be missing?)
2. What in this article is commentary or interpretation? How does the writer support her inferences — the conclusions she draws from what happened?

Talking, Listening, Writing

3. Does this article take you to a totally different world, or do you recognize familiar ways of thinking or familiar patterns of behavior? (Could these young people be among your friends or acquaintances?)
4. The following is one student's reaction to the article. How do you react to her reaction?

The real lesson to be learned from this article has to do with communication, specifically communication between children and their parents. Apparently, these boys did not consider simply telling Bootan's father what had happened and suffering the consequences. Cooney's and Bootan's parents had a great deal to do with this disaster. These young men didn't think they had the <u>option</u> of having their parents find out what happened to the car. In this respect, the parents failed, because they should have made sure that their sons understood they could always come to them, no matter what the problem was. I know a young woman who totaled her father's brand-new Corvette and worked at a hamburger joint all summer to pay the insurance deductible after she got out of the hospital. She now probably has a much greater respect for other people's cars than the average person as the result of her experience. The young men in this article failed to realize that their situation wasn't the end of the world, and this must have something to do with their upbringing.

5. Many columns or editorials take off from a striking incident that brings a current issue into focus. Write a guest editorial for *Time* or *Newsweek* (or for your campus newspaper) that takes off from the incident that is the subject of the *Time* article.

Projects

6. Do other newsmagazines use a formula similar to that of *Time*? Working alone or with a partner, try to find treatments of the same incident, event, or issue in two different newsmagazines. What are similarities or differences in approach, treatment, style, or interpretation?

THE ROYAL ANNIVERSARY: ELVIS PRESLEY'S FIFTIETH

Manuela Hoelterhoff

American pop culture creates cult figures ranging from the Beatles and Elvis Presley to Bob Dylan and Madonna. Legendary entertainers become the focus of a media circus of fan magazines, megatours, award ceremonies, and packaged and repackaged videos, CDs, and cassettes. As Muslim pilgrims journey to Mecca or Catholics to Lourdes, so fans journey to such shrines as Elvis Presley's Graceland in Memphis, Tennessee, where the "king" is buried next to his mother. Elvis Presley, whose recording of "You Ain't Nothing But a Hound Dog" sold seven million copies, had a meteoric rise to fame as a young rock musician and over the years slowly succumbed to glitz, obesity, and drugs. Manuela Hoelterhoff, a German-born arts editor and chief art critic for the Wall Street Journal, *visited Memphis on the occasion of the king's fiftieth birthday to visit the Presley mansion and talk to the faithful.*

Thought Starters: What is the attitude of this New York art critic toward American popular culture?

It was no place for blue suede shoes or even a hound dog. Piles of snow were falling out of the sky, and the only unchained melody audible on Elvis Presley Boulevard was the sound of wheels. They were spinning like upturned 45s on ice patches the size of Alaska. All shook up and close to paralyzed, we slithered toward Graceland, home of the king of rock 'n' roll, and now the Mecca, Lourdes, and sanctum sanctorum of his worshipers (and if you've dug out five song titles imbedded in this paragraph, you're probably a potential pilgrim).

Elvis, who churned up America and much of the world with his potent combination of country music, gospel, and rhythm and blues, would have been 50 years old today. Death hasn't dented his popularity or muffled his voice. At last count, the man had sold one *billion* records.

So late last week, the faithful headed to Memphis, where he lived and died. They braved a blizzard such as this town hadn't seen since 1968 and, given the absence of snow equipment, absolutely could not cope with. The roads were littered with ditched cars, with people striking Job-like poses and with alarmed drivers, among them the woman who suddenly found herself snoot to snoot with my igloo-like car after she made an involuntary U-turn. She wore a shower cap, a fashion must at the moment here, and it is also snowflake proof.

"You ever meet the king?" I asked, making conversation as we pushed her car. "Never did," she said, "but I know someone who knew someone he gave a Cadillac to."

Over a long weekend, I met a lot of people who knew people who got a car from the king. Friends knew a nurse who got a Cadillac for taking good care of him during a hospital stay; a longtime employee at the Peabody Hotel, this town's grand social center, recalled a young woman who gawked at a car he left outside the hotel. "You got a license?" Elvis reportedly asked. "Sure do," said she. "It's yours," he smiled, and gave her the keys. Aug. 16, 1977, the day a fat and fated Elvis succumbed to cardiovascular disease, hardened arteries and too many Nutty Buddies and Eskimo Pies topped off by Demerol, Valium, Quaaludes, Dexedrine, Percodan, Amytal and just about anything else that could be bottled and swallowed, was a black day for local car dealers.

There's more to this cotton town than the king. Memphis is regaining some vitality and grace, after racial strife and vicious urban renewal nearly blew the place off the map in the 1960s and '70s. Beale Street, where W. C. Handy tooted his famous horn, is being rebuilt; the gloriously refurbished Orpheum Theater features Leontyne Price on Jan. 18, and a great quintet arrives every morning to the tune of a Sousa march at the Peabody. They are five ducks who live in a little palazzo on top of the hotel, descend by elevator and then waddle along a red carpet fit for the king toward the atrium's marble fountain.

Elvis's D.A. hairdo probably was not inspired by the Peabody ducks, but they would look just fine at his 13-acre estate a few miles from downtown. Elvis bought this place in 1957 with a $100,000 check. He was 22 years old and had lived most of his life in a bungalow. A much-published photograph shows the young Elvis looking sweetly solemn, slender and somewhat suspicious in front of the columned entrance. It didn't take Elvis long to realize that the world was an enormous Piggly Wiggly store where he had limitless checking.

By the time he died, his balance was down to $1 million, and getting less by the minute because of Graceland's upkeep. (A substantial chunk of the $100 million he made landed in the capacious pockets of his handler, a sharpy named Col. Tom Parker, who sliced a whopping 50% off Elvis's earnings.) But since 1982, when Graceland was opened to the public, money has been soaking the estate like Kentucky rain.

Some 1.2 million people have passed through the note-adorned gates, among them the Soviet minister of tourism, a big Presley fan according to a Graceland executive. Typical visitors spend solemn minutes at the grave site (Elvis, his parents and grandmother are buried in the garden) and usually spend extra bucks to visit his airplane, which features a double bed with a huge safety belt. It is parked across the highway near shops selling Elvis memorabilia. Last year Graceland Enterprises grossed almost $5 million.

Graceland's hustle 'n' bustle is good news to a one-time resident who dropped by Thursday to give a news conference. This was "Dallas" personality Priscilla Presley, who is the host of a film about Graceland, the mother of Elvis's only child, Lisa Marie, and an executor of his estate. *10*

Beehived and bored, she got the heck out of Graceland and divorced Elvis in 1973, but this is glossed over in the warmly reverential film. A cranky journalist asked why there is no mention of Elvis's shortcomings. "Why do you want to bring out negativity?" responded a piqued Ms. Presley. *Zoop*, the press conference was over. Thus nobody got to ask the really important question: Ms. Presley, if you were living here today, would you redecorate?

Past the portals, the place is surprisingly small. But what a medley of shag carpets, mirrors, glass, marble, porcelain monkeys and chandeliers! Also cotton. "Seven hundred fifty yards of 100% cotton," announces the guide standing in front of the heavily draped billiards room, which looks like a walk-in oven glove. A gold-leafed piano gleams behind blue drapes in the music room. "Did he make these?" asks a visitor staring at some hulking carved chairs and tables in the den, also called the jungle room because of the tropical colors. "Absolutely not," informs the guide. Elvis picked them out personally in half an hour at a local store.

The tour then continues into the trophy room, which displays his many gold records and equally radiant outfits. (Lansky's, which pretty much dressed the king from cradle to crypt, is still on Beale Street, and continues to sell gallons of Lenel cologne, Elvis's scent).

Still, however small, Graceland is big enough to house the dreams of his fans. "I moved to Memphis just to be close to him," says Ruth Jones, a forthcoming, gray-haired woman, who works in a memorabilia shop across the highway at a counter filled with nail clippers, paperweights and key chains decorated with the king's face. She has visited Graceland some 30 times, meets Presley fans from all over the world and gets letters from Bangkok. She suggests persuasively that her life is now more interesting than it would have been in Loogootee, Ind.

In another part of the shopping arcade, several hundred fans were gathering for a birthday party — one of several events celebrating the 50th anniversary. It was a motley crowd, and by no means restricted to beehived, middle-aged fatsos reliving their youth. There, for instance, was peppy Melinda Lee of North Carolina, who first saw him in 1954 when she was 13 and now spends about $2,500 a year on Elvis memorabilia and trips to Graceland (two jobs help her buy). There, too, was young Grant Rice from Minnesota, who says he loses his shyness when "I put on an Elvis costume and sing." *15*

They deserved a better spread than the odds and ends served up for $10 a head by Graceland in two dreary, crowded rooms. But then a screen filled up with old clips of Elvis in his prime, smiling that crooked smile, tossing his pelvis and caressing the crowd with his extraordinarily vibrant voice. And once again the king worked his magic: He transformed an ordinary place and made everybody in it glow.

The Responsive Reader

1. What do you learn from this article about the appeal of the Presley legend, the mentality of the fans, and the commercial activity surrounding the Presley cult?
2. What is Hoelterhoff's attitude toward the Presley cult and the fans? Where or how does it show most clearly? Do you share it? (Why or why not?)
3. Do you think this critic responded to Presley's music?

Talking, Listening, Writing

4. Who do you think was the real person behind the media hype of the Presley legend?
5. Are you or could you have been an Elvis Presley fan? (Are you a "potential pilgrim"?)
6. Have you been an active fan of another legendary star or group? What was or is the history and appeal of your idol? What is the story of your involvement?
7. Would you call the Elvis Presley legend or the Presley cult typically American? (What features make it so?) Or is it an aberration?

Projects

8. Working with a small group, you may want to research the media legend surrounding one of the cult figures of American pop culture, such as John Lennon, Billie Holiday, Janice Joplin, Elvis Presley, Michael Jackson, or Madonna. How do the media create, fuel, and exploit the legend surrounding a popular idol?

SELLING OUR INNOCENCE ABROAD

Pico Iyer

> *A French film director recently said that young people in his country get their education about life, about attitudes and emotions, from American television series. The author of the following article lives in America, but his parents were from India and he was born and educated in England. He has made similar observations about the dominance of American popular entertainment in countries from Vietnam to Bhutan. As the world becomes "the global village," a global popular culture is developing that is made in America, with Hollywood as the true cultural capital of the world.*

Thought Starters: For some people, Hollywood stands for everything that is unreal, cheap, and gaudy in America. For others, it brings to mind the comedy classics of the silent screen, the great early movies, and legendary stars that became household words around the world. What associations and connotations does Hollywood have for you?

There is a genuine sense in many parts of the world that America is being left behind by the rise of a unified Europe and the new East Asian powers. The largest debtor nation in the world, where ten million blacks live in poverty and whose capital, run by a cocaine addict, had a murder rate during the Eighties higher than that of Sri Lanka or Beirut, seems an unlikely model for emulation. And yet America maintains a powerful hold on the world's imagination.

A visitor today in Vietnam, one of the last of America's official enemies, will find crowds in Hue, in waterside cafes, desperate to get a glimpse of Meryl Streep on video; at night, in Dalat, he will hear every last word of "Hotel California" floating across Sighing Lake. In Bhutan, where all the citizens must wear traditional medieval dress and all the buildings must be constructed in thirteenth-century style — in Bhutan, perhaps the most tightly closed country in the world, which has never seen more than 3,000 tourists in a single year — the pirated version of Eddie Murphy's *Coming to America* went on sale well before the video had ever come to America.

All this, of course, is hardly surprising and hardly new. Pop culture makes the world go round, and America makes the best pop culture. By now, indeed, such products represent the largest single source of America's export earnings, even as America remains the single most popular destination for immigrants. The more straitened or shut off a culture, the more urgent its hunger for the qualities it associates with America: freedom, wealth, and modernity. The Japanese may be the leaders in technology, the Europeans may have a stronger and more self-conscious sense of their aesthetic heritage, yet in the world of movies and songs and images America is still, and long will continue to be, the Great Communicator. The capital of the world, as Gore Vidal has said, is not Washington but Hollywood. And however much America suffers an internal loss of faith, it will continue to enjoy, abroad, some of the immunity that attaches to all things in the realm of myth. As much as we — and everyone else — assume that the French make the best perfumes and the Swiss the finest watches, the suspicion will continue that Americans make the best dreams.

As borders crumble and cultures mingle, more and more of us are becoming hyphenated. I, perhaps, am an increasingly typical example: entirely Indian by blood, yet unable to speak a word of any Indian language; a British citizen, born and educated in England, yet never having really worked or lived in the country of my birth; an American permanent resident who has made his home for two thirds of his life in America, in part because it feels so little like home; and a would-be resident of Japan. As people like me proliferate, and Filipinos in San Francisco marry Salvadorans, and Germans in Japan take home women from Kyoto, the global village becomes internalized, until more and more of us are products of everywhere and citizens of nowhere.

And though Paris, Tokyo, and Sydney are all in their way natural   5 meeting points for this multi-polar culture, America, as the traditional land of immigrants, is still the spiritual home of the very notion of integration. Everyone feels at home in only two places, Milos Forman has said: at home and in America. That is one reason why America's domination of pop culture is unlikely to subside, even if the reality of American power increasingly seems a thing of the past. The notion of America itself attracts more and more people to come and revive or refresh the notion of America. And the more international a culture is, the more, very often, it draws from the center of internationalism — the United States. The French may rail against cultural imperialism and try to enforce a kind of aesthetic protectionism by striving to keep out *le burger* and *le video*. But as soon as Madonna shows up in Cannes — so efficient is her command of all the media and so self-perpetuating her allure — she sets off the biggest stir in thirty years.

Madonna's global appeal is not unlike that of the Kentucky Fried Chicken parlor in Tiananmen Square: Both provide a way for people to align themselves, however fleetingly, with a world that is — in imagination at least — quick and flashy and rich. The lure of the foreign is quickened by the lure of the forbidden.

I got my own best sense of this in a friend's apartment in Havana some years ago. My friend was an intellectual dissident, fluent in several languages, eager to talk about Spinoza and Saroyan, and able to make a living by reading people's futures from their photographs and translating the latest Top 40 hits — recorded from radio stations in Miami — into Spanish. One night, trying to convey his desperation to escape, he pulled out what was clearly his most precious possession: a copy of Michael Jackson's album *Bad,* on which he had scrawled some heartfelt appeals to Jackson to rescue him. He did not, I suspect, know that Jackson was reclusive, eccentric, and about as likely to respond to political appeals as Donald Duck. What he did know was that Jackson was black, rich, and sexually ambiguous — all things that it is not good to be in Castro's Cuba. What he also knew was that Jackson had succeeded on his own terms, an individual who had proved himself stronger than the system. The less my friend knew about Jackson the man, the closer he could feel to Jackson the symbol. And so it is with America: Since the America that he coveted does not quite exist, it is immutable, a talisman that will fail him only if he comes here.

People everywhere, whatever their circumstances, will always have a hunger for innocence, and America seems to have a limitless supply of that resource. Somehow the moguls of Hollywood and Broadway and Nashville — perhaps because they were immigrants themselves, with half a heart on the streets they left — have never lost their common touch: *E. T.* and *Back to the Future* strike universal chords as surely as *Gone With the Wind* and *Casablanca* did half a century ago. These stories continue to affect us because they speak to our most innocent dreams. To renounce them would be to renounce our own innocence.

The Responsive Reader

1. What ideas do you associate with the buzzword of the "global village"? What evidence have you seen that "more and more of us are products of everywhere and citizens of nowhere"?
2. What, according to Iyer, are the qualities that people in other parts of the world associate with America? (Are you surprised? What would you have expected?) What, according to Iyer, is the worldwide appeal of media idols like Madonna or Michael Jackson?
3. Take a detailed look at one of the Hollywood products that Iyer claims satisfied for millions the "hunger for innocence." What does he mean when he says that they "speak to our most innocent dreams"? Take a good look at *E. T., Back to the Future, Gone With the Wind,* or *Casablanca* from this point of view. Or take a look at a more recent Hollywood product that might be said to satisfy the "hunger for innocence."

Talking, Listening, Writing

4. As a newspaper reader or watcher of television news, what evidence do you encounter that America, in areas other than popular culture,

"is left behind" by other parts of the world? Do the media tend to reinforce the idea that "the reality of American power increasingly seems a thing of the past"?

5. What picture of life on this planet would a visitor from outer space get from watching two or three of the currently most popular American television series? What might the alien conclude about our ways of thinking and feeling, about our traditions and values?

6. What accounts for Hollywood's reputation as the source of phony escapist entertainment? On the other hand, what makes observers like Iyer claim that for people around the world Americans are the best makers of dreams? Argue the pros and cons of Hollywood's reputation as the dream capital of the world.

Projects

7. Implantations like the new EuroDisney theme park outside Paris or the Moscow McDonald's have been test cases for foreign reactions to American popular culture. Working with others, you may want to check out the range of opinion and analyses as reported or available in this country.

Thinking about Connections

Intellectuals have often had a love-hate relationship with popular culture. Explore the range of attitudes in essays including Iyer's article and Manuela Hoelterhoff's "The Royal Anniversary" (p. 414), Joyce Carol Oates' "Rape and the Boxing Ring" (p. 535), and Sharon Olds' "The Death of Marilyn Monroe" (p. 442).

THE MYTH OF THE MATRIARCH
Gloria Naylor

> *Gloria Naylor has written on race issues and racial stereotypes for the*
> New York Times *and* Life *magazine. She is a novelist who has published*
> The Women of Brewster Place *(1982),* Linden Hills *(1985), and*
> Mama Day *(1988); the first of these won the American Book Award for*
> *first fiction in 1983. She was born in New York City and says that she "was*
> *part of a large extended family that had migrated from the rural South after*
> *World War II and formed a close-knit network"; aunts, uncles, cousins,*
> *friends, and neighbors came and went in the apartment in the building her*
> *family owned in Harlem. In the article that follows, Naylor focuses on the*
> *way the media create or perpetuate stereotypes. Her case in point is the*
> *stereotype of the black matriarch — the strong and loyal black woman who*
> *heads the fatherless black family and serves as a substitute mother for young*
> *white males in whose families she serves (or used to serve) as a nanny. Naylor*
> *remembers examples of the mythical strong black woman in the novels of*
> *William Faulkner, whose books from* The Sound and the Fury *to* Absa-
> lom, Absalom *are for many a cultural history of the South. She remembers*
> *her as the Mammy in* Gone With the Wind, *the Civil War epic (the book*
> *and the movie) that made Scarlett O'Hara and Rhett Butler household names.*
> *She remembers hearing her on radio and television shows like* Amos 'n'
> Andy.

Thought Starters: Naylor says that stereotypes are created in response
to a need; stereotypes and popular myths give people what they want or
need to hear. What needs did the myth of the black matriarch serve? What
is wrong with it?

The strong black woman: All my life I've seen her. In books she is   1
Faulkner's impervious Dilsey, using her huge dark arms to hold together
the crumbling spirits and household of the Compsons. In the movies she
is the quintessential Mammy, chasing after Scarlett O'Hara with forgotten sunbonnets and shrill tongue-lashings about etiquette. On television
she is Sapphire of *Amos 'n' Andy* or a dozen variations of her — henpecking
black men, herding white children, protecting her brood from the on-
slaughts of the world. She is the supreme matriarch — alone, self-sufficient
and liking it that way. I've seen how this female image has permeated the
American consciousness to the point of influencing everything from the
selling of pancakes to the structuring of welfare benefits. But the strangest
thing is that when I walked around my neighborhood or went into the
homes of family and friends, this matriarch was nowhere to be found.

I know the statistics: They say that when my grandmother was born at the turn of the century as few as 10 percent of black households were headed by females; when I was born at mid-century it had crept to 17 percent; and now it is almost 60 percent. No longer a widow or a divorcée as in times past, the single woman with children today probably has never married—and increasingly she is getting younger. By the time she is 18, one out of every four black unmarried women has become a mother.

But it is a long leap from a matrifocal home, where the father is absent, to a matriarchal one, in which the females take total charge from the males. Though I have known black women heading households in different parts of the country and in different social circumstances — poor, working class or professional — none of them has gloried in the conditions that left them with the emotional and financial responsibility for their families. Often they had to take domestic work because of the flexible hours or stay in menial factory or office jobs because of the steady pay. And leaving the job was only to go home to the other job of raising children alone. These women understood the importance of input from black men in sustaining their families. Their advice and, sometimes, financial assistance were sought and accepted. But if such were not forthcoming, she would continue to deal with her situation alone.

This is a far cry from the heartwarming image of the two-fisted black woman I watched striding across the public imagination. A myth always arises to serve a need. And so it must be asked, what is it in the relationship of black women to American society that has called for them to be seen as independent Amazons?

The black woman was brought to America for the same reason as   5 the black man—to provide slave labor. But she had what seemed to be contradictory roles: She did the woman's work of bearing children and keeping house while doing a man's work at the side of the black male in the fields. She worked regardless of the advanced stages of pregnancy. In the 19th century the ideal of the true woman was one of piety, purity, domesticity and submissiveness; the female lived as a wife sheltered at home or went abroad as a virgin doing good works. But if the prevailing belief was that the natural state of women was one of frailty, how could the black female be explained? Out in the fields laboring with their muscled bodies and during rest periods suckling infants at their breasts, the slave women had to be seen as different from white women. They were stronger creatures: they didn't feel pain in childbirth; they didn't have tear ducts. Ironically, one of the arguments for enslaving blacks in the first place was that as a race they were inferior to whites—but black women, well, they were a little *more* than women.

The need to view slavery as benign accounted for the larger-than-life mammy of the plantation legends. As a house servant, she was always pictured in close proximity to her white masters because there was nothing about her that was threatening to white ideas about black women. Her unstinting devotion assuaged any worries that slaves were discontented or harbored any potential for revolt. Her very dark skin belied any suspicions of past interracial liaisons, while her obesity and advanced age removed any sexual threat. Earth mother, nursemaid and cook, the mammy existed without a history or a future.

In reality, slave women in the house or the field were part of a kinship network and with their men tried to hold together their own precarious families. Marriages between slaves were not legally recognized, but this did not stop them from entering into living arrangements and acting as husbands and wives. After emancipation a deluge of black couples registered their unions under the law, and ex-slaves were known to travel hundreds of miles in search of lost partners and children.

No longer bound, but hardly equal citizens, black men and women had access to only the most menial jobs in society, the largest number being reserved solely for female domestics. Richard Wright wrote a terribly funny and satirical short story about the situation, "Man of All Work." His protagonist is unable to find a job to support his family and save his house from foreclosure, so he puts on his wife's clothes and secures a position as a housekeeper. "Don't stop me. I've found a solution to our problem. I'm an army-trained cook. I can clean a house as good as anybody. Get my point? I put on your dress. I looked in the mirror. I can pass. I want that job."

Pushed to the economic forefront of her home, the 19th century mammy became 20th century Sapphire. Fiery, younger, more aggressive, she just couldn't wait to take the lead away from the man of the house. Whatever he did was never enough. Not that he wanted to do anything, of course, except hang out on street corners, gamble and run around with women. From vaudeville of the 1880s to the advent of *Amos 'n' Andy,* it was easier to make black men the brunt of jokes than to address the inequities that kept decent employment from those who wanted to work. Society had not failed black women — their men had.

The truth is that throughout our history black women could depend 10 upon their men even when they were unemployed or underemployed. But in the impoverished inner cities today we are seeing the rise of the *unemployable.* These young men are not equipped to take responsibility for themselves, much less the children they are creating. And with the increasing youth of unwed mothers, we have grandmothers and grandfathers in their early thirties. How can a grandmother give her daughter's family the traditional wisdom and support when she herself has barely lived? And on the other side of town, where the professional black woman is heading a household, usually because she is divorced, the lack of a traditional kinship network — the core community of parents, uncles, aunts — makes her especially alone.

What is surprising to me is that the myth of the matriarch lives on — even among black women. I've talked to so many who believe that they are supposed to be superhuman and bear up under all things. When they don't, they all too readily look for the fault within themselves. Somehow they failed their history. But it is a grave mistake for black women to believe that they have a natural ability to be stronger than other women. Fifty-seven percent of black homes being headed by females is not natural. A 40 percent pregnancy rate among our young girls is not natural. It is heart-breaking. The myth of the matriarch robs a woman caught in such circumstances of her individuality and her humanity. She should feel that she has the *right* at least to break down — once the kids are put to bed — and do something so simple as cry.

The Responsive Reader

1. According to Naylor, what are key features in the stereotypical image of the black matriarch? (What are some of the historical and cultural associations of the terms *patriarch* and *matriarch*? What is the origin of the term *Amazon*?)
2. What, according to Naylor, are the roots of the myth in the contradictory roles black women played during slavery?
3. Why does Naylor call the stereotype a "myth"? What *support* for the myth does Naylor find in the realities of a black woman's role? What realities today *contradict* the myth?
4. Part of today's folklore about race is that black women often have a negative image of the black male. What is Naylor's perspective on black males and their relationship with black women?

Talking, Listening, Writing

5. What experiences or observations have shaped your own views of black women? Without adopting stereotypes, can you talk about any recurrent patterns, familiar traits, characteristic problems or concerns?
6. What has been your observation of or experience with strong or matriarchal women? What role do they play in the media? What role do they play in contemporary life?
7. Is there a special tension or antagonism between African American women and men? Try to interview a group of people who are in a position to know or who might have strong views on the subject.

Projects

8. Working alone or with a group, study the role of ethnic or cultural stereotypes in the media. For instance, you might focus on the stereotype of the hillbilly, blacks with "natural rhythm," the Cheech-and-Chong Mexican, the dumb blonde, the Jewish mother, the femme fatale. What role does the stereotype play in movies, television shows, news stories, or books? What seem to be its roots? What needs does it serve, or what is its appeal? How does the image it creates or perpetuates compare with the realities of American life today?

EROTICA AND PORNOGRAPHY
Gloria Steinem

> *Gloria Steinem is America's most widely known and admired (not to mention attacked) feminist. She is the granddaughter of a prominent American suffragist, or suffragette — a woman fighting for women's right to vote. Steinem grew up in poverty in Toledo, Ohio, and went from there to Smith College. She came to New York to work as a journalist and in 1972 became a cofounder and editor of* Ms. *magazine, the country's best-known feminist periodical, where the following article first appeared. She became an effective and influential lecturer, organizer, fund-raiser, and campaigner for the women's movement. Her apartment in New York City has been called "a stop on the underground railway" for international feminists. She published a collection of her essays,* Outrageous Acts and Everyday Rebellions, *in 1983, followed by a book about Marilyn Monroe,* Marilyn: Norma Jean. *In her best-selling* Revolution from Within: A Book of Self-Esteem *(1992), she turned from political activism to self-discovery and self-affirmation, searching for the "one true inner voice" that remains the constant in our changing roles, jobs, and relationships.*

Thought Starters: In Puritanical societies, sexual stimulation is considered sinful. In the following essay, Steinem tries to establish an essential distinction between acceptable and desirable "erotic" material and unacceptable pornography. What is the essence of the distinction she makes?

Human beings are the only animals that experience the same sex drive at times when we can — and cannot — conceive.

Just as we developed uniquely human capacities for language, planning, memory, and invention along our evolutionary path, we also developed sexuality as a form of expression; a way of communicating that is separable from our need for sex as a way of perpetuating ourselves. For humans alone, sexuality can be and often is primarily a way of bonding, of giving and receiving pleasure, bridging differentness, discovering sameness, and communicating emotion.

We developed this and other human gifts through our ability to change our environment, adapt physically, and in the long run, to affect our own evolution. But as an emotional result of this spiraling path away from other animals, we seem to alternate between periods of exploring our unique abilities to change new boundaries, and feelings of loneliness in the unknown that we ourselves have created; a fear that sometimes sends us back to the comfort of the animal world by encouraging us to exaggerate our sameness.

The separation of "play" from "work," for instance, is a problem only in the human world. So is the difference between art and nature, or an intellectual accomplishment and a physical one. As a result, we celebrate play, art, and invention as leaps into the unknown; but any imbalance can send us back to nostalgia for our primate past and the conviction that the basics of work, nature, and physical labor are somehow more worthwhile or even moral.

In the same way, we have explored our sexuality as separable from conception: a pleasurable, empathetic bridge to strangers of the same species. We have even invented contraception—a skill that has probably existed in some form since our ancestors figured out the process of birth—in order to extend this uniquely human difference. Yet we also have times of atavistic suspicion that sex is not complete—or even legal or intended-by-god—if it cannot end in conception.

No wonder the concepts of "erotica" and "pornography" can be so crucially different, and yet so confused. Both assume that sexuality can be separated from conception, and therefore can be used to carry a personal message. That's a major reason why, even in our current culture, both may be called equally "shocking" or legally "obscene," a word whose Latin derivative means "dirty, containing filth." This gross condemnation of all sexuality that isn't harnessed to childbirth and marriage has been increased by the current backlash against women's progress. Out of fear that the whole patriarchal structure might be upset if women really had the autonomous power to decide our reproductive futures (that is, if we controlled the most basic means of production), right-wing groups are not only denouncing prochoice abortion literature as "pornographic," but are trying to stop the sending of all contraceptive information through the mails by invoking obscenity laws. In fact, Phyllis Schlafly denounced the entire Women's Movement as "obscene."[1]

Not surprisingly, this religious, visceral backlash has a secular, intellectual counterpart that relies heavily on applying the "natural" behavior of the animal world to humans. That is questionable in itself, but these Lionel Tiger-ish studies make their political purpose even more clear in the particular animals they select and the habits they choose to emphasize.[2] The message is that females should accept their "destiny" of being sexually dependent and devote themselves to bearing and rearing their young.

Defending against such reaction in turn leads to another temptation: to merely reverse the terms, and declare that all nonprocreative sex is good. In fact, however, this human activity can be as constructive as destructive, moral or immoral, as any other. Sex as communication can

5

---

[1][Phyllis Schlafly became known for her strong antifeminist views and her campaign against the Equal Rights Amendment.]

[2][Lionel Tiger is a Canadian-born anthropologist who has written about the relation between biology and culture and who looks with a critical eye at current patterns of marriage and divorce.]

send messages as different as life and death; even the origins of "erotica" and "pornography" reflect that fact. After all, "erotica" is rooted in *eros* or passionate love, and thus in the idea of positive choice, free will, the yearning for a particular person. (Interestingly, the definition of erotica leaves open the question of gender.) "Pornography" begins with a root meaning "prostitution" or "female captives," thus letting us know that the subject is not mutual love, or love at all, but domination and violence against women. (Though, of course, homosexual pornography may imitate this violence by putting a man in the "feminine" role of victim.) It ends with a root meaning "writing about" or "description of" which puts still more distance between subject and object, and replaces a spontaneous yearning for closeness with objectification and a voyeur.

The difference is clear in the words. It becomes even more so by example.

Look at any photo or film of people making love; really making love. The images may be diverse, but there is usually a sensuality and touch and warmth, an acceptance of bodies and nerve endings. There is always a spontaneous sense of people who are there because they *want* to be, out of shared pleasure.

Now look at any depiction of sex in which there is clear force, or an unequal power that spells coercion. It may be very blatant, with weapons or torture or bondage, wounds and bruises, some clear humiliation, or an adult's sexual power being used over a child. It may be much more subtle: a physical attitude of conqueror and victim, the use of race or class difference to imply the same thing, perhaps a very unequal nudity, with one person exposed and vulnerable while the other is clothed. In either case, there is no sense of equal choice or equal power.

The first is erotic: a mutually pleasurable, sexual expression between people who have enough power to be there by positive choice. It may or may not strike a sense-memory in the viewer, or be creative enough to make the unknown seem real; but it doesn't require us to identify with a conqueror or a victim. It is truly sensuous, and may give us a contagion of pleasure.

The second is pornographic: its message is violence, dominance, and conquest. It is sex being used to reinforce some inequality, or to create one, or to tell us the lie that pain and humiliation (ours or someone else's) are really the same as pleasure. If we are to feel anything, we must identify with conqueror or victim. That means we can only experience pleasure through the adoption of some degree of sadism or masochism. It also means that we may feel diminished by the role of conqueror, or enraged, humiliated, and vengeful by sharing identity with the victim.

Perhaps one could simply say that erotica is about sexuality, but pornography is about power and sex-as-weapon—in the same way we have come to understand that rape is about violence, and not really about sexuality at all.

Yes, it's true that there are women who have been forced by violent   *15*
families and dominating men to confuse love with pain; so much so that
they have become masochists. (A fact that in no way excuses those who
administer such pain.) But the truth is that, for most women—and for
men with enough humanity to imagine themselves into the predicament
of women—true pornography could serve as aversion therapy for sex.

Of course, there will always be personal differences about what is
and is not erotic, and there may be cultural differences for a long time to
come. Many women feel that sex makes them vulnerable and therefore
may continue to need more sense of personal connection and safety before
allowing any erotic feelings. We now find competence and expertise erotic
in men, but that may pass as we develop those qualities in ourselves. Men,
on the other hand, may continue to feel less vulnerable, and therefore more
open to such potential danger as sex with strangers. As some men replace the need for submission from childlike women with the pleasure of
cooperation from equals, they may find a partner's competence to be
erotic, too.

Such group changes plus individual differences will continue to be
reflected in sexual love between people of the same gender, as well as
between women and men. The point is not to dictate sameness, but to
discover ourselves and each other through sexuality that is an exploring,
pleasurable, empathetic part of our lives; a human sexuality that is unchained both from unwanted pregnancies and from violence.

But that is a hope, not a reality. At the moment, fear of change is
increasing both the indiscriminate repression of all nonprocreative sex in
the religious and "conservative" male world, and the pornographic vengeance against women's sexuality in the secular world of "liberal" and
"radical" men. It's almost futuristic to debate what is and is not truly
erotic, when many women are again being forced into compulsory motherhood, and the number of pornographic murders, tortures, and woman-
hating images are on the increase in both popular culture and real life.

It's a familiar division: wife or whore, "good" woman who is constantly vulnerable to pregnancy or "bad" woman who is unprotected from
violence. *Both* roles would be upset if we were to control our own sexuality. And that's exactly what we must do.

In spite of all our atavistic suspicions and training for the "natural"   *20*
role of motherhood, we took up the complicated battle for reproductive
freedom. Our bodies had borne the health burden of endless births and
poor abortions, and we had a greater motive for separating sexuality and
conception.

Now we have to take up the equally complex burden of explaining
that all nonprocreative sex is *not* alike. We have a motive: our right to a
uniquely human sexuality, and sometimes even to survival. As it is, our
bodies have too rarely been enough our own to develop erotica in our own
lives, much less in art and literature. And our bodies have too often been

the objects of pornography and the woman-hating, violent practice that it preaches. Consider also our spirits that break a little each time we see ourselves in chains or full labial display for the conquering male viewer, bruised or on our knees, screaming a real or pretended pain to delight the sadist, pretending to enjoy what we don't enjoy, to be blind to the images of our sisters that really haunt us — humiliated often enough ourselves by the truly obscene idea that sex and the domination of women must be combined.

Sexuality *is* human, free, separate — and so are we.

But until we untangle the lethal confusion of sex with violence, there will be more pornography and less erotica. There will be little murders in our beds — and very little love.

The Responsive Reader

1. According to Steinem, how has human sexuality evolved, and what human purposes does it (or should it) serve?
2. What is the key difference between "erotica" and pornography? Where do you think Steinem states it most clearly or persuasively? What are striking or convincing examples? What is the major recurrent theme in this essay?
3. How does Steinem relate her discussion to both traditional and current trends in our culture? How does she relate it to the sexual politics of the right and the left?

Talking, Listening, Writing

4. What do you take to be the dominant attitude toward sex in our culture? Is our society ready for the view of human sexuality that Steinem presents? Should it be?
5. Would you call Steinem's a distinctly feminist point of view? Would you call it a distinctly female point of view? (Does the reader have to be feminist to sympathize with her view? Does the reader have to be a woman?)
6. Where would *you* draw the line between acceptable and unacceptable material with sexual content? Is it possible to draw the line?
7. What is the difference between art and pornography?

Projects

8. What is the current legal status of pornographic materials? As a possible research project, your class might want to choose an investigation of current legal definitions of pornography and their application.

Thinking about Connections

Campaigns against pornography raise the specter of censorship. The article by Susan Jacoby that follows discusses the First Amendment issues raised by attempts to control offensive materials.

PORNOGRAPHY AND THE FIRST AMENDMENT

Susan Jacoby

> *Susan Jacoby is a journalist who has frequently written on questions of women's rights. She has worked as an education reporter for the* Washington Post, *and she wrote the following article as a columnist for the* New York Times. The Possible She, *a collection of her columns and magazine essays, was published in 1979. She has also published several books about her observations while living for two years in the former Soviet Union. In the following article, she champions the protection that writers, printers, artists, and entertainers have historically enjoyed under the First Amendment. Adopted as part of the Bill of Rights in 1791, the First Amendment to the U.S. Constitution guarantees freedom of religion and the rights of assembly and petition. In addition, it stipulates that "Congress shall make no law . . . abridging the freedom of speech, or of the press."*

Thought Starters: Is freedom of speech an unconditional right? What about speech that incites to hate or violence? What about pornography that debases women? Are photographs or paintings (and also parades or cross burnings) "speech"?

It is no news that many women are defecting from the ranks of civil libertarians on the issue of obscenity. The conviction of Larry Flynt, publisher of *Hustler* magazine — before his metamorphosis into a born-again Christian — was greeted with unabashed feminist approval. Harry Reems, the unknown actor who was convicted by a Memphis jury for conspiring to distribute the movie *Deep Throat,* has carried on his legal battles with almost no support from women who ordinarily regard themselves as supporters of the First Amendment. Feminist writers and scholars have even discussed the possibility of making common cause against pornography with adversaries of the women's movement — including opponents of the equal rights amendment and "right to life" forces.

All of this is deeply disturbing to a woman writer who believes, as I always have and still do, in an absolute interpretation of the First Amendment. Nothing in Larry Flynt's garbage convinces me that the late Justice Hugo L. Black was wrong in his opinion that "the Federal Government is without any power whatsoever under the Constitution to put any type of burden on free speech and expression of ideas of any kind (as distinguished from conduct)." Many women I like and respect tell me I am wrong; I cannot remember having become involved in so many heated discussions of a public issue since the end of the Vietnam War. A feminist writer described my views as those of a "First Amendment junkie."

Many feminist arguments for controls on pornography carry the implicit conviction that porn books, magazines and movies pose a greater threat to women than similarly repulsive exercises of free speech pose to other offended groups. This conviction has, of course, been shared by everyone — regardless of race, creed or sex — who has ever argued in favor of abridging the First Amendment. It is the argument used by some Jews who have withdrawn their support from the American Civil Liberties Union because it has defended the right of American Nazis to march through a community inhabited by survivors of Hitler's concentration camps.

If feminists want to argue that the protection of the Constitution should not be extended to *any* particularly odious or threatening form of speech, they have a reasonable argument (although I don't agree with it). But it is ridiculous to suggest that the porn shops on 42nd Street are more disgusting to women than a march of neo-Nazis is to survivors of the extermination camps.

The arguments over pornography also blur the vital distinction be-   5
tween expression of ideas and conduct. When I say I believe unreservedly in the First Amendment, someone always comes back at me with the issue of "kiddie porn." But kiddie porn is not a First Amendment issue. It is an issue of the abuse of power — the power adults have over children — and not of obscenity. Parents and promoters have no more right to use their children to make porn movies than they do to send them to work in coal mines. The responsible adults should be prosecuted, just as adults who use children for back-breaking farm labor should be prosecuted.

Susan Brownmiller, in *Against Our Will: Men, Women and Rape,* has described pornography as "the undiluted essence of anti-female propaganda." I think this is a fair description of some types of pornography, especially of the brutish subspecies that equates sex with death and portrays women primarily as objects of violence.

The equation of sex and violence, personified by some glossy rock record album covers as well as by *Hustler,* has fed the illusion that censorship of pornography can be conducted on a more rational basis than other types of censorship. Are all pictures of naked women obscene? Clearly not, says a friend. A Renoir nude is art, she says, and *Hustler* is trash.[1] "Any reasonable person" knows that.

But what about something between art and trash — something, say, along the lines of *Playboy* or *Penthouse* magazines? I asked five women for

---

[1][Auguste Renoir (1841–1919) was a French impressionist painter who painted female nudes in such masterpieces as the *Baigneuses,* or "Women Bathing."]

their reactions to one picture in *Penthouse* and got responses that ranged from "lovely" and "sensuous" to "revolting" and "demeaning." Feminists, like everyone else, seldom have rational reasons for their preferences in erotica. Like members of juries, they tend to disagree when confronted with something that falls short of 100 percent vulgarity.

In any case, feminists will not be the arbiters of good taste if it becomes easier to harass, prosecute and convict people on obscenity charges. Most of the people who want to censor girlie magazines are equally opposed to open discussion of issues that are of vital concern to women: rape, abortion, menstruation, contraception, lesbianism — in fact, the entire range of sexual experience from a woman's viewpoint.

Feminist writers and editors and film makers have limited financial   10
resources: Confronted by a determined prosecutor, Hugh Hefner will fare better than Susan Brownmiller. Would the Memphis jurors who convicted Harry Reems for his role in *Deep Throat* be inclined to take a more positive view of paintings of the female genitalia done by sensitive feminist artists? *Ms.* magazine has printed color reproductions of some of those art works; *Ms.* is already banned from a number of high school libraries because someone considers it threatening and/or obscene.

Feminists who want to censor what they regard as harmful pornography have essentially the same motivation as other would-be censors: They want to use the power of the state to accomplish what they have been unable to achieve in the marketplace of ideas and images. The impulse to censor places no faith in the possibilities of democratic persuasion.

It isn't easy to persuade certain men that they have better uses for $1.95 each month than to spend it on a copy of *Hustler*? Well, then, give the men no choice in the matter.

I believe there is also a connection between the impulse toward censorship on the part of people who used to consider themselves civil libertarians and a more general desire to shift responsibility from individuals to institutions. When I saw the movie *Looking for Mr. Goodbar*, I was stunned by its series of visual images equating sex and violence, coupled with what seems to me the mindless message (a distortion of the fine Judith Rossner novel) that casual sex equals death. When I came out of the movie, I was even more shocked to see parents standing in line with children between the ages of 10 and 14.

I simply don't know why a parent would take a child to see such a movie, any more than I understand why people feel they can't turn off a television set their child is watching. Whenever I say that, my friends tell me I don't know how it is because I don't have children. True, but I do have parents. When I was a child, they did turn off the TV. They didn't expect the Federal Communications Commission to do their job for them.

I am a First Amendment junkie. You can't OD on the First Amend-   15
ment, because free speech is its own best antidote.

The Responsive Reader

1. Jacoby knew that her stand on this issue would be unpopular with many readers, especially women. How does she approach the issue? Where does she take her stand? What is her principal ammunition as she defends her position?
2. Jacoby once said, "Part of the process of writing is learning to think about your argument in other people's terms. . . . That process includes understanding other points of view besides the one you're taking in your argument." How does she anticipate and deal with counterarguments in her essay? (How, for instance, does she deal with the issue of kiddie porn or the issue of sex and violence?)
3. How does Jacoby define censorship as she begins to wind up her essay? What alternative does she suggest? (How workable is it?)

Talking, Listening, Writing

4. Do *you* consider the control of pornography advocated by women's groups censorship? Why or why not?
5. In an interview, Jacoby said about this article that she was "interested in writing about the question of censorship from the standpoint of a feminist. . . . The absolute substance of this essay is to reconcile feminism and civil libertarianism when pornography is degrading to women." Do you think a feminist position and "civil libertarianism" can be reconciled?
6. Would you support pulling magazines like *Playboy* or *Penthouse* off the shelves of college book stores? Try to do justice to the arguments pro and con.
7. Does the First Amendment mean anything to you personally? Have you had firsthand experience with censorship — for instance, of a high school or college paper, of reading materials for high school or college students, of student art in college galleries, or of artists in public museums? (Are you a "First Amendment junkie"?)

Projects

8. Disputes over alleged censorship have at times pitted the ACLU (American Civil Liberties Union) against NOW or other women's organizations. (In one case, the state affiliate of the ACLU asked the court to overturn a decision requiring male shipyard workers in Florida to remove nude pictures of women from their workplace.) Working alone or in a group, you may want to research the position of the national or regional ACLU on the issue of pornography or on other issues involving charges of censorship.

Thinking about Connections

Do Steinem and Jacoby represent radically opposed positions on the subject of pornography? Line up their arguments in pro and con fashion. Do they share common ground?

SKINNING FLINT
Penelope Mesic

> *Where, in the media, is the line between fact and fiction? Current trends are erasing the hazy borderline between news and entertainment, with news anchors groomed, coached, and pampered like film stars. Where is the line between documentaries and works of imagination, between history and history that is massaged for better ratings, or between biography and "fictionalized" biography? The following is a review of a documentary that was "made on a shoestring budget." The filmmaker aimed at airing some harsh truths about a manufacturing town caught in a downward spiral as part of the de-industrialization of America. To judge from this review by a movie reviewer for* Chicago *magazine, how successful was the filmmaker's effort?*

Thought Starters: Does anyone watch documentaries? Do people prefer entertaining fictions to sobering facts?

Roger & Me, a satiric documentary made on a shoestring budget, written, produced, and directed by Michael Moore, begins on a personal note, with shots from the quintessential fifties home movie. It shows a few quick wobbling images of Moore at the age of about seven, skinny and rambunctious in a Popeye mask, sandwiched between two fidgety, giggling sisters on a faded red couch. We hear Moore on the soundtrack — he has the slow, husky voice of a heavyset guy — as he speaks with carefully assumed naïveté about the good times 35 years ago, when the success of General Motors brought prosperity to his hometown of Flint, Michigan.

Scraps of news footage and advertisements, cut rapidly together, show us Flint as Moore remembers it. Pat Boone in his glossy 20s, teeth like piano keys, presents "the car I own and drive myself." A cheerful crowd observes the annual automotive parade, which features pretty girls dressed as spark plugs marching in formation. They're followed by a clunky, elaborate float saluting "the customer, Mr. and Mrs. America." The friendly, vanished innocence of all this, as well as the sheer dumbness of it, which Moore underlines by adding a soundtrack of the busy, inanely cheerful music that usually accompanies industrial training films, arouses a strange mixture of derision and longing. What person of the nineties, however cool or however much aware of the sins committed in the name of Mr. and Mrs. America here and abroad, doesn't feel the pull of a time when being ordinary, yourself, the customer, was a matter for congratulation?

While like most other documentaries the film follows events, it's thus clear from the beginning that this one also follows memory and opinion, political conviction and its maker's whims. What Moore gains by this is considerable: He's made a film about auto plant closings that's so quirky and personal that a general audience can sit through it. What he loses is also considerable: He is quite often flippant, disorganized, condescending, and inaccurate.

With commendable speed and humor he chronicles his own adolescent dream of "getting out of Flint, like the women who married Zubin Mehta and Don Knotts." Images of these weirdly juxtaposed celebrities flick by while Moore tells us about his own ticket out — the offer of a job in publishing in San Francisco. He accepts, although he pretends that as a Midwesterner he's baffled by the ethos of the place. Loss of his job ("I was asked to do an investigative report on herbal teas," he explains) sends him home to Flint, an event represented by B-movie footage of a soldier's emotional homecoming: "Hello, dad!" "Hello, son, it's been a long time!"

But the Flint that Moore returns to in 1987 is in crisis. The chairman   5
of General Motors, Roger Smith, appears on CBS news. His face, wrinkled like a kid glove, glows a violent shade of pink beneath flyaway white hair as fine as a baby's. Smith's announcement is as bland as his face is innocuous: He simply states that the company will be closing 11 "older" plants across the nation. "With profits in the billions," Moore tells us, "GM planned to open plants in Mexico where it would pay workers 70 cents an hour and buy Hughes Aircraft with the money it saved."

Interviewed by Moore, a GM spokesman shrugs off the company's responsibility to its workers, and describes Smith as "a warm person" with "a social conscience as strong as anybody's." "A warm man? Did I have Roger Smith all wrong just because he eliminated 30,000 jobs in my hometown?" Moore asks himself. He then states his mission: to track down the GM chairman and bring him to Flint to see the human consequences of his company's decision. Throughout the film, Moore thus follows "a trail of three-martini lunches" from country club to boardroom to corporate Christmas party, where he at last catches up with Smith and films him reading Dickens — an irony Dickens himself might have appreciated — to assembled employees.

The pursuit of Smith is intercut with scenes of economic and social disintegration. Footage of violent crime, abandoned stores and houses, and evictions alternate with shots of Flint officials proposing plans to revitalize the economy, none of which succeed in reversing the downward spiral. We also see visiting celebrities giving fatuous advice. Anita Bryant tells the unemployed to be grateful for the sunshine. Ronald Reagan, a Presidential candidate at the time, not President, as Moore says, takes a few ex-automotive workers out for a pizza and tells them he's heard there might be jobs in Texas. A wealthy local man at a *Great Gatsby* party talks as if being unemployed were a form of laziness. "Get up in the morning and do something," he advises. "Start your own motor." His empty, but appropriately automotive, metaphor is made to seem even more callously glib than it is by Moore's practice of moving directly from scenes of prosperity to those of privation—in this case to a pair of bolt cutters scissoring off a doorknob during the course of an eviction. You could make Mother Teresa look insensitive if you cut directly from her smiling face to bailiffs dumping householders' belongings in the street.

The black sheriff's deputy handling the eviction is mordantly described by Moore as "the one man in Flint with a secure job." The depths of the town's misery are casually revealed when the deputy remarks that at different times he's evicted 15 different families from a single house. A young man turned out of his apartment says, "I pity people who have children. They have bleak futures." Implicit is the young man's fear that he himself will never be able to afford to raise a family. On the sidewalk a brown-haired boy of about eight stands watching. "It's a rough time," he says conversationally, then adds, over his shoulder, as he walks away, "I got thrown out of my house once."

The consequences of the GM closing spread outward, like ripples in a pond. A U-Haul employee complains of problems caused by "so many of our trucks heading one way south out of here." A postal worker says she's handled 8,000 to 10,000 change-of-address cards. A former GM employee working as a prison guard talks uneasily about seeing guys from the plant who've become inmates. Moore bitterly observes that Flint may eventually solve its unemployment problem by having half of the population guard the other half.

Morale declines further when *Money* magazine declares Flint to be   10 the second worst place to live in the United States. Ted Koppel arranges to discuss the town's economic collapse, but his show is abruptly canceled after a truck containing its television equipment is stolen. A new five-story jail is built to hold a growing criminal population, and well-to-do citizens, some dressed in the striped suits of cartoon convicts, pay $100 a couple to spend the night behind bars at a slumber party celebrating the jail's opening. With actual events taking on the tone of a savage burlesque, Moore lets his contemptuous sense of satire grow recklessly broad.

Unwisely he fails to confine his scorn to those who might deserve it, and indulges his taste for the bizarre or incongruous to the point of insulting those whose cause he's trying to defend. One of the unemployed men Moore interviews, for example, is a blond-haired guy in his early 20s, standing in front of a plasma bank where he's just been paid for giving blood. He's a slight, aimless kid, with a red bandanna tied around his head à la Rambo. Moore prods him to express resentment about having to sell his own blood for money, but the kid only says, "Lots of people come down here. It's open Monday and Tuesdays." He thinks a minute and adds, "And Wednesdays, Thursday. And Friday. But Saturday and Sunday it's closed." The way the kid falters over explaining what most of us would sum up as "open weekdays" is funny in a cheap way, but laughing at someone who's kind of slow is not what you'd expect from a moral crusader. Moore then asks if the kid will show him the marks made by the needle at the plasma bank. The kid tells him it's nothing much. Moore insists, and the kid gives him a resentful look, then patiently reveals two unremarkable pinpricks. If Moore were seeking to demonstrate that someone who has been bullied and made passive by his economic circumstances can then be bullied by others, he couldn't have chosen a better example.

Much the same thing happens when Moore interviews a woman who supplements her social security check by raising rabbits, then sells them, according to her sign, as BUNNIES OR RABBITS/PETS OR MEAT. State inspectors have already warned her about unsanitary conditions, but she slaughters and skins one rabbit on camera — we suspect at Moore's request — while muttering over her shoulder, "I really shouldn't be doing this." She is a homely woman, tough, with lank dark hair and sinewy strong arms, living with few skills at the edge of poverty. It would take work to make us understand her life, and it's work Moore doesn't do. Instead, he makes her grotesque, which is easy enough, and uses her brutal simplicity to spice up his film.

Is the film a failure? Not at all. It's a sophomoric piece of work as slovenly as an unmade bed, but it does what its maker intended it to do, which is to focus attention on the social and economic problems caused by the lack of legislation governing the relocation of companies. You can wish that someone accurate and responsible had made this film, but it was Moore who wrote the script and sold his possessions to pay for its production. His inaccuracies are glaring, but are nothing compared with the central fact he gets right: that the power of GM in Flint is essentially "nondemocratic" and "hurts a lot of people." He is mischievous and cruel to those he interviews, but crusading satirists are commonly as much trouble to their friends as to their enemies. Even Voltaire's admirers sometimes referred to him as malicious, undignified, unscrupulous, and vain, while his enemies confessed that he was brilliant, audacious, and indefatigable in defense of the oppressed. By those standards Moore is certainly the Voltaire of Flint, Michigan.

The Responsive Reader

1. Does it sound to you as if the documentary told a truth the big-money media are not equipped to tell? (Or have you seen similar materials on network or cable TV?)
2. In the reviewer's account, what are some of the most telling details about the fate of the town and its people? What in this account is most telling about corporate policies and the behavior of company representatives?

3. The reviewer calls the filmmaker a small-town Voltaire. (Voltaire, eighteenth-century French writer, was admired and feared for his satirical barbs.) What was the role of satire in the documentary?
4. This reviewer aimed at writing what is called a "balanced review." What according to her are the weaknesses of the filmmaker's efforts? Do you think the negatives she cites are as important as the message of the movie? (Does the reviewer sound fair or unfair to you?)

Talking, Listening, Writing

5. How effective can efforts like this documentary be? Do you think the documentary as here described could influence your thinking on social and economic issues? (Did this review?)
6. Has media news or documentary material ever had a major impact on you? Why and how?

Projects

7. How much independent opinion finds its way into the media? What alternatives to network or cable news and to mainstream newspapers and magazines are available in your area? For instance, are there small independent newspapers or other publications? Are there radio or television stations that air unconventional or unpopular views? Does your college have unofficial or unauthorized student publications? Collaborating with others, you could check out the range of alternative outlets for ideas.

THE DEATH OF MARILYN MONROE
Sharon Olds

> *Sharon Olds is a widely published American poet who with uninhibited candor takes on the topics of a new generation: bad parenting, sex without love, sex with love, and the wars between mothers and daughters. In the following poem, Olds offers her own perspective on the myth of Marilyn Monroe, "goddess of the silver screen / the only original American queen" (Judy Grahn). In the popular imagination, Norma Jean or Marilyn Monroe, stereotypical sex bomb and dumb blonde, became the ultimate Hollywood creation. A male admirer called her "every man's love affair," whose voice "carried such ripe overtones of erotic excitement and yet was the voice of a little child" (Norman Mailer). Feminist writers have tried to rediscover the human being behind the stereotype, who "tried, I believe, to help us see that beauty has its own mind" (Judy Grahn).*

Thought Starters: What memories and associations does mention of Marilyn Monroe bring to mind? What do you remember about her career, her movies, her private life, her suicide?

The ambulance men touched her cold   1
body, lifted it, heavy as iron,
onto the stretcher, tried to close the
mouth, closed the eyes, tied the
arms to the sides, moved a caught   5
strand of hair, as if it mattered,
saw the shape of her breasts, flattened by
gravity, under the sheet,
carried her, as if it were she,
down the steps.   10

These men were never the same. They went out
afterwards, as they always did,
for a drink or two, but they could not meet
each other's eyes.

              Their lives took   15
a turn — one had nightmares, strange
pains, impotence, depression. One did not
like his work, his wife looked

different, his kids. Even death
seemed different to him — a place where she   *20*
would be waiting,

And one found himself standing at night
in the doorway to a room of sleep, listening to
a woman breathing, just an ordinary
woman   *25*
breathing.

The Responsive Reader

1. Poets often make us notice realities that to others might seem merely routine. In the account of the ambulance crew collecting the body, what details are striking, different, gripping, or unexpected?
2. Why did the death have such an impact on the ambulance men? How did it affect them and why?

Talking, Listening, Writing

3. A persona is an assumed identity that may serve as a mask hiding the real person. Have you ever discovered the private person or human being behind a public persona or media creation?
4. Has popular entertainment left the stereotype of the Hollywood blonde behind? Are other stereotypical females evident in the media today?

Projects

5. Macho Norman Mailer and Gloria Steinem, a leading feminist, have both published books about Marilyn Monroe. What accounts for the wide range of perspectives on her life, work, and person? Your class may want to farm out different treatments of the Marilyn Monroe legend to members of a group and then have them compare notes and pool their resources.

WRITING
WORKSHOP 8

Pro and Con

Thinking the matter through often means sorting out the pro and con. When we face a thorny issue, we weigh arguments for and against in the hope of arriving at a balanced conclusion. If we lean to one side, we listen to the other side so that we don't make up our minds prematurely, in ignorance of crucial facts. We listen to dissenting voices so that fair-minded listeners or readers cannot accuse us of being one-sided, of having a closed mind. Of course, no one is ever likely to have a totally open mind on a serious issue. Even open-minded people are likely to have at least tentative commitments on affirmative action, abortion, capital punishment, mandatory helmets for motorcycle riders, or army recruiting on campus. However, part of being a thinking, rational person is the ability to consider alternative views and to judge them on their merits.

Weighing the pro and con is not just a matter of helping you make up your own mind. To convince a fair-minded person, you need to show that you have looked at relevant evidence — without sweeping unwanted facts under the sofa. If readers suspect that you are prone to slant the evidence, you may lose your credibility. The more experienced your readers are, the more likely they are to be wary of being manipulated by someone who knows more than they do but is not telling.

Writing that honestly weighs the pro and con invites the reader to share in an intellectual journey. Writer and reader together embark on a journey of discovery. They look at the conflicting evidence together, trying to sort it out and make sense of it. Ideally, writer and reader will arrive at the same or similar conclusion. Readers then do not have to feel that they were browbeaten or bamboozled or talked into something they are not really in a position to judge. Pro-and-con writing gives you a chance to show that you respect your reader's intelligence.

TRIGGERING Many people's minds are set on controversial subjects. (Sometimes they seem set in cement.) Such people often voice their opinions confidently and sometimes at the top of the voice. But many other people are genuinely challenged by issues where there is something to be said on both sides. Here are examples of issues that you may want to think and write about:

- Traditionally, Americans have prided themselves on their opposition to censorship. However, we encounter situations that test our commitment to freedom of speech: snuff movies, hate literature circulated by neo-Nazis, rap songs endorsing the killing of cops, or art that seems blasphemous to religious groups. Where do we draw the line? Or is there a line? What do we learn from listening to those who radically oppose and those who seem to endorse censorship?

- We all pay lip service to equal educational opportunity. What happens when students reach college age whose previous schooling has been hampered by poverty, a violent environment, substandard schools? Do we apply the same admission standards to them as to preppies? (Do we "water down" our standards and our curriculum?) Or do we make allowance — taking "affirmative action"?

- Tempers on both sides of the abortion issue run high. However, it is ultimately the woman with an unwanted pregnancy who is facing an agonizing choice. What are the arguments for and against abortion?

GATHERING As with any other substantial paper, so with your pro-and-con paper, input has to come before output. You need to explore the issue — listening, reading, taking notes. The special difficulty we all face in preparing a pro-and-con presentation is to learn to listen to people we think are wrong. (The natural impulse is to ridicule them or shout them down.) What are they actually saying? *Why* do they disagree with us? What goes on in their minds? (What do they know that we don't know? What do they value that we disregard — and why?) It is good practice to try playing the "devil's advocate." To come to know an opposing view from the inside, try to present your opponents' position as if you were on their side.

In addition, you may want to make a special effort to listen to some voices that do *not* represent the opposing factions. Is there someone who is knowledgeable but above the fray? Can you find someone who might care but not have an axe to grind? You will realize early that you cannot take at face value the "facts" and arguments presented by interested parties, rah-rah advocates, or PR people promoting an agenda for a client for a fee. Who might be unbiased yet be in a position to know?

SHAPING As with other kinds of papers, there is no "one-size-fits-all" tried-and-true formula for writing a pro-and-con paper. To start getting your material under control, try lining up pro and con arguments in two separate facing columns. Preparing these two contrasting lists will help clarify the issue for you. It will at the same time be a big step toward structuring your paper.

By looking at what you have on each side of the issue, you can decide what organizational strategy might be more effective: Should you present and explain major arguments on one side first — and then look at those on the opposing side? This way the inner logic of each opposing position might become clear. Your readers would see how major planks in each opposing position are related, how they fit together. Or should you present one argument on one side at one time — and then immediately show what the other side would say in return? This way your readers could share in the excitement of the debate. They could become involved in the give-and-take of assertion and rebuttal.

Here is a tentative lining up of the pro and con on the issue of drug testing on the job: As a condition of employment, should people in sensitive occupations agree to submit to unannounced testing for illegal drugs? (Which side do you find yourself on when looking over these notes? Or are you torn between the two opposed positions?)

Pro

1. Pilots, engineers, and operators of heavy equipment literally take others' lives into their hands.

2. Drug users are responsible for absenteeism, low productivity, and high injury rates on the job.

3. "Recreational" drug users support a murderous drug trade responsible for unprecedented levels of crime.

4. Drug users in prestigious occupations are the worst possible role models for endangered American youth.

5. Testing is above-board and better than snooping and spying.

Con

1. The "war on drugs" makes no distinction between recreational drug users and addicts.

2. The tests are notoriously inaccurate (sesame seeds cause false positives) and ruin the careers of people falsely accused.

3. Employers become agents of a police state, poisoning employer-employee relations.

4. Drug testing undermines basic American traditions of due process and protection against self-incrimination.

5. We already have too much government meddling in people's private lives.

To help you explore the pro and con on an issue such as this, you might want to participate in a group writing activity. Different members of the class would suggest arguments to be lined up in two separate pro and con columns on the board. Or your class might want to stage a mock debate, with opposing speakers presenting arguments that members of the class would have to ponder in their pro-and-con papers.

REVISING In spite of your good intentions, a first draft is still likely to be too one-sided. It is likely to be too polemical—pushing your own side of the argument while giving a nod to the other (with too many barbs at those who disagree with you). The treatment of the other side is likely to be too brief—or too biased. A rule of thumb: Are the arguments for given roughly as much space as the arguments against?

Use your revision to tone down heated statements—to make your treatment more objective, more balanced. A sentence like "Again our First Amendment rights are encroached upon, ignored, and violated by the pro-censorship forces" is not likely to make the other side listen to your arguments (it is going to make them mad). *Extremists, lunatic fringe, safety nazis, gun nuts, femlibbers*—all such expressions generate more heat than light. (If any such appear in your paper, make sure to show that you are merely *quoting* them and that they are not yours.)

Study the following sample student paper. How successful is it? How good a model does it make?

SAMPLE PAPER

Warning: Material May Not Be Suitable for Members of Congress

We drink the vomit of priests, make love with the dying whore.
We suck the blood of the beast and hold the key to death's door.

This song by a heavy metal band shows the kind of lyrics that have brought organizations like the Parents' Music Resource Center (PMRC) into the censorship arena. With the aim of fighting explicit lyrics promoting violence, racism, suicide, sexual abuse, drugs, and alcohol, the PMRC has supported numerous bills mandating the labeling and censorship of offending recording artists and their albums. An in-house legal research service advised the U.S. Congress in 1987 that it has the "constitutional authority to regulate explicit sound recording lyrics and restrict minors' access to them." Senator Albert Gore, Democrat from Tennessee, went on record as saying that he would be "looking to find if there is some constitutional means to regulate lyrics." Phyllis Pollack, the executive director of Music in Action, an anti-censorship group, replied that "this is very dangerous, strange stuff. We've always said that the issue is not rock music; it's trying to take away freedom of speech. Once they convince people that censorship is O.K. in rock, they'll move on to other media."

The basic argument of the groups asking for warning labels on offensive recordings is that parents have the responsibility to bring up their children in a way that is acceptable to the parents' moral and ethical beliefs. Parents cannot exercise this responsibility when material diametrically opposite to their religious and moral views is everywhere easily accessible to their children. As one supporter of the labeling laws explained, our thoughts are influenced by the words and images we put in our minds. We should try to supply our minds with input that will promote healthy thoughts, "which in turn will produce healthy lives." Many supporters of warning labels for offensive material are members of the Christian right who attribute the rise of teenage suicides, teenage sex, and violence in our society to the constant presence of sex and violence in the media.

In rebuttal, defenders of rock musicians have challenged the alleged links between teen murderers or suicide victims and the rock lyrics that are being made the "scapegoat." As Jean Dixon, member of Congress from Missouri, said, there must have been something terribly wrong with these children before they listened to any particular song. The proposed laws would require large warning stickers or parental advisory labels on certain albums. Who would make the decisions? Retailers are not experts on the political and religious ideologies involved. More than one skeptic has warned, "a sticker may just entice kids to buy a record." Warning labels might actually encourage people to purchase records they otherwise would pass by.

As with similar issues, charges and countercharges are heated. Pro-censorship groups freely use terms like "filth" and "garbage of the mind." Anti-censorship forces call their opponents "book burners." What is the answer?

We are not going to control our children's minds. We cannot dictate what they can see and hear and think. The best we can hope for is open and honest communication between parents and their children. I agree we must help create positive images for our children. I also agree that there is much offensive or borderline material in today's popular music. However, if there is to be any labeling of recordings, it should be worked out on a voluntary basis by representatives of the industry and the artists concerned. The Federal, state, and local governments should keep their hands off. The basic challenge is to provide some voluntary system of rating, similar to the one used for movies. The music industry professionals should create their own system of labeling while protecting the free speech rights of their artists.

QUESTIONS How and how well does the student writer set up the issue? Do you think both sides are fairly represented in this paper? Are you willing to accept the writer's solution as a balanced, rational conclusion? Do you think the paper as a whole leads up to it effectively? Why or why not?

Topics for Pro-and-Con Papers (A Sampling)

1. Should public funds be used to support art that is offensive to the majority? (Study test cases like the Mapplethorpe exhibit, supported in part by funds from the National Endowment for the Arts, that put a Cincinnati art museum on the map.)
2. Should college bookstores take from the shelves magazines accused of being sexist or exploitative of women?

3. Should colleges have special admission standards for members of minority groups? (Should they lower their requirements for special groups?)
4. Should schools have "vocational" tracks that in practice have a disproportionate representation of minority students? (Does tracking shunt minorities away from pre-college work?)
5. Can anything be done to stem the flood of violence in movies and television programs?
6. Should television stations be required to make available "equal time" for representatives of smaller parties or for minority views?
7. Are the private lives and past histories of political candidates fair game for the news media?
8. Do people teaching minority literature have to be members of minority groups themselves? (Is a white teacher qualified to teach a course in African American literature, for instance?)
9. Is the government (or the post office) justified in conducting sting operations to combat child pornography? Or do such operations constitute entrapment?
10. Are the courts justified in banning school prayer? (Are they justified in banning invocations at ceremonies at public colleges or universities?)

9

Language: Bond or Barrier?

An education for freedom (and for the love and intelligence which are at once the conditions and the results of freedom) must be, among other things, an education in the proper uses of language.

Aldous Huxley

Languages are far-reaching realities. They go far beyond those political and historical structures we call nations.

Octavio Paz

Language is the greatest human invention. It almost always gives us more than neutral information of the kind that could be stored in a computer — or recited by a computerized voice. Words do not just give directions ("This way to the center of the city"). They tell us something about the speaker — as if a telephone while carrying a message were to tell us whether it liked its job. *Bureaucrat, politician, schoolmarm, welfare cheat, redneck,* and *woman driver* are not neutral labels like *detergent* or *soap.* They give vent to the speaker's feelings. They carry messages of dislike, of antagonism — they say, "I am not as dense or conniving or bigoted or incompetent as you are."

Many of the following selections raise the crucial human question about language: Is it boon or bane in relationships between individuals or groups? Does it further human understanding, or does it serve to muddy the waters or poison the wells? We like to think of language as a bond. It helps people to break out of their isolation, to break down the wall of separateness. In the dim prehistoric past, it enabled human beings to band together, to make plans, to coordinate their efforts. Language enables us to offer other human beings help and comfort. ("Be of good cheer; we will not abandon you" is chalked on a message board held up on a rescue vessel to comfort the people on a shipwrecked ship in one of Walt Whitman's poems.) However, language also carries messages of rejection, condescension, and contempt, as with words like *stud, slut, woman driver, dirty foreigner, greaser, dago* (and other racial or ethnic slurs too ugly to mention).

451

Language often reinforces divisions; it serves to outgroup people who are "not one of us." Language is the medium of love, but it is also the medium of quarrels, of hate propaganda, of incitement to violence.

Many people in our modern world have been suspicious of language—wary of its potential for abuse. Others have maintained their faith in the capacity of language to help human beings communicate. The critic Margaret Laurence said about the Nigerian novelist Chinua Achebe, author of *Things Fall Apart,*

> In Ibo villages, the men working on their farm plots in the midst of the rain forest often shout to one another—a reassurance, to make certain the other is still there, on the next cultivated patch, on the other side of the thick undergrowth. The writing of Chinua Achebe is like this. It seeks to send human voices through thickets of our separateness.

TALK IN THE INTIMATE RELATIONSHIP: HIS AND HERS

Deborah Tannen

Deborah Tannen is a linguistic scholar who has been both admired and criticized for going beyond the boundaries of conventional academic publishing to reach a large public. She has published two widely read books on the undercurrents and hidden messages in how people talk: You Just Don't Understand: Women and Men in Conversation *and* That's Not What I Meant: How Conversational Style Makes or Breaks Relationships *(1986). Her focus is on the* metamessages *we send — the messages that go beyond* what we say outright. *Literal-minded people miss much of what lies below surface meanings. The mere fact that people bother to talk to us already sends a message (they care enough to give us some of their time), just as their refusal to talk to us also sends a message.*

Thought Starters: Is it true that as far as language goes, boys and girls "grow up in different worlds"? Is a conversation between a man and a woman truly "cross-cultural" communication?

Male-female conversation is cross-cultural communication. Culture   *1*
is simply a network of habits and patterns gleaned from past experience, and women and men have different past experiences. From the time they're born, they're treated differently, talked to differently, and talk differently as a result. Boys and girls grow up in different worlds, even if they grow up in the same house. And as adults they travel in different worlds, reinforcing patterns established in childhood. These cultural differences include different expectations about the role of talk in relationships and how it fulfills that role.

Everyone knows that as a relationship becomes long-term, its terms change. But women and men often differ in how they expect them to change. Many women feel, "After all this time, you should know what I want without my telling you." Many men feel, "After all this time, we should be able to tell each other what we want."

These incongruent expectations capture one of the key differences between men and women. Communication is always a matter of balancing conflicting needs for involvement and independence. Though everyone has both these needs, women often have a relatively greater need for involvement, and men a relatively greater need for independence. Being understood without saying what you mean gives a payoff in involvement, and that is why women value it so highly.

If you want to be understood without saying what you mean explic-itly in words, you must convey meaning somewhere else—in how words are spoken, or by metamessages. Thus it stands to reason that women are often more attuned than men to the metamessages of talk. When women surmise meaning in this way, it seems mysterious to men, who call it "women's intuition" (if they think it's right) or "reading things in" (if they think it's wrong). Indeed, it could be wrong, since metamessages are not on record. And even if it is right, there is still the question of scale: How significant are the metamessages that are there?

Metamessages are a form of indirectness. Women are more likely to   5 be indirect, and to try to reach agreement by negotiation. Another way to understand this preference is that negotiation allows a display of solidarity, which women prefer to the display of power (even though the aim may be the same—getting what you want). Unfortunately, power and solidar-ity are bought with the same currency: Ways of talking intended to create solidarity have the simultaneous effect of framing power differences. When they think they're being nice, women often end up appearing def-erential and unsure of themselves or of what they want.

When styles differ, misunderstandings are always rife. As their dif-fering styles create misunderstandings, women and men try to clear them up by talking things out. These pitfalls are compounded in talks between men and women because they have different ways of going about talking things out, and different assumptions about the significance of going about it.

Sylvia and Harry celebrated their fiftieth wedding anniversary at a mountain resort. Some of the guests were at the resort for the whole weekend, others just for the evening of the celebration: a cocktail party followed by a sit-down dinner. The manager of the dining room ap-proached Sylvia during dinner. "Since there's so much food tonight," he said, "and the hotel prepared a fancy dessert and everyone already ate at the cocktail party anyway, how about cutting and serving the anniversary cake at lunch tomorrow?" Sylvia asked the advice of the others at her table. All the men agreed: "Sure, that makes sense. Save the cake for tomorrow." All the women disagreed: "No, the party is tonight. Serve the cake tonight." The men were focusing on the message: the cake as food. The women were thinking of the metamessage: Serving a special cake frames an occasion as a celebration.

Why are women more attuned to metamessages? Because they are more focused on involvement, that is, on relationships among people, and it is through metamessages that relationships among people are established and maintained. If you want to take the temperature and check the vital signs of a relationship, the barometers to check are its metamessages: what is said and how.

Everyone can see these signals, but whether or not we pay attention to them is another matter—a matter of being sensitized. Once you are sensitized, you can't roll your antennae back in; they're stuck in the extended position.

When interpreting meaning, it is possible to pick up signals that   10
weren't intentionally sent out, like an innocent flock of birds on a radar screen. The birds are there — and the signals women pick up are there — but they may not mean what the interpreter thinks they mean. For example, Maryellen looks at Larry and asks, "What's wrong?" because his brow is furrowed. Since he was only thinking about lunch, her expression of concern makes him feel under scrutiny.

The difference in focus on messages and metamessages can give men and women different points of view on almost any comment. Harriet complains to Morton, "Why don't you ask me how my day was?" He replies, "If you have something to tell me, tell me. Why do you have to be invited?" The reason is that she wants the metamessage of interest: evidence that he cares how her day was, regardless of whether or not she has something to tell.

A lot of trouble is caused between women and men by, of all things, pronouns. Women often feel hurt when their partners use "I" or "me" in a situation in which they would use "we" or "us." When Morton announces, "I think I'll go for a walk," Harriet feels specifically uninvited, though Morton later claims she would have been welcome to join him. She felt locked out by his use of "I" and his omission of an invitation: "Would you like to come?" Metamessages can be seen in what is not said as well as what is said.

It's difficult to straighten out such misunderstandings because each one feels convinced of the logic of his or her position and the illogic — or irresponsibility — of the other's. Harriet knows that she always asks Morton how his day was, and that she'd never announce, "I'm going for a walk," without inviting him to join her. If he talks differently to her, it must be that he feels differently. But Morton wouldn't feel unloved if Harriet didn't ask about his day, and he would feel free to ask, "Can I come along?," if she announced she was taking a walk. So he can't believe she is justified in feeling responses he knows he wouldn't have.

These processes are dramatized with chilling yet absurdly amusing authenticity in Jules Feiffer's play *Grown Ups*. To get a closer look at what happens when men and women focus on different levels of talk in talking things out, let's look at what happens in this play.

Jake criticizes Louise for not responding when their daughter, Edie,   15
called her. His comment leads to a fight even though they're both aware that this one incident is not in itself important.

Jake: Look, I don't care if it's important or not, when a kid calls its mother the mother should answer.
Louise: Now I'm a bad mother.
Jake: I didn't say that.

> *Louise:* It's in your stare.
> *Jake:* Is that another thing you know? My stare?

Louise ignores Jake's message — the question of whether or not she responded when Edie called — and goes for the metamessage: his implication that she's a bad mother, which Jake insistently disclaims. When Louise explains the signals she's reacting to, Jake not only discounts them but is angered at being held accountable not for what he said but for how he looked — his stare.

As the play goes on, Jake and Louise replay and intensify these patterns:

> *Louise:* If I'm such a terrible mother, do you want a divorce?
> *Jake:* I do not think you're a terrible mother and no, thank you, I do not want a divorce. Why is it that whenever I bring up any difference between us you ask me if I want a divorce?

The more he denies any meaning beyond the message, the more she blows it up, the more adamantly he denies it, and so on:

> *Jake:* I have brought up one thing that you do with Edie that I don't think you notice that I have noticed for some time but which I have deliberately not brought up before because I had hoped you would notice it for yourself and stop doing it and also — frankly, baby, I have to say this — I knew if I brought it up we'd get into exactly the kind of circular argument we're in right now. And I wanted to avoid it. But I haven't and we're in it, so now, with your permission, I'd like to talk about it.
> *Louise:* You don't see how that puts me down?
> *Jake:* What?
> *Louise:* If you think I'm so stupid why do you go on living with me?
> *Jake: Dammit! Why can't anything ever be simple around here?!*

It can't be simple because Louise and Jake are responding to different levels of communication. As in Bateson's example of the dual-control electric blanket with crossed wires, each one intensifies the energy going to a different aspect of the problem. Jake tries to clarify his point by over-elaborating it, which gives Louise further evidence that he's condescending to her, making it even less likely that she will address his point rather than his condescension.

What pushes Jake and Louise beyond anger to rage is their different perspectives on metamessages. His refusal to admit that his statements have implications and overtones denies her authority over her own feelings. Her attempts to interpret what he didn't say and put the metamessage into the message makes him feel she's putting words into his mouth — denying his authority over his own meaning.

The same thing happens when Louise tells Jake that he is being manipulated by Edie:

Louise: Why don't you ever make her come to see you? Why do you always go to her?

Jake: You want me to play power games with a nine year old? I want her to know I'm interested in her. Someone around here has to show interest in her.

Louise: You love her more than I do.

Jake: I didn't say that.

Louise: Yes, you did.

Jake: You don't know how to listen. You have never learned how to listen. It's as if listening to you is a foreign language.

Again, Louise responds to his implication — this time, that he loves Edie more because he runs when she calls. And yet again, Jake cries literal meaning, denying he meant any more than he said.

Throughout their argument, the point to Louise is her feelings — that Jake makes her feel put down — but to him the point is her actions — that she doesn't always respond when Edie calls:

Louise: You talk about what I do to Edie, what do you think you do to me?

Jake: This is not the time to go into what we do to each other.

Since she will talk only about the metamessage, and he will talk only about the message, neither can get satisfaction from their talk, and they end up where they started — only angrier:

Jake: That's not the point!

Louise: It's *my* point.

Jake: It's hopeless!

Louise: Then get a divorce.

American conventional wisdom (and many of our parents and English teachers) tell us that meaning is conveyed by words, so men who tend to be literal about words are supported by conventional wisdom. They may not simply deny but actually miss the cues that are sent by how words are spoken. If they sense something about it, they may nonetheless discount what they sense. After all, it wasn't said. Sometimes that's a dodge — a plausible defense rather than a gut feeling. But sometimes it is a sincere conviction. Women are also likely to doubt the reality of what they sense. If they don't doubt it in their guts, they nonetheless may lack the arguments to support their position and thus are reduced to repeating, "You said it. You did so." Knowing that metamessages are a real and fundamental part of communication makes it easier to understand and justify what they feel.

An article in a popular newspaper reports that one of the five most 20 common complaints of wives about their husbands is "He doesn't listen to me anymore." Another is "He doesn't talk to me anymore." Political scientist Andrew Hacker noted that lack of communication, while high on women's lists of reasons for divorce, is much less often mentioned by men. Since couples are parties to the same conversations, why are women more dissatisfied with them than men? Because what they expect is different, as well as what they see as the significance of talk itself.

First, let's consider the complaint "He doesn't talk to me."

One of the most common stereotypes of American men is the strong silent type. Jack Kroll, writing about Henry Fonda on the occasion of his death, used the phrases "quiet power," "abashed silences," "combustible catatonia," and "sense of power held in check." He explained that Fonda's goal was not to let anyone see "the wheels go around," not to let the "machinery" show. According to Kroll, the resulting silence was effective on stage but devastating to Fonda's family.

The image of a silent father is common and is often the model for the lover or husband. But what attracts us can become flypaper to which we are unhappily stuck. Many women find the strong silent type to be a lure as a lover but a lug as a husband. Nancy Schoenberger begins a poem with the lines "It was your silence that hooked me,/ so like my father's." Adrienne Rich refers in a poem to the "husband who is frustratingly mute." Despite the initial attraction of such quintessentially male silence, it may begin to feel, to a woman in a long-term relationship, like a brick wall against which she is banging her head.

In addition to these images of male and female behavior — both the result and the cause of them — are differences in how women and men view the role of talk in relationships as well as how talk accomplishes its purpose. These differences have their roots in the settings in which men and women learn to have conversations: among their peers, growing up.

Children whose parents have foreign accents don't speak with accents. They learn to talk like their peers. Little girls and little boys learn how to have conversations as they learn how to pronounce words: from their playmates. Between the ages of five and fifteen, when children are learning to have conversations, they play mostly with friends of their own sex. So it's not surprising that they learn different ways of having and using conversations. 25

Anthropologists Daniel Maltz and Ruth Borker point out that boys and girls socialize differently. Little girls tend to play in small groups or, even more common, in pairs. Their social life usually centers around a best friend, and friendships are made, maintained, and broken by talk — especially "secrets." If a little girl tells her friend's secret to another little girl, she may find herself with a new best friend. The secrets themselves may or may not be important, but the fact of telling them is all-important. It's hard for newcomers to get into these tight groups, but anyone who is admitted is treated as an equal. Girls like to play cooperatively; if they can't cooperate, the group breaks up.

Little boys tend to play in larger groups, often outdoors, and they spend more time doing things than talking. It's easy for boys to get into the group, but not everyone is accepted as an equal. Once in the group, boys must jockey for their status in it. One of the most important ways they do this is through talk: verbal display such as telling stories and jokes, challenging and sidetracking the verbal displays of other boys, and withstanding other boys' challenges in order to maintain their own story — and status. Their talk is often competitive talk about who is best at what.

Feiffer's play is ironically named *Grown Ups* because adult men and women struggling to communicate often sound like children: "You said so!" "I did not!" The reason is that when they grow up, women and men keep the divergent attitudes and habits they learned as children — which they don't recognize as attitudes and habits but simply take for granted as ways of talking.

Women want their partners to be a new and improved version of a best friend. This gives them a soft spot for men who tell them secrets. As Jack Nicholson once advised a guy in a movie: "Tell her about your troubled childhood — that always gets 'em." Men expect to *do* things together and don't feel anything is missing if they don't have heart-to-heart talks all the time.

If they do have heart-to-heart talks, the meaning of those talks may   30
be opposite for men and women. To many women, the relationship is working as long as they can talk things out. To many men, the relationship isn't working out if they have to keep working it over. If she keeps trying to get talks going to save the relationship, and he keeps trying to avoid them because he sees them as weakening it, then each one's efforts to preserve the relationship appear to the other as reckless endangerment.

If talks (of any kind) do get going, men's and women's ideas about how to conduct them may be very different. For example, Dora is feeling comfortable and close to Tom. She settles into a chair after dinner and begins to tell him about a problem at work. She expects him to ask questions to show he's interested; reassure her that he understands and that what she feels is normal; and return the intimacy by telling her a problem of his. Instead, Tom sidetracks her story, cracks jokes about it, questions her interpretation of the problem, and gives her advice about how to solve it and avoid such problems in the future.

All of these responses, natural to men, are unexpected to women, who interpret them in terms of their own habits — negatively. When Tom comments on side issues or cracks jokes, Dora thinks he doesn't care about what she's saying and isn't really listening. If he challenges her reading of what went on, she feels he is criticizing her and telling her she's crazy, when what she wants is to be reassured that she's not. If he tells her how to solve the problem, it makes her feel as if she's the patient to his doctor — a metamessage of condescension, echoing male one-upmanship compared to the female etiquette of equality. Because he doesn't volunteer information about his problems, she feels he's implying he doesn't have any.

His way of responding to her bid for intimacy makes her feel distant from him. She tries harder to regain intimacy the only way she knows

how — by revealing more and more about herself. He tries harder by giving more insistent advice. The more problems she exposes, the more
incompetent she feels, until they both see her as emotionally draining and
problem-ridden. When his efforts to help aren't appreciated, he wonders
why she asks for his advice if she doesn't want to take it. . . .

When women talk about what seems obviously interesting to them,
their conversations often include reports of conversations. Tone of voice,
timing, intonation, and wording are all re-created in the telling in order
to explain — dramatize, really — the experience that is being reported. If
men tell about an incident and give a brief summary instead of recreating
what was said and how, the women often feel that the essence of the
experience is being omitted. If the woman asks, "What exactly did he
say?," and "How did he say it?," the man probably can't remember. If she
continues to press him, he may feel as if he's being grilled.

All these different habits have repercussions when the man and the   35
woman are talking about their relationship. He feels out of his element,
even one down. She claims to recall exactly what he said, and what she
said, and in what sequence, and she wants him to account for what he said.
He can hardly account for it since he has forgotten exactly what was said —
if not the whole conversation. She secretly suspects he's only pretending
not to remember, and he secretly suspects that she's making up the details.

One woman reported such a problem as being a matter of her boyfriend's poor memory. It is unlikely, however, that his problem was poor
memory in general. The question is what types of material each person
remembers or forgets.

Frances was sitting at her kitchen table talking to Edward, when the
toaster did something funny. Edward began to explain why it did it.
Frances tried to pay attention, but very early in his explanation, she realized she was completely lost. She felt very stupid. And indications were
that he thought so too.

Later that day they were taking a walk. He was telling her about a
difficult situation in his office that involved a complex network of inter-
relationships among a large number of people. Suddenly he stopped and
said, "I'm sure you can't keep track of all these people." "Of course I
can," she said, and she retraced his story with all the characters in place,
all the details right. He was genuinely impressed. She felt very smart.

How could Frances be both smart and stupid? Did she have a good
memory or a bad one? Frances's and Edward's abilities to follow, remember, and recount depended on the subject — and paralleled her parents'
abilities to follow and remember. Whenever Frances told her parents about
people in her life, her mother could follow with no problem, but her father
got lost as soon as she introduced a second character. "Now who was
that?" he'd ask. "Your boss?" "No, my boss is Susan. This was my
friend." Often he'd still be in the previous story. But whenever she told
them about her work, it was her mother who would get lost as soon as she

mentioned a second step: "That was your tech report?" "No, I handed my tech report in last month. This was a special project."

Frances's mother and father, like many other men and women, had   40
honed their listening and remembering skills in different arenas. Their experience talking to other men and other women gave them practice in following different kinds of talk.

Knowing whether and how we are likely to report events later influences whether and how we pay attention when they happen. As women listen to and take part in conversations, knowing they may talk about them later makes them more likely to pay attention to exactly what is said and how. Since most men aren't in the habit of making such reports, they are less likely to pay much attention at the time. On the other hand, many women aren't in the habit of paying attention to scientific explanations and facts because they don't expect to have to perform in public by reciting them — just as those who aren't in the habit of entertaining others by telling jokes "can't" remember jokes they've heard, even though they listened carefully enough to enjoy them.

So women's conversations with their women friends keep them in training for talking about their relationships with men, but many men come to such conversations with no training at all — and an uncomfortable sense that this really isn't their event.

Most of us place enormous emphasis on the importance of a primary relationship. We regard the ability to maintain such relationships as a sign of mental health — our contemporary metaphor for being a good person.

Yet our expectations of such relationships are nearly — maybe in fact — impossible. When primary relationships are between women and men, male-female differences contribute to the impossibility. We expect partners to be both romantic interests and best friends. Though women and men may have fairly similar expectations for romantic interests, obscuring their differences when relationships begin, they have very different ideas about how to be friends, and these are the differences that mount over time.

In conversations between friends who are not lovers, small misun-   45
derstandings can be passed over or diffused by breaks in contact. But in the context of a primary relationship, differences can't be ignored, and the pressure cooker of continued contact keeps both people stewing in the juice of accumulated minor misunderstandings. And stylistic differences are sure to cause misunderstandings — not, ironically, in matters such as sharing values and interests or understanding each other's philosophies of life. These large and significant yet palpable issues can be talked about and agreed on. It is far harder to achieve congruence — and much more surprising and troubling that it is hard — in the simple day-to-day matters of the automatic rhythms and nuances of talk. Nothing in our backgrounds or in the media (the present-day counterpart to religion or grandparents' teachings) prepares us for this failure. If two people share so much in terms

of point of view and basic values, how can they continually get into fights about insignificant matters?

If you find yourself in such a situation and you don't know about differences in conversational style, you assume something's wrong with your partner, or you for having chosen your partner. At best, if you are forward thinking and generous minded, you may absolve individuals and blame the relationship. But if you know about differences in conversational style, you can accept that there are differences in habits and assumptions about how to have conversation, show interest, be considerate, and so on. You may not always correctly interpret your partner's intentions, but you will know that if you get a negative impression, it may not be what was intended — and neither are your responses unfounded. If he says he really is interested even though he doesn't seem to be, maybe you should believe what he says and not what you sense.

Sometimes explaining assumptions can help. If a man starts to tell a woman what to do to solve her problem, she may say, "Thanks for the advice but I really don't want to be told what to do. I just want you to listen and say you understand." A man might want to explain, "If I challenge you, it's not to prove you wrong; it's just my way of paying attention to what you're telling me." Both may try either or both to modify their ways of talking and to try to accept what the other does. The important thing is to know that what seem like bad intentions may really be good intentions expressed in a different conversational style. We have to give up our conviction that, as Robin Lakoff put it, "Love means never having to say 'What do you mean?'"

The Responsive Reader

1. Tannen once said that readers of her work reported an "Aha!" response. They found that what they thought was their personal problem was actually part of a larger pattern. Did you have an "Aha!" response to any part of this selection? Can you give examples from your own experience for the clashing assumptions or expectations that Tannen ascribes to men and women?
2. What are key examples that Tannen gives for the difficulties of communication between men and women? How real or convincing do they seem to you? (How convincing are the examples from the Feiffer play?) Do you interpret the examples the same way she does?
3. How does Tannen explain how misunderstandings "intensify" or escalate?
4. How familiar are the stereotypes about males that Tannen claims are widespread in our culture and shape male behavior? How strong are they?
5. Is there hope for miscommunicating couples? What is the gist of the positive advice, explicit or implied, that Tannen would give to couples who have trouble communicating?

Talking, Listening, Writing

6. There is much debate over what is truly "gender-specific" in our culture. Do you think Tannen exaggerates the differences between the talking styles of the sexes? Where and how?

7. Have you ever rebelled against a style of talking expected of you? Have you ever found yourself using language that was not "you"? What was the occasion or situation? What was the problem? What was the outcome?

Projects

8. Working alone or in a group, you may want to investigate the "women's language" of fashion sections or society pages. Or you may want to study the "men's language" of the sports pages. Or you may want to work out significant contrasts between the two.

CULTURAL ETIQUETTE: A GUIDE

Amoja Three Rivers

> Ms. *magazine published the following article as part of a series on race and women. The editors called it a "creative attempt to shed some light — and levity — on the serious task of dispelling racial myths and stereotypes." The author is a cofounder of the Accessible African Herstory Project and was described by the editors of* Ms. *as a "lecturer, herstorian, and craftswoman." Much of the article focuses on how language — ready-made phrases, loaded words — channel or distort our thinking. The article provides a guide to words that can raise hackles or short-circuit communication — in short, make people see red. This article should make you think about the power of words to shape our thinking and our views of other people.*

Thought Starters: Whatever the color of their skin, people tend to be thin-skinned when they encounter words that they perceive to be slurs on their group, religion, or background. Have you been a victim of any of the stereotyped assumptions and expressions discussed in this article? Are you guilty of using any of them yourself?

Cultural Etiquette is intended for people of all "races," nationalities,   1
and creeds, not necessarily just "white" people, because no one living in Western society is exempt from the influences of racism, racial stereotypes, race and cultural prejudices, and anti-Semitism. I include anti-Semitism in the discussion of racism because it is simply another manifestation of cultural and racial bigotry.

All people are people. It is ethnocentric to use a generic term such as "people" to refer only to white people and then racially label everyone else. This creates and reinforces the assumption that whites are the norm, the real people, and that all others are aberrations.

"Exotic," when applied to human beings, is ethnocentric and racist.

While it is true that most citizens of the U.S.A. are white, at least four fifths of the world's population consists of people of color. Therefore, it is statistically incorrect as well as ethnocentric to refer to us as minorities. The term "minority" is used to reinforce the idea of people of color as "other."

A cult is a particular system of religious worship. If the religious   5
practices of the Yorubas constitute a cult, then so do those of the Methodists, Catholics, Episcopalians, and so forth.

A large radio/tape player is a boom-box, or a stereo or a box or a large metallic ham sandwich with speakers. It is not a "ghetto blaster."

Everybody can blush. Everybody can bruise. Everybody can tan and get sunburned. Everybody.

Judaism is no more patriarchal than any other patriarchal religion.

Koreans are not taking over. Neither are Jews. Neither are the Japanese. Neither are the West Indians. These are myths put out and maintained by the ones who really have.

All hair is "good" hair. Dreadlocks, locks, dreads, natty dreads, et   *10* cetera, is an ancient traditional way that African people sometimes wear their hair. It is not braided, it is "locked." Locking is the natural tendency of African hair to knit and bond to itself. It locks by itself, we don't have to do anything to it to make it lock. It is permanent; once locked, it cannot come undone. It gets washed just as regularly as anyone else's hair. No, you may not touch it, don't ask.

One of the most effective and insidious aspects of racism is cultural genocide. Not only have African Americans been cut off from our African tribal roots, but because of generations of whites pitting African against Indian, and Indian against African, we have been cut off from our Native American roots as well. Consequently, most African Native Americans no longer have tribal affiliations, or know for certain what people they are from.

Columbus didn't discover diddly-squat.

Slavery is not a condition unique to African people. In fact, the word "slave" comes from the Slav people of Eastern Europe. Because so many Slavs were enslaved by other people (including Africans), their very name came to be synonymous with the condition.

Native Americans were also enslaved by Europeans. Because it is almost impossible to successfully enslave large numbers of people in their own land, most enslaved Native Americans from the continental U.S. were shipped to Bermuda, and the West Indies, where many intermarried with the Africans.

People do not have a hard time because of their race or cultural   *15* background. No one is attacked, abused, oppressed, pogromed, or enslaved because of their race, creed, or cultural background. People are attacked, abused, oppressed, pogromed, or enslaved because of racism and anti-Semitism. There is a subtle but important difference in the focus here. The first implies some inherent fault or shortcoming within the oppressed person or group. The second redirects the responsibility back to the real source of the problem.

Asians are not "mysterious," "fatalistic," or "inscrutable."

Native Americans are not stoic, mystical, or vanishing.

Latin people are no more hot-tempered, hot-blooded, or emotional than anyone else. We do not have flashing eyes, teeth, or daggers. We are lovers pretty much like other people. Very few of us deal with any kind of drugs.

Middle Easterners are not fanatics, terrorists, or all oil-rich.

Jewish people are not particularly rich, clannish, or expert in money   20
matters.

Not all African Americans are poor, athletic, or ghetto-dwellers.

Most Asians in the U.S. are not scientists, mathematicians, geniuses,
or wealthy.

Southerners are no less intelligent than anybody else.

It is not a compliment to tell someone: "I don't think of you as
Jewish/Black/Asian/Latina/Middle Eastern/Native American." Or "I
think of you as white."

Do not use a Jewish person or person of color to hear your confession   25
of past racist transgressions. If you have offended a particular person, then
apologize directly to that person.

Also don't assume that Jews and people of color necessarily want to
hear about how prejudiced your Uncle Fred is, no matter how terrible you
think he is.

If you are white and/or gentile, do not assume that the next Jewish
person or person of color you see will feel like discussing this guide with
you. Sometimes we get tired of teaching this subject.

If you are white, don't brag to a person of color about your overseas
trip to our homeland. Especially when we cannot afford such a trip.
Similarly, don't assume that we are overjoyed to see the expensive artifacts
you bought.

Words like "gestapo," "concentration camp" and "Hitler" are only
appropriate when used in reference to the Holocaust.

"Full-blood," "half-breed," "quarter-blood." Any inference that a   30
person's "race" depends on blood is racist. Natives are singled out for this
form of bigotry and are denied rights on that basis.*

"Scalping": a custom also practiced by the French, the Dutch, and
the English.*

Do you have friends or acquaintances who are terrific except they're
really racist? If you quietly accept that part of them, you are giving their
racism tacit approval.

As an exercise, pretend you are from another planet and you want an
example of a typical human being for your photo album. Having never
heard of racism, you'd probably pick someone who represents the majority of the people on the planet — an Asian person.

How many is too many? We have heard well-meaning liberals say
things like "This event is too white. We need more people of color." Well,
how many do you need? Fifty? A hundred? Just what is your standard for
personal racial comfort?

People of color and Jewish people have been so all their lives. Further,   35
if we have been raised in a place where white gentiles predominate, then

---

*Reprinted with permission from *The Pathfinder Directory,* by Amylee, Native American Indian Resource Center. [Author's note]

we have been subjected to racism/anti-Semitism all our lives. We are therefore experts on our own lives and conditions. If you do not understand or believe or agree with what someone is saying about their own oppression, do not automatically assume that they are wrong or paranoid or oversensitive.

It is not "racism in reverse" or "segregation" for Jews or people of color to come together in affinity groups for mutual support. Sometimes we need some time and space apart from the dominant group just to relax and be ourselves. If people coming together for group support makes you feel excluded, perhaps there's something missing in your own life or cultural connections.

The various cultures of people of color often seem very attractive to white people. (Yes, we are wonderful, we can't deny it.) But white people should not make a playground out of other people's cultures. We are not quaint. We are not exotic. We are not cool.

Don't forget that every white person alive today is also descended from tribal peoples. If you are white, don't neglect your own ancient traditions. They are as valid as anybody else's, and the ways of your own ancestors need to be honored and remembered.

"Race" is an arbitrary and meaningless concept. Races among humans don't exist. If there ever was any such thing as race, there has been so much constant crisscrossing of genes for the last 500,000 years that it would have lost all meaning anyway. There are no real divisions between us, only a continuum of variations that constantly change, as we come together and separate according to the movement of human populations.

Anyone who functions in what is referred to as the "civilized" world is a carrier of the disease of racism. 40

Does reading this guide make you uncomfortable? Angry? Confused? Are you taking it personally? Well, not to fret. Racism has created a big horrible mess, and racial healing can sometimes be painful. Just remember that Jews and people of color do not want or need anybody's guilt. We just want people to accept responsibility when it is appropriate, and actively work for change.

The Responsive Reader

1. The writer attacks stereotypes about hot-blooded Latins, inscrutable Asians, athletic blacks, rich Jews, Middle Eastern terrorists, and others. Which of these stereotypes have you encountered — where and how? Have they shaped your own thinking?
2. What are the author's objections to the terms *minority, exotic, cult, half-breed, reverse racism,* and *race* itself? What other uses of language does she ask you to reconsider? How serious or valid do her objections seem to you?
3. When conversations turn on sensitive subjects, it is easy to say the wrong thing. What advice does this guide to etiquette give for

conversations with people from different ethnic or cultural backgrounds? What pitfalls does Three Rivers warn against? How helpful or valid are her warnings?

4. The author uses weighty words like *ethnocentric, anti-Semitism, bigotry, genocide*. What do these words mean to you? How does the author use them?

5. The writer defends herself against the charge of being oversensitive — do you think she is?

Talking, Listening, Writing

6. The author says that "no one living in Western society is exempt from the influences of racism." Do you agree?

7. At the end, Three Rivers asks, "Does reading this guide make you uncomfortable? Angry? Confused? Are you taking it personally?" What are your answers to these questions?

8. What has been your own experience with the power of language to hurt people, to divide them, or to hold them back?

Projects

9. The African American writer Ossie Davis once wrote an article called "The English Language Is My Enemy." Sociolinguists (people who study how language works in societies) have noted that many of the expressions that use the word *black* have negative connotations or overtones (*black sheep, blackball*), whereas many expressions using the word *white* have positive associations. Working by yourself or with a group, study this "black and white" contrast in our language. How widespread is it — how many examples can you find? Are there exceptions? (For instance, to be in the red is bad, to be in the black is good.) Do you think our language unconsciously shapes our attitudes in this regard? What can or should be done to counteract these influences?

DEAF IN AMERICA:
A CHANGING CONSCIOUSNESS*

Carol Padden and Tom Humphries

The following is a chapter from a book titled Deaf in America: Voices from a Culture *(1988). Both authors are members of the Deaf community. Carol Padden is a professor of communication at the University of California in San Diego who was born into a deaf family. Tom Humphries is a community college administrator who became deaf as a child and did not meet other deaf people until he entered a college for deaf people. Both are teacher-scholars who have published research on the structure and uses of American Sign Language (ASL). Their aim in the book was to write about deaf people not as medical cases or people with disabilities but as people who share a rich culture, historically conditioned and transmitted across generations. In that culture, signed languages (sign languages or gesture languages) play a central role. The authors stress the "linguistic richness" of the languages of the deaf, describing them as "rich systems with complex structures that reflect their long histories."*

Thought Starters: What is the reaction of people in our society to the hearing-impaired? How are attitudes in our society changing toward people with disabilities?

David, an older member of the Deaf community, complained to us about a questionnaire he had been asked to fill out about his early language experience. He couldn't answer the questions, he said. One question asked what language he had used at home with his Deaf parents, and listed the following choices: speech, ASL, or one of the other modes of signing. But, he told us, none of the choices was correct. We were taken aback. Why wouldn't ASL be the correct answer, since his parents were Deaf and he had used the language from birth? "But we didn't call it 'ASL' back then. We didn't call it anything, we just did it. How can I call it one of these when we didn't call it any of them?"

In David's childhood, his family had never had a specific name for what they used to communicate with one another. The activity of signing had been called simply "sign language," or "manual language." But today there are names for different kinds of signing. The natural signed language used in the United States is called American Sign Language, or ASL; English-influenced signing has another name, Sign English; and then there are the various manual English systems, including those with pedagogically persuasive names such as Signing Exact English, or SEE.

As an adult David knew the new terminology, and could use it himself to talk about his own signing or that of others. Perhaps what distressed him about the questionnaire was that the names connote certain histories that he would have to weigh in his answer.

If he called the language he used at home ASL — the answer we expected him to choose — he might find himself accused of having an impoverished language background by those who believe ASL is inferior to English. As a Deaf man who had learned English well, he found such a suggestion offensive. He was no Tim Shalleck, no simple bartender, but a professional member of his community.

His reluctance to rename something familiar, even taken for granted, is understandable. The term "ASL" implies a particular history, one he was not sure he wanted to adopt. The best solution, he told us, was just to call it "the sign language," as he always had. But this choice was not listed. The new generation has names for what David and his contemporaries thought of as "just something we did." There are several possible names for the entire activity of signing, and the choice one makes among them depends not only on what type of activity one is referring to but also on its social and political implications.

These new tensions inspired Gilbert Eastman's *Sign Me Alice* (1974), a play modeled on George Bernard Shaw's *Pygmalion*. In the play a young woman, appropriately named Alice Babel, is promised riches and fame if she will abandon ASL and learn one of the artificial manual English systems, or to use Charles Krauel's description, if she will learn "all those IS kind of signs." She is taken under the wing of a Henry Higgins–type character who tutors her in the "better" way of signing. In her new world, she encounters language experiments, all using different forms of signing and manual activity — a virtual Tower of Babel. After learning her lessons, like Eliza in *Pygmalion,* she is taken to a ball, where she performs perfectly. But later she regrets having given up ASL and leaves her tutor.

The play was well received as a timely comment on a new situation. The audience could think about how things had changed: from the old days, when "the sign language" was all the terminology that was necessary, to today, with its dizzying array of new labels.

More important than these new labels — and perhaps in some ways even more bewildering to someone who was raised when "the sign language" was "just something we did" — is the new self-consciousness about signed language, the new way of thinking about the language. This new focus has come about along with recent scientific investigations into signed languages that have confirmed what in some sense Deaf people have known all along: that signed languages are human languages with the potential for rich expression.

We first understood this change in the way Deaf people talk about their language while watching "old home movies" that had recently been uncovered after years in storage. Dating from about 1940 to 1964, these are surprisingly good records of a variety of social activities of the Los Angeles Club for the Deaf (an edited version of this collection appears in *The LACD Story*, 1985), an organization that first provided a haven for newly arrived Deaf people during the war years and later remained an active social center for the community. We recognized typical club scenes, crowds milling about in the clubroom, sitting around the bar, playing group games at picnics, women in beauty contests, and, of course, popular entertainment: performances, songs, skits, and lectures.

The mainstay of club festivities was the signed performance. In one   10
scene from the 1940s we saw a young man signing a song that seemed to be about a young woman, her hair, her ample bust, concluding with a twirl of the body. But this, we were told, was the famous version of "Yankee Doodle" performed by the local favorite, Elmer Priester. We could see the crowds dancing around Priester and sometimes signing along with him, but it seemed to matter less whether everyone was in unison than that they were all joining in as part of a loud, joyous group.

We were reminded of today's Deaf performers, the poets and storytellers of our generation, and the kind of pleasure they bring to an audience, but it was also clear that since 1940 signed performance had changed. It was not simply that we had not recognized "Yankee Doodle."

The most significant difference is the one we have already mentioned: today's performers are much more self-conscious, what we would call analytical, about their language. A modern signed performance may focus on the elements of signed language; in this way, the language itself may be both the medium and the subject of the performance.

A good example of this is a "game" from *My Third Eye* (1973). Until the first performance of this play, all productions by the National Theatre of the Deaf had been signed translations of written works. The first season, for example, featured signed translations of Puccini's *Gianni Schicchi* and poetry by Lewis Carroll and Elizabeth Barrett Browning. It was not until the fourth season, when *My Third Eye* was put together, that members of the company began to experiment with creating their own pieces.

The game appears during a segment called "Manifest," a playful but expertly designed piece in which actors introduce the audience to their language. The game begins when an actor steps out to stage front and announces: "We will show you signs that all have the index finger!" Each actor gives a sign that has the index finger handshape: BLACK, WHO, SCOLD. After completing a round, the cast moves on to another handshape. For the "three" handshape, they demonstrate LOUSY, ELEGANT, and ROOSTER (figure 5.1).

LOUSY   ELEGANT   ROOSTER

Figure 5.1

The actors display yet another handshape, the index and middle   15
fingers in a vee — VISIT, STUPID, STUCK — and the game continues. The
game is fun to watch, although it tells no story and has no particular
dramatic impact apart from its animated listing of signs that share some
similarities. The objective of the game is simply to demonstrate a characteristic of signs: that they are made up of smaller parts, including the
handshape, its location, its movement, and the orientation of the hand
with respect to the body.

In creating this segment, the members of the NTD company discovered a new way of thinking about signs. The actors first look at the
audience but then slowly, by changing the direction of their gaze, invite
the audience to watch their hands instead of their bodies. As the actors
move around the stage, forming new groups for each demonstration, the
focus of the performance is on the signs themselves.

If we compare *My Third Eye* and other modern works with filmed
records of older performances, such as those found in the LACD collection
and in Charles Krauel's collection of old home movies of activities of the
National Fraternal Society of the Deaf (the Frat), we can see how much
both style and content have changed over the years.

One interesting observation about the older films is how little they
concentrate on recording signing. As Ted Supalla, the producer of the film
about Krauel, explains, Krauel saw himself as a documentarist whose
responsibility was to record events for those who were not fortunate
enough to attend. He enjoyed showing his films at the club as a kind of
local newsreel, narrowly aimed at the interests of his community. He
thought it important to note for the future the names of hotels where
national Frat conventions were held. He made careful film records of the
hotel, including shots of the marquee and the building itself. He took
shots of the city and the scenery. But he paid little attention to the detail of
signing. He did make good records of signed performances, but he devoted relatively little footage to causal signed conversations. Often only
short snatches of signed sentences can be seen as his camera pans over
groups of people.

In these films, signing is for commentary, to explain where events are taking place, to record names of friends, buildings and parks, or to orient the viewer to the film's content. Krauel did not choose to devote footage to recording signs or describing them. His films do include signed explanations: a friend introduces a couple celebrating their fiftieth wedding anniversary, a woodworking teacher proudly tells about the detailed airplane models his student has made. In the LACD film collection, too, signing is used to headline, explain, demonstrate, and guide. One scene in an LACD film features an animated advertisement for the club by the president: "Our policy is a good time. You'll never feel depressed or down around here!"

In *My Third Eye,* the actors began thinking about signing not as explanation but as object. In their self-conscious performances, they took their language out of the flow of everyday life and made it into an object for theater. Going one step further, they not only extracted the sign from the narrative flow but began to analyze its internal structure, and used the analysis to guide the game.

Priester, in contrast, cared about signing "Yankee Doodle" with patriotism and good cheer. He was not rigid in his sign selections; in fact he apparently took great liberties with his translation. His friends remembered his adult versions of the song, in which he used phallic substitutions for references to cannons. Unfortunately for us today, the filmmakers exercised their good judgment and we have only tasteful performances on record, but we know there was a lot of playfulness and creativity with the language. This intuitive creativity we do not dispute. What we could not find in any of the old films we watched was the focused, analytical sense of the language as object that we see in *My Third Eye.*

Along with "Yankee Doodle," the LACD and Krauel films include many signed performances of a certain type of popular song. This type of song was apparently widely performed in several parts of the United States, but its origin is unclear. In one version filmed by Krauel, a leader stands in front of a group, next to a large board with a list of animals. He leads the group through the list as they sign the song together in a simple rhythm. The trick is to stay in unison for each beat. After each animal sound, the group repeats the sign DARN three times:

> The birds sing, sing, sing, but I hear them not at all,
> Darn, Darn, Darn
> The cats meow, meow, meow but I hear them not at all,
> Darn, Darn, Darn
> The dogs bark, bark, bark but I hear them not at all,
> Darn, Darn, Darn
> The cows moo, moo, moo but I hear them not at all,
> Darn, Darn, Darn.[1]

---

[1] Translated by Ted Supalla.

The refrain "Darn, Darn, Darn" makes this song similar to another set of songs we found in both collections. In these songs, the repetition is done with a distinctive "one, two, one-two-three" rhythm, into which the performer inserts his own vocabulary.

One of the earliest performers of these songs seems to have been a pep-squad leader at Gallaudet College, George Kannapell, who continued his "one, two, one-two-three" routines after he graduated from college in 1930. Kannapell appears in one of Krauel's films with the following song, probably a narrative about going to a convention or on a group tour:

Boat, Boat, BoatBoatBoat
Drink, Drink, DrinkDrinkDrink
Fun, Fun, FunFunFun
Enjoy, Enjoy, EnjoyEnjoyEnjoy.[2]

In the LACD film collection we found a song created by Odean Rasmussen, or "Rasy" as his friends called him, who was the resident "one, two, one-two-three" singer at the LACD clubhouse:

Really, Really, ReallyReallyReally
Excited, Excited, ExcitedExcitedExcited
Packing, Packing, PackingPackingPacking
Farewell, Farewell, GoodbyeGoodbyeGoodbye
Taking the train, Taking the train (or)
　　MaybeMaybeMaybe
Hitchhike, Hitchhike, HitchhikeHitchhikeHitchhike
Hitchhike, Hitchhike . . .[3]

These songs all involve fitting a series of signs into the "one, two, one-two-three" rhythm. They all tell a story in some way, as in Rasy's story about leaving home or Kannapell's about the good times to be had at the convention. And they are all group songs, used to incite a crowd to good cheer and a sense of unity. Today they have all but disappeared. Possibly the only one still widely recited is the fight song of Gallaudet College:

Hail to our mighty bisons!
Snort, Snort, SnortSnortSnort
Spirit! And hail to our Gallaudet flag, the Buff and Blue!
Clap, Clap, ClapClapClap
All our enemies are afraid of our Gallaudet men
Because our Gallaudet men give them . . .
Damn, Damn! Hell, Hell, Hell!
Clap, Clap, ClapClapClap.[4]

[2]Translated by Ted Supalla.
[3]Translated by Carol Padden and Tom Humphries.
[4]Translated by Wilt McMillen from a poem by Robert Panara, "The Bison Spirit" (1945).

Between the time of the "one, two, one-two-three" songs and the creation of *My Third Eye,* as we have said, a major change took place in the way Deaf performers thought about and used their language. Contributing to this change was the development of new descriptions of signed language. One of the first steps toward this kind of analysis of signed language came from a radical proposal by William C. Stokoe for a new way to describe signs. Stokoe broke with the earlier tradition of describing signs as whole "picture" units. Drawing heavily on the work of structuralists like George Trager and Henry Smith, he suggested that each sign can instead be analyzed as being composed of smaller units: its handshape, its movement, and its location on the body. Signs can be decomposed into smaller parts which are then combined in limited ways, just as a spoken word is composed of a sequence of units called phonemes, arranged in rule-governed structures. Thus signed and spoken languages must be far more similar than previously thought, since, at least from the point of view of their internal analysis, there is no basis for treating them differently (Stokoe 1960).

To illustrate his point, Stokoe then published in 1965 a dictionary of "American sign language" "based on linguistic principles." (Note that this is a slight revision of the traditional label, "the sign language." The fully capitalized American Sign Language would not appear until later.) He organized signs not in the traditional way, according to their English translations or by categories such as "animals" or "food," but according to their handshapes, movements, and locations (Stokoe, Casterline, and Croneberg 1965). The dictionary's most innovative feature was a notation system for representing the handshape of the sign (for which he invented the term "dez"), and its movement and location. The entry for NIGHT reads as follows:

$\sqrt{\overline{B}}_\mathrm{B} \sqrt{B_v}^x$
(dez held so fingertips are lower than wrist, touches or taps across edge of tab; dez contact at heel of hand or inside of wrist) $_\mathrm{N}$ *night.*

Many considered this notation a bizarre idea. Stokoe's contention that "the sign language" warranted such extensive analysis created a minor stir among his colleagues and students at Gallaudet College. The campus newspaper, the *Buff and Blue,* dutifully reported Stokoe's various achievements, including grants from the American Council of Learned Societies and the National Science Foundation, but as one Deaf colleague, Gilbert Eastman, recalls, "I did not believe Dr. Stokoe would succeed in his project and I thought [his] two deaf assistants were wasting their time signing before the camera" (1980:19). The Deaf community for the most part still believed, much as Krauel did, that signs were best described in terms of how they "felt" and what "picture" they represented. J. Schuyler Long's standard dictionary, *The Sign Language: A Manual of Signs* (1918), had taken a typical approach:

NIGHT: Place the hands and arms in position as if about to sign for day but move the hand down and describe a semicircle below the arm from right to left, thus representing the course of the sun during the period of time from set of sun to its rising.

Stokoe, in contrast, wanted a dictionary of ASL that would, like a   30
dictionary of spoken language, list all possible lexical elements and their "pronunciations." Just as a dictionary of the oral language may include an inventory of the possible vowel and consonant combinations, Stokoe's dictionary listed the closed set of handshapes of ASL, with their locations and movements. As it turned out, Stokoe had gotten an early start on what would prove to be a science of signed language.

Coinciding with and contributing to the emergence of this science was a new generation of poets and performers and their art. The gradual convergence of art and science has had a strong impact on art forms. This can be seen in the performances of the actors of the National Theatre of the Deaf (NTD), as mentioned earlier. With funding from the Department of Health, Education and Welfare, the new NTD was established in 1967 with a mandate to bring to the public a new image of Deaf people. Deaf actors who had worked largely for their community, earning only occasional payments for their performances, were now continuously employed as part of a professional repertory. Faced with the task of creating a unique theater company with its own new productions, the performers turned within themselves and mined the rich resource of their language. As one founding member, Lou Fant, tells it, the task of translating material into signed language provoked serious arguments within the company about which "form" of the sign language should be used for the stage (Fant 1980).

The impact of the new way of thinking about the language can also be seen in the poetry of Dorothy Miles and Clayton Valli. In a preface to one of the poems in her book *Gestures,* Miles explains: "This poem developed from a discussion about the similarity between the signs for SHY, SHAME, and WHORE. When I finished writing it, I found that most of the signs I would use had the same handshape" (1976:37). In 1975, Miles visited Ursula Bellugi and her colleagues at the Salk Institute, who were involved in a scientific exploration of signed language structure. Her interaction with the group inspired her to develop more poetry (Miles 1976).

One of Miles's poems, "Total Communication," is an example of the way the language itself has become the subject of signed performance. In this poem we see some of the unusual devices Miles has developed, including her trademark "double translation," or poetry that works in either a signed or a spoken presentation. The poem is based on a handshape, that of the sign for the first person pronoun "I." The first four lines of "Total Communication" are written in English as follows:

You and I,
can we see aye to aye,
or must your I, and I
lock horns and struggle till we die?

In the third and fourth lines, Miles arranges the sequence of signs so all handshapes are the same. The sign I normally contacts the chest, but, using poetic license, Miles locates it in second-person space, and the result is YOUR-I. Next she maintains the same handshape and signs I, setting up the two hands to come together in the next sign, LOCK-HORNS. Compare the signs I and LOCK-HORNS (figure 5.2) with the line from the poem, "or must your I, and I / lock horns and struggle till we die?" This use of signs allows Miles to show, metaphorically, two people who come together and clash. The detail of keeping the same handshape across a line is small and subtle, and is characteristic of her poetry.

Elsewhere, instead of maintaining the same handshape, she manip-   35
ulates the location of signs. In her poem "Defiance," she again uses the sign I in an unfamiliar way:

If I were I
I would not say those pleasant things that I say;
I would not smile and nod my head
When you say
No!

Here Miles compares the "real I" and the "hypocritical I." In reference to the second I, the public self, she first signs HYPOCRITE, and then locates the next sign, I, not on the body as is usual but instead on the handshape of the sign HYPOCRITE — meaning "hypocritical I." The other meaning of I is signed normally, on the body, to represent the "real I," the private self.

The work of another modern poet, Clayton Valli, shows the same awareness of sign structure, as well as manipulation of a different kind. In

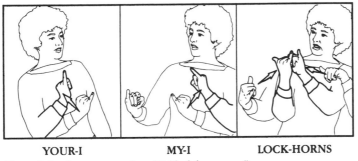

| YOUR-I | MY-I | LOCK-HORNS |

Figure 5.2   "or must your I, and I / lock horns . . ."

"Windy Bright Morning" (1985), Valli manipulates not only handshape and location but also the ways the two hands interact:

> Through the open window
> with its shade swinging, sunshine, playful
> taps my sleepy eyes.[5]

Some signs are made with one hand, like the sign I, and some with two hands, like LOCK-HORNS and HYPOCRITE. The beauty of this poem lies in the careful arrangement of one-handed and two-handed signs. Each segment of the poem is deliberately chosen to fit with segments before and after it. In the first line, Valli takes advantage of the fact that the sign WINDOW requires two hands. He sets up the sign WINDOW, then slowly but clearly he moves the hands out of the position for WINDOW and into position for the two one-handed signs WINDOWSILL and CURTAIN-EDGE-GENTLY-BLOWING. He simply changes the relation of the hands to each other, flowing into the next two signs without a break. The result is a very lyrical line with a soft rhythm.

Miles and Valli build their poetry around a detailed awareness of how signs are assembled and the relationship of structure to meaning. Compared to these poets, earlier performers like Priester and Kannapell seem to have taken their language for granted, just as our friend David said his family always had. For Priester, a performance was something one rehearsed and perfected, but not something one planned in the same conscious and careful way we see in the work of Miles and Valli.

But did the earlier performers have any knowledge about the structure of their language? We think so. Priester's adult version of "Yankee Doodle" suggests that he knew at least enough about the language to be able to select signs that subtly suggested another meaning, yet were similar enough to the original song so people would recognize the joke.

Another poem, first performed in 1939, makes it clear that sign performers of past generations did know, intuitively if not explicitly, about the structure of their language. This poem, when it was performed during the NTD's first season, stunned the audience, delighted the critics, and made its performer a national favorite. It is Eric Malzkuhn's translation of Lewis Carroll's "Jabberwocky."

Malzkuhn had first worked on the translation for a poetry contest while a student at Gallaudet College in 1939, and had taken the mixed reaction as evidence that he was attempting something new. He continued to perform the poem at various clubs, always changing the performance slightly according to his whim and the special characteristics of the club. For a Detroit Deaf club, for example, he turned the monsters in the poem into cars of varying sizes and features.

[5]Translated by Karen Wills and Clayton Valli.

In 1967 Malzkuhn joined the NTD as a coach, and his translation was assigned to a young actor, Joe Velez. Velez, with his lean and lithe style, imparted a new dimension to the performance, and became so well known for his "Jabberwocky" that today his name is inseparably linked to the poem. (Velez's performance can be seen in the film *Tyger, Tyger,* 1967.)

The art of the translation lies in the way Malzkuhn mirrors Carroll's word creations with equally fantastic sign creations. Just as Carroll formed words from parts of other words — "slithy," for example, from "slimy" and "lithe" — Malzkuhn recombined parts of ordinary signs. For the JubJub bird (figure 5.3), he first took parts of signs used for long, thin objects and combined them into one handshape, which he placed on top of the head, to characterize the bird's plumage. Next he recombined the parts of the sign WING to suggest an outlandish creature with double wings on each side of the body. All the other animals in the poem, including the Bandersnatch and the Jabberwock itself, he constructed by playing with various possible combinations of parts of signs such as JAW, MOUND, EYE, FANGS, and TEETH.

For other phrases in the poem, Malzkuhn again used combinations of signs. The sequence "gyre and gimble" involved using a part of a sign for flat surface, but combined with odd movements, suggesting an irregular and spooky wave. For "whiffling through the wood" (figure 5.4), Malzkuhn took parts of signs for broad-footed animals and combined them to form the legs, feet, and flaring eyes of a terrible animal thrashing its way through the brush.

Malzkuhn says he translated the poem strictly by "how it felt." But, as Ted Supalla first observed (1978), Malzkuhn had stumbled across a central structural property of ASL: the way its morphology, or word-forming system, works. *45*

In spoken languages each word is made up of at least one minimal unit of meaning, called a "morpheme." For example, in English the word "stick" has one morpheme, "stickpin" has two, and "stickpins" has three: "stick," "pin," and the plural "-s."

| BIRD | BEAK-LIKE | PLUMAGE |

Figure 5.3   "Jub-Jub bird"

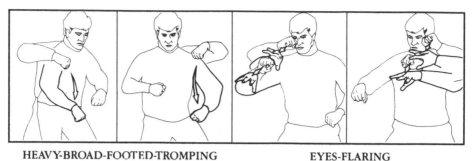

HEAVY-BROAD-FOOTED-TROMPING   EYES-FLARING

Figure 5.4   The Jabberwock whiffling through the wood

In his translation, Malzkuhn made clever use of the morphology of his language. To form his sign for "Jabberwock" he combined the morpheme TOOTH with the morphemes HUMP and JAW, resulting in a new combination used as the name for the creature. He exploited the combinative powers of the morphology to create new forms.

But he certainly would not have called his translation an experiment in the "morphology of ASL." In 1939, he had scarcely any idea that his language would be called "ASL," let alone that what he was doing was manipulating its morphology. It would not be until a later generation, when signing began to have names and when performers began to write poetry around sign structure, that Deaf people could think in this way.

Another game in *My Third Eye* also plays with the morphology of ASL. The actors have just finished their handshape game, and one of them, Freda Norman, announces that they will now demonstrate the different ways "we sign brightness." The actors form a line and wait their turns. This time the game is not to think of a sign with some handshape, but to think of a sign sentence that has something to do with brightness.

As the actors present their sentences, they use not the same sign but one of the same two morphemes, either FLASH or SHINE. FLASH is an opening to a spread hand and closing again. SHINE uses the middle finger of an open hand and an outward, wiggling movement. In order to form a sign, these morphemes must then be combined with other parts such as location. Patrick Graybill does BALD-HEAD SHINE, "my bald head shines." Tim Scanlon does SNOW SHINE-HERE SHINE-THERE, "the snow fell and light sparkled on it" (figure 5.5). Richard Kendall shows GUN POLISH-GUN GUN-SHINE, "I polished my gun" (figure 5.6).

Dorothy Miles does one with FLASH: LIGHTHOUSE-ON-HILL FLASH-AND-TURN FLASH-AND-TURN, "the lighthouse flashes in the night." Freda Norman shows PHOTOGRAPH CAMERA-CLICK FLASH, "a flashbulb on a camera went off" (figure 5.7), and Dorothy ends the scene with the delightful BUG FLASH-HERE FLASH-THERE FLASH-THERE CATCH-OBJECT, "I kept seeing a firefly out of the corner of my eye and finally caught it" (figure 5.8).

SNOW   SHINE   SHINE

Figure 5.5   "Snow fell and light sparkled on it"

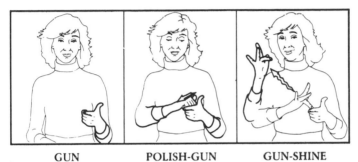

GUN   POLISH-GUN   GUN-SHINE

Figure 5.6   "I polished my gun"

PHOTOGRAPH   CAMERA-CLICK   FLASH

Figure 5.7   "A flashbulb on a camera went off"

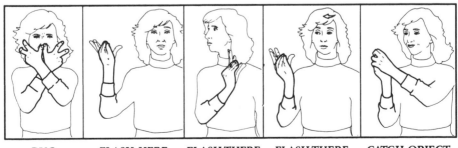

BUG   FLASH-HERE   FLASH-THERE   FLASH-THERE   CATCH-OBJECT

Figure 5.8   "I kept seeing a firefly out of the corner of my eye and finally caught it"

Here the actors are not only illustrating ASL morphology but have begun to talk about it directly. They understand that the same morpheme, FLASH, appears in both "the lighthouse flashes in the night" and "the kerosene lamp turns on and off." And the same morpheme that occurs in "my bald head shines" can be found in "the light sparkles on the snow."

If this kind of game were played in English, the actors might take turns thinking of English words containing, say, one of the morphemes "stick" and "sheet." Lipstick. Stickpin. Worksheet. Sheetrock. Pogo stick. Bedsheet. Stick shift. Sheet of steel. Stick of candy. Sheet of paper. Stick of wood. An actor might also try stretching the language to create new images: Sheet of snow on the road. Sheet of water flowing over the wall.

And now we see clearly the difference between Malzkuhn and the actors in MY THIRD EYE. In the game, the express purpose of doing the segment is to call the audience's attention to particular properties of the language. The actors use their new understanding of the language, that it is made up of smaller units of meaning, as an object for theater. Malzkuhn, in contrast, began with an English poem and built his performance around how to translate it. His translation shows an awareness of the way his language works, but not an analysis of it.

As we have said, the changes we have traced in the style and content of signed performance reflect profound changes in Deaf people's understanding of their language. The performers of the past, like Priester, Kannapell, Rasy, and Malzkuhn, clearly appreciated the creative potential of signed performance, just as their modern counterparts do. What is new is the idea that signs can be thought of—and are well worth thinking of—as objects in themselves.

What the more recent types of performance reveal is not only an emerging science of signed language but a new science of self. Deaf people today have a new self-consciousness about their own culture, including their performances. Where once their signed language and their culture were deeply embedded in larger contexts, they have now been extracted to become objects for analysis.

But it is important to repeat here, as we follow the history of signed performances, songs, and poetry, that Deaf people's deepest knowledge about their signed language has not changed—it has only been confirmed by science and affirmed by artistic expression. From Veditz's 1913 speech to Malzkuhn's playful "Jabberwocky" to Miles's and Valli's careful, measured poetry, all of the works we have quoted make clear, each in its own way, the rich potential of signed language. It is perhaps polemical to say that the performances of Deaf people showed that they always knew the potential of the language, but they did, after all, know. What we now see is a new reflectiveness about their language and a new vocabulary for describing it.

The Responsive Reader

1. Padden and Humphries are concerned to change common perceptions of the signed language of the deaf as a primitive gesture or signaling system. What do you learn from this essay about the signed language of the deaf as a language? What are key features it shares with spoken language? (Can you provide some instructive examples for each?)
2. What do you learn from this essay about the culture (or cultures) of the deaf?
3. What do you learn from this essay about poetry and the special challenges of translating it into signed language?
4. Drawing on the linguistic elements provided in the graphics with this essay, try to compose a few sentences or a simple story. How successful are you in communicating with your classmates?

Talking, Listening, Writing

5. What has been your experience with people with impaired sight, hearing, or mobility? How much do you know from firsthand experience or observation? How much is hearsay or stereotype?
6. How much progress has society made toward recognizing the needs and rights of the disabled?

Projects

7. Many colleges now employ interpreters who translate oral instruction into signed language. If you can, arrange for such a person to come and speak to your class about the language of the deaf.

BILINGUALISM: THE KEY TO BASIC SKILLS

Angelo Gonzalez

> *Angelo Gonzalez wrote the following* New York Times *article as executive director of ASPIRA, a civic organization in New York that is dedicated to advancing the cause of Hispanics, or Spanish-speaking Americans. In his article, Gonzalez takes a strong stand on an issue of special concern in areas with large Spanish-speaking school populations, such as New York City, Miami, Texas, or California. What is the mission of the schools in dealing with children whose proficiency in English is limited or nonexistent? The traditional policy had been total immersion (or, more informally, sink or swim). Everyone was taught all subjects in English, and the use of any other language even during recess was discouraged or banned outright. This policy was once credited with turning the children of Jewish, Polish, German, Armenian, or Czech immigrants into Americans after a few years of schooling. Today, however, this policy is blamed for the horrendous dropout rates among students for whom Standard English is a second language or a second dialect, different from the language of home and neighborhood. What is the alternative?*

Thought Starters: What is meant by "bilingual education"? How does this writer define it and explain the reasoning behind it?

If we accept that a child cannot learn unless taught through the language he speaks and understands; that a child who does not speak or understand English must fall behind when English is the dominant medium of instruction; that one needs to learn English so as to be able to participate in an English-speaking society; that self-esteem and motivation are necessary for effective learning; that rejection of a child's native language and culture is detrimental to the learning process; then any necessary effective educational program for limited or no English-speaking ability must incorporate the following:

- Language arts and comprehensive reading programs taught in the child's native language.
- Curriculum content areas taught in the native language to further comprehension and academic achievement.
- Intensive instruction in English.
- Use of materials sensitive to and reflecting the culture of children within the program.

The mastery of basic reading skills is the most important goal in primary education since reading is the basis for much of all subsequent learning. Ordinarily, these skills are learned at home. But where beginning reading is taught in English, only the English-speaking child profits from these early acquired skills that are prerequisites to successful reading development. Reading programs taught in English to children with Spanish as a first language wastes their acquired linguistic attributes and also impedes learning by forcing them to absorb skills of reading simultaneously with a new language.

Both local and national research data provide ample evidence for the efficacy of well-implemented programs. The New York City Board of Education Report on Bilingual Pupil Services for 1982–83 indicated that in all areas of the curriculum — English, Spanish and mathematics — and at all grade levels, students demonstrated statistically significant gains in tests of reading in English and Spanish and in math. In all but two of the programs reviewed, the attendance rates of students in the program, ranging from 86 to 94 percent, were higher than those of the general school population. Similar higher attendance rates were found among students in high school bilingual programs.

At Yale University, Kenji Hakuta, a linguist, reported recently on a study of working-class Hispanic students in the New Haven bilingual program. He found that children who were the most bilingual, that is, who developed English without the loss of Spanish, were brighter in both verbal and nonverbal tests. Over time, there was an increasing correlation between English and Spanish — a finding that clearly contradicts the charge that teaching in the home language is detrimental to English. Rather the two languages are interdependent within the bilingual child, reinforcing each another.

As Jim Cummins of the Ontario Institute for Studies in Education 5
has argued, the use and development of the native language makes an essential contribution to the development of minority children's subject-matter knowledge and academic learning potential. In fact, at least three national data bases — the National Assessment of Educational Progress, National Center for Educational Statistics High School and Beyond Studies, and the Survey of Income and Education — suggest that there are long-term positive effects among high school students who have participated in bilingual-education programs. These students are achieving higher scores on tests of verbal and mathematics skills.

These and similar findings buttress the argument stated persuasively in the recent joint recommendation of the Academy for Educational Development and the Hazen Foundation, namely, that America needs to become a more multilingual nation and children who speak a non-English language are a national resource to be nurtured in school.

Unfortunately, the Administration's educational policies would seem to be leading us in the opposite direction. Under the guise of protecting the common language of public life in the United States, William J.

Bennett, Secretary of Education, unleashed a frontal attack on bilingual education. In a major policy address, he engaged in rhetorical distortions about the nature and effectiveness of bilingual programs, pointing only to unnamed negative research findings to justify the Administration's retrenchment efforts.

Arguing for the need to give local school districts greater flexibility in determining appropriate methodologies in serving limited-English-proficient students, Mr. Bennett fails to realize that, in fact, districts serving large numbers of language-minority students, as is the case in New York City, do have that flexibility. Left to their own devices in implementing legal mandates, many school districts have performed poorly at providing services to all entitled language-minority students.

The harsh reality in New York City for language-minority students was documented comprehensively last month by the Educational Priorities Panel. The panel's findings revealed that of the 113,831 students identified as being limited in English proficiency, as many as 44,000 entitled students are not receiving any bilingual services. The issue at hand is, therefore, not one of choice but rather violation of the rights of almost 40 percent of language-minority children to equal educational opportunity. In light of these findings the Administration's recent statements only serve to exacerbate existing inequities in the American educational system for linguistic-minority children. Rather than adding fuel to a misguided debate, the Administration would serve these children best by insuring the full funding of the 1984 Bilingual Education Reauthorization Act as passed by the Congress.

The Responsive Reader

1. In his first paragraph, Gonzalez summarizes the assumptions on which the rest of his argument will be based. What are these assumptions? What does each imply or commit you to?
2. What is Gonzalez' definition of bilingual education? Are its major elements unexpected or familiar? What do they mean in practice?
3. A key issue in the debate over bilingual education is the need for accepting rather than rejecting the child's own language and cultural heritage. Why is this question crucial in the eyes of educators who share Gonzalez' views?
4. How does Gonzalez use authoritative sources and statistics? For instance, what evidence does he use to show that the two languages of a student will reinforce rather than interfere with one another?

Talking, Listening, Reading

5. What has been your own experience or what has shaped your own views on the issue of bilingualism? Is it an issue in schools you know? What explains the backlash that Gonzalez describes toward the end of his article?

Projects

6. Working with a group, you may want to research the nature and history of English-first movements in this country or in your area. What arguments and counter arguments have they generated? How effective have they been? Work with others to study brochures, articles, ballot propositions, and the like.

ARIA: A MEMOIR OF A BILINGUAL CHILDHOOD

Richard Rodriguez

> *Richard Rodriguez, in his autobiographical* Hunger of Memory *(1982), filed a strong dissent from the position held by advocates of bilingualism and bilingual education. For him, the transition from the private language of the home to the public language of school and work was a necessary rite of passage for members of minority groups who wanted to join fully in the American experience. He once wrote that children of immigrant parents are expected to "perch on a hyphen between two countries" but that sooner or later they tilt toward a new American identity and start losing the old ways. The son of Mexican immigrants in Sacramento, California, Rodriguez found himself on his first day of school as the only Mexican American in a class of white middle-class children. He went on to become a scholarship student; he studied English literature at Stanford, Berkeley, and the British Museum in London; and he became a successful writer and lecturer whose essays on the multicultural roots of America have appeared in publications like* Harper's *and* The American Scholar. *He frequently writes on the fruitful tension between the Catholic, Spanish, mestizo tradition of Mexico and the Protestant Anglo tradition of North America.*

Thought Starters: When and how do young people outgrow the ways of thinking and talking of family and home? How inevitable is the breaking away of the younger generation?

I remember, to start with, that day in Sacramento, in a California now nearly thirty years past, when I first entered a classroom — able to understand about fifty stray English words. The third of four children, I had been preceded by my older brother and sister to a neighborhood Roman Catholic school. But neither of them had revealed very much about their classroom experiences. They left each morning and returned each afternoon, always together, speaking Spanish as they climbed the five steps to the porch. And their mysterious books, wrapped in brown shopping-bag paper, remained on the table next to the door, closed firmly behind them.

An accident of geography sent me to a school where all my classmates were white and many were the children of doctors and lawyers and business executives. On that first day of school, my classmates must certainly have been uneasy to find themselves apart from their families, in the first institution of their lives. But I was astonished. I was fated to be the "problem student" in class.

The nun said, in a friendly but oddly impersonal voice: "Boys and girls, this is Richard Rodriguez." (I heard her sound it out: *Rich-heard Road-ree-guess.*) It was the first time I had heard anyone say my name in English. "Richard," the nun repeated more slowly, writing my name down in her book. Quickly I turned to see my mother's face dissolve in a watery blur behind the pebbled-glass door.

Now, many years later, I hear of something called "bilingual education" — a scheme proposed in the late 1960s by Hispanic-American social activists, later endorsed by a congressional vote. It is a program that seeks to permit non-English-speaking children (many from lower class homes) to use their "family language" as the language of school. Such, at least, is the aim its supporters announce. I hear them, and am forced to say no: It is not possible for a child, any child, ever to use his family's language in school. Not to understand this is to misunderstand the public uses of schooling and to trivialize the nature of intimate life.

Memory teaches me what I know of these matters. The boy reminds   5 the adult. I was a bilingual child, but of a certain kind: "socially disadvantaged," the son of working-class parents, both Mexican immigrants.

In the early years of my boyhood, my parents coped very well in America. My father had steady work. My mother managed at home. They were nobody's victims. When we moved to a house many blocks from the Mexican-American section of town, they were not intimidated by those two or three neighbors who initially tried to make us unwelcome. ("Keep your brats away from my sidewalk!") But despite all they achieved, or perhaps because they had so much to achieve, they lacked any deep feeling of ease, of belonging in public. They regarded the people at work or in crowds as being very distant from us. Those were the others, *los gringos.* That term was interchangeable in their speech with another, even more telling: *los americanos.*

I grew up in a house where the only regular guests were my relations. On a certain day, enormous families of relatives would visit us, and there would be so many people that the noise and the bodies would spill out to the backyard and onto the front porch. Then for weeks no one would come. (If the doorbell rang, it was usually a salesman.) Our house stood apart — gaudy yellow in a row of white bungalows. We were the people with the noisy dog, the people who raised chickens. We were the foreigners on the block. A few neighbors would smile and wave at us. We waved back. But until I was seven years old, I did not know the name of the old couple living next door or the names of the kids living across the street.

In public, my father and mother spoke a hesitant, accented, and not always grammatical English. And then they would have to strain, their bodies tense, to catch the sense of what was rapidly said by *los gringos.* At home, they returned to Spanish. The language of their Mexican past sounded in counterpoint to the English spoken in public. The words would come quickly, with ease. Conveyed through those sounds was the pleasing, soothing, consoling reminder that one was at home.

During those years when I was first learning to speak, my mother and father addressed me only in Spanish; in Spanish I learned to reply. By contrast, English (*inglés*) was the language I came to associate with gringos, rarely heard in the house. I learned my first words of English overhearing my parents speaking to strangers. At six years of age, I knew just enough words for my mother to trust me on errands to stores one block away — but no more.

I was then a listening child, careful to hear the very different sounds   10 of Spanish and English. Wide-eyed with hearing, I'd listen to sounds more than to words. First, there were English (gringo) sounds. So many words still were unknown to me that when the butcher or the lady at the drugstore said something, exotic polysyllabic sounds would bloom in the midst of their sentences. Often the speech of people in public seemed to me very loud, booming with confidence. The man behind the counter would literally ask, "What can I do for you?" But by being so firm and clear, the sound of his voice said that he was a gringo; he belonged in public society. There were also the high, nasal notes of middle-class American speech — which I rarely am conscious of hearing today because I hear them so often, but could not stop hearing when I was a boy. Crowds at Safeway or at bus stops were noisy with the birdlike sounds of *los gringos*. I'd move away from them all — all the chirping chatter above me.

My own sounds I was unable to hear, but I knew that I spoke English poorly. My words could not extend to form complete thoughts. And the words I did speak I didn't know well enough to make distinct sounds. (Listeners would usually lower their heads to hear better what I was trying to say.) But it was one thing for *me* to speak English with difficulty; it was more troubling to hear my parents speaking in public: their high-whining vowels and guttural consonants; their sentences that got stuck with "eh" and "ah" sounds; the confused syntax; the hesitant rhythm of sounds so different from the way gringos spoke. I'd notice, moreover, that my parents' voices were softer than those of gringos we would meet.

I am tempted to say now that none of this mattered. (In adulthood I am embarrassed by childhood fears.) And, in a way, it didn't matter very much that my parents could not speak English with ease. Their linguistic difficulties had no serious consequences. My mother and father made themselves understood at the county hospital clinic and at government offices. And yet, in another way, it mattered very much. It was unsettling to hear my parents struggle with English. Hearing them, I'd grow nervous, and my clutching trust in their protection and power would be weakened.

There were many times like the night at a brightly lit gasoline station (a blaring white memory) when I stood uneasily hearing my father talk to a teenage attendant. I do not recall what they were saying, but I cannot forget the sounds my father made as he spoke. At one point his words slid together to form one long word — sounds as confused as the threads of blue and green oil in the puddle next to my shoes. His voice rushed through what he had left to say. Toward the end, he reached falsetto notes, appealing to his listener's understanding. I looked away at the lights of passing automobiles. I tried not to hear any more. But I heard only too well the attendant's reply, his calm, easy tones. Shortly afterward, headed for home, I shivered when my father put his hand on my shoulder. The very first chance that I got, I evaded his grasp and ran on ahead into the dark, skipping with feigned boyish exuberance.

But then there was Spanish: *español,* the language rarely heard away from the house; *español,* the language which seemed to me therefore a private language, my family's language. To hear its sounds was to feel myself specially recognized as one of the family, apart from *los otros.* A simple remark, an inconsequential comment could convey that assurance. My parents would say something to me and I would feel embraced by the sounds of their words. Those sounds said: *I am speaking with ease in Spanish. I am addressing you in words I never use with los gringos. I recognize you as someone special, close, like no one outside. You belong with us. In the family. Ricardo.*

At the age of six, well past the time when most middle-class children   15 no longer notice the difference between sounds uttered at home and words spoken in public, I had a different experience. I lived in a world compounded of sounds. I was a child longer than most. I lived in a magical world, surrounded by sounds both pleasing and fearful. I shared with my family a language enchantingly private — different from that used in the city around us.

Just opening or closing the screen door behind me was an important experience. I'd rarely leave home all alone or without feeling reluctance. Walking down the sidewalk, under the canopy of tall trees, I'd warily notice the (suddenly) silent neighborhood kids who stood warily watching me. Nervously, I'd arrive at the grocery store to hear there the sounds of the gringo, reminding me that in this so-big world I was a foreigner. But if leaving home was never routine, neither was coming back. Walking toward our house, climbing the steps from the sidewalk, in summer when the front door was open, I'd hear voices beyond the screen door talking in Spanish. For a second or two I'd stay, linger there listening. Smiling, I'd hear my mother call out, saying in Spanish, "Is that you, Richard?" Those were her words, but all the while her sounds would assure me: *You are home now. Come closer inside. With us. "Sí,"* I'd reply.

Once more inside the house, I would resume my place in the family. The sounds would grow harder to hear. Once more at home, I would grow less conscious of them. It required, however, no more than the blurt of the doorbell to alert me all over again to listen to sounds. The house would turn instantly quiet while my mother went to the door. I'd hear her hard

English sounds. I'd wait to hear her voice turn to soft-sounding Spanish, which assured me, as surely as did the clicking tongue of the lock on the door, that the stranger was gone.

Plainly it is not healthy to hear such sounds so often. It is not healthy to distinguish public from private sounds so easily. I remained cloistered by sounds, timid and shy in public, too dependent on the voices at home. And yet I was a very happy child when I was at home. I remember many nights when my father would come back from work, and I'd hear him call out to my mother in Spanish, sounding relieved. In Spanish, his voice would sound the light and free notes that he never could manage in English. Some nights I'd jump up just hearing his voice. My brother and I would come running into the room where he was with our mother. Our laughing (so deep was the pleasure!) became screaming. Like others who feel the pain of public alienation, we transformed the knowledge of our public separateness into a consoling reminder of our intimacy. Excited, our voices joined in a celebration of sounds. *We are speaking now the way we never speak out in public — we are together,* the sounds told me. Some nights no one seemed willing to loosen the hold that sounds had on us. At dinner we invented new words that sounded Spanish, but made sense only to us. We pieced together new words by taking, say, an English verb and giving it Spanish endings. My mother's instructions at bedtime would be lacquered with mock-urgent tones. Or a word like *sí,* sounded in several notes, would convey added measures of feeling. Tongues lingered around the edges of words, especially fat vowels, and we happily sounded that military drum roll, the twirling roar of the Spanish *r.* Family language, my family's sounds: the voices of my parents and sisters and brother. Their voices insisting: *You belong here. We are family members. Related. Special to one another. Listen!* Voices singing and sighing, rising and straining, then surging, teeming with pleasure which burst syllables into fragments of laughter. At times it seemed there was steady quiet only when, from another room, the rustling whispers of my parents faded and I edged closer to sleep.

Supporters of bilingual education imply today that students like me miss a great deal by not being taught in their family's language. What they seem not to recognize is that, as a socially disadvantaged child, I regarded Spanish as a private language. It was a ghetto language that deepened and strengthened my feeling of public separateness. What I needed to learn in school was that I had the right, and the obligation, to speak the public language. The odd truth is that my first-grade classmates could have become bilingual, in the conventional sense of the word, more easily than I. Had they been taught early (as upper middle-class children often are taught) a "second language" like Spanish or French, they could have regarded it simply as another public language. In my case, such bilingualism could not have been so quickly achieved. What I did not believe was that I could speak a single public language.

Without question, it would have pleased me to have heard my teach-   20
ers address me in Spanish when I entered the classroom. I would have felt
much less afraid. I would have imagined that my instructors were somehow "related" to me; I would indeed have heard their Spanish as my
family's language. I would have trusted them and responded with ease.
But I would have delayed — postponed for how long? — having to learn the
language of public society. I would have evaded — and for how long? —
learning the great lesson of school: that I had a public identity.

Fortunately, my teachers were unsentimental about their responsibility. What they understood was that I needed to speak public English.
So their voices would search me out, asking me questions. Each time I
heard them I'd look up in surprise to see a nun's face frowning at me. I'd
mumble, not really meaning to answer. The nun would persist. "Richard,
stand up. Don't look at the floor. Speak up. Speak to the entire class, not
just to me!" But I couldn't believe English could be my language to use.
(In part, I did not want to believe it.) I continued to mumble. I resisted the
teacher's demands. (Did I somehow suspect that once I learned this public
language my family life would be changed?) Silent, waiting for the bell to
sound, I remained dazed, diffident, afraid.

Because I wrongly imagined that English was intrinsically a public
language and Spanish was intrinsically private, I easily noted the difference
between classroom language and the language at home. At school, words
were directed to a general audience of listeners. ("Boys and girls . . .")
Words were meaningfully ordered. And the point was not self-expression
alone, but to make oneself understood by many others. The teacher
quizzed: "Boys and girls, why do we use that word in this sentence? Could
we think of a better word to use there? Would the sentence change its
meaning if the words were differently arranged? Isn't there a better way
of saying much the same thing?" (I couldn't say. I wouldn't try to say.)

Three months passed. Five. A half year. Unsmiling, ever watchful,
my teachers noted my silence. They began to connect my behavior with
the slow progress my brother and sisters were making. Until, one Saturday morning, three nuns arrived at the house to talk to our parents. Stiffly
they sat on the blue living-room sofa. From the doorway of another room,
spying on the visitors, I noted the incongruity, the clash of two worlds,
the faces and voices of school intruding upon the familiar setting of home.
I overheard one voice gently wondering, "Do your children speak only
Spanish at home, Mrs. Rodriguez?" While another voice added, "That
Richard especially seems so timid and shy."

That Rich-heard!

With great tact, the visitors continued, "Is it possible for you and   25
your husband to encourage your children to practice their English when
they are home?" Of course my parents complied. What would they not
do for their children's well-being? And how could they question the
Church's authority which those women represented? In an instant they
agreed to give up the language (the sounds) which had revealed and

accentuated our family's closeness. The moment after the visitors left, the change was observed. "*Ahora,* speak to us only *en inglés,*" my father and mother told us.

At first, it seemed a kind of game. After dinner each night, the family gathered together to practice "our" English. It was still then *inglés,* a language foreign to us, so we felt drawn to it as strangers. Laughing, we would try to define words we could not pronounce. We played with strange English sounds, often overanglicizing our pronunciations. And we filled the smiling gaps of our sentences with familiar Spanish sounds. But that was cheating, somebody shouted, and everyone laughed.

In school, meanwhile, like my brother and sisters, I was required to attend a daily tutoring session. I needed a full year of this special work. I also needed my teachers to keep my attention from straying in class by calling out, "*Rich-heard*" — their English voices slowly loosening the ties to my other name, with its three notes, *Ri-car-do.* Most of all, I needed to hear my mother and father speak to me in a moment of seriousness in "broken" — suddenly heartbreaking — English. This scene was inevitable. One Saturday morning I entered the kitchen where my parents were talking, but I did not realize that they were talking in Spanish until, the moment they saw me, their voices changed and they began speaking English. The gringo sounds they uttered startled me. Pushed me away. In that moment of trivial misunderstanding and profound insight, I felt my throat twisted by unsounded grief. I simply turned and left the room. But I had no place to escape to where I could grieve in Spanish. My brother and sisters were speaking English in another part of the house.

Again and again in the days following, as I grew increasingly angry, I was obliged to hear my mother and father encouraging me: "Speak to us *en inglés.*" Only then did I determine to learn classroom English. Thus, sometime afterward it happened: one day in school, I raised my hand to volunteer an answer to a question. I spoke out in a loud voice and I did not think it remarkable when the entire class understood. That day I moved very far from being the disadvantaged child I had been only days earlier. Taken hold at last was the belief, the calming assurance, that I *belonged* in public.

Shortly after, I stopped hearing the high, troubling sounds of *los gringos.* A more and more confident speaker of English, I didn't listen to how strangers sounded when they talked to me. With so many English-speaking people around me, I no longer heard American accents. Conversations quickened. Listening to persons whose voices sounded eccentrically pitched, I might note their sounds for a few seconds, but then I'd concentrate on what they were saying. Now when I heard someone's tone of voice — angry or questioning or sarcastic or happy or sad — I didn't distinguish it from the words it expressed. Sound and word were thus tightly wedded. At the end of each day I was often bemused, and always relieved, to realize how "soundless," though crowded with words, my day in public had been. An eight-year-old boy, I finally came to accept what had been technically true since my birth: I was an American citizen.

But diminished by then was the special feeling of closeness at home.   *30* Gone was the desperate, urgent, intense feeling of being at home among those with whom I felt intimate. Our family remained a loving family, but one greatly changed. We were no longer so close, no longer bound tightly together by the knowledge of our separateness from *los gringos.* Neither my older brother nor my sisters rushed home after school any more. Nor did I. When I arrived home, often there would be neighborhood kids in the house. Or the house would be empty of sounds.

Following the dramatic Americanization of their children, even my parents grew more publicly confident — especially my mother. First she learned the names of all the people on the block. Then she decided we needed to have a telephone in our house. My father, for his part, continued to use the word gringo, but it was no longer charged with bitterness or distrust. Stripped of any emotional content, the word simply became a name for those Americans not of Hispanic descent. Hearing him, sometimes, I wasn't sure if he was pronouncing the Spanish word *gringo,* or saying gringo in English.

There was a new silence at home. As we children learned more and more English, we shared fewer and fewer words with our parents. Sentences needed to be spoken slowly when one of us addressed our mother or father. Often the parent wouldn't understand. The child would need to repeat himself. Still the parent misunderstood. The young voice, frustrated, would end up saying, "Never mind" — the subject was closed. Dinners would be noisy with the clinking of knives and forks against dishes. My mother would smile softly between her remarks; my father, at the other end of the table, would chew and chew his food while he stared over the heads of his children.

My mother! My father! After English became my primary language, I no longer knew what words to use in addressing my parents. The old Spanish words (those tender accents of sound) I had earlier used — *mamá* and *papá* — I couldn't use any more. They would have been all-too-painful reminders of how much had changed in my life. On the other hand, the words I heard neighborhood kids call their parents seemed equally unsatisfactory. "Mother" and "father," "ma," "papa," "pa," "dad," "pop" (how I hated the all-American sound of that last word) — all these I felt were unsuitable terms of address for *my* parents. As a result, I never used them at home. Whenever I'd speak to my parents, I would try to get their attention by looking at them. In public conversations, I'd refer to them as my "parents" or my "mother" and "father."

My mother and father, for their part, responded differently, as their children spoke to them less. My mother grew restless, seemed troubled and anxious at the scarceness of words exchanged in the house. She would question me about my day when I came home from school. She smiled at my small talk. She pried at the edges of my sentences to get me to say something more. ("What . . . ?") She'd join conversations she overheard, but her intrusions often stopped her children's talking. By contrast, my father seemed to grow reconciled to the new quiet. Though his English somewhat improved, he tended more and more to retire into silence. At dinner he spoke very little. One night his children and even his wife helplessly giggled at his garbled English pronunciation of the Catholic "Grace Before Meals." Thereafter he made his wife recite the prayer at the start of each meal, even on formal occasions when there were guests in the house.

Hers became the public voice of the family. On official business it was she, not my father, who would usually talk to strangers on the phone or in stores. We children grew so accustomed to his silence that years later we would routinely refer to his "shyness." (My mother often tried to explain: both of his parents died when he was eight. He was raised by an uncle who treated him as little more than a menial servant. He was never encouraged to speak. He grew up alone—a man of few words.) But I realized my father was not shy whenever I'd watch him speaking Spanish with relatives. Using Spanish, he was quickly effusive. Especially when talking with other men, his voice would spark, flicker, flare alive with varied sounds. In Spanish he expressed ideas and feelings he rarely revealed when speaking English. With firm Spanish sounds he conveyed a confidence and authority that English would never allow him.

The silence at home, however, was not simply the result of fewer words passing between parents and children. More profound for me was the silence created by my inattention to sounds. At about the time I no longer bothered to listen with care to the sounds of English in public, I grew careless about listening to the sounds made by the family when they spoke. Most of the time I would hear someone speaking at home and didn't distinguish his sounds from the words people uttered in public. I didn't even pay much attention to my parents' accented and ungrammatical speech—at least not at home. Only when I was with them in public would I become alert to their accents. But even then their sounds caused me less and less concern. For I was growing increasingly confident of my own public identity.

I would have been happier about my public success had I not recalled, sometimes, what it had been like earlier, when my family conveyed its intimacy through a set of conveniently private sounds. Sometimes in public, hearing a stranger, I'd hark back to my lost past. A Mexican farm worker approached me one day downtown. He wanted directions to some place. "*Hijito,* . . . " he said. And his voice stirred old longings. Another time I was standing beside my mother in the visiting room of a Carmelite convent, before the dense screen which rendered the nuns shadowy figures. I heard several of them speaking Spanish in their busy, singsong, overlapping voices, assuring my mother that, yes, yes, we were remem-

35

bered, all our family was remembered, in their prayers. Those voices echoed faraway family sounds. Another day a dark-faced old woman touched my shoulder lightly to steady herself as she boarded a bus. She murmured something to me I couldn't quite comprehend. Her Spanish voice came near, like the face of a never-before-seen relative in the instant before I was kissed. That voice, like so many of the Spanish voices I'd hear in public, recalled the golden age of my childhood.

Bilingual educators say today that children lose a degree of "individuality" by becoming assimilated into public society. (Bilingual schooling is a program popularized in the seventies, that decade when middle-class "ethnics" began to resist the process of assimilation — the "American melting pot.") But the bilingualists oversimplify when they scorn the value and necessity of assimilation. They do not seem to realize that a person is individualized in two ways. So they do not realize that, while one suffers a diminished sense of *private* individuality by being assimilated into public society, such assimilation makes possible the achievement of *public* individuality.

Simplistically again, the bilingualists insist that a student should be reminded of his difference from others in mass society, of his "heritage." But they equate mere separateness with individuality. The fact is that only in private — with intimates — is separateness from the crowd a prerequisite for individuality; an intimate "tells" me that I am unique, unlike all others, apart from the crowd. In public, by contrast, full individuality is achieved, paradoxically, by those who are able to consider themselves members of the crowd. Thus it happened for me. Only when I was able to think of myself as an American, no longer an alien in gringo society, could I seek the rights and opportunities necessary for full public individuality. The social and political advantages I enjoy as a man began on the day I came to believe that my name is indeed *Rich-heard Road-ree-guess.* It is true that my public society today is often impersonal; in fact, my public society is usually mass society. But despite the anonymity of the crowd, and despite the fact that the individuality I achieve in public is often tenuous — because it depends on my being one in a crowd — I celebrate the day I acquired my new name. Those middle-class ethnics who scorn assimilation seem to me filled with decadent self-pity, obsessed by the burden of public life. Dangerously, they romanticize public separateness and trivialize the dilemma of those who are truly socially disadvantaged.

If I rehearse here the changes in my private life after my Americani- *40* zation, it is finally to emphasize a public gain. The loss implies the gain. The house I returned to each afternoon was quiet. Intimate sounds no longer greeted me at the door. Inside there were other noises. The telephone rang. Neighborhood kids ran past the door of the bedroom where I was reading my schoolbooks — covered with brown shopping-bag paper. Once I learned the public language, it would never again be easy for me to hear intimate family voices. More and more of my day was spent hearing words, not sounds. But that may only be a way of saying that on the day I raised my hand in class and spoke loudly to an entire roomful of faces, my childhood started to end.

The Responsive Reader

1. What does Rodriguez say about the role of his first language in his childhood? What for him were the rewards and limitations of the private language of home? How did his parents use their first and their second language; how did they fare outside the home?
2. What were Rodriguez' first experiences with his second language, the public language of school? What phases did he go through in moving from the language of home to the language of school and the larger society? What were the stages in his slow alienation from the language and culture of his family?
3. The African American poet Imamu Amiri Baraka has said, "The price the immigrants had to pay for coming to America is that they had to become Americans." Rodriguez is eloquent on the price the children of immigrants pay for success in school. How would you sum up what he says about that price?
4. Where does Rodriguez seem to be at the end of his journey in his relation to his cultural and linguistic heritage?

Talking, Listening, Writing

5. What has been your experience with people whose private world is very different from their public personalities on the job or in school?
6. Rodriguez has said that by insisting on bilingualism Hispanics express their wish to "have it both ways" — to be full members of public America and yet also be separate and Hispanic. To judge from your own observation, is it possible in this country to "have it both ways"?
7. Many people take language for granted the way fish do the sea. Have you ever had problems with language? Have you ever had trouble finding the right language to use or overcoming barriers to communication?

Projects

8. How much official recognition is there in this country of the multi-lingual character of today's American society? How widespread are bilingual ballots, bilingual signs or instructions, or bilingual education? Collaborating with others, try to find answers to these questions.

Thinking about Connections

In the debate about bilingual education, does Rodriguez seem to have an answer or answers to the concerns raised by Gonzalez in "Bilingualism: The Key to Basic Skills"? Does Gonzalez seem to have an answer or answers to the questions raised by Rodriguez?

THE SECRETS OF CITIZENSHIP
Lawrence H. Fuchs

> *Lawrence H. Fuchs is Professor of American Civilization and Politics at Brandeis University and the author of* The American Kaleidoscope: Race, Ethnicity, and the Civic Culture. *The following is his extended review of Linda Chavez' 1992 book,* Out of the Barrio: Toward a New Politics of Hispanic Assimilation. *Fuchs, like other reviewers of books, uses his book review as a platform from which to expound his own views. He does not merely explain and discuss the author's thinking but he also fills in what the author allegedly omitted or sets straight what she perhaps misrepresented.*

Thought Starters: Does this review succeed in being fair to both sides in the arguments over bilingual education and affirmative action?

In his autobiography, *Barrio Boy,* Ernesto Galarza, a leader of the   1
Chicano movement in the 1950s and 1960s, tells of struggling to get out
of a Sacramento barrio by working hard in the fields in the summer, then
working his way through Occidental College, Stanford, and Columbia,
where he received his doctorate in economics. Hard work, as well as the
mastery of English, were also keys to escaping the barrio for Richard
Rodriguez, another Mexican-American whose memoir, *Hunger of Memory*
(1982), charted his emergence as a successful writer and teacher. It is a little
odd that Linda Chavez never mentions Galarza or Rodriguez in her book,
but their stories constitute remarkable testimonials to her argument that
Mexican-Americans and other Hispanics knew how to get out of the
barrio by studying, by working hard, and by participating in American civic life without the assistance of government-sponsored ethnic-
conscious policies such as bilingual education, which, in her view, do more
harm than good.

And their stories support her argument in other ways, too. For both
Galarza and Rodriguez, the mastery of English was a ticket to effectiveness and success that didn't erode their affection for Mexican culture.
Similarly, their love for *la raza* did not keep them from becoming patriotic
Mexican-Americans. When Galarza was attacked for his fight against the
exploitation of agricultural workers, he responded: "Can't they see? I love
this country in a way that people don't if they are born here." Chavez
loves this country, too. Unlike Galarza and Rodriguez, however, she has
not written about what it was like to live in a barrio, or about a personal
struggle to emerge from it. She has written something rather narrower,
an attack on Mexican-American leaders, on the "power brokers," who,

she charges, keep Mexican–Americans and other Hispanics in the barrio by practicing a politics of permanent victimization.

Such a politics, she correctly points out, often leads to a politics of separatism and divisiveness. Chavez argues that such leaders are substantially out of touch with large numbers of the people they purport to serve when they advocate language, affirmative action, welfare, and immigration policies that actually retard the upward mobility of Hispanics and alienate them from other Americans. The power brokers and their liberal allies, she maintains, are at least as self-interested as they are well-meaning. They have created an ethnic group advocacy industry, spinning off affirmative action and equal opportunity officers, bilingual teachers and supervisors, and immigration lawyers. They shamelessly buttress their arguments by manipulating statistics to show that little progress has been made by Hispanics in recent decades, neglecting to point out that statistics often include illegal aliens and recent immigrants who cannot be expected to have made much progress in education or employment compared with third-generation Mexican-Americans, who actually have done well.

But the attack on the self-interestedness of the professional elites is hardly worth the amount of attention that Chavez gives it. It is true that leaders of the Mexican-American Legal and Education Defense Fund (MALDEF) need cases and clients who have grievances, and rhetoric about victimization serves that need. But it is also true that there are clients with real grievances. What matters is whether or not the ethnic-conscious policies that the leaders advocate actually help Hispanics escape the barrio or hurt them, and whether they lead to a stronger, more unified nation or one that is torn by ethnic strife.

Chavez is so preoccupied with her attack on ethnic-conscious policies and the power brokers who advocate them that she tells us virtually nothing about the history of the Hispanic population in the United States, not even about its growth from fewer than 2 million in 1940 to 20 million in 1990. (The Hispanic population of the United States is projected to reach 31 million by 2010.) Prior to the 1960s that population was overwhelmingly of Mexican origin. Before the Mexican revolution in 1910, there were Hispanic families in the Southwest who traced their history in that area back to Spanish colonial times, before the accession of the northern half of Mexico by the United States in the Treaty of Guadalupe Hidalgo in 1848. Between 1910 and 1930 approximately 700,000 Mexican immigrants came to this country, but a considerable number returned to Mexico during the Depression. A large number of immigrants arrived in the 1950s and through the next three decades, giving the border cities, towns, and *colonias* or barrios that grew up around them a distinctive border culture.

The proportion of the total Hispanic population that was of Mexican origin declined from 70 percent in 1950 to 60 percent in 1980, due to the influx of Puerto Ricans, Cubans, and emigrants from Central and South

America. The 1950 census had counted only 70,000 persons of Puerto Rican background on the mainland, but by 1980 there were 2 million, concentrated heavily in New York City and New Jersey, and to a lesser extent in communities in more than a dozen other states. Mexicans and Mexican-Americans still were somewhat concentrated in the five southwestern states of Arizona, New Mexico, California, Colorado, and Texas (more than 50 percent lived in California and Texas in 1980), but they became much more widely dispersed during the 1970s, and by 1980 they constituted more than 5 percent of the population in the Northeast, 6 percent in the South, and 14.5 percent in the West. Although Cubans accounted for only 6 percent of the Spanish-origin population in 1980, they represented higher proportions in several states — 55 percent in Florida, 16 percent in New Jersey, 10 percent in Georgia, and 8 percent in both Maryland and Louisiana. And a rising proportion of the Spanish-origin population (21 percent in 1980) came from other Spanish-speaking countries, such as the Dominican Republic, El Salvador, Colombia, and Ecuador.

Chavez's failure to tell readers anything about barrios or *colonias,* as rural concentrations of Mexicans are often called in the Southwest, is even less excusable than her omission of any discussion of the history and the demography of the Latino population of this country. For what exactly is a barrio, and why would anyone want to get out of it? Stan Steiner, in *La Raza,* called it a "communal colony" over twenty years ago. He visited rural barrios on the outskirts of the cities, often the colonies of migrant workers who moved from one barrio to another, each with inadequate sewage, education, or other basic facilities and services. From such barrios there were nearly 2 million deportations of Mexicans in 1953 and 1954, most (but not all) illegal aliens. It was in such barrios that Cesar Chavez, the intrepid Mexican-American labor leader, grew up, attending more than thirty schools before the seventh grade.

The fast urbanization of the Southwest in recent decades absorbed Mexican-American barrios that had begun as agricultural labor communities. The barrios remained, but the population was no longer concentrated in agricultural work. Other barrios grew out of former labor camps that brought together Mexican-American railroad workers or miners. And there are central city barrios with large populations, such as the South Bronx and East Los Angeles, where by 1960 approximately 135,000 Mexican-origin persons made up more than three-quarters of the total population. Although Chavez never tells us what she means by a barrio, she cannot mean well-to-do Cuban-American neighborhoods in Miami or Mexican-American communities in San Antonio. She means the poor urban barrios of more than a dozen large and middle-sized cities and the rural *colonias* of the border cities and the rural areas around them. It is in such areas that Spanish-speaking immigrants and Latino Americans are plagued by unemployment, underemployment, and poor educational and health facilities. It is in such places that drugs often replace hope.

In making her case against ethnic-conscious policies, Chavez picks the two easiest targets: bilingual education and the amendments to the 1965 Voting Rights Act passed in 1982. The argument against the way the Bilingual Education Act has been implemented is a familiar one, resting on data and analysis developed by half a dozen scholars and polemicists over the past twenty years, most recently by Rosalie Pedalino Porter in her book *Forked Tongue*. To the considerable extent that the bilingual education industry has turned what was meant to be one of several strategies for helping youngsters deficient in English learn English into a program to maintain Spanish language and culture, it has often handicapped students rather than helped them move on to higher education and better jobs. And to the extent that it has packaged its approach in anti-assimilationist rhetoric, it has encouraged others to believe that Hispanics do not want to be Americans, an image that Chavez shows is absurdly untrue for most of them.

Still, her case would be stronger if she did not make the history of bilingual education sound as though it were a conspiracy to undermine American unity. "The purpose," she writes, "is not to assimilate Hispanic children, however, but to maintain and strengthen their ethnic identity." The movement certainly did not begin in a conspiracy. I remember collecting essays from Puerto Rican youngsters about twenty-five years ago and asking them to describe their earliest experiences in school before they learned English. They spoke of being sick to their stomachs, throwing up, and generally being miserable because they could not make themselves understood to their teachers. Today there are hundreds of bilingual teachers who support the philosophy of transition to English and teach accordingly. But Chavez is not one for presenting data that complicate her argument.

She is basically right, though, in stating that the bilingual education industry, which controls all but 25 percent of federal funds to help English-deficient children, has promoted the growth of maintenance programs. She would have applauded the remarks of Father Theodore Hesburgh, who, as chairman of the Select Commission on Immigration and Refugee Policy, listened carefully to a representative from MALDEF in 1980 testify that school was the only institution that could help youngsters maintain their ancestral languages and cultures. Hesburgh retorted: "I thought there already was an institution that was supposed to do that. It's called the family."

But Chavez's invocation of family self-help as the solution to the dismal predicament of many Hispanics is too simple. She writes that the immigrants "have no alternative but to work to provide for themselves and their families. But Puerto Ricans are well versed in public

10

assistance. . . . About 70 percent of all persons living in Puerto Rico receive some form of government assistance." She fails to analyze the destructive effect on Puerto Rican families of moving back and forth to and from the mainland; it is a major factor in the high rate of marital separation, which results in single parent female-headed households. Nor does she acknowledge the possibility that many Puerto Ricans who left poverty and moved to California or other parts of the country may have been saved at some point by food stamps, Head Start, a job training program for mothers, infants, and children. If Chavez has met any government program targeted specifically to help poor families, who happen to be disproportionately Hispanic and black, we don't learn of them here. . . .

What is wrong with Chavez's book is what is left out: the good, however limited or complicated, that has been done through race- and ethnic-conscious remedies in education, housing, and employment; the awareness of continuing prejudice and discrimination in those areas, particularly in housing, although less so against Hispanics than blacks; the failure to recognize that most of those who live in chronically poor ethnic communities, such as large numbers of Puerto Ricans in the Northeast, will not escape by bootstrapping alone; and the absence of any constructive suggestions for government's role in promoting opportunity for persistently poor Americans.

Also missing is an understanding of how much the struggles of contemporary immigrant-ethnic groups are similar to, not different from, those of other groups in American history, despite contemporary ethnic-conscious government policies. By insisting on their rights as Americans, by forming political groups, by emphasizing issues of particular interest such as immigration and language, and by combining a love and admiration for their ancestral culture with loyalty to their American citizenship, Hispanic-Americans are behaving much like the children and grandchildren of Irish, German, Scandinavian, Polish, Italian, and Jewish immigrants. Chavez greatly oversimplifies when she asserts that in contrast to ethnic group leaders in the past "now ethnic leaders demand that their groups remain separate." The leaders of MALDEF, LULAC, and several other groups are no less patriotic than the leaders of European ethnic groups were.

Chavez, who was staff director of the Civil Rights Commission during the Reagan administration, argues correctly that much of what is called affirmative action, including the two policies she targets, does not address the problems of chronically poor Puerto Ricans and other Hispanics. These policies also probably distract ethnic leaders and politicians from working more directly on those problems. But Chavez may not appreciate how much affirmative action policies have helped to desegregate fire and police departments and educational institutions, or to bring competent Hispanics and blacks to management positions in large corporations. Does anyone believe that in the Philadelphia construction indus- 15 try, where the concept of numerical goals and timetables was first applied during the Nixon administration, the percentage of minority construction workers would have risen from 1 to 12 between 1969 and 1981 without affirmative action? Does anyone doubt that this nation is a lot stronger because the number of black police officers nationwide increased from 24,000 in 1970 to 43,000 in 1980 partly because of affirmative action programs?

The Responsive Reader

1. To judge from this review, what is the substance of the charges that Chavez in her book brought against Mexican American leaders? Do you recognize and can you define key terms like *barrio, victimization, separatism, upward mobility,* and *ethnic group advocacy*?
2. What background or context does Fuchs fill in that helps you better understand the arguments over bilingualism and bilingual education? How instructive or thought-provoking are his historical facts and his statistics? What historical precedents does he recall to help us understand the situation of recent immigrants?
3. What balance does the review attempt to achieve between the strong supporters and the opponents of bilingual education? How reasonable or convincing does the reviewer's position appear?
4. What are Fuchs' basic arguments in favor of affirmative action?

Talking, Listening, Writing

5. Does this review make you rethink your own position on issues like bilingual education and affirmative action?
6. Have you encountered criticism of or attacks on leaders of minority groups or on advocates of minority rights? What do you know about ethnic leaders or politicians? Do you know any who have been challenged or discredited? Do you know any whom you particularly admire? Are you inclined to side with critics of their leadership?
7. Some years ago, Ralph Nader asked for a new definition of patriotism that would recognize the right to dissent and the duty to keep a watchful eye on the government as part of the birthright of a patriotic American. Should we redefine patriotism so as to make it compatible with a strong loyalty to a separate cultural or linguistic heritage?

Projects

8. How desegregated are fire and police departments and educational institutions in your community or your area? What is their record in hiring minorities, women, and the disabled? Whose figures or whose rationales would you trust? Your class may want to set up groups exploring different facets of this question.

WHAT'S WRONG WITH BLACK ENGLISH

Rachel L. Jones

"Ain't nobody gonna beat me at nuthin," says the girl telling her story in Tony Cade Bambara's short story "The Lesson." No problem of communication here — we get the point, and many of us will sympathize with the sentiment. However, the kind of language she uses to convey her message has been hotly debated among linguists and educators for several decades. First of all, there is no generally acceptable nonracist, nonpejorative label for the kind of language the girl talks. What do we call the language of her neighborhood and of the street? Nonstandard English? Black dialect? Street slang? (A patois, the author of the following article calls it — a regional variety of a language often spoken mainly by backcountry people or people in menial jobs.) Second, many linguists and educators agree that it alienates students and defeats the teacher's effort to call young people ignorant or illiterate for speaking the language they learned at their mother's knee. (The students will feel that the teacher is not just rejecting their language but them as people.) However, how would we react if the girl used the same kind of language in a job interview or in a talk with a college admissions officer? Assuming that in such situations the successful candidate needs to "talk white," is it possible for people to become bidialectal? Can people switch easily and naturally from a downhome or inner-city dialect to the standard English of school and office? When Jones wrote the following article for Newsweek, *she was a student at Southern Illinois University.*

Thought Starters: The author of this much-reprinted article took a position unpopular with advocates of the "students' right to their own language." What is the essence of her argument? Have you encountered the kinds of situations that the author describes?

William Labov, a noted linguist, once said about the use of black English, "It is the goal of most black Americans to acquire full control of the standard language without giving up their own culture." He also suggested that there are certain advantages to having two ways to express one's feelings. I wonder if the good doctor might also consider the goals of those black Americans who have full control of standard English but who are every now and then troubled by that colorful, grammar-to-the-winds patois that is black English. Case in point — me.

I'm a 21-year-old black born to a family that would probably be considered lower-middle class — which in my mind is a polite way of describing a condition only slightly better than poverty. Let's just say we rarely if ever did the winter-vacation thing in the Caribbean. I've often had to defend my humble beginnings to a most unlikely group of people for an even less likely reason. Because of the way I talk, some of my black peers look at me sideways and ask, "Why do you talk like you're white?"

The first time it happened to me I was nine years old. Cornered in the school bathroom by the class bully and her sidekick, I was offered the opportunity to swallow a few of my teeth unless I satisfactorily explained why I always got good grades, why I talked "proper" or "white." I had no ready answer for her, save the fact that my mother had from the time I was old enough to talk stressed the importance of reading and learning, or that L. Frank Baum and Ray Bradbury were my closest companions. I read all my older brothers' and sisters' literature textbooks more faithfully than they did, and even lightweights like the Bobbsey Twins and Trixie Belden were allowed into my bookish inner circle. I don't remember exactly what I told those girls, but I somehow talked my way out of a beating.

'White pipes.' I was reminded once again of my "white pipes" problem while apartment hunting in Evanston, Ill., last winter. I doggedly made out lists of available places and called all around. I would immediately be invited over — and immediately turned down. The thinly concealed looks of shock when the front door opened clued me in, along with the flustered instances of "just getting off the phone with the girl who was ahead of you and she wants the rooms." When I finally found a place to live, my roommate stirred up old memories when she remarked a few months later, "You know, I was surprised when I first saw you. You sounded white over the phone." Tell me another one, sister.

I should've asked her a question I've wanted an answer to for years: 5 how does one "talk white"? The silly side of me pictures a rabid white foam spewing forth when I speak. I don't use Valley Girl jargon, so that's not what's meant in my case. Actually, I've pretty much deduced what people mean when they say that to me, and the implications are really frightening.

It means that I'm articulate and well-versed. It means that I can talk as freely about John Steinbeck as I can about Rick James. It means that "ain't" and "he be" are not staples of my vocabulary and are only used around family and friends. (It is almost Jekyll and Hyde-ish the way I can slip out of academic abstractions into a long, lean, double-negative-filled dialogue, but I've come to terms with that aspect of my personality.) As a child, I found it hard to believe that's what people meant by "talking proper"; that would've meant that good grades and standard English were equated with white skin, and that went against everything I'd ever been taught. Running into the same type of mentality as an adult has confirmed the depressing reality that for many blacks, standard English is not only unfamiliar, it is socially unacceptable.

James Baldwin once defended black English by saying it had added "vitality to the language," and even went so far as to label it a language in its own right, saying, "Language [i.e., black English] is a political instrument" and a "vivid and crucial key to identity." But did Malcolm X urge blacks to take power in this country "any way y'all can"? Did Martin Luther King Jr. say to blacks, "I has been to the mountaintop, and I done seed the Promised Land"? Toni Morrison, Alice Walker and James Baldwin did not achieve their eloquence, grace and stature by using only black English in their writing. Andrew Young, Tom Bradley and Barbara Jordan did not acquire political power by saying, "Y'all crazy if you ain't gon vote for me." They all have full command of standard English, and I don't think that knowledge takes away from their blackness or commitment to black people.

Soulful. I know from experience that it's important for black people, stripped of culture and heritage, to have something they can point to and say, "This is ours, *we* can comprehend it, *we* alone can speak it with a soulful flourish." I'd be lying if I said that the rhythms of my people caught up in "some serious rap" don't sound natural and right to me sometimes. But how heartwarming is it for those same brothers when they hit the pavement searching for employment? Studies have proven that the use of ethnic dialects decreases power in the marketplace. "I be" is acceptable on the corner, but not with the boss.

Am I letting capitalistic, European-oriented thinking fog the issue? Am I selling out blacks to an ideal of assimilating, being as much like white as possible? I have not formed a personal political ideology, but I do know this: it hurts me to hear black children use black English, knowing that they will be at yet another disadvantage in an educational system already full of stumbling blocks. It hurts me to sit in lecture halls and hear fellow black students complain that the professor "be tripping dem out using big words dey can't understand." And what hurts most is to be stripped of my own blackness simply because I know my way around the English language.

I would have to disagree with Labov in one respect. My goal is not 10 so much to acquire full control of both standard and black English, but to one day see more black people less dependent on a dialect that excludes them from full participation in the world we live in. I don't think I talk white, I think I talk right.

The Responsive Reader

1. What are some of the incidents that made Jones "language-conscious"? What did she learn from them? What do you learn from them?
2. How was Jones' experience different from that of other black kids or other minority students? Do you think her own unusual experience

disqualifies her from speaking authoritatively on the issue of Black English?

3. Is Jones aware of the people who disagree with her? How does she answer them? Where does she state her own position most eloquently or effectively?

Talking, Listening, Writing

4. Has your way of talking ever caused difficulty for you or put obstacles in your path? Have you ever experienced ridicule because of your language? Have you ever made a conscious effort to change the way you speak?

5. What has been your observation of other people's foreign accents, regional dialects (Southern, for instance), or similar language differences? How do people who "talk funny" fare in our society? Is "talking different" ever an asset?

6. Do you know people who have two or more registers — different ways of talking for different groups or situations? When and how do they "shift gears"?

Projects

7. For further reading, examine the use of Black dialect or Black English in the writing of an African American author. For instance, study the use of language in a novel by Alice Walker or Toni Morrison or in a play by August Wilson. (Do all the characters speak the same kind of language? For instance, do the homeboy and the preacher in Wilson's *The Piano Lesson* speak the same way? Do the characters ever switch from one kind of language to another?)

THE LESSON
Toni Cade Bambara

> Toni Cade Bambara has been described as a "dancer, teacher, critic, editor, activist, and writer." She was born and educated in New York City, with degrees from Queens and City College. She started writing in the politically active sixties and has published two volumes of short stories — Gorilla, My Love (1972) and The Sea Birds Are Still Alive (1977) — and a novel, The Salt Eaters (1980). Critics commenting on her work have focused on her blend of politics and sexual politics; on the role of gender, family, and community in her stories; and on her awareness of the subjective, personal quality of the world we construct for ourselves. The following story, about black kids from a poor neighborhood coming downtown, makes us see affluent white society through their eyes. It thus turns the tables on the affluent majority, whose spokespersons endlessly study and analyze and report on the children of the poor. A major part of the contrast between the two worlds is set up by the tough street language of the young people, with the story told in what one editor has called "uncondescending, witty, poetic Black English."

Thought Starters: How much of our perception of people's personalities is shaped by the way people talk? Would the girl speaking in the following story be a different person if she talked differently?

Back in the days when everyone was old and stupid or young and   1
foolish and me and Sugar were the only ones just right, this lady moved on our block with nappy hair and proper speech and no makeup. And quite naturally we laughed at her, laughed the way we did at the junk man who went about his business like he was some big-time president and his sorry-ass horse his secretary. And we kinda hated her too, hated the way we did the winos who cluttered up our parks and pissed on our handball walls and stank up our hallways and stairs so you couldn't halfway play hide-and-seek without a goddamn gas mask. Miss Moore was her name. The only woman on the block with no first name. And she was black as hell, cept for her feet, which were fish-white and spooky. And she was always planning these boring-ass things for us to do, us being my cousin, mostly, who lived on the block cause we all moved North the same time and to the same apartment then spread out gradual to breathe. And our parents would yank our heads into some kinda shape and crisp up our clothes so we'd be presentable for travel with Miss Moore, who always looked like she was going to church, though she never did. Which is just one of the things the grownups talked about when they talked behind her

back like a dog. But when she came calling with some sachet she'd sewed up or some gingerbread she'd made or some book, why then they'd all be too embarrassed to turn her down and we'd get handed over all spruced up. She'd been to college and said it was only right that she should take responsibility for the young ones' education, and she not even related by marriage or blood. So they'd go for it. Specially Aunt Gretchen. She was the main gofer in the family. You got some ole dumb shit foolishness you want somebody to go for, you send for Aunt Gretchen. She been screwed into the go-along for so long, it's a blood-deep natural thing with her. Which is how she got saddled with me and Sugar and Junior in the first place while our mothers were in a la-de-da apartment up the block having a good ole time.

So this one day Miss Moore rounds us all up at the mailbox and it's pure-dee hot and she's knockin herself out about arithmetic. And school suppose to let up in summer I heard, but she don't never let up. And the starch in my pinafore scratching the shit outta me and I'm really hating this nappy-head bitch and her goddamn college degree. I'd much rather go to the pool or to the show where it's cool. So me and Sugar leaning on the mailbox being surly, which is a Miss Moore word. And Flyboy checking out what everybody brought for lunch. And Fat Butt already wasting his peanut-butter-and-jelly sandwich like the pig he is. And Junebug punchin on Q.T.'s arm for potato chips. And Rosie Giraffe shifting from one hip to the other waiting for somebody to step on her foot or ask her if she from Georgia so she can kick ass, preferably Mercedes'. And Miss Moore asking us do we know what money is, like we a bunch of retards. I mean real money, she say, like it's only poker chips or monopoly papers we lay on the grocer. So right away I'm tired of this and say so. And would much rather snatch Sugar and go to the Sunset and terrorize the West Indian kids and take their hair ribbons and their money too. And Miss Moore files that remark away for next week's lesson on brotherhood. I can tell. And finally I say we oughta get to the subway cause it's cooler and besides we might meet some cute boys. Sugar done swiped her mama's lipstick, so we ready.

So we heading down the street and she's boring us silly about what things cost and what our parents make and how much goes for rent and how money ain't divided up right in this country. And then she gets to the part about we all poor and live in the slums, which I don't feature. And I'm ready to speak on that, but she steps out in the street and hails two cabs just like that. Then she hustles half the crew in with her and hands me a five-dollar bill and tells me to calculate 10 percent tip for the driver. And we're off. Me and Sugar and Junebug and Flyboy hangin out the window and hollering to everybody, putting lipstick on each other cause Flyboy a faggot anyway, and making farts with our sweaty armpits. But I'm mostly trying to figure how to spend this money. But they all fascinated with the meter ticking and Junebug starts laying bets as to how much it'll read when Flyboy can't hold his breath no more. Then Sugar lays bets as to how much it'll be when we get there. So I'm stuck. Don't nobody want to go for my plan, which is to jump out at the next light and run off to the first bar-b-que we can find. Then the driver tells us to get the hell out cause we there already. And the meter reads eighty-five cents. And I'm stalling to figure out the tip and Sugar say give him a dime. And I decide he don't need it bad as I do, so later for him. But then he tries to take off with Junebug foot still in the door so we talk about his mama something ferocious. Then we check out that we on Fifth Avenue and everybody dressed up in stockings. One lady in a fur coat, hot as it is. White folks crazy.

"This is the place," Miss Moore say, presenting it to us in the voice she uses at the museum. "Let's look in the windows before we go in."

"Can we steal?" Sugar asks very serious like she's getting the ground 5 rules squared away before she plays. "I beg your pardon," say Miss Moore, and we fall out. So she leads us around the windows of the toy store and me and Sugar screamin, "This is mine, that's mine, I gotta have that, that was made for me, I was born for that," till Big Butt drowns us out.

"Hey, I'm goin to buy that there."

"That there? You don't even know what it is, stupid."

"I do so," he say punchin on Rosie Giraffe. "It's a microscope."

"Whatcha gonna do with a microscope, fool?"

"Look at things." 10

"Like what, Ronald?" ask Miss Moore. And Big Butt ain't got the first notion. So here go Miss Moore gabbing about the thousands of bacteria in a drop of water and the somethinorother in a speck of blood and the million and one living things in the air around us is invisible to the naked eye. And what she say that for? Junebug go to town on that "naked" and we rolling. Then Miss Moore ask what it cost. So we all jam into the window smudgin it up and the price tag say $300. So then she ask how long'd take for Big Butt and Junebug to save up their allowances. "Too long," I say. "Yeh," adds Sugar, "outgrown it by that time." And Miss Moore say no, you never outgrow learning instruments. "Why, even medical students and interns and," blah, blah, blah. And we ready to choke Big Butt for bringing it up in the first damn place.

"This here costs four hundred eighty dollars," says Rosie Giraffe. So we pile up all over her to see what she pointin out. My eyes tell me it's a chunk of glass cracked with something heavy, and different-color inks dripped into the splits, then the whole thing put into a oven or something. But for $480 it don't make sense.

"That's a paperweight made of semi-precious stones fused together under tremendous pressure," she explains slowly, with her hands doing the mining and all the factory work.

"So what's a paperweight?" asks Rosie Giraffe.

"To weigh paper with, dumbbell," say Flyboy, the wise man from 15 the East.

"Not exactly," say Miss Moore, which is what she say when you warm or way off too. "It's to weigh paper down so it won't scatter and make your desk untidy." So right away me and Sugar curtsy to each other and then to Mercedes who is more the tidy type.

"We don't keep paper on top of the desk in my class," say Junebug, figuring Miss Moore crazy or lyin one.

"At home, then," she say. "Don't you have a calendar and pencil case and a blotter and a letter-opener on your desk at home where you do your homework?" And she know damn well what our homes look like cause she nosys around in them every chance she gets.

"I don't even have a desk," say Junebug. "Do we?"

"No. And I don't get no homework neither," says Big Butt.   20

"And I don't even have a home," say Flyboy like he do at school to keep the white folks off his back and sorry for him. Send this poor kid to camp posters, is his specialty.

"I do," says Mercedes. "I have a box of stationery on my desk and a picture of my cat. My godmother bought the stationery and the desk. There's a big rose on each sheet and the envelopes smell like roses."

"Who wants to know about your smelly-ass stationery," say Rosie Giraffe fore I can get my two cents in.

"It's important to have a work area all your own so that . . ."

"Will you look at this sailboat, please," say Flyboy, cuttin her off   25
and pointin to the thing like it was his. So once again we tumble all over each other to gaze at this magnificent thing in the toy store which is just big enough to maybe sail two kittens across the pond if you strap them to the posts tight. We all start reciting the price tag like we in assembly. "Handcrafted sailboat of fiberglass at one thousand one hundred ninety-five dollars."

"Unbelievable," I hear myself say and am really stunned. I read it again for myself just in case the group recitation put me in a trance. Same thing. For some reason this pisses me off. We look at Miss Moore and she lookin at us, waiting for I dunno what.

"Who'd pay all that when you can buy a sailboat set for a quarter at Pop's, a tube of glue for a dime, and a ball of string for eight cents? It must have a motor and a whole lot else besides," I say. "My sailboat cost me about fifty cents."

"But will it take water?" say Mercedes with her smart ass.

"Took mine to Alley Pond Park once," say Flyboy. "String broke. Lost it. Pity."

"Sailed mine in Central Park and it keeled over and sank. Had to ask   30
my father for another dollar."

"And you got the strap," laugh Big Butt. "The jerk didn't even have a string on it. My old man wailed on his behind."

Little Q.T. was staring hard at the sailboat and you could see he wanted it bad. But he too little and somebody'd just take it from him. So what the hell. "This boat for kids, Miss Moore?"

"Parents silly to buy something like that just to get all broke up," say Rosie Giraffe.

"That much money it should last forever," I figure.

"My father'd buy it for me if I wanted it."   35

"Your father, my ass," say Rosie Giraffe getting a chance to finally push Mercedes.

"Must be rich people shop here," say Q.T.

"You are a very bright boy," say Flyboy. "What was your first clue?" And he rap him on the head with the back of his knuckles, since Q.T. the only one he could get away with. Though Q.T. liable to come up behind you years later and get his licks in when you half expect it.

"What I want to know is," I says to Miss Moore though I never talk to her, I wouldn't give the bitch that satisfaction, "is how much a real boat costs? I figure a thousand'd get you a yacht any day."

"Why don't you check that out," she says, "and report back to the   40 group?" Which really pains my ass. If you gonna mess up a perfectly good swim day least you could do is have some answers. "Let's go in," she say like she got something up her sleeve. Only she don't lead the way. So me and Sugar turn the corner to where the entrance is, but when we get there I kinda hang back. Not that I'm scared, what's there to be afraid of, just a toy store. But I feel funny, shame. But what I got to be shamed about? Got as much right to go in as anybody. But somehow I can't seem to get hold of the door, so I step away from Sugar to lead. But she hangs back too. And I look at her and she looks at me and this is ridiculous. I mean, damn, I have never ever been shy about doing nothing or going nowhere. But when Mercedes steps up and then Rosie Giraffe and Big Butt crowd in behind and shove, and next thing we all stuffed into the doorway with only Mercedes squeezing past us, smoothing out her jumper and walking right down the aisle. Then the rest of us tumble in like a glued–together jigsaw done all wrong. And people lookin at us. And it's like the time me and Sugar crashed into the Catholic church on a dare. But once we got in there and everything so hushed and holy and the candles and the bowin and the handkerchiefs on all the drooping heads, I just couldn't go through with the plan. Which was for me to run up to the altar and do a tap dance while Sugar played the nose flute and messed around in the holy water. And Sugar kept givin me the elbow. Then later teased me so bad I tied her up in the shower and turned it on and locked her in. And she'd be there till this day if Aunt Gretchen hadn't finally figured I was lyin about the boarder takin a shower.

Same thing in the store. We all walkin on tiptoe and hardly touchin the games and puzzles and things. And I watched Miss Moore who is steady watchin us like she waitin for a sign. Like Mama Drewery watches the sky and sniffs the air and takes note of just how much slant is in the bird formation. Then me and Sugar bump smack into each other, so busy gazing at the toys, specially the sailboat. But we don't laugh and go into

our fat-lady bump-stomach routine. We just stare at that price tag. Then
Sugar run a finger over the whole boat. And I'm jealous and want to hit
her. Maybe not her, but I sure want to punch somebody in the mouth.

"Watcha bring us here for, Miss Moore?"

"You sound angry, Sylvia. Are you mad about something?" Givin
me one of them grins like she tellin a grown-up joke that never turns out
to be funny. And she's lookin very closely at me like maybe she planning to do my portrait from memory. I'm mad, but I won't give her
that satisfaction. So I slouch around the store bein very bored and say,
"Let's go."

Me and Sugar at the back of the train watchin the tracks whizzin by
large then small then getting gobbled up in the dark. I'm thinkin about
this tricky toy I saw in the store. A clown that somersaults on a bar then
does chin-ups just cause you yank lightly at his leg. Cost $35. I could see
me askin my mother for a $35 birthday clown. "You wanna who that
costs what?" she'd say, cocking her head to the side to get a better view of
the hole in my head. Thirty-five dollars could buy new bunk beds for
Junior and Gretchen's boy. Thirty-five dollars and the whole household
could go visit Granddaddy Nelson in the country. Thirty-five dollars
would pay for the rent and the piano bill too. Who are these people that
spend that much for performing clowns and $1000 for toy sailboats? What
kinda work they do and how they live and how come we ain't in on it?
Where we are is who we are, Miss Moore always pointin out. But it don't
necessarily have to be that way, she always adds then waits for somebody
to say that poor people have to wake up and demand their share of the pie
and don't none of us know what kind of pie she talking about in the first
damn place. But she ain't so smart cause I still got her four dollars from
the taxi and she sure ain't gettin it. Messin up my day with this shit. Sugar
nudges me in my pocket and winks.

Miss Moore lines us up in front of the mailbox where we started
from, seem like years ago, and I got a headache for thinkin so hard. And
we lean all over each other so we can hold up under the draggy-ass lecture
she always finishes us off with at the end before we thank her for borin us
to tears. But she just looks at us like she readin tea leaves. Finally she say,
"Well, what did you think of F. A. O. Schwarz?"

Rosie Giraffe mumbles, "White folks crazy."

"I'd like to go there again when I get my birthday money," says
Mercedes, and we shove her out the pack so she has to lean on the mailbox
by herself.

"I'd like a shower. Tiring day," say Flyboy.

Then Sugar surprises me by sayin, "You know, Miss Moore, I don't
think all of us here put together eat in a year what that sailboat costs."
And Miss Moore lights up like somebody goosed her. "And?" she say,
urging Sugar on. Only I'm standin on her foot so she don't continue.

"Imagine for a minute what kind of society it is in which some people   50

WRITING
WORKSHOP 9

Writing to Define

Definition stakes out the territory a term covers. Key terms in a social or political argument often need definition. Even the boxes we are expected to check on a questionnaire may make us ask: "What do you mean?" Is a person with two French and two Hawaiian grandparents of "European descent"? Is a person with an Irish father and an African American mother white or black? Who is white or black in our society is a matter of definition.

To define means to draw the line. Who is poor in our society depends on where we draw the "poverty line." Who is a "qualified applicant" for a job or a promotion depends on the criteria applied by the people who do the hiring. (They are sometimes second-guessed by an arbitration board or by the courts.) What is obscene in our society depends on how explicit the treatment of sex has to become before viewers or readers stop saying, "This is sexy! This is hot!" and start saying, "This is disgusting! This is sick!" (Ultimately, what is obscene in our society depends on where the members of the United States Supreme Court draw the line.)

TRIGGERING Definition becomes an issue whenever someone says: "Just a minute—what exactly do we mean by this word?" The French philosopher Voltaire said, "Before you start arguing with me, define your terms!" Here are some typical situations where a writer might say: "Time out to define a key term!"

- We often need to spell out the core meaning of a term that can be used as a catch-all label. People we might identify as liberals or feminists or conservatives may be reluctant to use a label that might commit them to more than they bargained for. A person who says, "I'm not a feminist, but. . . ," often turns out to be a feminist—in the sense of someone promoting women's causes and standing up for women's rights. However, the person might not want to buy into some of the other positions that the label might imply — whether a generally negative attitude toward men, or a commitment to aggressive legal or political tactics. A definition of such a term can highlight the common core that qualifies a person—female or male— as a feminist. Such a definition can tell the reader: "This is what the term [whether *conservative, liberal, radical, feminist,* or *activist*] — basically means. Much else is optional!"

▪ Definition makes sure that words do not remain "just words." People who use the same terms often argue right past one another because the terms mean different things to them. The more sweeping and uplifting the terms are, the easier it is for everyone to pay lip service to them. Everyone today is an "equal opportunity employer." What does that mean? What equal opportunities can a student have who struggled to stay in school in a violence-prone neighborhood and a kid who grew up in a community where private security guards kept the riffraff out? If we commit ourselves to "equal opportunity," what if anything are we going to do to ensure the legendary "level playing field"? Are we going to provide the kind of second chance (or third chance) without which "equal opportunity" remains hot air?

GATHERING Student writers are often tempted to start a definition paper by saying, "*Webster's Dictionary* defines *equity* as the practice of being fair and equal." Noah Webster, of course, is dead, and several publishers of dictionaries have appropriated his name to help peddle their wares. (So what reference book are you quoting?) Moreover, the dictionary definition is often a **circular definition**: It tells us that being equitable means being fair but does nothing to make us see what that means in practice.

To make your readers see what a key word means in practice, you will have to become a word watcher. Who uses the word? in what situations? for what purpose? Are there several main uses? How are they related? Is there a common denominator — a common thread? What do you think is the prevailing or most useful meaning of the terms? What are possible abuses or dishonest uses?

Here are some categories a student might set up to collect material for a definition of the term *feminism.* Such categories serve as a **discovery frame,** charting a program for a systematic stock-taking of relevant material:

What popular associations (and misunderstandings) cluster around the term?

What is the history of the movement — what famous names and events are associated with it?

How do the media reflect changing definitions of gender roles?

Where have feminist issues played a role in my own experience?

What related terms (*women's liberation, emancipation, sexism, patriarchy*) cluster around the term?

What is the core meaning of the term?

SHAPING Strategies for presenting an **extended definition** — a definition in depth of a much-used important term — will vary.

▪ You may want to set your paper in motion by focusing on a common misunderstanding of the term — and then correcting it. You lead from the misuse or misunderstanding of the term to what you consider its true meaning. You then give several examples of situations where your definition fits especially well.

▪ You may want to focus on providing a historical perspective. For instance, you might trace key meanings of the term *democracy* from its original Greek meaning — "rule by the people" — to modern times. You move from the direct democracy of ancient Greece (with the electorate voting on major decisions) to the representative democracy of modern times (voting on major issues by proxy). From there, you move to the participatory democracy advocated by those who feel that democratic institutions have become too isolated from the people.

▪ You may want to examine several key examples of affirmative action to find what they have in common. Or you may want to focus on one extended case history that puts possible definitions of the term to the test.

What is the overall plan in the following student paper? What problems of definition does the writer recognize? What is the core definition that emerges from the paper?

Dem's Fightin' Words!

When does ordinary name-calling turn into offensive slurs? Where do we draw the line when people use racial epithets or demeaning language directed at other groups? What do we do about it?

"Faggot! Hope you die of AIDS! Can't wait till you die!" These words were shouted, not by an ignorant twelve-year-old, but by Keith R., a law student at Stanford University. Weeks later, when confronted, he said he had used offensive language on purpose in order to test the limits of freedom of speech at Stanford. Others doubt that his use of language was an experiment; they say it closely coincided with opinions he had expressed in The Stanford Review.

When dealing with abusive individuals like R., the natural impulse is to legislate, to pass ordinances, to enforce guidelines. If we could only ban offensive language, expel the offender, or shut down an offending magazine, we would get rid of the problem. Many colleges have tried this tack by instituting "Fighting Words" rules. Responding to the pain felt by the victims of racism, sexism, and homophobia, these schools have as necessary amended their constitutions to forbid certain offensive expressions. Violators may be reprimanded or even expelled. At Dartmouth, for instance, a student was called on the carpet for asking in class whether it was possible to "cure" homosexuals.

The objection to such rules is that they inevitably have what lawyers call "a chilling effect" on the free expression of ideas. These rules inevitably pose a problem of definition: Where do we draw the line? Who decides what is offensive, and to whom? Stanford's "Speech Code" made a brave attempt to minimize the problem by being very specific. It read in part: "Speech or other expression constitutes harassment or personal vilification if it: (1) intends to insult or stigmatize an individual or group of individuals on the basis of sex, race, color, handicap, religion, sexual orientation, or national or ethnic origin; (2) is addressed directly to the individual; (3) makes use of insulting or fighting words or gestures."

Nevertheless, drawing the line between offensive speech and legitimate expression is not easy. How would this rule apply to the speeches of Malcolm X, who for a time referred to whites as "white devils"? On the other hand, what set of rules could stop a person like Keith R. from being personally offensive? He could have expressed his hostility by gestures instead of words—a wink, a leer, a walk, humming a few bars of "Here Comes the Bride."

The British writer Christopher Isherwood (who often referred to himself as Christopher Swisherwood) insisted on using words like faggot and queer. He said that by using them and making them ordinary, he could help take away their power to insult and to hurt. Would Mr. Isherwood be censored today on Stanford's green and pleasant lawn? No, say supporters of the Speech Code, because his use of language was not intended to offend. But this puts the censors into the business of judging the intent of an expression—looking into people's heads to judge what made them say what they said. Who is going to say if an expression was used insultingly, kiddingly, or ignorantly?

At Stanford, the reaction to the incident was a petition condemning R.'s behavior, signed by almost five hundred students and faculty members. At the law school, a large poster read: "Exercise your right of free speech. Tell this law student what you think of his behavior. It may be legal, but it isn't right." This has to be the definition of offensive language in a free society: What bigots and racists say may be offensive, but they have the right to say it, and we have the right and duty to talk back to them. That is what free speech is all about.

If you take away the bigot's right to shout "Faggot!" you may also be taking away my right to say: "Shut up, you creep!" You may be taking away my right to call a religious fanatic a bigot or my gun-toting neighbor a redneck. Bad ideas and bad language cannot be legislated against; they must be driven out by better ideas.

Topics for Definition Papers (A Sampling)

1. What kind of group qualifies as a "minority"? (For instance, do white ethnics count as minority groups?)
2. When is "marital rape" rape? (Should it be a felony? a misdemeanor?)
3. What does *macho* mean?

4. What is meant by "welfare dependency"? Who uses the term and why?
5. Is the term *feminine* obsolete? Does anyone still want to be "feminine"?
6. Is there such a thing as an "ideal marriage"?
7. What is the difference between terrorists and freedom fighters?
8. Where would you draw the line between popular culture and "real" or highbrow culture?
9. Is there such a thing as "reverse racism"?
10. What is the difference between sexism and a healthy or normal antagonism between the sexes?

10

Violence: Living at Risk

Where have all the soldiers gone,
Long time passing?
Where have all the soldiers gone,
Long time ago?
Where have all the soldiers gone?
They've gone to graveyards, everyone.
Oh, when will they ever learn?

                       Pete Seeger

We live in a violent world. The twentieth century brought wars deploying an unprecedented technology of mass destruction. A generation of young men was killed in the trench warfare of World War I. In World War II, civilian casualties — from scorched-earth policies, bombings, and campaigns of extermination — rivaled the numbers of those killed in combat. Many Americans first came here as refugees — from Germany, Russia, Southeast Asia — carrying with them the scars, physical and psychological, of repression, starvation, and genocide. Young Americans (many from minority backgrounds) were sent to fight in North Africa, Italy, France, and the Pacific in World War II; in Korea, in Vietnam, and in Iraq. Thousands of veterans suffer from the disabilities and traumas left in the wake of their war experience overseas.

At home, American cities have rates of violent crime and murder unprecedented in the developed countries of the West. Serial murders, drive-by shootings, and gang wars are features of our news and entertainment. Americans live in fear of violence. Often that fear pits members of different racial or ethnic groups against one another. Are we going to live in a society where a white police officer is assumed to be the enemy of a black citizen? Are we going to live in communities where a Korean grocer and a customer from the barrio regard one another with hatred and distrust?

Have Americans come to accept violence as an inevitable fact of life? Do we have any blueprints for making ours a safer world?

EMOTIONS CLOUDING RATIONAL DECISIONS

Steven Musil

> *Steven Musil was an editor for a student newspaper when he wrote the following editorial about the loss of a friend. Like other writers of editorials and newspaper columns, he shares his thoughts and feelings, but these are grounded in what he knows. He writes as a witness — someone who took in and cared about something that for many newspaper readers was just a statistic.*

Thought Starters: Musil writes as a witness trying to sort out his thoughts and feelings about a traumatic event. Do you understand what he thinks and feels?

"An eye for an eye and the whole world goes blind." — Ghandi

The following is an open letter to a lost friend.

Dear Dennis,

It has been two-and-a-half years since we last spoke. I'm sorry that I haven't written to you before but I wasn't sure where to send this. I haven't seen you since two days before your funeral and I'm sure you must have many questions. First off, you probably know by now that Tony was your killer. Last week, a jury found him guilty and sentenced him to life in prison without the possibility of parole.

All the articles in the newspaper got me thinking about the whole mess again. I watched some of the trial downtown and a couple days ago I visited your memorial in front of Chili's. It has been hard to forget lately.

Many of us who were working at Chili's at the time of the murder were hoping for the death sentence. We wanted to see him die in the gas chamber for what he did to you. Some of us even felt sorry for him before we realized that he murdered you. The autopsy reported that you were shot once in the back of the head with a sawed-off .22-caliber rifle and then twice in the face after you fell to the floor.

The coroner said that you probably didn't know what was happening and you died instantly without suffering. Is that true? The sheriff found the rifle and about $1,600 in cash in his apartment on the day of your funeral. I was one of the last to be told.

The jury "let him off" because he had "no prior convictions of violent crimes or anything of that sort," according to the jury foreman.

Everyone at Chili's liked you Dennis. Even Tony. He testified that he was in a confused, cocaine-induced trance and needed the money to cover some debts. He said that he knew he would have to kill whoever was in the restaurant at the time. You weren't even scheduled to work that day, but were doing another manager a favor. I'm thankful no one else was there.

It just seemed so unfair. You were so young. So nice, so gentle. I regret the hard time we gave you at the Fourth of July party the night before. Do you remember? We were kidding you because you were the only married manager without children. The night before you died you said that it was time to have a child.

They closed the store for a couple of days for the investigation and to clean up. With all the extra time, some of the cooks decided to go camping, stay together. We had a real hard time dealing with it so we just took off. We ended up on a beach south of Santa Cruz. We bought a couple cases of beer, built a bonfire and toasted your memory all night until the sun came up the next day.

That night we made a pact to visit the campsite every year in your honor. A year later, I was the only one that returned. Many of those people don't work at Chili's anymore and are hard to get a hold of. I'm sure they haven't forgotten you.

It touched some people so that they revised their personal stance on   10
capital punishment. After your murder there were people stating that they had rethought the issue and now supported the death penalty, gun control, and assorted other related causes. I admit that I too made my gun control decision based on the emotional aftershock. I'm not sure if someone can make a rational decision of such importance based on an emotionally traumatic event.

Anyway, I don't have a lot of room to write to you. I have to tell you that I'm putting this behind me and you probably won't hear from me again. Know that we haven't forgotten you just because we are going on with our lives. Somehow I think you would have wanted it that way. Take care of yourself.

Your friend,
Steven

The Responsive Reader

1. What are the bare facts in this case? What are allegations, theories, or excuses?
2. What does this "letter to a lost friend" accomplish? What did it do for the writer? What does it do for the reader?

Talking, Listening, Writing

3. Who or what is to blame? What if anything can be done to help prevent a similar tragedy? Does this editorial make you rethink your

position regarding the "death penalty, gun control, and assorted other related causes"?

4. Musil says, "I'm not sure if someone can make a rational decision . . . based on an emotionally traumatic event." Don't we have a right to be emotional about events like the one that is the occasion for this editorial? Shouldn't we be emotional? What would a "rational" reaction be to what happened in this case?

5. A tired joke has it that when the students at one college were asked whether they were concerned about apathy concerning social issues, 87 percent responded: "I don't care." Do you think students of your generation or on your campus are guilty of apathy?

6. Write your own personal response to the author of this "letter to a lost friend."

Projects

7. For one of several possible research projects related to issues in this chapter, you might choose to collaborate with others to find out about the movement toward victims' rights. What are reasons, initiatives, accomplishments? What are possible roadblocks, pitfalls, objections?

WHY HANDGUNS MUST BE OUTLAWED

Nan Desuka

> *In spite of attempts to place restrictions on the free sale — being sold like groceries — of lethal weapons, more guns are in circulation (and in use) in the United States than in any other country in the world. American citizens, and especially young Americans, are killed by firearms at a rate unheard of in civilized countries. One city councillor trying to get a gun control ordinance passed discovered that anyone regardless of criminal record or medical history could buy a gun but that the local sheriff tried to screen out angry wives who might use the guns to shoot their husbands. The councillor's initiative, like many before and after, was defeated after an organized campaign by the National Rifle Association. Nan Desuka, the author of the following article on gun control, was born in Japan but came to the United States with her parents when she was two. She knows how to listen, how to take in what people on the other side of an issue have to say.*

Thought Starters: Is there any point in listening one more time to the arguments about gun control? Is this kind of article going to change anyone's mind? Is anything going to be done?

"Guns don't kill people — criminals do." That's a powerful slogan, much more powerful than its alternate version, "Guns don't kill people — people kill people." But this second version, though less effective, is much nearer to the whole truth. Although accurate statistics are hard to come by, and even harder to interpret, it seems indisputable that large numbers of people, not just criminals, kill, with a handgun, other people. Scarcely a day goes by without a newspaper in any large city reporting that a child has found a gun, kept by the child's parents for self-protection, and has, in playing with this new-found toy, killed himself or a playmate. Or we read of a storekeeper, trying to protect himself during a robbery, who inadvertently shoots an innocent customer. These killers are not, in any reasonable sense of the word, criminals. They are just people who happen to kill people. No wonder the gun lobby prefers the first version of the slogan, "Guns don't kill people — criminals do." This version suggests that the only problem is criminals, not you or me, or our children, and certainly not the members of the National Rifle Association.

Those of us who want strict control of handguns — for me that means the outlawing of handguns, except to the police and related service units — have not been able to come up with a slogan equal in power to "Guns don't kill people — criminals do." The best we have been able to come up with is a mildly amusing bumper sticker showing a teddy bear, with the words "Defend your right to arm bears." Humor can be a powerful weapon (even in writing *on behalf* of gun control, one slips into using the imagery of force), and our playful bumper sticker somehow deflates the self-righteousness of the gun lobby, but doesn't equal the power (again the imagery of force) of "Guns don't kill people — criminals do." For one thing, the effective alliteration of "*criminals*" and "*kill*" binds the two words, making everything so terribly simple. Criminals kill; when there are no criminals, there will be no deaths from guns.

But this notion won't do. Despite the uncertainty of some statistical evidence, everyone knows, or should know, that only about 30 percent of murders are committed by robbers or rapists. For the most part the victims of handguns know their assailants well. These victims are women killed by jealous husbands, or they are the women's lovers; or they are drinking buddies who get into a violent argument; or they are innocent people who get shot by disgruntled (and probably demented) employees or fellow workers who have (or imagine) a grudge. Or they are, as I've already said, bystanders at a robbery, killed by a storekeeper. Or they are children playing with their father's gun.

Of course this is not the whole story. Hardened criminals also have guns, and they use them. The murders committed by robbers and rapists are what gave credence to Barry Goldwater's quip, "We have a crime problem in this country, not a gun problem." But here again the half-truth of a slogan is used to mislead, used to direct attention away from a national tragedy. Different sources issue different statistics, but a conservative estimate is that handguns annually murder at least 15,000 Americans, accidentally kill at least another 3,000, and wound at least another 100,000. Handguns are easily available, both to criminals and to decent people who believe they need a gun in order to protect themselves from criminals. The decent people, unfortunately, have good cause to believe they need protection. Many parts of many cities are utterly unsafe, and even the tiniest village may harbor a murderer. Senator Goldwater was right in saying there is a crime problem (that's the truth of his half-truth), but he was wrong in saying there is not also a gun problem.

Surely the homicide rate would markedly decrease if handguns were outlawed. The FBI reports that more than 60 percent of all murders are caused by guns, and handguns are involved in more than 70 percent of these. Surely many, even most, of these handgun killings would not occur if the killer had to use a rifle, club, or knife. Of course violent lovers, angry drunks, and deranged employees would still flail out with knives or baseball bats, but some of their victims would be able to run away, with few or no injuries, and most of those who could not run away would nevertheless survive, badly injured but at least alive. But if handguns are

5

outlawed, we are told, responsible citizens will have no way to protect themselves from criminals. First, one should remember that at least 90 percent of America's burglaries are committed when no one is at home. The householder's gun, if he or she has one, is in a drawer of the bedside table, and the gun gets lifted along with the jewelry, adding one more gun to the estimated 100,000 handguns annually stolen from law-abiding citizens. (See Shields, *Guns Don't Die — People Do,* 1981.) Second, if the householder is at home, and attempts to use the gun, he or she is more likely to get killed or wounded than to kill or deter the intruder. Another way of looking at this last point is to recall that for every burglar who is halted by the sight of a handgun, four innocent people are killed by handgun accidents.

Because handguns are not accurate beyond ten or fifteen feet, they are not the weapons of sportsmen. Their sole purpose is to kill or at least to disable a person at close range. But only a minority of persons killed with these weapons are criminals. Since handguns chiefly destroy the innocent, they must be outlawed — not simply controlled more strictly, but outlawed — to all except to law-enforcement officials. Attempts to control handguns are costly and ineffective, but even if they were cheap and effective stricter controls would not take handguns out of circulation among criminals, because licensed guns are stolen from homeowners and shopkeepers, and thus fall into criminal hands. According to Wright, Rossi, and Daly (in *Under the Gun,* 1983), about 40 percent of the handguns used in crimes are stolen, chiefly from homes that the guns were supposed to protect.

The National Rifle Association is fond of quoting a University of Wisconsin study that says, "gun control laws have no individual or collective effect in reducing the rate of violent crime" (cited in Smith, 1981, p. 17). Agreed — but what if handguns were not available? What if the manufacturer of handguns is severely regulated, and if the guns may be sold only to police officers? True, even if handguns are outlawed, some criminals will manage to get them, but surely fewer petty criminals will have guns. It is simply untrue for the gun lobby to assert that all criminals — since they are by definition lawbreakers — will find ways to get handguns. For the most part, if the sale of handguns is outlawed, guns won't be available, and fewer criminals will have guns. And if fewer criminals have guns, there is every reason to believe that violent crime will decline. A youth armed only with a knife is less likely to try to rob a store than if he is armed with a gun. This commonsense reasoning does not imply that if handguns are outlawed crime will suddenly disappear, or even that an especially repulsive crime such as rape will decrease markedly. A rapist armed with a knife probably has a sufficient weapon. But *some* violent crime will almost surely decrease. And the decrease will probably be significant if in addition to outlawing handguns, severe mandatory punishments are imposed on a person who is found to possess one, and even severer mandatory punishments are imposed on a person who uses one while committing a crime. Again, none of this activity will solve "the crime problem," but neither will anything else, including the "get tough with criminals" attitude of Senator Goldwater. And of course any attempt to reduce crime (one cannot realistically talk of "solving" the crime problem) will have to pay attention to our systems of bail, plea bargaining, and parole, but outlawing handguns will help.

What will the cost be? First, to take "cost" in its most literal sense, there will be the cost of reimbursing gun owners for the weapons they surrender. Every owner of a handgun ought to be paid the fair market value of the weapon. Since the number of handguns is estimated to be between fifty million and ninety million, the cost will be considerable, but it will be far less than the costs — both in money and in sorrow — that result from deaths due to handguns.

Second, one may well ask if there is another sort of cost, a cost to our liberty, to our constitutional rights. The issue is important, and persons who advocate abolition of handguns are blind or thoughtless if they simply brush it off. On the other hand, opponents of gun control do all of us a disservice by insisting over and over that the Constitution guarantees "the right to bear arms." The Second Amendment in the Bill of Rights says this: "A well-regulated militia being necessary to the security of a free State, the right of the people to keep and bear arms shall not be infringed." It is true that the founding fathers, mindful of the British attempt to disarm the colonists, viewed the presence of "a well-regulated militia" as a safeguard of democracy. Their intention is quite clear, even to one who has not read Stephen P. Halbrook's *That Every Man Be Armed,* an exhaustive argument in favor of the right to bear arms. There can be no doubt that the framers of the Constitution and the Bill of Rights believed that armed insurrection was a justifiable means of countering oppression and tyranny. The Second Amendment may be fairly paraphrased thus: "*Because* an organized militia is necessary to the security of the State, the people have the right to possess weapons." But the owners of handguns are not members of a well-regulated militia. Furthermore, nothing in the proposal to ban handguns would deprive citizens of their rifles or other long-arm guns. All handguns, however, even large ones, should be banned. "Let's face it," Guenther W. Bachmann (a vice president of Smith and Wesson) admits, "they are all concealable." In any case, it is a fact that when gun control laws have been tested in the courts, they have been found to be constitutional. The constitutional argument was worth making, but the question must now be regarded as settled, not only by the courts but by anyone who reads the Second Amendment.

Still, is it not true that "If guns are outlawed, only outlaws will have guns"? This is yet another powerful slogan, but it is simply not true. First, we are talking not about "guns" but about handguns. Second, the police will have guns — handguns and others — and these trained professionals are 10 the ones on whom we must rely for protection against criminals. Of course the police have not eradicated crime; and of course we must hope that in the future they will be more successful in protecting all citizens. But we must also recognize that the efforts of private citizens to protect themselves with handguns has chiefly taken the lives not of criminals but of innocent people.

The Responsive Reader

1. Where does Desuka take her stand on this controverted issue? How is her stance similar to or different from other positions on this issue that you know?
2. Desuka uses the "Yes, but" technique — taking in carefully what other people have to say, agreeing with them in part, but then trying to show that their arguments are only half-truths. What slogans does she take on that often cloud this issue? How does she deal with them?
3. On an issue where emotions often drown out rational argument, Desuka makes a special effort to show that she is well informed. Where and how does she use authoritative sources? How does she use and interpret statistics? Do you interpret them the same way?
4. How does Desuka deal with the "constitutional argument"? How does she make you reread the language of the Second Amendment?

Talking, Listening, Writing

5. What for you are Desuka's strongest arguments? Which seem to you weakest? (Where is she most persuasive, where least?)
6. What do you know about the National Rifle Association? Where and how does this author take on the NRA? With what success?
7. Do you think there are other more effective ways to support gun control? Are there precedents of successful gun control initiatives?
8. Write a "Yes, but" reply to Desuka's arguments.

Projects

9. Collaborating with others, you may want to study news reports in your area over a period of time to determine the role different kinds of firearms play in local crime.

SHOOTING HOLES IN GUN LAWS
Mike Royko

> *Mike Royko is a Chicago columnist whose writing about his city has won him a large following. He prides himself on dealing in a blunt no-nonsense style with drugs, muggings, and other civic ills. He wrote this column when the increasing use of automatic weapons by drug dealers and youth gangs was reopening the debate about the need for controls vs. the right to bear arms.*

Thought Starters: Is there anything new in the following column? Or does the columnist put a familiar issue in a new light?

It was just a short news story, tucked away in the back pages, but it caused me to slightly alter my views on gun control laws. 1

The story was about a young woman who lives on the South Side of Chicago. A few nights ago, she was waiting for a bus. She had been visiting a friend, and it was after midnight.

Instead of a bus, a car pulled up. A man got out. He was holding a knife. He told the woman to get into the car or he would cut her. She got into the car. The man drove to an alley and spent the next two hours raping her.

Then he drove her a few blocks from her home and dumped her out of the car. She began walking home, intending to call the police.

But before she got home, another man walked up to her. He, too, 5 had a knife. He walked her to an abandoned building, where he raped her. After he finally let her go, she made it to a friend's house, the police were called, and she was hospitalized.

Now, we've all heard of gang rapes, and of women being held prisoner and raped by whichever two-legged animal happens to wander along.

But this is the first case I've come across of a woman being yanked off the street and raped by two different men within a matter of hours.

So what does this have to do with my views on gun controls?

If that woman had a pistol in her purse or coat pocket, knew how to use it, and was alert to danger, it's doubtful that the first rapist would have been able to get her into his car.

As soon as he got out of his car and approached her with his knife, 10 she could have had the gun out, pointed it at his chest, and said something like: "Go away or die." My guess is that his libido would have quickly cooled. But if it didn't, he would have had a new hole in his anatomy.

Of course, if the woman had a gun in her purse, she would have been violating the law that forbids carrying a concealed weapon. That's a part of the gun laws that I think should be changed.

I still believe all guns should be registered. I'm against the selling of the mini-machine guns that allow deranged people to blow away kids in schoolyards or their former co-workers. I also believe in cooling-off periods before guns are sold and background checks of those who want to buy guns.

But I think the law concerning carrying a concealed weapon should be amended so that a woman who has no serious criminal background or history of mental disorders and lives or works in or near a high-crime area of a city should be able to legally tote a pistol in her purse or pocket.

As long as gun ownership is legal in our society, it doesn't make much sense that I should be able to keep a couple of fully loaded pump-action shotguns in my home, but a woman on a dark street in a dangerous neighborhood is forbidden by law to carry a pistol in her purse.

Who is in greater danger? Me, with my doors double-locked, my 15 dog and my shotguns? Or a woman in a neighborhood where rape and other assaults are almost as common as church pancake parties in small towns?

I'm not saying that a gun in a purse would put an end to all of it. But I don't doubt that after a few mugs suddenly find they have an extra navel, those of similar inclinations might ponder what that lady coming down the street might have in her purse.

Of course, I don't really expect the gun laws to be changed to permit women to protect themselves.

So I have another suggestion for females. Get a gun and carry it in your purse anyway. If you put a hole in some thug who pops out of a doorway or a car with a knife, I doubt if a judge will do more than deliver a lecture.

These days, there's always a good chance that the same judge put the guy with the knife back out on the street in the first place.

The Responsive Reader

1. Like other columnists, Royko often builds a column around a provocative current news story. How does he use the story on which this column is based? Do you agree with his discussion and his conclusions? Would you accept his advice?

Talking, Listening, Writing

2. What do you think of citizens arming themselves in self-defense? Do you think they have the right to use their guns? In what situations?

3. Write a letter to the editor in support of or in rebuttal of Royko's column.

4. For a student newspaper, write a column that discusses a current news story involving violence and tries to spell out the lessons to be learned from it.

Projects

5. For further reading, you may want to study the role violence plays in the columns of one widely read columnist, such as George Will, Mike Royko, Ellen Goodman, Anna Quindlen, or a widely read local writer. Check a series or a sampling of columns spread over a period of several months. Do you find recurrent themes or often repeated arguments? How influential do you think are the columnist's opinions or advice?

Thinking about Connections

In writing about gun control, do Desuka and Royko share any common assumptions or commitments? Where is their basic disagreement? Which of the two do you find more persuasive?

RAPE AND THE BOXING RING

Joyce Carol Oates

> *Joyce Carol Oates is a prolific and provocative novelist and writer of short stories who has published at least forty books. In stories like "Stalking" (p. 113) she shows an uncanny sense of what ails people in our materialistic, soulless modern society. In the following article, she focuses on the kind of media event that, for a time, brings a simmering social issue to a boil. Mike Tyson, the former heavyweight champion with a previous reputation for abusing women, was charged with rape by an eighteen-year-old beauty pageant contestant and convicted.*

Thought Starters: Is there any connection between the cult of violence perpetuated by our media or American sports and the prevalence of rape and violence directed against women in our society?

Mike Tyson's conviction on rape charges in Indianapolis was a minor tragedy for the beleaguered sport of boxing, but a considerable triumph for women's rights. For once, though bookmakers were giving 5-1 odds that Tyson would be acquitted, and the mood of the country seemed distinctly conservative, a jury resisted the outrageous defense that a rape victim is to be blamed for her own predicament. For once, a celebrity with enormous financial resources did not escape trial and a criminal conviction by settling with his accuser out of court.

That boxing and "women's rights" should be perceived as opposed is symbolically appropriate, since of all sports, boxing is the most aggressively masculine, the very soul of war in microcosm. Elemental and dramatically concise, it raises to an art the passions underlying direct human aggression; its fundamentally murderous intent is not obscured by the pursuit of balls or pucks, nor can the participants expect help from teammates. In a civilized, humanitarian society, one would expect such a blood sport to have died out, yet boxing, sponsored by gambling casinos in Las Vegas and Atlantic City, and broadcast by cable television, flourishes: had the current heavyweight champion, Evander Holyfield, fought Mike Tyson in a title defense, Holyfield would have earned no less than $30 million. If Tyson were still champion, and still fighting, he would be earning more.

The paradox of boxing is that it so excessively rewards men for inflicting injury upon one another that, outside the ring, with less "art," would be punishable as aggravated assault, or manslaughter. Boxing belongs to that species of mysterious masculine activity for which anthropologists use such terms as "deep play": activity that is wholly without utilitarian value, in fact contrary to utilitarian value, so dangerous that no amount of money can justify it. Sports-car racing, stunt flying, mountain climbing, bullfighting, dueling — these activities, through history, have provided ways in which the individual can dramatically, if sometimes fatally, distinguish himself from the crowd, usually with the adulation and envy of the crowd, and traditionally, the love of women. Women — in essence, Woman — is the prize, usually self-proffered. To look upon organized sports as a continuum of Darwinian theory — in which the sports-star hero flaunts the superiority of his genes — is to see how displays of masculine aggression have their sexual component, as ingrained in human beings as any instinct for self-preservation and reproduction. In a capitalist society, the secret is to capitalize upon instinct.

Yet even within the very special world of sports, boxing is distinct. Is there any athlete, however celebrated in his own sport, who would not rather reign as the heavyweight champion of the world? If, in fantasy at least, he could be another Muhammad Ali, or Joe Louis, or indeed, Mike Tyson in his prime? Boxing celebrates the individual man in his maleness, not merely in his skill as an athlete — though boxing demands enormous skill, and its training is far more arduous than most men could endure for more than a day or two. All athletes can become addicted to their own adrenaline, but none more obviously than the boxer, who, like Sugar Ray Leonard, already a multimillionaire with numerous occupations outside the ring, will risk serious injury by coming back out of retirement; as Mike Tyson has said, "Outside of boxing, everything is so boring." What makes boxing repulsive to many observers is precisely what makes boxing so fascinating to participants.

Blood sacrifice: This is because it is a highly organized ritual that   5
violates taboo. It flouts such moral prescriptions as "Thou shalt not kill." It celebrates, not meekness, but flamboyant aggression. No one who has not seen live boxing matches (in contrast to the sanitized matches broadcast over television) can quite grasp its eerie fascination — the spectator's sense that he or she is a witness to madness, yet a madness sanctioned by tradition and custom, as finely honed by certain celebrated practitioners as an artist's performance at the highest level of genius, and, yet more disturbing, immensely gratifying to the audience. Boxing mimics our early ancestors' rite of bloody sacrifice and redemption; it excites desires most civilized men and women find abhorrent. For some observers, it is frankly obscene, like pornography; yet, unlike pornography, it is not fantasy but real, thus far more subversive.

The paradox for the boxer is that, in the ring, he experiences himself as a living conduit for the inchoate, demonic will of the crowd: the expression of their collective desire, which is to pound another human being into absolute submission. The more vicious the boxer, the greater the acclaim. And the financial reward — Tyson is reported to have earned $100 million. (He who at the age of 13 was plucked from a boys' school for juvenile delinquents in upstate New York.) Like the champion gladiators of Roman decadence, he will be both honored and despised, for, no matter his celebrity, and the gift of his talent, his energies spring from the violation of taboo and he himself is tainted by it.

Mike Tyson has said that he does not think of boxing as a sport. He sees himself as a fantasy gladiator who, by "destructing" opponents, enacts others' fantasies in his own being. That the majority of these others are well-to-do whites who would themselves crumple at a first blow, and would surely claim a pious humanitarianism, would not go unnoted by so wary and watchful a man. Cynicism is not an inevitable consequence of success, but it is difficult to retain one's boyish naiveté in the company of the sort of people, among them the notorious Don King, who have surrounded Tyson since 1988, when his comanager, Jim Jacobs, died. As Floyd Patterson, an ex-heavyweight champion who has led an exemplary life, has said, "When you have millions of dollars, you have millions of friends."

It should not be charged against boxing that Mike Tyson *is* boxing in any way. Boxers tend to be fiercely individualistic, and Tyson is, at the least, an enigma. He began his career, under the tutelage of the legendary trainer Cus D'Amato, as a strategist, in the mode of such brilliant technicians as Henry Armstrong and Sugar Ray Robinson. He was always aware of a lineage with Jack Dempsey, arguably the most electrifying of all heavyweight champions, whose nonstop aggression revolutionized the sport and whose shaved haircut and malevolent scowl, and, indeed, penchant for dirty fighting, made a tremendous impression upon the young Tyson.

In recent years, however, Tyson seems to have styled himself at least partly on the model of Charles (Sonny) Liston, the "baddest of the bad" black heavyweights. Liston had numerous arrests to his credit and served time in prison (for assaulting a policeman); he had the air, not entirely contrived, of a sociopath; he was always friendly with racketeers, and died of a drug overdose that may in fact have been murder. (It is not coincidental that Don King, whom Tyson has much admired, and whom Tyson has empowered to ruin his career, was convicted of manslaughter and served time in an Ohio prison.) Like Liston, Tyson has grown to take a cynical pleasure in publicly condoned sadism (his "revenge" bout with Tyrell Biggs, whom he carried for seven long rounds in order to inflict maximum damage) and in playing the outlaw; his contempt for women, escalating in recent years, is a part of that guise. The witty obscenity of a prefight taunt of Tyson's — "I'll make you into my girlfriend" — is the boast of the rapist.

Perhaps rape itself is a gesture, a violent repudiation of the female, *10* in the assertion of maleness that would seem to require nothing beyond physical gratification of the crudest kind. The supreme macho gesture — like knocking out an opponent and standing over his fallen body, gloves raised in triumph.

In boxing circles it is said — this, with an affectionate sort of humor — that the heavyweight champion is the 300-pound gorilla who sits anywhere in the room he wants; and, presumably, takes any female he wants. Such a grandiose sense of entitlement, fueled by the insecurities and emotions of adolescence, can have disastrous consequences. Where once it was believed that Mike Tyson might mature into the greatest heavyweight of all time, breaking Rocky Marciano's record of 49 victories and no defeats, it was generally acknowledged that, since his defeat of Michael Spinks in 1988, he had allowed his boxing skills to deteriorate. Not simply his ignominious loss of his title to the mediocre James (Buster) Douglas in 1990, but subsequent lackluster victories against mediocre opponents made it clear that Tyson was no longer a serious, nor even very interesting, boxer.

The dazzling reflexes were dulled, the shrewd defensive skills drilled into him by D'Amato were largely abandoned: Tyson emerged suddenly as a conventional heavyweight like Gerry Cooney, who advances upon his opponent with the hope of knocking him out with a single punch — and does not always succeed. By 25, Tyson seemed already middle aged, burnt out. He would have no great fights after all. So, strangely, he seemed to invite his fate outside the ring, with sadomasochistic persistence, testing the limits of his celebrity's license to offend by ever-escalating acts of aggression and sexual effrontery.

The familiar sports adage is surely true, one's ultimate opponent is oneself.

It may be objected that these remarks center upon the rapist, and not his victim; that sympathy, pity, even in some quarters moral outrage flow to the criminal and not the person he has violated. In this case, ironically, the victim, Desiree Washington, though she will surely bear psychic scars through her life, has emerged as a victor, a heroine: a young woman whose traumatic experience has been, as so few traumas can be, the vehicle for a courageous and selfless stand against the sexual abuse of women and children in America. She seems to know that herself, telling *People* magazine, "It was the right thing to do." She was fortunate in drawing a jury who rejected classic defense ploys by blaming the victim and/or arguing consent. Our criminal-justice system being what it is, she was lucky. Tyson, who might have been acquitted elsewhere in the country, was unlucky.

'Poor guy': Whom to blame for this most recent of sports disgraces   *15* in America? The culture that flings young athletes like Tyson up out of obscurity, makes millionaires of them and watches them self-destruct? Promoters like Don King and Bob Arum? Celebrity hunters like Robin Givens, Tyson's ex-wife, who seemed to have exploited him for his money and as a means of promoting her own acting career? The indulgence generally granted star athletes when they behave recklessly? When they abuse drugs and alcohol, and mistreat women?

I suggest that no one is to blame, finally, except the perpetrator himself. In Montieth Illingworth's cogently argued biography of Tyson, "Mike Tyson: Money, Myth and Betrayal," Tyson is quoted, after one or another public debacle: "People say 'Poor guy.' That insults me. I despise sympathy. So I screwed up. I made some mistakes. 'Poor guy,' like I'm some victim. There's nothing poor about me."

The Responsive Reader

1. What, for Oates, makes boxing an outstanding fitting symbol for the masculine drive toward aggression and war? What, in her view, are similar symbolic sports? What to her is the "sexual component" in these and similar sports?
2. How does the ritual of boxing violate basic taboos? What is the relationship between the boxer and the crowd?
3. What, to Oates, is the connection between boxing and rape?
4. What, to Oates, were the causes of Tyson's decline as a champion? How does she explain the connection between his decline as a boxer and his behavior outside the ring?
5. How does Oates relate to Tyson's victim? How does she explain the outcome of the trial?
6. How does Oates deal with the question of blame? Does she see extenuating circumstances in Tyson's background? Does she consider the role of society, of his handlers, or of the women in his life?

Talking, Listening, Writing

7. Is Oates prejudiced against boxers generally? Or is Tyson for her a special case? (Does she show an understanding or appreciation of the sport?)
8. Does Oates anywhere raise the question of race? (Does it matter to her that both the champion and the victim were African American? Should it have mattered to her?)
9. Do you think this article promotes an adversarial relationship between men and women, encouraging hostility between the sexes?
10. Do you think violent sports should be blamed for contributing to the prevalence of violence in American society?

Projects

11. Is it true that there has been a shift in the assumptions and procedures that help determine the outcome of rape trials? Working with others, you may want to investigate the situation in courts in your area or state. Try to talk to lawyers, victims, suspects, journalists, social workers, or others in a position to know.

Thinking about Connections

What is the connection between Oates' analysis of boxing and rape and the discussion of violence in Gloria Steinem's "Erotica and Pornography" (p. 426)?

A DOSE OF DISCIPLINE FOR FIRST OFFENDERS

Joseph L. Kane

The following article demonstrates a newsmagazine format that Time *magazine perfected long ago. A new way of trying to deal with young criminals is treated* Timestyle: *The article zeros in on a news development that is striking, provocative, or thought-provoking — and can therefore be dramatized or jazzed up. Early in the article, there is a handle, a striking phrase or slogan ("shock incarceration," in this instance). The early paragraphs provide a snappy capsule account of the phenomenon. Some striking firsthand examples and quotes from people in the know give the article an "insider's" feel. There is a conscientious attempt to balance the pro and con, as both advocates and skeptics have their say. There is a reasonable (and safe) conclusion that allows the magazine to rise above partisanship and the heat of controversy.*

Thought Starters: What makes the issue raised in this article timely? What answer does the writer give to what he calls the big question: "Does any of this work?" How effective is the writer in getting you interested in the topic? Do you agree with his conclusion?

Time was when what used to be called juvenile delinquents were offered a stark choice: join the service or go to jail. A dose of military discipline was supposed to make a man out of a boy and set him on the path to respectable citizenship. But the all-volunteer armed forces eliminated that option for what are now called youthful offenders. In a growing number of states, however, the purported benefits of paramilitary discipline are being showered on young criminals through programs known as "shock incarceration."

Nine states have such programs, and 30 more are considering them. Usually the programs fence off parts of state prisons into "boot camps," where 17-to-25-year-old first offenders convicted of drug or property crimes are held for three to six months. Between head shaving, close-order drills and servile work, the youthful felons are screamed and hollered at by correctional officers skilled in the art of humiliation. They are compelled to rise at dawn, eat meals in silence, speak only when spoken to ("Sir, yessir"). The hope is that the rough treatment they experience will produce a permanent "change of attitude" that will survive after the inmates are released.

A typical boot camp is the Al Burruss Correctional Training Center in Forsyth, Ga., where 150 inmates are housed in two-level, spartan, modern facilities. A scene one recent morning: correctional officer Eddie Cash greets burglar Robert Parker and three other new inmates with a stream of profane abuse.

"Let's get something straight right now, chumps. Anything you do in the next 90 days must go through me," shouts Cash, from a distance of no more than four inches from Parker's ear. "I am God around here, and I am going to see to it that none of you ever gets out of here. You've got a problem with me. I am a certified psycho. I hate this job, and I hate you. I got too much responsibility for a psycho." The tirade continues. "You're in here for burglary," he shrieks at Parker. "You are stupid, you know that? I wish it had been my house. You'd be pushing daisies right now. You don't want to tick me off 'cause I'll snatch your head off and shove it down your throat."

By now Cash is soaking with sweat and stomping the floor. His neck   5
veins are popping and his eyes are bulging as he works his way from inmate to inmate, delivering a series of blistering, nose-to-nose tongue-lashings. At the end of Cash's 45-minute outburst, the frightened inmates run right out of their shoes into a dressing room — and another bout of humiliation. As if on cue, an aide shows up with electric clippers and shaves the young men's heads. The inmates then strip naked, and an assistant sprays them with delousing fluid. All the while, Cash keeps up his string of personal insults.

The new inmates soon become immersed in the boot-camp routine. The day begins at 5 A.M., when correctional officer Robert Richards mashes down on a bank of toggle switches, unlocking the cell doors. "On line, on line, let's go!" he shouts, as bleary-eyed inmates appear at attention in the doorways. Then there is cell clean-up, a shower and marching off to breakfast. Any inmate who deviates even slightly from the prescribed regimentation is ordered to drop to the ground and "give me 50" — meaning 50 push-ups.

The remainder of the day is filled with menial labor: whacking weeds, swabbing floors, painting walls, marching in formation. As they half-step, an officer asks, "What is the word for the day?" The platoon answers, "Self-discipline. We like it. We love it. We want more of it, sir!" At 10 P.M., it is lights out.

"We really don't want to show them any respect," says Cash as one platoon trudges by. "Why should we? They are criminals. Most dropped out of the tenth grade. They come to us and then go back to their old environment. The inmate will be in that environment longer than he will be with us. This program is definitely worth having unless I see a better way. It is better than warehousing them and teaching them to be better criminals."

The big question is, Does any of this work? In Georgia, where boot camps were invented in 1983, boosters claim that it costs only $3,400 to house and revamp one inmate in 90 days, in contrast to the $15,000 annual bill for housing a prisoner in the state penitentiary. Boot camps provide one unquestioned benefit: they get the youthful offenders off the street and give them a taste of the debasement of prison life while offering them a startling "one last chance" to straighten out.

But in Georgia, experts say 35% of boot-camp graduates are back in   *10* prison within three years, roughly the same rate as for those paroled from the general prison population. Blitzing young people into acceptable be- havior through terror has been tried before and has failed. Ohio experi- mented with "shock probation" in 1965, sentencing first offenders to the penitentiary for 90 days. The disastrous results were indolence, sodomy and violence. Prisoners at the East Jersey State Prison in Rahway played real-life roles in which they confronted juvenile offenders on probation to demonstrate the violence behind the walls. Subsequent studies by Rutgers University showed that the 1978 film *Scared Straight* frightened the lesser punks into proper living, but the more sophisticated toughs came to view the inmates as role models.

The inherent fault with such scare tactics, says David C. Evans, Georgia's commissioner of corrections, is expecting too much from them. Says he: "Too many middle-class whites see it as the answer, a panacea." But with minimal counseling or after-shock guidance, the boot-camp experience "is just a car wash for criminals who are supposed to be cleansed for life," says Pat Gilliard, executive director of the Clearing- house on Georgia Prisons and Jails. Edward J. Loughran, commissioner of the department of youth services in Massachusetts, dismisses the whole idea of shock therapy because "you cannot undo 15 to 17 years of a life of abuse by barking into a kid's face and having him do push-ups."

Drug czar Bennett agrees with those correctional officers who be- lieve shock incarceration is no cure-all for street crime, though it can help "build character." It seems to have the most effect on nonviolent young men for whom crime has not become a hardened way of life. The program appears to work best for youngsters who might have been helped just as much by a resolute kick in the pants and some productive community service and victim reparation. Perhaps that is a more realistic way of coping with the burgeoning problem of youthful crime.

The Responsive Reader

1. What would you include in a capsule description of "shock incarcer- ation"? What are key features or striking details? (What struck or impressed you most in this article?)

2. How does this article present the pro and con? What are the arguments in favor of the program? What counterarguments are cited after the *but* that provides the turning point of the article?
3. The writer leads up to a conclusion that he expects reasonable readers to accept. Do you agree with him? Why or why not?

Talking, Listening, Writing

4. What has shaped your own thinking on this topic? What firsthand observation or experience, if any, has shaped your views of first offenders, young criminals, or their treatment by the justice system?
5. As an oral presentation or in writing, present a proposal for dealing with young offenders. Present a plea for one of the alternatives examined in this article or for one *not* included.
6. Write an imaginary letter to the authorities from one of the young people in a "shock incarceration" program.

Projects

7. What is the local system for dealing with young people in trouble with the law? For one of several possible research projects related to issues in this chapter, you may choose to work with classmates to examine the juvenile justice system in your local jurisdiction. How accessible are the people in charge, lawyers or public defenders, offenders and their families, victims of juvenile crime?

TOUR OF DUTY

Larry Heinemann

> *The Vietnam War was a traumatic chapter in this country's history. It*
> *shaped the outlook of a generation of Americans — whether they were actually*
> *sent to Vietnam or whether they joined the growing antiwar protest at home.*
> *In the following essay, a Vietnam War veteran writes as an eyewitness who*
> *shared the "blunt and heartfelt bitterness" of those who felt they "had been*
> *lied to and used by arrogant and selfish men." Prize-winning author Larry*
> *Heinemann was born in Chicago in 1944. He graduated from Columbia*
> *College and later came back there to teach writing. He said almost twenty*
> *years after the war, "I have been thinking and talking and reading about the*
> *war since I got back in 1968." He had served as a sergeant in the infantry,*
> *and he published his novel,* Close Quarters, *based on his experience, in*
> *1977. In the following excerpt from an article first published in 1985, he*
> *reported on his interviews with other veterans. When he published this article,*
> *he said, "Tens of thousands of GIs got chewed up in Vietnam, and there are*
> *tens of thousands on whom the war still chews."*

Thought Starters: Is the Vietnam War ancient history for the current
generation of young Americans? What ideas, assumptions, or memories
do you as a reader bring to the subject? How much do you learn from this
eyewitness account about "how it was"?

During World War I, the Allied military, and the British especially,   *1*
weren't interested in attributing the soldiers' responses to battle and butch-
ery to any unmanly newfangled psychological or emotional causes.
Rather, it was believed that the very shock, the concussion, from an artil-
lery round had an irresistible effect upon the body itself. "Shell shock"
seemed a perfectly reasonable explanation for what happened to the men
in the trenches.

During World War II, the troops suffered "combat fatigue" — the
boys were just tired. World War II veterans did not escape the effects
associated with delayed stress. The psychiatric casualties were 300 percent
higher in the early years of World War II than in World War I. But the way
soldiers fought in World War II, and the way they stopped fighting after
it, were different from what happened in Vietnam — and this difference
would prove crucial. During World War II, a unit trained together and
shipped overseas together. You humped North Africa, Italy and Sicily,
then France and Germany, or you island-hopped from Tarawa and Guadal-
canal and Peleliu to Iwo Jima and Okinawa. You were in for the duration,
as the saying went. After the war, waiting to be shipped home, you had

time to share the sympathetic support of men with whom you had a particular intimacy not often permitted in this culture. (It wasn't "buddies," the dead-flat, shopworn newspaper cliché that trivialized a complex and powerful relationship. "Buddy-up" was something you did at Boy Scout camp, when everyone would mosey down to the lake for a swim. Boy Scout camp may be many things, but it ain't the straight-leg, ground-pounding infantry.)

Waiting, you got to work some of the war out of your system; to release the grief for men long dead; to feel keenly, perhaps for the first time, your survivor's guilt; to feel as well the sharp personal guilt for murdering prisoners, say, or for shelling villages good and hard that you later discovered were filled with women and children, or for firebombing Dresden; to recognize the delight you took in destruction (what the Bible calls "lust of the eye") and the warm, grim satisfaction of your firm and bitter anger. Waiting, you had time for crying jags, public and private; you had time for fistfights to settle old scores once and for all. By the time your ship docked, you had worked much of the stress out of your system, though the annual depressions (usually coinciding with anniversaries), the periodic screaming, thrashing nightmares (vivid and colorful recollections of the worst times of your life), and the rest would linger for years — delayed stress (though no one yet called it by that name) a permanent fixture in your life.

In the Vietnam War, everyone served a one-year tour — the assumption being that any dipstick could keep his buttons buttoned *that* long — though you could volunteer to stay as long as you liked. (United States Marine Corps esprit dictated that every Marine would serve one year and one month. *Semper Fi,* Mac.) But the one-year tour created a reverberating and lingering turmoil of emotional problems unlike anything known after World War II.

Vietnam was a war of individuals. You went through Basic Training 5 with one group, Advanced Individual Training with another. You shipped overseas with a planeload of total strangers, and when you reached your outfit — a rifle company out in the middle of nowhere, say — the astonishment on your face and the bright sheen of your uniform pegged you as a 'cruit, the newbee, the fucking new guy.

You have never seen those people before in your life. Everyone avoids you (dumb guys never last, we used to say). At the very least, you have replaced a highly experienced and valuable man whose tour was up. He was as smooth as silk when he took the point, and no John Wayne. You, on the other hand, have hardly seen an M-16 and do not know your ass from a hole in the ground. The heat and humidity are withering, and you're so exhausted by ten in the morning, pouring sweat, that when they call a break in place you can't even stand up to piss.

As you begin your tour, the short-timers finish theirs, mount their choppers and leave, and are never heard from again; other FNGs arrive.

Your first firefight is a bloody, nasty mess, and it is a pure wonder you are not killed. Slowly you become accustomed to the weather and the work — the *grinding,* backbreaking humps, the going over the same ground day in and day out, aboard choppers and on foot. More short-timers leave; more FNGs arrive. This is the ugliest, most grueling, and most spiritless work you have ever done. But you soon discover you're a pretty good tunnel rat or booby-trap man, or especially canny and efficient on night ambush. You come to know the ground around your base camp and firebases like the back of your hand. In camp, on standdown, you smoke dope in earnest; you drink like a fish; you party with a serious frenzy.

More short-timers leave; more FNGs arrive. With every firefight the men around you drop like flies. You endure jungle rot, heat exhaustion, crabs and head lice, and an endless diarrhea from the one-a-day malaria pills. You take your five-day R&R in Bangkok, a culinary and sexual rampage. When you get back to the field more short-timers have disappeared; more FNGs have replaced them. You are sprayed with Agent Orange; the dust is in your hair, in your water, on your food. They send you to sharpshooter school; you return with an M-14 with scope and carrying case and a $500 pair of field glasses — the company sniper. You can draw a bead and drop a VC — man, woman, or child — in his tracks at 500 meters, and he never knows what hit him. You have many kills. More short-timers leave; more FNGs arrive. You are promoted to sergeant and made a squad leader. Your platoon leader, an ROTC first lieutenant, admires and trusts you: you will go anywhere and do anything. Humping is a snap, and you live in the midst of an alien ease.

The firefights and ambushes are bloody and nasty, businesslike massacres with meat all over everything. The one-year tour is the topic of endless conversation; you know exactly when your tour will end, and *that* is what keeps you going. You don't care about anything but finishing your tour — you just don't care.

Then one morning you wake up and it is finally your turn — not a day too soon, you understand. You say your goodbyes, hop in your chopper, and leave. You will never see or hear of these men again. The next morning you hitch a ride to the airfield in time to catch the plane to Saigon. You have hacked it, but you are exhausted. Your body is as tight as a drum. The plane finally comes: a Boeing 707. The replacements file off and you and your fellow passengers walk across the tarmac, and load up — a ritual unbelievably ordinary and benign.

On the plane you sit in a space both anonymous and claustrophobic, more glad and more guilty than tongue can tell. Sick, lame or lazy, blind, crippled or crazy — you just want out. The plane ride is nineteen hours of canned music and beach-blanket movies. At Oakland Army Terminal you're mustered out — given a bum's rush of a physical and a new baggy, smelly uniform, and issued your outstanding pay in greenback cash. You are free to go.

10

Your entire family meets you at the airport and takes you home to the house where you grew up. Yesterday or the day before you were surrounded by men who humped guns and grenades, up to their eyeballs in bloody murder (mean and evil sons-of-bitches, you bet). Now you're dumped into a maelstrom — walk/don't-walk lights, Levi's and daytime TV; mom and dad and the dog on the couch — that bears no relationship to anything you're accustomed to. You're with people who love you, but they don't have the faintest inkling how to help you. You want to sit and tell them what happened — what you saw, what you did, what you became — but more often than not they don't want to hear about it. Your father, a World War II Marine, perhaps, shrugs his shoulders and, struggling with his own residual delayed stress, says, Everybody did those things, grow up, forget it (it's all right). But you sit in that clean kitchen, smelling the eggs and bacon, and warming your hands on a cup of coffee, and it is not all right.

And no "validating" ritual — no parade or Vietnam War memorial — will make it so.

And make no mistake: if you have any healthy impulses left at all, you want to find a woman and take her to bed. Skip the date; skip the dinner; skip the movie. You want to feel good in your body and reestablish those powerful human feelings. Maybe you manage it, but just as likely you don't: some women refuse to date veterans, and then brag to them about it.

You get your old job back (it's the law) stocking shelves at the A&P. 15 The work is easy and dull, and the money's decent, but the petty harassment is galling. The boss doesn't want you around, the way you *stare* when the customers ask their endlessly stupid questions. You drift from job to job. Sometimes, as soon as you mention you're a veteran, the clerk behind the counter tells you to beat it; they don't need junkies and they don't need freaks.

You cannot concentrate. You begin having nightmares; you jerk out of sleep, pouring sweat. You drink to anesthetize yourself against the dreams and the daydream flashbacks (drunks don't dream very well). You try to stay up as long as you can. You know you will dream about the night you shivved that wounded VC who kept waving his hands in your face, shaking his head and whispering man to man, "No, no," while he squirmed against your knife with all his might.

You cannot stand crowds or people walking too close behind you. You discover an abrupt and furious temper; you startle into a crouch at the damnedest things. You become self-destructive, picking fights and driving your car crazily. There is the nagging thought that you didn't do enough, that you never should have left Vietnam. Everyone you came to trust has disappeared from your life, dead by now, for all you know. How does that make you feel? You withdraw into isolation. Why put up with the grief?

The Responsive Reader

1. Why does Heinemann start with a discussion of earlier wars? What essential contrasts is he setting up?
2. Heinemann sets out to make you understand veterans who felt misunderstood, stereotyped, or rejected. What is his major point or central thesis? Does he succeed in making you understand the way the veterans felt?
3. What are the major waystations or mileposts in the author's "tour of duty"?
4. What is the mix of personal experience and other sources in this essay?

Talking, Listening, Writing

5. Many people would prefer to forget the war experience and move on to the challenges of the present. Do you agree or disagree with them, and why?
6. How does Heinemann use slang or obscenities? Do you find his use of language offensive?
7. Write about a traumatic period in your life or in the life of someone close to you.
8. During and after the Vietnam War, there was much protest activity designed to keep army recruiters or ROTC units off campus. What arguments would you present to support or reject such initiatives?

Projects

9. How does our society treat its veterans? Working with a group, you may want to research one limited area of this larger subject. For instance, choose the treatment or reception of the veterans of the Gulf War; the story of the Vietnam War Memorial in Washington, D.C.; medical or counseling services for Vietnam veterans; the reception of American prisoners of war returning from Vietnam; or the treatment of Vietnam veterans in the media.

CAMBODIAN BOYS DON'T CRY

Rasmey Sam

Many Americans first came to this country as refugees. They fled from repression, revolution, famine, or war. They made it to a ship going to America barely ahead of the kaiser's or the tsar's police. Like the Irish during the great famine, they left a country in which there seemed to be no hope of freedom or even survival. They crossed a border to temporary safety before the Gestapo sealed off the last routes of escape. Like many of the boat people leaving Vietnam after the war, some perished in the attempt. Some were turned back, sometimes to prison or death. Some spent years in crowded refugee camps — unwanted, undesirable. Many others, finally, found sanctuary and a chance to start a new life. The student who wrote the following essay in a basic writing class in an American college is the survivor of the genocide in Cambodia, a small country in Southeast Asia that was nominally neutral during the Vietnam War. But the American government accused the Vietnamese Communists of using Cambodia as a staging area and conducted heavy bombing raids. When the Americans lost the war, the Cambodian Communist guerrillas, the Khmer Rouge, took over the country.

Thought Starters: How much do you already know about the "killing fields" of Cambodia? From the following account, what do you learn that you didn't know? How do you react to Rasmey Sam's story?

Cambodia is a small country that is about the size of the state of Missouri; it is a land of great contrasts. One still sees in the people and in their ways of living an awareness of an ancient heritage of greatness. Cambodians have pride in their language: pride in their music, dancing, visual arts, and pride in being Cambodian.

Cambodia came prominently to the attention of United States policy makers in the early 1970s, when the United States actively supported the noncommunist Lon Nol government against the communist Khmer Rouge regime. Cambodia again became an important issue after 1978, when the Soviet Union backed a Vietnamese invasion that toppled the Khmer Rouge regime.

I was a little boy eating some greasy chicken, on a dark, cloudy summer night when suddenly the air became calm and cool. The countryside was silent as if there were no people there. Some people were heading to their homes from a hard day of work. The breeze was starting to pick up and leaves were falling from the tall, healthy trees to the ground in my front yard. It seemed like the rain was coming toward our direction. It was only about six o'clock, but it seemed like almost midnight. The restless insects were starting to make extremely loud noises across the innocent, quiet villages. The insects seemed to cry horribly loud as the night went on. Maybe the insects were crying for the rain to come down, or maybe it was just something else. The clouds became thicker and thicker all over my house and the beautiful, small countryside. The wooden houses in the village were clustered together so as to help each other survive better. The houses had roofs made of dried palm tree leaves that were tied together to provide protection from rain. The sound of lightning was almost like the sound of guns shooting toward my house, while the white light flashed all over the villages. As I sat down on the rocker in front of my parents' house and gazed at the rice fields, I wondered what could possibly happen that night. The fields fascinated me. Low earthen dikes divided them into a pattern like irregular checkerboards, with paddies instead of squares, and trees rose here and there where dikes met. As I watched the darkness and the lightning, my imagination began to wonder about a ghost that I dreamed of the previous night. My body suddenly started to chill. Without wasting any more time, I got up and ran inside the house.

It was ten till eleven o'clock when, suddenly, a heavy sound exploded approximately a quarter of a mile away from my house. It seemed like my whole house was moving. I had never heard anything like this before. I was very curious to see what was going on out there. Since the filthy dogs started to bark and chickens cackled, the village seemed to become a jungle. Standing in front of the house, I immediately looked to my left, and, sure enough, there was a big fire flashing all over the village. It looked to me as if the village was on fire. While I stood there wondering what could possibly cause the fire to burn the village, there were two more bombs dropped right after one another as close as fifty yards away from my back yard. As I watched a small house of wood and palm trees, I noticed that part of its back was destroyed. As I stood alone in front of the house, the images of violence burned harder and harder. My heart started to pound. I was nervous and panicked through the whole event. The night of the countryside was filled with light and burning fire. The people were screaming for help. The bombs continually exploded while the sounds of the guns were so loud that my ears hurt. I began to cry for my parents, but I didn't remember where they were. Because of the sound of explosions, I was unable to hear my parents call me. Although all my family was inside the house, my parents were trying to find where I was. Somehow, I was running to my next door neighbor's house. In a short time, the village became a war zone. The airplanes, helicopter and tanks were all over the countryside. People were hit by bombs left and right. The bodies of my neighbors were lying all over their walkways. The moment the bombs were dropped, I could feel the ground move. Suddenly, a dark cloudy summer night became a lightning war zone. My father finally found me and took me inside the bomb shelter.

Two days later, the Cambodian communist government that called   5
itself the Khmer Rouge took over Cambodia. The war was finally ended
and many people were anguished to know about our new government.
The symbol of the red flag was rising everywhere. People were wondering
how this communist government was going to control people and the
country. The soldiers were everywhere, and everything seem confused.
As the people began to settle down and start their new lives, the Khmer
Rouge government forced people to go to work every day and every night.
They gave us very little food and there was nothing we could do about it.
Whenever we received a small amount of rice, we ate it gladly. Human
life had no meaning and people were treated like animals. Some people
couldn't work because they were hungry or sick. The Khmer Rouge
government punished them and shot them.

As I remember, on one cold winter season, the rains were constantly
dropping down every day and night. I was forced to stay in a boys home
that was almost falling apart. I was sick and hungry while lying down on
the wet dirt floor. No one was allowed to take care of me, not even my
parents. That didn't matter anyway, because I was separated from my
parents the day the Khmer Rouge took over the power. It was almost three
years since I saw my parents, but I could never forget. When the rainy
season brought its heavy storms, teams of men and women transplanted
the seedlings to the rest of the paddies. One day I was working behind a
skinny woman with long black hair, brown eyes and a black torn outfit. It
seemed as though the wind could easily have blown her away. She seemed
as if she was thinking of something that made her appear worried. She
turned around and looked straight into my eyes and said "Rasmey son." I
was confused and didn't realize it was my mother. I slowly looked up to
my mother's face and stood there with a somber smile—I didn't have any
word to say. I was shocked; my heart began to pound inside of me. My
tears started to drip down my sweaty face as fast as I could blink. My
skinny, skeleton-body became weaker and weaker from staring into her
crying eyes. Being a lonely boy who was standing in the mud that was
overcrowded with blood-sucking leeches, I could barely hold my body
straight up from excitement. I finally got to see my beloved mother whom
I had admired and respected for so long. I thought it was just a dream. But
either way, I am grateful to have a vivid picture of her in my mind. I didn't
want the Khmer Rouge to see, and I quickly walked away to another rice
field and continued to work.

I can't remember the day or month when one of the leaders of the
Khmer Rouge came and dragged me to work. I was so sick and hungry
that I didn't care what he would do to me. He kicked me while I was lying
down and pointed his gun toward my head and said "either you go to
work, or I'll shoot you right now." I had no choice but with my long
skeleton's body, I got up slowly and went to work with the rest of the
people.

During the next four years, three to four million innocent hard working people were murdered by the Khmer Rouge. Many houses, automobiles, trees and many more things were destroyed during the war under the Khmer Rouge's power. My father, grandfather, sister and many other close relatives were killed by the Khmer Rouge. The picture of one of the most beautiful countries in South East Asia became the jungle of the killing field. The skeletons and the bodies of the innocent human beings were lying all over the rice fields and the bushes. I found myself believing, for at least a few moments at a time, that the Khmer Rouge had done it, that the people of Cambodia had nothing left, except the memories of the most brutal, inhumane and senseless killings that ever happened; it will stay with them — forever.

It was a happy day when I learned that my mother, two brothers and one sister were still alive. The country was now under Vietnamese rule and my surviving family in no danger of being killed, since this new communist government was non-violent.

I am a student in Cal State San Bernardino, but nothing has shaped   10
my life as much as surviving the Khmer Rouge regime. I am a survivor of the Cambodian holocaust. That's who I am.

The Responsive Reader

1. Can you identify with the student telling this story? Why or why not?
2. How much does the writer reveal of his feelings? Do you think he is holding back some of what he thinks and feels?

Talking, Listening, Writing

3. When something defeats our attempts at understanding, we may give up and call it senseless or irrational. Is there any rational explanation for what happened to Rasmey's people?
4. People in the West have become jaded by reports of upheavals in distant countries and by the flood of refugees asking for asylum. Assuming your vote counted, would you have voted to admit people like Rasmey Sam to the United States? Why or why not?

Projects

5. Social scientists and psychologists have studied the physical and psychological scars of survivors of holocaust or genocide. For further reading, you may want to study the published testimony of survivors. (Or conduct some firsthand interviews if you can.) What do survivors remember? How do survivors cope? What do they want us to learn from their experience?

THE BUCK PRIVATE (*SOLDADO RAZO*)

Luis Valdez

> *If you can sing, dance, walk, march, hold a picket sign,*
> *play a guitar or harmonica or any other instrument, you can*
> *participate! No acting experience required.*
> — *from a recruiting leaflet for the* Teatro Campesino

Luis Valdez (born 1940) founded the Teatro Campesino, *which has been honored in both the United States and Europe. (A* campesino *is someone who works in the fields.) Valdez himself was working in the fields by the time he was six years old, with the much interrupted schooling of the children of America's migrant workers. He eventually accepted a scholarship at San Jose State University and graduated with a B.A. in English in 1964. The theater group that Valdez founded in 1965 began by performing* actos — *short, one-act plays — in community centers, church halls, and in the fields in California. Under his leadership, the* Teatro Campesino *explored the lives of urban Chicano youth, Mexican Indian legend and mythology, and materials from Third World sources. At the beginning of his play* Los Vendidos (The Sellouts, *1967), a secretary from the governor's office comes to Honest Sancho's Used Mexican lot to look for a suave, not-too-dark Chicano to become a token Mexican American at social functions in the state capital. In 1987, Valdez wrote and directed the movie* La Bamba, *a biography of the Chicano rock 'n' roll singer Ritchie Valens. His PBS production of* Corridos: Tales of Passion and Revolution, *with Linda Ronstadt, won the Peabody Award.* Soldado razo, *or* The Buck Private, *was first performed by the* Teatro Campesino *in 1971.*

Thought Starters: What is the history of minorities in the American military? Have the least privileged in our society borne a disproportionate share of the burden of defending it?

Characters

Johnny	The Mother
The Father	Cecilia
Death	The Brother

DEATH (*enters singing*). I'm taking off as a private, I'm going to join the ranks . . . along with the courageous young men who leave behind beloved mothers, who leave their girlfriends crying, crying, crying their farewell. Yeah! How lucky for me that there's a war. How goes   *1* it, bro? I am death. What else is new? Well, don't get paranoid because I didn't come to take anybody away. I came to tell you a story. Sure, the story of the Buck Private. Maybe you knew him, eh? He was killed not too long ago in Vietnam.

[JOHNNY *enters, adjusting his uniform.*]

DEATH. This is Johnny, The Buck Private. He's leaving for Vietnam in the morning, but tonight — well, tonight he's going to enjoy himself, right? Look at his face. Know what he's thinking? He's thinking (Johnny *moves his lips*) "Now, I'm a man!"

[THE MOTHER *enters.*]

DEATH. This is his mother. Poor thing. She's worried about her son, like all mothers. "Blessed be God," she's thinking; (The Mother *moves her mouth*) "I hope nothing happens to my son." (The Mother *touches* Johnny *on the shoulder.*)

JOHNNY. Is dinner ready, mom?

MOTHER. Yes, son, almost. Why did you dress like that? You're not leaving until tomorrow. 5

JOHNNY. Well, you know. Cecilia's coming and everything.

MOTHER. Oh, my son. You're always bringing girlfriends to the house but you never think about settling down.

JOHNNY. One of these days I'll give you a surprise, ma. (*He kisses her forehead. Embraces her.*)

DEATH. Oh, my! What a picture of tenderness, no? But, watch the old lady. Listen to what she's thinking. "Now, my son is a man. He looks so handsome in that uniform."

JOHNNY. Well, mom, it's getting late. I'll be back shortly with Cecilia, okay? 10

MOTHER. Yes, son, hurry back. (*He leaves.*) May God take care of you, mom's pride and joy.

[JOHNNY *re-enters and begins to talk.*]

DEATH. Out in the street, Johnny begins to think about his family, his girl, his neighborhood, his life.

JOHNNY. Poor mom. Tomorrow it will be very difficult for her. For me as well. It was pretty hard when I went to boot camp, but now? Vietnam! It's a killer, man. The old man, too. I'm not going to be here to help him out. I wasn't getting rich doing fieldwork, but it was something. A little help, at least. My little brother can't work yet because he's still in school. I just hope he stays there. And finishes. I never liked that school stuff, but I know my little brother digs it. He's smart too — maybe he'll even go to college. One of us has got to make it in this life. Me — I guess I'll just get married to Cecilia and have a bunch of kids. I remember when I first saw her at the Rainbow Ballroom. I couldn't even dance with her because I had had a few beers. The next week was pretty good, though. Since then. How long ago was that? June . . . no, July. Four months. Now I want to get hitched. Her parents don't like me, I know. They think I'm a good for nothing. Maybe they'll feel different when I come back from Nam. Sure, the War Veteran! Maybe I'll get wounded and come back with tons of medals. I wonder how the dudes around here are going to think about that? Damn neighborhood — I've lived here all my life. Now I'm going to Vietnam. (*Taps and drum*) It's going to be a drag, man. I might even get killed. If I do, they'll bring me back here in a box, covered with a flag . . . military funeral like they gave Pete Gomez . . . everybody crying . . . the old lady — (*Stops*) What the hell am I thinking, man? Damn fool! (*He freezes.*)

[DEATH *powders* JOHNNY'S *face white during the next speech.*]

DEATH. Foolish, but not stupid, eh? He knew the kind of funeral he wanted and he got it. Military coffin, lots of flowers, American flag, women crying, and a trumpet playing taps with a rifle salute at the end. Or was it goodbye? It doesn't matter, you know what I mean. It was first class all the way. Oh, by the way, don't get upset about the makeup I'm putting on him, eh? I'm just getting him ready for what's coming. I don't always do things in a hurry, you know. Okay, then, next scene. (Johnny *exits.*)

[JOHNNY *goes on to* CECILIA'S *and exits.*]

DEATH. Back at the house, his old man is just getting home.   15

[THE FATHER *enters.*]

FATHER. Hey, old lady, I'm home. Is dinner ready?

[THE MOTHER *enters.*]

MOTHER. Yes, dear. Just wait till Juan gets home. What did you buy?
FATHER. A sixpack of Coors.
MOTHER. Beer?
FATHER. Well, why not? Look — This is my son's last night.   20
MOTHER. What do you mean, his last night? Don't speak like that.
FATHER. I mean his last night at home, woman. You understand — hic.
MOTHER. You're drunk, aren't you?
FATHER. And if I am, what's it to you? I just had a few beers with my buddy and that's it. Well, what is this, anyway . . . ? It's all I need, man. My son's going to war and you don't want me to drink. I've got to celebrate, woman!
MOTHER. Celebrate what?   25
FATHER. That my son is now a man! And quite a man, the twerp. So don't pester me. Bring me some supper.
MOTHER. Wait for Juan to come home.

FATHER. Where is he? He's not here? Is that so-and-so loafing around again? Juan? Juan?

MOTHER. I'm telling you he went to get Cecilia, who's going to have dinner with us. And please don't use any foul language. What will the girl say if she hears you talking like that?

FATHER. To hell with it! Who owns this damn house, anyway? Aren't I   *30* the one who pays the rent? The one who buys the food? Don't make me get angry, huh? Or you'll get it. It doesn't matter if you already have a son who's a soldier.

MOTHER. Please. I ask you in your son's name, eh? Calm down. *(She exits.)*

FATHER. Calm down! Just like that she wants me to calm down. And who's going to shut my trap? My son the soldier? My son . . .

DEATH. The old man's thoughts are racing back a dozen years to a warm afternoon in July. Johnny, eight years old, is running toward him between the vines, shouting: "Paaa, I already picked 20 trays, paaapá!"

FATHER. Huh. Twenty trays. Little bugger.

[THE BROTHER *enters.*]

BROTHER. Pa, is Johnny here?   *35*

DEATH. This is Johnny's little brother.

FATHER. And where are you coming from?

BROTHER. I was over at Polo's house. He has a new motor scooter.

FATHER. You just spend all your time playing, don't you?

BROTHER. I didn't do anything.   *40*

FATHER. Don't talk back to your father.

BROTHER *(shrugs)*. Are we going to eat soon?

FATHER. I don't know. Go ask your mother.

[THE BROTHER *exits.*]

DEATH. Looking at his younger son, the old man starts thinking about him. His thoughts spin around in the usual hopeless cycle of defeat, undercut by more defeat.

FATHER. That boy should be working. He's already fourteen years old.   *45* I don't know why the law forces them to go to school till they're sixteen. He won't amount to anything, anyway. It's better if he starts working with me so that he can help the family.

DEATH. Sure, he gets out of school and in three or four years, I take him the way I took Johnny. Crazy, huh?

[JOHNNY *returns with* CECILIA.]

JOHNNY. Good evening, pa.

FATHER. Son! Good evening. What's this? You're dressed as a soldier?

JOHNNY. I brought Cecilia over to have dinner with us.

already knows what her son is going to say. So does the father. And even little brother. They are all thinking: "He is going to say: Cecilia and I are getting married!"

JOHNNY. Cecilia and I are getting married!   110

MOTHER. Oh, son!

FATHER. You don't say!

BROTHER. Really?

MOTHER. When, son?

JOHNNY. When I get back from Vietnam.   115

DEATH. Suddenly a thought is crossing everybody's mind: "What if he doesn't come back?" But they shove it aside.

MOTHER. Oh, darling! (*She hugs* Cecilia.)

FATHER. Congratulations, son. (*He hugs* Johnny.)

MOTHER (*hugging* Johnny). My boy! (*She cries.*)

JOHNNY. Hey, mom, wait a minute. Save that for tomorrow. That's   120
enough, ma.

FATHER. Daughter. (*He hugs* Cecilia *properly.*)

BROTHER. Heh, Johnny, why don't I go to Vietnam and you stay here for the wedding? I'm not afraid to die.

MOTHER. What makes you say that, child?

BROTHER. It just came out.

FATHER. You've let out too much already, don't you think?   125

BROTHER. I didn't mean it! (The Brother *exits.*)

JOHNNY. It was an accident, pa.

MOTHER. You're right; it was an accident. Please, sweetheart, let's eat in peace, ha? Juan leaves tomorrow.

DEATH. The rest of the meal goes by without any incidents. They discuss the wedding, the tamales, and the weather. Then it's time to go to the party.

FATHER. Is it true there's going to be a party?   130

JOHNNY. Just a small dance, over at Sapo's house.

MOTHER. Which Sapo, son?

JOHNNY. Sapo, my friend.

FATHER. Don't get drunk, okay?

JOHNNY. Oh, come on, dad, Cecilia will be with me.   135

FATHER. Did you ask her parents for permission?

JOHNNY. Yes, sir. She's got to be home by eleven.

FATHER. Okay. (Johnny *and* Cecilia *rise.*)

CECILIA. Thank you for the dinner, ma'am.

MOTHER. You're very welcome.   140

CECILIA. The tamales were really good.

JOHNNY. Yes, ma, they were terrific.

MOTHER. Is that right, son? You liked them?

JOHNNY. They were great. (*He hugs her.*) Thanks, eh?

MOTHER. What do you mean thanks? You're my son. Go then, it's getting late. 145

FATHER. Do you want to take the truck, son?

JOHNNY. No thanks, pa. I already have Cecilia's car.

CECILIA. Not mine. My parents' car. They loaned it to us for the dance.

FATHER. It seems like you made a good impression, eh?

CECILIA. He sure did. They say he's more responsible now that he's in the service. 150

DEATH (to audience). Did you hear that? Listen to her again.

CECILIA (repeats sentence, exactly as before). They say he's more responsible now that he's in the service.

DEATH. That's what I like to hear!

FATHER. That's good. Then all you have to do is go ask for Cecilia's hand, right, sweetheart?

MOTHER. God willing. 155

JOHNNY. We're going, then.

CECILIA. Good night.

FATHER. Good night.

MOTHER. Be careful on the road, children.

JOHNNY. Don't worry, mom. Be back later. 160

CECILIA. Bye!

[JOHNNY and CECILIA exit. THE MOTHER stands at the door.]

FATHER (sitting down again). Well, old lady, little Johnny has become a man. The years fly by, don't they?

DEATH. The old man is thinking about the Korean War. Johnny was born about that time. He wishes he had some advice, some hints, to pass on to him about war. But he never went to Korea. The draft skipped him, and somehow, he never got around to enlisting. (The Mother turns around.)

MOTHER (She sees Death). Oh, my God! (Exit)

DEATH (ducking down). Damn, I think she saw me. 165

FATHER. What's wrong with you? (The Mother is standing frozen, looking toward the spot where Death was standing.) Answer me, what's up? (Pause) Speak to me! What am I, invisible?

MOTHER (solemnly). I just saw Death.

FATHER. Death? You're crazy.

MOTHER. It's true. As soon as Juan left, I turned around and there was Death, standing — smiling! (The Father moves away from the spot inadvertently.) Oh, Blessed Virgin Mary, what if something happens to Juan.

FATHER. Don't say that! Don't you know it's bad luck? 170

[They exit. DEATH re-enters.]

[*The Greyhound Bus Depot.*]

DEATH. The next day, Johnny goes to the Greyhound Bus Depot. His mother, his father, and his girlfriend go with him to say goodbye. The Bus Depot is full of soldiers and sailors and old men. Here and there, a drunkard is passed out on the benches. Then there's the announcements: THE LOS ANGELES BUS IS NOW RECEIVING PASSENGERS AT GATE TWO, FOR KINGSBURG, TULARE, DELANO, BAKERSFIELD AND LOS ANGELES, CONNECTIONS IN L.A. FOR POINTS EAST AND SOUTH.

[JOHNNY, FATHER, MOTHER, *and* CECILIA *enter*. CECILIA *clings to* JOHNNY.]

FATHER. It's been several years since I last set foot at the station.
MOTHER. Do you have your ticket, son?
JOHNNY. Oh, no, I have to buy it.
CECILIA. I'll go with you.   175
FATHER. Do you have money, son?
JOHNNY. Yes, pa, I have it.

[JOHNNY *and* CECILIA *walk over to* DEATH.]

JOHNNY. One ticket, please.
DEATH. Where to?
JOHNNY. Vietnam. I mean, Oakland.   180
DEATH. Round trip or one way?
JOHNNY. One way.
DEATH. Right. One way. (*Applies more makeup.*)

[JOHNNY *gets his ticket and he and* CECILIA *start back toward his parents.* JOHNNY *stops abruptly and glances back at* DEATH, *who has already shifted positions.*]

CECILIA. What's wrong?
JOHNNY. Nothing. (*They join the parents.*)   185
DEATH. For half an hour then, they exchange small talk and trivialities, repeating some of the things that have been said several times before. Cecilia promises Johnny she will be true to him and wait until he returns. Then it's time to go: THE OAKLAND-VIETNAM EXPRESS IS NOW RECEIVING PASSENGERS AT GATE NUMBER FOUR. ALL ABOARD PLEASE.
JOHNNY. That's my bus.
MOTHER. Oh, son.
FATHER. Take good care of yourself then, okay, son?
CECILIA. I love you, Johnny. (*She embraces him.*)   190
DEATH. THE OAKLAND-VIETNAM EXPRESS IS IN THE FINAL

BOARDING STAGES. PASSENGERS WITH TICKETS ALL ABOARD PLEASE. AND THANKS FOR GOING GREYHOUND.

JOHNNY. I'm leaving, now.

[*Embraces all around, weeping, last goodbyes, etc.* JOHNNY *exits. Then parents exit.* THE MOTHER *and* CECILIA *are crying.*]

DEATH (*sings*). *Goodbye, Goodbye*
       Star of my nights
       A soldier said in front of a window
       I'm leaving, I'm leaving
       But don't cry, my angel
       For tomorrow I'll be back . . .

So Johnny left for Vietnam, never to return. He didn't want to go and yet he did. It never crossed his mind to refuse. How can he refuse the government of the United States? How could he refuse his family? Besides, who wants to go to prison? And there was the chance he'd come back alive . . . wounded maybe, but alive. So he took a chance — and lost. But before he died he saw many things in Vietnam; he had his eyes opened. He wrote his mother about them.

[JOHNNY *and* THE MOTHER *enter at opposite sides of the stage.* JOHNNY *is in full battle gear. His face is now a skull.*]

JOHNNY. Dear mom.

MOTHER. Dear son. 195

JOHNNY. I am writing this letter.

MOTHER. I received your letter.

JOHNNY. To tell you I'm okay.

MOTHER. And I thank the heavens you're all right.

JOHNNY. How's everybody over there? 200

MOTHER. Here, we're all doing fine, thank God.

JOHNNY. Ma, there's a lot happening here that I didn't know about before. I don't know if I'm allowed to write about it, but I'm going to try. Yesterday we attacked a small village near some rice paddies. We had orders to kill everybody because they were supposed to be V-C's, communists. We entered the small village and my buddies started shooting. I saw one of them kill an old man and an old lady. My sergeant killed a small boy about seven years old, then he shot his mother or some woman that came running up crying. Blood was everywhere. I don't remember what happened after that but my sergeant ordered me to start shooting. I think I did. May God forgive me for what I did, but I never wanted to come over here. They say we have to do it to defend our country.

MOTHER. Son what you are writing to us makes me sad. I talked to your father and he also got very worried, but he says that's what war is like. He reminds you that you're fighting communists. I have a candle lit and everyday I ask God to take good care of you wherever you are and that he return you to our arms healthy and in one piece.

JOHNNY. Ma, I had a dream the other night. I dreamed I was breaking into one of the hooches, that's what we call the Vietnamese's houses. I went in firing my M-16 because I knew that the village was controlled by the gooks. I killed three of them right away, but when I looked down it was my pa, my little brother and you, mother. I don't know how much more I can stand. Please tell Sapo and all the dudes how it's like over here. Don't let them . . .

[DEATH *fires a gun, shooting* JOHNNY *in the head. He falls.* THE MOTHER *screams without looking at* JOHNNY.]

DEATH. Johnny was killed in action November 1965 at Chu Lai. His body lay in the field for two days and then it was taken to the beach and placed in a freezer, a converted portable food locker. Two weeks later he was shipped home for burial. 205

[DEATH *straightens out* JOHNNY'S *body. Takes his helmet, rifle, etc.* THE FATHER, THE MOTHER, THE BROTHER, *and* CECILIA *file past and gather around the body. Taps plays.*]

The Responsive Reader

1. Death plays a major role in Mexican folklore and custom. What is the role of Death in this play? What is the role of the soldier's family?
2. Does this play make a political statement about the war? Where and how?
3. In your judgment, would this play appeal primarily to Mexican Americans? Or does it have universal appeal?
4. How do you relate to the humor in this play? What are its targets? How does it affect the tone of the play?

Talking, Listening, Writing

5. Are the people in this play too passive in their acceptance of what is in store for them?
6. Have people in our society become jaded about the arguments of antiwar or pacifist groups? What would you say to a group of people to make them pay renewed attention to warnings about war? Or what would you answer if someone approached you with a plea to join an antiwar group?
7. Have you lost someone close to you as the result of war, illness, accident? Write a tribute to the person.

Projects

8. Valdez' text is well suited for a mini-production designed to bring the play to life for an audience and help them get into the spirit of the play. (One class production changed the GI in the Valdez play to a young woman and the war to the "Desert Storm" war against Iraq.) You and your classmates may want to organize a group project to stage your own reenactment of the Valdez play.

whole scene, a car pulled up with three men inside. One of the men in the car shot him, putting a bullet through his head. Art is now partially paralyzed in his left leg and arm, and he has restricted speech and vision.

Because there is little or no restriction on the purchase or use of guns, innocent people are killed or maimed every day. . . .

▪ *Persuasive writers appeal to shared values.* They compile examples and statistics that will arouse the indignation or activate the loyalties of the reader. Look at the following skeleton of a paper attacking the huge damage awards assessed against businesses and individuals accused of negligence. What are the standards or values that the writer appeals to in each successive section of the paper?

Are You Insured?

Courts are going out of their way to do away with traditional standards of fairness and shared responsibility. Increasingly, courts are disallowing the traditional defense of contributory negligence. One case involved a man who strapped a refrigerator on his back and ran a stunt footrace. One of the straps failed, and he collected $1 million from the strap manufacturer.

Little attention is paid to the limited financial resources of small businesses or of individuals. The costs of litigation and the enormous damage awards are driving small companies to the wall. . . .

The effects on the pharmaceutical industry are especially harmful. Liability for rare side effects is driving many manufacturers out of the vaccine market, even in cases where medical opinion agrees that the good the vaccines do far outweighs the possible harm. Vaccines (such as those for diphtheria and tetanus) for children are steadily climbing in price. . . .

Who benefits from the inflation of damage awards? The big winners (in case you had any doubts) are the lawyers. A Rand study found that a typical court case costs $380,000, of which $125,000 went to the defense lawyers, $114,000 to the plaintiff's lawyers, and $141,000 in net compensation to the plaintiff.

▪ *Persuasive writers often use a key example to clinch an argument.* They discuss a test case in graphic detail. A reader who is already predisposed to think of tests as culturally biased is likely to remember a striking example like the following:

Consider this question from a standardized group IQ test. "No garden is without its _____." The desired answer is one of these five: "sun–rain–tool–work–weeds." A child who happens to know the expression will recognize the missing word (weeds) and complete the sentence "correctly." If he doesn't have that piece of information, he'll have to figure out the answer. He might explain to a tester, "It isn't 'tools' because I once planted a garden with my hands." But there is no tester to tell. He might continue, "I don't know how to choose between sun and rain, so I won't use either one." Again there's no tester to hear his reasoning. "So it's either 'work' or 'weeds.'" Another pause. "Well, if a gardener worked hard, maybe he wouldn't have any weeds — but, if he doesn't work at all, he won't have any garden!" Triumphantly, the clever, logical, analytical young mind has selected — the wrong answer!

When a computer grades that test, "work" will simply be marked wrong, and no one will be there to explain the thought process to the computer. Nor will anyone point out the differences between the child who has personal experience with gardens and the child whose closest contact may be the city park, ten blocks away from his fire escape.   *Arlene Silberman, "The Tests That Cheat Our Children,"* McCall's

▪ *Persuasive writers exploit the weaknesses of the opposition.* They look for contradictions. They look for a contrast between public pronouncements and actual practice. The author of the following excerpt took aim at an ironic discrepancy he saw between enlightened humanitarian ideals and personal behavior:

Among trendy young professionals in our major cities, there is no stigma attached to using cocaine. In particular, the hip lawyers, doctors, movie stars, and so on who use the drug are not deterred, or even bothered much, by the mere fact that it happens to be illegal. But perhaps they will be receptive to a more fashionable approach. After all, many cocaine consumers are the same sort of people who will boycott lettuce or grapes because farm workers are underpaid, or a cosmetic because the company tortures rabbits, or tuna to protest the killing of dolphins. . . .

Murder is as much a part of cocaine culture as tiny silver spoons and rolled-up hundred-dollar bills. There is seldom a major coke bust that doesn't also turn up an arsenal of automatic weapons. In a recent year in Miami, the cocaine capital of the Northern Hemisphere, a quarter of the city's 614 murders were committed with machine guns.   *— David Owen, "Boycott Cocaine,"* Harper's

SHAPING A basic strategy in much persuasive writing (as in advertising and propaganda) is insistence. Often a writer will pile on graphic examples, keeping after the reader. Sooner or later, even a reluctant reader may begin to say: "I see what you mean. I didn't realize things were this bad or the needs this great."

To make your plea as effective as possible, try to spell out the heart of your message in pointed, memorable language:

Of all the drug problems afflicting our society, heroin is the most deadly. Once addicted, the user needs cash to feed the habit. The males steal and rob. The women become shop lifters and prostitutes.

Remember that much effective persuasion builds to a climax. The writer leads up to a high point or saves an especially telling example for the last. A paper pleading for allowing the terminally ill to "go in peace" took up in turn the traditions of the medical profession and the cases of a hypothetical comatose patient, a braindead accident victim, and a patient with terminal cancer. But the paper saved for the end the case of a person close to the student writer:

My grandmother asked what I would do when it came time for her to die. I told her I would weep for her and be very sad, but I would remember how she lived. For me, this means that I could not let her linger in a life in between with machines and tubes. I must respect her wishes concerning how she wants to die. She must be able to go in peace the way she plans, not the way a doctor plans. She chose the way she lived, and with my help she will choose the way she dies.

REVISING Pleas written in the heat of passion or indictments written in the first flush of anger are best allowed to cool a day or two. Take time to focus your enthusiasm or to channel your anger. Remember that a strong plea may seem shrill and biased when sent out unedited. When revising a persuasive paper, consider advice like the following:

- Reconsider strongly charged language. When we are passionately committed to a cause, we naturally use emotional language. But consider that wildly enthusiastic language can seem immature or overdone. Abusive language can weaken your cause when it alienates fair-minded readers. Revise any labels that might be considered condescending or offensive.

- Do not make weighty charges lightly. Use strong words like *corruption* or *deceit* only after due deliberation and when you are sure of your target.

- Revise *ad hominem* attacks — arguments directed "against the person." Broad hints about an opponent's divorce, troubled private life, or medical history may gain an advantage, but they may also alienate fair-minded people. Do without remarks about a person's baldness, obesity, or limp.

How persuasive is the following sample paper? How much depends on the audience? What is the overall pattern or strategy adopted by the writer? Does anything in the paper have a special effect on you?

Justice

Three years ago I signed up to be a Big Sister to an eight-year-old girl through the Big Brothers/Big Sisters agency of the county. When the caseworker matched me with Sonia she warned me that Sonia's mother had decreed two topics as taboo for Sonia: sex and her father. I could somewhat understand the mother's prudery about sex, although I disagreed with it. But I was surprised and intrigued when the caseworker told me that Sonia's father was in a state prison, sentenced to death. I pitied the girl, wondering how she felt about having a father who brought her shame.

Sonia has rarely mentioned sex, so that part of the agreement was easy to keep. However, although I never brought up the subject of her father, I discussed how she felt about him whenever she wanted to discuss him. After about three months of seeing each other, Sonia told me that she had been to the movie Pinocchio as a very little girl but she didn't remember it. She explained that she had fallen asleep in the car and her father had carried her into the theater, held her as she slept through the movie, and carried her out again. I was astonished that she had a warm memory of trusting a man who had raped and brutally killed two teenage girls. Then she said that she liked visiting him in jail because she and her brothers got to eat a lot at the prison. I didn't discourage her from talking; I was discovering that she loved her father and was not ashamed of him.

Not only does Sonia love her father, but she has the same need to idealize him as all children need to admire their parents. I remember being moved once when she startled me as we were driving downtown by pointing to a tall building and exclaiming, "There's my daddy's cell." I was confused, so I asked her to explain. She told me that he wasn't there at that time but he had spent some time in jail in the city and she remembered visiting him there. She had pointed with pride to a building she associated with her father, just as another child might say excitedly, "There's my daddy's office." I realized that her father, a vicious killer, was loved and needed. If capital punishment is reinstated in the state, she will lose her father and she will have to shift through an immense burden of conflicting feelings—grief, anger, shame, confusion. His death would help no one. His victims are already dead and his death can't bring them back. Perhaps their relatives want justice, but his death is not justice. It would simply be vengeance. By killing him, we can't bring back the innocent; we can only hurt more innocent people.

I have always been opposed to capital punishment. I believe that, as a society, our role is to care for and protect each other. When one of our members hurts others, we remove him or her from the rest. But killing that person as punishment seems to be sinking to a low level of ethics. Policies of vengeance and "an eye for an eye" morality serve only to escalate violence. We forbid people from killing each other, yet as a legal institution, society dictates that killing is acceptable only when it deems it necessary, as in times of war and as punishment for crimes. I believe that if, as a society, we refuse to accept violence among ourselves and refuse to punish the violent with death, we are carrying out a commitment to peace and non-violence.

Sonia has two pictures hanging in her bedroom that her father painted for her while imprisoned. One is of an Indian girl and the other of an eagle flying above a canyon. Sonia has told me that her father has painted a mural at the prison, as well. Perhaps she idealizes him in her ignorance; most people are guilty of idealizing imperfect people. Yet Sonia will be faced with the much harder job of reconciling her love for her father with the reality that he is a criminal. Most children only have to realize that their caretakers aren't strong, all-knowing, and perfect. To increase this child's pain for the sake of saving tax dollars or of satisfying the understandable, but impossible to achieve, needs for revenge that some people have, would be tragic. Allowing Sonia's father to live would save his family more pain, and it would allow our society to rise above ethics based on violence and revenge.

Topics for Persuasion Papers (A Sampling)

1. Write a fund-raising letter to help support a cause to which you are committed.
2. Have there been recent initiatives concerning gun control in your community or state? Write a persuasive paper designed to influence votes on this issue.
3. Do you have strong feelings about the "right to die"? Present your position, trying to persuade those who might disagree.
4. Do you feel strongly about an issue like rape prevention, the treatment of rape victims, or marital rape? Write a paper designed to influence readers who in your opinion are too unconcerned or uncommitted on the issue.
5. What would you say to young people who have gang affiliations or who might get involved in youth gangs?
6. Write a letter to officials in which you call for stricter supervision of, or more official support for, the local police.
7. What can be done about child abuse?
8. Should Americans endorse the use of military force to fight oppression or crimes against humanity abroad? Try to change the minds of readers who disagree with you.
9. What needs to be done to lessen violence in our communities? Try to persuade a skeptical or disillusioned reader.
10. Should anything be done to counteract Americans' addiction to violent sports or violent entertainment?

11

Environment: Participating in Nature

> *There is power in an antelope, but not in a goat or in a sheep, which holds still while you butcher it, which will eat your newspaper if you let it. There was a great power in a wolf, even in a coyote. You have made him into a freak — a toy poodle, a Pekingese, a lap dog.*
>
> *John (Fire) Lame Deer*

A central goal of Western culture has been to tame and control nature. Progress meant advances in freeing humanity from hunger, from disease, and from back-breaking toil in the fields to wrest meager crops from the earth. Without technology, one of its defenders has said, a human being would be a naked ape — at the mercy of droughts, floods, blights, and epidemics. Cities would cease to exist, with bands of survivors roaming the countryside and plundering and scrounging for food.

In recent times, however, many thinkers and writers have voiced second thoughts about the mixed blessings of our technological civilization. Our technology, our modern lifestyle, has increasingly isolated us from contact with the natural world. Air-conditioned buildings isolate us from the changing winds and the fresh air; we walk on asphalt and concrete rather than on sand or grass; we fly over prairies and rivers and mountains with the windows closed, watching a Hollywood movie. The toxic by-products of our technological civilization are poisoning the rivers, the oceans, the air.

Many have turned to other cultural traditions to search for a different sense of the relationship between humanity and nature. Other cultures have envisioned a more organic relation between human civilization and the natural world. They have or had a better sense of the interdependence of creatures. Some cultures have taught human beings to look at all living things with reverence. Their myths or religious traditions kept people aware of their roots in the natural world.

Is it true that Western industrial civilization is at war with nature and is bound to destroy our natural environment? Is it possible for people in the modern world to live in harmony with nature?

LISTENING TO THE AIR

John (Fire) Lame Deer and Richard Erdoes

In the lore of the West, Native Americans have been seen through changing prisms reflecting contradictory images. They were often seen as "savages" needing the blessings of Western culture to become civilized and fully human. However, they have also been seen as people living close to nature, with a respect for the land and for the animals that nourished them, and with a reverence for the life-giving forces of the natural world that the exploitative technocratic, technology-dominated white culture had lost. John (Fire) Lame Deer, who published Lame Deer, Seeker of Visions *with John Erdoes in 1972, is one of many voices asking other Americans to reexamine their assumptions about the superiority of the dominant white civilization. Richard Erdoes, an illustrator and photographer, met Lame Deer when on an assignment for* Life *magazine on a Sioux reservation. Lame Deer mentions the Washita Massacre in what is now Oklahoma (1868), the Sand Creek Massacre in Colorado (1864), and the battle at Wounded Knee in South Dakota (1890) — encounters in which the U.S. Cavalry or local militia broke the resistance of the Cheyenne and the Sioux, killing men, women, and children. Lame Deer compares these massacres to the killings at My Lai in Vietnam, where American GIs "wasted" several hundred Vietnamese, many of them women and their children.*

Thought Starters: Do you feel cut off from nature? How do you feel about poodles or Pekingese dogs? How do you feel about wolves or coyotes?

Let's sit down here, all of us, on the open prairie, where we can't see   1
a highway or a fence. Let's have no blankets to sit on, but feel the ground with our bodies, the earth, the yielding shrubs. Let's have the grass for a mattress, experiencing its sharpness and its softness. Let us become like stones, plants, and trees. Let us be animals, think and feel like animals.

Listen to the air. You can hear it, feel it, smell it, taste it. *Woniya waken* — the holy air — which renews all by its breath. *Woniya, woniya waken* — spirit, life, breath, renewal — it means all that. *Woniya* — we sit together, don't touch, but something is there; we feel it between us, as a presence. A good way to start thinking about nature, talk about it. Rather talk to it, talk to the rivers, to the lakes, to the winds as to our relatives.

You have made it hard for us to experience nature in the good way by being part of it. Even here we are conscious that somewhere out in those hills there are missile silos and radar stations. White men always pick

the few unspoiled, beautiful, awesome spots for the sites of these abomi-
nations. You have raped and violated these lands, always saying, "Gimme,
gimme, gimme," and never giving anything back. You have taken 200,000
acres of our Pine Ridge reservation and made them into a bombing range.
This land is so beautiful and strange that now some of you want to make
it into a national park. The only use you have made of this land since you
took it from us was to blow it up. You have not only despoiled the earth,
the rocks, the minerals, all of which you call "dead" but which are very
much alive; you have even changed the animals, which are part of us, part
of the Great Spirit, changed them in a horrible way, so no one can recognize them. There is power in a buffalo—spiritual, magic power—but
there is no power in an Angus, in a Hereford.

There is power in an antelope, but not in a goat or in a sheep, which
holds still while you butcher it, which will eat your newspaper if you let
it. There was great power in a wolf, even in a coyote. You have made him
into a freak—a toy poodle, a Pekingese, a lap dog. You can't do much
with a cat, which is like an Indian, unchangeable. So you fix it, alter it,
declaw it, even cut its vocal cords so you can experiment on it in a laboratory without being disturbed by its cries.

A partridge, a grouse, a quail, a pheasant, you have made them into   5
chickens, creatures that can't fly, that wear a kind of sunglasses so that
they won't peck each other's eyes out, "birds" with a "pecking order."
There are some farms where they breed chickens for breast meat. Those
birds are kept in low cages, forced to be hunched over all the time, which
makes the breast muscles very big. Soothing sounds, Muzak, are piped
into these chicken hutches. One loud noise and the chickens go haywire,
killing themselves by flying against the mesh of their cages. Having to
spend all their lives stooped over makes an unnatural, crazy, no-good bird.
It also makes unnatural, no-good human beings.

That's where you fooled yourselves. You have not only altered, de-
clawed, and malformed your winged and four-legged cousins; you have
done it to yourselves. You have changed men into chairmen of boards,
into office workers, into time-clock punchers. You have changed women
into housewives, truly fearful creatures. I was once invited into the home
of such a one.

"Watch the ashes, don't smoke, you stain the curtains. Watch the
goldfish bowl, don't breathe on the parakeet, don't lean your head against
the wallpaper; your hair may be greasy. Don't spill liquor on that table: it
has a delicate finish. You should have wiped your boots; the floor was just
varnished. Don't, don't, don't . . ." That is crazy. We weren't made to
endure this. You live in prisons which you have built for yourselves,
calling them "homes," offices, factories. We have a new joke on the reservation: "What is cultural deprivation?" Answer: "Being an upper-middle-
class white kid living in a split-level suburban home with a color TV."

Sometimes I think that even our pitiful tar-paper shacks are better
than your luxury homes. Walking a hundred feet to the outhouse on a

clear wintry night, through mud or snow, that's one small link with nature. Or in the summer, in the back country, leaving the door of the privy open, taking your time, listening to the humming of the insects, the sun warming your bones through the thin planks of wood; you don't even have that pleasure anymore.

Americans want to have everything sanitized. No smells! Not even the good, natural man and woman smell. Take away the smell from under the armpits, from your skin. Rub it out, and then spray or dab some nonhuman odor on yourself, stuff you can spend a lot of money on, ten dollars an ounce, so you know this has to smell good. "B.O.," bad breath, "Intimate Female Odor Spray"—I see it all on TV. Soon you'll breed people without body openings.

I think white people are so afraid of the world they created that they   10 don't want to see, feel, smell, or hear it. The feeling of rain and snow on your face, being numbed by an icy wind and thawing out before a smoking fire, coming out of a hot sweat bath and plunging into a cold stream, these things make you feel alive, but you don't want them anymore. Living in boxes which shut out the heat of the summer and the chill of winter, living inside a body that no longer has a scent, hearing the noise from the hi-fi instead of listening to the sounds of nature, watching some actor on TV having a make-believe experience when you no longer experience anything for yourself, eating food without taste—that's your way. It's no good.

The food you eat, you treat it like your bodies, take out all the nature part, the taste, the smell, the roughness, then put the artificial color, the artificial flavor in. Raw liver, raw kidney—that's what we old-fashioned full-bloods like to get our teeth into. In the old days we used to eat the guts of the buffalo, making a contest of it, two fellows getting hold of a long piece of intestines from opposite ends, starting chewing toward the middle, seeing who can get there first; that's eating. Those buffalo guts, full of half-fermented, half-digested grass and herbs, you didn't need any pills and vitamins when you swallowed those. Use the bitterness of gall for flavoring, not refined salt or sugar. *Wasna*—meat, kidney fat, and berries all pounded together—a lump of that sweet *wasna* kept a man going for a whole day. That was food, that had the power. Not the stuff you give us today: powdered milk, dehydrated eggs, pasteurized butter, chickens that are all drumsticks or all breast; there's no bird left there.

You don't want the bird. You don't have the courage to kill honestly—cut off the chicken's head, pluck it and gut it—no, you don't want this anymore. So it all comes in a neat plastic bag, all cut up, ready to eat, with no taste and no guilt. Your mink and seal coats, you don't want to know about the blood and pain which went into making them. Your idea of war—sit in an airplane, way above the clouds, press a button, drop the bombs, and never look below the clouds—that's the odorless, guiltless, sanitized way.

When we killed a buffalo, we knew what we were doing. We apologized to his spirit, tried to make him understand why we did it, honoring with a prayer the bones of those who gave their flesh to keep us alive, praying for their return, praying for the life of our brothers, the buffalo nation, as well as for our own people. You wouldn't understand this and that's why we had the Washita Massacre, the Sand Creek Massacre, the dead women and babies at Wounded Knee. That's why we have Song My and My Lai now.

To us life, all life, is sacred. The state of South Dakota has pest-control officers. They go up in a plane and shoot coyotes from the air. They keep track of their kills, put them all down in their little books. The stockmen and sheepowners pay them. Coyotes eat mostly rodents, field mice and such. Only once in a while will they go after a stray lamb. They are our natural garbage men cleaning up the rotten and stinking things. They make good pets if you give them a chance. But their living could lose some man a few cents, and so the coyotes are killed from the air. They were here before the sheep, but they are in the way; you can't make a profit out of them. More and more animals are dying out. The animals which the Great Spirit put here, they must go. The man-made animals are allowed to stay — at least until they are shipped out to be butchered. That terrible arrogance of the white man, making himself something more than God, more than nature, saying, "I will let this animal live, because it makes money"; saying, "This animal must go, it brings no income, the space it occupies can be used in a better way. The only good coyote is a dead coyote." They are treating coyotes almost as badly as they used to treat Indians.

The Responsive Reader

1. What is Lame Deer's advice to help us get closer to our natural roots? Does it make sense?
2. What, for you, are the major charges in Lame Deer's indictment of white civilization? Can you explain his charges? Are they fair?
3. The buffalo and the coyote play a major role in Native American tradition. What role do they play in this account?

Talking, Listening, Writing

4. Have you observed, or participated in, attempts to bring people closer to unspoiled countryside and animals in the wild? What did you learn from your observations or experiences?
5. What would you say in defense of domesticated animals and pets?
6. Do you agree with people who say that the extermination or displacement of the Native American tribes was "inevitable" — no different from other nations' striking out in search of new lands for their people?

Projects

7. How much has been preserved of Native American myth or folklore (and by whom)? How accessible is it? What light does it shed on the relationship of the tribes to nature, to the land, to the animals? (For instance, what is the role of the coyote in Native American lore?) Working with a group, try to find answers to questions like these. Your group may want to prepare a presentation of poems, songs, and stories from authentic Native American sources.

THE LAST OF THE WILD SALMON

Marie De Santis

We tend to be armchair ecologists who know the threatened wildlife of our planet mostly from television specials. The author of the following article knows the life of the oceans and rivers from close personal observation. De Santis worked for eight years as a commercial fisherwoman and the captain of her own boat. She told her story of the lure of the sea and of the hard work and dangers faced by those who make a living from the sea in her book Neptune's Apprentice *(1984). In the following excerpt from her book* California Currents *(1985), she pays tribute to the wild salmon who are endangered by the destruction of their spawning grounds and the obstacles that dams and polluted or diverted rivers present to their age-old journey upstream. She hated to see the wild salmon replaced by artificially bred fish "no more suited to the stream than a poodle is to the woods." She addressed her book to those who "wish to continue living in a world with real animals" and who want future generations to "see more than the broken spirits of the animals of the zoo."*

Thought Starters: Why is the author of the following article fascinated by the life cycle of the salmon? What for her makes the salmon a symbol of the threatened life on our endangered planet?

In a stream so shallow that its full body is no longer submerged in the water, the salmon twists on its side to get a better grip with its tail. Its gillplate is torn, big hunks of skin hang off its sides from collisions with rocks, there are deep gouges in its body, and all around for miles to go there is only the cruelty of more jagged rocks and less and less water to sustain the swim. Surely the animal is dying!

And then the salmon leaps like an arrow shot from a bow; some urge and will and passion ignores the animal body and focuses on the stream.

Of all the extremes of adaptation to the ocean's awful toll on the young, none is more mythic in proportion than the salmon's mighty journey to the mountain streams: a journey that brings life to meet death at a point on a perfect circle, a return through miles of narrowing waters to the exact gravel-bedded streamlet of its birth. A journey to spawning and death, so clear in its resemblance to the migrations of the sperm to the egg as to entwine their meanings in a single reflection.

On every continent of the northern hemisphere, from the temperate zone to the arctic, there is hardly a river that hasn't teemed with the salmon's spawn: the Thames, the Rhine, the rivers of France and Spain, Kamchatka and Siberia, Japan (which alone has more than 200 salmon rivers) and the arctic streams of Greenland. From the Aleutians to Monterey Bay, through the broadest byways to the most rugged and narrow gorge, the salmon have made their way home. There are many journeys for which the salmon endure more than 1000 miles.

As soon as the ice melts on the Yukon, the king salmon enter the river's mouth, and for a month, the fish swim against the current, 50 miles a day for a total of 1500. And like every other salmon on its run, the king salmon fasts completely along the way. In other rivers, salmon scale vertical rocks up to 60 feet high, against hurtling waterfalls.

The salmon gets to spawn once in life, and maybe that's reason enough. The salmon's instinct to return to the place of its birth is so unmodifiable and of such purity as to have inspired hundreds of spiritual rites in as many societies of human beings.

The salmon arrives battered and starved, with a mate chosen along the way, and never has passion seemed less likely from two more wretched-looking beings. But, there in the gravel of the streamlet, the female fans out a nest with the sweep of her powerful tail and the male fends off intruders. The nest done, the two fish lie next to each other suspended in the water over the nest; their bodies quiver with intense vibrations, and simultaneously they throw the eggs and the sperm. Compared with the millions of eggs thrown by a cod in a stream, the salmon need throw only 2000 to 5000. Despite the predators and other hazards of the stream, these cold mountain waters are a sanctuary compared with the sea. For the next two or three days, the pair continue nesting and spawning until all the eggs are laid. Then the salmon, whose journey has spanned the ocean and the stream, lies by the nest and dies.

Soon the banks of the streams are stacked with ragged carcasses, and the animals of the woods come down for a feast. The stream lies quiet in the winter's deepening cold. But within a month two black eyes appear through the skin of each egg. And two weeks later, the water is again alive with the pulsing of millions of small fish feeling the first clumsy kicks of their tails. The fingerlings stay for a while, growing on the insects and larvae that have been nurtured by the forest. Then, one day, they realize what that tail is for and begin their descent to the sea, a journey mapped in their genes by the parents they left behind.

The young salmon arrive in the estuary facing the sea, where they linger again and learn to feed on shrimp, small crustaceans and other creatures of the brine. Here, also, their bodies complete an upheaval of internal and external changes that allow them to move on to the saltier sea. These adaptations require such extraordinary body transformations that when the same events occur on the stage of evolution they take millions and millions of years. In the life of the salmon, the changes take place in only a matter of months. One of life's most prohibitive barriers—

that between fresh and salt water — is crossed, and the salmon swim back and forth, in and out of the sea, trying it on for size.

Then one day, the youngsters do not return. The stream is only a   10
distant memory drifting further and further back in the wake of time, only different — a memory that will resurrect and demand that its path be retraced.

So accessible is the salmon's life in the stream that more is known about the reproduction of this fish than any other ocean animal. With the ease of placing cameras underwater, there isn't any aspect of this dramatic cycle that hasn't been captured in full color in some of the most spectacular film footage ever made.

But once the salmon enters the sea, the story of its life is a secret as deep and dark as the farthest reaches of the ocean it roams. The human eye with its most sophisticated aids, from satellite to sonar, has never caught more than a glance of the salmon at sea. Extensive tagging programs have been carried out, but they tell us little more than that the salmon is likely to be found anywhere within thousands of miles of its origins, and even this is only a sliver of the picture because the tags are recovered only when the salmon is caught by fishermen, who work solely within the narrow coastal zone. Along with a few other pelagic fishes, like the tuna, that claim vast stretches of sea for their pasture, the salmon's life remains one of the most mysterious on earth.

The Responsive Reader

1. What makes the stage of the salmon's life cycle that she describes at the beginning the symbolic high point for the author?
2. What are the major stages of the salmon's life journey? What are key events or striking details at each stage?

Talking, Listening, Writing

3. For you, does the salmon's life cycle make a good symbolic representation of life on this planet? Why or why not?
4. What plant or animal with an especially rich or varied life cycle have you studied or do you know well? Trace it in rich authentic detail, emphasizing major stages.
5. Do people, institutions, or ideas have life cycles similar to those De Santis observed in the natural world? Focus on one central example, and bring it to life for your reader.

Projects

6. How successful is the struggle to restore life to lakes and streams poisoned by pollution? What have been notable successes and notable failures? What in particular is the current status of attempts to

save the wild salmon? For a possible research project, work with a group to collect and collate data from authoritative sources.

Thinking about Connections

Is the attitude toward nature in this article similar to or different from the attitude toward nature that John (Fire) Lame Deer talks about in "Listening to the Air"?

THE FEMINIZATION OF EARTH FIRST!

Judi Bari

> *What animals or plants have become symbols for you of the endangered life on planet Earth? People in many countries banded together to save the whales. Ecologists are fighting what may be a losing battle to preserve the elephants threatened by poachers and shrinking habitat. For many people in the Western United States, a powerful symbol of our threatened natural heritage is the giant redwood trees* (Sequoia sempervirens) *that reach a height of 360 feet. Many of those still standing were already growing at the time of the birth of Christ. In an ominous note, Webster's Ninth New Collegiate Dictionary calls the redwood a "commercially important" timber tree, and for years ecologists and nature lovers have done battle with the logging interests to save the remaining stands of original growth. (Ronald Reagan, then governor of California, once said that if you have seen one redwood you have seen them all.) In the following article from* Ms. *magazine, a committed feminist talks about the "Redwood Summer," with radical ecologists blocking logging roads and living off the ground in the trees in a desperate last-ditch attempt to save the remnants of the ancient forests.*

Thought Starters: What has been your experience or contact with the ecology movement? Do you think you would have joined in the efforts to save the redwood trees?

It is impossible to live in the redwood region without being profoundly affected by the massive destruction of this once-magnificent ecosystem. Miles and miles of clearcuts cover our bleeding hillsides. Ancient forests are being strip-logged to pay off corporate junk bonds. Log trucks fill our roads, heading to the sawmills with loads ranging from 1,000-year-old redwoods, one tree trunk filling an entire logging truck, to six-inch-diameter baby trees that are chipped for pulp.

So it is not surprising that I, a lifelong activist, would become an environmentalist. What is surprising is that I, a feminist, single mother, and blue-collar worker, would end up in Earth First!, a "no compromise" direct action group with the reputation of being beer-drinking ecodudes. Little did I know that combining the feminist elements of collectivism and nonviolence with the spunk and outrageousness of Earth First! would spark a mass movement. And little did I know that I would pay for our success by being bombed and nearly killed, and subjected to a campaign of hatred and misogyny.

I was attracted to Earth First! because its activists were the only people willing to put their bodies in front of the bulldozers and chain saws to save the trees. They were also funny and irreverent, and they played music. But it was the philosophy of Earth First! that ultimately won me over. This philosophy, known as biocentrism or deep ecology, states that the Earth is not just here for human consumption. All species have a right to exist for their own sake, and humans must learn to live in balance with the needs of nature instead of trying to mold nature to fit the needs of humans.

I see no contradiction between deep ecology and ecofeminism, but Earth First! was founded by five men, and its principal spokespeople have all been male. As in all such groups, there have always been competent women doing the real work behind the scenes. But they have been virtually invisible behind the public Earth First! persona of "big man goes into big wilderness to save big trees." I certainly objected to this. Yet despite the image, the structure of Earth First! was decentralized and nonhierarchical, so we could develop any way we wanted in our local northern California group.

In many ways the northwest timber country resembles Appalachia 5 more than California. It is sparsely populated and set in mountainous terrain. Some of the more isolated communities are located hours away from the nearest sheriff, and have become virtually lawless areas, with a wild West mentality. The economy is dominated by a few large timber corporations. Louisiana-Pacific, Georgia-Pacific, and Maxxam are the most powerful, and in our impoverished rural communities local government, police, schools, and others all bow to the economic blackmail of King Timber. The town of Scotia, one of the last actual company towns in the U.S., is owned and operated by Maxxam, and you are not allowed to rent a house in Scotia unless you work for the company.

For years the strategy of Earth First!, under male leadership, had been based on individual acts of daring. "Nomadic action groups" of maybe ten people would travel to remote areas and bury themselves in logging roads, chain themselves to heavy equipment, or sit in trees. There were certainly brave and principled women who engaged in these actions. But by and large, most of the people who had the freedom for that kind of travel and risk-taking were men.

I have nothing against individual acts of daring. But the flaw in this strategy is the failure to engage in long-term community-based organizing. There is no way that a few isolated individuals, no matter how brave, can bring about the massive social change necessary to save the planet. So we began to organize with local people, planning our logging blockades around local issues. And we began to build alliances with progressive timber workers based on our common interests against the big corporations. As our success grew, more women and more people with families and roots in the community began calling themselves Earth First!ers in our area.

But as our exposure and influence grew, so did the use of violence against us. At one demonstration a 50-year-old nonviolent woman was punched so hard her nose was broken. In another incident, my car was rammed Karen Silkwood–style by the same logging truck that we had blockaded less than 24 hours earlier. In both these cases, as in other instances of violence against us, local police refused even to investigate our assailants.

Earth First! had never initiated any violence. But I felt we needed a much more explicit nonviolence code in the face of an increasingly volatile situation on the front lines. So, drawing on the lessons of the civil rights movement, we put out a nationwide call for Freedom Riders for the Forest to come to northern California and engage in nonviolent mass actions to stop the slaughter of the redwoods. We called the campaign Redwood Summer and, as it became clear that we were sucessfully drawing national interest, the level of repression escalated again.

I began to receive a series of increasingly frightening death threats, obviously written on behalf of Big Timber. The most frightening was a photo of me with a rifle scope and cross hairs superimposed on my face and a yellow ribbon (the timber industry's symbol) attached. My complaints to the local police and to the county board of supervisors were ignored. Finally, on May 24, 1990, as I was driving through Oakland on a concert tour to promote Redwood Summer, a bomb exploded under my car seat. I remember my thoughts as it ripped through me. I thought, this is what men do to each other in wars.

The bomb was meant to kill me, and it nearly did. It shattered my pelvis and left me crippled for life. My organizing companion, Darryl Cherney, who was riding with me in the car, was slightly injured. Then, adding to the outrage, police and the FBI moved in immediately and arrested Darryl and me, saying that it was our bomb and we were knowingly carrying it. For eight weeks they slandered us in the press, attempting to portray us as violent and to discredit Redwood Summer, until they finally admitted there was no evidence against us.

There were indications in advance that the attack on me was specifically misogynist. One of the death threats described Earth First!ers as "whores, lesbians, and members of NOW." But soon after the bombing a letter was received that left no doubt. It was signed "The Lord's Avenger," and it took credit for the bombing. It described the bomb in exact detail and explained in chilling prose why the Lord's Avenger wanted me dead.

It was not just my "paganism" and defense of the forest that outraged him. The Lord's Avenger also recalled an abortion clinic defense I had led years ago, and quoted Timothy 2:11: "Let the woman learn in silence with all subjection. But I suffer not a woman to teach, nor to usurp authority over the man, but to be in silence."

Meanwhile, out in the forest, Redwood Summer went on without me. Before the bombing I was one of very few women leaders in Earth First! But after the bombing it was the women who rose to take my place.

10

Redwood Summer was the feminization of Earth First!, with three quarters of the leadership made up of women. Our past actions had drawn no more than 150 participants. But 3,000 people came to Redwood Summer, blocking logging operations and marching through timber towns in demonstrations reminiscent of civil rights protests against the Klan in the South. Despite incredible provocation, and despite the grave violence done to me, Earth First! maintained our nonviolence throughout the summer.

Being the first women-led action, Redwood Summer has never gotten the respect it deserves from the old guard of Earth First! nationally. But it has profoundly affected the redwood region. The 2,000-year-old trees of Headwaters Forest, identified, named, and made an issue of by Earth First!, are now being preserved largely due to our actions. And the movement here, recently renamed Ecotopia Earth First!, is probably the only truly gender-balanced group I have ever worked in.   15

I recently attended a workshop in Tennessee on violence and harassment in the environmental movement. As the 32 people from all over the country shared their stories, I was struck by the fact that the most serious acts of violence had all been done to women. This is no surprise because it is the hatred of the feminine, which is the hatred of life, that has contributed to the destruction of the planet. And it is the strength of women that can restore the balance we need to survive.

The Responsive Reader

1. Does Bari succeed in making the loss of the redwoods seem urgent to you? What images or details in her account are most likely to overcome the apathy of readers?
2. Bari says that the activists of Earth First! used to be mainly male. What does she admire them for; why or how does she criticize them?
3. The struggle to save the redwoods is often presented as a struggle between "ecofreaks" and logging workers who need jobs. What is Bari's take on the economic dimension of the struggle? What are her views of the workers and the corporations?
4. What did Bari see as her special role or contribution as a woman? What does she mean by the "feminization" of the movement? What does she say about the role of misogyny in the attacks on her and her associates?

Talking, Listening, Writing

5. Can you see yourself as a radical ecologist? (Or would you limit yourself mainly to making contributions to genteel organizations like the Sierra Club?) Where do you draw the line?
6. Where do you stand on the issue of violence or nonviolence in efforts to bring about social change?
7. Where do *you* think the emphasis or the priorities should be in the effort to save the environment?

Projects

8. For a possible research project, you might consider the following:

   - In the struggle between ecologists and economic interests, charges and countercharges surround violent incidents like the explosion of a bomb in Bari's car. The police charged that a bomb she and her companion were transporting went off accidentally. Bari filed a lawsuit against the FBI and other police agencies, alleging civil rights violations stemming from her arrest after the incident. Working with a group, can you try to get at the truth behind the accusations and countercharges?

   - Bari mentions the Karen Silkwood case. Who was she? What are the controversies surrounding her case?

   - Greenpeace activists were charged with the sinking of a French ship in Australia. What happened?

SAVING NATURE, BUT ONLY FOR MAN

Charles Krauthammer

> *Charles Krauthammer is a conservative columnist who is a frequent contributor to* Time. *As the 500th anniversary of Columbus' voyage to the New World was approaching, Krauthammer published a* Time *essay titled "Hail Columbus, Dead White Male." As is his custom, he skewered what he considers the intellectual fashions of the "politically correct" American left: He attacked the "sentimental" glorification of the natives by writers "singing of the saintedness of the Indians in their pre-Columbian Eden, a land of virtue, empathy, ecological harmony." In the* Time *essay that follows, Krauthammer raises the familiar question of the economic cost of our current commitment to ecology and urges the setting of priorities.*

Thought Starters: How does Krauthammer distinguish between "environmental luxuries" and "environmental necessities"?

Environmental sensitivity is now as required an attitude in polite society as is, say, belief in democracy or aversion to polyester. But now that everyone from Ted Turner to George Bush, Dow to Exxon has professed love for Mother Earth, how are we to choose among the dozens of conflicting proposals, restrictions, projects, regulations and laws advanced in the name of the environment? Clearly not everything with an environmental claim is worth doing. How to choose?

There is a simple way. First, distinguish between environmental luxuries and environmental necessities. Luxuries are those things it would be nice to have if costless. Necessities are those things we must have regardless. Then apply a rule. Call it the fundamental axiom of sane environmentalism: Combatting ecological change that directly threatens the health and safety of people is an environmental necessity. All else is luxury.

For example: preserving the atmosphere — stopping ozone depletion and the greenhouse effect — is an environmental necessity. In April scientists reported that ozone damage is far worse than previously thought. Ozone depletion not only causes skin cancer and eye cataracts, it also destroys plankton, the beginning of the food chain atop which we humans sit.

The reality of the greenhouse effect is more speculative, though its possible consequences are far deadlier: melting ice caps, flooded coastlines, disrupted climate, parched plains and, ultimately, empty breadbaskets. The American Midwest feeds the world. Are we prepared to see Iowa acquire New Mexico's desert climate? And Siberia acquire Iowa's?

Ozone depletion and the greenhouse effect are human disasters.   5
They happen to occur in the environment. But they are urgent because
they directly threaten man. A sane environmentalism, the only kind of
environmentalism that will win universal public support, begins by un-
ashamedly declaring that nature is here to serve man. A sane environmentalism is entirely anthropocentric: it enjoins man to preserve nature, but
on the grounds of self-preservation.

A sane environmentalism does not sentimentalize the earth. It does
not ask people to sacrifice in the name of other creatures. After all, it is
hard enough to ask people to sacrifice in the name of other humans.
(Think of the chronic public resistance to foreign aid and welfare.) Ask
hardworking voters to sacrifice in the name of the snail darter, and, if they
are feeling polite, they will give you a shrug.

Of course, this anthropocentrism runs against the grain of a contemporary environmentalism that indulges in earth worship to the point of
idolatry. One scientific theory — Gaia theory — actually claims that Earth
is a living organism. This kind of environmentalism likes to consider itself
spiritual. It is nothing more than sentimental. It takes, for example, a
highly selective view of the benignity of nature. My nature worship stops
with the April twister that came through Kansas or the May cyclone that
killed more than 125,000 Bengalis and left 10 million (!) homeless.

A nonsentimental environmentalism is one founded on Protagoras'
maxim that "Man is the measure of all things." Such a principle helps us
through the thicket of environmental argument. Take the current debate
raging over oil drilling in a corner of the Alaska National Wildlife Refuge.
Environmentalists, mobilizing against a bill working its way through the
U.S. Congress to permit such exploration, argue that Americans should
be conserving energy instead of drilling for it. This is a false either/or
proposition. The U.S. does need a sizable energy tax to reduce consumption. But it needs more production too. Government estimates indicate a
nearly fifty-fifty chance that under the ANWR lies one of the five largest
oil fields ever discovered in America.

The U.S. has just come through a war fought in part over oil. Energy
dependence costs Americans not just dollars but lives. It is a bizarre senti-
mentalism that would deny oil that is peacefully attainable because it risks
disrupting the calving grounds of Arctic caribou.

I like the caribou as much as the next man. And I would be rather   10
sorry if their mating patterns are disturbed. But you can't have everything.
And if the choice is between the welfare of caribou and reducing an oil
dependency that gets people killed in wars, I choose man over caribou
every time.

Similarly the spotted owl in Oregon. I am no enemy of the owl. If it
could be preserved at no or little cost, I would agree: the variety of nature
is a good, a high aesthetic good. But it is no more than that. And sometimes aesthetic goods have to be sacrificed to the more fundamental ones.

If the cost of preserving the spotted owl is the loss of livelihood for 30,000 logging families, I choose family over owl.

The important distinction is between those environmental goods that are fundamental and those that are merely aesthetic. Nature is our ward. It is not our master. It is to be respected and even cultivated. But it is man's world. And when man has to choose between his well-being and that of nature, nature will have to accommodate.

Man should accommodate only when his fate and that of nature are inextricably bound up. The most urgent accommodation must be made when the very integrity of man's habitat — e.g., atmospheric ozone — is threatened. When the threat to man is of a lesser order (say, the pollutants from coal- and oil-fired generators that cause death from disease but not fatal damage to the ecosystem), a more modulated accommodation that balances economic against health concerns is in order. But in either case the principle is the same: protect the environment — because it is man's environment.

The sentimental environmentalists will call this saving nature with a totally wrong frame of mind. Exactly. A sane — a humanistic — environmentalism does it not for nature's sake but for our own.

The Responsive Reader

1. What is the essence of Krauthammer's "sane environmentalism"? What are the test cases that help him expound his thesis? (What does he mean by "anthropocentrism"?)
2. What is Krauthammer's basic philosophical difference with what he calls "sentimental" environmentalism?

Talking, Listening, Writing

3. Prepare an oral presentation or write an essay to support or rebut Krauthammer's position. Support your point of view with detailed examples or cases in point.

Projects

4. Scientists like Carl Sagan sounded the alarm concerning the loss of the protective ozone layer in the atmosphere and the resultant global warming — the "greenhouse effect." What is the current state of scientific knowledge concerning global warming? Has there been preventive action by this country or other nations? Your class may want to farm out different aspects of this issue for research by small groups.

WHAT'S WRONG WITH ANIMAL RIGHTS

Vicki Hearne

The animal rights movement has led many to rethink their relationship with the animal world. The movement has led to crusades to rehabilitate and protect animals of the wild like the wolf and the coyote. It has focused attention on the suffering and destruction of animals in medical and military research. Animal rights activists have challenged the unnatural conditions under which chickens and calves, for instance, are raised for food. They have made zoo-keepers reexamine the unnatural conditions under which animals are confined. By the same token, the animal rights movement has put hunters, trainers, and pet owners on the defensive, making them justify practices that they had long taken for granted. Vicki Hearne, the author of the following article, is an animal trainer and the author of Bandit: Dossier of a Dangerous Dog *(1991). In this article, written for* Harper's Magazine, *she explores the "symbiotic" relationship — the close organic interdependence — of human beings and the animals they keep. Her article is followed by a sampling of the letters to the editor it triggered from people who disagree with her views.*

Thought Starters: Do animals have feelings? Do animals have rights? Do animal trainers and pet owners have the right to do what they do?

Not all happy animals are alike. A Doberman going over a hurdle   1
after a small wooden dumbbell is sleek, all arcs of harmonious power. A basset hound cheerfully performing the same exercise exhibits harmonies of a more lugubrious nature. There are chimpanzees who love precision the way musicians or fanatical housekeepers or accomplished hypochondriacs do; others for whom happiness is a matter of invention and variation — chimp vaudevillians. There is a rhinoceros whose happiness, as near as I can make out, is in needing to be trained every morning, all over again, or else he "forgets" his circus routine, and in this you find a clue to the slow, deep, quiet chuckle of his happiness and to the glory of the beast. Happiness for Secretariat is in his ebullient bound, that joyful length of stride. For the draft horse or the weight-pull dog, happiness is of a different shape, more awesome and less obviously intelligent. When the pulling horse is at its most intense, the animal goes into himself, allocating all of the educated power that organizes his desire to dwell in fierce and delicate intimacy with that power, leans into the harness, and MAKES THAT SUCKER MOVE.

If we are speaking of human beings and use the phrase "animal happiness," we tend to mean something like "creature comforts." The emblems of this are the golden retriever rolling in the grass, the horse with his nose deep in the oats, the kitty by the fire. Creature comforts are important to animals — "Grub first, then ethics" is a motto that would describe many a wise Labrador retriever, and I have a pit bull named Annie whose continual quest for the perfect pillow inspires her to awesome feats. But there is something more to animals, a capacity for satisfactions that come from work in the fullest sense — what is known in philosophy and in this country's Declaration of Independence as "happiness." This is a sense of personal achievement, like the satisfaction felt by a good wood-carver or a dancer or a poet or an accomplished dressage horse. It is a happiness that, like the artist's, must come from something within the animal, something trainers call "talent." Hence, it cannot be imposed on the animal. But it is also something that does not come *ex nihilo*. If it had not been a fairly ordinary thing, in one part of the world, to teach young children to play the pianoforte, it is doubtful that Mozart's music would exist.

Happiness is often misunderstood as a synonym for pleasure or as an antonym for suffering. But Aristotle associated happiness with ethics — codes of behavior that urge us toward the sensation of getting it right, a kind of work that yields the "click" of satisfaction upon solving a problem or surmounting an obstacle. In his *Ethics,* Aristotle wrote, "If happiness is activity in accordance with excellence, it is reasonable that it should be in accordance with the highest excellence." Thomas Jefferson identified the capacity for happiness as one of the three fundamental rights on which all others are based: "life, liberty, and the pursuit of happiness."

I bring up this idea of happiness as a form of work because I am an animal trainer, and work is the foundation of the happiness a trainer and an animal discover together. I bring up these words also because they cannot be found in the lexicon of the animal-rights movement. This absence accounts for the uneasiness toward the movement of most people, who sense that rights advocates have a point but take it too far when they liberate snails or charge that goldfish at the county fair are suffering. But the problem with the animal-rights advocates is not that they take it too far; it's that they've got it all wrong.

Animal rights are built upon a misconceived premise that rights were created to prevent us from unnecessary suffering. You can't find an animal-rights book, video, pamphlet, or rock concert in which someone doesn't mention the Great Sentence, written by Jeremy Bentham in 1789. Arguing in favor of such rights, Bentham wrote: "The question is not, Can they *reason?* nor, can they *talk?* but, can they *suffer?*"

The logic of the animal-rights movement places suffering at the iconographic center of a skewed value system. The thinking of its proponents — given eerie expression in a virtually sado-pornographic sculpture of a tortured monkey that won a prize for its compassionate vision — has collapsed into a perverse conundrum. Today the loudest voices calling for — demanding — the destruction of animals are the humane organizations. This is an inevitable consequence of the apotheosis of the drive to relieve suffering: Death is the ultimate release. To compensate for their contradictions, the humane movement has demonized, in this century and the last, those who made animal happiness their business: veterinarians, trainers, and the like. We think of Louis Pasteur as the man whose work saved you and me and your dog and cat from rabies, but antivivisectionists of the time claimed that rabies increased in areas where there were Pasteur Institutes.

An anti-rabies public-relations campaign mounted in England in the 1880s by the Royal Society for the Prevention of Cruelty to Animals and other organizations led to orders being issued to club any dog found not wearing a muzzle. England still has her cruel and unnecessary law that requires an animal to spend six months in quarantine before being allowed loose in the country. Most of the recent propaganda about pit bulls — the crazy claim that they "take hold with their front teeth while they chew away with their rear teeth" (which would imply, incorrectly, that they have double jaws) — can be traced to literature published by the Humane Society of the United States during the fall of 1987 and earlier. If your neighbors want your dog or horse impounded and destroyed because he is a nuisance — say the dog barks, or the horse attracts flies — it will be the local Humane Society to whom your neighbors turn for action.

In a way, everyone has the opportunity to know that the history of the humane movement is largely a history of miseries, arrests, prosecutions, and death. The Humane Society is the pound, the place with the decompression chamber or the lethal injections. You occasionally find worried letters about this in Ann Landers's column.

Animal-rights publications are illustrated largely with photographs of two kinds of animals — "Helpless Fluff" and "Agonized Fluff," the two conditions in which some people seem to prefer their animals, because any other version of an animal is too complicated for propaganda. In the introduction to his book *Animal Liberation,* Peter Singer says somewhat smugly that he and his wife have no animals and, in fact, don't much care for them. This is offered as evidence of his objectivity and ethical probity. But it strikes me as an odd, perhaps obscene, underpinning for an ethical project that encourages university and high school students to cherish their ignorance of, say, great bird dogs as proof of their devotion to animals.

I would like to leave these philosophers behind, for they are inept 10
connoisseurs of suffering who might revere my Airedale for his capacity to scream when subjected to a blowtorch but not for his wit and courage,

not for his natural good manners that are a gentle rebuke to ours. I want to celebrate the moment not long ago when, at his first dog show, my Airedale, Drummer, learned that there can be a public place where his work is respected. I want to celebrate his meticulousness, his happiness upon realizing at the dog show that no one would swoop down upon him and swamp him with the goo-goo excesses known as the "teddy-bear complex" but that people actually got out of his way, gave him room to work. I want to say, "There can be a six-and-a-half-month-old puppy who can care about accuracy, who can be fastidious, and whose fastidiousness will be a foundation for courage later." I want to say, "Leave my puppy alone!"

I want to leave the philosophers behind, but I cannot, in part because the philosophical problems that plague academicians of the animal-rights movement are illuminating. They wonder, do animals have rights or do they have interests? Or, if these rightists lead particularly unexamined lives, they dismiss that question as obvious (yes, of course, animals have rights, prima facie) and proceed to enumerate them, James Madison style. This leads to the issuance of bills of rights — the right to an environment, the right not to be used in medical experiments — and other forms of trivialization.

The calculus of suffering can be turned against the philosophers of festering flesh, even in the case of food animals, or exotic animals who perform in movies and circuses. It is true that it hurts to be slaughtered by man, but it doesn't hurt nearly as much as some of the cunningly cruel arrangements meted out by "Mother Nature." In Africa, 75 percent of the lions cubbed do not survive to the age of two. For those who make it to two, the average age at death is ten years. Asali, the movie and TV lioness, was still working at age twenty-one. There are fates worse than death, but twenty-one years of a close working relationship with Hubert Wells, Asali's trainer, is not one of them. Dorset sheep and polled Herefords would not exist at all were they not in a symbiotic relationship with human beings.

A human being living in the "wild" — somewhere, say, without the benefits of medicine and advanced social organization — would probably have a life expectancy of from thirty to thirty-five years. A human being living in "captivity" — in, say, a middle-class neighborhood of what the Centers for Disease Control call a Metropolitan Statistical Area — has a life expectancy of seventy or more years. For orangutans in the wild in Borneo and Malaysia, the life expectancy is thirty-five years; in captivity, fifty years. The wild is not a suffering-free zone or all that frolicsome a location.

The questions asked by animal-rights activists are flawed, because they are built on the concept that the origin of rights is in the avoidance of suffering rather than in the pursuit of happiness. The question that needs to be asked — and that will put us in closer proximity to the truth — is not, do they have rights? or, what are those rights? but rather, what is a right?

Rights originate in committed relationships and can be found, both   *15*
intact and violated, wherever one finds such relationships — in social com-
pacts, within families, between animals, and between people and nonhuman animals. This is as true when the nonhuman animals in question are
lions or parakeets as when they are dogs. It is my Airedale whose excellen-
cies have my attention at the moment, so it is with reference to him that I
will consider the question, what is a right?

When I imagine situations in which it naturally arises that A defends
or honors or respects B's rights, I imagine situations in which the relationship between A and B can be indicated with a possessive pronoun. I might
say, "Leave her alone, she's my daughter" or, "That's what she wants, and
she is my daughter. I think I am bound to honor her wants." Similarly,
"Leave her alone, she's my mother." I am more tender of the happiness of
my mother, my father, my child, than I am of other people's family
members; more tender of my friends' happinesses than your friends' happinesses, unless you and I have a mutual friend.

Possession of a being by another has come into more and more
disrepute, so that the common understanding of one person possessing
another is slavery. But the important detail about the kind of possessive
pronoun that I have in mind is reciprocity: If I have a friend, she has a
friend. If I have a daughter, she has a mother. The possessive does not bind
one of us while freeing the other; it cannot do that. Moreover, should the
mother reject the daughter, the word that applies is "disown." The form
of disowning that most often appears in the news is domestic violence.
Parents abuse children; husbands batter wives.

Some cases of reciprocal possessives have built-in limitations, such
as "my patient / my doctor" or "my student / my teacher" or "my
agent / my client." Other possessive relations are extremely limited but
still remarkably binding: "my neighbor" and "my country" and "my
president."

The responsibilities and the ties signaled by reciprocal possession
typically are hard to dissolve. It can be as difficult to give up an enemy as
to give up a friend, and often the one becomes the other, as though the
logic of the possessive pronoun outlasts the forms it chanced to take at a
given moment, as though we were stuck with one another. In these bindings, nearly inextricable, are found the origin of our rights. They imply a
possessiveness but also recognize an acknowledgment by each side of the
other's existence.

The idea of democracy is dependent on the citizens' having knowl-   *20*
edge of the government; that is, realizing that the government exists and
knowing how to claim rights against it. I know this much because I get
mail from the government and see its "representatives" running about in
uniforms. Whether I actually have any rights in relationship to the government is less clear, but the idea that I do is symbolized by the right to vote.
I obey the government, and, in theory, it obeys me, by counting my
ballot, reading the *Miranda* warning to me, agreeing to be bound by the

Constitution. My friend obeys me as I obey her; the government "obeys" me to some extent, and, to a different extent, I obey it.

What kind of thing can my Airedale, Drummer, have knowledge of? He can know that I exist and through that knowledge can claim his happinesses, with varying degrees of success, both with me and against me. Drummer can also know about larger human or dog communities than the one that consists only of him and me. There is my household — the other dogs, the cats, my husband. I have had enough dogs on campuses to know that he can learn that Yale exists as a neighborhood or village. My older dog, Annie, not only knows that Yale exists but can tell Yalies from townies, as I learned while teaching there during labor troubles.

Dogs can have elaborate conceptions of human social structures, and even of something like their rights and responsibilities within them, but these conceptions are never elaborate enough to construct a rights relationship between a dog and the state, or a dog and the Humane Society. Both of these are concepts that depend on writing and memoranda, officers in uniform, plaques and seals of authority. All of these are literary constructs, and all of them are beyond a dog's ken, which is why the mail carrier who doesn't also happen to be a dog's friend is forever an intruder — this is why dogs bark at mailmen.

It is clear enough that natural rights relations can arise between people and animals. Drummer, for example, can insist, "Hey, let's go outside and do something!" if I have been at my computer several days on end. He can both refuse to accept various of my suggestions and tell me when he fears for his life — such as the time when the huge, white flapping flag appeared out of nowhere, as it seemed to him, on the town green one evening when we were working. I can (and do) say to him either, "Oh, you don't have to worry about that" or, "Uh oh, you're right, Drum, that guy looks dangerous." Just as the government and I — two different species of organism — have developed improvised ways of communicating, such as the vote, so Drummer and I have worked out a number of ways to make our expressions known. Largely through obedience, I have taught him a fair amount about how to get responses from me. Obedience is reciprocal; you cannot get responses from a dog to whom you do not respond accurately. I have enfranchised him in a relationship to me by educating him, creating the conditions by which he can achieve a certain happiness specific to a dog, maybe even specific to an Airedale, inasmuch as this same relationship has allowed me to plumb the happiness of being a trainer and writing this article.

Instructions in this happiness are given terms that are alien to a culture in which liver treats, fluffy windup toys, and miniature sweaters are confused with respect and work. Jack Knox, a sheepdog trainer originally from Scotland, will shake his crook at a novice handler who makes a promiscuous move to praise a dog, and will call out in his Scottish accent,

"Eh! Eh! Get back, get BACK! Ye'll no be abusin' the dogs like that in my clinic." America is a nation of abused animals, Knox says, because we are always swooping at them with praise, "no gi'ing them their freedom." I am reminded of Rainer Maria Rilke's account in which the Prodigal Son leaves — has to leave — because everyone loves him, even the dogs love him, and he has no path to the delicate and fierce truth of himself. Unconditional praise and love, in Rilke's story, disenfranchise us, distract us from what truly excites our interest.

In the minds of some trainers and handlers, praise is dishonesty. 25 Paradoxically, it is a kind of contempt for animals that masquerades as a reverence for helplessness and suffering. The idea of freedom means that you do not, at least not while Jack Knox is nearby, helpfully guide your dog through the motions of, say, herding over and over — what one trainer calls "explainy-wainy." This is rote learning. It works tolerably well on some handlers, because people have vast unconscious minds and can store complex pre-programmed behaviors. Dogs, on the other hand, have almost no unconscious minds, so they can learn only by thinking. Many children are like this until educated out of it.

If I tell my Airedale to sit and stay on the town green, and someone comes up and burbles, "What a pretty thing you are," he may break his stay to go for a caress. I pull him back and correct him for breaking. Now he holds his stay because I have blocked his way to movement but not because I have punished him. (A correction blocks one path as it opens another for desire to work; punishment blocks desire and opens nothing.) He holds his stay now, and — because the stay opens this possibility of work, new to a heedless young dog — he watches. If the person goes on talking, and isn't going to gush with praise, I may heel Drummer out of his stay and give him an "Okay" to make friends. Sometimes something about the person makes Drummer feel that reserve is in order. He responds to an insincere approach by sitting still, going down into himself, and thinking, "This person has no business pawing me. I'll sit very still, and he will go away." If the person doesn't take the hint from Drummer, I'll give the pup a little backup by saying, "Please don't pet him, he's working," even though he was not under any command.

The pup reads this, and there is a flicker of a working trust now stirring in the dog. Is the pup grateful? When the stranger leaves, does he lick my hand, full of submissive blandishments? This one doesn't. This one says nothing at all, and I say nothing much to him. This is a working trust we are developing, not a mutual-congratulation society. My backup is praise enough for him; the use he makes of my support is praise enough for me.

Listening to a dog is often praise enough. Suppose it is just after dark and we are outside. Suddenly there is a shout from the house. The pup and I both look toward the shout and then toward each other: "What do you think?" I don't so much as cock my head, because Drummer is growing up, and I want to know what he thinks. He takes a few steps toward the house, and I follow. He listens again and comprehends that it's just Holly, who at fourteen is much given to alarming cries and shouts. He shrugs at me and goes about his business. I say nothing. To praise him for this performance would make about as much sense as praising a human being for the same thing. Thus:

A. What's that?
B. I don't know. [Listens] Oh, it's just Holly.
A. What a goooooood human being!
B. Huh?

This is one small moment in a series of like moments that will culminate in an Airedale who on a Friday will have the discrimination and confidence required to take down a man who is attacking me with a knife and on Saturday clown and play with the children at the annual Orange Empire Dog Club Christmas party.

People who claim to speak for animal rights are increasingly devoted   30
to the idea that the very keeping of a dog or a horse or a gerbil or a lion is in and of itself an offense. The more loudly they speak, the less likely they are to be in a rights relation to any given animal, because they are spending so much time in airplanes or transmitting fax announcements of the latest Sylvester Stallone anti-fur rally. In a 1988 *Harper's* forum, for example, Ingrid Newkirk, the national director of People for the Ethical Treatment of Animals, urged that domestic pets be spayed and neutered and ultimately phased out. She prefers, it appears, wolves — and wolves someplace else — to Airedales and, by a logic whose interior structure is both emotionally and intellectually forever closed to Drummer, claims thereby to be speaking for "animal rights."

She is wrong. I am the only one who can own up to my Airedale's inalienable rights. Whether or not I do it perfectly at any given moment is no more refutation of this point than whether I am perfectly my husband's mate at any given moment refutes the fact of marriage. Only people who know Drummer, and whom he can know, are capable of this relationship. PETA and the Humane Society and the ASPCA and the Congress and NOW — as institutions — do have the power to affect my ability to grant rights to Drummer but are otherwise incapable of creating conditions or laws or rights that would increase his happiness. Only Drummer's owner has the power to obey him — to obey who he is and what he is capable of — deeply enough to grant him his rights and open up the possibility of happiness.

The Responsive Reader

1. Where in this article do you get a glimpse of the animal rights arguments that put Hearne on the defensive and that she is trying to refute? What are some of her central objections?

2. How successful is Hearne in showing that animals can achieve a quasi-human work ethic and a satisfaction from performance? (What are key examples? How persuasive are they?)
3. What is the gist of her discussion of rights?

Talking, Listening, Writing

4. Do you think Hearne reads too many quasi-human qualities into the behavior of the animals she knows?
5. Would you say that Hearne loves animals? Do you think it is true that Hearne cares more about animals than her opponents do?
6. Write an indictment or a defense of hunters, zookeepers, animal trainers, or people who keep pets.

Projects

7. For a possible research project, you may choose to investigate the motives, procedures, and successes or failures of one major initiative to protect the animal creation. For instance, you may decide to investigate one of the following:

   - the movement to protect the wolf
   - the conflict between ranchers and environmentalists over the coyote
   - the campaign against barbaric practices in raising calves for veal
   - the movement to replace traditional zoos with more natural habitats for captive animals
   - efforts to save wildlife threatened by oil spills

ANIMAL RIGHTS, WRONGED

The following is a sampling of the outpouring of letters provoked by Hearne's "What's Wrong with Animal Rights." What in her article triggered the reactions of the letter writers? What is the range of opinion? What are the assumptions about the relation between animals and human beings implied in the arguments?

Thought Starters: Is there any common ground shared by Hearne and the letter writers? What are the most basic disagreements?

Vicki Hearne is so wrapped up in defining happiness for Drummer, her Airedale ["What's Wrong with Animal Rights," September], that she neglects to examine the most crucial argument advanced by proponents of animal rights. Despite Hearne's complaint, it is only the most extreme animal-rights activists who suggest that domestic pets be "phased out." The remainder of those concerned with the plight of animals, like myself, focus instead on what Hearne only alludes to: suffering.

Few would agree that training a show dog or putting a horse to work is cruel. Surely Hearne takes good care of her own dog, as do most pet owners. Countless acts of animal neglect do exist, however, and are preventable. The wanton destruction of laboratory rats to test cosmetics or the obsessive shooting of cats to study gunshot wounds *is* cruel and unusual. These blatant abuses outrage the majority of animal-rights activists and fuel their sympathies. Much as it may surprise Hearne, these activists are not losing sleep over her playing fetch with her loyal Drummer.

Furthermore, Hearne twists logic when she suggests that since the Humane Society destroys animals, the entire animal-rights movement is rotten to the core. This is old, tired rhetoric. The Humane Society destroys unwanted animals so that they will not suffer. Moreover, by writing that "the wild is not a suffering-free zone," Hearne infers that any pain an animal incurs in a domestic situation (home or laboratory) is somehow, in her view, legitimated. Here, she fails to isolate intention from her clever "calculus of suffering." Does Mother Nature *intend* to hurt, maim, and kill, or are these effects simply part of a larger cyclical design? Clearly the answer is the latter. The wolf tears apart the frail and sick caribou not only to ensure its own survival but to maintain the balance of nature. Humankind, however, is not compelled to shock the monkey. Must we infect, injure, and inject in our quest for luscious lipstick, thicker eyelashes, more efficient handguns? Does this research ensure our survival? Although some animal experimentation does provide useful data, much of it provides only superfluous pain for animals.

1

True, the notion of animal rights per se is troubling: Who really knows what animals desire or need? Although Hearne pretends to possess the secrets of the animal world, the truth is that we will never know the true essence of animal happiness. No human is Doctor Doolittle. No one, not even the dog lovers among us, can speak to or for animals' sensibilities. But does this insurmountable communication gap permit us to act without empathy? To disregard decency and common sense? If animal suffering can be prevented, without significant detriment to whatever useful scientific knowledge animal testing purports to produce, then perhaps our own species will have progressed.

Ethan Gilsdorf
Baton Rouge, La.

Happiness, as dog trainer Vicki Hearne defines it, comes to animals in the course of being trained and "getting it right." Thus, the draft horse is happy only when it strains against an unbearable weight, and the trained rhino is happy only when it perches on a tiny stool and mimics ballet steps. What Hearne has recognized, and then twisted, is the very real desire of some animals to please humans. Rowlf, in Richard Adams's *The Plague Dogs,* puzzles about why the whitecoats drown and revive him over and over again. He finally hits upon an explanation: He was trying to "get it right," but he just couldn't. Hearne's hellish, whitecoat logic is as follows: Animals like to please humans. Therefore, animals are happiest when they are fulfilling humans' whims, however cruel. Therefore, in order to contribute to animals' happiness, humans should force animals to fulfill human whims. If it pleases a vivisector to pour oven cleaner into a rabbit's eye, the rabbit is happiest with oven cleaner in his eye. If it pleases a deep-sea fishing guide to use a live kitten for bait, the kitten is happiest impaled on a fishing hook.

Hearne concludes by revealing the philosophical underpinnings of her theory: "Only [an animal's] owner has the power . . . to grant him his rights. . ." Jefferson, whose name Hearne blasphemously evokes in support of a theory that would sicken him, knew better. He recognized that rights are inalienable, their existence self-evident. A rabbit's right not to have oven cleaner poured in its eye is inherent. It exists whether the state recognizes it or not. If our government repeals the Thirteenth Amendment tomorrow, slavery may once again be legal, but it will still be wrong. Pouring oven cleaner in rabbits' eyes is wrong. It always has been; it always will be. One day, the law will conform to this truth.

Elizabeth L. DeCoux
Jackson, Miss.

To select an animal trainer to write on animal rights is like asking a butcher to write on vegetarianism. To train an animal means, first of all, to subdue it. The methods used by trainers to do this subduing are, for the most part, kept secret from the public.

Most wild animals are trained by withholding their food, that is, if the subduer is "kind." Another more common method is beating in the face—as is done to the so-called trained orangutans in one Las Vegas nightclub. Elephant trainers use an implement with brightly colored fibers that disguise a sharp steel hook. When a trainer sticks this training tool into the aural cavity or other delicate parts of the elephant's body, the pain is so severe that the elephant will do *anything*—stand on its head, dance on its hind legs in a tutu, etc. These are not actions that any elephant would perform if permitted to retain its moral rights.

With our longtime domesticated animals, such as the dog and horse, training may not have to be this severe, but it is still plenty tough. It doesn't take a dog long to learn that not minding means being brought up suddenly and hard by a choke chain, having its paws stepped on if it walks ahead of its trainer, or being denied its dinner. A dressage horse that makes a misstep catches on quickly when it gets a sharp stab in the belly from its trainer's spurs.

Hearne speaks of the "extended" lives of animals in captivity. An   10
orca whale that ordinarily lives forty or fifty years in the wild lives approximately eight years in our various Sea Worlds. Even if they lived only eight years in the wild, they would be free to travel through the hundreds of miles of ocean natural to them rather than be confined to the tiny pools in which they are made prisoners at Sea Worlds. How much better for all captive animals to have even a few natural years in the wild than a longer lifetime of incarceration, boredom, and "training."

Mary Sternberg
Escondido, Calif.

The Responsive Reader

1. The first letter writer is concerned to establish a rational, middle-of-the-road position, distancing himself from "extreme animal rights activists." Why, where, how, and with what effect? What, nevertheless, is his basic quarrel with Hearne?
2. How does the second letter writer show that she has taken in some of Hearne's key arguments? How does she turn the tables on Hearne?
3. How does the third letter writer aggressively attack and rebut key parts of Hearne's position?

Talking, Listening, Writing

4. Letters to the editors are expected to include a fair share of crank letters—written by opinionated people who predictably rise to the bait whenever a writer seems to question one of their pet theories.

How reasonable do these correspondents seem to you? Does one of them come close to voicing your own sentiments or reactions?

5. Where do you stand on the current animal rights movement? Do you sympathize—all or in part? Do you think animal righters tend to be unrealistic or extreme?

6. Write your own letter to the editor in response to Hearne's original article.

Projects

7. Investigate the range of opinion in the letters-to-the-editor column of your local newspaper. What issues or topics seem to generate the most mail—or the most heat? Do you recognize familiar approaches, kinds of argument, or ploys?

THE SNOW WALKER

Farley Mowat

Farley Mowat is a Canadian ethnologist — a student of cultures different from our own. When Mowat was fourteen, a great-uncle introduced him to Canada's vast Arctic territories. After serving in the Canadian army in World War II, Mowat lived for two years among the Ihalmuit tribe of the Eskimo, or Inuit, of the North. His People of the Deer *(1952) was highly critical of the Canadian government's treatment of the dying tribe. In* Never Cry Wolf, *Mowat championed the cause of a species threatened with extinction. The following is the lead story of his* The Snow Walker *(1975), a collection of stories about the native peoples of the Arctic. The story makes us reexamine one of the cherished myths of Western civilization — the myth of European cultures bringing the blessings of civilization to the backward peoples of the world.*

Thought Starters: In this story, what is the life of the native peoples before the arrival of the white man? What is their relationship with nature? What does the arrival of white civilization bring for the peoples of the North?

After death carried the noose to Angutna and Kipmik, their memory 1
lived on with the people of the Great Plains. But death was not satisfied and, one by one, he took the lives of the people until none was left to remember. Before the last of them died, the story was told to a stranger and so it is that Angutna and Kipmik may cheat oblivion a little while longer.

It begins on a summer day when Angutna was only a boy. He had taken his father's kayak and paddled over the still depths of the lake called Big Hungry until he entered a narrow strait called Muskox Thing. Here he grounded the kayak beneath a wall of looming cliffs and climbed cautiously upward under a cloud-shadowed sky. He was hunting for *Tuktu,* the caribou, which was the source of being for those who lived in the heart of the tundra. Those people knew of the sea only as a legend. For them seals, walrus and whales were mythical beasts. For them the broad-antlered caribou was the giver of life.

Angutna was lucky. Peering over a ledge he saw three caribou bucks resting their rumbling bellies on a broad step in the cliffs. They were not sleeping, and one or other of them kept raising his head to shake off the black hordes of flies that clung to nostrils and ears, so Angutna was forced to crawl forward an inch or two at a time. It took him an hour to move

twenty yards, but he moved with such infinite caution that the bucks
remained unaware of his presence. He had only a few more yards to crawl
before he could drive an arrow from his short bow with enough power
to kill.

Sunlight burst suddenly down through the yielding grey scud and
struck hot on the crouched back of the boy and the thick coats of the deer.
The warmth roused the bucks and one by one they got to their feet. Now
they were restless, alert, and ready to move. In an agony of uncertainty
Angutna lay still as a rock. This was the first time he had tried to stalk
Tuktu all by himself, and if he failed in his first hunt he believed it would
bode ill for his luck in the years ahead.

But the burst of sunlight had touched more than the deer and the   5
boy. It had beamed into a cleft in the cliffs overhanging the ledge where it
had wakened two sleeping fox pups. Now their catlike grey faces peered
shortsightedly over the brilliant roll of the lake and the land. Cloudy black
eyes took in the tableau of the deer and the boy; but in their desire to see
more, the pups forgot the first precept of all wild things — to see and hear
but not to be seen or heard. They skittered to the edge of the cleft, shrilling
a mockery of the dog fox's challenge at the strange beasts below.

The bucks turned their heavy heads and their ears flopped anxiously
until their eyes found the pups scampering back and forth far over their
heads. They continued to watch the young foxes, and so they did not see
the boy move rapidly closer.

The hard twang of the bow and the heavy thud of an arrow striking
into flesh came almost together. The deer leapt for the precipitous slope
leading to the lake, but one of them stumbled, fell to his knees, and went
sliding down on his side. In a moment Angutna was on him. The boy's
copper knife slipped smoothly between the vertebrae in the deer's neck,
and the buck lay dead.

The curiosity of the pups had now passed all bounds. One of them
hung so far out over the ledge that he lost his balance. His hind legs
scrabbled furiously at the smooth face of the rocks while his front feet
pushed against air. The rocks thrust him away and he came tumbling in a
steep arc to pitch into the moss almost at Angutna's feet.

The pup was too stunned to resist as the boy picked him up by the
tail. Angutna put a tentative finger on the small beast's head, and when it
failed to snap at him he laughed aloud. His laughter rang over the hills to
the ears of the mother fox far from her den; it speeded the flight of the two
surviving bucks, and rose to the ears of a high-soaring raven.

Then the boy spoke to the fox: 10
"*Ayee!* Kipmik — Little Dog — we have made a good hunt, you and
I. Let it be always this way, for surely you must be one of the Spirits-Who-
Help."

That night in his father's skin tent Angutna told the tale of the
hunting. Elder men smiled as they listened and agreed that the fox must

indeed be a good token sent to the boy. Tethered to a tent pole, the pup lay in a little grey ball with his ears flat to his head and his eyes tightly shut, hoping with all his small heart that this was only a dream from which he would wake to find solace at the teats of his mother.

Such was the coming of the white fox into the habitations of men. In the days that followed, Angutna shared most of his waking hours with Kipmik who soon forgot his fears; for it is in the nature of the white fox to be so filled with curiosity that fear can be only a passing thing.

While the pup was still young enough to risk falling into the lean jaws of the dogs that prowled about the camp, he was kept tethered at night; but during the days, fox and boy travelled the land and explored the world that was theirs. On these expeditions the pup ran freely ahead of the boy over the rolling plains and hills, or he squatted motionless on the precarious deck of a kayak as Angutna drove the slim craft across the shining lakes.

Boy and fox lived together as one, and their thoughts were almost as one. The bond was strong between them for Angutna believed the fox was more than a fox, being also the embodiment of the Spirit-Who-Helps which had attached itself to him. As for Kipmik, perhaps he saw in the boy the shape of his own guardian spirit.   *15*

The first snows of the year came in late September and soon after that Kipmik shed the sombre grey fur of youth and donned the white mantle of the dog fox. His long hair was as fine as down and the white ruff that bordered his face framed glistening black eyes and the black spot of his nose. His tail was nearly as long and as round as his body. He was small compared to the red foxes who live in the forests, but he was twice as fleet and his courage was boundless.

During the second winter they spent together, Angutna came of age. He was fifteen and of a strength and awareness to accept manhood. In the time when the nights were so long they were almost unbroken, Angutna's father spoke to the father of a young girl named Epeetna. Then this girl moved into the snowhouse of Angutna's family and the boy who was now a man took her to wife.

During the winters life was lived without much exertion in the camps of the barrenland people for the deer were far to the south and men lived on the fat and meat they had stored up from the fall slaughter. But with the return of the snowbirds, spring and the deer came back to the plains around the Big Hungry and the camps woke to new and vigorous life.

In the spring of the first year of his marriage, Angutna went to the deer-hunting places as a full-fledged hunter. With him went the white fox. The two would walk over the softening drifts to reach rocky defiles that channelled the north-flowing deer. Angutna would hide in one of the ravines while the fox ran high up on the ridges to a place where he could overlook the land and see the dark skeins of caribou approaching the ambush. When the old doe leading a skein approached the defile, she would look carefully around and see the little white shadow watching from above. Kipmik would bark a short greeting to Tuktu, and the herd would move fearlessly forward believing that, if danger lurked, the fox would have barked a cry of alarm. But Kipmik's welcoming bark was meant for the ears of Angutna, who drew back the arrow on the bent bow and waited.

Angutna made good hunts during that spring and as a result he was   *20* sung about at the drum dances held in the evenings. The fox was not forgotten either, and in some of the songs the boy and the fox were called the Two Who Were One, and that name became theirs.

In the summer, when the deer had passed on to the fawning grounds far to the north, the fox and the boy sought other food. The Two Who Were One took the kayak down the roaring rivers that debouched over the scarred face of the plains, seeking the hiding places of the geese that nested in that land. After midsummer the adult geese lost their flight quills and had to stay on the water, and at such times they became very shy. The kayak sought out the backwaters where the earthbound geese waited in furtive seclusion for the gift of flight to return.

While Angutna concealed himself behind rocks near the shore, Kipmik would dance on the open beach, barking and squealing like a young pup. He would roll on his back or leap into the air. As he played, the geese would emerge from their hiding places and swim slowly toward him, fascinated by this peculiar behaviour in an animal they all knew so well. They had no fear of the fox for they knew he would not try to swim. The geese would come closer, cackling to one another with necks outstretched in amazement. Then Angutna's sling would whir and a stone would fly with a angry hiss. A goose would flap its wings on the water and die.

It was an old trick Kipmik played on the geese, one used by foxes since time began . . . but only Kipmik played that game for the benefit of man.

So the years passed until there were two children in the summer tent of Angutna — a boy and a girl who spent long hours playing with the soft tail of the fox. They were not the only young to play with that white brush. Every spring, when the ptarmigan mated on the hills and the wild dog foxes barked their challenges as an overtone to the sonorous singing of the wolves, unrest would come into the heart of the fox that lived in the houses of men.

On a night he would slip away from the camp and be gone many   *25* days. When he returned, lean and hungry, Angutna would feed him special tidbits and smilingly wish good luck to the vixen secreted in some newly dug den not far away. The vixen never ventured into the camp, but Kipmik saw to it that she and her pups were well fed, for Angutna did not begrudge the fox and his family a fair share of the meat that was killed. Sometimes Angutna followed the fox into the hills to the burrow. Then Angutna might leave a fresh fish at its mouth, and he would speak kindly to the unseen vixen cowering within. "Eat well, little sister," he would say.

As the years slipped by, stories of the Two Who Were One spread through the land. One of them told of a time when Angutna and his family were camped alone by the lake called Lamp of the Woman. It was a very bad year. In midwinter there was an unbroken month of great storms and the people used up all the meat stored near the camp but the weather was too savage to permit the men to travel to their more distant caches. The people grew hungry and cold, for there was no more fat for the lamps.

Finally there came a day without wind. Angutna hitched up his team and set out for a big cache lying two days' travel to the west. The dogs pulled as hard as their starved muscles would let them while the fox, like a white wraith, flitted ahead, choosing the easiest road for the team. The sled runners rasped as if they were being hauled over dry sand, for the temperature stood at fifty or sixty degrees below freezing.

On the second day of the journey the sun failed to show itself and there was only a pallid grey light on the horizon. After a while the fox stopped and stared hard into the north, his short ears cocked forward. Then Angutna too began to hear a distant keening in the dark sky. He tried to speed up the dogs, hoping to reach the cache, which lay sheltered in a deep valley, before the storm broke. But the blizzard exploded soon after, and darkness fell with terrible swiftness as this great gale, which had swept a thousand miles south from the ice sea, scoured the frozen face of the plains. It drove snow before it like fragments of glass. The drifting granules swirled higher and higher, obscuring the plodding figures of man, fox and dogs.

Kipmik still moved at the head of the team but he was invisible to Angutna's straining, snowcaked eyes, and many times the anxious white shadow had to return to the sled so that the dogs would not lose their way. Finally the wind screamed to such a pitch that Angutna knew it would be madness to drive on. He tried to find a drift whose snow was firm enough for the making of a snowhouse, but there was none at hand and there was no time to search. Turning the sled on its side facing the gale, he dug a trench behind it with his snowknife — just big enough for his body. Wrapping himself in his robes he rolled into the trench and pulled the sled over the top of the hole.

The dogs curled abjectly nearby, noses under their tails, the snow   30
drifting over them, while Kipmik ran among them snapping at their shoulders in his anxiety to make them continue on until some shelter was found. He gave up when the dogs were transformed into white, inanimate mushrooms. Then the fox ran to the sled and burrowed under it. He

wormed in close, and Angutna made room so that he might share the warmth from the little body beside him.

For a day and a night nothing moved on the white face of the dark plains except the snow ghosts whirling before the blast of the gale. On the second day the wind died away. A smooth, curling drift shattered from within as Angutna fought free of the smothering snows. With all the haste his numbed body could muster, he began probing the nearby drifts seeking the dogs who were sealed into white tombs from which they could no longer escape by themselves.

He had little need of the probe. Kipmik ran to and fro, unerringly sniffing out the snow crypts of the dogs. They were all uncovered at last, and all were alive but so weak they could barely pull at the sled.

Angutna pressed on. He knew that if no food was found soon, the dogs would be finished. And if the dogs died, then all was lost, for there would be no way to carry the meat from the cache back to the camp. Mercilessly Angutna whipped the team on, and when the dogs could no longer muster the strength to keep the sled moving, he harnessed himself into the traces beside them.

Just before noon the sun slipped over the horizon and blazed red on a desolate world. The long sequence of blizzards had smoothed it into an immense and shapeless undulation of white. Angutna could see no landmarks. He was lost in that snow desert, and his heart sank within him.

Kipmik still ran ahead but for some little while he had been trying to swing the team to a northerly course. Time after time he ran back to Angutna and barked in his face when the man persisted in trudging into the west. So they straggled over that frozen world until the dogs could go no farther. Angutna killed one of the dogs and fed it to the others. He let them rest only briefly, for he was afraid a new storm would begin.

The sun was long since gone and there were no stars in the sky when they moved on; therefore Angutna did not notice as, imperceptibly, Kipmik turned the team northward. He did not notice until late the next morning when the dawn glow showed him that all through the long night they had been travelling into the north.

Then Angutna, who was a man not given to rage, was filled with a terrible anger. He believed it was all finished for him and his family. He seized his snowknife from the sled and with a great shout leapt at the fox, his companion of so many years.

The blow would have sliced Kipmik in two but, even as he struck, Angutna stumbled. The blade hissed into the snow and the fox leapt aside. Angutna stayed on his knees until the anger went from him. When he rose to his feet he was steadfast once more.

"Ayorama!" he said to the fox who watched him without fear. "It cannot be helped. So, Little Pup, you will lead us your way? It is a small matter. Death awaits in all directions. If you wish, we will seek death to the north."

35

It is told how they staggered northward for half a day, then the fox *40*
abandoned the man and the dogs and ran on ahead. When Angutna caught
up to Kipmik it was to find he had already tunnelled down through the
snow to the rocks Angutna had heaped over a fine cache of meat and fat in
the fall.

A year or so later a great change came to the world of the plains
dwellers. One winter day a sled drove into the camps by the Big Hungry
and a man of the sea people came into the snowhouses. Through many
long nights the people listened to his wondrous tales of life by the salt
water. They were particularly fascinated by his accounts of the wonders
that had been brought to that distant land by a white man come out of the
south. Their visitor had been commissioned by the white man to acquaint
the plains people with the presence of a trading post on the eastern edge of
the plains, and to persuade them to move closer to that post and to trap
furs for trade.

The idea was much talked about and there were some who thought
it would be a good thing to go east for a winter, but most of the people
were opposed. By reason of his renown as a hunter, Angutna's opinions
carried weight and one night he spoke what was in his mind.

"I think it is to be remembered that we have lived good lives in this
land, knowing little evil. Is it not true that *Tuktoriak* has fed and clothed
us from before the time of the father's fathers? *Eeee!* It is so. And if we
turn from the Deer Spirit now to seek other gifts, who can say what he
may do? Perhaps he will be angry and speak to his children, the deer, and
bid them abandon our people. And then of what value would be the
promises made by this man on behalf of the Kablunait? . . . Those promises would be dead sticks in our hands."

So spoke Angutna, and most agreed with him. Still, when the
stranger departed, there were two families who went with him. These
returned before the snows thawed in the spring and they brought such
wealth as a man could hardly credit: rifles, steel knives, copper kettles and
many such things.

But they also brought something they did not know they were *45*
bringing.

It was a sickness that came into men's lungs and squeezed the life
from their bodies. It was called the Great Pain and it flung itself on the
plains people like a blazing wind. In one season it killed more than half of
those who lived in that land.

Panic struck many of the survivors who, believing the land was now
cursed, fled to the east to seek help from the white man. From him they
learned a new way of life, becoming trappers of fur and eaters of white
man's food. And, instead of Tuktu, the beast they now pursued was
Terriganiak — the white fox. During all time that had been, the plains
people had known the white fox as a friend in a land so vast and so empty

that the bark of the fox was often the only welcoming sound. Since time began, foxes and men had shared that land and there had been no conflict between them. Now men turned on Terriganiak and lived by the sale of his skin.

For a time Angutna and a few other men and their families tried to continue living the old life in the old places, but hunger came more often upon them and one autumn the deer failed to appear at all. Some said this was because of the great slaughter of deer resulting from the new rifles in the hands of all northern people, Indian and Innuit; but Angutna believed it was due to the anger of Tuktoriak. In any event, the last few people living on the inland plains were forced to follow those who had already fled to the east and become trappers of fox.

When the survivors of that long trek came to the snowhouses which stood a few miles away from the house of the trader at the mouth of the River of Seals, they expected to be greeted with warmth and with food, for it had always been the law of the land that those who have food and shelter will share with those who have not.

Disappointment was theirs. White foxes, too, were scarce that win- *50* ter and many traps stood empty. Those people who had chosen to live by the fox were nearly as hungry as the people who journeyed out of the west.

Angutna built a small snowhouse for his family, but it was a dark place filled with dark thoughts. There was no fuel for the lamps and almost no fuel for the belly. Angutna, who had once been such a great hunter, was now forced to live on the labours of others because, even if he had so wished, he could not have trapped foxes. He could not have done so because Terriganiak was his Spirit-Who-Helps and, for him, the lives of all foxes were sacred. Other men went to their traps and, when they were lucky, caught foxes whose pelts they bartered for food. Sometimes a portion of that food was given to Angutna's wife; but Angutna had nothing to give in return.

The new way of life was as hard for Kipmik as for Angutna. The fox who had always been free now lay, day and night, tethered to a stick driven into the floor of the snowhouse. All around that place steel traps yawned for his kind and there were many men with rifles who, to help feed their families, would not have hesitated to put a bullet through him, for although Kipmik was growing old, his pelt was still thicker, softer and longer than that of any fox that had ever been seen before.

As the winter drew on, the remaining foxes deserted that part of the country and then hunger was the lot of all who had tried to live by the fox. There were no more gifts to the family of Angutna, who had himself become so emaciated that he could do little but sit like a statue in his cold house, dreaming of other times, other days. Sometimes his gaze would fix on the curled ball of white fur that was Kipmik, and his lips would move, but silently, for he was addressing a plea to the Spirit-Who-Helps.

Sometimes the fox would raise its head and stare back into the eyes of the man, and perhaps he too was pleading . . . for the freedom that once had been his.

The trader heard about the fabulous fox who lived in the houses of men and one day he drove his dogs to the camps of the people to see for himself whether the stories were true. He entered Angutna's snowhouse, and as soon as he saw Kipmik curled up on the floor he wished to possess that magnificent pelt.

It distressed him to see the big, staring eyes and the swollen bellies 55 of Angutna's children. He felt pity for the people who were starving that winter. But what could he do? He did not own the food that lay in his storehouse. It belonged to the company that employed him, and he could not part with a pound unless there was payment in fur.

Angutna greeted the visitor with a smile that tautened the skin that was already stretched too tightly over the broad bones of his face. Even though he be in despair, a man must give a good greeting to those who visit his house. It was otherwise with the fox. Perhaps he smelled the death stink from the skins of so many of his kind this stranger had handled. He pulled away to the side of the snowhouse as far as his tether would reach and crouched there like a cat facing a hound.

The white man spoke of the hard times that lay on the people; of the shortage of foxes and the absence of deer. Then he turned to look at Kipmik again.

"That is a fine fox you have there. I have never seen better. If you will sell it to me, I can pay . . . as much as three sacks of flour and, yes, this I can do, ten, no, fifteen pounds of fat."

Angutna still smiled, and none knew the thoughts that swirled behind the masked face. He did not answer the white man directly, but spoke instead of trivial things while he wrestled with himself in his mind: food . . . food enough to ensure that his wife and children would live until spring. Perhaps he even believed his Spirit-Who-Helps had something to do with the miraculous hope the white man extended. Who will know what he thought?

The trader knew better than to say anything more about Kipmik, 60 but when he went outside to his waiting sled he ordered his Eskimo helper to take a small bag of flour into Angutna's snowhouse. Then he returned to his trading post at the mouth of the River of Seals.

That night the woman, Epeetna, made a small fire of willow twigs in the tunnel entrance and she and her children ate unleavened bread made of flour and water. She passed a cake of it to Angutna where he sat unmoving on the sleeping ledge, but he did not taste it. Instead he threw it to the fox. Kipmik bolted it down, for he too was starving. Then Angutna spoke, as it seemed, to himself.

"This is the way it must be."

Epeetna understood. The woman let her hair loose so that it hung down over her face. The acrid smoke from the fire clouded the four figures sitting on the high ledge. The small flames gave hardly enough light for Angutna to see what he was doing, but his fingers needed no light as he carefully plaited the Noose of Release.

When it was finished, Angutna slipped Kipmik's tether, and the fox leapt up to the ledge and stood with its paws braced against the chest of the man—free once again. The black eyes were fixed on the eyes of the man, in wonder perhaps, for the fox had never seen tears in those eyes before. Kipmik made no move when the noose fell over his neck. He made no move until Angutna spoke.

"Now, Little Pup, it is time. You will go out onto the plains where 65 the deer wait our coming."

And so Kipmik passed into that country from which nothing returns.

Next morning when the trader opened his door he found the frozen pelt of the fox suspended from the ridge of his porch by a strangely plaited noose. The pelt swayed and spun in the breath of the wind. The trader was delighted, but he was uneasy too. He had lived in that land long enough to know how little he knew. He wasted no time ordering his helper to load the promised food on a sled and take it to the snowhouse of Angutna.

The payment was received by Epeetna. Angutna could not receive it, for the Noose of Release was drawn tight at his throat. He had gone to join the one he had lost.

His grave still stands on the bank of the River of Seals. It is no more than a grey cairn of rocks with the decayed weapons of a hunter scattered among the quiet stones. Inside the grave lies Angutna, and beside him lies the fox who once lived in the houses of men.

The two are still one. 70

The Responsive Reader

1. What does Mowat want the reader to learn about the setting, the climate, and the relation of Angutna and his people to the cycles of the seasons and the habits of the wildlife?
2. Does Mowat seem to romanticize the life of Angutna's people or his relationship with the fox?
3. What changes does the arrival of white men bring for Angutna's people? Which are physical; which relate to ways of living and thinking? How do Angutna and his people interpret them and react to them?
4. What is the role of the white trader in this story? Is he the villain?

Talking, Listening, Writing

5. At the end of his conversation with Angutna, the trader "knew better than to say anything more." Epeetna "understood" but said

little. If Angutna had felt the need to share his thoughts and feelings at the end, what might he have said?

6. If the white trader could have had the last word, what do you think he might have said in reply to Angutna? (Your class may want to stage an imaginary dialog between the two.)

7. What to you is the most essential difference between the native lifestyle that Mowat re-creates in this story and the outlook and way of life brought by the white traders?

Projects

8. What is the current status of the people Mowat wrote about? What can you find out about recent developments in Canada's treatment of the indigenous tribes of the North?

Thinking about Connections

How does Mowat's perspective relate to the controversy about animal rights represented by Vicki Hearne's article (p. 591) and the letters it inspired (p. 600)? Do you think his story would tend to lend support to one side or the other?

THE DEATH OF AN ELEPHANT

Gianfranco Pagnucci

Gianfranco Pagnucci's poem was first published in Northeast *magazine
and appears in his collection* Face the Poem *(1979). It pays tribute to one
of the species endangered by the relentless march of human civilization.*

Thought Starters: Why has the elephant, threatened by poachers and a
shrinking habitat, had a special hold on our collective imagination?

a transformation	1
She stood	
apart from the grazing herd	
motionless,	
except for a slowed	5
curl of her trunk,	
her head lowered,	
her great ears flopped forward	
like a closing umbrella	
as the bull	10
came to sniff.	
When she dropped to her haunches,	
the herd	
screaming and trumpeting,	
thundered,	15
a fallen half-moon	
around her.	
Her forelegs collapsed	
and she slumped to her belly,	
a Dagon come tumbling down.	20
Only the young ones	
were allowed	
to touch her now:	
one laid his trunk on her back;	
one nuzzled her ear;	25
one strained at her great fallen rump	
as if pushing toward life	
and learning of death.	

Then the great bull,
head lowered,   30
tried to lift her with a roar.
He moved to her head and tried to lift her.
He tore a trunkful of dry grass
and stuffed it in her mouth
over the dust on her sagged lip   35
to lift her.
He tried to mount her into life.
She heaved to her side
and was dead.

It was sunset   40
late African spring
and December,
as a restless
feeding herd came
one by one to the gray body   45
and moved off
together over the ridge
into the dusk.

The Responsive Reader

1. How does this poem make us see ourselves as in a mirror as we watch our cousins of the animal world? What features of kinship are we made to recognize?

Talking, Listening, Writing

2. What, to you, is the essential difference between animals and humans?

Projects

3. Robinson Jeffers, in his poem "Hurt Hawks," said that he would sooner, except for the penalties, kill a man than a hawk. Your class may want to stage a reading of poems that express a special sense of empathy for the animal world. You might consider poems ranging from D. H. Lawrence's "Snake" to Emily Dickinson's "A Narrow Fellow in the Grass" or Howard Nemerov's "The Great Gull."

WRITING
WORKSHOP 11

The Investigative Writer

Honest writing always results from a process of investigation, of discovery. However, in some kinds of writing, the emphasis on investigation, on finding out, is especially strong. Journalists and others writing about current affairs today pride themselves on not being satisfied with official pronouncements, press releases, or campaign handouts. They aim at getting out the real story. They dig and probe; they believe in the public's right to know.

When investigative writing turns especially aggressive, it becomes **exposé** — the bringing out into the open of shortcomings or wrongdoings that have been kept from the public.

TRIGGERING Investigative writing is triggered when someone says: "There is more to this than meets the eye. The truth is probably not easy to establish, but it is worth ferreting out." Situations like the following might set an investigative writer to work:

▪ A highly placed administration official talks to an audience of developers about costly restrictions on logging mandated to preserve the habitat of the spotted owl. He claims that environmentalist legislation restricting logging has added between three thousand and five thousand dollars to the cost of the homes they are building. How much of this is true? What is the economic cost of protecting endangered species? Who is in a position to make informed estimates?

▪ Environmentalists and other local organizations are protesting against experiments with bacteria produced by gene-splicing. At issue are bacteria, produced by biogenetic engineering, that promise to reduce frost damage to temperature-sensitive crops. Some concerned scientists warn that the release of these new organisms may have unforeseen and dangerous consequences. Are they alarmists? Are their warnings, as one academic said, "ridiculous"?

▪ A watchdog group charges that local industry continues to discharge toxic materials into local waterways in violation of state and federal law. Spokespersons for concerned companies state that their firms are in compliance with applicable legislation. Who is lying?

GATHERING An investigative writer needs some of a detective's curiosity and perseverance — while often getting little cooperation from people who might have something to hide. Here are some hints for the apprentice sleuth:

• Read up on the subject — check out relevant *background*. Assume you are trying to find out what is behind current arguments over biology textbooks and the theory of evolution. Doing your background reading, you might find out that Tennessee, site of the original "Monkey Trial," still has a law called the Butler Act on the books. Texas for a time banned books that taught evolution. In California, on the other hand, it was against the law to hint at a divine hand in creation.

• Get as close as possible to *insiders,* to people vitally concerned. Establish them as authorities. When you investigate current efforts to weaken tough drunk-driving laws, you might introduce one of your key sources as follows:

> Three years ago a 23-year-old man with a blood alcohol nearly three times the 0.10 legal limit, crashed head-on into a car carrying Jackie Masso, her husband Patrick, her daughter Patty, and a friend at 4:30 in the afternoon. Today Jackie Masso faces two to three more operations on her legs. Her husband must get his lungs pumped about three times a year because of congestive heart failure and her 21-year-old daughter, after having her crushed nose broken and reset two times, faces yet more plastic surgery.
>
> Masso got MADD. She and her husband are co-presidents of the local chapter of Mothers Against Drunk Driving, which has 400–500 paying members and 1,000 on a mailing list.
>
> Masso said she has noticed something in the many courtrooms where she has sat with families who have had a son or daughter killed or badly injured. She has noticed that the drunken drivers with multiple offenses tend to always blame their car, the weather, or the other driver but never themselves.
>
> "I've never heard a drunken driver say he's sorry," she said.

• Pros know how to seek out revealing or privileged information. They will search for internal memos rather than official press releases. They will listen to people recalling informal conversations behind closed doors rather than rationalizations presented in a public meeting.

SHAPING Many investigative papers start by documenting a public misunderstanding or a questionable official version. Typically, the writer's assumption is that there is more than one side to the story. The paper will thus often play off an unauthorized, unofficial version against the established or familiar view. It may then sift testimony for and against the "revisionist" hypothesis. Finally, the paper may try to present a balanced conclusion.

Often an investigative paper will try to reenact the excitement of the search, of the hunt. It may create an air of mystery by first hints of something misrepresented or amiss. It may build suspense as the paper examines additional clues. It may lead up to a climax where a clinching admission or discovery provides the high point.

REVISING Investigative writers are known for their zeal. Like other zealous persons they at times get carried away, leaving the skeptical reader behind. Revision gives you a chance to rewrite your paper to side-step familiar pitfalls.

- *Check the credibility of your sources.* You are likely to strengthen a paper if you jettison or play down what is mere hearsay or what is clearly biased or partisan testimony. (Readers may not be impressed by a flack's defense of agency policy, a fired employee's disgruntled remarks, or a CEO's lauding the integrity of the company's balance sheet.)
- *Guard against charges of having slanted the evidence.* If you filter out all doubt, dissent, or disagreement, your readers will start reading your tract as one-sided propaganda (and many will discount it accordingly). Take on and try to rebut major objections or doubts that are likely to arise in your readers' minds. Make sure you cite both management and workers when investigating a labor dispute.
- *Give facts and credible testimony a chance to speak for themselves.* There is a strong temptation to call evildoers the names they deserve. Some writers keep up a steady drumfire of labels like *inexcusable, self-interested, incompetent, maniacal, capricious, greedy for profits,* and *using political ploys.* (As someone said about one writer, this is just what he called the editor!) Save weighty words and serious charges for places where you have clearly earned the right to use them by the careful presentation of evidence.
- *Watch out for innuendo.* Innuendos or insinuations are damaging charges that are never openly made but only hinted at — and therefore not really supported or defended. ("Politician X attended the same fund-raiser as alleged mobster Y." Yes? What are you hinting or implying?)

The following is a paper investigating the controversy over new "let-it-burn" policies in the country's national parks. How and how well does the paper bring the controversy into focus? How does the paper establish the writer's authority? How informative is the paper? Is more than one side heard?

The Fire Seeder

As we drove along the west shore of Yellowstone Lake, we could see the island in the middle of the lake to our right, its angular shape paralleling our own approach to the inn at the foot of the lake. We watched one lodgepole pine after another turn into a flaming orange-red torch, shooting skyward through the island's black smoke like a fireworks display on a foggy night in San Francisco. The fire swept through the island leaving much of it unscathed before it ran pell-mell into the lake, drawing its last destructive breath in a billowing gasp of steam and black smoke.

We had entered the "burn-area" mid-afternoon in the general area of Grant Village. A park attendant flagged us down, told us to turn on our lights and not to stop for any pictures. About two miles down the road, the first fumes of smoke filled our nostrils, irritated our eyes, and besmudged what had been a beautiful blue sky. Around a bend, we encountered the result of the fire's frenetic activity several hours earlier, its erratic path and shape reminding me of a giant baker run amuck with a cookie cutter. Gray ash covered the burnt-out patches of forest, and red-hot coals smoldered in the "snags," the smoking stumps that had once been towering, majestic lodgepole pines.

As we drove through Yellowstone across the north end of Yellowstone Lake to the "Fishing Bridge," the lodgepole pines everywhere caught my attention. With their limbs wrapped around each other, they made a canopy so thick that for miles all I could see were lodgepole pines set onto a surreal landscape, their deceased members creating beautiful artistic forms as they cluttered the barren forest floor. At those times when the road wound out of the forest and into a clearing, we could see smoke rising from the top of another forest grove far in the distance, a part of the more than nine-tenths of Yellowstone which is wilderness and can only be reached on foot or on horseback.

I was unfamiliar with the park's "natural burn" policy. This policy had been in effect for sixteen years and allows fires caused by lightning to burn themselves out, except where they threaten towns or park buildings. During our swing through the park, fire had already destroyed 15,000 acres. Before it ended, however, the inferno had raged over half of Yellowstone's 2.2 million acres and cost more than $100 million to fight and clean up. The logging industries and the tourist industries, incensed over the park's "natural burn" policy, started their own political firestorm: Wyoming's U.S. Senators called for the resignation of the head of the Park Service. The logging industries wanted to reforest the burned areas to give wooded areas in Yellowstone a "five-year jump" on natural regrowth of the woods and to "get it green again," according to Willamette Industries' general manager for Western timber logging operations. The tourist industry suffered enormous losses because of the fire's adverse publicity. In an average year, 2.5 million tourists visit the park. In August, with fires out of control, the tourist trade was off 30% according to published reports. When the fire finally subsided, public opinion seemed to be questioning a policy that could allow such a degree of devastation and destruction to Yellowstone Park, our oldest national park and the largest wildlife preserve in the United States.

But as the fire subsided, as the media and television turned their eyes toward more immediate "fires," a calm and rational voice could be heard soothing the public's fears about one of its national treasures. In his article in The Wall Street Journal entitled "Back to Life: Yellowstone

Park Begins Its Renewal," Scott McMurray interviewed Research Biologist Donald Despain, who teaches us all an invaluable lesson about ecosystems and the lodgepole pine's regenerative role in the forest's rebirth. Their tiny quarter-inch seeds, or "wings" as Despain calls them, are slowly released from rock-hard pine cones only after the cones have been seared by the passing flames; they require a fire to propagate themselves. The little wings act like the rotary blades of a helicopter in dispersing the seeds which, according to Despain's count, "works out to one million seeds an acre." The burnt "snags," as the charred tree trunks are called, vary in age from a relatively young Civil War period fire to the lodgepole stands that burned which were 250 to 400 years old. According to Despain, it is no coincidence that most burnt trees here were senior citizens and susceptible to fire. As they age, they lose their natural resistance to disease and insects. Dead trees fall to the forest floor, joined by others blown over by the strong winds howling down from surrounding peaks. The thinning canopy, in turn, lets in more light to the forest floor, dormant grass and shrub seeds fill in the open spaces between the trees; the ground clutter thickens; more trees fall; and, with the help of a prolonged drought, "the old forest creates its own funeral pyre."

As John Varley, Yellowstone's chief of research said, "We see what's going on here not as devastation and destruction, but rather, rebirth and renewal of these ecosystems."

Topics for Investigative Papers (A Sampling)

1. Are people who warn against global warming alarmists?
2. Are toxic dumps a danger in your community? Who is responsible?
3. Was the publicity about acid rain destroying forests a passing media scare?
4. What are current projections for the fate of the rain forests in South America? What are responsible estimates of the consequences?
5. What is the record or current stance of the U.S. government concerning efforts to safeguard the variety of living species?
6. Can and should oil spills be prevented?
7. Is overgrazing of public lands a major environmental threat?
8. Are there employment barriers for minorities in local police and fire departments? Who or what is responsible?
9. In your community or state, are charges of police brutality exaggerated?
10. What are the living conditions for illegal aliens in your area or community?

12

Future Shock: Dream or Nightmare

Any day now I'll reach that land of freedom
Yes, o yes
Any day now, that promised land.
                                        Traditional Spiritual

Since the Greek philosopher Plato's time 2,500 years ago, writers projecting our common future have written Utopias. (Literally, a Utopia is a place that exists "nowhere" — only in our dreams). Often these Utopias were imaginary commonwealths in which human beings had outgrown their tendencies toward selfishness, conflict, and war. They had learned to live in harmony, to share the wealth, to marry sagely and raise their children without traumas. They had learned to follow wise leaders (or to do without leaders altogether).

However, gradually, apprehension and disillusionment seeped in: Writers wrote *dys*topias — the opposite of books projecting an ideal future state. Dystopias took readers to nightmare worlds where people were faceless nobodies in beehive societies. All pleasure or satisfaction came from artificial stimulants. Books were likely to be banned, and their owners persecuted. Big Brother (or the big master computer) did the thinking for everybody.

How optimistic or how pessimistic are we as Americans about the society of the future? What kind of world are we going to leave for future generations? What are our projections for the future state of economic warfare, women's rights, racial divisions, or health catastrophes like AIDS?

PRO-CHOICE, NOT PRO-ABORTION

Mary R. Callahan

After a gradual movement in many Western countries toward legalizing abortion, active antiabortion campaigns have reopened the issue. In this country, state legislatures and the United States Supreme Court have weighed new initiatives restricting a woman's right to abortion, provoking bitter debate between pro-life and pro-choice groups. Groups like Operation Rescue have taken to the streets in their attempt to stop the work of abortion clinics. Politicians have had to take or change sides; a candidate's stand on abortion became a major concern in the selection of new Supreme Court justices. The following editorial from a student newspaper was written on the abortion issue by a young woman who was the city editor of the paper.

Thought Starters: Is it possible to say anything new on the subject of abortion? Has everyone heard all the arguments pro and con? Is everyone's mind made up for good?

This is my last statement on abortion and related issues. Promise. 1

Based on some of the mail I've received recently, it seems clear there is still a widespread misconception that "pro-choice" is synonymous with "pro-abortion."

The truth is, no one likes abortion. It is not a good thing. Most who encounter abortion personally are faced with a painful and traumatic dilemma, and anyone who thinks those who choose abortion do so without intense thought and consideration are wrong.

No. The pro-choice movement is not about favoring abortions. It is about preserving the right of the individual to decide whether to carry a child from conception to birth.

As for graphic photographs some pro-life groups distribute portray- 5 ing fetuses purportedly mutilated through abortion, I agree with their revulsion. It is an ugly, abhorrent vision these photographs represent. But most abortions are performed in the very early stages after conception and do not produce the results depicted in such pictures.

And I acknowledge, too, that a woman who chooses abortion may suffer long-lasting emotional repercussions.

But the vast range of variables that exist in each individual life, that influence the decisions different people make, must be taken into consideration. No one can say just what forces are at work in another person's life or how that person will react upon pursuing a course of action.

These are the very reasons we should trust the individual to weigh the options and to select what is best for her- or himself. All of us feel remorse at one time or another. Each day we make decisions, many of them wrong. But we, as the individuals affected, more than anyone else, are in the best position to make those decisions.

The morality issue is not a simple one. It is easy to view the world as black and white — and quite frankly, we do that all too often.

But it doesn't work. Because we are individuals, our views of life and the world vary from one to the next. And as our body of knowledge and experience changes over time, so too does our sense of morality. *10*

Still, it remains individual.

I, for example, am morally offended by racial slurs. But I would be loathe to suggest that government officials establish laws forbidding this sort of expression. That is a job to be accomplished through improved education and social pressure.

I find it morally repugnant that we, as a nation, are fat and eat expensively produced foods while whole countries go hungry because of our greed. Farbeit from me to force my fellow-Americans to renounce all but the most economical foods until the rest of the world is fed.

The point is, one cannot dictate morality or obligation for the individual, particularly where abortion is concerned.

Instead of battling over where the decision of abortion lies, we should devote our energy to education and family planning and strike at the very root of abortion. Though no form of birth control is 100 percent effective, it is possible to limit unwanted pregnancies and to reduce the need for women to make what may be the most difficult choice of their lives. *15*

The Responsive Reader

1. Where does Callahan take her stand? (Does her position seem familiar or predictable?) What is the heart of her argument? How does she support her position, and how effectively?
2. How does Callahan show that she is aware of the ongoing debate?

Talking, Listening, Writing

3. What does the future hold as far as the abortion issue is concerned? What is the strength of the forces opposing abortion? Which side seems more effective in promoting its cause?
4. Is abortion a woman's issue? Is there a developing consensus among women on the issue?
5. Where do you stand personally? Write an editorial for a real or imaginary student newspaper on the abortion issue.

Projects

6. Much of the abortion debate focuses on legal points and medical distinctions concerning the termination of pregnancy. Working with a group, you may want to research the legal distinctions and medical criteria that an informed voter would need to gauge the significance of recent or proposed legislation.

LIFEBOAT ETHICS

Garrett Hardin

> *In the seventies and eighties, a neoconservative movement broke with the official rhetoric of America's good intentions around the world. New voices began to substitute a tough, hard-nosed prognosis of what was needed for national survival in an increasingly overpopulated world. Garrett Hardin is a leading neoconservative intellectual who in his widely published and debated writings attacks the traditional humanitarian views of the "guilt-ridden," "conscience-stricken" liberal. He has a doctorate in biology from Stanford University, has taught at the University of California at Santa Barbara, and has lectured at other universities. He is the author of books and articles on "human ecology" — the study of how human life is sustained on our planet.*

Thought Starters: Key metaphors — striking, thought-provoking imaginative comparisons — can help shape our thinking. What assumptions and attitudes are implied when we think of ourselves as passengers on the Spaceship Earth? What assumptions and attitudes are implied in the contrasting metaphor of the lifeboat?

Environmentalists use the metaphor of the earth as a "spaceship" in trying to persuade countries, industries and people to stop wasting and polluting our natural resources. Since we all share life on this planet, they argue, no single person or institution has the right to destroy, waste, or use more than a fair share of its resources.

But does everyone on earth have an equal right to an equal share of its resources? The spaceship metaphor can be dangerous when used by misguided idealists to justify suicidal policies for sharing our resources through uncontrolled immigration and foreign aid. In their enthusiastic but unrealistic generosity, they confuse the ethics of a spaceship with those of a lifeboat.

A true spaceship would have to be under the control of a captain, since no ship could possibly survive if its course were determined by committee. Spaceship Earth certainly has no captain; the United Nations is merely a toothless tiger, with little power to enforce any policy upon its bickering members.

If we divide the world crudely into rich nations and poor nations, two thirds of them are desperately poor, and only one third comparatively rich, with the United States the wealthiest of all. Metaphorically each rich nation can be seen as a lifeboat full of comparatively rich people. In the ocean outside each lifeboat swim the poor of the world, who would like to get in, or at least to share some of the wealth. What should the lifeboat passengers do?

First, we must recognize the limited capacity of any lifeboat. For example, a nation's land has a limited capacity to support a population and as the current energy crisis has shown us, in some ways we have already exceeded the carrying capacity of our land. So here we sit, say 50 people in our lifeboat. To be generous, let us assume it has room for 10 more, making a total capacity of 60. Suppose the 50 of us in the lifeboat see 100 others swimming in the water outside, begging for admission to our boat or for handouts. We have several options: we may be tempted to try to live by the Christian ideal of being "our brother's keeper," or by the Marxist ideal of "to each according to his needs." Since the needs of all in the water are the same, and since they can all be seen as our "brothers," we could take them all into our boat, making a total of 150 in a boat designed for 60. The boat swamps; everyone drowns. Complete justice, complete catastrophe.

Since the boat has an unused excess capacity of 10 more passengers, we could admit just 10 more to it. But which 10 do we let in? How do we choose? Do we pick the best 10, the neediest 10, "first come, first served"? And what do we say to the 90 we exclude? If we do let an extra 10 into our lifeboat, we will have lost our "safety factor," an engineering principle of critical importance. For example, if we don't leave room for excess capacity as a safety factor in our country's agriculture, a new plant disease or a bad change in the weather could have disastrous consequences.

Suppose we decide to preserve our small safety factor and admit no more to the lifeboat. Our survival is then possible, although we shall have to be constantly on guard against boarding parties.

While this last solution clearly offers the only means of our survival, it is morally abhorrent to many people. Some say they feel guilty about their good luck. My reply is simple: "Get out and yield your place to others." This may solve the problem of the guilt-ridden person's conscience, but it does not change the ethics of the lifeboat. The needy person to whom the guilt-ridden person yields his place will not himself feel guilty about his good luck. If he did, he would not climb aboard. The net result of conscience-stricken people giving up their unjustly held seats is the elimination of that sort of conscience from the lifeboat.

This is the basic metaphor within which we must work out our solutions. Let us now enrich the image, step by step, with substantive additions from the real world, a world that must solve real and pressing problems of overpopulation and hunger.

The harsh ethics of the lifeboat become even harsher when we consider the reproductive differences between the rich nations and the poor nations. The people inside the lifeboats are doubling in numbers every 87 years; those swimming around outside are doubling, on the average, every

35 years, more than twice as fast as the rich. And since the world's resources are dwindling, the difference in prosperity between the rich and
the poor can only increase.

As of 1973, the U.S. had a population of 210 million people, who
were increasing by 0.8 percent per year. Outside our lifeboat, let us
imagine another 210 million people (say the combined populations of
Colombia, Ecuador, Venezuela, Morocco, Pakistan, Thailand, and the
Philippines), increasing at a rate of 3.3 percent per year. Put differently,
the doubling time for this aggregate population was 21 years, compared
to 87 years for the U.S.

Now suppose the U.S. agreed to pool its resources with those seven
countries, with everyone receiving an equal share. Initially the ratio of
Americans to non-Americans in this model would be one-to-one. But
consider what the ratio would be after 87 years, by which time the Americans would have doubled to a population of 420 million. By then, doubling every 21 years, the other group would have swollen to 354 billion.
Each American would have to share the available resources with more
than eight people.

But, one could argue, this discussion assumes that current population trends will continue, and they may not. Quite so. Most likely the rate
of population increase will decline much faster in the U.S. than it will in
the other countries, and there does not seem to be much we can do about
it. In sharing with "each according to his needs," we must recognize that
needs are determined by population size, which is determined by the rate
of reproduction, which at present is regarded as a sovereign right of every
nation, poor or not. This being so, the philanthropic load created by the
sharing ethic of the spaceship can only increase.

The fundamental error of spaceship ethics, and the sharing it requires, is that it leads to what I call "the tragedy of the commons." Under
a system of private property, people who own property recognize their
responsibility to care for it, for if they don't they will eventually suffer. A
farmer, for instance, will allow no more cattle in a pasture than its carrying
capacity justifies. If he overloads it, erosion sets in, weeds take over, and
he loses the use of the pasture.

If a pasture becomes a commons open to all, the right of each to use   *15*
it may not be matched by a corresponding responsibility to protect it.
Asking everyone to use it with discretion will hardly do, for the considerate herdsman who refrains from overloading the commons suffers more
than a selfish one who says his needs are greater. If everyone would restrain
himself, all would be well; but it takes only one less than everyone to ruin
a system of voluntary restraint. In a crowded world of less than perfect
human beings, mutual ruin is inevitable if there are no controls. This is
the tragedy of the commons.

One of the major tasks of education today should be the creation of
such an acute awareness of the dangers of the commons that people will

recognize its many varieties. For example, the air and water have become polluted because they are treated as commons. Further growth in the population or per-capita conversion of natural resources into pollutants will only make the problem worse. The same holds true for the fish of the oceans. Fishing fleets have nearly disappeared in many parts of the world; technological improvements in the art of fishing are hastening the day of complete ruin. Only the replacement of the system of the commons with a responsible system of control will save the land, air, water and oceanic fisheries.

In recent years there has been a push to create a new commons called a World Food Bank, an international depository of food reserves to which nations would contribute according to their abilities and from which they would draw according to their needs. This humanitarian proposal received support from many liberal international groups, and from such prominent citizens as Margaret Mead, the U.N. Secretary General, and Senator Edward Kennedy.

A world food bank appeals powerfully to our humanitarian impulses. But before we rush ahead with such a plan, let us ask if such a program would actually do more good than harm, not only momentarily but also in the long run. Those who propose a food bank usually refer to a current "emergency" or "crisis" in terms of world food supply. But what is an emergency? Although they may be infrequent and sudden, everyone knows that emergencies will occur from time to time. A well-run family, company, organization or country prepares for the likelihood of accidents and emergencies. It expects them, it budgets for them, it saves for them.

What happens if some organizations or countries budget for accidents and others do not? If each country is solely responsible for its own well-being, poorly managed ones will suffer. But they can learn from experience. They may mend their ways, and learn to budget for infrequent but certain emergencies. For example, the weather varies from year to year, and periodic crop failures are certain. A wise and competent government saves out of the production of the good years in anticipation of bad years to come. Joseph taught this policy to Pharaoh in Egypt more than 2,000 years ago. Yet the great majority of the governments in the world today do not follow such a policy. They lack either the wisdom or the competence, or both. Should those nations that do manage to put something aside be forced to come to the rescue each time an emergency occurs among the poor nations?

"But it isn't their fault!" some kind-hearted liberals argue. "How can we blame the poor people who are caught in an emergency? Why must they suffer for the sins of their governments?" The concept of blame is simply not relevant here. The real question is, what are the operational consequences of establishing a world food bank? If it is open to every country every time a need develops, slovenly rulers will not be motivated to take Joseph's advice. Someone will always come to their aid. Some countries will deposit food in the world food bank, and others will withdraw it. There will be almost no overlap. As a result of such solutions to food shortage emergencies, the poor countries will not learn to mend their ways, and will suffer progressively greater emergencies as their populations grow.

On the average, poor countries undergo a 2.5 percent increase in population each year; rich countries, about 0.6 percent. Only rich countries have anything in the way of food reserves set aside, and even they do not have as much as they should. Poor countries have none. If poor countries received no food from the outside, the rate of their population growth would be periodically checked by crop failures and famines. But if they can always draw on a world food bank in time of need, their population can continue to grow unchecked, and so will their "need" for aid. In the short run, a world food bank may diminish that need, but in the long run it actually increases the need without limit.

Without some system of worldwide food sharing, the proportion of people in the rich and poor nations might eventually stabilize. The overpopulated poor countries would decrease in numbers while the rich countries that had room for more people would increase. But with a well-meaning system of sharing, such as a world food bank, the growth differential between the rich and the poor countries will not only persist, it will increase. Because of the higher rate of population growth in the poor countries of the world, 88 percent of today's children are born poor, and only 12 percent rich. Year by year the ratio becomes worse as the fast-reproducing poor outnumber the slow-reproducing rich.

A world food bank is thus a commons in disguise. People will have more motivation to draw from it than to add to any common store. The less provident and less able will multiply at the expense of the abler and more provident, bringing eventual ruin upon all who share in the commons. Besides, any system of "sharing" that amounts to foreign aid from the rich nations to the poor nations will carry the taint of charity, which will contribute little to the world peace so devoutly desired by those who support the idea of a world food bank.

As past U.S. foreign-aid programs have amply and depressingly demonstrated, international charity frequently inspires mistrust and antagonism rather than gratitude on the part of the recipient nation.

The modern approach to foreign aid stresses the export of technology and advice, rather than money and food. As an ancient Chinese proverb goes: "Give a man a fish and he will eat for a day; teach him how to fish and he will eat for the rest of his days." Acting on this advice, the Rockefeller and Ford Foundations have financed a number of programs for improving agriculture in the hungry nations. Known as the "Green Revolution," these programs have led to the development of "miracle rice" and "miracle wheat," new strains that offer bigger harvests and greater resistance to crop damage. 25

Whether or not the Green Revolution can increase food production as much as its champions claim is a debatable but possibly irrelevant point. Those who support this well-intended humanitarian effort should first consider some of the fundamentals of human ecology. Ironically, one man who did was the late Alan Gregg, a vice president of the Rockefeller Foundation. Two decades ago he expressed strong doubts about the wisdom of such attempts to increase food production. He likened the growth and spread of humanity over the surface of the earth to the spread of cancer in the human body, remarking that "cancerous growths demand food, but, as far as I know, they have never been cured by getting it."

Every human born constitutes a draft on all aspects of the environment: food, air, water, forests, beaches, wildlife, scenery and solitude. Food can, perhaps, be significantly increased to meet a growing demand. But what about clean beaches, unspoiled forests, and solitude? If we satisfy a growing population's need for food, we necessarily decrease its per capita supply of the other resources needed by people.

India, for example, now has a population of 600 million, which increases by 15 million each year. This population already puts a huge load on a relatively impoverished environment. The country's forests are now only a small fraction of what they were three centuries ago, and floods and erosion continually destroy the insufficient farmland that remains. Every one of the 15 million new lives added to India's population puts an additional burden on the environment, and increases the economic and social costs of crowding. However humanitarian our intent, every Indian life saved through medical or nutritional assistance from abroad diminishes the quality of life for those who remain, and for subsequent generations. If rich countries make it possible, through foreign aid, for 600 million Indians to swell to 1.2 billion in a mere 28 years, as their current growth rate threatens, will future generations of Indians thank us for hastening the destruction of their environment? Will our good intentions be sufficient excuse for the consequences of our actions?

Without a true world government to control reproduction and the use of available resources, the sharing ethic of the spaceship is impossible. For the foreseeable future, our survival demands that we govern our actions by the ethics of a lifeboat, harsh though they may be. Posterity will be satisfied with nothing less.

The Responsive Reader

1. Why did "Spaceship Earth" become an effective slogan of the environmental movement? What attitudes and assumptions does it imply? What, according to Hardin, is wrong with it?
2. How does Hardin use the lifeboat metaphor to help us see our present situation and to make us chart a different course for the future? What attitudes and actions are implied in the lifeboat analogy?

How does Hardin use projections concerning population growth to support his points?

3. A second key metaphor Hardin uses is the idea of the "commons." (A widely read article by Hardin was called "The Tragedy of the Commons.") What is the original history and meaning of the term? How does Hardin apply the idea of the commons to our current situation? How well does it fit?

4. How does Hardin's discussion of the Green Revolution differ from more familiar views of it?

5. Hardin is a formidable controversialist. How does he appropriate "liberal" ideas like the protection of the environment and the need for safeguarding the quality of life? How does he use loaded connotative language like "misguided idealists," "boarding parties," "guilt-ridden person," or "spread of cancer"? (How are they supposed to steer the reactions of the reader?)

Talking, Thinking, Writing

6. For you, which of the three basic survival metaphors — the spaceship, the lifeboat, the commons — provides the best guide to our common future? How would you defend your choice?

7. Would you call Hardin's position realism, pragmatism, or cynicism — or none of the above? (Are these terms different labels for the same basic attitude? What sets them apart?)

8. Write a profile of Hardin's ideal reader. Then write a profile of a hostile reader who is in basic disagreement with Hardin. (What basic assumptions, attitudes, or experiences would you expect to find represented by each type? Would you want to call the one a typical "conservative," the other a typical "liberal"? Why or why not?)

Projects

9. Can you update Hardin's statistics? Your class may want to set different groups to work on areas like population growth, the Green Revolution, or immigration. (Do Hardin's projections seem to be coming true?)

THE NEW ECONOMICS OF HIGH TECH

Lester C. Thurow

Most experts agree that in the global economic warfare of the future the United States will be at a competitive disadvantage. However, the experts tend to disagree on the causes and remedies. What are the root causes of America's failure to compete successfully with leading industrial nations like Japan and Germany? In the following article, Lester C. Thurow, dean of the Sloan School of Management at MIT in Cambridge, Massachusetts, tries to give a new and unstereotyped answer to that question. This selection is from his book Head to Head: Coming Economic Battles among Japan, Europe, and America *(1992). What is his advice on topics like the allocation of research and development (R&D) funds, the reassessment of American executives, or the training of the workforce?*

Thought Starters: Why are the cars, computers, VCRs, television sets, and Walkmen that Americans buy manufactured overseas or south of the border?

In the past, the nations that succeeded economically were those *1*
whose businesses invented new products. The British in the nineteenth century and the Americans in the twentieth century got rich by doing this. In the twenty-first century, sustainable competitive advantage will come not from new-product technologies but from new-process technologies — those that enable industries to produce goods and services faster, cheaper, and better.

American firms currently spend two-thirds of their R&D money on new products and one-third on new processes. The Japanese do exactly the opposite — one-third on new products, two-thirds on new processes. Not surprisingly, both sets of firms do well where they concentrate their talent: The Americans earn higher rates of return on new-product technologies; the Japanese earn higher rates of return on new processes.

Someone, however, is making a mistake. Both strategies cannot be correct. In this case, the someone is the United States. Its spending patterns are misguided, reflecting economic thinking that is thirty years out of date. In the early 1960s the rate of return on investment in new-product R&D was almost always higher than that on new-process R&D. A new product gave the inventor the monopoly power to set higher prices and earn higher profits. With a new product, there were no competitors.

In contrast, a new manufacturing or production process left the inventor to fend for himself in an existing, competitive business. Competitors also knew how to make the product, and they would always lower their prices to match the inventor's. It was simply rational to spend most of a firm's R&D money on new-product development.

But while Americans focused on product technologies, Japan and Germany focused on process technologies. They did so not because they were smarter than Americans but because the United States had such a technological advantage in the 1950s and 1960s that it was virtually impossible for either Japan or Germany to become leaders in the development of new products. They could only hope to compete in existing markets. As a result, Japan and Germany invested more heavily in process R&D. They had no choice.

But what was a good American strategy thirty years ago—a focus on product technologies—is today a poor strategy. Levels of technical sophistication in Germany, Japan, and the United States are not very different, and reverse engineering—the art of developing a new manufacturing process for an existing product—has become a highly developed art form. The nature of the change can be seen in the economic history of three of the most successful products introduced into the mass consumer market in the past two decades—the video recorder, the fax, and the CD player. Americans invented the video recorder and the fax; Europeans (the Dutch) invented the CD player. But measured in terms of sales, employment, and profits, all three have become Japanese products.

The moral of the story is clear. Those who can make a product cheaper can take it away from the inventor. In today's world it does very little good to invent a new product if the inventor is not also the cheapest producer of that product. What necessity forced upon Germany and Japan thirty years ago happens to be the right long-run R&D strategy today.

This reality will eventually force the United States to alter its R&D spending patterns, but it also requires a much more difficult shift in human-resource allocation. Over time, the pay and promotion curve for American managers and engineers in production has fallen behind that in other parts of a firm. Since production isn't seen as the key to a firm's success, it has ceased to be the route to the top. Only 4 percent of American CEOs come from production; America's best and brightest, aware of this trend, have not gone into processes. Reversing this allocation of talent is now very difficult, since traditional salary scales and promotion practices will have to be disrupted.

In order to profit from technological advancement, firms need CEOs who understand process technologies. Large investments in revolutionary technologies will only be made quickly if the man or woman at the top appreciates those technologies. Yet American CEOs are much less likely to be technologically aware than those in either Japan or Europe. In those countries 70 percent of CEOs have technical backgrounds; in the United States 30 percent do. This difference in educational background is not unrelated to the fact that in industry after industry, American firms have been slow to adopt revolutionary new-process technologies. One striking example: Twenty-five years ago the leaders of the American steel industry failed to comprehend the technology revolution that was under way and chose not to make the massive investments in oxygen furnaces and continuous casters being made elsewhere in the world. American steel companies have been playing an unsuccessful game of catch-up ever since.

The management of technology is usually seen as something of   10
relevance to manufacturing but not to the rest of the economy. Here again, what was historically true is no longer true. In the twenty-first century there will be high-tech and low-tech products, but almost every product will be produced with high-tech processes. The automobile is a low-tech product; the robots that make it are high-tech. Gaining an edge in high-tech processes will be important in almost every industry — from fast food to textiles — and mastering process technologies will become central to the success of almost every firm.

The new information and telecommunication technologies that are being developed are also going to make most service industries into high-tech process industries. In retailing, those who survive will have the inventory-control systems that best reduce costs. Stores will be directly linked to suppliers to minimize the time lags between the customer's purchase of some particular item and the restocking of that item. Even now, American firms such as The Limited, a clothing retailer, are converting retailing into a high-tech competition. The Limited's inventory-control, telecommunication, and CAD–CAM (computer-aided design/computer-aided manufacturing) systems allow it to know what women are buying and to put precisely those clothes in their stores within twenty-eight days; their competitors take as long as six months. The result: They win, and their slower competitors lose.

While technology creates competitive advantage, seizing that advantage requires a work force skilled from top to bottom. When the route to success is inventing new products, the education of the smartest 25 percent of the labor force is critical: Someone in that top group can be counted on to invent the new products of tomorrow. But when success depends on being the cheapest and best producer of products, the education of the bottom 50 percent of the population becomes a priority. This is the part of the population that must operate those new processes. If the bottom 50 percent cannot learn what must be learned, new high-tech processes cannot be employed.

Information technologies need to be integrated into the entire production process, from initial designs through marketing to final sales and supporting services such as maintenance. To do this requires workers in the office, the factory, the retail store, and the repair service to have levels of education and skill that they have never had to have in the past.

If sustainable competitive advantage depends on work-force skills, American firms have a problem. Human-resource management is not traditionally seen as central to the competitive survival of the firm in the United States. Skill acquisition is considered an individual responsibility. Labor is simply another factor of production to be hired — rented at the lowest possible cost — much as one buys raw materials or equipment.

The lack of importance attached to human-resource management can be seen in the corporate pecking order. In an American firm the chief financial officer is almost always second in command. The post of head of human-resource management is usually a specialized job, off at the edge of the corporate hierarchy. The executive who holds it is never consulted on major strategic decisions and has no chance to move up to CEO. By way of contrast, in Japan the head of human-resource management is central — usually the second most important executive, after the CEO, in the firm's hierarchy.

While American firms often talk about the vast amounts spent on training their work forces, in fact they invest less in the skills of their employees than do either Japanese or German firms. The money they do invest is also more highly concentrated on professional and managerial employees. And the limited investments that are made in training workers are also much more narrowly focused on the specific skills necessary to do the next job rather than on the basic background skills that make it possible to absorb new technologies.

As a result, problems emerge when new breakthrough technologies arrive. If American workers, for example, take much longer to learn how to operate new flexible manufacturing stations than workers in Germany (as they do), the effective cost of those stations is lower in Germany than it is in the United States. More time is required before equipment is up and running at capacity, and the need for extensive retraining generates costs and creates bottlenecks that limit the speed with which new equipment can be employed. The result is a slower pace of technological change. And in the end the skills of the bottom half of the population affect the wages of the top half. If the bottom half can't effectively staff the processes that have to be operated, the management and professional jobs that go with these processes will disappear.

The Responsive Reader

1. How would you sum up Thurow's central message? What makes it new or different?
2. Can you help explain some of Thurow's key terms and basic distinctions — and show why they are important? For instance, help explain such concepts as new-product technologies, new-process technologies, reverse engineering, and human-resource allocation.

3. According to Thurow, what is wrong with the way this country selects and promotes executives? What is wrong with the way this country trains workers? What is wrong with the American system of education?

Talking, Listening, Writing

4. What other reasons are often given for the competitive advantage enjoyed by Japan and Europe? How do these reasons differ from the causes identified by Thurow? Or how are they related to them?
5. Does Thurow think the adverse trends and causes he describes can be remedied? Do you? To judge from this article, what is the outlook for the country's economic future?
6. What chance does the average voter have to evaluate arguments like those presented in this article? Is there any part of this article you want to challenge on the basis of your observation, experience, or reading?

Projects

7. What has been the fate of "Buy-American" campaigns? Who initiates them? (Who opposes them?) How successfully do they reach the buying public? Your class may want to assign different groups to investigate such different areas as public relations campaigns, the role of organized labor, or the history of related legislation.

THE NEXT WAVE

Barbara Ehrenreich

> *What is the future of the women's movement? How will it build on its successes? What has it learned from its setbacks? How should it chart its course? Barbara Ehrenreich is a trend watcher who examines these questions in an article she wrote as a contributing editor to* Ms. *magazine. A Ph.D. from Rockefeller University and a fellow of the Washington Institute of Policy Studies, she frequently writes on topics of special interest to career women or working women. Her books include* For Her Own Good: 150 Years of the Experts' Advice to Women *(1978),* The Hearts of Men: American Dreams and the Flight from Commitment *(1983), and* Worst Years of Our Lives: Irreverent Notes from a Decade *(1991).*

Thought Starters: What have been the successes of the feminist movement? What obstacles has it encountered? What lies ahead?

Of all the charges leveled against feminism — that it is selfish, disruptive of the family, conducive to poor grooming, or disrespectful of the laws of biology — probably nothing rankles more than the well-worn accusation that it is "just a middle-class movement." I used to have a half-dozen rebuttals ready at hand: I'd list all the famous feminists I could think of with bona fide low-income backgrounds (not to mention all the less famous ones with certifiably low-income *foregrounds*). I'd make elaborate arguments about the inadequacy of class in understanding women's status. (Is the wife of a doctor "middle class" if a divorce can pitch her into poverty?) Finally, I'd deliver my coup de grace: so what! 1

But I have begun to think that it does matter. If by middle class we mean someone who is college-educated, who expects to have a "career" rather than a job, and who enjoys a standard of living defined by credit cards and touch-tone appliances, then the women's movement — at least, the visible, organized women's movement — had indeed been disproportionately middle class. This, in itself, is no cause for shame. The abolition movement was middle class by the standards of the day; so too, on the average, is the contemporary peace movement, the environmental movement, and the resurgent student movement. In the clichéd explanation, only the middle class has the time and energy to sit in at bomb test sites or fritter away whole evenings debating bylaws and agenda items. The working class is, by definition, otherwise occupied.

Only a funny thing is happening in the women's movement today. The middle-class movement, which is pretty much the movement as we've known it, has been showing disturbing signs of lethargy. Meanwhile, something vast and angry and inspired seems to be brewing among the women of the pink-collar ghettos and the blue-collar suburbs, the housing developments and the trailer parks. And I think it may be nothing less than the next great wave of feminism.

To begin with what could be called, loosely but by no means pejoratively, the "middle-class" movement: one of the early signs of lethargy was Betty Friedan's 1981 book, *The Second Stage.* In some complex way, Friedan is still the mother of us all, so when she announced that the battle was over and it was time to refocus on home and husband, it was clear that we had turned a significant corner. The signs were everywhere. Among rank-and-file career women, consciousness-raising groups gave way to "networks," and even these began to unravel as the upwardly mobile discovered that the people one really needed to network with were *men.* In academe, women's studies — long the most reliable reproductive organ of middle-class feminism — began, in some quarters, to take on a remote and esoteric air. Reviewing an important new anthology of highbrow feminist scholarship, Catharine Stimpson — herself a leading pioneer of women's studies — found the contributions unaccountably tired and "uneasy in spirit." . . .

All of these may be taken as signs of simple exhaustion. In the last   5
decade, organized feminism has faced the mortal challenge of the antifeminist right, and on the whole I believe we have done remarkably well. If we have not been able to advance our agenda as much as we would have liked to, neither has the other side. Even in the area of economic rights for low-income women, we were able to stymie the administration's efforts to all but eliminate food stamps, welfare, and Medicaid. And prominent among the "we" in this case was a loose coalition of distinctly middle-class organizations, including the League of Women Voters, the American Association of University Women, and the National Federation of Business and Professional Women's Clubs. Perhaps, after so many defensive struggles, a certain weariness is to be expected; a bit of a breather, richly earned.

But there is one disturbing sign that cannot be chalked up to battle fatigue, and that is the so-called postfeminism of young, educated, career-oriented women. I don't want to contribute to the exaggeration of this phenomenon; even the most elite campuses are still generating feminist activists as well as corporate clones. But it *is* there, especially on the elite campuses: the assured conviction that, whatever indignities women may have suffered in the remote past (for example, 1970), the way is now clear for any woman of spirit to rise straight to the top of whatever fascinating, lucrative profession she chooses.

For a long time I asked myself: where did we go wrong? Surely, considering the totality of the feminist agenda, it is too early to be exhausted, or too soon to be smug. Then it occurred to me. The problem is not that we (the organized, publicly visible, largely middle–class feminist movement) failed, but that we *succeeded,* at least in one absolutely critical area: the doors to the professions are now open to women. Not all the way, and certainly not all the way to the top, but they are open. Consider the numbers. In 1970, fewer than 8 percent of the nation's physicians were female; today, 14.6 percent are female and approximately 30 percent of our medical students are women, and the gains are of the same magnitude in law and business.

This may be, all things considered, the most momentous achievement since suffrage. A young woman who was born in the same year as this magazine [1972] will not have to secure her membership in the middle class through the tenuous pact of marriage. She doesn't have to marry a doctor; she can be one. And she knows it; and so do we who are old enough to be her mother, her chemistry professor, or her guidance counselor. In this one crucial way, we have it made.

Some of us, anyway. Because the chief beneficiaries of the opening up of the professions and upper-middle management are women who were born to the middle class. This is one of the nasty little secrets of the American class system: that the people who get ahead are, by and large, the ones who start out ahead, that is, who have the advantages of good schools, an encouraging home life, and the money and leisure for higher education. A 1976 study showed, for example, that the influx of women into medical school did not change the *class* composition of the medical student body. Most of the women, as well as the men, were the children of the approximately 20 percent of the population in the professions. If the recent *glasnost* in the professions has been feminism's greatest victory, it is a victory whose sweetness the majority of American women will never taste.

Now let us consider that sub-yuppie female majority — the women who are *not* M.B.A.s or surgical residents or assistant professors. It is these "average women," and especially the working women among them, who I believe hold the key to a feminist renewal. According to long-standing feminist myth, the "average" working-class woman is in the "I'm no women's libber, but . . ." category: perhaps a fellow traveler but never an actual feminist. Well, consider the results of a poll conducted by The Gallup Organization, Inc., in the spring of 1986. Asked "Do you consider yourself a feminist?" a stunning 56 percent of American women answered yes. (Incidentally, only 4 percent considered themselves "anti-feminists." So if you're wondering who won the gender wars of the seventies and eighties, the score is in.)

But the result that surprised even the pollsters was that working-class women (blue and pink collar) were at least as likely to call themselves feminists as were women in the "professional and business" category. If anything, feminist consciousness appears to rise as one descends the socioeconomic scale. Fifty-five percent of women with family incomes of over $40,000 a year are self-identified feminists, compared to 57 percent of women with family incomes of under $20,000 a year. This 2-percentage point difference is not statistically significant, but it is probably significant that 41 percent of the upper-income group consider themselves *not* to be feminist, compared to only 26 percent of the lower-income group. "Non-white" women (what a colorless, negative category) were the most feminist of all, with 64 percent declaring themselves feminist. What the statistics seem to be saying for anyone who cares to listen, is that the women who are most favorably disposed to feminism today are the ones who have gained the least from the movement so far, and hence have the most to gain from the struggles that lie ahead.

And for the working-class feminist majority, most of the victories still do lie ahead. True, there have been some gains in opening up the better-paying, blue-collar occupations to women, but one is struck at once by how minute they are when measured against women's advance into the professions. While the percentage of women in professional training rose from 10 to 30 or 40 percent, the percentage of women carpenters, machinists, and mechanics has not even risen *to* 10 percent. As a result, the average working woman is still pretty much where she always was: waiting on tables, emptying wastebaskets, or pounding a keyboard for an hourly wage in the mid-single-digit range. When she looks out — at television or the dressed-for-success-style magazines — she sees more fortunate women bounding ahead. But when she looks around her, she sees women like herself, going nowhere.

Somewhere in this collision of rising expectations and unchanging conditions lie the seeds of the next feminist upsurge. According to Joyce Miller, president of the Coalition of Labor Union Women,

> Thirteen years ago, when CLUW was formed, working women tended to see feminism as something for the college-educated suburban set. Since then, they've been taking up feminist ideas and translating them into economic issues. Issues like sexual harassment, pay equity, and child care have brought blue-collar women closer to feminism.

The signs are all around us. Think of the TWA flight attendants picketing with neatly printed posters announcing, WE ARE BREADWINNERS! (TWA boss Carl Icahn was reported to have suggested that flight attendants, being mostly women rather than, as he saw it, breadwinners, could stand to take a larger pay cut than other TWA workers.) Think of the strike of over 1,800 clerical and technical workers at Yale two years ago. Fighting for pay equity, the strikers reached out for support from NOW and campus women's groups. "We are coming together around our common interests as women . . ." one striker wrote, in words that could be a preamble to a feminist manifesto anywhere, anytime. Or, for a

slightly different kind of example, think of the pink-collar wife of a striking meat packer from Minnesota: "At first we told our husbands, 'We're
right behind you,'" she told a strike-support rally in New York, "but now
we say to them, 'We're right *next* to you, all the way.'"

These examples come from strike situations, union activities, and   15
indeed, how else are most working women to seek the rapid redress
of economic injustice? For now, unions are the main beneficiaries of
working-class women's increasing assertiveness. Most new union members, for the past few years, have been women; and in 1985 American
unions' slow decline in membership (a result of deindustrialization and the
loss of blue-collar manufacturing jobs) began to turn around — mostly
due to the influx of 70,000 new female members. Trade unions are notoriously masculine institutions, the home of hard hats and cigar-chomping
bosses, but their future depends, for the first time in history, on the feminist consciousness of a female constituency. I think of an exchange that
occurred on a clerical workers' picket line not far from where I live. A
male union official asked, jokingly, if any of the "girls" wanted to go for
coffee. "Hey, what d'you think we're out here for?" shot back a middle-
aged woman. "We're not 'girls' and we don't get coffee!"

But the future of the feminist movement, as opposed to the trade
union movement, depends on the ability and willingness of low-income
women to carve out, create, or join autonomous *women's* organizations.
There has already been an impressive start. Since 1980, about a half-dozen
brand-new regional and statewide organizations representing low-income
women's economic interests have emerged — notably the California Wom-
en's Economic Agenda Project, Women for Economic Justice in Massachusetts, and Women's Agenda in Pennsylvania. These organizations tend
to be traditional in their tactics — lobbying, public education, organizing — but distinctly nontraditional in their composition. The first national
conference of the new, low-income women's organizations convened in
California last spring, bringing together workplace organizers, welfare
rights activists, and all-purpose community heroines from all ethnic
groups and corners of the country. I was there, too, and I came away
feeling I had seen the feminist future, and that it is far more richly diverse,
and perhaps even more militant and deeply aggrieved, than anything in
the feminist past.

But the big question may be whether the emergent working-class
feminist insurgency will be able to find a home in the infrastructure of
feminist institutions and organizations that have been created, to a large
extent, by middle-class activists. For though feminist movements may be
of one class or another at one time or another, the feminist *vision* belongs
to all women — from the cleaning "lady" to the lady of leisure, from the
lowest paid keyboard operator to the woman law partner. If the vision and
the movement are to come together, for all women, organized feminism
may have some soul searching to do. Do our issues too narrowly reflect
our own economic status? Do our ways of talking and working together

covertly exclude women who are poorer, who have had less formal education, or who may simply be unfamiliar with the decorum of meetings and "feminist process"? How open are *we* to new ideas, how ready to embrace new sisters without the self-indulgence of guilt or the insult of condescension?

I say "we" with a trace of embarrassment, knowing that already many of you will read it as "they." But if we are clear about differences now — and prepared to be open and sisterly — perhaps there will be no "us" and "them" in the next great wave of feminism.

The Responsive Reader

1. What assumptions does Ehrenreich make about her audience? Why would terms like *abolition, suffrage,* and *postfeminism* have a special meaning for her intended readers?
2. Where does Ehrenreich first spell out the trend that is the focus of her essay? How does her introduction lead up to it? How does she handle the issue of class and the women's movement?
3. Where does she turn for evidence? What statistics, examples, or quotations best support her thesis?

Talking, Listening, Writing

4. Does Ehrenreich have a plan for action? Does she offer good advice?
5. Is there a backlash to the feminist movement? Does Ehrenreich recognize it? How important or significant is it?
6. Do you think working-class women will be the next wave of feminism? Why or why not?

Projects

7. Can you update some of Ehrenreich's statistics and poll results? Working with a group, try to compile current data that could be compared with hers. (How accurate a trend watcher is she proving to be?)

Thinking about Connections

Committed feminists represented in this book, in addition to Ehrenreich, include Patty Fisher (p. 307), Alice Walker (p. 338 and p. 379), Gloria Steinem (p. 426), and Judi Bari (p. 583). When you look back over their writing, what seem to be topics of paramount concern? What are basic shared values or goals? What are significant differences in perspective?

HUMANITY'S BETTER MOMENTS
Barbara Tuchman

> *During much of the twentieth century, historians, sociologists, and writers of imaginative literature have been pessimistic about the prospects for humankind. As one of America's best-known historians, Barbara Tuchman did her share of chronicling the great catastrophes. After graduating from Radcliffe, she worked as a foreign correspondent, reporting on the Spanish Civil War from Madrid in 1937. Her Pulitzer Prize–winning* The Guns of August *(1962) reexamined the events leading up to the outbreak of World War I. Her book* A Distant Mirror *(1978) chronicled the calamities of Europe in the fourteenth century — the age of the plague, an age of "depopulation and disaster, extravagance and splendor." However, although much of her own work dealt with catastrophe, war, and disease, in a lecture (abridged here) she gave in 1980, she tried to counteract the "negative overload" of recorded history. Paying tribute to achievements and inspirational acts, she tried to counterbalance the historian's emphasis on "the bad side" — on "evil, misery, contention, and harm."*

Thought Starters: When you look ahead to the future, do you tend to be a pessimist or an optimist about the prospects of the human species?

For a change from prevailing pessimism, I should like to recall some   1
of the positive and even admirable capacities of the human race. We hear very little of them lately. Ours is not a time of self-esteem or self-confidence — as was, for instance, the nineteenth century, when self-esteem may be seen oozing from its portraits. Victorians, especially the men, pictured themselves as erect, noble, and splendidly handsome. Our self-image looks more like Woody Allen or a character from Samuel Beckett.[1] Amid a mass of worldwide troubles and a poor record for the twentieth century, we see our species — with cause — as functioning very badly, as blunderers when not knaves, as violent, ignoble, corrupt, inept, incapable of mastering the forces that threaten us, weakly subject to our worst instincts; in short, decadent.

The catalogue is familiar and valid, but it is growing tiresome. A study of history reminds one that humanity has its ups and downs and

---

[1][Samuel Beckett's best-known play is *Waiting for Godot* (1954), in which two tramps spend much of their time in aimless conversation, vacillating between self-pity and self-disgust.]

during the ups has accomplished many brave and beautiful things, exerted stupendous endeavors, explored and conquered oceans and wilderness, achieved marvels of beauty in the creative arts and marvels of science and social progress; has loved liberty with a passion that throughout history has led men to fight and die for it over and over again; has pursued knowledge, exercised reason, enjoyed laughter and pleasures, played games with zest, shown courage, heroism, altruism, honor, and decency; experienced love; known comfort, contentment, and occasionally happiness. All these qualities have been part of human experience, and if they have not had as important notice as the negatives nor exerted as wide and persistent an influence as the evils we do, they nevertheless deserve attention, for they are currently all but forgotten.

Among the great endeavors, we have in our own time carried men to the moon and brought them back safely — surely one of the most remarkable achievements in history. Some may disapprove of the effort as unproductive, too costly, and a wrong choice of priorities in relation to greater needs, all of which may be true but does not, as I see it, diminish the achievement. If you look carefully, all positives have a negative underside — sometimes more, sometimes less — and not all admirable endeavors have admirable motives. Some have sad consequences. Although most signs presently point from bad to worse, human capacities are probably what they have always been. If primitive man could discover how to transform grain into bread, and reeds growing by the riverbank into baskets; if his successors could invent the wheel, harness the insubstantial air to turn a millstone, transform sheep's wool, flax, and worms' cocoons into fabric — we, I imagine, will find a way to manage the energy problem.

Consider how the Dutch accomplished the miracle of making land out of sea. By progressive enclosure of the Zuider Zee over the last sixty years, they have added half a million acres to their country, enlarging its area by eight percent and providing homes, farms, and towns for close to a quarter of a million people. The will to do the impossible, the spirit of can-do that overtakes our species now and then, was never more manifest than in this earth-altering act by the smallest of the major European nations. Today the *Afsluitdijk,* or Zuider Zee road, is a normal thoroughfare. To drive across it between the sullen ocean on one side and new land on the other is for that moment to feel optimism for the human race.

Even when the historical tide is low, a particular group of doers may   5 emerge in exploits that inspire awe. Shrouded in the mists of the eighth century, long before the cathedrals, Viking seamanship was a wonder of daring, stamina, and skill. Pushing relentlessly outward in open boats, the Vikings sailed south, around Spain to North Africa and Arabia, north to the top of the world, west across uncharted seas to American coasts. They hauled their boats overland from the Baltic to make their way down Russian rivers to the Black Sea. Why? We do not know what engine drove them, only that it was part of the human endowment.

What of the founding of our own country, America? We take the *Mayflower* for granted — yet think of the boldness, the enterprise, the determined independence, the sheer grit it took to leave the known and set out across the sea for the unknown where no houses or food, no stores, no cleared land, no crops or livestock, none of the equipment or settlement of organized living awaited.

Equally bold was the enterprise of the French in the northern forests of the American continent, who throughout the seventeenth century explored and opened the land from the St. Lawrence to the Mississippi, from the Great Lakes to the Gulf of Mexico. They came not for liberty like the Pilgrims, but for gain and dominion, whether in spiritual empire for the Jesuits or in land, glory, and riches for the agents of the King; and rarely in history have people willingly embraced such hardship, such daunting adventure, and persisted with such tenacity and endurance. They met hunger, exhaustion, frostbite, capture and torture by Indians, wounds and disease, dangerous rapids, swarms of insects, long portages, bitter weather, and hardly ever did those who suffered the experience fail to return, re-enter the menacing but bountiful forest, and pit themselves once more against danger, pain, and death.

Above all others, the perseverance of La Salle in his search for the mouth of the Mississippi was unsurpassed. While preparing in Quebec, he mastered eight Indian languages. From then on he suffered accidents, betrayals, desertions, losses of men and provisions, fever and snow blindness, the hostility and intrigues of rivals who incited the Indians against him and plotted to ambush or poison him. He was truly pursued, as Francis Parkman wrote, by "a demon of havoc."[2] Paddling through heavy waves in a storm over Lake Ontario, he waded through freezing surf to beach the canoes each night, and lost guns and baggage when a canoe was swamped and sank. To lay the foundations of a fort above Niagara, frozen ground had to be thawed by boiling water. When the fort was at last built, La Salle christened it Crèvecoeur — that is, Heartbreak. It earned the name when in his absence it was plundered and deserted by its half-starved mutinous garrison. Farther on, a friendly Indian village, intended as a destination, was found laid waste by the Iroquois with only charred stakes stuck with skulls standing among the ashes, while wolves and buzzards prowled through the remains.

When at last, after four months' hazardous journey down the Great River, La Salle reached the sea, he formally took possession in the name of Louis XIV of all the country from the river's mouth to its source and of its tributaries — that is, of the vast basin of the Mississippi from the Rockies to the Appalachians — and named it Louisiana. The validity of the claim,

---

[2][Francis Parkman (1823–1893), author of *The Oregon Trail* and *Pioneers of France in the New World,* was the leading nineteenth-century historian of the American frontier.]

which seems so hollow to us (though successful in its own time), is not the point. What counts is the conquest of fearful adversity by one man's extraordinary exertions and inflexible will.

Our greatest recourse and most enduring achievement is art. At its 10 best, it reveals the nobility that coexists in human nature along with flaws and evils, and the beauty and truth it can perceive. Whether in music or architecture, literature, painting or sculpture, art opens our eyes, ears, and feelings to something beyond ourselves, something we cannot experience without the artist's vision and the genius of his craft. The placing of Greek temples, like the Temple of Poseidon on the promontory at Sunion, outlined against the piercing blue of the Aegean Sea, Poseidon's home; the majesty of Michelangelo's sculptured figures in stone; Shakespeare's command of language and knowledge of the human soul; the intricate order of Bach, the enchantment of Mozart; the purity of Chinese monochrome pottery with its lovely names — celadon, oxblood, peach blossom, clair de lune; the exuberance of Tiepolo's ceilings where, without picture frames to limit movement, a whole world in exquisitely beautiful colors lives and moves in the sky; the prose and poetry of all the writers from Homer to Cervantes to Jane Austen and John Keats to Dostoevski and Chekhov — who made all these things? We — our species — did.[3]

If we have (as I think) lost beauty and elegance in the modern world, we have gained much, through science and technology and democratic pressures, in the material well-being of the masses. The change in the lives of, and society's attitude toward, the working class marks the great divide between the modern world and the old regime. From the French Revolution through the brutal labor wars of the nineteenth and twentieth centuries, the change was earned mainly by force against fierce and often vicious opposition. While this was a harsh process, it developed and activated a social conscience hardly operative before. Slavery, beggary, unaided misery, and want have, on the whole, been eliminated in the developed nations of the West. That much is a credit in the human record, even if the world is uglier as a result of adapting to mass values. History generally arranges these things so that gain is balanced by loss, perhaps in order not to make the gods jealous.

The material miracles wrought by science and technology — from the harnessing of steam and electricity to anesthesia, antisepsis, antibiotics, and woman's liberator, the washing machine, and all the labor-savers that go with it — are too well recognized in our culture to need my emphasis. Pasteur is as great a figure in the human record as Michelangelo or

[3][In her list of great artists, the author includes, along with those who are universally known, the Italian painter Tiepolo (1696–1770); the Spanish novelist Cervantes (1547–1616), author of the mock-heroic *Don Quixote;* the British novelist Jane Austen (1775–1817), author of *Pride and Prejudice;* and the Russian short-story writer and dramatist Anton Chekhov (1860–1904), author of *The Cherry Orchard.*]

Mozart — probably, as far as the general welfare is concerned, greater.[4] We are more aware of his kind of accomplishment than of those less tangible. Ask anyone to suggest the credits of mankind and the answer is likely to start with physical things. Yet the underside of scientific progress is prominent and dark. The weaponry of war in its ever-widening capacity to kill is the deadly example, and who is prepared to state with confidence that the over-all effect of the automobile, airplane, telephone, television, and computer has been, on balance, beneficent?

Pursuit of knowledge for its own sake has been a more certain good. There was a springtime in the eighteenth century when, through knowledge and reason, everything seemed possible; when reason was expected to break through religious dogma like the sun breaking through fog, and man, armed with knowledge and reason would be able at last to control his own fate and construct a good society.

Although the Enlightenment may have overestimated the power of reason to guide human conduct, it nevertheless opened to men and women a more humane view of their fellow passengers. Slowly the harshest habits gave way to reform — in treatment of the insane, reduction of death penalties, mitigation of the fierce laws against debtors and poachers, and in the passionately fought cause for abolition of the slave trade.

The humanitarian movement was not charity, which always carries   15
an overtone of being done in the donor's interest, but a more disinterested benevolence or altruism, motivated by conscience. It was personified in William Wilberforce, who in the later eighteenth century stirred the great rebellion of the English conscience against the trade in human beings. In America the immorality of slavery had long troubled the colonies. By 1789 slavery had been legally abolished by the New England states followed by New York, New Jersey, and Pennsylvania, but the southern states, as their price for joining the Union, insisted that the subject be excluded from the Constitution.

In England, where the home economy did not depend on slave labor, Wilberforce had more scope. His influence could have carried him to the Prime Minister's seat if personal power had been his goal, but he channeled his life instead toward a goal for humanity. He instigated, energized, inspired a movement whose members held meetings, organized petitions, collected information on the horrors of the middle passage, showered pamphlets on the public, gathered Nonconformist middle-class sentiment into a swelling tide that, in Trevelyan's phrase, "melted the hard prudence of statesmen."[5] Abolition of the slave trade under the British flag was won in 1807. The British Navy was used to enforce the ban by searches on the

[4][Louis Pasteur (1822–1895) was the French chemist who pioneered the prevention of disease through inoculation and after whom the process of pasteurization is named.]
[5][The Nonconformists were English protestants who refused to conform to the official Anglican state church and who commanded a strong following among the middle class. G. M. Trevelyan, long a professor of history at Cambridge University, first published his widely read *History of England* in 1926.]

high seas and regular patrols of the African coast. When Portugal and Spain were persuaded to join in the prohibition, they were paid a compensation of £300,000 and £400,000 respectively by the British taxpayer. Violations and smuggling continued, convincing the abolitionists that, in order to stop the trade, slavery itself had to be abolished. Agitation resumed. By degrees over the next quarter-century, compensation reduced the opposition of the West Indian slave-owners and their allies in England until emancipation of all slaves in the British Empire was enacted in 1833. The total cost to the British taxpayer was reckoned at £20 million.

Through recent unpleasant experiences we have learned to expect ambition, greed, or corruption to reveal itself behind every public act, but, as we have just seen, it is not invariably so. Human beings do possess better impulses, and occasionally act upon them, even in the twentieth century. Occupied Denmark, during World War II, outraged by Nazi orders for deportation of its Jewish fellow citizens, summoned the courage of defiance and transformed itself into a united underground railway to smuggle virtually all eight thousand Danish Jews out to Sweden, and Sweden gave them shelter. Far away and unconnected, a village in southern France, Le Chambon-sur-Lignon, devoted itself to rescuing Jews and other victims of the Nazis at the risk of the inhabitants' own lives and freedom. "Saving lives became a hobby of the people of Le Chambon," said one of them. The larger record of the time was admittedly collaboration, passive or active. We cannot reckon on the better impulses predominating in the world, only that they will always appear.

The strongest of these in history, summoner of the best in us, has been zeal for liberty. Time after time, in some spot somewhere on the globe, people have risen in what Swinburne called the "divine right of insurrection" — to overthrow despots, repel alien conquerors, achieve independence — and so it will be until the day power ceases to corrupt, which, I think, is not a near expectation.

The ancient Jews rose three times against alien rulers, beginning with the revolt of the Maccabees against the effort of Antiochus to outlaw observance of the Jewish faith.[6] Mattathias the priest and his five sons, assembling loyal believers in the mountains, opened a guerrilla war which, after the father's death, was to find a leader of military genius in his son Judah, called Maccabee or the Hammer. Later honored in the Middle Ages as one of the Nine Worthies of the world, he defeated his enemies, rededicated the temple, and re-established the independence of Judea. In the next century the uprising of the Zealots against Roman rule was fanatically and hopelessly pursued through famines, sieges, the fall of Jerusalem and destruction of the temple until a last stand of fewer than a thousand on the rock of Masada ended in group suicide in preference to surrender.

[6][The revolt of the Maccabees against the Syrians under King Antiochus took place in the second century B.C. Hadrian was the Roman emperor at the time of the final Jewish rebellion against Roman rule in the second century A.D.]

After sixty years as an occupied province, Judea rose yet again under Simon Bar Kochba, who regained Jerusalem for a brief moment of Jewish control but could not withstand the arms of Hadrian. The rebellion was crushed, but the zeal for selfhood, smoldering in exile through eighteen centuries, was to revive and regain its home in our time.

The phenomenon continues in our own day, in Algeria, in Vietnam, although, seen at close quarters and more often than not manipulated by outsiders, contemporary movements seem less pure and heroic than those polished by history's gloss — as, for instance, the Scots under William Wallace, the Swiss against the Hapsburgs, the American colonies against the mother country.[7]   *20*

I have always cherished the spirited rejoinder of one of the great colonial landowners of New York who, on being advised not to risk his property by signing the Declaration of Independence, replied, "Damn the property; give me the pen!" On seeking confirmation for purposes of this essay, I am deeply chagrined to report that the saying appears to be apocryphal. Yet not its spirit, for the signers well knew they were risking their property, not to mention their heads, by putting their names to the Declaration.

Is anything to be learned from my survey? I raise the question only because most people want history to teach them lessons, which I believe it can do, although I am less sure we can use them when needed. I gathered these examples not to teach but merely to remind people in a despondent era that the good in humanity operates even if the bad secures more attention. I am aware that selecting out the better moments does not result in a realistic picture. Turn them over and there is likely to be a darker side, as when Project Apollo, our journey to the moon, was authorized because its glamour could obtain subsidies for rocket and missile development that otherwise might not have been forthcoming. That is the way things are.

Whole philosophies have evolved over the question whether the human species is predominantly good or evil. I only know that it is mixed, that you cannot separate good from bad, that wisdom, courage, and benevolence exist alongside knavery, greed, and stupidity; heroism and fortitude alongside vainglory, cruelty, and corruption.

It is a paradox of our time in the West that never have so many people been so relatively well off and never has society been more troubled. Yet I suspect that humanity's virtues have not vanished, although the experiences of our century seem to suggest that they are in abeyance. A century that took shape in the disillusion which followed the enormous effort and hopes of World War I, that saw revolution in Russia congeal into the same

---

[7][William Wallace (1272–1305) led the Scots in their fight for independence from English rule. Switzerland has through the centuries been the symbol of a small country that successfully defended its independence against powerful neighbors, such as the Austrian-Hungarian empire ruled by the House of Hasburg.]

tyranny it overthrew, saw a supposedly civilized nation revert under the Nazis into organized and unparalleled savagery, saw the craven appeasement by the democracies, is understandably marked by suspicion of human nature. A literary historian, Van Wyck Brooks, discussing the 1920s and '30s, wrote that whereas Whitman and Emerson "had been impressed by the worth and good sense of the people, writers of the new time" were struck by their lusts, cupidity, violence, and had come to dislike their fellow men. The same theme reappeared in a recent play in which a mother struggled against her two "pitilessly contemptuous" children. Her problem was that she wanted them to be happy and they did not want to be. They preferred to watch horrors on television. In essence this is our epoch. It insists upon the flaws and corruptions, without belief in valor or virtue or the possibility of happiness. It keeps turning to look back on Sodom and Gomorrah; it has no view of the Delectable Mountains.[8]

We must keep a balance, and I know of no better prescription than a   25 phrase from Condorcet's eulogy on the death of Benjamin Franklin: "He pardoned the present for the sake of the future."

The Responsive Reader

1. Do you recognize the modern self-image that Tuchman sets out to balance or counteract? What features of it do you recognize? What evidence of it have you seen?
2. Early in her essay, Tuchman discusses examples of the "spirit of can-do," from engineering marvels to journeys of exploration. Which are familiar accomplishments to you? Which are most impressive? What do they have in common?
3. Tuchman celebrates art as the most enduring human achievement. How does she define the role it plays in human culture?
4. Tuchman pays tribute to the spirit of humanitarian reform and to a changing attitude toward the working class as the great legacies of an enlightened political tradition going back to the eighteenth century, or Age of Reason. What does she say about the forces at work and the impact of the changes they wrought?
5. In the final part of her essay, does Tuchman succeed in counteracting the modern pessimism about politics? Why or why not?

Talking, Writing, Thinking

6. Tuchman keeps reassuring her readers that she is aiming at a balanced picture. Where and how does she deal with the "darker side"? Do you think the overall picture she paints is too optimistic?
7. What event or achievement would you nominate for one of "humanity's better moments"?

[8][a symbol for salvation or the promise of eternal life]

8. Write a paper to attack or defend optimism, pessimism, pragmatism, skepticism, or a similar –ism of your choice.

Projects

9. How widespread is pessimism about the future in your generation
   or on your campus? Working with others, organize a survey and
   interpret the results.

THE MYTHS OF RACIAL DIVISION

Andrew Hacker

Andrew Hacker is a professor of political science; according to a reviewer in Newsweek, *he "is known for doing with statistics what Fred Astaire did with hats, canes, and chairs." In 1992, he published a book called* Two Nations: Black and White, Separate, Hostile, Unequal *that attracted wide media attention. To gauge the current state of race relations in this country, he drew on statistics from such agencies as the Census Bureau and the Bureau of Labor Statistics and on his own observations in the multiethnic setting of Queens College in New York City. Although he does not like to be labeled a pessimist, his figures document the lack of real progress in such areas as the gap between average incomes of blacks and whites. He has been criticized for writing a book that is all diagnosis with no remedies, let alone a panacea or a quick fix. In the following article, he uses some materials from his book.*

Thought Starters: How pervasive are the effects of racism in holding back African Americans? How much real progress has there been in race relations?

The urge to emphasize racial division in America is hard to resist. *1*
Few nations have etched so deep a black-and-white separation as our own. Even South Africa allows for Coloureds, while Latin countries have mulattos and mestizos, as well as Creoles and quadroons. But here even children of mixed marriages end up regarded as black. And while citizens may cherish their European origins, being white retains primacy in most of their minds. At times, race seems to surpass even gender as our major schism.

It shouldn't. We now have information about how much impact race has in areas such as school achievement, hiring, family life, and crime — and it should spur us to rethink the actual impact of race and ethnic separatism. If anything, there is evidence that race is becoming a *less* salient factor for growing groups of Americans. Here follows a brief debunking of a variety of black-and-white myths, which, upon inspection, turn out to be grayer realities.

The black family is disintegrating, while the white family remains intact. Since Daniel Patrick Moynihan's 1965 report found black families trapped in a "tangle of pathology," conditions seem to have gotten worse. Two-thirds of black babies are now born outside of wedlock, and more than half of black homes are headed by women. A majority of black youngsters live only with their mother; and in most of these households she has never been married.

Almost everyone agrees that the increases in nonmarital births and female-headed households are causes for dismay. But why should race be the crucial variable? Readily available reports show that low income and education outweigh race in causing family instability. Absent fathers abound in depressed counties where the residents are almost wholly white. In rural Maine, for example, out-of-wedlock rates exceed those for blacks in several states.

As it happens, extramarital births and households headed by women are subject to social trends, which touch all races and classes in similar ways. The Census figures for female-headed families for the last four decades show that both black and white families have disintegrated at virtually identical rates. In 1950, 17.2 percent of black families were headed by single women, against 5.3 percent of white families (a black-white multiple of 3.2). In 1990, the figures are 56.2 percent and 17.3 percent respectively (a black-white multiple of 3.2). Plainly, what we have been seeing are not so much race-based differences as concurrent adaptations to common cultural conditions. True, the black figure has always been three times larger, and here is where "racial" reasons have an influence of their own. But those forces were at work well before 1950, prior to talk about "pathology." Of course, the current 56.2 percent rate for black households is depressingly high. But then the 1990 figure for whites is almost identical to the one for blacks lamented in Moynihan's report.

The point here is not whether family structure is important, but whether its dynamic over the last thirty years has been different along racial lines. It hasn't been. Given the ubiquity of absent fathers — black and white — little will be gained by lecturing one race on its duties. To call on black Americans to show greater discipline would seem to suggest that only they have deviated from national norms. Black families will become more stable when all households evolve a stronger structure.

Where out-of-wedlock births are concerned, there is actual racial convergence. What we hear most is that 66 percent of black births are to girls and women who are not married. However, close study of the figures reveals that the black-white multiple is less than half of what it was forty years ago. So while black out-of-wedlock births are at an all-time high, the white ratio has been ascending at a far faster rate. Even in typical mid-American cities such as Davenport, Iowa, and Dayton, Ohio, the current white figures are 27.8 percent and 31.4 percent. In 1950, 16.8 percent of black births were out of wedlock, while 1.7 percent of white births were (a black-white multiple of 9.9). In 1970, the proportions were 37.6 percent and 5.7 percent respectively (a multiple of 6.6). Today, the figures are 66 percent and 16 percent (a multiple of 4.1). The chief reason for the decrease in the multiple is the availability of abortion. Although black women constitute only 13 percent of women of childbearing age, they account for more than 30 percent of the pregnancies terminated each year.

Blacks are far more likely to commit crimes than whites. When we hear allusions to "crime," our first image tends to be of violent assaults — rape, robbery, murder — not insider trading or embezzling. And "black crime" conjures up Willie Hortons, whose acts of terror forever scar their victims' lives. By every measure we have, black felons commit far more than their share of the most dreaded crimes. While constituting only about 12 percent of the population, they account for 43.2 percent of arrests for rape, 54.7 percent of murders where the perpetrator is known, and 69.3 percent of reported robberies.

Does this mean that blacks on the whole are less law-abiding? Bruce Wright, a black New York judge, came close to saying just that when he argued that felons of his own race are simply breaking "a social contract that was not of their making in the first place." In fact, we know much less about offenses by whites, since their crimes tend to be office-based, or involve insurance claims or tax evasion, fewer of which are uncovered or apprehended. Although white-collar crooks can and do end up behind bars, many more do not. There is reason to believe that larcenous proclivities exist in members of every race but since more alternatives are open to whites, they have less need for thievery that threatens physical harm. (Class constraints are also more likely to make whites repress hatred or rage that could propel them to rape or murder.)

Because we fear more for our bodies than our bank accounts, violent   10
crimes are more apt to bring prison terms, which explains the disproportionate number of blacks behind bars. But how far is their race the reason? What we can say with some assurance is that people who end up as inmates tend to be lower class, and represent a rougher and tougher element within that economic stratum. The prison rolls in West Virginia and Idaho are overwhelmingly white, and most inmates were convicted of crimes that in other states tend to be associated with blacks. (While West Virginia's and Idaho's overall crime rates are relatively low, their ratios of violent to non-violent crimes do not differ significantly from those of states having larger black populations.)

Blacks now outnumber whites in our penal institutions, but this was not always so. In 1930, 76.7 percent of inmates were white; as recently as 1970 the number was 60.5 percent. In contrast, blacks made up 22.4 percent of the prison population in 1930 and now make up a staggering 45.3 percent. This would suggest that black men were much more law-abiding half a century ago, since most then lived in the South, where they could have been sent to the chain gang with relative ease. In fact, controls exerted by churches, the authority of elders, and community pride combined to deter conduct that could land black men in trouble. Given the depth of poverty and endless humiliations, this discipline is all the more striking.

At the same time, the past had a much larger class of whites who used or threatened violence. The Jimmy Cagneys of New York's Hell's Kitchen and the George Rafts who filled the cells at Sing Sing portrayed an actual segment of the population. Indeed, what is often seen today as "black crime" used to be predominantly white. Since those days many if not most whites have moved up to the middle class, so those who are drawn to larceny have less need to commit face-to-face felonies. The flip side is that blacks now constitute a much larger share of the poor, and more of them live in urban centers where earlier controls no longer apply. As a result, they preponderate among those being charged and imprisoned for the kinds of crimes poorer people are more likely to commit.

Blacks score less well on objective IQ tests. Ours is an age of machine-graded tests, so much so that a single score can determine a person's future. The Scholastic Aptitude Test, which more than a million high school seniors take every year, is the first thing colleges consider when assessing applicants. Do the tests discriminate? Quite obviously they do. Children from better-off families usually do better, since they go to schools that familiarize them with the format. Students with a mathematical bent usually score well throughout the SAT, as do those with a flair for solving puzzles at a one-a-minute rate.

The problem is that black Americans as a group do not do well on standardized tests. This holds true for job applicants and civil service promotions, even when special courses have been arranged. An analysis of the SAT results shows that blacks still lag behind other groups even when they come from homes with comparable incomes and parental educations. The average SAT scores for students whose parents earn between $50,000 and $60,000 are 955 for Asians, 947 for whites, 879 for Hispanics, and 790 for blacks. For those whose parents have a graduate degree, the average SAT scores are 1053 for Asians, 1018 for whites, 897 for Hispanics, and 830 for blacks. Can there be a bias in the SAT that hampers even privileged blacks?

The first answer is that if there is a bias, it is not "white" in character. 15 As the scores show, Asians rank ahead of whites when backgrounds are held constant, just as Hispanics outperform blacks. Asians and Hispanics do better on this American test because they study longer and harder, pay attention to the rules, and are less likely to cavil about the oddities of the test. If there is a bias to the multiple-choice matrix, it favors what might be called a technocratic mentality, which is emerging in Seoul and Bogotá as much as in Seattle or Baltimore.

But why so visible a black gap at every social level? Here the causes are explicitly racial, in that they stem from the segregation that affects even black youngsters from professional homes. Simply stated, the intellectual processes most black children learn, which tend to be at odds with technocratic modes, are reinforced by spending much of their time among people of their own race. The persistence of segregation — residential and social — draws a sharp dividing line between blacks and whites of all classes. In consequence, black intellectual styles remain more discursive than linear, which can be a drawback when facing a multiple-choice format. Indeed, one of the early arguments for integration was that in mixed classes, black students would learn "white" modes of interpretation and analysis, thus eroding the SAT gap. Yet white scores have been on the decline for at least twenty years, so whites may not be the best model.

Whites have been hurt by affirmative action. Whether affirmative action involves "quotas" or "goals," in practice it means exempting some people from customary requirements and qualifications. In fact, such policies have been around for a long time. For example, colleges occasionally decide to admit some students from Montana, to ensure a diverse entering class. Even if their grades aren't very good, coming from a distant state is seen as a compensatory credential. And to make room for them, abler applicants from other states end up being turned down. Today affirmative action aims at raising black ratios in education and employment. As with coming from Montana, being black becomes a credential.

No one can say with certainty how many white Americans have been bypassed or displaced because of preferential policies. Alan Bakke sued a University of California medical school because he believed that a place he deserved had gone to a minority applicant. He obviously felt injured. But if his record was creditable, he would probably have been admitted to some other schools, which should have cushioned the blow. With this caveat in mind, we can try to gauge how far affirmative action has been edging out whites.

At last count, ten top-rated schools — Amherst, Brown, Cornell, Dartmouth, Harvard, MIT, Northwestern, Princeton, Stanford, and Yale — had a total of 9,555 black, Hispanic, and Native American students out of an overall 107,409 enrollment. Unfortunately, colleges do not report academic records for subgroups. So for present purposes, using nationwide SAT figures, I will assume that three-fifths of the minority students accepted had records that were inferior to those of other applicants who were turned away. Three-fifths of 9,555 works out to 5,733 unadmitted whites and Asians, who had to settle for lesser schools. (Had these colleges imposed their customary criteria, their aggregate minority ratio would have stood at 3.6 percent, rather than the 8.9 percent they attained through affirmative action.) Still, 101,676 whites and Asians *were* admitted, a fairly hefty number. And in many if not most cases, those rejected simply traded down within the Top Ten. It's also worth considering that not all admitted whites are potential Phi Beta Kappas. In addition to Montana residents, even the Iviest schools bend rules for alumni offspring, and even Harvard has been known to favor football players.

White displacement in employment is less easy to compute, since   20
hirings and promotions are more apt to involve intangible judgments. Still, figures for occupations yield some answers. In most professional, white-collar, and craft fields, recent years have seen an increased bloc of blacks; and affirmative action has undoubtedly played some role. There is much talk about whites who feel they are being bypassed, with not a few filing lawsuits. In the academic world, white men seeking instructorships have good reason to believe that their résumés will be relegated to the bottom of the pile. After all, it is hard to find a department that has not given high priority to recruiting a black colleague.

The blue-collar world has young men who aspire to careers as police officers or fire fighters, often to carry on a long family tradition. Although not usually studious, they cram hard for the tests; but those who pass at the margin see appointments going to blacks with lower scores.

But how typical are stories like these? The Census and Bureau of Labor Statistics collate figures on racial distributions within various occupations. As the accompanying table shows, despite all the efforts of medical schools and college faculties, the black proportions of physicians and professors have barely budged over twenty years. Indeed, blacks filled only 6.3 percent of the new faculty positions created between 1970 and 1990. So if white men haven't gotten posts, it wasn't due to extensive black hiring, but rather to a preference for women, who received more than half of the new academic openings. Among doctors and lawyers, black gains were even smaller, in part because expansions in both professions brought in even more whites. Nor are all advances by blacks due to preferential policies. There are more black bus drivers and bank tellers; while one reason is that blacks have been upgrading their skills, another may be that fewer whites find they are attracted to those jobs.

BLACK REPRESENTATION IN OCCUPATIONS

	1970	*1990*	*Share of New Jobs*
Physicians	2.2%	3.0%	3.8%
Lawyers	1.3%	3.2%	4.3%
College Professors	3.5%	4.5%	6.3%
Electricians	3.0%	6.2%	12.7%
Bank Tellers	4.3%	9.9%	16.3%
Bus Drivers	14.3%	24.4%	33 8%
Police Officers	6.3%	13.5%	41.1%
Total Work Force	9.6%	10.1%	11.0%

Although the percentage of black electricians doubled, it yielded them little more than their overall share of new jobs, so hardly any whites lost out. The real shift was in police selection, where blacks received more than 40 percent of the 100,000 new posts in law enforcement. Here, clearly, affirmative action has worked against white applicants. Unlike the students rejected by Amherst, who go on to Lehigh, whites who don't make it into the police haven't as consoling a second option. But in the end black Americans remain a relatively small minority, so there are limits to how many whites they can displace even with aggressive affirmative action recruiting. At the college level, the real competition for whites comes from Asians, who are winning places not through preferential policies but on academic merit.

Overall, persons with racial identities—black and white Americans—constitute a declining portion of the population. Since 1970 individuals of European ancestry, or Caucasoid stock, have declined from 83.3 percent to 75.3 percent of the national total. And during these decades, Americans of African ancestry, or the Negroid race, rose by only one percentage point—from 10.9 to 11.9 percent—and that was largely due to new arrivals from the Caribbean. By the next census, it is likely that blacks will have lost out to Hispanics—whose share of the population has more than doubled in the last twenty years—as America's largest minority group. Indeed, this has already happened in twenty states, including Massachusetts, California, and Colorado.

The nation's fastest-growing groups are rejecting racial designa-   25
tions. For example, we hardly ever hear allusions to the "yellow" or "Mongoloid" race, just as "Oriental" has all but disappeared. Chinese and Japanese and Koreans have chosen to emphasize their separate national identities rather than evoke a common heritage. Unfortunately the media have adopted the umbrella term "Asian," which tells us little about those under it, since they could equally well be Afghans or Laotians or Filipinos.

Hispanics are also finding no need for a racial category. This, too, is a recent development. In responding to the 1970 census, fully 98 percent said they wanted to be classified as black or white. In 1990, however, over half shunned those racial options and chose to check "Other." By doing this, they were signaling that their Hispanic identity was all they wanted or needed. Even less than Asians, Hispanics are hardly a race. If anything, Latin America has been the world's leading melting pot, yielding every possible mixture of European and African and indigenous strains. Even Latino lobbyists limit themselves to calling for preserving regional histories, languages, and cultures rather than racial roots.

In the past, also, many persons of indigenous stock would report that they were white, perhaps hoping to gain such benefits as that designation might bring. Recently we have seen displays of pride among these groups, reflected in what they tell the census. Since 1970 persons listing themselves as Native Americans, Hawaiians, Aleuts, or Eskimos have increased by almost 90 percent, which comes to seven times the increase for the nation as a whole. Moreover, these affinities tend to be tribal or regional, rather than racial.

Of course, it could be argued that it doesn't much matter if the "disuniting of America" — Arthur Schlesinger's phrase — is along racial or other lines. Blacks and Puerto Ricans and Aleuts all claim preference under affirmative action; and supposed disadvantages can have varied sources. Still, my own observations have been that Asians and Hispanics and others who want to make it on their own have seen the harm that being "racial" can do. To define oneself as black or white — or to have those origins assigned to you — assigns overwhelming weight to a primordial ancestry. With race can come a genetic determinism, often suggesting higher or lower locations on an evolutionary ladder. Hence the choice of Asians to put their nationalities first, while Hispanics prefer to stress the culture they created and sustain as a matter of choice. They are also aware of the hostilities and tensions dividing blacks and whites, and have chosen not so much a middle ground as seats off to the side.

If the United States becomes less racial, does this mean it will emerge as a more "multiethnic" society? Don't bet on it. The great majority of recent immigrants, like their counterparts in the past, intend to become mainstream Americans. They did not make the trek here to change the rules and regimens of a society in which they want to succeed. Too much heed has been paid to Latino and kindred publicists, who make careers calling for the preservation of what are essentially folktales and folkways. (They get as much attention as they do by playing on white guilt, which regards tribal rites in the same vein as the spotted owl.)

Statistically, the advent of Hispanics and Asians — joined by new   *30* immigrants from the Middle East — will spell further white decline. Yet if most of those arriving have no wish to become white, not many see themselves as "people of color." They want their children to get traditional American educations and graduate to assimilated suburbs. As recent books by Linda Chavez and Rosalie Pedalino Porter have shown, Hispanic students tend to be shunted into special classes by self-serving bureaucrats rather than at the behest of their parents. And the families of my immigrant students in Queens regard the borough as a way-station prior to a suburban move. Moreover, once they become middle-class, they will have little or no difficulty entering what were once all-white neighborhoods. (For that reason, they are at pains to dissociate themselves from black Americans; just listen to some of their remarks.) In return, middle-class America is prepared to absorb newcomers who show a willingness to adapt. Even George Bush boasts of his Hispanic daughter-in-law, and she is one of almost 30 percent of Hispanics who marry outside their culture.

But that hardly matters, since most people come here to become Americans, and they have a good eye and ear for how and where to adapt.

The Responsive Reader

1. What are key statistics in Hacker's analysis of the disintegration of the family — black or white? What "spin" does Hacker give to these statistics? What is he trying to prove? Is he successful?
2. How does Hacker turn the tables on those who assume that blacks are more prone to crime than whites? What, to Hacker, is the key difference in the crime rates attributed to blacks and whites? (Is his analysis here similar to his analysis of the deteriorating family?)
3. What conclusions do you draw from Hacker's discussion of tests? What, according to Hacker, are the root causes of poor performance on tests by African American students?
4. What results from Hacker's analysis of the effect of affirmative action? According to him, how much discrimination against whites has it produced? (Where has affirmative action been most effective?)
5. What, according to Hacker, are the causes and effects of the movement away from stressing race or racial identity? What is taking the place of race? What are the implications for the future of the country?

Talking, Listening, Writing

6. Do you disagree anywhere with the way Hacker interprets his statistics?
7. Hacker writes in the American tradition of the maverick, who does not follow a party line and delights in challenging the received wisdom. Reviewers have found it hard to pigeonhole him in ideological terms. Can you place him on a political or ideological spectrum? Can you think of a label that would fit him? How would you justify it?
8. Reviewers have missed in Hacker's writing a program for action or advice for the future. How would you spell out any program or advice for the future that seems implied in his statistics and analyses?
9. Have you personally observed or experienced any progress in race relations?

Projects

10. What statistics concerning race and ethnicity are kept at your school and in your community? Who collects them? Who uses

them, and for what purpose? How are racial or ethnic criteria employed? What are the pitfalls in collecting and interpreting them? Your class may want to parcel out different aspects of this question to small groups.

_____

Thinking about Connections

Current writing about race relations often mentions or quotes Andrew Hacker and Shelby Steele ("White Guilt," p. 321) in similar contexts. What connections or points of contact are there between the articles of the two writers? How do their perspectives compare on topics like racism, academic performance of black students, or affirmative action?

_____

AIDS AND ADOLESCENTS: WORDS FROM THE FRONT

Victoria A. Brownworth

> *AIDS has dramatized for a wide public the limitations of medical science. It is a frightening throwback to times when whole populations were ravaged by epidemics for which physicians had no cure. The author of the following selection joins the chorus of those sounding the alarm about the unchecked spread of the AIDS epidemic. In an article first published in* SPIN *magazine, a monthly published in New York, she cites informed opinion from an array of people in the know — medical experts, counselors, community workers. Like other concerned authorities, she takes aim at the stereotypes, traditional attitudes, and complacencies that stand in the way of effective prevention.*

Thought Starters: Are people heeding the warnings about the spread of AIDS? Are they too used to disaster news or too apathetic to pay attention?

At 17, Jarrod had everything he wanted: good grades, acceptance at   1
two colleges of his choosing, a steady girlfriend, and parents who wanted him to have the best.

But when Jarrod began having recurrent cases of tonsillitis in the beginning of his senior year in high school, everything changed. He was told by his doctor that the tonsils should be removed. The surgery would be routine; Jarrod would be out of the hospital and on his feet in a matter of days.

What Jarrod's doctor hadn't factored in was his patient's HIV status: Jarrod was seropositive.

"At first nobody knew how I had gotten it. My girlfriend and I practiced safe sex because we were concerned about pregnancy. Neither of us slept with anyone else — and she has tested HIV negative and doesn't do any drugs. Then I finally realized that it was me. I was the one doing drugs and I didn't even realize it."

Jarrod is one of an increasing number of young men in the U.S.   5
getting HIV through sharing needles when using anabolic steroids. A high school athlete and weight lifter, Jarrod was introduced to what he calls "occasional" steroid use by fellow athletes at the gym where he was working at bodybuilding.

"It really was one of those things — 'Everybody's doing it' — so I did it, too," he says.

According to Dr. Karen Hein, director of the Adolescent AIDS Program at Montefiore Medical Center in the Bronx and one of a handful of experts on adolescent AIDS and HIV in the world, a story like Jarrod's is not unusual. "Teenagers are the next wave of the epidemic," Hein says. "These kids are the AIDS generation. AIDS is everywhere we look. HIV is popping up in the middle of the teenage community."

The Centers for Disease Control put the number of cases of AIDS among adolescents at less than 3 percent of the total, but experts like Hein note that few adolescents are tested, adolescents are the least likely group to be suspected of having HIV by their family physicians, and poor adolescents frequently have little access to health care until they are seriously ill.

"What we *are* seeing," says Belinda Rochelle, program director of the AIDS Action Council in Washington, D.C., "is increased numbers among adolescents in areas where there is high risk to begin with. If you look at the numbers in cities like New York, Newark, and Miami, for example, they are very high. They might be much lower in, say, Iowa, but they could be as high as 20 and 30 percent in some eastern cities."

The numbers recently released by the Job Corps, the only government agency dealing with adolescents that regularly tests for HIV (the agency requires all entrants to submit to HIV testing), showed that approximately 1 in 40 applicants tested HIV positive. "Now this isn't a cross section of the population, obviously," says Anna Forbes of the AIDS Activities Coordinating Office in Philadelphia, "but it does tell you what is happening with inner-city youth." 10

However, inner-city youth have long been classified by experts in the field of HIV disease as "high-risk" youth — teens with multiple sex partners, drug habits, and possible links with prostitution. What the statistics don't illuminate is the fact that the number of cases of teen AIDS *doubles every 14 months* in the U.S. In 1990, according to the CDC HIV/AIDS Surveillance Report, there was a *49 percent increase* in the number of cases of adolescent women with AIDS from the previous year.

Dale Orlando, former director of the Fenway Health Center in Boston and consultant for the recent TV film about teens and AIDS, *In the Shadow of Love,* points out that the refusal of parents to acknowledge that their children are at risk for HIV is a major contributing factor. "Many kids find out that they are HIV positive through pregnancy," says Orlando. "A teenage girl gets pregnant, has her baby, and that baby tests HIV positive. Others find out when they get sick and can't get better. But parents aren't educating their children about the risk of AIDS because they still view it as a disease of somebody else's kids. It isn't.

"There may still be high numbers among street youth and gay youth, but more and more we are going to be seeing cases of the boy and girl next door."

Orlando is not alone in this perception. Brad Brusavich is the coordinator for youth services at the Gay and Lesbian Community Service Center in Los Angeles. The center works with a variety of youth, including runaways and throwaways, as well as gay and lesbian youth. "It's important that we remember where a lot of these kids came from. They weren't *born* homeless — and many of them come from a middle-class environment. About 25 percent of our clients come through HIV positive and not all of those youth got HIV on the streets."

According to Hein and other experts, the majority of youth with *15* HIV are getting it through heterosexual transmission. Over 85 percent of all adolescent women (defined by the CDC as 13 to 19 years old) with HIV contracted it through heterosexual contact, rather than intravenous drug use. Adolescent males who contract HIV are still predominantly drug users, but many are like Jarrod — teens who don't realize that passing a needle, any needle, puts them at risk.

William Cannon, outreach coordinator for the Montefiore adolescent AIDS program, notes that "bisexual sexual activity and the use of these drugs are definitely components in spreading AIDS into the middle-class teen environment. You can't just say it is street kids anymore, or gay kids. With such a high percentage of our youth sexually active and/or involved in drug use of some kind, it is no wonder we are in the midst of a new and very frightening epidemic. It is very difficult to watch kids die of this disease."

Yet in spite of the growing rate of HIV disease among teens and in spite of the CDC's own statistic that nearly 25 percent of the recent cases of HIV among those in their 20s and early 30s were contracted during adolescence, there are almost no national programs — or local programs — to deal with the epidemic.

Philadelphia was the first city in the nation to adopt a program to distribute free condoms in the city's high schools after a school district survey in 1989 showed that at least one third of the high school students in that city were sexually active with more than one partner, and 67 percent of that third were sexually active with one partner. The survey estimated that about five percent of the city's 51,000 high school students were HIV infected.

But it took nearly a year to get the program implemented — only after repeated protests by groups such as ACT UP (AIDS Coalition to Unleash Power) and local AIDS organizations. At the end of 1991, only four schools were distributing the condoms: Three of the schools are largely nonwhite and one is a former boys-only high school, with few female students.

New York City adopted a similar program in November 1991, but *20* Hein points out the problems with these programs. "This is not just about condoms," she says. "It's about saturating our whole society with talk about the epidemic. We've got to look at some new strategies, not just keep hauling out the old ones like telling kids not to have sex. Wishful thinking and 'Just say no' ought to be part of the past history of the first decade of the AIDS epidemic. We need very bold steps to address the epidemic."

The problem with condom distribution, say experts like Hein and Orlando, is parental resistance. "Nobody wants the schools taking charge of their kids' sexual life," says Orlando, "and that is the way condom distribution is perceived. Everybody sees it as licensing kids to have sex. What they don't seem to understand is that kids *are* having sex. And now they're dying from it."

But that argument doesn't hold for many resisting the condom distribution movement. Public Health Service director Dr. James Mason told *SPIN* that condom distribution "is perceived as promoting sexual activity among teenagers. And since they are at such high risk for the disease, we do not want to support such programs. Abstinence is the only safe approach for teens today. They have to remember that every boy or girl they have sex with is like having sex with every other person that boy or girl had sex with. How can we responsibly promote that?"

Steve Ashkinazy, director of the Harvey Milk High School in New York, the nation's only lesbian and gay high school, sees the problem quite differently. "We are not looking at our youth as whole people — which means *sexual* people. There is a lot of experimentation that goes on with teens — if kids experiment with sex, it shouldn't kill them. But the lack of counseling in the schools that is proactive just serves to isolate these kids further."

Ashkinazy says that lesbian and gay youth are particularly susceptible. "There is no safe sex for gay kids taught in high schools, there is no effort being made to address these kids and that makes them even more isolated than heterosexual kids in high schools. And it very well could be killing them."

CDC statistics support Ashkinazy's claim. In studies conducted in San Francisco, safe sex practices within the gay male community have resulted in a steady decrease in the number of new AIDS cases among gay men. But in the 15- to 19-year age group, the cases were *increasing*. Mason says, "The message is not getting through to this segment of the gay population." But Ashkinazy notes that there is no avenue for the safe-sex message to get through to gay youth.

"Few kids are secure enough in their sexual identity to go to their high school counselor and ask for safe sex information when they are *heterosexual*. It's that much harder for gay youth. And even if they did ask, how many counselors are trained to give the right information? We could soon have a whole new epidemic of HIV in a new generation of gay youth."

And the adolescent epidemic of AIDS and HIV in the '90s is beginning to look alarmingly similar to the first wave of the AIDS epidemic of the '80s. In New York City, cases of AIDS among 13- to 20-year-olds represent almost 25 percent of adolescent cases of AIDS nationwide. The numbers are also very high in cities that are AIDS hot spots: Los Angeles, Miami, Boston, and Philadelphia. In New York and New Jersey, AIDS has become the leading cause of death among adolescent African-American and Hispanic women. And in those states AIDS is the leading cause of death for Hispanic children between the ages of one and four, many, according to the U.S. surgeon general's office, born to teenage mothers infected with the disease.

Hein thinks that adolescents are the most secretive and frightened about HIV. "For those young people in our program who are living with HIV, the veil of secrecy, of having the virus, they say is the biggest burden of all."

Orlando cautions that the worst is yet to come. "Now is the time for people to be shaping their programs for teens because we are on the verge of a tremendous explosion of teens and people in their early 20s with AIDS or HIV. The kids are getting younger and younger. With adolescents it's very hard to trace where the infection came from in the first place. And that's why we have to have very comprehensive programs of education and information. Condoms are a good first step, but much more is needed."

For Jarrod, who says he always used condoms with his girlfriend, condom distribution wouldn't have changed his HIV status. "What would have helped me," he says, "is knowing that there's a lot of other dangers out there that you don't even consider. I didn't know I could get AIDS from using steroids. Here I was, trying to make my body better, and now I'll probably die. I just wished *somebody* had told me."   *30*

The Responsive Reader

1. How does Brownworth try to reach readers who feel: "This issue does not concern me"? How effective do you think her approach is in reaching the apathetic majority?
2. What are her most thought-provoking statistics and testimonies?
3. How does she analyze the attitudes standing in the way of programs aimed at prevention?

Talking, Listening, Writing

4. Has AIDS become for you more than a matter of statistics? Has anything brought the human reality of the disease home for you?
5. Are the people you know changing their thinking and behavior in response to warnings like those in this article?

6. Susan Sontag once divided the lives people live into two large categories, which she called "the kingdom of the sick" and "the kingdom of the well." What have been your travels in or to the kingdom of the sick?

Projects

7. What prevention programs are in place in your school or community? How do they operate? How effective do you think they are?

_____

Thinking about Connections

What goals and assumptions does the author of the poem on page 669 share with Brownworth? How do they differ in attitude, tone, or strategy?

_____

AN ALARMING NEW DEVELOPMENT
Ron Schreiber

Many heterosexuals have assumed that, barring a transfusion of infected blood, they were shielded from the ravages of AIDS. How does the following bitter poem deal with this attitude? The poet was born in Chicago and raised in Dayton, Ohio. He has been in Japan (with the army) and has lived in places including New York City, Amsterdam, and Cambridge, Massachusetts. He has edited an anthology of 31 New American Poets *and published two collections of his own poetry:* False Clues *(1978) and* Tomorrow Will Really Be Sunday *(1984). A later book,* John, *was published by Hanging Loose Press and Gay Presses of New York.*

Thought Starters: What have been assumed to be the "high-risk groups" for AIDS? What inklings have you had that AIDS would spread beyond them?

Heterosexuals can get AIDS too   1
—not just the smaller "high risk

groups," but what doctors & newscasters
call "all of us." All of *them,*

say the Haitians, all of *them,*   5
say the queers. If *they (all of us)*

can get it too, then maybe they
will begin to take it seriously:

that most people in the world
have been high risk groups for   10

years & years; maybe now "the majority
of Americans" is beginning to feel

at risk—their jobs, their planet,
& (now) even "our" disease is reaching

them. "Welcome," we will tell them,   15
"we were wondering how long it

would take for you to come out
as members of the species. It's not

easy here, but if you learn to behave
yourselves & stop trying to kill   *20*

the rest of us, we have room for you,
& we will try to teach you how to

survive while you're dying."

The Responsive Reader

1. What is the role in the poem of the key pronouns — *us, them*? Where in the poem does the person speaking in the poem align himself or take sides?
2. As seen from the perspective of this poem, how are "they" trying to kill "the rest of us"?

Talking, Listening, Writing

3. When it comes to subjects like AIDS, are you a fatalist? What needs to be done and can be done? What does the future hold?

Projects

4. In many areas, AIDS has savaged the artistic community. Your class may want to consider collecting tributes in memory of people lost to the disease.

WRITING
WORKSHOP 12

The Documented Paper

In a documented paper, you furnish the data a reader would need to verify your sources. Where did you find the information? in what book? written by whom? published where, when, and by whom? On what page did this particular passage occur? If a quotation came from a magazine article, what was the date of the issue and the exact page number? if from a newspaper story, what edition (morning, evening, or regional)? what section of the paper?

TRIGGERING Authors provide full documentation when they think that their procedures and their findings might be challenged. When you work on a documented paper, you keep a complete record of where you found your material — so that the reader can retrace your steps and check your sources. Documentation is for readers who do not just accept someone else's say-so. They like to check things out for themselves. They may want to know more than you chose to tell them.

Full and accurate documentation reassures readers who might have questions like the following:

"Did author X really say this — are you sure it was not somebody else? Are you sure this source is not misquoted — an important word or important words left out?"

"Maybe this is what your source *said* — but what was the context? What was the overall intention?"

"Are you sure your source did not acknowledge possible objections to this theory — possible weaknesses in this line of argument?"

"Is this all you are going to say on this subject? I want to know more — let me read more about this in the original source."

GATHERING Writers develop their own ways of recording the materials for a documented research paper or library paper. You may use handwritten or typed note cards (which can be easily shuffled and put in the order in which you will use them in your paper). You may rely on files in your word processor (where you can transfer typed quotations and the like directly to the body of your paper, without the need for retyping).

You may rely heavily on newspaper clippings and photocopies of whole articles or key pages. To ensure maximum usefulness of your notes, remember:

- *Start each note with a tag or "descriptor."* Show where the material tentatively fits into your paper. Use headings like the following:

```
AZTECS—sacrificial rites
AZTECS—myths about light-skinned gods
INCAS—conquests of other tribes
```

- *Clearly mark — with quotation marks — all direct quotation.* Distinguish clearly between direct quotation (material quoted exactly word for word) and paraphrase (where you put less important material in your own words, often in slightly or severely condensed form).
- *Make sure each note shows the exact source.* Include all publishing information you will need later: exact names, titles and subtitles, publishers or publications, as well as dates and places. Register exact page numbers: the specific page or pages for a quotation, but also the complete page numbers for an article.

SHAPING As you start to draft your paper, you will be grappling with familiar issues: What is going to be your focus? What will be the point of your paper as a whole? What will be your organizing strategy? How will you lay out your material in an order that will make sense to your readers?

However, in writing a documented paper, you will also be paying special attention to matters of format and style. In the paper itself, you will use **parenthetical documentation**: You will give, in parentheses, exact page references — and quick identification of sources as needed. Then, at the end of your paper, you will provide an alphabetic list of **Works Cited**, giving complete information about your sources. Study the way parentheses, italics, quotation marks, colons, and other punctuation features are used in sample passages and sample entries.

Remember a few pointers: *Italicize* (underline on an old-fashioned typewriter) the titles of books and other complete publications: *The Color Purple*. Put in quotation marks the titles of poems, articles, and other pieces that are *part* of a publication: "Stopping by Woods."

Samples of Parenthetical Documentation

- simple page reference when you have identified the source:

```
Octavio Paz has called the meeting of the Indian and the Spaniard
the key to the Mexican national character (138).
```

- author's name and page reference when you have *not* identified the source:

A prominent Latin American writer has called the meeting of the Indian and the Spaniard the key to the Mexican national character (Paz 138).

- more than one author:

Tests and more tests have often been a substitute for adequate funding for our schools (Hirsenrath and Briggers 198).

- abbreviated title added when you quote more than one source by same author:

Lin, who has called the homeless problem the result of "social engineering in reverse" ("Homeless" 34), examines current statistics in a scathing indictment of official neglect (On the Street 78–81).

- a source you found quoted by someone else:

Steinbeck said he admired "strong, independent, self-reliant women" (qtd. in Barnes 201).

- a reference to preface or other introductory material, with page numbers given in lower-case roman numerals:

In his preface to The Great Mother, Neumann refers to the "onesidedly patriarchal development of the male intellectual consciousness" (xliii).

Note: References to the Bible typically cite chapter and verse instead of page numbers (Luke 2:1); references to a Shakespeare play usually cite act, scene, and line (*Hamlet* 3.2.73–76). After block quotations, a parenthetical page reference *follows* a final period or other terminal mark. (See sample paper on pages 677–679 for examples.)

Sample Entries for "Works Cited"

Indent the second line of an entry five spaces. Leave two spaces after periods marking off chunks of information.

- newspaper article with date and section of paper:

Lamensa, Juan. "Pre-Aztec Art." Fremont Times 15 Aug. 1992: B7–8.

- magazine article identified by date with complete page numbers (the + sign shows that article is continued later in the same issue):

Foote, Stephanie. "Our Bodies, Our Lives, Our Right to Decide." The Humanist July/Aug. 1992: 2–8+.

- article with volume number (for a magazine with continuous page numbering through several issues):

Herzberger, David K. "Narrating the Past: History and the Novel of Memory in Postwar Spain." PMLA 106 (1991): 34–45.

- professional journal with separate page numbering for each issue of the same volume (volume number is followed by number of issue):

Winks, Robin W. "The Sinister Oriental Thriller: Fiction and the Asian Scene." Journal of Popular Culture 19.2 (1985): 49–61.

- coauthored article (last name first for first author only):

Elkholy, Sharin, and Ahmed Nassef. "Crips and Bloods Speak for Themselves: Voices from South Central." Against the Current July/ August 1991: 7–10.

- article with more than three authors — *et al.* for "and others":

Martz, Larry, et al. "A Tide of Drug Killings." Newsweek 16 Jan. 1989: 44–45.

- unsigned editorial — author not identified (alphabetize under first word other than *A, An,* or *The*):

"At the Threshold: An Action Guide for Cultural Survival." Editorial. Cultural Survival Quarterly Spring 1992: 17–18.

- letter to the editor:

Carraciola, Joseph. "Children at Risk." Letter. San Jose Mercury News 18 Nov. 92: C3.

- standard entry for a book:

Tan, Amy. The Kitchen God's Wife. New York: Putnam's, 1991.

- later edition of a book:

Mayfield, Marlys. Thinking for Yourself: Developing Critical Thinking
 Skills Through Writing. 2nd ed. Belmont, CA: Wadsworth, 1991.

- material edited or collected by someone other than the author (or
 authors):

Shockley, Ann Allen, ed. Afro-American Women Writers 1746–1933: An
 Anthology and Critical Guide. Boston: G. K. Hall, 1988.

Barrett, Eileen, and Mary Cullinan, eds. American Women Writers: Diverse
 Voices in Prose Since 1845. New York: St. Martin's, 1992.

- material translated from another language:

Neruda, Pablo. Selected Poems of Pablo Neruda: A Bilingual Edition.
 Trans. Ben Belitt. New York: Grove, 1961.

- special imprint (special line of books) of a publisher:

Acosta, Oscar Zeta. The Revolt of the Cockroach People. New York:
 Vintage-Random, 1989.

- article that is part of a book:

Gutierrez, Irene. "A New Consciousness." New Voices of the Southwest.
 Ed. Laura Fuentes. Santa Fe: Horizon, 1992. 123–34.

- one of several volumes:

Woolf, Virginia. The Diary of Virginia Woolf. Ed. Anne Olivier Bell. New
 York: Harcourt, 1977. Vol. 1.

- personal interview:

Milecik, Sonja. Personal Interview. 29 Jan. 1993.

- audio or video source:

The Endangered Planet. Narr. Karen Coleman. Writ. and prod. Loren
 Shell. WXRV, Seattle. 7 Nov. 1992.

Creation vs. Evolution: Battle of the Classrooms. Videocassette. Dir. Ryall
 Wilson. PBS Video, 1982. 58 min.

- computer software:

Naruba, Mark. The Strategic Writer. Vers. 1.3. Computer Software.
  Pentrax, 1993. Mac, 128K, disk.

- additional entry by same author (substitute three hyphens for name):

Steinem, Gloria. Outrageous Acts and Everyday Rebellions. New York:
  Holt, 1983.
–––. Revolution from Within: A Book of Self-Esteem. Boston: Little,
  Brown, 1992.

REVISING A number of common revision strategies are especially to the point when you revise a paper that has brought together a mass of information and quotation. (Remember that if *you* get lost in the maze of your materials, your *readers* will have no chance to find their way.)

- *Strengthen the overall framework.* Do not allow the reader to feel lost in a Sahara of bit facts. Make sure that the three or four major stages of your paper or the major steps in your argument are clear in your own mind — and that the reader can see how they structure your paper.

- *Strengthen transitions.* Highlight connections between one part of the paper and the next. Check whether a *however, on the other hand,* or *finally* is needed to clarify a logical link between two points.

- *Revise for clear attribution.* Who said what? Repeat the name of the quoted author if a *he* or *she* might point to the wrong person.

- *Integrate undigested chunk quotations.* If you have too many block quotations, break them up. Work partial quotations into your own text for a smoother flow.

- *Do a final check of documentation style.* Teachers and editors of scholarly writing or research–based writing are sticklers for detail. Use capitals, indents, spacing, colons, parentheses, quotation marks, and the like exactly as the style guide for your class or for your publication says.

Writers and readers of documented papers may lose sight of the larger purposes of a writing project as they grapple with the technicalities of research and documentation. As you study the following sample paper, pay attention to the larger questions of purpose, content, strategy, and use of evidence. Who would make a good audience for this paper? (Who would be the ideal reader?) What use has the writer made of his sources? How clear or helpful is his attribution and documentation of the sources? How balanced or persuasive are his conclusions?

A Flawed Saint

"Just as the Christian Jesus said, 'Forgive them, for they know not what they do,' we pray, 'Forgive them, Great Spirit, for they know not what they do.'" These words were spoken by Anthony Miranda, a Costanoan Native American in the basilica of the Carmel Mission in California on the same day that its founder, Father Junipero Serra, was being proposed for sainthood in Rome. His words drew "shocked gasps and stares at what many of the worshipers considered a sacrilege." A man in the back of the basilica loudly called out, "Why don't you take your pagan rites and get out of this church?" The group of twenty Native Americans carrying ceremonial rattles, feathers, and abalone shells filled with burning sage retreated to the church cemetery. They assembled at the foot of a crude wooden cross that marks the graves of "2,364 Christian Indians and 14 Spaniards," buried there between 1771 and 1833 (O'Neill 17).

Junipero Serra has been called "California's founding father" and "the most overlooked man in American history" by one of the leading religious magazines in the United States. In 1984, the Reagan administration issued a postage stamp in his honor (Fay 71). It has been said that "his devotion to his work was an inspiration to those who followed in his footsteps" (Krell 310). After he died, we are told, his parishioners "flocked to the church where his body lay, bearing bouquets of flowers and weeping inconsolably" (Fink 48).

However, Serra has also been accused of enslaving and torturing his converts, sending out search parties to hunt down those who escaped from his churches, and committing genocide. His proposed canonization (raising to official recognition as a saint) provoked a storm of criticism from the American Indian Historical Society. According to an article in U.S. News & World Report, "records are replete with documentation of whippings and other harsh treatment" of the indigenous people under his jurisdiction ("Question" 24). Can both parties to this controversy be speaking of the same person?

According to Augusta Fink's Monterey: The Presence of the Past, Father Serra was born Miguel Joseph Serra in the humble town of Petra on the island of Majorca, Spain, in 1713. In 1749, he realized his dream of becoming a missionary when he was sent to Mexico to help convert the Indians to Christianity. During the next twenty years, he founded and guided a mission among the Pame tribe in northern Mexico and often preached in Mexico City (4–8). According to an article in Life magazine, Serra arrived in California in 1769 and began his work of founding the California Missions. "Unlike the Spanish military and many of the clergy, he immediately made friends with the local tribes." Serra died "cradled in the arms of some of his 6,000 Christian converts." According to the author of the article, "Serra has been the unofficial state 'saint' for generations" (Fay 68–71).

Much recent work has painted a less saintly picture of the Spanish priest. Alma Villanueva, a professor at the University of California at Santa Cruz, spoke to me of "mass graves" of Indians unearthed near several of the California missions and used the term genocide. In the book The Missions of California: A Legacy of Genocide, the American Indian Historical Society has circulated the same charges. The book provides numerous documented reports of the indigenous inhabitants being subjected to "forced conversion," "forced labor," and "physical punishment." It includes an account of an early settler who wrote, "For the slightest things they receive heavy floggings, are shackled and put in stocks, and treated with so much cruelty that they are kept whole days without a drink of water" (Costo 69).

In his book, The Ohlone Way: Indian Life in the San Francisco–Monterey Bay Area, Malcolm Margolin quotes the explorer La Perouse, who compared the missions in Father Serra's charge to slave colonies he had seen in Santo Domingo:

> We declare with pain that the resemblance [to the Santo Domingo slave colonies] is so exact that we saw both the men and the women loaded with irons, while others had a log of wood on their legs. . . . Corporal punishment is inflicted on the Indians of both sexes who neglect their pious exercises. (162)

Margolin quotes a visitor to the mission at Santa Clara about the confinement of young unmarried women by the padres "to assure the chastity of their wards":

> We were struck by the appearance of a large quadrangular building, which, having no windows on the outside, resembled a prison for state criminals. . . . The dungeons are opened two or three times a day, but only to allow the prisoners to pass to and from the church. I have occasionally seen the poor girls rushing out eagerly to breathe the fresh air and driven immediately into the church like a flock of sheep, by an old ragged Spaniard with a stick. After mass, they are in the same manner hurried back into their prisons. (161)

Fink's book reports that the last few years of Serra's life were "difficult ones." There were "few new converts and many runaways among the Indians, and a series of plagues, which were probably smallpox, had decimated the small Christianized group that remained" (48). Margolin says that "300 or more Indians out of a thousand might die during a severe epidemic year" (163).

To judge Father Serra's role in these events, we need to remember how badly the Spaniards and the Indians misunderstood each other. They represented two vastly different cultures. In the words of another book about the California missions,

> The California Indian has often been criticized because he lived a life of slothfulness, not stirring himself to raise crops, herd

flocks, or practice other disciplined forms of food production characteristic of more advanced cultures. . . . Ironically, the civilized Spaniards, who looked down upon the childlike Indians, suffered famines after they first settled in the same environment when their imported foodstuffs failed to arrive on time. (Krell 50)

Serra probably never doubted the rightness of his actions. As Fink points out, the Native Americans "resisted conversion to the Christian faith, which required complete separation from the pagan community. Children presented for baptism had to live at the mission under the supervision of the padres" (43). It must be noted, however, that not even his countrymen always took his side. Governor Neve "refused to round up Indian fugitives from the missions, who, Serra felt, had broken the contract they made at baptism" (48).

The historical evidence makes one thing clear: Serra's methods were overzealous by twentieth-century standards. Some would argue that he was overzealous by anyone's and anytime's standards. When we read that Indians wept and brought flowers to his grave, we have to wonder how many others were overjoyed at the news of his death. When we are faced with documented accounts of what happened to many indigenous inhabitants under his authority, it is hard to consider Father Serra worthy of being made a saint. In the words of Jack Norton, a Native American professor at Humboldt State University, a candidate for sainthood "should epitomize virtue and kindness" (qtd. in "Question" 24).

Works Cited

Costo, Rupert, and Jeanette H. Costo, eds. The Missions of California: A Legacy of Genocide. San Francisco: Indian Historical Society, 1987.

Donohue, John W. "California's Founding Father." America 11 May 1985: 306.

Fay, Martha, Linda Gomez, and Wilton Wynn. "So You Want To Be a Saint." Life Sept. 1987: 68–71.

Fink, Augusta. Monterey: The Presence of the Past. San Francisco: Chronicle Publishing, 1972.

Krell, Dorothy, and Paul C. Johnson, eds. The California Missions: A Pictorial History. Menlo Park, CA: Lane, 1979.

Margolin, Malcolm. The Ohlone Way: Indian Life in the San Francisco–Monterey Bay Area. Berkeley: Heyday, 1978.

O'Neill, Ann W. "Confrontation at the Mission." San Jose Mercury News 26 Sept. 1987: B17–19.

"A Question of Faith in California." U.S. News & World Report 11 May 1987: 24.

Villanueva, Alma. Personal Interview. 26 June 1989.

Topics for Documented Papers (A Sampling)

1. Susan Faludi's book *Backlash: The Undeclared War against American Women* explores the obstacles or reversals encountered by the women's movement. Can you find additional sources that would tend to confirm or challenge her findings?
2. Naomi Wolf's *The Beauty Myth* is part of the current criticism of the media ideal of beauty. Can you find additional current sources dealing with this issue?
3. What is the role of computer-assisted learning in our schools? What are the expectations of its advocates? How much of what they aim at has come true?
4. Are Americans getting poorer? What statistics are available, and how should they be interpreted? What sources other than statistics throw light on this question?
5. What is the current state of women's sports in the colleges? What progress has been made? (Who keeps score?)
6. What is the status of legal rights or protections for gays and lesbians? What have been recent initiatives in this area, and how have they fared?
7. Have racial or ethnic minorities made progress during the past decade? Focus on one group, such as Latinos, African Americans, or Asian Americans. Can you find authoritative sources? What do they report?
8. Is there a pattern in recent court cases involving tribal rights of Native Americans? What are the implications of these cases for the future of Native Americans?
9. Is AIDS spreading to the heterosexual population? What authoritative data and informed opinion are available on this issue?
10. What is behind recent initiatives to give parents more choice in where to send their children to school? (What, for instance, is the motivation and possible impact of plans for issuing vouchers to parents?)

A GLOSSARY OF TERMS

Abstraction A general idea (often *very* general) that "draws us away" from the level of specific data or observations; large abstractions are concepts like justice, dignity, and freedom

Ad Hominem Getting personal in an argument; distracting from the merit of ideas by attacking the person, character, or private life of an opponent (Latin for "directed at the person")

Allusion A brief mention that brings a whole story or set of associations to the reader's mind

Analogy A close comparison traced into several related details, often used to explain the new in terms of the familiar

Analysis Explaining a complex phenomenon by identifying its major parts, stages, or causes

Bandwagon Trying to sway people by claiming that the great majority is on the speaker's or writer's side (and that he or she must therefore be right)

Brainstorming Freely calling up memories, data, or associations relevant to a topic, without at first editing or sorting them out

Cause and Effect The logical connection between actions and their consequences, making us focus on reasons and results

Claim What we assert in an argument and then need to support with evidence or examples

Classification The setting up of categories that help us sort out a mass of data

Cliché A tired, overused expression that may have been clever or colorful at one time but has long since lost its edge

Cluster A network or web of ideas centered in a key term or stimulus word, from which various strands of ideas and associations branch out

Comparison Tracing connections to demonstrate similarities and contrast differences

Connotation The attitudes, emotions, or associations a word carries beyond its basic factual meaning (or denotation)

Context What comes before and after a word or a statement and helps give it its full meaning; the setting or situation that helps explain what something means

Data Facts, observations, or statistics that provide the input for reasoning or interpretation

Deduction The kind of reasoning that applies general principles to specific situations

Definition Staking out the exact meaning of a possibly vague, ambiguous, or abused term

Dialectic The kind of reasoning that makes ideas emerge from the play of pro and con; ideally, dialectic proceeds from thesis (statement) to antithesis (counterstatement) and from there to synthesis (a balanced conclusion)

Discovery Frames Sets of questions that help a writer explore a topic

Doublespeak A verbal smokescreen designed to cover up unpleasant facts (such as calling an airplane crash "unscheduled contact with the ground")

Draft A possibly unfinished or tentative version of a piece of writing, subject to revision

Fallacy A common pattern of faulty logic, leading to wrong conclusions

Figurative Language Language using imaginative comparisons, such as calling someone a gadfly (metaphor) or punctual as a clock (simile)

Image Something we can vividly visualize; something that appeals vividly to our senses

Induction The generalizing kind of reasoning that finds the connecting thread or common pattern in a set of data

Inference The logical jump from facts or observations to what we interpret them to mean

Hasty Generalization Generalizing from a limited sample, such as labeling a brand of cars defective because two that you know about were

Jargon Pretentious, overblown pseudo-scientific or unnecessarily technical language

Metaphor An imaginative comparison that treats one thing as if it were another, without using a signal such as *like* or *as* ("he *surfed* to the speaker's table on a *wave* of applause")

Narrator In fiction, the person—real or imaginary—telling the story

Paraphrase Putting a statement or passage into one's own words

Peer Review Feedback given to a writer by classmates or fellow writers

Persona The identity assumed or the public role played by a writer in a piece of writing (the persona may be different from the writer's private personality)

Post Hoc Fallacy Short for *post hoc ergo propter hoc*, Latin for "it happened after this; therefore it's because of this"; blaming something on a highly visible recent event rather than on true long-range causes (there was an earthquake after a nuclear test; therefore the test triggered the earthquake)

Premise A basic shared assumption on which an argument is built

Rationalization A creditable, reasonable-sounding explanation that clears us of blame

Rhetoric The practice or the study of effective strategies for speech and writing (sometimes used negatively to mean empty or deceptive use of language)

Simile An imaginative comparison signaled by such words as *like* or *as* ("the library had bare solid walls *like a prison*")

Slanting Presenting only evidence or testimony that favors your own side

Syllogism A formal deductive argument that moves from the major premise ("mammals need air to breathe") through the minor premise ("whales are mammals") to a logical conclusion ("whales need air to breathe")

Thesis The central idea or unifying assertion that a paper as a whole supports; the claim a paper stakes out and defends

Valid Logically correct (but logically correct reasoning may lead to untrue conclusions if based on faulty premises)

ACKNOWLEDGMENTS

Maya Angelou, *I Know Why the Caged Bird Sings.* © 1979 by Maya Angelou. Reprinted by permission of Random House, Inc.

"Animal Rights, Wronged," © 1991 by *Harper's* Magazine. All rights reserved. Reprinted from the December issue by special permission.

Arthur Ashe, "A Black Athlete Looks at Education," *Time*, February 6, 1977. © 1977 by The New York Times Company. Reprinted by permission.

Toni Cade Bambara, "The Lesson," from *Gorilla, My Love.* Copyright © 1972 by Toni Cade Bambara. Reprinted by permission of Random House, Inc.

Judi Bari, "The Feminization of Earth First!" reprinted by permission of *Ms* Magazine, © 1992.

Sylvan Barnet and Hugo Bedau, *Current Issues and Enduring Questions: Methods and Models of Argument.* Copyright © 1990. Reprinted by permission of St. Martin's Press, Inc.

Mary Kay Blakely, "Memories of Frank," from *Wake Me When It's Over.* Copyright © 1989 by Mary Kay Blakely. Reprinted by permission of Time Books, a division of Random House, Inc.

Victoria A. Brownworth, "AIDS and Adolescents: Words from the Front." *Spin*, Vol. 7, Number 12, 1992.

Fox Butterfield, "Why They Excel." *Parade*, January 21, 1990. Reprinted with permission of *Parade*. Copyright © 1990.

Mary R. Callahan, "Pro-choice, Not Pro-Abortion," from *The Spartan Daily*, November 9, 1989. Reprinted by permission of the publisher.

Gregory Cerio, "Were the Spaniards That Cruel?" from *Newsweek*, Special Issue, Fall/ Winter 1991. Copyright © Newsweek, Inc. Reprinted by permission. All rights reserved.

Lorna Dee Cervantes, "Freeway 280," from *Emplumada*, 1981. Reprinted by permission of the publisher, *Latin American Literary Review*, Vol. 5, No. 10, 1977, Pittsburgh, PA.

Frank Chin, *Donald Duk*, Coffee House Press, 1991. Copyright © 1991 by Frank Chin. Reprinted by permission of the publisher.

Mary Crow Dog and Richard Erdoes, from *Lakota Woman* by Mary Crow Dog with Richard Erdoes. Copyright © 1990 by Mary Crow Dog and Richard Erdoes. Used by permission of Grove Press, Inc.

Marie de Santis, "Last of the Wild Salmon," from *This World*, San Francisco Chronicle, July 21, 1985. Reprinted by permission of the author.

Barbara Ehrenreich, "The Next Wave," from *Ms* Magazine, July/August 1987. Reprinted by permission of the author.

Lars Eighner, "My Daily Dives in the Dumpster," from *Harper's* Magazine, December 1991. Reprinted by permission of the author.

Louise Erdrich, "Indian Boarding School: The Runaways," from *Jacklight*. Copyright © 1984 by Louise Erdrich. Reprinted by permission of Henry Holt and Company, Inc.

David Eyler and Andrea Barison, "Far More Than Friendship." Reprinted with permission from *Psychology Today*. Copyright © 1992 Sussex Publishers, Inc.

Patty Fisher, "The Injustice System." Reprinted with permission of the San Jose Mercury News, March 25, 1992.

"Five Friends in a Car," from *Time* Magazine, July 11, 1988. Copyright © 1988 by Time Warner, Inc. Reprinted by permission.

683

Lawrence H. Fuchs, "The Secrets of Citizenship," March 23, 1992, p. 37, *The New Republic*. Reprinted by permission of the publisher. Copyright © 1992, The New Republic, Inc.

Herbert Gold, "Addict Is Finally a Star at His Own Funeral," from the San Francisco Chronicle, September 4, 1988. Reprinted by permission of the author. (Gold's novels include *Fathers, Family* and *A Girl of Forty*, and the non-fiction books *Best Nightmare on Earth: A Life in Haiti* and *Cool Days, Hot Company*, a memoir of the bohemian life.)

Angelo Gonzales, "Bilingualism: The Key to Basic Skills," *Time*, November 10, 1985. Copyright © 1985 by The New York Times Company. Reprinted by permission.

Ellen Goodman, "We Are What We Do." Copyright © 1984, The Boston Globe Newspaper Co./Washington Post Writers Group. Reprinted with permission.

Judy Grahn, "Nadine, Resting on Her Neighbor's Stoop," from *The Work of a Common Woman: Collected Poems* (1964–1977). Reprinted by permission of The Crossing Press.

Rose D. Guilbault, "Americanization Is Tough on 'Macho,'" *This World*, San Francisco Chronicle, August 20, 1989. Rose Del Castillo Guilbault is a contributing writer to the San Francisco Chronicle, and Pacific News Service. She is the Editorial and Public Affairs Director at KGO-TV in San Francisco. She was raised in the Salinas Valley in California.

Joe Gutierrez, "On the Job," from *Race* by Studs Terkel, 1991. Reprinted by permission of The New Press.

Andrew Hacker, "The Myths of Racial Division," March 23, 1992. Reprinted by permission of *The New Republic*. Copyright © 1992 The New Republic, Inc.

Garrett Hardin, "Lifeboat Ethics: The Case Against Helping the Poor." Reprinted with permission from *Psychology Today*. Copyright © 1974 Sussex Publishers Inc.

Suzan Shown Harjo, "I Won't Be Celebrating Columbus Day," from *Newsweek*, Special Issue, Fall/Winter, 1991. Reprinted by permission of Suzan Shown Harjo (Cheyenne & Hodulgee Muscogee).

Vicki Hearne, "What's Wrong with Animal Rights?" Copyright © 1991 by *Harper's* Magazine. All rights reserved. Reprinted from the September 1991 issue by special permission.

William Least Heat Moon, from *Prairyerth*. This excerpt was published in *Atlantic Monthly*. Copyright © 1991 by William Least Heat Moon. Reprinted by permission of Houghton Mifflin Co. All rights reserved.

Larry Heinemann, "Just Don't Fit," from *Harper's* Magazine, April 1985. Reprinted by permission of Larry Heinemann. Copyright © 1985 by Larry Heinemann.

Manuela Hoelterhoff, "The Royal Anniversary: Elvis Presley's Fiftieth," from *The Wall Street Journal*, January 8, 1985. Reprinted with permission of The Wall Street Journal. Copyright © 1989 Dow Jones & Company, Inc. All rights reserved.

"Homeless Woman Reveals Misery of Living in Car," *San Jose Mercury News*, December 8, 1991. (Anonymous)

Garrett K. Hongo, "Yellow Light," from *Yellow Light*. Copyright © 1982 by Garrett Kaoru Hongo. Reprinted by permission of the University Press of New England.

Lois Phillips Hudson, "Children of the Harvest," originally appeared in *The Reporter*, October 16, 1958. Reprinted by permission of the author.

Zora Neale Hurston, "How It Feels to Be Colored Me," from *The World Tomorrow*. Reprinted by permission of Lucy Ann Hurston.

Pico Iyer, "Selling Our Innocence Abroad," from *The Contagion of Innocence* by Pico Iyer in the Fall issue of *New Perspectives Quarterly*, 1991. Reprinted by permission of the publisher.

Steven Musil, "Emotions Clouding Rational Decision," *The Spartan Daily*, December 12, 1989. Reprinted by permission of the publisher.

Gloria Naylor, "The Myth of the Matriarch." Copyright © 1988 by Gloria Naylor. Reprinted by permission of Sterling Lord Literistic, Inc.

John G. Neihardt, "The Earth Is All That Lasts," from *Black Elk Speaks*, 1959.

"The New Drug Vigilantes." Copyright © May 9, 1988, *US News & World Report*. Reprinted by permission of the publisher.

Joyce Carol Oates, "Stalking." Copyright © 1972 by Joyce Carol Oates. Reprinted by permission of the author and Blanche C. Gregory, Inc. "Rape and the Boxing Ring" from *Newsweek*, February 24, 1992. Reprinted by permission of the author and Blanche C. Gregory, Inc. Copyright © 1992 by The Ontario Review, Inc.

Sharon Olds, "The Death of Marilyn Monroe," from *Dead & The Living*. Copyright © 1983 by Sharon Olds. Reprinted by permission of Alfred A. Knopf, Inc.

Tillie Olsen, "I Stand Here Ironing," from *Tell Me a Riddle*. Copyright © 1956, 1957, 1960, 1961 by Tillie Olsen. Used by permission of Delacorte Press/Seymour Lawrence, a division of Bantam Doubleday Dell Publishing Group, Inc.

Simon Ortiz, "Kaiser and the War," from *New World Literature: Tradition and Revolt in Latin America* by Arturo Torres Rioseco. Copyright © 1949 Regents of the University of California, renewed 1977 Arturo Torres Rioseco. Reprinted by permission of the publisher.

Gianfranco Pagnucci, "The Death of an Elephant." Copyright © 1979 by Gianfranco Pagnucci. First appeared in *Northeast*, Series III, Number 6, Winter 1978-79.

Kathleen Parker, "Divorce: The End That Never Quite Does," reprinted by permission of the Orlando Sentinel.

Anna Quindlen, "Public & Private: Making the Mosaic," November 20, 1991. Copyright © 1991 by The New York Times Company. Reprinted by permission.

Diane Ravitch, "Multiculturalism: E Pluribus Plures." Reprinted from *The American Scholar*, Vol. 59, No. 3, Summer 1990. Copyright © 1990 by Diane Ravitch. Reprinted by permission of the publisher and author.

Richard Rodriguez, "Aria: A Memoir of a Bilingual Childhood." Reprinted by permission of Georges Borchardt, Inc.

Richard Rodriguez, excerpt from "Children of a Marriage," copyright © 1988 by Richard Rodriguez. Reprinted by permission of Georges Borchardt, Inc. for the author.

Mike Royko, "Shooting Holes in Gun Laws," November 1989. Reprinted by permission of Tribune Media Services.

Rasmey Sam, "Cambodian Boys Don't Cry," from *The Compost HEAP*, Vol. 2, No. 3. Reprinted by permission of the author.

Ron Schreiber, "An Alarming New Development," first published in *Bay Windows*. It is included in *Gay and Lesbian Poetry in Our Time*. Reprinted by permission of the author.

Shelby Steele, "White Guilt," from *American Scholar*, Autumn 1990.

Gloria Steinem, "Erotica and Pornography," from *Ms* Magazine, November 1978, pp. 53-54, 75, 78. Copyright © 1978 Gloria Steinem. Reprinted by permission of the author.

Irving Stone, "Death Valley Earns Its Name," from *Men to Match My Mountains*. Copyright © 1956 by Irving Stone. Used by permission of Doubleday, a division of Bantam Doubleday Dell Publishing Group, Inc.

Deborah Tannen, "Talk in the Intimate Relationship: His and Hers," from *That's Not What I Meant!* by Deborah Tannen, Ph.D. Copyright © 1986 by Deborah Tannen, Ph.D. Reprinted by permission of William Morrow & Company, Inc.

Amoja Three Rivers, "Cultural Etiquette: A Guide," from *Ms* Magazine, September/ October, 1991.

Lester C. Thurow, "The New Economics of High Tech," from *Head to Head: Coming Economic Battles Among Japan, Europe and America*, by Lester C. Thurow. Copyright © 1992 by Lester C. Thurow. Reprinted by permission of William Morrow & Company, Inc. This selection appears as edited for the March 1992 issue of *Harper's* magazine.

Barbara Tuchman, "Mankind's Better Moments." Copyright © 1980 by Barbara Tuchman. Reprinted by permission of Russell & Volkening as agents for the Estate of Barbara Tuchman.

Luis Valdez and Teatro Campesino (Hollister), *The Buck Private*, English version as printed in Charles Tatum, *Mexican American Literature*, Harcourt Brace Jovanovich, Inc. Reprinted by permission of the author.

Camilo Jose Vergara, "Hell in a Very Tall Place." Copyright © 1989 by Camilo Jose Vergara, as originally published in *The Atlantic*, September 1989. Reprinted with permission.

Nora Villagren, "Victor Villaseñor and the Long Road North," reprinted by permission of the *San Jose Mercury News*, September 17, 1991.

Alice Walker, "Women" from *Revolutionary Petunias & Other Poems*. Copyright © 1970 by Alice Walker. Reprinted by permission of Harcourt Brace Jovanovich, Inc. "In Search of Our Mothers' Gardens" from *In Search of Our Mothers' Gardens*. Copyright © 1974 by Alice Walker, reprinted by permission of Harcourt Brace Jovanovich, Inc. "Everyday Use," from *In Love & Trouble*. Copyright © 1973 by Alice Walker. Reprinted by permission of Harcourt Brace Jovanovich, Inc.

Jade Snow Wong, excerpt from Thomas C. Wheeler, ed., *The Immigrant Experience*. Copyright © 1971 by The Dial Press.

Hisaye Yamamoto, "Seventeen Syllables," from *Partisan Review*, Vol. XVI, No. 11, November, 1949. Reprinted by permission of the publisher.

INDEX OF AUTHORS AND TITLES

ABOUT THE EDITORS

Dolores laGuardia teaches at University of San Francisco, where she has developed a humanities sequence titled "American Voices: Ourselves and Each Other," with courses focused on African Americans, Asian Americans, Latinos, Native Americans, religious minorities, and alternative lifestyles. From 1990 to 1992, she served as the writing specialist for a large Federal grant designed to improve writing instruction at the community college level. In the summer of 1992, she conducted a workshop on computer education at the prestigious Troitsk Institute outside Moscow.

Hans P. Guth (San Jose State University) has worked with writing teachers and spoken at professional meetings in most of the fifty states. He spoke on "Redefining the Canon" at the 1991 NCTE Convention in Seattle. He is co-author of *Discovering Literature* (Blair Press, 1993) and the author of numerous composition texts, including *The Writer's Agenda, Student Voices,* and *New English Handbook.* He is co-director and program chair of the annual Young Rhetoricians' Conference in Monterey.